FREUD: LIVING AND DYING

FREUD: LIVING AND DYING

MAX SCHUR, M.D.

INTERNATIONAL UNIVERSITIES PRESS, INC.
New York

Library of Congress Catalog Card Number: 71-143379
ISBN: 0-8236-2025-5
Second Printing 1972

Manufactured in the United States of America

The author's research in the writing of this book was supported by grants from: Foundation for Research in Psychoanalysis, Beverly Hills, California; The Commonwealth Fund, New York, N. Y.; Chapelbrook Foundation, Boston, Massachusetts; New-Land Foundation, Inc., New York, N. Y.; and The Robert P. Knight VFR Fund, New Haven, Connecticut.

CONTENTS

v

Contents

Part III

ILLNESS AND DEATH

In Lebensfluten, im Tatensturm
Wall ich auf und ab,
Webe hin und her!
Geburt und Grab,
Ein ewiges Meer,
Ein wechselnd Weben,
Ein glühend Leben,
So schaff ich am sausenden
    Webstuhl der Zeit
Und wirke der Gottheit lebendiges Kleid.

In the floods of life, in the storm of deeds
I surge and ebb,
Weaving to and fro,
An eternal sea,
A changing weaving,
A glowing life,
I create at the whirring loom of Time
And work the deities' living garb.

Goethe, *Faust*, Act I, Scene 1.

Notes on Documentation

1. All letters to Wilhelm Fliess published in *The Origins of Psycho-analysis* will be referred to by the letter number, e.g., L. 10.

All unpublished letters to Fliess are given in the original German in the notes collected in the Appendix. Numbers in brackets refer to these notes.

2. Letters contained in *Letters of Sigmund Freud,* edited by E. L. Freud, are referred to by numbers followed by an asterisk, e.g., L. 224.*

3. All other letters, unless otherwise identified, are referred to by the addressee and date. The various collections of Freud's correspondence are listed in the Bibliography as, e.g., Freud/Abraham, Freud/Pfister, etc.

4. All previously unpublished material is presented in the original German in the Appendix. While I have retained Freud's antiquated spelling, I have occasionally added punctuation to facilitate the reading and have also spelled out abbreviated words.

5. All the translations of unpublished letters are my own. In general, I have sacrificed elegance of language to accuracy. It needs to be stressed, however, that the translation of letters presents a particularly difficult problem because Freud used many uncommon phrases, unusual metaphors, sometimes slang. In addition, his particular attitude may have been known to the person to whom he wrote, but is no longer available. Yet, this attitude often defines the choice of word. To give an example: In *Beyond the Pleasure Principle* Freud refers to "[die] grossartige Konzeption von W. Fliess" (*Ges. Werke,* 13:47). I began by translating this as "grand" conception; Jones used "grandiose"; Strachey, "large"; and someone else, coming upon this isolated sentence would be justified to adopt "magnificent."

PREFACE

At the time of my husband's death, in October 1969, this book had been completed insofar as its content was concerned. However, editorial work was still needed to ensure the continuity of the main theme within each chapter and throughout the book. Since great care was taken not to change the original content, some passages, which from an editorial point of view might have benefited from shortening, remain.

Contributions to the form and content of this book have come from many sources, and a complete list of acknowledgements could only have been made by the author himself. However, I would like to thank the following for their help to me in readying for publication a work which occupied the heart and mind of Max Schur for many years: Mrs. Lucille Osterweil, who has devotedly worked on this study since its inception in an editorial and translating capacity; Mrs. Lottie M. Newman, who did extensive editorial work and offered many valuable suggestions; Dr. Joseph Goldstein, who read the manuscript and provided very useful advice; Dr. Roy Lilleskov, who not only helped to improve the book from a stylistic point of view but—more important —made certain that the theoretical interpretations remained as originally intended; and last but not least, Dr. Gertrud M. Kurth, who saw the book through to its final and most crucial editing, helping to make certain that the work which appeared in print was the work its author had in mind.

Helen Schur, M.D.

INTRODUCTION

To write a book which deals not only with the process of living but more particularly with the problem of death and dying of a particular human being is of necessity a most delicate undertaking. For a physician to write such a book about a patient of his, a person whom he also loved and revered, is even more difficult. It is a formidable task if this patient was a man like Freud. To explain why I consider it not only necessary but an obligation on my part to undertake such a task, I must first give a short history of the origin of this book.

THE HISTORY OF THIS BOOK

Psychoanalysis has taught us that human events are less often determined by chance than is generally believed. And yet chance has its place in our lives. It was by chance that in the fall of 1915, when I had just entered medical school, a charming cousin of mine, who had studied psychology with Claparède in Geneva and was now stranded in Vienna because of the war, suggested that I join her in attending Freud's lectures, which were later to be published as the *Introductory Lectures to Psycho-Analysis.*

There were a few medical students attending these lectures. The audience was composed for the most part of Freud's students, "intellectuals," and curiosity seekers. The medical students who attended had to submit their "Index" to the lecturer for his signature. This was a booklet listing all courses attended. Freud made it a point to meet each student, exchange a few words with him, and shake his hand.

1

Most impressive was the searching look which accompanied the hand-shake. Little did I dream at that moment that thirteen years later I would become Freud's personal physician.

I attended every lecture that year and the next. It is not easy to explain why this was such a unique, unforgettable experience, nor is this the place to do so. At 18 I was certainly not equipped to integrate the content of the lectures. It probably was the total harmony of content and delivery which created the impact. It has been a taxing experience for any translator of Freud's works, including Strachey, and of course myself, to find that the difficulty of this task was comparable to that of translating poetry.

Attending the Introductory Lectures could not fail to evoke in me an intense interest in psychoanalysis. While, for various reasons I decided to specialize in internal medicine, I started my personal analysis in 1924.

Then chance intervened once again. In 1927, an older colleague and fatherly friend with whom Marie Bonaparte[1] had consulted, sent me to her to take a blood specimen. We engaged in conversation and she was pleasantly surprised to meet a psychoanalytically oriented internist. In 1928, during one of her repeated stays in Vienna, she became acutely ill and I treated her for many weeks.[2] It was she who then persuaded Freud to appoint me as his personal physician. I functioned in this role until his death in 1939.

Thus I came to know Freud the teacher, the scientist, and the *pater familias* in the circle of his family. I treated his family, many of his patients, and often had to discuss them with him at length. I saw him suffer pain and sorrow. I saw him show scorn and contempt for brutality and stupidity as well as tender love and concern for those close to him. He was always a deeply human and noble man, in the fullest meaning of the word. And I saw him face dying and death as nobly as he had faced living.

After Freud's death I came to this country, where many friends, colleagues, magazine and book publishers, and even movie producers inquired, not if, but when I would "let the public share" my experiences with Freud. I resisted this idea for many years, not only because a respect for privacy was part of Freud's honored tradition, but also

[1] Marie Bonaparte, a patient-student of Freud, eventually became a prominent psychoanalyst in her own right.

[2] I remained her physician, or at least her medical advisor and friend, up to the time of her death.

because I knew that I had to gain some distance in order to acquire the necessary objectivity. I would have to approach the topic in a manner which would have been acceptable to Freud himself.

In 1950 *The Origins of Psychoanalysis* was published. It is somewhat redundant to reaffirm the momentous importance of this event. The preservation and partial publication of Freud's correspondence with Wilhelm Fliess and the manuscripts attached to them, in particular the "Project for a Scientific Psychology" greatly increased our understanding of the unfolding of Freud's personality and work. All this has been ably pointed out by Ernst Kris in his introduction to *The Origins,* Ernest Jones in *The Life and Work of Sigmund Freud,* and others. Through *The Origins* we have gained a most intimate view of the development and the workshop of a genius. We see that Freud arrived at his insights not only by flashes of brilliant intuition, but by trial and error and by unflagging honesty, determination, and courage.

Anyone who has tried to engage in psychoanalytic research and has therefore delved into Freud's writings is struck again and again by the fact that many of the concepts which Freud formulated during the later periods of his life were already alluded to or clearly discernible in his early writings. It is for this reason that the systematic study of Freud's writings remains even today an essential part of teaching and research in psychoanalysis. Even in such early works as the "Project" (1895) and especially *The Interpretation of Dreams* (1900) we find at least the elements of most of the ideas developed later not only by Freud but by the subsequent generations of psychoanalysts.

It was the particular intent of Ernst Kris's introduction and footnotes to the published Fliess correspondence to compare the development of ideas reflected in these letters with that evidenced in Freud's published works during the same period. Beyond this, Kris also endeavored to trace many of the ideas expressed in the Fliess letters to much later formulations in Freud's works. Other ideas remained dormant until Freud accumulated the necessary confirming evidence, which was forthcoming only after decades of self-analysis and analyses of patients. Pertinent examples are the concepts of ego and superego, or the reformulation of the theory of anxiety.

I have mentioned respect for privacy as a barrier against the publication of intimate biographical details. However, Freud himself overcame this wish for privacy when he deemed it necessary for the sake of science. In *The Interpretation of Dreams* and *The Psychopathology of Everyday Life* he did not hesitate to discuss with utter frankness highly intimate details of his life, thoughts, and fantasies, which he had uncovered only through his self-analysis. Of course, in writing *The Interpretation of Dreams,* Freud exercised the right of selection, of a certain "censorship"—not so in the Fliess correspondence. Freud himself said in one of his letters to Fliess that it was the unrestricted frankness and sharing of thoughts which made this correspondence so precious to him. It is not surprising that Freud was deeply disturbed by the prospect of the publication of these letters when they were unexpectedly acquired by Marie Bonaparte. Her correspondence with Freud reveals the conflict between the individual's wish for privacy and the demands of the scientific community. Thus Marie Bonaparte wrote to Freud (see Schur, 1965, pp. 14, 16):

> Perhaps you yourself . . . do not perceive your full greatness. You belong to the history of human thought, like Plato, shall we say, or Goethe. What a loss it would have been for us, their poor posterity, if Goethe's conversation with Eckermann had been destroyed, or the *Dialogues* of Plato. . . .

To which Freud replied:

> It is disappointing that my letters to Fliess are not yet in your hands, but are still in Berlin. . . . I cannot easily accept your opinion and the comparisons you draw. I just tell myself that after 80 or 100 years interest in this correspondence will be notably less marked than in our own time.

The editors of the Fliess correspondence were well aware of this conflict and spoke of it in their introduction. And yet, the correspondence was published, though only in part.

The publication of the Fliess correspondence not only opened up new perspectives on the unfolding of Freud's scientific concepts, but also made available an invaluable source of biographical material and permitted us at least a glimpse into Freud's most astonishing feat—his self-analysis.

The Fliess correspondence has had a very special impact on everyone who knew Freud, myself included. To compare the Freud I knew from the Introductory Lectures and from personal contact during the last eleven years of his life with the Freud who emerges so vividly from the correspondence was an experience both illuminating and poignant. Moreover, there was a point of special interest for me in this correspondence. From my personal experience with Freud and from reading his works I was familiar with his attitudes toward living, illness, and death. I knew his behavior during the years of his most severe suffering and as a dying patient. Freud had told me in general terms that he had had some cardiac symptoms before he was forty. There were a few scattered references to this in some of Freud's scientific and autobiographical works. There were also a few indications of a preoccupation with prospective death dates, which had a mildly superstitious-obsessive character. I did not know, however, that this cardiac episode had been serious, and that Freud had actually lived for at least two years with the prospect of an early cardiac death. This episode will be discussed in detail in Chapter 2.

The published Fliess correspondence covered the period from 1887 to 1902. Of this period the years 1893-1900 were in many respects the most dramatic in Freud's life. In 1893 Breuer and Freud published their preliminary communication "On the Psychical Mechanism of Hysterical Phenomena," and in the same year Freud also had his first anginal symptoms; in 1900 Freud published *The Interpretation of Dreams*.

We learned a great deal from the publication of some of the Fliess correspondence, but many questions remained unanswered. I myself arrived at the conclusion that my own data, concerning mainly the last 10½ years of Freud's life, would eventually have to be published. I composed a rough draft of my material, most of which was recorded for the Sigmund Freud Archives by Dr. K. R. Eissler.

At this time Ernest Jones was preparing his biography of Freud. The Freud family gave support to this work to the fullest extent. Jones was given access to a great part of Freud's extensive correspondence, including even his betrothal letters, which had been preserved unread by his family.

With the authorization of the Freud family, I therefore decided to make available to Jones all my own material as well as the notes taken by the late Professor Dr. Hans Pichler, the oral surgeon who treated Freud from 1923 to 1938. These notes (on 80 closely typed pages) covered every single visit and contained a detailed description of more than 30 surgical interventions,[3] pathology and X-ray reports, and so forth. I also supplied copies of all letters written by Freud to me. It was my intention to turn all this material over to Jones before he started on the last volume of his biography. I did this because I wished to make a contribution to scientific biography and, on a more

---

[3] I am grateful to Professor Dr. Hans Pichler, Jr., for letting me have this material.

personal level, to cooperate with a man who had obtained an English visa for me and my family as well as a permit to function as Freud's personal physician even before I had passed the necessary examinations.

In 1953, Volume 1 of Jones's biography appeared. This contained a large amount of hitherto unknown material, including, for example, a selection of Freud's betrothal letters. The high quality and merits of Jones's work have been amply acknowledged. All three volumes will remain an invaluable source of material for later historians and biographers. It also proved to me the need for contributions to Freud's biography by contemporaries who had been in close contact with him.

I was disturbed, however, by several points in Volume 1. Principally, I did not agree with Jones's evaluation of Freud's physical symptoms. Jones had simply designated Freud's cardiac episode an "anxiety hysteria." He also spoke of Freud's "frequent attacks" of *Todesangst* (dread of dying) during the Fliess period, for which I had found no proof in the published Fliess correspondence. Nor could I agree with Jones's somewhat schematic interpretation of certain aspects of Freud's relationship to Fliess, which he saw as originating mainly from infantile sexuality, especially the oedipal conflict. This presentation failed to appreciate fully all the intricate elements of this unique relationship.

At that time I had already recognized that any examination of Freud's changing attitude toward illness and death hinged on the evaluation of both his physical symptoms and their intertwining with Freud's self-analysis and his relationship to Fliess.

After the publication of Volume 1, which covered the period up to 1902, I therefore rewrote what Jones later called my "essay" and incorporated into it some of my divergent opinions, principally those concerning Jones's evaluation of Freud's physical symptoms.

Before sending this to Jones, I submitted it, in 1954, for Miss Anna Freud's approval, which she expressed in a letter that said more than I could have hoped for: "Der Patient selbst hätte Sie sehr gelobt, wenn er es lesen könnte." ("The patient himself would have praised you highly had he been able to read it.") I decided to send the manuscript to Jones when he was ready to start on Volume 3.

In the meantime I had engaged in extensive correspondence with him concerning many details of his work. We then arrived at the agreement that my "essay" would be published under my own name as the last chapter of the biographical section of Volume 3, with the title "The Last Chapter." Jones changed this plan for a number of reasons, and incorporated certain portions of my material into the body of his work, of course giving me due credit. Nevertheless, a great deal was left unsaid. In the long run, however, I was glad of this change of plan. I came to realize first that Freud's attitude toward death as a biological, physiological, and psychological problem represented an integral part of his work; that it had its own development paralleling that of the science he had created; that this development was part and parcel of his self-analysis, which continued throughout Freud's life. Having arrived at this conclusion, I recognized that much more was needed than "the last chapter." An attempt had to be made to retrace the path which had led to that chapter.

I expressed earlier my initial reluctance to write a biographical study of Freud and gave as one of the reasons that the "respect for privacy was part of Freud's honored tradition." Some clarification of this statement is necessary. I have indicated that Freud divulged in *The Interpretation of Dreams* and other works intimate details of his private life. He did so unsparingly because it was essential for the understanding of dreams or the "psychopathology of everyday life."

Freud was, throughout his life, very liberal in discussing his private thoughts in his correspondence, above all with Fliess, but also with many friends and associates. Yet in all these instances it was he who set the limits of disclosure. Moreover, he did not assume—at least consciously—that all this material would be used by future biographers. Hence, in 1936, his initial reaction of horror to the news that Marie Bonaparte had acquired the Fliess correspondence.

When Freud emerged at the turn of the century from his partly self-enforced isolation, and gradually became an internationally famous man, he hated publicity and interviews with the press.

It is known that from the time of his single visit to the United States in 1909 Freud felt a certain prejudice against this country. One of the reasons for this was probably the easygoing intimacy between casual acquaintances and professional colleagues which was so common among Americans. There were very few friends with whom Freud conversed or corresponded on the *Du* level, the German expression of personal intimacy.

What was Freud's attitude toward biographical studies? Here we must draw a distinction between Freud's attitude to biographical studies of others and those making him the subject. Freud himself did not hesitate to apply psychoanalytic interpretations to works of art as well as to their creators. The list of such examples would be a long one: *Oedipus Rex, Hamlet, King Lear,* the novels of C. F. Meyer, Jensen's *Gradiva,* and the Moses of Michelangelo, among others. He wrote biographical essays on Goethe, Dostoevsky, and Leonardo da Vinci.

A letter written to Havelock Ellis on September 12, 1926, after he had received the latter's autobiography, reveals Freud's awareness of a contrast between his curiosity concerning the life of a prominent man and his own reluctance to share such information with others. Freud expressed this as follows:

> I also see a sign of your magnanimity in your readiness to place so much personal material at the disposal of a biographer. For this I would lack all incentive [L. 224*].[4]

Freud responded in different ways to the biographical studies written about himself by F. Wittels (1924) and Stefan Zweig (1931, 1933).

He received the prepublication copy of the German edition of Wittels's book in December, 1923, shortly after his second radical cancer operation (see Chapter 13). Freud's written response combined sharp criticism with an acknowledgment of some positive points. He stated, for instance:

> Needless to say, I would never have desired or promoted such a book. It seems to me that the world has no claim on my person and that it will learn nothing from me so long as my case . . . cannot be made fully transparent [L. 205*].

One of Freud's main criticisms was that Wittels, being a student of Stekel, could not have presented the reasons for Freud's break with the latter with the necessary objectivity (see Jones, Vol. 2, Chapter 5).

Freud also enclosed a list of inaccuracies, which he expected Wittels to correct in a later edition. He ended the letter with the following sentence:

> Please look upon this communication as a sign that although I cannot approve of your effort I by no means wish to underestimate it.

The published version of this letter does not contain a paragraph in which Freud responded to an interpretation of Wittels with the statement: "Probability is not always the truth" (Jones, Vol. 3, p. 41).

[4] See Note on Documentation.

After having received the English translation of Wittels's book, which apparently contained only some of the changes suggested by him, Freud wrote on August 15, 1924:

> I still maintain that someone who knows as little about a person as you do about me is not entitled to write a biography about that person. One waits till the person is dead, when he cannot do anything about it and fortunately no longer cares [L. 209*].

Freud objected specifically to Wittels's inaccurate presentation of the cocaine episode (see Chapter 1), but even more to his interpretation of the final break with Fliess (L. 209*). Nevertheless, the following year Freud gave his consent to the readmission of Wittels to the Vienna Psychoanalytic Society.

We can see that Freud expressed in these letters his basic dislike of biographical studies written about him, and that he mostly demanded of them strict adherence to the truth. That "probability is not always the truth" applies of course to many hypotheses and interpretations. In spite of this basic disinclination he provided even this very critical biographer with advice and corrections.

Freud reacted much more favorably to a biographical study about him by Stefan Zweig. He said:

> That one doesn't like one's own portrait, or that one doesn't recognize oneself in it, is a general and well-known fact. I therefore hasten to express my satisfaction at your having recognized correctly the most important feature in my case. Namely, that in so far as achievement is concerned it was less the result of intellect than of character. This seems to be the core of your opinion, and one in which I myself believe. . . .
>
> The fellow is actually somewhat more complicated: your description doesn't tally with the fact that I too have had my splitting headaches and attacks of fatigue like anyone else, that I was a passionate smoker (I wish I still were), that I ascribe to the cigar the greatest share of my self-control and tenacity in work, that despite my much vaunted frugality I have sacrificed a great deal for my collection of Greek, Roman and Egyptian antiquities, have actually read more archaeology than psychology, and that before the war and once after its end I felt compelled to spend every year at least several days or weeks in Rome, and so on [L. 258*].

Freud dealt most directly with the problems inherent in writing about "great men" in his acceptance address written for the presentation of the Goethe Prize in 1930. He said:

I am prepared for the reproach that we analysts have forfeited the right to place ourselves under the patronage of Goethe because we have offended against the respect due to him by trying to apply analysis to him himself: we have degraded the great man to the position of an object of analytic investigation. But I would dispute at once that any degradation is intended or implied by this.

We all, who revere Goethe, put up, without too much protest, with the efforts of his biographers, who try to re-create his life from existing accounts and indications. But what can these biographies achieve for us? Even the best and fullest of them could not answer the two questions which alone seem worth knowing about. It would not throw any light on the riddle of the miraculous gift that makes an artist, and it could not help us to comprehend any better the value and the effect of his works. And yet there is no doubt that such a biography does satisfy a powerful need in us. We feel this very distinctly if the legacy of history unkindly refuses the satisfaction of this need—for example in the case of Shakespeare. . . . But how can we justify a need of this kind to obtain knowledge of the circumstances of a man's life when his works have become so full of importance to us? People generally say that it is our desire to bring ourselves nearer to such a man in a human way as well. Let us grant this; . . .

All the same, we may admit that there is still another motive-force at work. The biographer's justification also contains a confession. It is true that the biographer does not want to dispose of his hero, but he does want to bring him nearer to us. That means, however, reducing the distance that separates him from us: it still tends in effect toward degradation. And it is unavoidable that if we learn more about a great man's life we shall also hear of occasions on which he has in fact done no better than we, has in fact come near to us as a human being. Nevertheless, I think we may declare the efforts of biography to be legitimate. Our attitude to fathers and teachers is, after all, an ambivalent one since our reverence for them regularly conceals a component of hostile rebellion. That is a psychological fatality; it cannot be altered without forcible suppression of truth and is bound to extend to our relations with the great men whose life histories we wish to investigate [1930a, p. 211f.].

These passages depict clearly the conflicts and limitations which face any biographer. To be aware of them is the latter's duty. And yet Freud declared—reluctantly—that "the efforts of biography are legitimate." No biographical study written by a psychoanalyst can refrain from applying the tools of psychoanalysis to its object. Hence biography has become one of the fields of what is generally called applied psychoanalysis.

Freud addressed himself to this problem in another context as well. Arnold Zweig, with whom Freud was engaged in an intensive correspondence during the last decade of his life (see Chapters 20-27) had been preoccupied since 1930 with the idea of writing a study comparing and contrasting the work and personalities of Freud and Nietzsche.

In 1934 Arnold Zweig sent Freud a first draft of what he called a "novel" centered on Nietzsche's mental derangement (*Umnachtung*). In a series of letters he then presented Freud with the outline of his plan, which was essentially biographical fiction.[5]

Freud responded with a thoughtful letter, in which he discussed the "problem of historical license versus historical reality." Freud granted that wherever there was a hopeless gap between history and biography, a poet was justified in bridging this gap with his imagination. Freud cited such examples as Shakespeare's Macbeth, Schiller's Don Carlos, and Goethe's Egmont. Freud postulated, however, using the metaphor of a portrait, that in the case of a person like Nietzsche, who was still exerting much influence on our time, the emphasis of an author writing a biographical study should be on creating a maximum of resemblance (Freud/Zweig, May 12, 1934). Freud called Zweig's attention in a subsequent letter to two obstacles which a biographer must face in the case of Nietzsche. First of all, relatively little is known about his sexual "constitution." More important, during at least the last twelve years of his life Nietzsche suffered from general paresis, and there was no way of knowing when the destructive illness had started. Freud raised the question of whether it was permissible for the poet to "refantasize the gross facts of pathology" (July 15, 1934).

Freud also commented that he could not believe even half of the praise which Zweig had expressed about him in his book, *Bilanz der deutschen Judenheit: ein Versuch* (1934).

In spite of his objection to Zweig's plan Freud asked Lou Andreas-Salomé (who was one of the important women in Nietzsche's life) whether she would be willing to supply Zweig with some information about Nietzsche. She refused adamantly to have anything to do with such a study. We can see that Freud's main objection to Zweig's plan was the lack of solid information.[6]

Freud expressed the most objective—scientific—opinion about psychoanalysis as applied to biography when he said in his Goethe Prize address:

[5] Zweig was at that point preoccupied mainly with tracing the fatal influence of Nietzsche's ideas on the development of Nazi Germany.

[6] Zweig then published a much more modest essay under the title "Apollon bewältigt Dionysos" (1936) on the occasion of Freud's 80th birthday.

When psycho-analysis puts itself at the service of biography, it naturally has the right to be treated no more harshly than the latter itself. Psycho-analysis can supply some information which cannot be arrived at by other means, and can thus demonstrate new connecting threads in the 'weaver's masterpiece'[7] spread between the instinctual endowments, the experiences and the works of an artist [1930a, p. 212].

This statement also applies to any biographical study of Freud which uses the psychoanalytic method. I shall therefore refrain in general from making any interpretations which are not warranted by Freud's own revelations, in his letters, his personal communications, the interpretation of his dreams, his autobiographical writings, his works and some biographical material as, for instance, the recently published actuarial data (see Chapter 1). To paraphrase Freud's statement in the earlier quoted letter to Wittels: probability is not *always* the truth, but it may be the truth. This has to be weighed carefully.

In writing my own study I had to consider yet another question, perhaps the most difficult one: I was Freud's physician, and in my book I also present Freud's medical case history. This question of whether this was permissible had already been answered in principle when I made available to Jones all my material for his biography. I earlier stated my reason for doing so. In this book, however, I shall present the case history *in toto*. It was Freud who "disturbed the sleep of the world" (see Chapter 11) by exposing the awesome aspect of our instinctual life by uncovering the illusion we harbor about im-mortality, and by explicating our inability to fathom the thought of our own death (see Chapters 5, 10, 11, 14, 18). I therefore consid-ered it to be in the spirit of Freud, who always insisted on knowing the whole truth, however painful this might be, not to withhold any of the tragic details of his prolonged suffering and dying.

SOURCE MATERIAL

Several of Freud's essays were directly autobiographical, as for ex-ample "Screen Memories" (1899), and "An Autobiographical Study" (1925b). A paper written in 1936 ("A Disturbance of Memory on the Acropolis") is basically a part of Freud's self-analysis and can easily be traced back to events of 1899 and 1904, and to some of

---

[7] A quotation from Mephistopheles's description of the fabric of thought, in *Faust,* Part I, Scene 4.

Freud's dreams (see Chapters 5, 7, 12 and 14). Others were indirectly autobiographical, such as *The Interpretation of Dreams* (1900) and *The Psychopathology of Everyday Life* (1901b) in which Freud revealed a good deal of personal material and supplied us with important reconstruction of his earliest childhood. Some pertinent new material about this early period has recently been unearthed by Sajner (1968). These facts throw an important light on Freud's reconstructions and on some of his most controversial hypotheses.

Most important were Freud's letters. The Fliess correspondence showed that in many instances Freud's letters were more revealing than his works. In 1956, a year before the appearance of Jones's Volume 3, Binswanger published the *Erinnerungen an Sigmund Freud* (later translated as *Sigmund Freud: Reminiscences of a Friendship*). Many of Freud's letters published in this beautiful little volume were highly pertinent to the topic of my study. Many other important letters were scattered throughout Jones's three volumes, along with much other invaluable information.

In 1960 Ernst L. Freud published a wide selection of Freud's letters. In 1961 Marie Bonaparte consented to my studying her intensive correspondence with Freud, which she had deposited for safekeeping in London with the Freud family.

Jones had amassed from all available sources a great deal of information. Freud's betrothal letters, of which 93 were published in the 1960 letter selection, also fill an important gap in the years from 1901 on, for which we have no source material comparable to the Fliess correspondence. However, the number of recipients of Freud's letters grew steadily. Freud's correspondence with Ferenczi, which is particularly rich in information, is being prepared for publication by Dr. M. Balint and Mr. Ernst L. Freud.[8] I am indebted to Dr. Michael Balint for putting copies of these letters at my disposal. Freud's own publications during those next three decades contained much pertinent material (see Chapters 8-14).

In addition to Jones, a number of Freud's student patients, Lou Andreas-Salomé, Binswanger, H. D., H. Sachs, F. Wittels, S. Zweig, and Freud's son Martin, to mention only the most important ones, and other contemporaries have also published biographical studies or memoirs, each of which has added to our knowledge of the many facets of

[8] *Editor's note:* Since this was written, both Dr. Balint and Mr. Freud have died.

Freud's personality. From 1928-1939 my own eyewitness reports can be added to the source material.

Fortunately Freud was a prolific letter writer, and most of his correspondence was preserved. In 1963 I went to London, where I was given access to all the correspondence and material of the Freud Copyright, Ltd. which included, among others, Freud's correspondence with Abraham, Lou Andreas-Salomé, Eitingon, Jones, Jung, Arnold Zweig, and Stefan Zweig.[9] In 1964 I was given transcripts of the entire Fliess correspondence.[10] For all this I am especially indebted to Mr. Ernst L. Freud and to Miss Anna Freud.

SELECTION OF CONTENT

When in 1964 I delivered the Fourteenth Freud Anniversary Lecture of the New York Psychoanalytic Society under the title: "The Problem of Death in Freud's Writings and His Life" I was able to deal with the topic in a highly condensed way only. The lecture was given before I could fully integrate the total impact of the unabridged Fliess correspondence. Even then I tried to approach my topic by a comparison and correlation of the three dimensions: Freud's behavior in everyday life, his letters, and his work. I have maintained this approach while expanding the topic of my book.

In the letter to me from Miss Anna Freud, which I mentioned earlier, she remarked that my first "essay" was much more than a case history, that it was actually a piece of biography. I realized then that the title of my Freud Anniversary Lecture, which I had originally planned to use for this book, covered too narrow a field. The problems of life and death cannot be separated. The wish to live and all the elements which sustain it, the fear of death, which can gradually change into acceptance, and even into a wish to die, the conflict and shifting balance of these opposing wishes are all part of human existence. My book, as its title indicates, will therefore attempt to deal with all these elements as they are reflected in the life of one man. However, the choice of material is highly selective and many of Freud's works and events in his life are not discussed.

In the discussion I shall dwell on the so-called "Fliess" period (see Jones, Volume 1, Chapter 13) because it was the period of the *Origins*

[9] Freud's correspondence with Abraham, Lou Andreas-Salomé, and Arnold Zweig has since been published.

[10] An unabridged publication of the Fliess correspondence is being prepared.

of Psychoanalysis, during which Freud underwent the most crucial changes as a result of his self-analysis. Above all, it was the period about which we know the most from Freud's own writing. I shall deal at great length with the material furnished by the correspondence, at the risk of being accused of using an "exegetic" method, which will have to include extensive verbatim quotations.

I shall consider in detail the multiple factors which contributed to the development of Freud's ideas about living and dying: his physical —primarily cardiac—symptoms; his nicotine addiction; his precarious financial situation; his promethean struggle for insight into the uncharted region of "the unconscious"; his proclivity for alternating between a generally depressive mood involving a certain letdown in creativity and a feverish "frenzy of activity." I shall discuss some phobic and obsessive-compulsive mechanisms and, above all, Freud's self-analysis which, along with the complex relationship to Fliess, generated not only thoughts about death but a preoccupation with specific aspects of the end of life. There was such an intricate interplay of all these factors that no one of them can be investigated entirely by itself, and an overlapping of these subjects will be unavoidable in the discussion that follows.

With the help of the unabridged Fliess correspondence and its correlation with some of Freud's dreams and their interpretations, reported in *The Interpretation of Dreams,* I shall trace some aspects of Freud's self-analysis which were important in his later life. I shall outline the multiple specific determinants of Freud's preoccupation with the "deadlines" of his life, and the persistence of this preoccupation, despite the fact that he gradually turned toward an objective inclusion of the problem of death in his scientific work and his credo of a scientific *Weltanschauung,* reflected in a personal attitude of supreme serenity and fortitude, devoid of illusions and denial. That such a transition did not take a linear course, but rather emerged from an unremitting battle between conflicting tendencies, could be expected. Although I shall consider many of Freud's writings in their relation to this topic, I shall discuss some of Freud's later works, such as *Beyond the Pleasure Principle* (1920), in which he first formulated the death instinct theory, and some of his metapsychological concepts about death, formulated in *The Ego and the Id* (1923), "The Economic Problem of Masochism" (1924a), and *Inhibitions, Symptoms and Anxiety* (1926a) in a different perspective.

ORGANIZATION

Freud applied psychoanalysis to such diverse fields as education, anthropology, literature, and sociology, to name only a few. This application of psychoanalytic concepts has mushroomed in the last decade, especially in the United States, where it has been extended to all the branches of the humanities. Consequently this book addresses itself not only to students of the behavioral sciences, but to all those interested in the above-mentioned fields, a consideration which in turn created certain difficulties in the organization of the book.

In writing this book I had the choice of either adopting Jones's method of separating biographical material from the discussion of Freud's writings of a given period, or utilizing in the main a chronological presentation. I chose the latter for many reasons, mainly because, as far as my topic is concerned, Freud's life and his works are so intimately interconnected.

In correlating the events of Freud's life with his letters and works it was necessary to include some highly technical material not easily understandable to readers unfamiliar with psychoanalytic theory. This is, for instance, particularly true with regard to my critical discussion of Freud's death instinct theory.

Another difficulty arose from the fact that my book, although a biographical study, is *not a full-scale biography*. The general reader may not be as familiar with the most pertinent facts of Freud's biography. Hence, I shall refer to most of the available source material, and I shall include such biographical data as are essential.

The three parts into which the book is divided correspond to the three phases in the development of Freud's attitudes toward the problems of illness, dying, and death, and the manner in which he related these attitudes to his life and work.

Part I

PER ASPERA AD ASTRA

1

BACKGROUND

Biographical studies are rarely complete. In the intensive search to increase our understanding new facts emerge continually. So it was that, only quite recently, information became available (Sajner, 1968) which shed new light on important experiences that occurred during the early and most formative years in Freud's life. It is on those that I shall focus first in some detail.

EARLIEST CHILDHOOD, THE FIRST YEARS IN FREIBERG

Freud's father, Jakob, was born in 1815 in Tysmenica in Eastern Galicia. This little town had about 6,000 inhabitants divided more or less equally between Poles, Jews, and Ukrainians.[1]

Jakob Freud was a wool merchant. His business consisted in exchanging various textile products between Galicia and Moravia,[2] provinces of the Austro-Hungarian Empire. Because life in Tysmenica was for many reasons rather precarious, the family moved the center of its business to Freiberg.[3]

---

[1] Galicia as a whole had a Polish majority, but the Eastern part had a strong Ukrainian minority. Tysmenica was the Polish name of the little town. Its German name, which appears in most sources, is Tysmenitz.

[2] It was an "uncanny coincidence" to discover in the data quoted by Sajner that Jakob Freud was an agent of a merchant in Stanislawow, my birthplace, who was none other than my great-grandfather.

[3] According to R. Gicklhorn (1969), Jakob Freud settled in Freiberg in 1844 and not in 1840 as Sajner (1968) stated.

There are striking differences between the data reported by Jones[4] about Freud's father and his family, and the actuarial data given by Sajner. According to Jones,[5] Freud's father, at the age of 16, married a girl named Sally Kanner. They had two sons, Emanuel, born 1832, and Philipp, born 1836. After Sally's death in 1852, Jakob Freud crisscrossed Germany for about a year and then reached Vienna, where he married Freud's mother, Amalia (who was born on August 18, 1835), on July 29, 1855.

Neither Jones nor Alexander Freud had at their disposal the actuarial data quoted by Sajner, who made an extensive study of the birth, marriage, travel, and death registers. Sajner also provides us with a detailed description of the living quarters in which Freud spent the first three years of his life.

The facts that emerge from all the available sources are as follows: Jakob and his sons Philipp and Emanuel[6] settled in Freiberg in 1840 and made their permanent residence there until some time in late 1859 or early 1860. But there is no mention of the presence of Jakob Freud's first wife Sally in Freiberg. There is no entry of Sally's death. There is no indication of exactly when Sally had died.[7]

In the register of Jewish inhabitants for the year 1852, the following members of the family are listed: Jakob Freud, age 38; *his wife Rebekka,* age 32; his son Emanuel, age 21; the latter's wife Maria, age 18; and Jakob's son Philipp, age 16. This entry proves that Rebekka could not have been Jakob's first wife; that is, Rebekka and Sally were not the same person, because Rebekka was not old enough to have been Emanuel's mother. In the register of alien Jewish inhabitants living in Freiberg in 1854, Rebekka is no longer listed. Thus, by 1854, Rebekka had apparently also died, unless the marriage ended by divorce.

The house in which Sigmund Freud was born belonged to the same family for four generations, all of them locksmiths. The workshop was located on the main floor. The second floor had only two rooms.

---

[4] Jones's chief informant was Freud's younger brother, Alexander (1868-1943).

[5] I am referring here to the German translation of his biography, the first volume of which was published in 1960, while the first volume of Jones's original biography was published in 1953. The German edition provides some additional details about the "migration" of the Freud family (1960, p. 18f.).

[6] The birth certificate of Emanuel Freud's daughter Bertha (born on February 22, 1859) establishes that Emanuel was the son of Jakob Freud and Sally, born Kanner.

[7] (We do not know who supplied Jones with the information that she died in 1852.) In a family tree given to me by Mr. Harry Freud, the son of Alexander Freud, only the year of her marriage to Jakob—1831—is listed.

In one of them the owner lived with his family.[8] Crowded into the second room, lived the Freud family, Jakob, Amalia, and the children: Sigmund (born on May 6, 1856), Julius (who was born sometime late in 1857 and died on April 15, 1858) and Anna (born on December 31, 1858). The older sons lived nearby, Philipp across the street, Emanuel with his wife and children (John, born 1854 or 1855; Pauline, born 1856; Bertha born on February 22, 1859) lived on a different street. The Freud women frequently worked in the warehouse of the family business, packing the goods, while all the children were cared for by a maid.

The information unearthed by Sajner is highly significant. Not only does it help us to understand some of the early environmental influences on Freud's development, but it shows us the discrepancies between the "family legend" and the "actuarial" truth.[9] Discrepancies between a family legend and actuarial history may develop either through distortion or the complete blotting out of certain facts. It would seem, for instance, that the existence of Jakob Freud's second wife was subjected to such a blotting-out mechanism.

Obvious questions now arise: who *must* have known about the marriage and who *probably* knew about it? In addition to Jakob Freud, his two sons Philipp and Emanuel as well as Emanuel's wife must have known. It is possible, but not likely, that Freud's mother, Jakob's third wife, was completely unaware of the second marriage. There would have been no reason for her not to have been told about this previous marriage, unless there were some special reasons for secrecy. We know, however, that it is very difficult to keep such information secret in a family and in a small community. Even if such a secret is successfully kept, an "air" of secrecy is nearly always present.

Did Freud know about his father's second wife? Most likely not consciously. The fact of this secret is important enough, however, to warrant our searching carefully through Freud's reports about his self-analysis, his letters, reconstructions, and dreams. It also warrants scrutinizing his theoretical formulations concerning the meaning of

[8] According to Sajner, the owner was a Mr. Johann Zajíc (1850-1924), whose daughter supplied the above information. According to her, her father remembered Freud as a lively youngster who liked to play in the workshops and to make small toys of metal scraps. Mr. Zajíc allegedly used to visit Freud whenever he went to Vienna.

[9] Freud and his students (e.g., Rank) later tried to unravel the relationship between myths, legends and historiography. Freud also tried eventually to find the core of historical truth in myths and legends, for example, in *Totem and Taboo* (1913b) and his last work, *Moses and Monotheism* (1939).

death to small children and the repercussion of deaths experienced in early childhood in order to search for traces of this "secret" which might have codetermined his thinking.

Another, more important, discrepancy between "legend" and actuality concerns the living quarters of Freud's family in Freiberg. The actuarial data also point to certain inaccuracies in Freud's reconstruction of early childhood memories, which he derived mainly from the interpretation of his own dreams during his self-analysis. I shall discuss these discrepancies, the questions they raise and the answers they permit in detail in Chapters 4, 5, and 9 of this book.

Freud commented on his early years in Freiberg not only in his autobiographical works (1899, 1925b) but also in the Fliess correspondence, in which he reported many of his reconstructions, in *The Interpretation of Dreams* (1900), and in *The Psychopathology of Everyday Life* (1901b). In later years he had nostalgic thoughts about those early days in Freiberg. He missed the natural surroundings, the walks through the meadows and woods, and he obviously felt the loss of his first playmates. He returned to Freiberg for a short vacation trip at the age of 16, a visit which he described in detail in his paper on "Screen Memories" (1899).

Before Freud was 4 years old his father decided to leave Freiberg (most likely, late in 1859; the exact time is unknown). Jakob Freud probably first tried to settle in Germany, but eventually, in 1860, he settled in Vienna.

We do not know what kind of business he conducted, but it is likely that he tried to continue as a wool merchant. From much later remarks in Freud's betrothal letters (1882-1886), we do know that in later years Jakob often engaged in somewhat unrealistic ventures, none of them very successful. It was not easy to take care of seven children (two sons and five daughters) born between 1856 and 1866 (not including Julius, born in 1857, who died in 1858). Somehow the family managed to make ends meet. It is probable that Emanuel and Philipp, who had moved to Manchester and had become relatively prosperous there, helped out. The family, therefore, always led a marginal existence, occasionally even quite a precarious one.

THE EAST-EUROPEAN JEWISH BACKGROUND AND ITS INFLUENCE ON FREUD

Jones believed that anti-Semitism was one of the reasons for Jakob Freud's emigration from Freiberg. However, we have no documented proof for this. Bernfeld and Bernfeld (1944) attributed this move mainly to economic reasons, and Sajner (1968) strongly concurred in this opinion. However, the whole situation of being Jewish, with its attendant problems, was an environmental factor which played an important role in Freud's development.

I have mentioned the fact that Tysmenica, the birthplace of Jakob Freud, had a high percentage of Jewish inhabitants. Jews living in such a small town were usually what one calls "observant": the language of communication between them was Yiddish, but most Jews spoke and wrote German as well. They were also obliged to know some Polish. All Jews learned Hebrew, and most of the intelligent and not too poor Jewish children reached a level on which they were able to read and understand some parts of the Bible in Hebrew. At that time most Jews also wore the traditional caftan.

In Moravia orthodoxy was less generally accepted and widespread. Jakob Freud was a liberal, enlightened man, who remained proud of his Jewishness, without strictly adhering to the rules.[10] Freud himself always felt and expressed pride in being Jewish, as the following two examples will show. Freud said in his preface to the Hebrew translation of *Totem and Taboo* (1913b, p. xv):

> No reader of [the Hebrew version of] this book will find it easy to put himself in the emotional position of an author who is ignorant of the language of holy writ, who is completely estranged from the religion of his fathers—as well as from every other religion—and who cannot take a share in nationalist ideals, but who has yet never repudiated his people, who feels that he is in his essential nature a Jew and who has no desire to alter that nature. If the question were put to him: 'Since you have abandoned all these common characteristics of your countrymen, what is there left to you that is Jewish?' he would reply: 'A very great deal, and probably its very essence.' He could not now express that essence clearly in words; but some day, no doubt, it will become accessible to the scientific mind.
>
> Thus it is an experience of a quite special kind for such an author when a book of his is translated into the Hebrew language and put into the hands of readers for whom the historic idiom is a living tongue: a book, moreover, which deals with the origin of religion and morality, though it adopts no Jewish standpoint and makes no exceptions in favour of Jewry. This author hopes, however, that he will be at one with his readers in the conviction that unprejudiced science cannot remain a stranger to the spirit of the new Jewry.

[10] I am using the term rules instead of dogma, because dogma in its strict meaning plays a lesser role in Judaism than, for instance, in Catholicism.

Nearly 20 years later on May 8, 1932, Freud wrote to Arnold Zweig, who had just settled in what was then still called Palestine: "and we hail from there . . . our ancestors lived there perhaps for half, perhaps for a whole millennium . . . and it is impossible to say how much of the life in that country we carry as a heritage in our blood and nerves (as it is mistakenly said)." (See also Chapter 21.)

Nothing can express Jakob Freud's attitude better than an inscription in a Bible which he presented to his son Sigmund on his 35th birthday:

> My dear Son,
>   It was in the seventh year of your age that the spirit of God began to move you to learning. I would say the spirit of God speaketh to you: "Read in My book; there will be opened to thee sources of knowledge and of the intellect." It is the Book of Books; it is the well that wise men have digged and from which lawgivers have drawn the waters of their knowledge.
>   Thou hast seen in this Book the vision of the Almighty, thou hast heard willingly, thou hast done and hast tried to fly high upon the wings of the Holy Spirit. Since then I have preserved the same Bible. Now, on your thirty-fifth birthday I have brought it out from its retirement and I send it to you as a token of love from your old father [Jones, Vol. 1, p. 19].

This inscription tells us something about father and son. The father too must have grown up with that conviction which alone explained the survival of the Jewish people through centuries of exile, migration, and persecution, namely, that the Jews were the "people of the Book."

The difference between the "learned ones"—and learning was literally synonymous with studying the Bible and its commentaries—and those who "did not know" constituted perhaps the most important class distinction among many generations of Jews. The man who wrote this inscription must have shared the wish of so many Jewish fathers that their sons might be among the learned ones, even if they themselves were not. This fatherly wish found fulfillment in Freud, who did become a man of the Book, a seeker of the truth.

In a sentence added in 1935 to his "Autobiographical Study," Freud said: "My deep engrossment in the Bible story (almost as soon as I had learnt the art of reading) had, as I recognized much later, an enduring effect upon the direction of my interest" (1925b, p. 8).

We might add that a man who could write such a message to his son was, as Freud put it after his father's death, a man of "deep wisdom." In this area, Freud was able to find in his father an object for identification and ego-ideal formation. This mechanism provides a more convincing explanation of some of Freud's characteristics than his "visionary" statement about carrying the heritage of the ancient land in his "blood and nerves."

However, some other aspects of Freud's East-European Jewish background are pertinent. Every culture has its own idiomatic language, which finds expression in such things as jokes as well as in certain superstitions. Freud made extensive use of Jewish jokes as he did of literary quotations, to illustrate scientific points he was discussing.

Some common superstitions in this cultural environment were linked to the Bible or to the use of the Hebrew alphabet, as both an orthographic and numerical system. An example of a Bible-linked superstition was the distinction between "good" and "bad" days of the week. Monday, the second day of the week was considered a bad day, because God did not state, after describing the second day of creation, that "it was good." In contrast, after describing the creation of man on the sixth day, God said that it was "very good." Thus Friday was a very good day. This superstition implied, for instance, a warning against starting a journey or making an important decision on a Monday.

There were typical superstitions about certain numbers, which were linked to words formed by substituting words for letters. For example, 18 could be spelled out as the Hebrew word for "life" and hence was a very good number. The number 17 could be spelled out as the Hebrew word for good. Jones (Vol. 3, p. 379) mentioned as an example of Freud's superstitiousness that he told his bride how as a boy he had chosen the number 17 in a lottery that allegedly would reveal his character and out came the word "constancy" (in German *Beständigkeit*—persistence, steadfastness, faithfulness), and the engagement took place on the 17th day of the month. For years they celebrated this day (see also Jones, 1962). I would strongly suspect that the old Jewish superstition was behind the fact that Freud chose the number 17 in the first place.

The number 52 could be spelled out as the Hebrew word for dog— hence a bad number—and the 52nd birthday was considered a "critical" one, especially for men (see also Chapter 5).

If someone was asked about the age of a member of the family or any important person, he would state the age and then add "until 120," implying his hope that the person in question would live until that age.

Another important number was 36, which corresponded to the combination of the Hebrew letters *Lamed* and *Vov*. According to a Hasidic legend, there must always be 36 just (holy) people living on earth. When one of them dies, God selects another one—usually a poor young boy of humble background—to succeed. The presence of these 36 holy men protects humanity from destruction because of its sinfulness. If somebody was an especially virtuous and learned man, he was called a *Lamedvovnik,* meaning a personification of the two letters *Lamed* and *Vov,* which stood for the number 36. The 36 men remained anonymous. Thirty-six is, of course, two times 18, the latter standing, as mentioned earlier, for life.

It can be assumed that a family stemming from Tysmenica would be well acquainted with this type of knowledge because Tysmenica was the seat of one of the several dynasties of Hasidic rabbis.

It will be necessary to discuss at length Freud's preoccupation with prospective dates of his death, and it seems likely that such "cultural" superstitions were among the many determinants for this preoccupation. In a letter which described an episode of intensive preoccupation of this kind, Freud himself remarked: "you will find confirmation . . . of the specifically Jewish nature of my mysticism"[11] (see Chapter 5). In this context, one memory of an incident important for my topic is reported by Freud in *The Interpretation of Dreams.* I shall quote only the pertinent part of the dream and of Freud's association to it:

> I went into a kitchen in search of some pudding. Three women were standing in it; one of them was the hostess of the inn and was twisting something about in her hand, as though she was making *Knödel* [dumplings]. She answered that I must wait till she was ready. . . . I felt impatient and went off with a sense of injury. . . . When I began analyzing this dream, I thought quite unexpectedly of the first novel I ever read (when I was thirteen, perhaps). . . . I have a vivid memory of its ending. The hero . . . kept calling out the names of the three women who had brought the greatest happiness and sorrow into his life. . . . In connection with the three women I thought of the three Fates who spin the destiny of man, and I knew that one of the three

[11] Bakan (1958) devoted a study to the influence of the Jewish mystical tradition on Freud. Within the framework of this book, I cannot discuss Bakan's assumptions. It is, however, pertinent to my discussion about the cultural sources of Freud's preoccupation with numbers that Bakan specifically relates the Cabalistic gematria, which deals with the cryptographic significance of words, to Freud's numerology. It may also be pertinent that Freud began the same letter to Jung, in which he alluded to the specifically Jewish nature of his mysticism with a remark that he had "anointed" Jung to be his successor.

women—the inn-hostess in the dream—was the mother who gives life, and furthermore (as in my own case) gives the living creature its first nourishment. Love and hunger, I reflected, meet at a woman's breast. . . . One of the Fates, then, was rubbing the palms of her hands together as though she was making dumplings; a queer occupation for a Fate, and one that cried out for an explanation. This was provided by another and earlier memory of my childhood. When I was six years old and was given my first lessons by my mother, I was expected to believe that we were all made of earth and must therefore return to earth. This did not suit me and I expressed doubts of the doctrine. My mother thereupon rubbed the palms of her hands together—just as she did in making dumplings, except that there was no dough between them—and showed me the blackish scales of *epidermis* produced by the friction as a proof that we were made of earth. My astonishment at this ocular demonstration knew no bounds and I acquiesced in the belief which I was later to hear expressed in the words: '*Du bist der Natur einen Tod schuldig.*'[12] So they really were Fates that I found in the kitchen when I went into it—as I had so often done in my childhood when I was hungry, while my mother, standing by the fire, had admonished me that I must wait till dinner was ready [p. 204f.].

In view of Freud's statement from his autobiography quoted earlier, we may assume that he knew the lines from Genesis: "Dust thou art, and into dust shalt thou return" before he read Shakespeare. Thus the inevitability of death was early brought home to him—and this by his mother!

And the theme of the Three Fates remained a repetitive one in Freud's writing.

THE PREANALYTIC PERIOD

We know very little about Freud's life between 1860 and 1873, the year he finished the gymnasium. He was an excellent student, in most years at the top of his class. At the end of this phase of studies every student had to pass a rigorous written and oral examination called the *Matura* before he could enter any faculty of the University.

Freud mentioned in his autobiography (1925b) that in the early years of his gymnasium studies, under the influence of an older friend,[13]

---

12 We shall see that Freud used this same quotation (with the same error) in some of his letters.

Footnote added by Strachey: " 'Thou owest Nature a death.' Evidently a reminiscence of Prince Hal's remark to Falstaff in *Henry IV*, v. 1: 'Thou owest God a death' " (p. 205n.).

13 Viktor Adler, who later became the leader of the Social-Democratic party in Austria.

he had thought of studying law and engaging in social activities. He attributed to the influence of Darwin's works and to Goethe's "Essay on Nature" the fact that he entered medical school instead.

His course as a medical student did not follow the usual routine. While still in the first year, he took a course on Biology and Darwinism given by the zoologist, Carl Claus, a follower of Haeckel, one of the first and most enthusiastic adherents of Darwin's doctrine of evolution. It was Haeckel who formulated the fundamental biogenetic law that "ontogeny recapitulates phylogeny"—a concept which later played a great role in Freud's genetic thinking.

It took Freud 8 years, instead of the usual 5 to 5½, to complete his medical studies, because he began to do research while he was still a student, first at Claus's Institute for Comparative Anatomy and then from 1876 on at the Physiological Institute directed by Brücke. It was at Claus's Institute that Freud wrote his first papers (see Bernfeld, 1949), and at the Physiological Institute that he established important relationships with Brücke and his associate, Fleischl. It was there, too, that he met Josef Breuer.

In this work at Brücke's Institute, Freud came quite close to the discovery that the neurone (the unit comprising the nerve cell and the fiber emerging from it) was the anatomical and functional unit of the nervous system, a discovery which later gained Waldeyer world fame.

Freud received his M.D. degree on March 31, 1881, but remained at Brücke's Institute for another year. Eventually, he had to leave the Institute for the simple reason that there was no future for a young physician who had no private funds and who, moreover, was a Jew. An academic career was hopeless for the same reasons. Brücke confronted him quite frankly with these facts. Thus he would have had to leave the haven of the Institute where he felt very much at home, even if he had not fallen in love with young Martha Bernays and become engaged on June 17, 1882.

Freud's engagement and Brücke's confrontation forced Freud at that point to make other plans for his future. He started on what would now be called a rotating internship at the Allgemeines Krankenhaus, and on January 1, 1884 became the equivalent of a resident in the Department of Neurology. At the same time he worked in the laboratory of Meynert, the renowned neurologist. His goal was now to become a *Privatdozent* (Lecturer) in neuropathology, and to establish a private practice.

The title of Lecturer meant a great deal in Vienna. It established one as a specialist and consultant entitled to higher fees. Freud achieved this goal in 1885 and in the same year received a stipend to spend 6 months in Paris at the famous Saltpêtrière, the hospital headed by Charcot, the most famous European neuropsychiatrist at that time.

Some of the papers which Freud wrote during this period revealed a sharp mind, a faculty for seeing wider implications in a simple detail, and a thoroughness and tenacity. Freud was also engaged in a scientific venture which was far afield from his main area of interest. This was an investigation into the pharmacological properties of cocaine.

He soon discovered its analgesic potentiality, its capacity to influence the general mood, and its anesthetic qualities. The first two properties interested him more than the last. He had high hopes that it might prove to be applicable to a wide-ranging number of complaints such as gastric upset; seasickness; "neurasthenia," a frequently diagnosed condition at that time, involving such symptoms as lassitude, fatigue, and mild depression; trigeminal (facial) neuralgia; sciatica, etc. Freud also hoped that it might have an effect on morphine addiction, and tried it out on his admired friend, Fleischl, the aforementioned associate of Brücke. Freud did not yet know that cocaine too could be addictive, with even more dangerous consequences than morphine addiction.

Not being interested himself in the anesthetic qualities of cocaine, Freud spoke about the drug to two ophthalmologist friends, Königstein and Koller. The latter was the first to use it and thus became the "father" of local anesthesia.

Freud was subsequently bitterly attacked for having introduced a dangerous drug, and for a while he stubbornly denied its addictive properties. For a few years he took it himself on occasion. Later, he used it as a local application for sinusitis. Freud rightly assumed that only a person with certain mental characteristics would develop a cocaine addiction, and these he fortunately did not have.[14]

Did Freud at this stage of his life and career show any indication of becoming within a decade a man who would change the course of human events? Did he himself feel then that his destiny was to "reach for the stars?" His scientific work did not yet show such indications,

[14] This topic will be discussed further on in connection with Freud's nicotine addiction.

but we can detect hints of this in his letters.[15] One of the letters published in the 1960 collection, written to a childhood friend when Freud was 17, just between the written and oral finals *(Matura)* of the Gymnasium, already gives evidence of Freud's faculty of introspection:

> You take my "worries about the future" too lightly. People who fear nothing but mediocrity, you say, are safe. Safe from what? . . . Surely not safe and secure from being mediocre? What does it matter whether we fear something or not? Isn't the main question whether what we fear exists? Admittedly more powerful intellects are also seized with doubts about themselves; does it therefore follow that anyone who doubts his virtues is of powerful intellect? In intellect he may be a weakling yet at the same time an honest man by education, habit, or even self-torment. I don't mean to suggest that if you find yourself in a doubtful situation, you should mercilessly dissect your feelings, but if you do you will see how little about yourself you are sure of. The magnificence of the world rests after all on this wealth of possibilities, except that it is unfortunately not a firm basis for self-knowledge [L. 1*].

The second letter tells us that even as a medical student Freud knew that he would be not only a man of the Book, but also of the pen. He sent to a friend two reprints of his first publications, writing:

> I am . . . sending you herewith my collected works, not my complete ones as I have reasons to suspect, for I am awaiting the correction of a third, and a fourth and fifth keep appearing in my prescient mind, which is startled by them like Macbeth by the ghosts of the English kings: "What! Will the line stretch out to the crack of doom?" [L. 2*].

The years from 1882-1886 were, among other things, the period of Freud's betrothal. To the dismay of the lovers, but to the delight of future biographers and critics, Freud and his beloved Martha were separated most of this time. Freud wrote to her practically every day.[16] These letters have been acclaimed as treasures of the art of letter writing, as were many other of his letters. (Freud, who did not receive many public honors during his lifetime, was awarded the Goethe

---

[15] A large selection of Freud's letters was published in 1960. Letters quoted from this collection will be identified by number, followed by an asterisk. Letters from the Fliess correspondence are identified only by number.

[16] Freud's wife, Martha, had kept all of them and took them with her when Freud, in 1938, was forced to leave Vienna. Many excerpts were published by Jones in Vol. 1 of his Freud biography and 93 letters were published in the above-mentioned collection (1960a).

prize for literature in 1930.) Some of them illustrate Freud's literary gift for bringing people to life with a few strokes. Others provide the biographer with a fascinating possibility of tracing the continuity of development, and of finding ideas which were fully formulated only decades later.

At this time Freud was mainly involved with greatest tenacity in his research. And yet he also considered the possibility of settling in a smaller city as a general practitioner in order to speed up his marriage for he was constantly faced with real want. Fortunately, he found friends who were only too glad to help him financially: Breuer, his old high school teacher of religion, Hammerschlag, and his colleagues and friends Paneth and Fleischl.

When he mentioned such plans to Martha, she urged him to wait rather than to sacrifice his career as a scientist. Such conflicts are expressed, for instance, in the following passages, written in April, 1884:

> Most certainly you can take seriously what I said, and please don't believe for a moment that I am making any sacrifices for you which you cannot think about with a free heart. Believe me, it is only natural that I should object more than you to the protracted waiting; I just stand it less well; it is a general rule that brides are happier than bridegrooms. So it is more for my own sake that I have decided on a short-term career. . . . I haven't got particularly far, and in the two years we still have to wait nothing very decisive is likely to happen. At best a slight change in my position in society. It won't cost me any effort. . . . Add to this . . . that in one field of science I am independent enough to make contributions without any further contacts or assistance, by which I mean my knowledge of the nervous system. . . . So the world will not be allowed to forget my name just yet. The trouble is I have so little ambition. I know I am someone, without having to be told so.
>
> By a German region[17] I was of course thinking of Lower Austria, Moravia or Silesia.
>
> For the time being anyhow I am still quite ready to fight and have no intention of breaking off my battle for a future in Vienna. The "struggle for existence" still means for me a struggle for existence here. This past week the chances of being a *Dozent* next winter have, I must admit, seemed very remote [L. 42*].

Such swings of mood within a single letter were quite frequent later on when Freud was struggling with the formulation of his new discoveries and mainly during his self-analysis. Freud disclaimed that he was ambitious, but did so in terms of not requiring to be told that he

---

17 Regarding the possibility of starting a practice there.

was "someone," as long as he knew this himself. True ambition to him meant to live up to his high inner standards.

A year later he had the chance to get a somewhat higher and more secure position in the hospital in which he was working; he also had an opportunity to get the stipend he had applied for to work at Charcot's clinic in Paris. This would mean foregoing the "safe" job. He wrote: "lots of people would say it is sheer folly to turn down a job I applied for a month ago. But a human being's demon is the best part of him, it is himself. One shouldn't embark on anything unless one feels whole-hearted about it" [L. 60*]. In later years he would often speak of his inner demon.

There was also illness and sorrow during this time. Freud allegedly had in 1882 a mild case of typhoid.[18] In 1884 he suffered for a few weeks from sciatica. He had been told to rest in bed for a few weeks, but he soon became tired of this and decided "not to have sciatica any more." In view of later claims that Freud was rather hypochondriacal, Freud's description of this episode is pertinent:

Her Highness the Princess deigns to look out at me from her plush as if she had guessed again what I did today. Well, I bet she hasn't guessed right. Be prepared for the most unlikely thing you ever heard. In the morning I lay there in the vilest pain and looked at myself in the mirror till I shuddered at the sight of my wild beard. My rage rose and rose until finally it boiled over. I decided not to have sciatica any more, to become human again, and to abandon the luxury of being ill. In no time I was dressed and sitting at the barber's, literally breathed a sigh of relief as I looked once more like a well-trimmed garden hedge, and as the weather was so glorious I walked for a while in the courtyard. It grew more and more easy, after a warm bath I could walk quite well, then I dashed into the laboratory, made up my mind to start work again, in the afternoon played chess in the coffeehouse, and on receiving a brief visit from Prof. Hammerschlag I decided to return it in the evening. This I did; of course they were all rather concerned and soon threw me out again, but here I am in the saddle once more, have no pains despite the long day, only feelings of fatigue which is understandable, can work again and am immensely, immensely pleased that I have recovered by my own decision. I can't really explain it to myself, but it is a fact. Not that I expect the pains and difficulties in walking to have completely disappeared by tomorrow, but if they are no worse than they were after my bold attempt today, I will be able to work and soon it will be gone for good.

[18] At that time no bacteriological and serological tests for typhoid were available and many gastrointestinal febrile diseases were diagnosed as "mild typhoid."

Goodnight, my little princess, and not another word about my sciatica . . . [L. 39*].

In April 1885, Freud allegedly[19] had a "light case of smallpox." This is how Freud described it:

Saturday, April 25, 1885

My beloved Marty:

Lustgarten, my doctor, found a way for me to write to you. This letter with the envelope will be placed for a few hours in a dry sterilizer at 120 centigrade, in which it is supposed to lose all its dangerous properties. You agree this kind of censorship will not do us any harm? . . .

I do have genuine smallpox, but not the right one, you know, not the one that you would imagine from your childhood recollection. I do not have a single pustule, perhaps five characteristic small pimples [Freud used the Viennese *Wimmerl*] and a dozen smaller nodules. No disfiguration, scars, fever, and so on. I have not even been in bed. But I am nevertheless sick, at times extraordinarily weak, my food has no taste at all, and I can read only in the morning. The afternoon becomes excruciating, because I am faint, unable to work and restless; toward the evening I feel better again . . . on the whole I am quite glad in spite of it all, in the first place because my previous exhaustion was not psychological, but the consequence of an illness, and in the second place because this wretched illness, with which as a physician I must after all come to terms, has treated me so kindly [1].

After this episode Freud had to go through some kind of quarantine. Perhaps this was the precipitating reason for his decision to "destroy" all his notes and manuscripts. Freud wrote on April 28, 1885:

This has been a bad, barren month. How glad I am it is soon coming to an end! I can do nothing all day; sometimes I browse in Russian history, and now and again I torture the two rabbits which nibble away at turnips in the little room and make a mess of the floor. One intention as a matter of fact I have almost finished carrying out, an intention which a number of as yet unborn and unfortunate people will one day resent. Since you won't guess what kind of people I am referring to, I will tell you at once: they are my biographers. I have destroyed all my notes of the past fourteen years, as well as letters, scientific excerpts, and the manuscripts of my papers. As for letters, only those from the family have been spared. Yours, my darling, were never in danger.

---

[19] Here, too, I say "allegedly." Cases of smallpox were more frequent at that time and could be diagnosed clinically without any special tests. However, it is very rare that even mild cases would not leave any scars ("pockmarks"). Freud's description could fit one of many various infections accompanied by skin lesions, or a greatly attenuated case of smallpox in a person who had been vaccinated but not at sufficient intervals to give him full protection.

. . . I couldn't have matured or died without worrying about who would get hold of those old papers. Everything, moreover, that lies beyond the great turning point in my life, beyond our love and my choice of profession, died long ago and must not be deprived of a worthy funeral. As for the biographers, let them worry, we have no desire to make it too easy for them. Each one of them will be right in his opinion of "The Development of the Hero," and I am already looking forward to seeing them go astray [L. 61*].

Does this not sound as though Freud somehow knew that some time in the future he would be the subject of many biographers? Unfortunately, Freud repeated this "auto-da-fé" ceremony several times in his life: in 1915 he burned a number of his metapsychological manuscripts, and before leaving Vienna in 1938 he destroyed a great deal of correspondence and manuscripts.

Freud also encountered death and suicide during this period and commented on it. Martha's sister Minna was engaged to a friend of Freud's, Schönberg, who contracted tuberculosis.[20] In June 1885, Freud recognized that Schönberg was incurable—tuberculosis had already affected his larynx, the beginning of the last stage. He had visited with Minna for the last time, and Martha, too, recognized that Schönberg was doomed. In his letter to Martha of June 23, 1885, Freud wrote:

I have just received your long-awaited letter with the sad, anticipated news . . . there is probably no great divergence in our views. He [Schönberg] cannot marry her now, this is clear for every possible reason; he will not be able to marry her if he dies from his illness, and he ought not to see her as someone else's wife if he remains alive. There just isn't any decision to be made, is there? It decides itself. To break off an engagement now in view of a probable event for which one can only wait—surely this isn't necessary. As for Minna herself, she won't want to do anything but stand by Schönberg, as long as there is such a person. And you wouldn't behave differently, wouldn't leave me before I died, if it looked as though I were going to die. And I certainly wouldn't give up what is most precious to me as long as I am alive . . . [L. 71*].

Several weeks later, Freud wrote:

As you have seen him [Schönberg] recently I won't describe to you what he looks like now—without blood or flesh, without voice or

---

[20] So apparently did Freud's friend and benefactor, Paneth. Tuberculosis was very frequent in Vienna. Even at the time I was a student it was called "Morbus Vindobonensis." It was *the* dreaded disease.

breath. One of his lungs is completely destroyed, and the other probably riddled with disease. I consider him a lost man; how fast or how slowly the miserable remains will take to burn themselves out, I don't know. . . .

For us in any case he is lost. His wretched soul is weary; enthusiasm for an aim, passion, the halo with which one surrounds the woman of one's choice, all these are the products of health. When the breath comes short, interest narrows, the heart abandons all desire, nothing remains but a tired, resigned philosopher . . . in need of peace. . . . He said: "You agree, don't you, with my having broken off the engagement?" . . . I suddenly realized I was wrong and that his love had died before him. What has brought him to the point of renouncing everything he has clung to for so long—work and position, independence from his brother, and his own willfulness—I don't know. Is this the end of a long, hard struggle or a symptom of the psyche going to sleep? [L. 78*].

Schönberg then passed through a short period of euphoria, which occasionally occurs in the terminal phase of tuberculosis. He spoke about his hope that Minna would be able to forget him, explaining, "Don't you think that the psychic burden of such a relationship is too great for me? My egotism is beginning to assert itself. All I really want is to keep going for a few years." Freud commented:

The final prognosis of his condition remains the same, in spite of the present improvement.

In the evening I kept thinking that if serious illness made it impossible for us to marry, we two would behave differently. I have been looking upon you for a long time as my own, and I would never set you free; I would accept the fact that you suffered with and about me, and I doubt that you, my little woman, would do otherwise. A human being is so miserable when all he wants is to stay alive [L. 80*].

After Schönberg's death early in 1886, Freud wrote to Minna:

Your sad romance has come to an end, and when I think it over carefully I can only consider it fortunate that the news of Schönberg's death should reach you after such a long time of estrangement and cooling off. . . . In my opinion the most terrible aspect of this disease is that it destroys a human being before it makes him suffer. Can you visualise the change he must have undergone before he could misunderstand his condition as much as he did during his last months? Everyone suffering from this disease lives in the certain hope of recovering in the immediate future. Whenever a patient in the hospital asked to be discharged because he was feeling so well, we knew that he would be dead within twenty-four hours. Nature isn't always so charitable toward her victims. . . . [L. 95*].

Nature was not so "charitable" to Freud when his time came, but then he would not have wanted this charity any longer.

While, on the one hand, in these letters we recognize the Freud of later years, on the other some letters reveal pervasive feelings of insecurity. Freud described how he gained Charcot's attention by showing his familiarity with the latter's publications. Charcot then asked one of his assistants to study a case together with Freud. Freud continues:

> . . . since then the assistant's behavior toward me has changed. . . . After we had decided to postpone the final observation till 4 P.M., the assistant invited me (!!) to lunch with him and the other hospital doctors in the Salles des Internes—as their guest, of course. And all this in response to one nod from the Master! But how hard this little victory has been for me, and how easy for Ricchetti! I consider it a great misfortune that nature has not granted me that indefinite something which attracts people. I believe it is this lack more than any other which has deprived me of a rosy existence. It has taken me so long to win my friends, I have had to struggle so long for my precious girl, and every time I meet someone I realize that an impulse, which defies analysis, leads that person to underestimate me. This may be a question of expression or temperament, or some other secret of nature, but whatever it may be it affects one deeply. What compensates me for all this is the devotion shown to me by all those who have become my friends [L. 93*].

Martha must have protested against his low self-esteem and Freud answered with a much more intimate analysis of his personality:

> You write so charmingly and sensibly and every time you speak your mind about something I feel soothed. I don't know how to thank you. . . .
> . . . I will go on writing and comment on your criticism of my wretched self. Do you realize how strangely a human being is constructed, that his virtues are often the seed of his downfall and his faults the source of his happiness? . . . But if today were to be my last on earth and someone asked me how I had fared, he would be told by me that in spite of everything—poverty, long struggle for success, little favor among men, oversensitiveness, nervousness, and worries—I have nevertheless been happy simply because of the anticipation of one day having you to myself and of the certainty that you love me. I have always been frank with you, haven't I? I haven't even made use of the license usually granted to a person of the other sex—of showing you my best side. . . .
> Do you really find my appearance so attractive? Well, this I very much doubt. I believe people see something alien in me and the real

reason for this is that in my youth, I was never young and now that I am entering the age of maturity I cannot mature properly. There was a time when I was all ambition and eager to learn, when day after day I felt aggrieved that nature had not, in one of her benevolent moods, stamped my face with that mark of genius which now and again she bestows on men. Now for a long time I have known that I am not a genius and cannot understand how I ever could have wanted to be one. I am not even very gifted; my whole capacity for work probably springs from my character and from the absence of outstanding intellectual weaknesses. But I know that this combination is very conducive to slow success, and that given favorable conditions I could . . . possibly reach the level of Charcot. By which I don't mean to say that I will get as far as that, for these favorable conditions no longer come my way, and I don't possess the genius, the power, to bring them about. Oh, how I run on! I really wanted to say something quite different. I wanted to explain the reason for my inaccessibility to and gruffness with strangers, which you mentioned. It is simply the result of suspicion due to my having learned that common or bad people treat me badly, but this is bound to disappear to the extent to which I grow stronger and more independent, and don't have to fear them any more. I always comfort myself with the fact that people subordinate to or on a par with me have never considered me unpleasant, only superiors or people otherwise above me. One would hardly guess it from looking at me, and yet even at school I was always the bold oppositionist, always on hand when an extreme had to be defended and usually ready to atone for it. As I moved up into the favored position of head boy, where I remained for years and was generally trusted, people no longer had any reason to complain about me. You know what Breuer told me one evening? I was so moved by what he said that in return I disclosed to him the secret of our engagement. He told me he had discovered that hidden under the surface of timidity there lay in me an extremely daring and fearless human being. I had always thought so, but never dared tell anyone. I have often felt as though I had inherited all the defiance and all the passions with which our ancestors defended their Temple and could gladly sacrifice my life for one great moment in history. And at the same time I always felt so helpless and incapable of expressing these ardent passions even by a word or a poem. So I have always restrained myself, and it is this, I think, which people must see in me [L. 94*].

Freud always claimed that he owed his success to his tenacity and his intellectual and moral courage which prevented him from retreating from any obstacle.

In a letter written to Fliess Freud referred to himself as having the temperament of a "conquistador" with the necessary curiosity, audacity, and tenacity (see Chapter 6).

That Freud at that time would think of himself as lacking the qualities of attracting people might seem surprising. It is even more surprising that he expressed similar feelings much later. In a letter written to Jung in 1907 he said: "I have invariably found that something in my personality, my words and ideas strike people as alien, whereas to you all hearts are open" (L. 126*). It was not success but the unrelenting process of self-analysis which freed Freud from such feelings of insecurity.

One more letter must be mentioned. In 1883 a colleague of Freud's committed suicide a month after his wedding. Freud described the incident to Martha at length. He summed up his evaluation by saying that this "madly vain man . . . died from the sum total of his qualities, his pathological self-love coupled with the claims he made for the higher things of life" (L. 22*). I quote this letter because of the opinion voiced by some long after Freud's death that he could have contemplated suicide when he was stricken by cancer.

Freud married in September, 1886, and with this event started a new chapter in his life. What followed was a relatively long period of consolidation and gradual germination of ideas. Freud himself described this transitional state in two of his autobiographical studies (1914a, 1925b) and Jones (Vol. 1, pp. 221-251) has discussed it extensively. I shall therefore mention only the main factors that were active during this period.

Foremost in importance was the influence of Josef Breuer who conducted, between 1880 and 1882, what can be called the first systematic psychotherapy of a case of severe hysteria. (This patient would probably now be diagnosed as a "borderline case.") Jones stated that Freud certainly overestimated Breuer's significance for his work.

We do not know whether Freud had really *overestimated* Breuer's significance, but perhaps out of his deep sense of fairness he may have *overstated* it. Probably, Jones underestimated Breuer's contribution. It was Breuer who conveyed to Freud the concept of psychic determinism in the etiology of hysteria, and also the fact that the precipitating trauma was unconscious. Breuer told Freud a great deal about the case, and let him read his extensive notes. That the psychological revolution developed from this seed is, of course, due to Freud's genius and his indomitable courage and determination.

From Charcot Freud learned that hysteria had to be taken seriously, that it was something quite different from malingering, and that its symptoms could be reproduced in hypnosis. He also learned that there was nothing disreputable about studying hypnosis seriously. It was a sign of his stubborn determination, and perhaps also of his protest against the entrenched authority of the medical "establishment" in Vienna and Germany, that he went, in 1889, to Strasbourg and spent several weeks studying hypnotism with Bernheim—a decision which at that time, when Freud was just starting to make ends meet, was a serious financial sacrifice. There he not only improved his technique of hypnotism, but also "received the profoundest impression of the possibility that there could be powerful mental processes which nevertheless remained hidden from the consciousness of men" (1925b, p. 17). Freud at first practiced hypnotic suggestion, but soon followed Breuer's example and induced his patients to speak about their past in the hypnotic trance.

He patiently gathered material while publishing during this period his translation of the works of Bernheim (1888-1889 and 1892); his important monograph *On Aphasia* (1891), which was fully appreciated only much later; and finally a monograph on cerebral palsey in children, written with O. Rie (1891). Only after he had gathered sufficient clinical material did he approach Breuer and persuade him to collaborate on the joint publication of the *Studies on Hysteria* (1893-1895).

Psychoanalysis as a science was initiated with this book. As a technique of treatment it began when Freud abandoned hypnosis and introduced free association. The next eight years were to be times of dramatic progress achieved not without agonizing doubts.

2

FREUD'S CARDIAC EPISODE: THE BATTLE AGAINST NICOTINE ADDICTION

One of the aims of this study is to trace the gradual development of different responses used by Freud to prevent situations of great stress and danger from becoming traumatic and to discover the ways which Freud utilized to achieve mastery without resorting to denial.

In my Introduction I referred to Freud's correspondence with Fliess and emphasized its importance for our understanding of the development of psychoanalysis as a science and of Freud as a person. I have also stressed the special importance of Freud's self-analysis during the years from 1892 to 1902.

Freud's relationship to Fliess, as it is reflected in this correspondence, was a very complex and intense one and played a great role in Freud's self-analysis; and we can consider that Freud's most intimate exchange of letters with Fliess during this period came often very close to the free association in an analytic session.[1]

The development of any relationship has many variables: we have learned from Freud that it has genetic roots in early childhood and that early childhood experiences leave their imprint on all later friendships. Human relationships also depend on the life situation that exists

[1] Compare Freud's letter of January 10, 1937 to Marie Bonaparte concerning the preservation of the Fliess correspondence (Schur, 1965).

when the two people meet and, of course, on the specific character-istics of the persons.[2]

However, one additional factor gave a certain direction to his rela-tionship with Fliess. During a period of serious physical illness when Freud was justified in his doubt about its outcome, Fliess became his trusted physician. This period of serious physical illness is of course especially relevant to my main topic.[3]

In many of his letters to Fliess Freud spoke of many physical symp-toms: headaches, which he described as "migraine attacks" (an afflic-tion which he had in common with Fliess); nasal symptoms, which may or may not have been due to a chronic sinus infection; some rather vague gastrointestinal symptoms. However, the most important by far were his cardiac symptoms. I found Freud's first allusion to his cardiac symptoms in an unpublished letter dated October 18, 1893, which indicates that he must have discussed these with Fliess during one of their recent meetings. This and later letters make it obvious that Fliess initially either attributed Freud's symptoms mainly to his smoking, or at least felt that they were greatly exacerbated by nicotine. Whatever his reasoning, Fliess apparently insisted quite firmly that Freud give up smoking. This started an endless series of attempts to abstain from nicotine. As we shall see, these attempts were nearly always determined by the frequency or intensity of his cardiac symp-toms. Freud wrote:

> I would have a lot to write about the nose and sexuality (two topics). However, that you do not see much of that sort does indicate a prior selection of material. There is at present not a great rush [in my prac-tice], yet I have the most beautiful cases and I have even gone a step further. Next time I am going to send you an observation of migraine with scotoma in onanists, unfortunately *without* any nasal findings. . . .
>
> I have no intention of running out on you with my heart condition. At the moment it is much better, though not through any merit of mine since I am smoking wickedly owing to all the excitement which was plentiful in these last days.[4] I believe it [the heart condition] will flare up again badly in the near future. As far as smoking is concerned, I

[2] Most of these factors were discussed with great perspicacity by Ernst Kris in his Introduction to the Fliess correspondence (1950) and by Jones in his biography of Freud.

[3] Kris, whose Introduction to the Fliess correspondence was mainly concerned with the scientific background of this relationship, did not discuss this aspect, and Jones, who discussed this illness, did so largely as a manifestation of Freud's neurosis.

[4] There is no reference in other letters of the same month to the source of this excitement, except for certain hints about Freud's difficulties with Breuer.

shall follow your prescription painstakingly [literally: "painfully"] as I did once before when you expressed an opinion on the subject (while we were waiting at the railway station). Obviously I have missed it badly. A severe [crossed out] acute cold has not made things any worse [1].

These few sentences tell a great deal about Freud's attitudes toward Fliess and toward smoking: he promised not to smoke but used the word *peinlich* with its double meaning of "painstakingly" and "painfully." He promised not to "run out" on Fliess, but at the same time threatened an imminent worsening of the heart condition (an expectation which was to be fulfilled). This may have been a thought of dying, but also of disobeying Fliess and refusing to accept the latter's belief in the connection between the cardiac symptoms and the smoking. Indeed, Freud indicated that he felt better *in spite of* his intensive smoking. Such ambivalence obviously had many determinants.

The theme of smoking reappeared in the next letter (November 17, 1893). This time a new motif was added, which came up again and again when the question whether to smoke or not was no longer an academic one. It expressed a certain mood but also a most painful conflict.

I am not obeying your smoking prohibitions; do you really consider it such a great boon to live a great many years in misery? [2]

This theme reappeared in a somewhat different context a few months later when Freud wrote on February 7, 1894 (L. 16):

Billroth's[5] death is the event of the day here. It is an enviable thing not to survive oneself.[6]

Freud's prediction that the cardiac symptoms would return with greater intensity proved to be accurate. On April 19, 1894 (L. 17) he wrote:

After your kind letter I shall not hold back and spare you any longer, and I feel that I have a right to write you about my health. Scientific and personal matters will come at the end.

As everyone must come under the influence of someone else's sug-

[5] Theodor Billroth, a famous surgeon and fine musician; one of the most intimate friends of Brahms. Freud admired him for his many-sided talents and interests.

[6] Freud was to express the same thought sixteen years later, somewhat misquoting Macbeth: "Let us die in harness."

gestions in order to escape his own criticism, from that time on (three weeks ago today) I have had nothing lit between my lips and now can actually watch others smoking without envying them and conceive of living and working without it. I have just reached this point, and the misery connected with abstinence has been unexpectedly great, but that is really obvious.

What is perhaps less obvious is my state of health in other respects. For a few days after depriving myself I felt moderately well and began to write down for you my present position on the question of neurosis. Then suddenly there came a severe cardiac oppression [*Herzelend,* literally: "cardiac misery"], greater than I had before giving up smoking. I had violent arrhythmia, with constant tension, pressure, and burning in the heart region, burning pains down the left arm, some dyspnea— suspiciously moderate, as though organic—all occurring in attacks lasting continuously for two thirds of the day, accompanied by depression which took the form of visions of death and departure in place of the normal frenzy of activity. The organic discomforts have lessened during the past two days, but the hypomanic mood persists, having the courtesy, though, to let up suddenly (as it did last evening and at noon today), leaving behind a human being who looks forward confidently again to a long life and undiminished pleasure in smoking.

It is painful for a medical man, who spends every hour of the day struggling to achieve an understanding of the neuroses, not to know whether he himself is suffering from a reasonable or a hypochondriacal depression. In such a situation one needs help. So last evening I went to see Breuer and told him my opinion that the heart trouble was not due to nicotine poisoning, but that I had a chronic myocarditis which could not tolerate smoking. I remember that arrhythmia occurred quite suddenly in 1889 after my attack of influenza. I had the satisfaction of being told that it might be one or the other of these things, and that I should have myself examined. I promised to do so, but I know that these examinations generally do not turn up anything. I do not know how far it is possible to differentiate between the two things, but I think that it should be possible to do so on the basis of subjective symptoms and events, and that you people know what to make of it all. I am suspicious of you this time because this heart trouble of mine is the first situation in which I have ever heard you contradict yourself. Last time you explained it as being nasal, saying that the percussive signs of a nicotine heart were missing; this time you show great concern over me and forbid me to smoke. I can explain this inconsistency only by assuming that you wish to conceal the true state of affairs from me, and I appeal to you not to do so. If you can tell me anything definite, please do. I have no exaggerated opinion either of my responsibilities or of my indispensability, and should endure with dignity the uncertainty and shortened life expectancy connected with a diagnosis of myocarditis. I might even benefit from it in making arrangements for the remainder of my life and enjoying fully what was left for me. . . .

There is hardly a sentence in this letter which is not pertinent to my topic. It shows one of Freud's typical attitudes: that only under special circumstances would he "impose" upon someone else with personal complaints, and he had to apologize for such an imposition and for the fact that scientific topics were made to wait until the end of the letter. It expresses the thought that self-criticism, or rather self-evaluation, must yield occasionally to "suggestion," and it refers to the struggle with his addiction, to submitting to Fliess's injunctions, but without inner conviction. In it Freud also describes most vividly both his attacks of cardiac distress and his reaction to them, stating that this time his "cardiac misery" had been much worse than ever as a result of smoking.

Freud clearly suffered from repeated attacks of tachycardia with "most violent" *(tollster)* arrhythmia *(delirium cordis),* chest pain irradiating into the left arm, and dyspnea. These attacks were intense and frequent, and persisted for a number of days at a time. Without discussing, for the moment, the etiological possibilities, we may assume from Freud's description that he was suffering from attacks of paroxysmal tachycardia, probably with auricular fibrillation, and such signs of "coronary insufficiency" as anginal pain and dyspnea.

Freud's *reactions* to these attacks were manifold. He himself describes his depressive moods accompanied by visions *("Malereien")* of death and leave-taking.

But we can detect in the same paragraph of the April 19 letter certain other—not conscious—manifestations of Freud's reactions. Anyone who is acquainted with Freud's mastery and elegance in the use of the German language cannot fail to recognize that the sentence in which he describes his symptoms contains distorted or at least quite uncommon versions of several words, somewhat suggestive of neologisms, and that it reveals an awkward sentence structure. Because these changes cannot be detected in the English translation, I shall quote this sentence in German:

> Tollste Arrhythmie, beständige Herzspannung—*Pressung—Brennung,* heisses Laufen in den linken Arm, etwas Dyspnoe von verdächtig *organischer Mässigung,* das alles eigentlich in Anfällen, d.h. über 2/3 des Tages in continuo erstreckt und dabei ein Druck auf die Stimmung, der sich in Ersatz der gangbaren Beschäftigungsdelirien durch Todten- und Abschiedsmalereien äusserte [italics added].

The words *Pressung* and *Brennung* actually do not exist. The meaning of the first word is obviously "pressure" (in German, *Druck* or *Beklemmung*) and perhaps Freud intended to use the somewhat unusual noun version of the verb *pressen* (to press, oppress, strain). He used this word only on one other occasion in a letter which also dealt with his symptoms.

As for *Brennung*, what is meant is *Brennen* (burning sensation); *"heisses Laufen in den linken Arm"* would have to be translated literally as "hot flow into the left arm," i.e., pains down the left arm (this is the translation used in the English edition) or "intense (hot, burning) irradiation into the left arm."

The phrase (translated literally) "some dyspnea of suspiciously organic moderation," is not clear either. There seems to be no reason why a *moderate* dyspnea should indicate an organic cause.

The phrase *"über 2/3 des Tages in continuo erstreckt"* is part of the clumsy sentence structure referred to above, which has been incorrectly translated in the published English version as "occurring in two or three attacks lasting continuously throughout part of the day."

Such a distorted sentence from a writer of Freud's caliber, can be understood only as a manifestation of intense stress in a situation which, in Freud's own terminology (1926a), would be termed "traumatic."

Of further evidence is the fact that this paragraph contains several meaningful parapraxes (a very rare occurrence in Freud's letters or handwritten manuscripts). After having vividly described his suffering and the depressive—perhaps even desperate—"visions of death and leave-taking," Freud wrote: "The hypomanic mood persists, having courtesy though, to let up suddenly. . . ." By turning "depressive" into its opposite "hypomanic," Freud was using denial.[7] However, in addition to the denial of the depressive mood, this parapraxis also expresses the anticipation of the lifting of the depression—and thus the resumption of smoking ("leaving behind a human being who looks forward confidently again to a long life and undiminished pleasure in smoking"): The denial, therefore, had a certain adaptive quality.[8]

[7] A mechanism which, much later, was described as characteristic of "hypomania" (Lewin, 1932, 1950; H. Deutsch, 1933).

[8] It is also quite striking that this sentence containing the parapraxis which *anticipates* the hypomanic reaction is again written in Freud's masterful German, in marked contrast to the garbled sentence describing the traumatic situation. That this adaptive regaining of mastery required both denial and a parapraxis is an indication of the depth of the conflict. Nearly 45 years later Freud was to express a last desperate attempt at denial in another parapraxis (see letter to Arnold Zweig of March 5, 1939).

Another parapraxis can be found at the end of this paragraph.[9] Freud obviously intended to say (as does the translation) that he looked forward to a long life and undiminished pleasure in smoking *(Rauchlust)*. However, what Freud actually wrote was *"Rauflust"*— "pugnacity"! The meaning of this parapraxis is not hard to understand. With the lifting of the depression, Freud was no longer dejected and was now ready to *fight* for his right to smoke (as evidenced by the rest of the letter)!

This paragraph, then, gives us in a condensed fashion a description of Freud's illness, his response to a traumatic situation, and his mode of mastering that situation. That is why it has been subjected to what might seem like a Talmudic exegesis, although close attention to details is really in the psychoanalytic tradition.[10]

The next paragraph already shows us the trend of this development. Freud wanted to know the truth—chiefly whether his depression *("Verstimmung"),* and his fears, we might add—were a response to an organic illness or a sign of "hypochondriasis." He wanted to know whether he was suffering from nicotine toxicity or a chronic myocarditis which could not tolerate nicotine. This was on the one hand a fine diagnostic distinction and on the other an admission of the painful recognition that smoking was plainly not good for his heart.

Not convinced that Breuer (the "X" of the published letters) would tell him the truth, and fearing that even Fliess wanted to hide the diagnosis from him, Freud appealed to the latter to be honest with him.[11] In his state of uncertainty he searched for diagnostic clues of his own, remembering attacks of arrhythmia after a bout of influenza in 1889, which may be important for our reconstruction of the diagnostic possibilities.

We frequently hear assertions from patients that they can accept with full dignity the knowledge of serious and even fatal illness, but find that they actually do *not* wish to know the truth, and may even

---

[9] It is noteworthy that despite the legibility of this handwritten letter, the typed transcript and the published German text contain some misleading errors in this paragraph (for example: "über zwei zu drei des Tages" instead of "2/3 des Tages") as well as at the end of the third paragraph (where a parapraxis was "corrected"), whereas other letters much more difficult to decipher were faithfully reproduced.

[10] See K. R. Eissler's (1959) excellent discussion of the function of details in the interpretation of works of literature.

[11] The tragic events of the year 1923 (see Chapter 13) were to confirm Freud's uneasiness about this lack of truthfulness. See also L. 104, written to Fliess on February 6, 1899.

break down under its impact. Freud, however, meant what he said, as he was subsequently to prove.

Thus we see in this letter the entire conflict at work. One part of Freud still had to practice denial. But the supremacy of the ego—Freud's goal in life and also the principal goal of therapy—was beginning to assert itself.[12]

How fully Freud was able to regain his composure during the writing of this letter is evidenced by the light, witty, even slightly flippant tone of some unpublished passages:

> I shall bear your remark about the diary[13] in mind. You are right.
> I too didn't much like Frau Dr. Fr. Perhaps I am doing her an injustice when I classify her as meat dish: "goose"; vegetable dish: *Zwiderwurzen*.[14] I readily believe that analysis was unpleasant for her. In this way she just confirms my concept of defense. Also she ran away from me the third time. . . .
> The many new things which you announce are obviously indicative of almost uninterrupted well-being on your part. I have pondered about the etiology of your second headache. I do not really believe it. Wouldn't you rather stick to ethnoidal sinuses?[15]
> My rascals and my wife are fine. The latter is not a confidante of my death deliria. Probably superfluous from every point of view [3].[16]

Thus, the entire letter is very much like a transcript of an analytic session during which the productions of the analysand run the whole

---

12 Here Freud was already giving utterance to thoughts similar to those he expressed so beautifully twenty years later in his paper on "Transience" (1916a): "Transience value is scarcity value" (see Chapter 11).

13 Fliess had apparently advised Freud to keep a diary of his symptoms.

14 An untranslatable Viennese slang word meaning an obnoxious person. Only the ending "-*wurzen*," reminiscent of *Wurzel* (root) permits the jocular association to a vegetable.

15 This is an allusion to Fliess's very frequent bouts of headache which he attributed to nasal pathology, and later also to the "laws of periodicity." Fliess underwent a series of extensive surgical interventions within the next few years. As we shall see, these repeated "attacks" were the subject of many letters. They placed a great strain on Freud's unfolding relationship of perfect trust, which demanded that Fliess be stable, strong, and hale. The fact that Freud at this point could reciprocate Fliess's advice with some of his own also indicates that he had overcome the traumatic situation.

16 This last sentence already gives evidence of the attitude which Freud was to adopt during his fight against cancer many years later. He did not want to be a burden to those around him by making them aware of his suffering (see letter to Eitingon of April 1, 1925, quoted in Chapter 15). The words "from every point of view" clearly meant: "If my worry is unfounded, why let my wife participate in it? If I really am suffering from a fatal illness, why cause her anguish years ahead of time?"

gamut of emotions and express various ego states. This was to be the characteristic tone of much of Freud's correspondence with Fliess.

This letter (of April 19, 1894) also indicated the vexing problem which subsequently ran like a red thread through the course of Freud's life and was reflected in a good deal of his correspondence—his nicotine addiction. Although the "traumatic situation" had been mastered, Freud's cardiac symptoms, his doubts about the diagnosis, and his conflict about nicotine remained the leitmotif of his correspondence with Fliess for many years.

Fliess must have stuck to his belief that nicotine was the chief culprit and not a myocarditis, for Freud wrote:

My dear Friend,

You have written so charmingly that I cannot let you wait until I have something to say,[17] but must send you a note about everyday events.

I certainly consider you more competent than anyone else to make the differential diagnosis of these ticklish problems, and I am once again at a loss what to make of my condition. Breuer quietly accepted the possibility of a nontoxic heart condition.[18] Apparently I do not have a dilation [of the heart], [but] split heart sounds [an important sign of an "organic" lesion], arrhythmia, etc., continue despite my abstinence.[19] The libido has long since been subdued. One gram of digitalis every two days[20] has considerably diminished the subjective symptoms and presumably also influenced the arrhythmia, which however I always am aware of when I find some resonance of my pulse. My depressive mood, fatigue, inability to work, and the mild dyspnea have gotten rather worse.

That is the *"status idem."* That I do not leave this beautiful world without summoning you for a personal farewell has been settled in my mind since I began to feel ill. I do not think, however, that I shall be in a position to take you up on your offer in the near future, but the torture and the fruitless slipping away of the present hurt me more than any possible unsatisfactory prognosis.

In a few days I shall send you several pages of raw material, a quickly sketched analysis in which one can perceive the root of neurosis.

[17] This introduction is characteristic of Freud; to write only about his own person is not having "something to say" that is really worthwhile.

[18] See the preceding letter. Breuer must have examined Freud in the meantime. The fact that Freud's relationship to Breuer had by then lost its earlier intimacy (see Jones, Vol. 1, pp. 220-267) was making Freud doubly dependent on Fliess's advice and support during these months of severe strain.

[19] We can see Freud's conflict here: from a prognostic point of view Fliess's assumption about nicotine toxicity was obviously more acceptable than Breuer's tacit admission of the possibility of a myocarditis, but this would mean more abstinence!

[20] A good-sized dose.

I have not yet been able to pull myself together to make a summary[21] for you, about which I am very angry with myself. Things really used to be different. The social and scientific dead calm[22] is causing me all kinds of worries. I feel best when I am in the midst of my daily work.

I hope that you, at least, are well. I believe that for one hour during these last days I enjoyed my illness after all. That must have been when I received your letter.

I send you and your dear Ida cordial greetings in which my family also joins.

> Yours,
> Dr. Sigm. Freud [4]

Only a few days later doubt about the diagnosis returned. On May 6, 1894 (his 38th birthday) Freud wrote:

I have so far not been able to finish the outline of the neuroses. I feel better, at times even much better, but I have not been free of symptoms for as much as half a day, and my mood and ability to work are really at a low ebb. I still do not believe all this is from nicotine; having by chance seen *a good deal of this same thing in* my practice, I think it is rheumatic myocarditis, something one never really gets rid of. During the last years I have repeatedly had rheumatic muscle nodes on other parts of my body.

During the summer I would like to go back[23] to anatomy for a while; that is after all the only gratifying thing [5].

This last sentence is indicative of the interplay of the many factors that influenced Freud's mood: his illness, abstinence, isolation, the lonely struggle which had begun with his attempt to uncover the roots of neurosis, gradually leading him to the realization that what he was actually trying to do was unravel the working of the human mind. While he was at this point just putting the finishing touches on his contribution to the *Studies on Hysteria,* he was already far ahead of himself, so to speak. He was soon to recognize that each patient confronted him with new discoveries, and that these discoveries could be confirmed and understood only when he made them anew by becoming his own patient.

The struggle demanded at least a minimum of physical well-being,

[21] An allusion, perhaps, to a provisional "Summary" (see L. 18) and the manuscript D (*ibid.,* pp. 86-88).

[22] This probably refers on the one hand to the social and scientific isolation in which Freud found himself at that time, and on the other hand to the temporary interruption of his creative productivity.

[23] In the original German text Freud made a slip. He first wrote: "zur Anatomie zurückfahren," which he corrected to "zurückkehren."

and apart from his cardiac symptoms the abstinence from nicotine was depriving him of the one external stimulant that remained essential to him throughout his life.

It is not surprising, then, that Freud should express, at least in a letter, his longing to return to the safe haven of anatomy, to the laboratory, the microscope, and that he should have needed so badly at least one sounding board, especially on his birthday. This aspect of his utter loneliness is reflected in the next letter, part of which has already been published (L. 18, May 21, 1894). From the unpublished part I shall quote only a few paragraphs.

> Dearest Friend,
> Dearest, in earnest, because I am touched that at a time when you are either very busy or not well—or perhaps both—you should so thoroughly trouble yourself with my symptoms. There was a gap in your letters which was beginning to look quite uncanny to me. . . . Then came your letter with its meticulous repudiation of my "internist-dilettante" fantasies, but without a word about your own health. I have recognized for quite some time that you tolerate suffering better and with more dignity than I, who endlessly vacillate between moods.
>
> I promise to send you shortly a detailed progress report; I am feeling better, but far from well; at least I am working again. Today I shall afford myself one good hour and chat only about science with you. It is obviously not a special favor of fate that I can have only five hours or so a year to exchange thoughts with you, when I can barely exist without the other person, and you are the only other person, the *alter*.[24]
>
> Tomorrow I shall send the hen with the five little chicks to Reichenau,[25] and during the lonely, sad time that follows . . . I shall more often carry out my resolution at least to write to you.
>
> Wasn't M. D.[26] a jewel? She will not be included in the collection [of case histories I am making] with Breuer, since the second level, that of the sexual motives, will not be disclosed there. The case history I am writing now—a cure—belongs to my most difficult pieces of work.[27] You will get it before Breuer if you mail it back quickly.
>
> Among the gloomy thoughts of the past few months there is one that is in second place, right after wife and children—namely, that I shall not be able to prove the sexual thesis any more. After all one does not want to die either immediately or completely [6].

[24] The letter indicates quite clearly that Freud was by then in a frame of mind resembling what we now call the "analytic situation," and was using Fliess as a transferencelike figure, promising himself and "the other," the *alter* ego, a "good [analytic] hour."

[25] A mountain resort 40 miles from Vienna.

[26] One of Freud's cases, with which Fliess must have been familiar.

[27] Probably the case history of Elisabeth von R., the last of Freud's clinical contributions to the *Studies on Hysteria*.

The beginning of the next paragraph gives the essence of Freud's situation.

I am pretty much alone here in the elucidation of the neuroses. They look upon me as pretty much of a monomaniac, while I have the distinct feeling that I have touched upon one of the great secrets of nature.

This was one of the rare statements (see also, for example, L. 137) in which Freud acknowledged the greatness of his discoveries. The promised "progress report" took another month to materialize. On June 22, 1894 Freud wrote Fliess.[28] He began by saying that he was going to write a long letter about "theory and life," and went on:

Today I am sending you the last case history. You will notice from my style that I have been ill. Between pages 4 and 5 is a confession of my long-concealed troubles. The material itself is obviously very instructive, [and that] was decisive for me.

I shall welcome the summer if it brings what I have been longing for for years—a few days with you without serious interference. . . . Most of the time life appears so uncertain to me that I am more inclined not to postpone long-held wishes any longer. Other trips will have to be relinquished in favor of this one because this year has been in many respects a bad one, which in addition to illness also brought financial loss. I could of course come for a few days in any event. I have given up [mountain] climbing "with a heavy heart"—how meaningful colloquial usage is! If you can accommodate me so that I do not have to travel too far and then can really be alone with you (this always includes your wife), then we shall meet this year thanks to my dislike of any further delay.[29]

Now follows my case history, the unvarnished truth, with all the details that seem important to a wretched patient and yet probably do not deserve it.

I have not smoked for seven weeks, since the day of your injunction. At first I felt, as expected, impossibly [literally: prohibitively] bad—cardiac symptoms with depression plus the horrible misery of abstinence. The latter wore off after approximately 3 weeks, the former improved after about 6 weeks, but I remained completely incapable of working,[30] a beaten man. After 7 weeks, contrary to my promise to you, I began smoking again, influenced by the following factors:

1) During this time I saw patients of the same age with nearly identical conditions, who either had not smoked at all (two women) or

28 Only the first two and the last paragraphs of this letter were included in the published version.
29 The meeting took place in mid-August of 1894.
30 This is in contradiction to the report Freud gave of his activities in the previous letters.

had given up smoking. Breuer, to whom I repeatedly said that I did not attribute my condition to nicotine poisoning, finally agreed and also referred to the women. Thus I was deprived of the motivation which you so aptly characterized in one of your previous letters: a person can give up something only if he is firmly convinced that it is the cause of his illness.

2) Since the first few cigars I was able to work and was the master of my mood; before that life was unbearable.[31] Nor have I noticed that the symptoms got any worse after one cigar.

I am now smoking moderately, having gradually increased to 3 *pro die*,[32] I feel much better than before, actually progressively better, but of course not yet well. I shall describe the condition:

Some arrhythmia always seems to be present, but increases to a delirium cordis[33] with oppression, occurs only with attacks, lasting now less than an hour, almost regularly after lunch.[34] The moderate dyspnea during stair-climbing is gone; the left arm has been free of pain for weeks; the chest wall is still quite tender; [an illegible word], the feeling of oppression, and the burning sensation have not let up for a single day. No objective evidence can apparently be found, but then I do not really know. Sleep and all other functions have not been disturbed. I am in good control of my moods, on the other hand I feel aged, sluggish, not healthy. Digitalis has helped me tremendously.[35]

What tortures me is the uncertainty as to how to evaluate the whole story. It would embarrass me to reveal a hypochondriacal evaluation, but I have no criteria by which to decide this. I am very dissatisfied with the way I am being treated here. Breuer is full of apparent contradictions. When I say that I am feeling better, the answer is: "You don't know *how* glad I am to hear that." This would point to a serious condition. If another time I ask what it actually is, I get the answer: "Nothing; in any event something that is already over." Moreover, he does not pay any attention to me at all, does not see me for 2 weeks at a stretch. I do not know whether this is policy, genuine indifference, or fully justified. On the whole I notice that I am being treated evasively and dishonestly as a patient instead of having my mind set at rest by being told everything there is to tell in a situation of this kind, namely, whatever is known.

It would be a tremendous relief if I had been able to share your opinion or to share it now; even a new weaning period [from smoking]

---

[31] Note the contradiction to the preceding paragraph where Freud claimed that he had overcome the misery of abstinence after three weeks, but had remained incapable of working.

[32] The common Latin phrase used on prescriptions, like "t.i.d."

[33] The Latin term used then for what corresponded to a paroxysmal tachycardia with auricular fibrillation.

[34] This was the main meal of the day in Vienna. Postprandial "oppression" is a common sign of anginal syndrome.

[35] The diagnostic importance of this remark will be discussed at the end of this Chapter.

would be less difficult now, but this seems to me like a *sacrificio d'intelletto*. For the first time I have an opinion that differs from yours on some matter. This is easier for me with Breuer; he does not voice any opinion.

The example of Kundt frightened me less, since anyone who could guarantee me the 13 years until my 51st birthday would not have spoiled my pleasure in cigars.[36] My compromise opinion, for which I have no scientific basis, is that I shall suffer for about 4 to 5 to eight years from various complaints, have good and bad periods, and then between 40 and 50 shall perish nicely and suddenly from a rupture of the heart; if it is not too close to 40, it is not so bad at all.

I would be immensely indebted to you, though, if you gave me definite information, since I secretly believe that you know very well what it [the illness] is, and that you have been so absolute and strict in your smoking prohibition, the merit of which is after all relative, only because of its educational and soothing effect.

Well, now, enough of this; it is very sad to have to be so preoccupied with oneself when there are so many more interesting things to write about.

I read between the lines of your letter that you are not very happy about your headaches, and I am angry at our ignorance. You write nothing about your work; evidently it appears to you that I have no interest in it. I beg you to take it for granted that it is just that I have no opinion about these matters, which certainly are based on facts [7].

The last paragraph of the published portion of this letter is pertinent in the whole context:

Actually, I spend the whole day thinking only about the neuroses, but since the scientific contact with Breuer came to an end I have been thrown back completely on my own resources, which is why progress is so slow.

Fliess obviously responded to this letter with a "command" for further abstinence from nicotine, to which Freud replied on July 14, 1894:

---

36 This is the first mention of the number 51 as an anticipated and dreaded "deadline" of Freud's life. In this letter no allusion is made to Fliess's periodicity theory with which, however, this number was linked (the combination of the "feminine" and "masculine" periods 28 and 23). Instead, Freud referred to "the example" of the famous German physicist Kundt, the successor to Helmholtz in the chair of experimental physics at the University of Berlin, one of whose students was Brücke, Freud's former superior. Kundt had died on May 21, 1894, a few weeks before this letter was written. We may assume that Fliess had written to Freud about the event. The context of Freud's reference indicates that Fliess had probably linked Kundt's premature death to his heavy smoking.

What is strange, however, is that although Freud linked Kundt's death to the feared "deadline" of 51, Kundt was actually 54½ when he died. For a discussion of this point in a somewhat different context, see Chapter 5.

Dearest Friend,

Your praise is nectar and ambrosia to me, because I know full well how hard it is for you to bestow it—no, to be more precise, how genuinely you mean it when you do bestow it. Since then, I have, preoccupied with abstinence, produced little; another draft of the anxiety neurosis, which I gave, however, to Breuer. Miss Elisabeth von R. has meanwhile become engaged.

My condition—I now feel obliged not to arouse the suspicion that I might want to withhold something from you—is as follows: since your letter of 2 weeks ago last Thursday [June 28], abstinence which lasted eight days;[37] on the following Thursday in an indescribably bleak moment, one cigar; then again 8 days of abstinence; on the following Thursday again one cigar; since then, peace again [this letter was written on the Saturday after the last cigar]. Briefly, a pattern has established itself—one cigar a week to commemorate your letter which again deprived me of the enjoyment of tobacco. In practical terms, this may not be considerably different from abstinence. . . .

Condition is unchanged. At the end of last week I again had to resort to digitalis; the pulse was again delirious [i.e., fast and completely irregular]. . . . With digitalis it is better, but not really comfortable. Should I take digitalis frequently or rarely? I promise to obey. . . .

Your headache makes me feel helplessly[38] outraged. . . .

> With most cordial regards . . .
> Sigm. Freud [8]

This letter obviously elicited an even stronger command from Fliess to abstain from smoking, to which Freud replied in an undated letter (a rare occurrence), grudgingly accepting another, limited period of abstinence.

Dear Wilhelm,

I understand far too little about these matters to be able to evaluate so firm a rebuttal, but evidence tells me that I have enough physiological grounds to comply with your orders, so I am starting today on a second period of abstinence, which I hope will last until we meet in August.

> Cordial greetings,
> Your S. [9]

These letters marked at least temporarily the end of a crisis. Although Freud had occasional symptoms throughout 1895, an optimistic attitude was reflected in a letter written upon his return from a meeting with Fliess in August, 1894. On August 18, 1894, Freud wrote:

[37] Colloquially, eight days was frequently used for a week.
[38] *"Ohnmächtig"* has a double meaning: helpless and impotent, and fainting; in any event, a very unusual usage.

Having returned home and after getting a charming reception from the whole gang of flourishing rascals, and with the aftertaste of the beautiful days in Munich in mind—there is again a moment when one can take pleasure in life [L. 20].

and further:

From now on I shall prophesy only good things, and these will prove to be as right as did my last bad predictions [10].[39]

A longer letter written on August 23, 1894 furnished more details about the improvement in Freud's cardiac symptoms:

On the Thursday after our parting,[40] I was forced by circumstances to take a four-hour hike from Weissenbach to Ischl—night, loneliness, pouring rain, hurry—and I tolerated it very well [11].

A review of this crisis, and of Freud's response to it, is pertinent for many reasons, especially if looked at from the perspective of his evolving attitudes toward illness and death, which, when finally developed, prevailed during the last 25 years of his life.

In attempting an evaluation of the medical aspects of this episode, I am of course aware how difficult it is to arrive at a valid differential diagnosis some 75 years after the events. We can base such a diagnosis only on the following facts: (1) Freud's very detailed description of his symptoms, given in the above-quoted letters to Fliess; (2) Freud's later—rather scanty—references to these episodes made to me during the time I acted as his physician (1928-1939) and which I could subsequently compare with his descriptions in the Fliess correspondence; (3) Freud's later cardiac history; (4) Freud's reports about Breuer's findings; (5) Freud's favorable response to digitalis; and, of course, (6) our general knowledge of cardiac pathology, its etiology and symptoms.

We learn from Freud's letters that he first noticed "arrhythmia" after a febrile illness, presumably influenza, in 1889. Apparently Freud neither suffered subjectively from this nor paid undue attention

[39] This statement is actually highly ambiguous. On the one hand, Freud was alluding to his premonition about falling ill, which did prove to be correct. On the other hand, he had also prophesied that he would die within a few years from a "rupture of the heart," and this prophecy was now being annulled by happy premonitions.

[40] On his way back from the meeting with Fliess, which had taken place in Salzburg, Freud stopped to visit his parents, who were spending their vacation in Ischl. This was two years before the death of Freud's father.

to it. He just remembered it at the height of his symptoms in April, 1894.

No mention is made of cardiac symptoms until the fall of 1893. During the summer of 1891 Freud had climbed the Dachstein (nearly 10,000 feet high, requiring combined ice and rock climbing and hence complete fitness on the part of the climber). Some time before October 18, 1893 Freud must have developed cardiac symptoms and been advised by Fliess to give up his heavy cigar smoking. This letter tells us nothing about the nature of Freud's symptoms, but we get the first insight into Freud's battle against his nicotine addiction. His ambivalence regarding the prohibition against smoking is clear.

In the spring of 1894 the cardiac symptoms became acute. Freud's letters dated April 19 and 25, May 6, and June 22, 1894 tell us much more than was heretofore known about the nature of his symptoms. For weeks he had apparently had frequent daily attacks of severe arrhythmia and tachycardia ("delirium cordis") with anginal pain and dyspnea, which greatly limited his physical activity. We may assume from Freud's description that during the most severe attacks Freud had paroxysmal tachycardia, probably with auricular fibrillation.

Freud, Breuer, and Fliess saw two main possibilities: a "chronic myocarditis" and a nicotine toxicity or hypersensitivity. Breuer, an excellent, experienced clinician, probably leaned toward the first hypothesis; Fliess persistently blamed the nicotine. Freud himself—as we have seen from his letters—was alternately inclined to agree with each of them. Subjective reasons made it extremely difficult for him to arrive at an objective evaluation: to agree with Fliess meant a much more favorable prognosis, but necessitated abstinence, with all the misery that it entailed. Acceptance of what he assumed was Breuer's diagnosis—an organic illness—made the prognosis rather unfavorable. As far as abstinence was concerned, Freud knew and indicated in his letters that even with myocarditis heavy smoking *might* be a contributory factor, but complete abstinence would seem less essential, especially in the light of the possible rationalization: If one is suffering from an incurable disease, why shouldn't one enjoy life as long as it lasts?

There are further diagnostic possibilities to be considered: the diagnosis "chronic myocarditis" is extremely vague. It is indicative of the nonexistence of such diagnostic procedures as EKG, X-rays, etc. Contemporaries of Freud knew the symptomatology of angina pec-toris; Nothnagel, who held the chair in internal medicine and was one of the few faculty members of the Vienna Medical School who supported Freud's career, not only had studied its manifestations, but subsequently furnished a graphic example by describing his own fatal attack up to the moment of losing consciousness. But the frequency of coronary thrombosis, its varied symptomatology, and particularly its incidence in younger individuals were still unknown. Anyone who reads Freud's description of his symptoms during the spring of 1894 must at least consider the possibility that Freud had suffered a coronary thrombosis at that point.

Freud's mention of "painful nodules" in his muscles does not justify the assumption that he was suffering from "rheumatic fever" with involvement of the heart. Nothing in his later cardiac status justifies such a conclusion. However, an acute postinfectious myocarditis of unspecific origin is another (rather remote) possibility which must be given consideration.

The syndrome of paroxysmal tachycardia with or without auricular fibrillation is well known. It may occur *without* any noticeable indication of "organic" lesion. Its symptomatology is not dissimilar to the one described by Freud. The anginalike pain and the dyspnea can be explained by "coronary insufficiency" brought about by the longer-lasting attacks.

It is typical, however, for paroxysmal tachycardia to occur at various intervals over a lifetime. We hardly ever hear from a patient who lives long enough that he had such attacks for only a certain number of weeks or months without any recurrence at a later age. The individual attacks can be precipitated by various causes, such as a heavy meal or severe exertion. A colleague of mine would get such an attack whenever he became seasick. We know that attacks can occasionally be precipitated by extreme anxiety (see Schur, 1953), and these are then considered to be anxiety equivalents.

During the year 1895, Fliess, who by then had widened the scope of his speculations about nasal reflex neuroses, came up with a new hypothesis: that Freud's cardiac symptoms were all of "nasal origin." This hypothesis has two aspects, neither of them tenable: (1) the idea of a "nasal reflex" and (2) the idea of a "focal infection" producing generalized severe disturbances.

As to the first, we know that in patients prone to "vasovagal reflex" many types of circulatory disturbances can be precipitated by a wide variety of sensory stimuli and by emotional stress. The most common symptoms of such origin are blushing, profuse sweating, fainting spells, and, less frequently, various types of arrhythmia such as extrasystoles. In persons prone to idiopathic paroxysmal tachycardia such attacks can be precipitated by reflexes of this kind. In a patient suffering from angina pectoris, an anginal attack can be precipitated by such a "reflex."

Apart from circulatory symptoms, we encounter such reactions as nausea, vomiting, diarrhea, or signs of a spastic or "irritable" colon, including mucous colitis. We know that Freud had several fainting spells during his life, and I shall discuss these incidents and their determinants in detail. Freud also had an "irritable," spastic colon.

It is characteristic of such "reflex" symptoms, however, that they are *acute* occurrences. Fliess's notion that a host of functional and organic syndromes could be caused by a local "process" in the nasal mucosa in the region of the turbinate bone, and that these could be treated successfully by local cocaine applications and/or by surgical procedures on the turbinal bones has since been subjected to critical appraisal through largely unbiased controls and proven to be completely unfounded (see also Ernst Kris's introduction and footnotes to Freud, 1950).[41]

Freud's fainting spells (we know of four or five) always occurred in a situation of acute stress. During the years Freud was under my care, his "irritable," spastic colon attacks and short periods of frequent extrasystoles were prevalently precipitated by excessive smoking and were relieved promptly by a small dose of Belladonna (an anticholinergic) along with a reduction in smoking.

From the Fliess correspondence, it is not quite clear whether Fliess and Freud were also giving consideration to the "focal infection" concept in evaluating the latter's cardiac symptoms. This is questionable because the hypothesis that many diseases, especially various types of polyarthritis, neuritis, bronchial asthma, etc., were due to "focal infections," primarily of the teeth, tonsils, and nasal sinuses as well as the appendix, became fashionable only in the first decades of the twentieth century, when innumerable innocent organs were mutilated on the basis of this assumption. Certainly, a "focal infection" could not have been responsible for Freud's initial severe cardiac symptoms.

Which of all the possible diagnoses indicated above is the most likely one? That Freud's condition was due *exclusively* to an acute

---

[41] Fliess did not stop with this aspect of his speculations. He went on to conclude that the nasal pathology, with all of its consequences, was in turn determined by so-called "critical periods."

nicotine toxicity without organic changes, or to nicotine hypersensitivity is not too likely. Acute nicotine toxicity may also produce cardiovascular symptoms, but in the absence of organic changes such symptoms subside within days or weeks after the patient stops smoking. While Freud was not too persistent in his abstinence, his symptoms neither disappeared during the weeks of abstinence nor became consistently worse upon his resumption of smoking.

The assumption of a special hypersensitivity to nicotine in the absence of an organic lesion is an even less convincing explanation for Freud's prolonged symptoms. If such were the case, the intense attacks would have coincided more or less regularly with the resumption of heavy smoking, and severe cardiovascular reactions would have recurred frequently throughout the rest of his life, because Freud remained a persistently heavy smoker.

What about the diagnosis of an "idiopathic" paroxysmal tachycardia? The previously mentioned fact that such attacks usually occur at various intervals throughout life speaks against this. Freud lived for another 45 years and never had another attack of paroxysmal tachycardia with auricular fibrillation.

At this point we must consider still another possibility, which was proposed by Jones, who stated in his biography of Freud that the latter suffered from a "very considerable psychoneurosis" (Vol. 1, p. 304), the severe stage of which Jones placed in the second half of the 1890s. Jones writes: "There seem to have been no 'conversion' physical symptoms, and he [Freud] would later doubtless have classified it as an anxiety hysteria" (p. 305). After quoting Freud's description of his attacks, Jones arrives at the following conclusion:

> Looking back one would come to the conclusion that all these troubles were in the main special aspects of his psychoneurosis, possibly slightly localized by the effect of nicotine. There was assuredly no myocarditis. . . . Subsequent events were to show that Freud had an exceptionally sound heart, and also that he could tolerate considerable quantities of nicotine [p. 311].

Jones does not elaborate on this statement. If he does not assume the existence of " 'conversion' physical symptoms," how does he explain the psychoneurotic character of "all these troubles"? Does he assume that there was an "organ neurosis," a somatization of conflicts and/or anxiety, something we would now call a "psychosomatic" state? Or did he believe that it was a plainly hypochondriacal elaboration of some occasional extrasystoles?

Jones based his interpretation in the main on the Fliess correspondence. The samples already quoted by me, with more to come, reflect much that can be labeled "neurotic."[42] However, neurotic *anxiety* was much less pronounced in Freud than excessive swings of mood, which at their low ebb had a definitely depressive quality. An obsessive preoccupation not only with death in general but with dying at a specific age recurs frequently. This preoccupation, which will be discussed in detail, persisted for long periods and in varying degrees of intensity throughout Freud's life. However, only twice in the entire published and unpublished Fliess correspondence did Freud express a fear of dying: once in his letter of April 19, 1894, where he described his most severe attacks, saying that "visions of death and departure" were replacing the more usual "deliria" about one's everyday occupations; once he specifically mentioned attacks of *Todesangst* (fear of dying), occasioned by the death of the contemporary sculptor Tilgner from a heart attack (see letter of April 16, 1896 and the ensuing discussion, Chapter 4). All such manifestations, especially the depressive mood, were quite prominent at the height of his cardiac symptoms. However, if a person expresses pessimistic views, is depressed and even afraid of death during a period of severe cardiovascular distress, this in no way proves that these symptoms represent the somatization of an unconscious conflict or of excessive, uncontrolled anxiety.[43]

We also have no indications from the Fliess correspondence that during the months when his cardiac symptoms were at their peak, Freud was exposed to greater stresses than at other times. Nor did he show more signs of "neurosis" during this period than in the months following his father's death (October, 1896) or at the beginning of his systematic self-analysis in the spring of 1897. It is during these later years that his cardiac symptoms were mild, transient, atypical, and more convincingly related to intensified stress and conflict.

Is it possible that Freud suffered from an organic heart ailment, specifically a coronary thrombosis in a small artery? The symptoms

[42] An example of a localized neurotic symptom would be Freud's moderate travel phobia, which, however, never actually prevented him from traveling.

[43] Such logically invalid assumptions are frequently made in the evaluation of somatic symptoms, especially during analysis. It is often very difficult to make a careful distinction between somatization of responses which lead to structural pathology and secondary responses to an "organic," "structural" process, especially if these are exaggerated and add to the somatic symptom. The failure to make such a distinction too often has tragic consequences.

which Freud described so vividly are typical of anginal attacks: the severe pain, radiating into the left arm, the feeling of oppression. Attacks of tachycardia and arrhythmia are a common occurrence in this ailment. During this period Freud also showed such signs of slight left ventricular failure as shortness of breath or what he later described as "motoric insufficiency" (see letter of March 28, 1895, Chapter 3). The fact that Freud responded favorably to repeated series of digitalization, which he took at various intervals for over a year, is highly suggestive of an organic lesion with temporary left ventricular failure.

It is well known that coronary thrombosis can occur at a relatively early age (Freud was 38 in 1894). Moreover, if such a thrombosis occurs in a small artery, with no involvement of the remaining arterial system, the patient may remain free of anginal symptoms for decades and retain a normally functioning heart. I have personally known many patients who, after coronary episodes, have resumed mountaineering, skiing, and other athletic activities.

During the manifestation of any organic cardiac lesion, sensitivity to nicotine may be heightened. This I observed in Freud with great regularity in later years.

It was Freud's contention, based on his own experience, which I could later only confirm, that he needed nicotine during periods of creative writing or the preparation for such activity. And when was Freud not at such a stage? As is true with any addiction, it is extremely difficult to decide whether Freud could have achieved without nicotine the concentration necessary for problem solving of the highest order, either because the consequences of the withdrawal would have interfered with his ability to sustain attention, or because, in Freud's case at least, the specific pharmacological effect of nicotine seemed to be conducive to optimal achievement.

Those who might object to my use of the term "addiction" in connection with Freud's use of nicotine need only consult Freud's letters, where his treatment of this subject provides a glowing example of his unfailingly honest self-scrutiny:

> I have gained the insight that masturbation is the one great habit that is a "primary addiction," and that the other addictions, for alcohol, morphine, tobacco, etc., enter into life only as a substitute for and a withdrawal [symptom] from it. This addiction plays an enormous role in hysteria, and perhaps my great unsurmounted obstacle is wholly, or in part, to be found in it. The doubt of course arises whether such an

addiction is curable, or whether analysis and therapy must stop short at this point and remain content with transforming a hysteria into a neurasthenia [December 22, 1897; L. 79].

The following letter best summarizes Freud's lifelong attitude toward smoking.[44] It is revealing not only for the facts about Freud's smoking habits, but also shows that Freud remained convinced that the cardiac episode which I have been discussing was due to organic causes, and it points to Freud's identification with this habit (or vice, as he called it) of his father's. As we shall see, the age of 81½ at which his father died was to play an important role in Freud's obsessive-superstitious preoccupation with the time of his prospective death.

February 12, 1929

I began smoking at the age of 24, first cigarettes but soon exclusively cigars, and am still smoking now (at 72½), and very reluctant to restrict myself in this pleasure. Between the ages of 30 and 40 I had to give up smoking for a year and a half because of heart trouble which may have been [due to] the effect of nicotine, but was probably a sequel to influenza. Since then I have been faithful to my habit or vice, and believe that I owe to the cigar a great intensification of my capacity to work and a facilitation of my self-control. My model in this was my father, who was a heavy smoker and remained one till his 81st year.

Sigm. Freud [12]

To sum up: We have no valid reason for subscribing to Jones's theory that "all these troubles were . . . special aspects of his psychoneurosis" (Vol. 1, p. 311). I am inclined to the opinion that between late 1893 and 1896 Freud suffered from attacks of paroxysmal tachycardia, with anginal pain and signs of left ventricular failure; that these attacks reached their peak during April, 1894, at which point he suffered an organic myocardial lesion, most likely a coronary thrombosis in a small artery, or perhaps a postinfectious myocarditis, with temporarily increased nicotine sensitivity.

---

[44] I am indebted to the Arents Collection of the New York Public Library for permission to publish this letter which was written in answer to a questionnaire directed to many outstanding contemporary figures regarding their smoking habits. I am also indebted to Dr. A. Grinstein of Detroit for having called my attention to this letter.

3

THE FRIENDSHIP WITH FLIESS:
EARLY PHASE

At the time when his cardiac symptoms became more intense Freud was not yet 38. He was supporting his wife and five children, the oldest born in 1887, the youngest in 1892. He also had to provide for other members of his family. His practice was far from consolidated, as a result of which he had great difficulty making ends meet. There were still old debts to pay from his desperately poor student years, and he had no savings. Anyone who in later years knew Freud's generosity and pride could understand his humiliation at being forced into debt. Freud used to remark repeatedly how hard it was for someone to overcome a certain basic insecurity after he had been forced actually to worry about his daily bread. Thus he wrote to Fliess (September 21, 1899; L. 119):

> My state of mind also depends very much on my earnings. . . . Something I remember from my boyhood is that when wild horses on the pampas have once been lassoed, they retain a certain anxiousness for life. In the same way I once knew helpless poverty and have a constant fear of it.

ISOLATION—GENIUS IN SEARCH OF A CAUSE

When Freud embarked on the treatment of neurosis by using his new method exclusively, he was burning his bridges behind him. He not only was exposing himself to ostracism, but was also risking the financial security of his family.

Under these circumstances the prospect of illness and possible death would have placed anyone under great stress, but even more so a physician who was well aware of the diagnostic possibilities and the dubious prognosis in his case. The most tormenting burden, however, as we learn from his letters, was the realization that he was on the threshold of monumental discoveries and that these discoveries could not be rushed. His search was of a kind in which time was of the essence. He would have to wait until his patients—among whom he now had to count himself with his dreams, phobic symptoms, and fluctuations in mood—supplied him with the answers. No one but he held the key. Would he have the precious years he needed?

Freud behaved under these circumstances as he was to do again in the tragic years beginning with 1923: he refused to burden his family with his pain and worry. Like so many physicians, he had no doctor to whom he could turn with full confidence, assured of his colleague's competence, trustworthiness about revealing the truth, and ability to keep his judgment unclouded by personal factors. Freud had complete trust in his friend Dr. Oskar Rie, but the latter was a pediatrician and not a cardiologist.

The person Freud turned to then was Breuer, who did have the necessary experience and knowledge. Unfortunately it was just at this point that their ways were beginning to part. From the Fliess correspondence we learn that during the most critical weeks and months of the cardiac episode Breuer saw Freud at infrequent and irregular intervals. We have no way of knowing to what extent this was Freud's doing, perhaps caused by his reluctance to be a "complainer." But in his letters Freud spoke of Breuer's contradictory statements, his not caring, and so on.

It was Fliess who became his trusted physician, "the healer," the "magician" (see letters of April 20, 26, 1895 cited later in this Chapter). Fliess was an E.N.T. specialist who, pursuing his far-reaching interests and hypotheses, did not limit his practice to his specialty. Freud's letters disclose that Fliess "took over," claiming with full authority that Freud did not have a myocarditis but was suffering only from a nicotine hypersensitivity. With this pronouncement he gave Freud a new lease on life. Years later Freud acknowledged what Fliess had done for him at that time. As their friendship was drawing to a close, Freud wrote in a letter (June 9, 1901) that was tantamount to a farewell:

You have reminded me of that beautiful and difficult time when I was forced to believe that I was very close to the end of my life, and it was your confidence that kept me going [M. Schur, 1966a, p. 71].

Every close patient-physician relationship has aspects whose roots and manifestations are similar to those of the transference relationship in the psychoanalytic situation. During those difficult months Fliess's support was essential to Freud. In spite of painful symptoms caused by abstinence from nicotine, in spite of Freud's awareness of the logical flaws in Fliess's reasoning—there was no direct relationship between the intensity of Freud's symptoms and his indulgence in or abstinence from smoking—Freud's basic trust and belief in Fliess as his "healer" never wavered. Clearly, his heart was getting better and he did not have the progressive heart ailment that Breuer's diagnosis of a myocarditis would have implied.

During this same period Freud's relationship to Breuer became strained. Freud was all the more hurt by Breuer's inability to concur fully in his discoveries because Freud had always given credit to the decisive stimulus that Breuer's earlier work on hysteria had provided for the development of psychoanalysis. Nor had Freud forgotten Breuer's financial support during times of real want. Breuer, in turn, never doubted Freud's genius. In a letter to Fliess written in the summer of 1895, Breuer said: "Freud's intellect is operating full force. I am already lagging behind him like a hen following a falcon" (see Kris, 1950, p. 13, n. 1). But Breuer, like so many after him, could not overcome his inner resistance to the findings of Freud, who in turn could foresee nothing but animosity or at best skepticism from Breuer.

Ernst Kris (1950), and Jones, have discussed several factors that contributed to Freud's relationship with Fliess. Both authors link the development of that relationship to the increasing estrangement between Freud and Breuer and their mounting differences of opinion (see also Wittels, 1924).

Freud himself, however, subsequently linked both the positive and the negative, hostile aspects of his relationship to Fliess—with all the ambivalence that these created in him—to his early childhood experiences (see Chapters 4 and 5). The validity of such genetic links is one of the important tenets of psychoanalysis. We know, however, although this is occasionally overlooked (even by Freud), that new relationships and conflicts, while following infantile experiences, are never exact replicas of them. They have a life of their own, which they acquire through the most intricate interplay of inner and environmental circumstances.

We learn from the Fliess correspondence what a profound impression Fliess made on Freud from the moment of their first encounter. In the opening paragraph of his first published letter to Fliess, Freud wrote:

> While my letter today is occasioned by business, I must introduce it with the confession that I hope to remain in contact with you and that you left a deep impression on me, which could easily induce me to tell you frankly in what class [*Rangordnung*] of men I must place you.

This was in November, 1887, long before Freud's estrangement from Breuer had begun to develop, before he had started to apply Breuer's method to the treatment of hysteria or even before he had begun to utilize hypnotherapy.

Kris believed that an additional important factor in the development of the friendship between Freud and Fliess was the similarity of their intellectual background and their shared interest in research and literature. This would not explain the intensity of the impact described in the above-quoted letter. Nor could this impact be ascribed solely to the genetic roots of Freud's readiness to form friendships and to react enthusiastically at that given moment. We must assume that there was, in addition, something in Fliess's personality that greatly facilitated (or possibly invited) such a reaction and also permitted its effusive expression. There must have been something fascinating, scintillating about Fliess. In a letter (written in circumstances that will be discussed below) Freud said: ". . . for me you remain the healer, the prototype of the man into whose hands one confidently entrusts one's life and that of one's family" (April 20, 1895) [5].

Freud was not alone in feeling this way about Fliess. Within a relatively short time Fliess had developed an extensive medical practice, which did not remain limited to his E.N.T. specialty. Moreover, Fliess developed a highly original hypothesis which linked a great variety of diverse symptoms.[1] Because Fliess believed strongly in his

---

[1] In Fliess's hypothesis about the "nasal reflex neurosis" swellings of the nasal mucosa and pathology of the turbinate bones and the sinuses were held responsible for such diverse symptoms as: pain in most parts of the body, migraine and other types of headaches, "neuralgic" pain of the head, thorax, abdomen, extremities, etc., disturbed functioning of the heart, the respiratory organs (resulting particularly in bronchial asthma), the gastrointestinal system, and finally the female genitals, causing dysmenorrhea, miscarriage, etc.

claims, and because the patients he treated by his method frequently did suffer from various types of psychoneurosis, and because Fliess had a "magnetic" personality, he was apparently able to help his patients considerably, which in turn contributed to his firm conviction that his hypotheses were sound.

That Fliess had a gift for impressing his friends and patients with the wealth of his biological knowledge, his far-reaching imagination, and his unflagging faith in his therapeutic abilities can be concluded from the intense loyalty of his patients which was evident from Freud's correspondence with him. Even a patient who, as we shall see, suffered dangerous consequences from a grave "slip" committed by Fliess remained loyal to him for the rest of her life.[2] It is particularly impressive that even so sound and sober a scientist as Karl Abraham fell under Fliess's spell during the terminal phase of his illness of 1925 (see Chapter 16).

The biographies of "geniuses" show a wide divergence in the age range at which these persons began their significant work or at least showed a valid promise of their later achievement. Many composers and painters—for example, Mozart and Leonardo da Vinci—showed their creativity very early. Goethe's mastery was evidenced in his early 20's (see Eissler, 1963). Einstein formulated his theory of relativity at the age of 26. The case was different with Darwin, whose *Notebooks* and *Diary of the Voyage of the H.M.S. "Beagle"* tell us of finding "somewhere" in his mind ideas which he fully conceptualized and

---

Initially Fliess placed the blame on structural nasal pathology, although this was occasionally of an insignificant order; later he believed that "functional," "vasomotor" disturbances could have the same results. At that point Fliess made a logical "jump" when he claimed that "neurasthenic complaints, in other words the neuroses with a sexual aetiology, so frequently assume the form of the nasal reflex neurosis" (see Kris, 1950, p. 5).

Whatever objective validity there was to Fliess's widely exaggerated claims was based on the following facts:

(a) Fliess was right in asserting that a certain structural similarity exists between the corpus cavernosum of the nose and the corpus cavernosum of the penis.

(b) The occurrence of nosebleeds along with or in place of menstruation ("vicarious menstrual bleeding") is an established fact.

(c) It is well known (see, for example, Travell and Bigelow, 1947) that the treatment of certain "trigger points" in the muscles by local anesthetics can relieve neuralgiform pain in a wide area of the nervous distribution.

(d) Sinus infections can account for various types of headaches and cause some general symptoms, as do other local infections.

(e) Finally, unimpaired nasal breathing is important for a variety of reasons to patients with bronchial asthma.

Obviously, these facts furnish backing for only a *very small* percentage of Fliess's claims.

[2] Personal communication.

published only years later, at the age of 50. It seems highly unlikely
that anyone would become a "genius" at an advanced age. But certain
people who fall in this category exemplify what Goethe and Freud
called *daimon kai tyche,* the interaction of the innate and the acquired.
This situation probably held true for Freud more than for most extraordinary men.

There are still others with unusual endowment who never encounter the kind of *tyche* necessary for the full unfolding of their "givens."

When Freud met Fliess in 1887, at the age of 31, he was a "genius
in search of a cause." None of Freud's scientific achievements described by me in Chapter 1 was tantamount to solving one of the big
riddles of life. Being a rebel, Freud was contemptuous of the "Old
Guard" at the medical school of the University of Vienna—the
Hofräte—who had been awarded honorary titles either because they
were chairmen of departments, or were noted for some special achievement, or had merely arrived at a certain seniority and "knew the right
people."

After giving up his work in Brücke's laboratory, Freud became
more or less of an outsider. Charcot, the master of the Saltpêtrière,
and Bernheim, who had made hypnosis respectable, were much more
congenial to the brilliant young rebel than his old professors.

From Freud's autobiographical essays, and the writings of Kris,
Jones, Bernfeld, and others, we know the stage of development Freud
had reached when he met Fliess. Breuer, Freud's senior colleague and
friend, who had also abandoned an academic career and become a
highly successful internist, had told Freud of the successful treatment
of Anna O., described in the *Studies on Hysteria* (see Chertok, 1968).
Freud planned to call Charcot's attention to this new method, but
Charcot showed no interest in it. Freud was at that point both deeply
infatuated with his fiancée Martha and fascinated by Charcot and his
teachings, so that he did not follow up Breuer's idea.

After his return from Paris Freud delivered a report in 1886 to the
Vienna Medical Society about Charcot's work on hysteria, dwelling
particularly on the manifestation of hysteria in males. When this view-
point was challenged Freud presented a case of male hysteria, only to
arouse the violent opposition of Meynert, the chief of the Neurological
Institute, thereby losing his last foothold in an academic institute.

As Freud encountered more psychoneuroses than organic illnesses
in his neurological practice, he began to make use of hypnosis and
eventually "remembered" Breuer's case. Although he initially used this

newly discovered approach for the treatment of hysterias, Freud recognized its great importance for the treatment and understanding of other types of psychoneuroses as well. We might say, as is true of many discoveries, that Freud "stumbled" upon the great importance of sexuality in the etiology of neurosis. But once this first step had been taken, Freud met his real destiny. He found himself in completely uncharted territory where his teacher and friend, Breuer, could neither show him the way nor follow him.

It was then that his genius found its cause and its destiny, although Freud did not yet know where it would lead him. At this time he also met Fliess.

Here was another independent, lonely rebel, who, on the basis solely of hunches and clinical observation, had dared to create a set of hypotheses which sounded somewhat fantastic but were nevertheless very impressive by their sheer boldness. His hypotheses and Freud's budding ideas on hysteria and other psychoneuroses converged in that vague region where the mind "meets" the body.

It may also have appealed to Freud that Fliess based his whole hypothesis on the therapeutic effect of local applications of cocaine, the anesthetic action of which had been discovered by Freud. We also learn from a letter of July 10, 1893 that Fliess had some years earlier been a "student" of Freud's, participating in a course given by the latter on hysterical paralyses. This brilliant, fascinating man was ready to accept Freud as a friend and to listen to him, and expected to be listened to in turn. Moreover, Fliess lived in another city, so that their relationship was relatively unencumbered by the petty details of everyday life, while their meetings ("congresses," as Freud called them) were held at specially chosen places, lasted as a rule only two or three days, and apparently took place in an atmosphere of the highest intellectual concentration, with both men pouring out their ideas.

After Freud found his "cause," which possessed him to such a degree that in one letter (February 19, 1899; see Chapter 5) he was to call it his "neoplasm," the correspondence between the two men became more intensive and more intimate. Freud was overflowing with ideas, which he formulated and reformulated in drafts of papers that he sent to Fliess. He also encouraged Fliess to publish a preliminary report on his concept of the nasal reflex neuroses, read the manuscript, suggested changes, and even proposed the publication of a joint paper.

Freud could not but be awed and frightened by his own findings at this time, and it was therefore highly important for him to find a man like Fliess who listened and praised him, probably in part because he himself needed an audience for his even bolder hypotheses.

Freud was very much isolated at this time by the indifference and hostility of his professional colleagues. Some of the letters previously quoted reflect this situation. His letter of April 25, 1894 spoke of "the social and scientific dead calm" by which he was surrounded; the letter of May 21, 1894 stated "I am pretty much alone here in the elucidation of the neuroses. They look upon me as pretty much a monomaniac. . . ." On June 22, 1894 Freud commented: "since the scientific contact with Breuer came to an end I have been thrown back completely on my own resources, which is why progress is so slow." Freud's correspondence and meetings with Fliess broke the isolation and provided encouragement and stimulation (see letter of July 14, 1894).

It is unfortunate that the letters written by Fliess to Freud were not preserved. When Fliess's widow demanded their return from Freud, he was unable to find them. Referring to this in a letter written to Marie Bonaparte in 1937, when she had just acquired Freud's letters to Fliess from a dealer who had smuggled them out of Germany, Freud said: "I don't know till this very day whether I destroyed them, or only hid them ingeniously. . . . Our correspondence was of the most intimate nature, as you can surmise" (see Schur, 1965, p. 13). We thus do not know to what extent Fliess was able to follow Freud's ideas, but we may deduce from Freud's own letters, especially those written during his intensive work on *The Interpretation of Dreams,* that Fliess was not merely an interested, but to a certain degree an understanding—albeit critical—listener and reader. While this understanding had its limitations, Fliess's praise was very important to Freud, who alternated between doubt and conviction as to the worth of his work.[3]

I shall consider later when, why, and how Fliess's and Freud's points of view were bound to clash head on. During this period, however, we see Freud's relationship with Fliess growing in intensity, his praise of Fliess becoming more expansive as his insight into the com-

---

[3] Fliess's understanding attitude changed into one of complete rejection when he recognized that it was not possible to believe simultaneously in psychic determinism and the absolute dominance of some mysterious inner clock. Nevertheless, we have learned from such sources as the correspondence between Freud and Abraham and from the personal communications of Dr. Marianne Kris, the daughter of Dr. Oskar Rie, that Fliess apparently retained an interest in psychoanalysis to the very end, reading Freud's publications and referring patients for psychoanalytic treatment.

plexities of the neuroses increased and he began to understand the ubiquitous validity of certain psychic mechanisms.

Freud was given to swings of mood, periods of enthusiasm and highly intensive work alternating with periods of letdown, as was already evident in his betrothal letters, which show clearly those pendulum fluctuations that Goethe described as characteristic of a state of infatuation:

> Rejoicing to the heavens,
> Grieved to death.[4]

However, such fluctuations are frequently found in persons blessed with supreme creativity, who produce some of their best work in spurts of intense, concentrated effort of relatively short duration. Freud's creative activity was characterized by periods of this kind. Works of the greatest complexity—to mention only the "Project" (1895), Chapter VII of *The Interpretation of Dreams* (1900), and most of his papers on metapsychology (1915a, 1915b, 1915c)—were written in the span of a few weeks. Such creative effort was frequently followed by a period of letdown, which sometimes carried with it an undervaluation of his achievement.

However, during the Fliess period the determinants of such swings of mood were much more complex. They depended in part on Freud's physical condition (which I discussed in Chapter 2). His creativity and capacity for intensive, concentrated work were obviously impaired during the period of his most distressing cardiac symptoms. It is a well-known phenomenon that angina pectoris and attacks of paroxysmal tachycardia are nearly always accompanied by a greater or lesser amount of anxiety; so much so, in fact, that before the tools for cardiac diagnosis had been refined to their present level, anxiety was considered a diagnostically important sign.[5]

Anxiety in these cases is due partly to that particular feeling of oppression which Freud described so vividly in his letter of April 19, 1894, partly to the suddenness and unpredictability of the onset of the attack. Therefore what Freud subsequently described as the core of a

---

[4] Goethe, *Egmont,* "Klärchenlieder":
Himmelhoch jauchzend
Zu Tode betrübt.
[5] Many patients who suffered from angina pectoris described it as an iron ring constricting their chest so that they felt suffocated even in the absence of actual dyspnea. Reflex-shock phenomena such as "cold sweat," etc., increase the feeling of terror, which in turn can significantly contribute to the actual danger of the attack.

"traumatic" situation—the ego's utter helplessness in the face of over-whelming danger (1926a, p. 166ff.)—applies to this affliction. A physician's awareness of the meaning of these symptoms adds another determinant of anxiety in his own case.

However, what Freud described in connection with his attacks was not so much the terror involved. As indicated earlier, only once in his letters did he mention an attack of fear of dying (see Chapter 4). We may assume that given the complete frankness and intimacy shown in his letters, Freud would have confessed to such feelings if he had had them. Without claiming, therefore, that Freud did not dread death, especially during this period, or that he did not link apprehension about renewed attacks with the fear that one of them might mean the end, we may say that Freud's main reaction was a depressive mood, entailing obsessive thoughts about how long he still had to live. This reaction, freely expressed in his letters, was inseparably linked with questions which might be phrased as follows: "Was the task which I undertook too great? Did I dare too much? Will I live long enough at least to come in sight of the Promised Land?" (He subsequently ex-pressed this thought in one of his last letters to Fliess; see Chapter 6.) The depressive mood following his attacks interfered with the progress of his work, which added greater urgency to these questions. But more than this: it is inconceivable that when his mood was low, and prog-ress in the treatment of his patients was slow, Freud was not beset by doubts about the validity of his findings.

BEGINNING OF SELF-ANALYSIS

Freud's inner conflicts were far from resolved at that time. He still had to discover through his self-analysis the overriding importance of early childhood experiences, the oedipal conflict, the many determi-nants of ambivalence and guilt feelings, etc. Certain phobic symptoms such as his travel phobia and the preoccupation with aging and the anticipation that his own death would come at a particular age were manifestations of such conflicts.

Freud was on the threshold of monumental discoveries. What had started as a method of treating hysteria involved him in a search in which he gradually realized that he had touched upon one of the great mysteries of nature. The closer he came to the solution of the riddle, the greater were the obstacles. Progress was painfully slow, and was achieved by trial and error. He depended on the production of his patients, but was forced to recognize that something within himself would not allow him to approach the riddle through methods he had learned in the laboratory. The correspondence with Fliess indicates that Freud's *systematic* self-analysis did not begin until 1897.

We must distinguish between the *motivations* for the self-analysis and the proof that Freud had started it. The motivations were manifold. Freud had become aware that he, too, was not free of neurotic symptoms or "hysterias," as he called them in his correspondence with Fliess. He increasingly became aware of the fact that certain phenomena he saw in his patients might be only distortions and exaggerations of phenomena characteristic of the psychic functioning of all men. For a man of Freud's integrity what was more natural than to look at himself to determine whether his hypotheses about the working of the mind were really sound and applicable to others besides his patients? Certainly, there was one phenomenon that was ubiquitous: dreaming. Freud's patients had begun to tell him about their dreams, and he had come to realize that these were meaningful. It was therefore a logical step for Freud to investigate his own dreams.

There was additional motivation. During the course of the constant, highly intensive study of his patient's psychic manifestations, Freud became aware that whenever he thought he had found the key to the development of their symptoms, he was forced to recognize the existence of still another level that remained hidden. His correspondence with Fliess, especially the theoretical drafts enclosed in the letters, reveals the constant shifting of his formulations and his realization that the "traumatic" experiences of his patients had to be sought earlier and earlier in their lives. He gradually began to appreciate the powers of repression and resistance long before coining these terms. And so it dawned on him that perhaps he himself was subject to these same phenomena.

I now return to Freud's interest in dreams. We know the date of the dream of "Irma's Injection"—the "specimen dream of psychoanalysis" (July 24, 1895)—about which Freud later wrote in a letter to Fliess of June 12, 1900: "Do you actually suppose that some day this house will have a marble plaque with the inscription: 'Here, on July 24, 1895, the mystery of dreams revealed itself to Dr. Sigm. Freud'?" This interpretation may have been Freud's first *systematic* dream analysis in the sense that he set down the associations to *each* element of the dream, compared them carefully with each other, and in this way discovered the modes of operation of the dream work, as he later called it. However, such a systematic procedure must have been preceded by a long series of analyses of Freud's own dreams and those of his patients. In a letter to Fliess of March 4, 1895 (more than three and a half months *before* the Irma dream) Freud mentioned the dream of Rudi Kaufmann,[6] a young physician who was reluctant to get up early and therefore had a "hallucinatory" dream in which he saw himself in the hospital (see L. 22, and 1900, p. 125). This letter indicates not only that Freud had already conceived of the wish-fulfilling function of the dream, but also that friends and colleagues must have been aware of Freud's interest in dreams and were collecting samples for him.

I assume that in analogy to the gradual development of dream analysis, which eventually culminated in the application of a specific technique, Freud's systematic self-analysis also went through an even longer, introductory phase, before he took it up in a planned fashion. It is pertinent that the analysis of Freud's own dreams played a prominent role in it. I am also making the assumption that some aspects of this preliminary phase started as early as 1893.

We rightly consider Freud's self-analysis as a unique and unsurpassable feat. This statement requires an explanation for those not familiar with the obstacles that everyone who enters analysis has to overcome. (We must bear in mind however that such an analysis is conducted by an expert who himself has had to go through the same procedure in his training analysis.) The obstacles arise in the form of resistances against the uncovering of manifold conflicts through which we all have to pass during our formative years; against recovering painful memories of the past; finding that we all harbor thoughts and wishes which are considered evil, base, dangerous, and have even committed deeds of that kind; by the reluctance to change deeply ingrained character traits and even to give up painful symptoms. The resistances are also commensurate with the strength of the defenses through which we have dealt more or less successfully with all our conflicts. Resistances are as much a part of the "secrets of nature" which Freud had discovered as are the forces against which the resistances (and defenses) are directed.

Let us now contrast Freud's task of self-analysis. It can be compared with the situation of an explorer who sets out on a voyage not knowing

---

[6] Rudolf Kaufmann, who became one of Vienna's foremost cardiologists. He was a nephew of Breuer.

his destination, having neither maps nor compass, unsure of what tools he will need once having set out on his trip.[7]

We know that one of the important ingredients of every analysis is the "transference." The analysand develops a very special relationship to the analyst, which reflects all his intense relationships to important figures of the past, as, for instance, parents and siblings. A transference relationship is therefore essentially a repetition of the past, but it also reflects the vicissitudes which such relationships have undergone under the influence of the exigencies of life. The analysis of "transference manifestations" gives important clues to the understanding of drives, fantasies, conflicts, and also actual events of the past. We distinguish between "positive" and "negative" transference phenomena. The analysand may develop very intense positive feelings toward his analyst, which run the whole range of trust, infatuation, sexual fantasies, unrealistic overvaluation of his qualities, equally unrealistic "magic" expectations about the result of the analysis, etc.; and on the other hand the analysand goes also through periods of intense resentments, hatred, death wishes, and disappointment.

The intense sexual transference which Breuer's first patient developed made him recoil from the further pursuit of this method of therapy. Freud recognized that the positive transference—when managed properly—is an important vehicle for the development of a relationship of trust. He also recognized the essential importance of analyzing this positive transference. It took Freud much longer to recognize that the development of the negative transference is not only a resistance, but an essential repetition of the past. Briefly the transference is an essential part of analysis.

How does this aspect of an analysis, the development of a transference, apply to Freud? Freud was his *own* analyst, and yet the essential need, which becomes a yearning, for a transference object, manifested itself even in his self-analysis and was reflected in his relationship to Fliess.

It is idle speculation to ask whether Freud could have accomplished his self-analysis without such an object. All we can state with certainty is that the self-analysis was crucial for the solution of his own conflicts *and* for the development of his concepts. For this reason it is important for us to gain as much understanding of Freud's self-analysis as is

[7] I am purposely using here a metaphor similar to the one which Freud used in a letter to Fliess in which he described his plan for writing *The Interpretation of Dreams* (L. 114).

possible and to examine how it entered into and was influenced by his relationship to Fliess. In doing so I follow the example of Freud, who, as late as 1912, reported in his correspondence that certain episodes of his life which he submitted to self-analysis were related to his relationship with Fliess.

A certain personal distance between analysand and analyst is an important condition for the development of a typical transference in a regular analysis. In the latter, of course, the analyst provides the interpretations, including those of all transference manifestations, and thus influences in a subtle way the course of the analysis. Most of this was different in Freud's case. It was Freud who had to provide the interpretations of unknown psychological mechanisms, that he discovered only in this process. No wonder that he occasionally found himself in a blind alley. He wrote, for instance, on November 14, 1897: "My self-analysis is still interrupted. I can only analyze myself with objectively acquired knowledge (as if I were a stranger); self-analysis is impossible, otherwise there would be no illness." Freud did not add that he was *the* exception, and he did not give up.

Nothing can convey better the interplay between Freud's self-analysis and his relationship to Fliess than his own words. When he heard from Marie Bonaparte that she was about to acquire the Fliess correspondence he wrote to her:

> In view of the intimate nature of our relationship, these letters cover all kinds of things, factual as well as personal topics; and the factual ones, which indicate all the presentiments and blind alleys of the budding psychoanalysis, are also quite personal in this case. . . . For these reasons, it would be so desirable for me to know that this material was in your hands [Schur, 1965, p. 16].

I have already discussed several factors which may have contributed to the development of Freud's relationship to Fliess. I will recapitulate them now, adding some factors not previously discussed:

The genetic links rooted in Freud's infantile relationships which manifested themselves in his relationship to Breuer and Charcot; Freud's increasing estrangement from Breuer.

His more or less complete social and intellectual isolation; his growing awareness that he had not merely discovered a new treatment for hysteria but was about to find a key to the mysteries of the human mind; the urgent need for a sympathetic "alter ego" who would listen with empathy and understanding; all the specific qualities of Fliess's personality, his interests and the audacity of his hypotheses.

Freud's prolonged cardiac episode, during which Fliess gradually assumed the role of the trusted physician, the "arbiter" over life and death, the strict frustrator, the enforcer of abstinence. There is no doubt that this contributed not only to the rapid intensification of their relationship but also to its stormy course. The repeated surgical procedures which Fliess performed on Freud's nose and sinuses.

Fliess's response which apparently not only permitted a certain type of relationship to develop but invited and fostered it.

Which aspects of Freud's relationship to Fliess were comparable to a transference relationship in the analytic situation? First, the extreme overvaluation of the object which blunts the critical evaluation of the latter's qualities, work, scientific accomplishments, etc.; then, an exaggerated need for approval and praise; a tendency to deny any negative feelings (see Chapters 4 and 5); an alternation between submissiveness and defiance indicating the ambivalence which is unavoidable in any regular analysis.

Sudden eruptions of hostility which can be expressed in slips, dreams, and even quite openly in veiled, displaced guilt feelings, or in symptom formation (see Chapters 4, 5, 6, and 7); the sexualization of the relationship. This aspect Freud recognized—or at least acknowledged—only later (see Chapters 5, 6, and 9).

In order to keep the distinction between a transference in a regular analysis and the phenomena reminiscent of a transference occurring during Freud's self-analysis, I shall speak of "transferencelike phenomena" and of a "transferencelike relationship." These factors began to emerge during the year 1893.

It is characteristic of the need to preserve a somewhat exalted image of the analyst that any sign of weakness is both resented and feared. This also applies to a physical illness of the analyst, and any such illness, especially if its details are known to the analysand, is apt to create a strain on the transference relationship.

This element was quite pronounced during the prolonged introductory phase of Freud's self-analysis. Although we are not in possession of direct information about Fliess's illnesses, Freud's letters are replete with pertinent information. Fliess apparently suffered from very severe headaches. He attributed them, on the one hand, to pathology of the nose and sinuses; on the other hand, he linked them, once he had developed his periodicity theory, to the "critical periods" during which such headaches could recur with or without the reappearance of nasal pathology. For the diagnosis and treatment of these symptoms Fliess consulted many prominent specialists in the field and underwent quite a few operations, some of them rather extensive and—in view of the high incidence of serious postoperative complications at that time —quite risky.

Freud was deeply concerned about Fliess's symptoms, and his initial response was worry and sympathy. In a letter of February 7, 1894 Freud wrote:

> I feel reassured about your headache since I received an opinion from Scheffer [an E.N.T. man who treated Fliess in Bremen] which holds out the promise of a complete cure. I was brazen enough to contact him directly [1].

In the letter of April 19, 1894 where Freud described his most severe heart attack and thus could have been expected to voice his deepest need of Fliess, he also voiced his first doubts about the origin of his friend's headaches (see Chapter 2). During their meeting in August, 1894 Fliess, who had undergone surgery earlier that summer, must have discussed his headaches with Freud. In the previously quoted letter written on August 23, 1894 the conflict aroused in Freud by Fliess's symptoms became manifest:

> Dearest Friend,
> You are having severe headaches and are anticipating further surgery; this might sound gloomy and disagreeable if I did not fully share your expectation that the course you have undertaken will free you of *your* headaches. Just promise me one thing right now, and that is not to forget the factor which immediately precedes the knot[ty problem] "headache," and which is of a purely nervous nature. In other, and for once also plainer, words, promise me this time to let months go by [literally: "pass over the scar," i.e., allow for complete healing] before you go back to work in Berlin.
> We shall write or talk about this further [2].

The conflict became even more apparent in the unpublished passage of Letter 21 written on August 29, 1894:

> Dearest Friend,
> Now that is really too much; are you going to turn completely into pus on me? The devil with having surgery again and again; just be done with it once and for all. So that old woman[8] who did not like

8 This reference is not identifiable.

your headaches years ago, and who wrote me that peculiar letter, was actually quite right! But what shall I do about it? I wish I were a "doctor," as people say, a physician and magical healer in order to understand such matters and not have to leave you in strange hands under such circumstances. Unfortunately, I am nothing of the sort, as you well know. I must rely on you in this as in all the rest [of things]; I must hope that you also know how to treat *yourself* and that you will be successful in *your* own case as in those of others (myself included).

The fact that our meeting will fall through because of that is not very nice either. A temporary hope leaves behind something like an unfulfilled claim [3].

The conflicting emotions expressed in these paragraphs are quite transparent: anger, disappointment, pain, a definitely critical attitude, followed by a protestation of complete confidence. Other parts of this letter expressed even more painful conflicts which were to return in years to come, and which played a very important part in some of Freud's dreams. Among them was the fact that Freud was about to leave on a trip with his wife; should he abandon his plans and hurry to the bedside of his sick friend? He chose the trip, which was very enjoyable; and when he learned that Fliess had undergone surgery in Munich, his letters expressed guilt and halfhearted offers to hurry there for a visit.

No wonder his relationship with Fliess was sometimes severely strained and at a crisis point! Each of these crises was due to a combination of factors originating both from Fliess's actions, behavior, and opinions and the simultaneous expansion of Freud's insight into the working of the mind gained from his own analysis and that of his patients.

In a normal analysis the transference manifestations, both positive and negative, are subjected to constant scrutiny. At that time Freud was already becoming aware of the importance of an erotized transference, but he had not yet recognized the complexity of positive and negative transference phenomena. It is therefore not surprising that Freud remained for several years oblivious to the very existence, not to speak of the intensity, of the ambivalence conflict in his relationship to Fliess.

THE EMMA EPISODE

This ambivalence was especially prominent during an episode which dominated their correspondence during March and April of 1895 and which influenced the manifest content, the associations, and the interpretation of Freud's "specimen dream," which took place during the night of July 23-24, 1895. This episode was concerned with the case of Emma (see Schur [1966a] for a complete discussion and most of Freud's letters pertaining to this event).

Freud was treating a patient, Emma, for hysteria. He had asked Fliess (as he had also done in the case of many other patients), to examine her for any pathology of the turbinate bones and the sinuses which might be a factor contributing to her hysterical abdominal symptoms. Fliess diagnosed some pathology and suggested surgery. Upon the insistence of Freud who, as he said, wanted "only the best" for his patient, Fliess came from Berlin in February, 1895 to operate on Emma, although he could not stay in Vienna long enough to attend to her aftercare.

Following the surgery Freud's patient had persistent pain, fetid secretions, and some bleeding. Freud initially attributed her complaints to her hysteria, but gradually he became genuinely concerned about her symptoms. After some attempts had been made to improve the drainage of the wound, an E.N.T. specialist was called in who found that Fliess had inadvertently left a half-meter strip of iodoform gauze in the cavity (which had obviously been created by the removal of the turbinal bone and the opening of a sinus). Upon the removal of the gauze the patient had a severe hemorrhage and went into shock for a few seconds until a new packing staunched the flow of blood. Freud, who was present, felt sick and had to leave the room; he recovered after drinking some cognac.

Subsequently the patient had to undergo additional surgery and had repeated hemorrhages, one of them so severe that ligation of the carotid artery was considered. She required packing for a long period during which the danger of infection was ever present. It took many weeks before she was out of danger.

After the discovery that Fliess had committed one of the not too uncommon surgical "parapraxes," thereby causing unforeseeable complications, Freud hesitated for a day before writing the news to Fliess, and then sent him a long letter starting with a vivid description of the "dénouement"—the discovery of the iodoform gauze, the cause of the foul odor, pain, bleeding, etc. Then followed a solemn protestation of Freud's unshaken trust in Fliess, and the reassurance that no one could or would blame Fliess for what had happened, a confession of Freud's own shame at his momentary hesitation over writing the letter, and an assertion of his conviction that Fliess could certainly take such news in stride, etc. Freud attributed his spell of faintness after the hemorrhage not to the smell and sight of the blood, but to the emotions which had flooded him when he thought in a flash of all these aspects of the situation. "Only" ten minutes later was he able to realize that it was the E.N.T. man who was to blame for the hemorrhage! The reason, or rather the rationalization, for the displacement of the blame was that the gauze had been removed in the patient's home instead of in a hospital, where the wound could have been widened (as it was later) before the gauze was removed.

At a later stage of his analytic work Freud recognized the meaning of parapraxes—and the fact that protestations and negations such as his invariably expressed their opposite. We may therefore state with certainty that Freud unconsciously knew very well that Fliess was responsible for the critical complications and blamed him for them, so that his trust in Fliess had been deeply shaken.

All this came out clearly in later letters, at a time when Emma's condition was really critical, through a series of subtly disguised reproaches whose wording barely hid Freud's attitude. Yet consciously Freud apparently knew nothing of this attitude. The explanation is obvious. At that time Freud could not afford to abandon his positive relationship which had to be protected by denial and a displacement of the accusation. Torn between needing and blaming Fliess, Freud's actions were highly revealing throughout the period of crisis. Freud needed Fliess because he was in the midst of momentous discoveries and decisions about the direction his work was to take. Moreover, he was not yet quite secure about his own health.

The correspondence during this whole period, from the beginning of the Emma episode in February, 1895 to the day of the Irma dream (July 23-24), documents a change not only in Freud's physical symptoms, but also in his response to them, which was closely paralleled by a shift in his relationship to Fliess.

Fliess had evidently changed his evaluation of Freud's cardiac symptoms and was now assigning an important role to nasal pathology, but without rescinding his injunction against smoking. During the winter of 1895 Freud had had one of his frequent colds and probably a chronic sinus infection. When Fliess came to Vienna to operate on Emma at the end of February, he saw a good deal of Freud, and treated him by one or more of the methods he often used during other "congresses"—local application of cocaine to the nose and cauterization (on at least one later occasion he performed some surgery on the turbinate bone).

It is hard to judge whether Fliess's emphasis on Freud's nasal pathology as the cause of his cardiac symptoms was due to his expanding views on the nasal reflex neurosis or represented a new way of attempting to allay Freud's concern about his heart. It may also have been influenced by Fliess's constant preoccupation with his own "nasal" symptoms.

Fliess underwent another surgical procedure late in March, or early in April. Freud responded with mixed feelings as he had done in 1894. He wrote to Fliess on April 11, 1895:

> Science is proceeding half-way, i.e., nothing new, no ideas and no observations. I thoroughly overworked myself with the psychology, and am letting it lie for the time being. Only the book with Breuer [*Studies on Hysteria*] is progressing, and will be finished in about three weeks. . . .
>
> Thus far nothing has been said about you. I gather that you have just begun to feel like yourself again. This time keep it up for a while! So your head is all right after all. *This* has been accomplished, can I now really believe it? [4]

In these last sentences Freud expressed both his hopes and his doubts about the final success of Fliess's various nasal and sinus surgeries. As we shall see, this hope, which was essential to Freud's positive feelings for Fliess, especially at the time he wrote this letter, was not fulfilled.

A letter written on April 20, 1895 clearly indicated the meshing of the Emma affair with both Freud's own health problems and the complex manifestations of his ambivalence conflict concerning Fliess (see also Schur, 1966a, p. 65f). At one point, when Emma's condition was highly critical, Freud had let Fliess know that one of the many E.N.T. men called in to treat Emma had connected her repeated hemorrhages with something Fliess had done during that first operation. This theme of "telling on" someone was to run like a thread through many of Freud's dreams, and I shall discuss it extensively further on.

Fliess apparently reacted with great indignation and demanded some kind of retraction. Freud answered on April 20:

> The writer of this is still very miserable, but is also quite offended that you should deem it necessary to have a testimonial from G. for your rehabilitation. Even if G. should have the same opinion of your skill

as Weil, for me you remain the healer, the prototype of the man into whose hands one confidently entrusts one's life and that of one's family. I wanted to tell you of my misery, perhaps ask you for some advice about Emma, but not reproach you for anything. This would have been stupid, unjustified, in clear contradiction to my feelings. . . .

In the same letter Freud discussed his health and in particular Fliess's assumptions about the nasal origin of his cardiac symptoms.

With regard to my condition, I would like you to be right in thinking that the nose has a large share in it, and the heart a small one. Only a very strict judge would take it amiss that with this kind of pulse and the insufficiency I often believe the opposite. I cannot accept your proposal that I come to Berlin *now*. I am not in a position to allow myself 1000-1500 florins [$400-$600] or even half that amount for my own health, and I am not sufficiently demoralized to take up your hint about sparing me the loss.[9] I also think that it is not necessary. If the empyema [of the sphenoidal sinus; see letter of April 26, 1895] is the main problem, then the vantage point of danger is eliminated and a few more months of discomfort will not kill me. If, however, a cardiac lesion is the main trouble, then you can only relieve discomfort and I shall then have to face the danger without any warning, which I do not want.

Today I can write because I have more hope. I pulled myself out of a miserable attack [of nasal, not cardiac discomfort] with a cocaine application. I cannot guarantee that I shall not come for a day or two for cauterization or galvanization [Freud meant either chemical or electrical cauterization], but even that is not possible at the moment. *What I would like most is for you to agree to want to know nothing more about the topic heart* [my italics].

I am happy that I now have a claim to hear from you again, and a good deal more.

Most cordially
Your
Sigm. [5]

This last letter is especially revealing. Freud was obviously becoming less and less concerned about his heart. Despite the continuing intimacy and cordiality of his relationship with Fliess, he was also showing much more independence by rightly refusing to undergo any radical procedures—perhaps with Emma's complications in mind. His concern over the potential financial drain of an unessential trip to Berlin was probably connected in part with his wife's pregnancy.

---

[9] Fliess probably offered financial help for this trip.

On April 26, 1895 Freud wrote again

Strangely enough, I have not felt bad at all. I put an end to the last horrible attack with cocaine; since then things are fine and a great deal of pus is coming out. I evidently have an empyema of the sphenoidal bone, which naturally makes me very happy.[10] She, my and your tormentor, also seems to be doing well now [6].

[And on April 27:] (1) I am feeling well; (2) am secreting lots of pus; (3) I am feeling *very* well. Thus I want to have no more of a heart condition, just the "treatment" through nicotine.[11] Really, I have gone through a great deal and I still cannot get away now, all the more so if the diagnosis is more harmless rather than more serious. But I shall come and let myself be helped by you [7].

[Finally, on May 25, Freud wrote:] Now, about my nasal condition. I secreted abundant masses of pus and throughout it I felt splendid. Now the secretion has nearly stopped and I still feel very well [8].

THE FIRST TRIUMPH

Throughout this dramatic period when Freud was alternating between deep sympathy for his patient, Emma, whom he had come to like, and guilt for what had been done to her by Fliess who had been called in at his behest, he was engaged in writing his contributions to the *Studies on Hysteria,* which merely meant setting down on paper what he had found two years earlier. In addition, Freud was working on a paper on anxiety neurosis. However, neither represented the area of his main efforts, which he described in two letters written a month apart. The first one was written on April 27, a day after the above-quoted letter; the second, the more revealing of the two, was written on May 25, 1895.[12] In these letters we can see the germination of a nexus of crucial ideas, and the conflict and mental anguish which they engendered. Freud was making a first attempt to arrive at a general psychology, which in the first of these two letters he still somewhat modestly called a "psychology for the neurologist." In doing so he was torn between the temptation to formulate his hypothesis within the framework of neurophysiology and the growing recognition that he would have to develop his concepts within a purely psychological framework. The first line of thought led in the fall of 1895 to the

[10] Freud was obviously "happy" because the more nasal pathology he had, the more he was inclined to believe Fliess's theory concerning the "nasal reflex" etiology of his cardiac symptoms. It is much more likely, of course, that he was recovering from a mild coronary episode unrelated to a recurrent sinusitis.

[11] I.e., through abstinence from nicotine.

[12] Both letters were published only in part in *The Origins of Psychoanalysis.*

"Project"; the second, after four more years of trial and error, to Chapter VII of The *Interpretation of Dreams*.

There were more immediate results, however. Freud had begun to realize that a satisfactory understanding of psychic pathology could be attained only by basing it on a real comprehension of normal psychic functioning. On the other hand, he saw that a greater understanding of normal mental functioning could be achieved through a study of psychopathology. The postulate that psychoanalysis had to be an integral part of a general psychology was being born.

That Freud's self-analysis was already a part of this extremely creative period is suggested by his description of his mode of activity in the letter to Fliess of May 25, 1895:

> Actually a satisfactory general conception of neuropsychotic disturbance is impossible if one cannot link it with clear assumptions about normal mental processes. During recent weeks I have devoted every free minute to such work. I have spent the hours of the night between eleven and two in fantasying, transposing, interpreting, and following hunches, and stopping only when somewhere I came up against an absurdity [L. 24].

It was this state of mind which in subsequent letters Freud described as his self-analysis.

Apparently he was also on the verge of discovering the dream work —that mental phenomenon in which "normal" and "pathological" processes are most closely linked. Freud must have been preparing the ground by analyzing dreams and also by fashioning a technique, for such a systematic analysis as the one he utilized for the Irma dream is not created in a day. However, that day, July 24, 1895, represented a milestone in the development of the new science.

Freud did not fail to devote half of his May 25th letter (most of it unpublished) to Fliess's own work, and expressed his enthusiasm about Fliess's possible "solution" to the problem of conception (or rather its prevention), which probably involved the postulation of a period of increased fertility at a certain point in the menarche.[13] In an almost parenthetical remark, Freud let Fliess know that his wife was pregnant. Conception had occurred immediately before the Emma episode.

---

13 Fliess seems to have had an idea similar to the one developed later by the Austrian gynecologist Knauss, which became the basis of the "rhythm" method of contraception. Fliess arrived at it while developing his idea of periodicity, which had apparently begun to occupy him at that time. It is interesting that Fliess evidently failed to follow up this valid and biologically sound idea.

(Four weeks after this letter Freud received the news that Fliess's wife too was pregnant!)

Despite the frantic pace of his work and his concern over Emma, Freud was in a very good and confident mood. On June 12, 1895, he became bold and resumed smoking. He wrote to Fliess:

> I have started smoking again, because I have always missed it (after fourteen months of abstinence)[14] and because I must treat this psychic fellow well or else he won't work for me. I demand a great deal of him. Most of the time the torment is superhuman [L. 25].[15]

Freud apparently discussed his decision to resume smoking with his friend Dr. Rie, who "told on" him in a letter to Fliess written the same day as Freud's—June 12—which was preserved among the letters from Freud to Fliess. Fliess promptly insisted on continued abstinence, and Freud submitted grudgingly, but even this frustration did not detract from his well-being. He greeted with enthusiasm the news of Mrs. Fliess's first pregnancy, not without adding an ironic comment on Fliess's discoveries about contraception!

> Hail, dear Wilhelm!
> May your dear, good, and strong wife, for whom until now hope and fulfillment have always coincided, remain the darling of fate as a mother as well. . . .
> So I shall come early in September. How I will manage to do without you afterward, I don't know. I am having enough troubles with the smoking. . . .
> Given full credit for your discovery, you would be the strongest man, in your hands you would hold the reins of sexuality which rules humanity, you could do everything and prevent everything. Therefore, I do not yet believe the second piece of glad tidings.[16] The first one I do believe; it is certainly easier . . . [9].

Fliess did not answer for some time, and Freud finally sent him a letter on the day following his Irma dream. In an earlier publication (1966a) I have discussed at length the striking relationship between the details of the Emma episode, the manifest content, associations,

---

[14] Freud made a slip here: he had informed Fliess in his long medical report of June 22, 1894—not quite a year before—that he had started to smoke again, and he also had smoked intermittently during periods of "abstinence" (e.g., the "Thursday cigar").

[15] Reading about Freud's constant struggle against his nicotine addiction, I understood better why I was not more successful when I tried to persuade him to give up smoking more than 30 years later.

[16] Fliess's birth control discoveries.

and interpretations of the Irma dream, Freud's self-analysis, and the transferencelike aspect of his relationship to Fliess. I shall therefore repeat only some of the pertinent data here.

According to Freud's own interpretation (1900, pp. 106-120, 292-296), the main theme of the Irma dream was his wish to exculpate himself from any responsibility for his patient's continuing symptoms. If she still had any, these must have been due to some organic illness. The exculpation required him to prove that his professional conscientiousness was beyond reproach. To achieve this he displaced all blame onto his friend Otto (Dr. Oskar Rie), who had apparently questioned his results with Irma in a conversation with Breuer, and who, as we know, had also "told on" Freud in his letter of June 12 to Fliess. In the dream Freud also put M. (Breuer) in a rather disparaging position, making the latter look foolish. Freud's associations also included Fliess, and he delineated two groups of people to whom he attached opposing sets of ideas. One group consisted of those who "didn't know"; who made silly diagnoses; who, like Otto, gave injections with dirty syringes; who gave presents of smelly liqueur; who, like M., made silly remarks while examining the patient. The second group actually consisted of just one person—the exalted figure of his friend Fliess, "whose agreement" Freud recalled "with satisfaction" whenever he "felt isolated in his opinions"; who *did* understand Freud and "played so large a part" in his life; who "had a special knowledge of the consequences of affections of the nose and its accessory cavities"; who had drawn Freud's attention "to some very remarkable connections between the turbinal bones and the female sex organs." Freud's associations also included his concern about Fliess because the latter suffered from suppurative rhinitis, which might cause pyemia.

Freud also mentioned that he had had Irma examined by Fliess to rule out such nasal pathology as a possible cause of her abdominal symptoms. All these connections with the Emma episode indicate that the main wish behind Freud's Irma dream was not to exculpate *himself* but Fliess. It was a wish not to jeopardize his positive relationship with Fliess.

On July 24, 1895 Freud discovered "the riddle of the dream" (see L. 137). On that day he wrote to Fliess, but did not mention the dream or his analysis:

You demon! Why don't you write to me? How are you? Don't you care at all any more what I'm doing? What's happening with the nose, menstruation, labor pains, neuroses, your dear wife and the budding little one? This year I am sick after all and must come to you. What will happen if by chance both of us should remain healthy for a whole year? Are we only friends in misfortune? Or do we also want to share the experiences of calmer times with each other?

Where will you spend the month of August? We are living very contentedly in "Heaven."[17]

Heartiest greetings,
Your
Sigm. [10]

Freud, who later emphasized that *daimon kai tyche* (fate and accident) determine the development of all individuals, here addressed Fliess as his *demon* (or fate)—that force that drives us on according to its own law and that cannot be escaped.[18] Yet—to repeat—he wrote this letter on the day which he subsequently and triumphantly proclaimed as the day of his great discovery.

With the interpretation of the Irma dream and the writing of this letter, a chapter in Freud's life came to an end. Freud had begun it as a brilliant, curious, troubled man. From that day on he knew that whatever misfortunes the future might bring, he had radically changed the interpretation, and thus to some extent the course, of human events. Whenever doubts beset him, he could fall back on the analysis of dreams, which constantly reconfirmed his discoveries, although it took another four years before he fully formulated his concepts in *The Interpretation of Dreams.*

Freud states this repeatedly, for instance, in a letter to Jung written on September 2, 1907:

I would like . . . to tell you . . . of my many years of honorable but painful isolation which started after I had had my first glimpse into the new world; of my closest friends' lack of interest and understanding; of the anxious periods when I myself believed I had been mistaken and wondered how I could still turn to advantage a bungled life for the sake of my family; of the gradually growing conviction that kept clinging to the interpretation of dreams as to a rock in a stormy sea, and of the calm assurance that finally took possession of me . . . [L. 126*].

Obviously, in 1895, Freud had not yet achieved this "calm assurance."

---

[17] The Bellevue, where Freud and his family were spending the summer, was situated on Himmelstrasse (Heaven Street), a steep road in a suburb of Vienna.
[18] Cf. Goethe, Urworte, Orphisch. *Gesammelte Werke,* Vol. 15, p. 180f.

The interpretation of the first dream not only was a milestone in the development of psychoanalysis, it also became *the* important vehicle in Freud's self-analysis and with it in his personal development. While the Irma dream had at the moment also made it possible for Freud to deny any hostile, accusatory feelings toward Fliess, or any doubt about the latter's "greatness," such feelings had nonetheless taken root in Freud's unconscious. From that point on one part of Freud realized that it was *he* who was probing some of the great riddles of life, while Fliess was on the way to losing himself in more and more fantastic speculations. The firm knowledge that he now had such a potent tool for future research provided Freud with the great incentive to continue his self-analysis in order to deepen his understanding of the working of the mind. The unavoidable dissolution of the transferencelike element in his relationship was to be a slow and difficult process. What made this last aspect of his effort so painful and caused it to have lingering repercussions was the fact that, in contrast to the normal process of an analysis, this dissolution was both enhanced and complicated by external events and therefore resulted eventually in a total break.

The role that the Irma dream played in Freud's personal life does not in the least detract from its importance in the history of psychoanalysis. Here Freud recognized for the first time that every element of the manifest dream content had meaning and that the latent content of the dream could be unraveled by associating freely to each of these elements. In connection with this dream Freud also discovered and described the operation of the dream work; it involved condensation and displacement mechanisms, which he later described as typical of the mental processes operating in the "unconscious," or the "id."

What Freud had not yet realized was the transference aspect of the dream, especially the negative transference and the defenses against it which operate in dream formation.

Freud did not mention his important discovery of the dream work in the letter of July 24, 1895, and merely hinted at it in a letter of August 6, 1895. He was saving the news for their "congress," hoping that Fliess's treatment of his nose would leave him with enough energy to talk about it all.

As usual, after a tremendous creative effort, there was a letdown, but Freud was able to deal with it without becoming depressed. He wrote on August 16: "Bowling and picking mushrooms are certainly much healthier [than psychology]" (L. 27).

This letter of August 16 contained a "leitmotif" which subsequently was repeated more explicitly. It was the composite image of Jacob wrestling with the Angel and Moses seeing the Promised Land only from afar, at the top of a high mountain:

> Shortly after . . . one of the foothills had been climbed, I saw new difficulties before me and did not think that my breath would hold out for the new effort.

While the context (preceding sentence) clearly indicates that Freud was referring to his work on the "Psychology," this was probably also an allusion to his persisting shortness of breath and his inability to climb mountains during that period.

In September, 1895 Freud visited Fliess in Berlin. In the train on the way back to Vienna he started to write his "Project for a Scientific Psychology," which he completed within a few weeks. Although this was a fragmentary work, it is only now, after 70 years, that we are beginning to understand all of its implications for the past and future development of psychoanalysis as a general psychology, and to correlate it with newer findings in neurophysiology.

Unfortunately, Fliess had again operated on Freud's ethmoidal bone during that meeting. No wonder Freud not only reported on the progress of the "Project" in his letter of September 23, 1895, and mentioned further confirmation of his findings on the dream work, but also complained that since his return from the visit to Fliess he had been feeling progressively more miserable!

In addition to describing the tremendous difficulties he encountered in his attempt to finish the "Project," Freud's letters of this period also reflect the turmoil created by his self-analysis and the flood of new ideas about neurosogenesis, paralleled by a new upsurge in positive feelings for Fliess, obviously intensified by their meeting in September.

On October 8, 1895 Freud wrote to Fliess:

> Dearest Wilhelm,
> News from you had already become a necessity for me because I had already come to the same wrong conclusion: that your silence was indicative of headache. I began to feel more comfortable when—after a long interval—I again had a piece of your scientific material in my hands. I have so far only had a glimpse at it, and I fear that the respect for so much honest and sophisticated material will put my theoretical fantasies to shame.

Freud then expressed the intensity of his longing for Fliess, which this time had developed only after his feverish effort to write the "Project," but then had erupted full force. He ended the letter by saying:

How am I doing heartwise?[19] Not especially well, but not as badly as during the first two weeks. This time *my attention has not been with it at all* [my italics] [11].

This last sentence again shows that Freud had acquired at least temporarily the ability not to pay undue attention to physical discomfort. During the years to come this ability was developed to the point of mastery. However, in 1895 he had not yet achieved this mastery. Only eight days later (October 16, 1895) Freud complained again about his miserable physical state. He was struggling with the formulation of his "Project" and the final answers were eluding him. He pleaded with Fliess: "If I send you . . . a few more pages of philosophical stammering (not especially what I consider well done), I hope this will put you in a more conciliatory mood" (L. 31). Was Freud trying a few sentences later to appease Fliess, who had always insisted on Freud's not smoking and who had probably "scolded" him during their meeting in Berlin?

. . . I have entirely given up smoking again, so as not to have to reproach myself for my bad pulse and to be rid of the miserable struggle with the craving for a fourth or fifth [cigar]; I prefer having my struggle over the first one. The abstinence is probably also not very conducive to psychic satisfaction.

Freud was able to adhere to not smoking for only a few weeks. By November 8, 1895 he had to confess:

I have not been able to go through with complete abstinence. With my load of theoretical and practical worries the increase in psychical hyperasthesia has been unbearable [L. 35].

Freud's cardiac symptoms did not last long, and from this point on they gradually seemed to subside, even though Freud was engaged in the most intense period of his self-analysis. This was two years after the symptoms had begun, and about 20 months after the most severe attacks of anginal pain and paroxysmal tachycardia, a timetable which

---

[19] Literally: in the direction of the heart.

fits in well with my assumption that Freud had suffered a mild coronary thrombosis in the spring of 1894.

Freud temporarily abandoned his work on the theoretical formulation of a general psychology and devoted his full energy to his empirical observations. He reported feelings of physical well-being and the ability to sustain his working capacity at its top level. On November 29, 1895 Freud wrote to Fliess:

> Dearest Wilhelm,
> I feel amazingly well, as I have not *since the beginning of the whole affair*. I no longer have any pus either, just a lot of mucous secretion. I have, by the way, never doubted the success of your *small* [surgical] interventions, and thus have earned my well-being [my italics] [12].

From this point on the physical symptom mentioned most frequently in the correspondence was "migraine" headaches from which both Freud and Fliess suffered, and which soon became enmeshed in Fliess's speculations about periodicity.

For Freud the year ended on an optimistic note. His sixth child arrived on December 3, 1895, and "evidently brought fortune" (L. 38) because thereafter Freud's practice nearly doubled.

4

SELF-ANALYSIS

Freud began the new year (1896) with a long letter which was a kind of summary of his latest attempts to conceptualize his findings. To some extent it also marked the end of a period. From then on (with certain exceptions such as *Beyond the Pleasure Principle* in 1920 and "A Note upon the 'Mystic Writing Pad' " in 1925) Freud abandoned his efforts to formulate concepts in terms of neuroanatomy and neurophysiology, and relied mainly on formulations couched in psychological terms. During this time Fliess was apparently already deeply involved in his "periodicity" hypotheses.

BEGINNING OF DIFFERENCES WITH FLIESS

It is significant and characteristic of the remarkable continuity of Freud's work that in this letter of January 1, 1896 he expressed a thought which he restated in nearly identical terms almost 40 years later (in the Postscript to his *Autobiographical Study* (1925b, p. 71).

> I see that via the detour of being a physician, you have attained your first ideal—the understanding of man through physiology; while I secretly nurse the hope of reaching by the same path my original goal of philosophy. For that is what I wanted originally, when I did not yet know the purpose of my being in this world [L. 39].

There now followed a period of intensive work in which ideas and findings were consolidated, while the self-analysis remained dormant. In a letter of February 13, 1896, Freud used the term "metapsychol-

93

ogy" for the first time in connection with his attempt to formulate a general psychology "in depth." Concerning his health he wrote:

> My state of health does not deserve to be a topic of inquiry. The suppuration on the left side [from the old empyema of the sinuses] has recurred during the past week; migraines [are] rather frequent. The necessary abstinence is scarcely helping me much either. I have rapidly turned grey [1].

During this time we can also detect a certain shift in Freud's relationship with Fliess—away from the previously prevalent transference-like manifestations with their effusive admiration and hidden, denied ambivalence.

A week after writing the letter of February 13, Freud received the manuscript of Fliess's book, *Die Beziehungen zwischen Nase und weiblichen Geschlechtsorganen in ihren biologischen Bedeutungen dargestellt,* which was to be published in 1897. This manuscript already contained many of Fliess's farfetched speculations about periodicity, which he formulated in the introduction to the book as follows:

> Woman's menstrual bleeding [is the expression] of a process which affects both sexes and the beginning of which goes back beyond puberty. . . .
>
> The facts before us compel us to emphasize another factor. They teach us that, apart from the menstrual process of the twenty-eight day type, another group of periodic phenomena exists with a twenty-three day cycle, to which people of all ages and both sexes are subject.
>
> Consideration of these two groups of periodic phenomena points to the conclusion that they have a solid inner connection with both male and female sexual characteristics. And if both—only with a different emphasis—are present in both man and woman, that is only consistent with our bisexual constitution.
>
> Recognition of these things led to the further insight that the development of our organism takes place by fits and starts in these sexual periods, and that the day of our death is determined by them as much as is the day of our birth. The disturbances of illness are subject to the same periodic laws as are these periodic phenomena themselves.
>
> A mother transmits her periods to her child and determines its sex by the period which is first transmitted. The periods then continue in the child, and are repeated with the same rhythm from generation to generation. They can no more be created anew than can energy, and their rhythm survives as long as organized beings reproduce themselves sexually. These rhythms are not restricted to mankind, but extend into the animal world and probably throughout the organic world. The wonderful accuracy with which the period of twenty-three, or, as the case

may be, twenty-eight whole days is observed permits one to suspect a deeper connection between astronomical relations and the creation of organisms [quoted by Kris (1950, p. 7f.)].

Freud had given Fliess, in return for the latter's interest and encouragement, effusive admiration and praise for his work. He had been ready to accept—or at least tried to accept—farfetched theories. He even tried to apply to his own life Fliess's main hypotheses concerning, first, the nasal reflex neurosis and, later, the periodicity of all biological events.

What probably appealed to Freud in the nasal reflex neurosis hypothesis was that Fliess related many of the symptoms presumably connected with nasal pathology to vasomotor disturbances of sexual origin, which he treated, and claimed to cure, by local applications of cocaine, a form of therapy based on Freud's cocaine research.

It is more difficult to understand what induced Freud to accept Fliess's speculations about the periodicity of biological events. We can only speculate about the reasons for Freud's acceptance, hesitant though it was, of this "number game."[1] In any event, Fliess's speculations about the influence of certain periods on dates of illness and death played into Freud's obsessive (so akin to superstitious) preoccupation with his own death and the date on which it would occur.

Freud's first reaction to Fliess's new work showed that he was greatly impressed by its flight of imagination. However, he did try in his letter of March 1, 1896 (L. 42) to offer Fliess some constructive, carefully worded criticism, and to correlate some of Fliess's speculations with his own theory of neurosis. Freud originally believed that there was an area in which Fliess's periodicity hypothesis could provide some sort of "organic," physiological basis for the periodicity of the anxiety attacks which occur in anxiety neuroses. At that time he did not foresee that precisely this point would become one of the critical areas of incompatibility between Fliess's theories and his own observations. Fliess increasingly came to view the "critical periods" as *the* decisive etiological factor, whereas Freud emphasized the importance of psychic conflict as the precipitating factor of neurosis.

Freud's letter of March 1 contained an unpublished passage that is especially meaningful in this context. Did it indicate that Freud already anticipated the eventual rupture of their friendship and knew

---

[1] See, however, my discussion of the significance of numbers in the Jewish cultural tradition (Chapter 1).

just why this would happen? After some bitter remarks about the growing estrangement between himself and Breuer, he wrote:

> The fact that one must pay so dearly for everything one has enjoyed in life is decidedly not a nice arrangement. Will the *same thing* happen to both of us *too?* [2; italics added]

As time went on, Freud became increasingly reluctant to acquiesce in Fliess's ever more fanciful hypotheses, and the resultant strain in the relationship between the two men eventually led to a break between them. At this time, however, as a sign of cooperation with Fliess, Freud enclosed some complex formulas applying periodicity related to personal matters. This cooperation continued, with a number of ups and downs, for more than three years.

Fliess's latest hypotheses created a new complication; migraine and other types of headache suffered by Fliess were now projected and anticipated at certain "critical" dates, and of course they frequently materialized. Soon, to Freud's dismay, even the dates of their "congresses" had to fit into "noncritical" periods. In the unpublished portion of his letter of March 16, 1896, Freud was quite outspoken in his annoyance about this:

> I have not yet really overcome the depression about your headache calendar. I can be somewhat glad that Easter is far away from the period which you have underlined as the most critical one. As for the rest, I can see, unfortunately, that every third day brings you a headache. However, just as emperors undoubtedly exert an influence on the weather, I was able, by my presence, to have a favorable influence on [dispose of] your headaches, and therefore I hope for good weather for ɔur meeting [3].

Freud rarely went so far in implying that Fliess's firm belief in "critical" periods was in itself enough to cause the headaches.

Freud was now making plans to write a number of books which would occupy him for years to come. He indicated their nature and scope in the above-quoted letter to Fliess (L. 42). His growing confidence in the importance of his contributions was expressed in his letter of April 2 (L. 44):

> If a few more years of quiet work are granted to the two of us, we shall certainly leave something behind that can justify our existence. In short, in that knowledge I feel myself to be strong enough to cope with all the everyday worries and toil. As a young man I knew no longing

other than that for philosophical insight, and I am now in the act of achieving this by steering from medicine to psychology.

Even the meeting with Fliess which took place about a week after this letter and which apparently was followed by a resumption of the self-analysis, did not basically change Freud's increasing feelings of self-confidence and independence. This was revealed in the following letter of April 16, 1896:

Dearest Wilhelm,

. . . with my head full of periods and hunches about summations, proud of having achieved some recognition, and with a bold feeling of independence, I returned with a real sense of well-being, and have been very lazy ever since, for that state of semimisery[2] which is essential for intensive work will not re-establish itself. I have to record only a few dawning hunches (from my daily work) about the in-between realm,[3] and in general a reinforcement of the impression that *everything* is as I surmise it to be and that everything will become clear. Among these, a completely surprising explanation of Emma's hemorrhages, which will give you great satisfaction. I have already guessed what the story is, but I shall wait with communicating it until the patient herself has caught up.

Following your suggestion [literally: invitation] I have started to isolate myself completely and find it easy to bear. However, there is still one prior commitment I have to honor—a lecture at the Psychiatric Society on Tuesday. . . .

As far as I am concerned, I note migraines, nasal secretion, and attacks of fear of death, such as today, for example, *although Tilgner's cardiac death is probably more responsible for that than the time period* [my italics].[4] You have helped me a great deal toward achieving moderation with regard to nicotine, and altogether I feel more settled and put-together since our meeting. It was very good for me and very necessary. I shall probably surprise you shortly with some psychologi-

[2] *Mittelelend* was another of the unusual word combinations coined by Freud. *Mittelelend* also was a pun, an allusion to *Mittelschmerz,* the pain experienced by many women at the time of ovulation, which usually occurs in the middle of a menstrual cycle. This topic was of great interest to Fliess. Freud repeatedly referred to the fact that he was most creative during periods of mild physical discomfort. This had first been called to his attention by Fliess. However, it was not quite accurate. The mood Freud describes here was actually characteristic of periods of waiting before new material in his work or in his self-analysis came up, as the rest of the letter shows.

[3] Freud coined the term *Zwischenreich,* combining *zwischen* (between, in-between) and *Reich* (realm, state, empire). This probably refers to the unconscious, and also to his self-analysis. It also applies to the mind-body problem which preoccupied both Freud and Fliess (see also Stewart, 1967).

[4] Tilgner was a prominent Viennese sculptor. For a detailed discussion of his death and Freud's reaction to it, see the following section in this chapter.

cal scraps; at the moment I am exceedingly lazy about writing. By the way, any drop of alcohol makes me completely stupid [4].

This letter is truly remarkable. It is rare to find such seemingly contradictory expressions of mood and descriptions of Freud's physical condition in one letter. Such contradictions are usually indicative of conflict. They manifest themselves chiefly in the following areas:

In the first part of the letter Freud declared his independence and characterized his feeling as "*frech*," which may be translated as "bold" but more often has the meaning of "fresh, insolent, defiant, impudent." Freud then expressed his conviction that *all* of his assumptions were gradually being confirmed. He also made some veiled allusions to the confusing aspect of Fliess's complex manipulations of time. At the same time, he assured Fliess that he was submitting to the latter's suggestion with regard to breaking off all social and scientific contacts. On the one hand, some letters of this period indicate that Freud was keeping notes about himself and his family to check on the validity of the "periods," and on the other hand he belittled Fliess's hypotheses once again by stating that his attacks of fear of death had nothing to do with their timing (i.e., "the time period"), only to exclaim in the next sentence how much good his meeting with Fliess had done him.

Add to this the seeming contradictions between the initial statement of physical well-being and the enumeration of symptoms such as migraine, nasal secretion, and attacks of fear of death. However, this apparent contradiction can easily be explained: at that particular moment when the dominant mood was pride in his achievements, Freud's sense of general physical well-being was not affected by these ailments. On the other hand, as has already been stated, references to migraines played an important role in the letters of the two men. Migraine and nasal secretion were symptoms from which both Freud and Fliess suffered and in the etiology of which both were interested.[5]

---

[5] Migraine is a complex syndrome. Even now there are many theories about its causes, and this is not the place for an exhaustive consideration of their merits. To mention just one factor: migraine can be precipitated by changes in atmospheric pressure and ion concentration. Many of Freud's fellow migraine sufferers who lived on the northern or southern slopes of the Alps, in Vienna or Trieste, for example, got their migraine attacks either exclusively or primarily before or during a sudden change of temperature and atmospheric pressure caused by a change in the direction of the prevailing winds. Such winds are called *Föhn* on the northern slopes and *Sirocco* on the southern. These sufferers were frequently able to predict the arrival of *Föhn*—which may last for several days—with more accuracy than a barometer. During a period of *Föhn,* most frequent in the spring, there was also an increased incidence and mortality from coronary thrombosis and a much higher incidence than usual of pulmonary hemorrhage in tuberculosis.

Fliess originally attributed migraine largely to pathology of the nose and its sinuses. Later he also tried to link the dates of migraine attacks with his calculations of the laws of periodicity.

Freud's ideas concerning the causes of migraine and the factors precipitating such attacks mirrored his own development, in particular the vicissitudes of his relationship to Fliess, his self-analysis with the resultant solution of his neurotic conflicts, and the progress made in his conceptualizations.

During the 1890s, Freud frequently mentioned migraine attacks and colds. He was prone to relate his headaches to the nose, with the result that he not only made frequent local applications of cocaine, but also permitted Fliess to perform several cauterizations and perhaps some surgery of the turbinate bone in the course of their "congresses." When Fliess began to make calculations about the laws of "periodicity," Freud tried at least to ascertain whether any periodic recurrence of his migraine was discernible. However, he simultaneously became aware of the connection between migraine and neurotic conflict, and several of the manuscripts accompanying his letters were devoted to clinical examples and theoretical formulations about migraine. These formulations changed in accordance with his deepening insight. While Freud frequently included this symptom under the heading of hysteria, he was actually describing what we would now call a "psychosomatic" symptom.

But here Freud ran into conflict with his psychological findings, the hypotheses of Fliess, and his personal feelings for Fliess. Was he to assign more importance to "psychogenic" factors, to nasal pathology, or—alas!—to periodicity calculations? For a time he compromised; the "nose" and, more and more reluctantly, the "periods" were acknowledged as "givens" (either genetic or acquired through nasal infections), and the neurotic conflict was viewed as the precipitating factor; however, the importance of the latter grew in Freud's estimation, and not only with regard to migraine. In his own case, which provides an example of the multiple determinants of a somatic symptom in itself neither too important nor distressing, we can trace the varying factors through Freud's physical and emotional development.

Freud did have frequent head colds, possibly a recurrent sinusitis. He was very sensitive to changes in weather, especially to *Föhn* and *Sirocco*. On the basis of his correspondence with Fliess we may assume that during the decade of their close relationship many of Freud's migraine attacks were in fact precipitated by intense stress, especially in his self-analysis. After the analysis had freed him not only of such overt symptoms as his travel phobia, his excessive preoccupation with the—not too distant—date of his own death, and above all his transferencelike conflicts, the migraine attacks were of no great import, and Freud's interest in migraine as a psychosomatic symptom consequently receded. However, during the years I acted as his physician, he still had migraine on days of *Föhn*. Yet despite the fact that after his radical surgery in 1923 he suffered from chronic sinusitis, this condition never precipitated a migraine attack.

Last, we must ask whether Freud's attacks during the Fliess period showed the true migraine syndrome, which usually begins with prodromal visual signs—"flickering," scotoma, etc.—and is generally unilateral. Freud's correspondence with Fliess does not contain a detailed description of his headaches. As far as Fliess was concerned, Freud usually just referred to "headaches."

Todesangst—The Tilgner Episode

In the remarkable letter of April 16, 1896, Freud had also mentioned attacks of fear of death. On this specific occasion, *he had recognized that it was neurotic, based on a neurotic identification with the dead sculptor Tilgner.* I fortunately have been able to obtain material substantiating my hunch.[6] It is so pertinent to my topic that I think it is justifiable to interrupt the chronological sequence at this point to consider the facts and their meaning for Freud.

Victor Tilgner was a sculptor who had gained considerable renown in Vienna. His biography and certain details of the last weeks of his life were, from many points of view, "made to order" for a neurotic identification with him, so that Freud's reaction to the news of Tilgner's death—in essence: "There but for the grace of God go I"—was not surprising.

Freud usually wrote his letters, as this one to Fliess, late in the evening, so that he had had an opportunity to learn about Tilgner's death from the early afternoon edition of the *Neue Freie Presse,* which Freud read faithfully every evening, and which contained a long obit-

---

[6] I am very indebted to Dr. K. R. Eissler for obtaining for me a lengthy obituary on Victor Tilgner published in the leading Viennese daily of the time, the *Neue Freie Presse,* April 16 and 17, 1896. This obituary contains the biographical data which I present in the following pages.

uary giving Tilgner's life history and many details about his last weeks, including an extensive description of his mortal attack—a typical coronary thrombosis which in many respects was a replica of Freud's own attacks as described in his letter of April 19, 1894. Freud may already have been familiar with details contained in this and a subsequent obituary, because Tilgner had been a popular figure in the intellectual circles of Vienna.

In assessing the impact of Tilgner's death on Freud, we must consider a variety of factors of greater or lesser importance.

Tilgner's first name—Victor—was the same as that of Adler, one of the founders and leaders of the Social-Democratic Party, who had played a role in Freud's development during his student years. Freud had admired Adler, but had attacked him with somewhat undue severity during a philosophical discussion, an incident which had then figured in one of Freud's dreams (see Freud, 1900, p. 213). It was in Adler's former apartment in the Berggasse that Freud was now living.

Victor Tilgner's life and work had in some respects paralleled Freud's. Born in 1844 (12 years before Freud) he had come to Vienna at the age of two and spent his childhood in great poverty. He had shown artistic talent early and had been granted a stipend to study sculpture at the Vienna Academy of Arts; although he received many medals, he had had to fight hard for his daily bread. Finally, the International Exposition of 1874 in Vienna brought him recognition, and he soon became one of the most renowned sculptors of his time, both at home and abroad. He was noted for his reluctance to compromise his artistic credo in response to public criticism.

Throughout his career Tilgner stressed how much he owed to two people—a sculptor in whose studio he had worked as a young man; and a painter who, at a time when no one had yet recognized his talent, was responsible for his success at the International Exposition when the official judges were by no means taken by his novel realistic art.

Even when Tilgner had achieved moderate success as a sculptor, he did not yet dare to try his hand at the monuments and statues which by the time of his death were to populate the palaces, theaters, parks, and squares of Vienna. To do this he felt he would first have to visit Italy, the country of his dreams. The trip was made possible by the generous gift of a wealthy industrialist who not only supplied the necessary funds, but also stipulated: "if one day you happen to see me in the street and do not feel like greeting me—don't do so. This will prove only that by accepting the gift you have not taken on the slightest obligation."

Freud's letters to Fliess, as well as his dreams, were full of his longing to see Italy, especially Rome. He managed to see Tuscany and northern Italy before 1897, but he went to Rome only in 1901. In a letter to Fliess of August 31, 1898 he expressed a witty but meaningful fantasy:

> The great news of the day, the Tsar's manifesto, also stirred me personally. Many years ago I made the diagnosis that the young man is suffering from obsessional ideas. . . . If I could be put in touch with him, two people could be helped. I'll go to Russia for a year and cure him. . . . After that you and I would have three congresses a year, on Italian soil *only,* and I could treat all my patients for nothing [L. 95].

The theme of smarting under financial indebtedness (which Tilgner presumably escaped) also figured in Freud's life. In 1896 he still owed money to some of his friends, especially Breuer, and this bothered him excessively. In later years he could not tolerate owing money to anyone.

During the last years of his life, Tilgner concentrated more and more on the creation of monuments. When the city of Vienna decided to place a large statue of Mozart in a square situated between the Opera House and the Albertina Museum, Tilgner competed for the commission and won it. The last year of his life was devoted largely to the creation of this monument, which he felt would be his *magnum opus.* When he developed anginal symptoms, his physicians advised him to limit his activity drastically. Nevertheless he continued to work incessantly, and consented to take a brief vacation on the Semmering only after his work was ready to be transferred from his studio to the square. He began to be beset by anxious doubts and premonitions, stating: "My gratification will be complete only if I can see [the statue] free and fully unveiled." This was countered with: "Of course, there isn't the slightest doubt that I shall live to see my Mozart free, in full daylight." After a moment of silence came the assertion that after the festivities were over, he would go to Italy instead of dying in his studio.

Freud, in his two letters to Fliess preceding the one in which he spoke of Tilgner's death, had referred to the works he was planning to write if a few more years of life were granted to him. His anxious queries to Fliess: "Will I live long enough—and earn enough—to see Rome?" were comparable to his asking: "Will I live to see the Promised Land?" with which he later referred to the completion of *his magnum opus*—the dream book. Freud feared that, like Moses, he would die within sight of his goal.

This is what actually did happen to Tilgner. The unveiling of the Mozart statue was scheduled to take place on April 21, 1896, in the presence of the Emperor, followed by a gala Mozart concert. Late in the afternoon of April 15, Tilgner gave final instructions for engraving a few bars from Mozart's *Don Giovanni* on the base of the monument. He then spent the evening playing Tarok, Freud's favorite card game and one of his few means of relaxation. During the night Tilgner had repeated attacks of very intense pain in the region of the heart, accompanied by shortness of breath. At first he responded to treatment, but then died in the morning during another attack.

Curiously enough, Freud, who was anything but a music lover, was very fond of Mozart's operas, particularly of *Don Giovanni*. The bars to be engraved on the monument were taken from the final scene of the opera: the scene in which the ghost of the Commandere, whom Don Giovanni had murdered after having seduced his daughter, appears before the villain who dies under the impact of the apparition. It was hardly an accident that Tilgner chose this theme at a time when he was torn by conflicting expectations of ultimate artistic triumph and death. Regardless of whether or not Freud had already learned about this detail when he had his anxiety attack, we know that some of the determinants of such states are rooted in the same ubiquitous conflicts. Freud had not yet reached the point where he could face the ultimate, unfathomable reality with full serenity. Moreover, his own father was aging rapidly, and in fact became mortally ill only a few months later. In addition, Freud was coming ever closer to the discovery of the oedipal conflict. In Mozart's opera the crime of seduction which leads to punishment by the avenging father may have such a powerful impact on us because the oedipal motif reaches us through the senses, heightened by its musical expression.

It is not surprising that reading about all the details of Tilgner's life and death evoked in Freud an attack of dread of dying. Moreover, he recognized his reaction as a neurotic response, and did not exhibit any symptoms of this kind after his self-analysis.

It is also significant that Freud should mention Tilgner's death and his reaction to it in a letter which mirrored his severe ambivalence toward Fliess.[7] Freud mentioned no cardiac symptoms in this connection, and it is remarkable that in the many descriptions of his cardiac attacks he often spoke of his depression and gloomy foreboding but never of any actual fear of death.

For this reason Freud could say at this point that he felt well, because he was not concerned about migraine and nasal secretion, and in general he was increasingly able *not* to be concerned with slight physical discomfort. *He could master his fear of death as long as he understood its cause.*

We may therefore attribute both apparent contradictions—the one between proud independence of and grateful submission to, Fliess, and the one between physical well-being and various physical symptoms and neurotic fears—to the progress of his self-analysis which was only hinted at by Freud in his reference to new hunches in the "in-between sphere."

As Freud mentioned in his letter of April 16, 1896, he had one commitment left to fulfill before retreating into complete isolation—a lecture at the Psychiatric Society. He described this experience in a letter to Fliess started on April 26 and continued on April 28:

> A lecture on the etiology of hysteria at the Psychiatric Society met with an icy reception from the asses, and from Krafft-Ebing the peculiar evaluation: "It sounds like a scientific fairy tale." And this after one has demonstrated to them the solution to a more than thousand-year-old problem—a "source of the Nile"! [5].

ILLNESS AND DEATH OF FREUD'S FATHER

Freud had passed his 40th birthday, an age which two years earlier he had been doubtful of reaching. In a letter to Fliess written on May 17, 1896 Freud alluded to his having passed a critical date, adding that he had no more vital energy. Thus one part of him had accepted Fliess's speculations. Yet Freud had unveiled the riddle of the dream. He had taken decisive steps not only toward achieving a new method of treating certain psychoneuroses, but toward developing a general psychology. His health had improved. His relationship to Fliess had on the one hand become more independent and on the other more per-

---

[7] Although Jones did not know the background factors that provide insight into the impact of Tilgner's death on Freud, he took this one letter of the entire Fliess period in which Freud mentioned an attack of *Todesangst* as proof that Freud was suffering from a typical anxiety hysteria.

meated by unconscious doubts and conflicts. It was at this point in his development that Freud reported to Fliess (on June 30, 1896) that his 81-year-old father was very ill, suffering from heart failure, urinary symptoms, etc. He introduced the letter as follows:

> My dear Wilhelm,
> You have taught me that an element of truth lurks behind all popular madness, and I can supply you with an example of this. Certain things should not even be mentioned in jest, otherwise they come true. Thus I wrote you recently that there was no real need for a congress and today I must report to you a serious obstacle which stands in the way of the next one—or at least in the way of fixing its date [6].

This was one of the few direct expressions of superstition ever set down by Freud.

Prior to this, Freud's father had hardly been mentioned in the correspondence with Fliess. Now Freud told Fliess how gloomy *(verdüstert)* he felt not, surprisingly, how badly he needed him.

> I am looking forward to the congress as to the slaking of hunger and thirst [L. 48].

The following passage, especially the last paragraph, illustrates not only Freud's reactions to the impending death of his father, but also his attitude toward the process of dying.

> My dear Wilhelm,
> Just received your letter and was greatly pleased about all the things I shall be hearing from you. It's just a pity that I am not sure when. This is the situation: the old man has paralysis of the bladder and rectum, his nutrition is failing, and at the same time he is mentally overalert and euphoric. I really think that these are his last days, but I do not know his final day [term] and do not dare to leave, least of all for two days and for a pleasure which I would like to indulge in fully. To meet you in Berlin, hear about the new magic from you for a few hours, and then suddenly have to rush back during the day or night because of news which might turn out merely to have been a false alarm—that is something I would like to avoid, and to this fear I sacrifice the burning desire once again to live fully, with both head and heart, to be a *Zoon Politikon,* and in addition to that to see you. . . .
> By the way, the old man's condition does not depress me. I do not begrudge him the well-deserved rest, as he himself desires it. He was an interesting human being, intrinsically very happy. He is suffering very little now, and is fading with decency and dignity. I do not wish

him a prolonged illness, nor [do I wish that for] my unmarried sister who is nursing him and suffering while doing so [7].

Since the condition of Freud's father remained unchanged, Freud did go away on a vacation. For the first time since his cardiac illness he was able to climb a mountain of 5000 feet or so, and he declared himself cured. Freud and Fliess met briefly in August, 1896, and Freud even went on a short trip to northern Italy with his brother Alexander (see Jones, Vol. 1, p. 333). On September 29, he wrote to Fliess:

My dear Wilhelm,
I hope that you with your wife and son are again installed most comfortably in the beautiful rooms of Heydtstrasse, [and] you are busily observing and calculating new periods of 28 and 23. . . . I write to you only today because an influenza with fever, pus, and cardiac symptoms suddenly shattered my well-being, so that I have begun to have an inkling of possible health only today. I would so much like to hold out until that famous age limit of approximately 51,[8] but one day [among them] was so bad that it did not seem very probable. The infection caught up with me on the last critical date, September 24, so that I was hoarse and breathless on September 25.[9] Simultaneously Martin went to bed with tonsillitis. But now I can breathe freely again. . . . I have taken the wife of my friend R.[10] into treatment and see again how everything fits and tallies in hysteria, so that it is a sheer pleasure. . . .
My father lies on his death bed. He is at times confused and is steadily shrinking toward pneumonia and a fateful date [literally: a great term, end].

With very cordial greetings,
Your
Sigm. [8]

The letter reflects a wide range of conflicting feelings. One part of him still needed Fliess, hence the expression of love and admiration, and even the acceptance of Fliess's arithmetical acrobatics. Freud had just passed through an illness and, in addition, was facing his father's imminent death. There was a resurgence of his preoccupation with his own death date, a preoccupation that recurred at various times in his life even after he had achieved complete serenity in his attitude toward death. Thus at this particular moment he was, so to speak, pleading

---

[8] For a discussion of Freud's "critical" age ($51 = 28 + 23$), see Chapter 5.
[9] Freud made two slips here. He started with: 26/9, corrected it to: 24/9, continued: 23/9, and changed it to: 25/9.
[10] An E.N.T. man who had figured in the Emma episode.

with fate—and with Fliess: "Let me live at least till 51, since I didn't die at 40."

Yet there is also a fine hidden vein of irony in this letter, as if another part of Freud were saying: "I need you; you are my friend, my 'alter,' my sounding board. My father is dying. I know that all these calculations are mental acrobatics which do not make sense, but I also know that I am racing against time; I am only human."

This part of Freud not only did not want to die young, but wanted assurances about the eventual date. "I want to know—but there are things one cannot know, you no more than anyone else. And so only one 'fateful date' is sure—the one toward which my father is now 'steadily shrinking.'"

Only upon reading the last sentence of the September 29 letter did I begin to understand the full meaning, with all its fatal overtones of Greek tragedy, of one of the last conversations I had with Freud some 43 years after this letter had been written (see Chapter 27).

There was still another part of Freud writing this letter—the one which could triumphantly proclaim that everything was tallying and falling into place, and which could therefore declare: "Give me a few more years and this earth won't be the same."

Freud's father died a slow death, lingering for nearly four weeks more. Only in the frame of mind arising from this situation could Freud have written on October 9, 1896:

> My state of health has really not improved very much. The cardiac symptoms in particular do not play a large role; I see no reason to ask you for immediate treatment. . . .
>
> The condition of my old father will probably keep my participation [in the celebration of the marriage of Oscar Rie to Mrs. Fliess's sister] to a minimum. . . .
>
> You know that I do not laugh at fantasies such as those about historical periods, and that is so because I do not see any grounds for it.[11] There is something to such ideas; it is the symbolic presentiment of unknown realities, with which they have something in common. Since then not even the organs are the same, one can no longer evade the acknowledgment of heavenly influences. I bow before you as honorary astrologer [9].

Here for once Freud was giving free rein to speculation—we might even say, wild speculation. In a similar, though much more restrained

---

[11] This is a subtly ambiguous formulation; it may mean either no grounds or reasons for ridicule or no grounds for such fantasies.

fashion, Freud speculated about the "creation and transformation of organs through the power of unconscious ideas over one's own body" when he attempted a possible explanation of Lamarck's theory of the inheritance of acquired characteristics (see Freud's correspondence with Abraham; letter of November 11, 1917; see also *Totem and Taboo* [1913b], and *Moses and Monotheism* [1939]). Such speculations figure to a lesser degree in Freud's death-instinct theory and in the papers on extrasensory perception. Yet the ambiguous reassurance he gave Fliess about the reality of historical periods and the title of honorary astrologer which he bestowed on his friend have a tongue-in-cheek quality, an irony which was also self-irony.

The tone of the remainder of this letter is in marked contrast to that in the preceding sentences:

> I am now very satisfied with [the results of] my cures; another year or two and I can express the matter in formulations that can be told to everyone. This prospect and the satisfaction about what has already been achieved keep my confidence high in many a dark hour [9].

Freud was in effect telling Fliess: What I am going to tell the world will be solid, so that everyone can understand it without resorting to wild flights of imagination. He knew he would succeed as long as he had a few more years.

In a letter of October 26, 1896, Freud announced his father's death, describing the fever, repeated spells of unconsciousness, and the final attack of pulmonary edema before the end. He added: "All this happened during my own critical period,[12] and I am really quite downhearted as a result." An unpublished final sentence reads: "I learned only this year that your birthday is on October 24" [10].

In his preface to the second edition of *The Interpretation of Dreams* Freud was to write:

> During the long years in which I have been working at the problem of the neuroses I have often been in doubt and sometimes have been shaken in my convictions. At such times it has always been the *Interpretation of Dreams* that has given me back my certainty.
>   . . . this book has a further subjective significance for me personally —a significance which I only grasped after I had completed it. It was, I found, a portion of my own self-analysis, my reaction to my father's death—that is to say, to the most important event, the most poignant loss, of a man's life [1900, p. xxvi].

---

[12] Freud's father died on October 23, about two weeks before Freud reached the age of 40½.

A few days after the first announcement Freud described his feelings in a letter of November 2, 1896 (L. 50):

> By one of the obscure routes behind the official consciousness the old man's death affected me deeply. I valued him highly, understood him very well indeed, and with his peculiar mixture of deep wisdom and fantastic light-heartedness he meant a great deal in my life. By the time he died his life had long been over, but in one's inner self the whole past is of course awakened by such an event.
> I now feel quite uprooted.

Yet in the same letter Freud reported that he had been late for the funeral because he had had to wait at the barber's! In a pertinent sentence omitted from the published version of the letter, Freud said: "With heart and nose I am satisfied again" [11].

In this letter we can already detect the stirrings of Freud's *systematic* self-analysis. Although Freud called *The Interpretation of Dreams* a portion of his self-analysis, i.e., his reaction to his father's death, this was true only in part, but that part was essential. Only after this event was Freud able to fathom the ubiquity of ambivalence in man's relationship to beloved and revered parents, and eventually to discover the oedipus complex and the "guilt of the survivor" (see Chapter 5).

Freud's father, especially in connection with his last illness and death, comes up frequently in the dreams and associations which Freud reported in *The Interpretation of Dreams*. We learn of Freud's various reactions not only to his father's death but also to certain aspects of the final illness such as the prolonged intestinal paralysis with incontinence of urine and stool (see letter of July 15, 1896). Freud had thus had to undergo the agonizing experience of watching someone waste away—shrink, as he had put it—so that he was "lived out" ("the candle had burned down") long before he was physiologically dead. It was probably then that Freud acquired his wish to prolong his life but not his death. We shall find this theme repeated in various ways through the decades that followed, right to the bitter end.

On November 22, Freud wrote to Fliess:

> Dearest Wilhelm,
> You are the first one to whom I am writing from my new quarters. . . .[13]
> The studies on hysteria are progressing satisfactorily. I am now making arrangements for four new cases, but probably none of these will materialize. However, I am busier [in my practice]. Good mood and

[13] Freud had moved to a larger apartment in the same house.

zest in living are wholly absent. Instead, I am diligently noting down the occasion when I must occupy myself with the state of affairs after my death. Another topic one ought not to deal with too extensively if one loves one's friend and only correspondent. . . .

Martha has again handled things splendidly, so that I have not had to miss any office hours.[14] Now the disorder is upstairs. The second generation is very satisfying [12].

Thus after the death of his father, Freud turned to the "state of affairs" which would follow his own death. The wording of the letter could mean: "I have a big family I must provide for during my lifetime and afterward." And yet, the tone of the letter and the mood it reflects say more than this. The big question which he *must* be preoccupied with is the "afterward"—the "hereafter."

SYSTEMATIC SELF-ANALYSIS

Only a few days later we find two letters, written just 48 hours apart (December 4 and 6, 1896), which bubble over with ideas, discoveries, and plans for the future. The following pertinent words were omitted from the first sentence in the published version of L. 51:

My bad time has run its course in typical fashion . . . and I am not at all interested in life after death [13].

The first letter of the new year (January 3, 1897) started in a similar vein:

We shall not fail. Instead of the passage we seek, we may find oceans whose fuller exploration will be left to those who come after us. . . . *Nous y arriverons.* Give me ten more years and I shall finish the neuroses and the new psychology. . . . In spite of the symptoms you allude to, no previous new year has found both of us so rich and so mature. When I happen to have no fears, I am always ready to take on all devils, and you still know no fear at all [L. 54].

Despite the last sentence, the whole passage indicates a subtle but important change in Freud's attitude. It is now he who is reassuring his friend!

Freud had obviously reached a phase during which both his self-analysis and the analyses of his patients were furnishing abundant new material. The optimistic vein continued.

14 Freud's wife—the "Frau Professor"—was an exemplary housewife. Freud's needs, adjusted to his working hours and habits, were always given priority and everything was run as smoothly as possible. This was true for the early, lean years as well as the later period of fame and comfortable prosperity.

The letter of January 24 ended with: "I believe I have now passed the age boundary; my state [of health and mind] is so much more stable" (L. 57). In a letter written on February 8, Freud contrasted Fliess's help and understanding with Breuer's criticism, and stated: "You must know that I am the 'nobody' in Vienna who believes in your periods" [14].[15]

The letters of this period, which began on December 4, 1896 and continued throughout 1897 (see L. 51-80), were filled with indications of constant progress and also of struggle.

While a great deal of the material contribution to Freud's new insights was "given" to him by his patients, his ongoing self-analysis must certainly have been a very important factor. By that time in 1897 Freud had come much closer to developing the technique of free association, a technique which constitutes one of his most outstanding contributions. He had completely abandoned hypnosis, and demanded of his patients that they withhold nothing.

Thus psychoanalytic technique developed hand in hand with psychoanalytic theory and practice. Freud's accomplishments during this period derived from his listening with utmost attention to his patients' productions. In this scanning process he had already recognized that *whatever* they told him was meaningful. During his periods of rapid progress, he combined the functions of psychoanalyst, creative thinker of the highest order, and patient.[16]

The process started, as I have already indicated, long before Freud was to speak of himself as his own patient.[17] By this time Freud knew that he had to wait not just for the productions of his patients but for his own as well. It was during such waiting periods that he needed Fliess, sometimes quite badly.

During March, 1897 Freud's inner struggle was intensified by his deep concern over the illness of his oldest daughter Mathilde, who had a severe case of diphtheria.[18] On March 29, he wrote to Fliess:

---

15 Someone, probably Breuer, must have declared that no one in Vienna believed in Fliess's periods. Again the theme of "telling"! Freud had already told Fliess that Breuer's whole circle considered the recurrences of 28 and 23 in various aspects of human life to be mere coincidences, and many of Breuer's friends were engaged in finding mathematical formulas to disprove Fliess's theory.

16 This discussion supplements my remarks about Freud's self-analysis in Chapter 5.

17 Here I disagree with Ernst Kris.

18 Although a diphtheria antitoxin had been discovered by von Behring in 1892 and soon thereafter began to be used extensively, the consultant called in to attend Mathilde refused to use it, even though Freud seems to have suggested that he do so. Diphtheria was then still one of the most dreaded diseases of childhood.

My dear one,

. . . Many thanks for your lecture. It reveals an incredible power of condensing ideas and takes one in 20 minutes through the universe. . . . I yearn for the days in Prague . . . [15].[19]

In his letter of May 16, 1897 Freud told Fliess: "Something is fermenting and seething within me. I am only waiting for a new surge." It was in this letter that he first mentioned the project of the dream book. It had become obvious by then how much more Freud was getting out of the relationship than Fliess. In the first unpublished sentences of a letter dated May 2, 1897, written on his return from their congress, Freud had said:

Card and telegram received in the meantime and regret that the congress did not bring you what it did me—pleasure and refreshment. Since then I have been in a continuous state of euphoria and am working like a young man [16].

Now, in the letter of May 16, Freud made it clear how much he still needed Fliess as an audience, remarking very frankly:

I could tell from your letter how refreshed you are. I hope you will now remain your old self for a long time and allow me to go on taking advantage of you as a kindly disposed audience. Without this I really cannot yet work [L. 62].

Freud's letter of May 31, 1897 indicated that he had already discovered the importance of hostile impulses against parents, and had had the first inkling about the sources of taboos against incest, before he consciously and "officially" began his self-analysis. However he had to pay a price for having Fliess as an audience for his discoveries, as he indicated on June 22, 1897.[20] Fliess had sent him news about his own new "discoveries" and expected a favorable response, which Freud found difficult to provide:

Never before have I faced your communications so expectantly stupidly [*erwartungsvoll blöde*], but I hope the world will not hear about it before I do, and that instead of a short article you will within a year present us with a small book which will reveal the organic secrets in periods of 23 and 28.

---

[19] The intended meeting place for their Easter congress, which actually took place in Nuremberg. The congress had the desired effect on Freud.

[20] Erroneously dated as June 12 (L. 65). While the date of the letter is difficult to read in the original, the letter starts: "Tuesday, . . ." June 12 was a Saturday, whereas June 22 was a Tuesday.

This plea of ignorance and incomprehension of mathematical formulas became Freud's expression of "resistance." Yet, as Freud became more deeply engulfed in his self-analysis, he also longed for a new congress. He wrote on June 18, 1897:

I look forward longingly to the end of the season. . . . Little by little it becomes permissible to tackle the question when we can see each other during the summer. I need a new impetus from you; after a while I am spent. Nuremberg kept me going for 2 months [17].

The summer meeting did not take place. The self-analysis was taking all of Freud's time and energy. He frequently experienced something akin to "paralysis" and among all "the masses of riddles staring" at him, only the "illumination of the dream" seemed to have "the most solid foundation" (July 7, 1897; L. 66). On August 14, Freud stated:

This analysis is more difficult than any other. It is also that which paralyzes my mental capacity to formulate and communicate what I have learned so far. Nevertheless I believe it must be done and is an essential intermediary step in my work [L. 67].

It is understandable that Freud spoke of a systematic psychoanalysis only at this point; that he later stated (in the previously quoted preface to the second edition of *The Interpretation of Dreams*) that both his self-analysis and his book had to a large extent been precipitated by the death of his father; and that he now consciously recognized that "something from the deepest depths of my own neurosis had ranged itself against any progress in the understanding of neuroses and you [Fliess] have somehow become involved in this" (July 7, 1897; L. 66). That was the first of many occasions on which Freud freely revealed such thoughts to Fliess.

Freud was behaving here as we would expect a patient in analysis to behave. He did not hesitate to convey to his "analyst" any thoughts about the latter—even hostile, deprecatory ones. The "analyst" in turn, as in any analysis, was expected to be prepared for this and not to take it "personally." We may ask ourselves, however, how Fliess actually responded to such remarks, especially later on when Freud conveyed much more hostile thoughts connected with his dreams.

Freud was now approaching what he later called the core of the neurotic conflict. In quick succession he understood the nature of infantile sexual fantasies and sibling rivalry, which in his case involved death wishes against his younger brother that subsequently had become an important source of guilt feelings. He recognized that the infantile sources of ambivalence formed the basis of his ambivalence toward his friends, including Fliess (L. 70, October 3, 1897). Finally, he gained insight into the oedipus complex as a universal phenomenon in human development (L. 71; October 15, 1897). Throughout these months Freud was subject to sharp swings of mood and periods of intently waiting for new material to which he referred as "peculiar states not accessible to consciousness, twilight thoughts, veiled doubts [*Schleierzweifel*—a new word combination]; occasionally here and there a flicker of light" (L. 65).

One of the first important results of the self-analysis was the realization that the early "seductions" by relatives reported by patients were in most cases fantasies. He cheerfully reported this to Fliess on September 21, 1897 (L. 69). Much later, in 1914, Freud described his discovery as follows:

> Influenced by Charcot's view of the traumatic origin of hysteria, one was readily inclined to accept as true and aetiologically significant the statements made by patients in which they ascribed their symptoms to passive sexual experiences in the first years of childhood—to put it bluntly, to seduction. When this aetiology broke down under the weight of its own improbability and contradiction in definitely ascertainable circumstances, the result at first was helpless bewilderment. Analysis had led back to these infantile sexual traumas by the right path, and yet they were not true. The firm ground of reality was gone. At that time I would gladly have given up the whole work, just as my esteemed predecessor, Breuer, had done when he made his unwelcome discovery. Perhaps I persevered only because I no longer had any choice and could not then begin again at anything else. At last came the reflection that, after all, one had no right to despair because one has been deceived in one's expectations; one must revise those expectations. If hysterical subjects trace back their symptoms to traumas that are fictitious, then the new fact which emerges is precisely that they create such scenes in *phantasy,* and this psychical reality requires to be taken into account alongside practical reality [1914a, p. 17].

With the above-mentioned letter of September 21, 1897 began what was perhaps the most dramatic period of Freud's life. Within three months his self-analysis uncovered memories from earliest childhood, leading to the discoveries that had radical influence on the future of human thought (L. 69-79).

After his discovery that "the firm ground of reality was gone," which might well have deterred a lesser man from pursuing his work any further, Freud's whole seduction theory of hysteria had fallen apart. Yet he was able to declare that he was proud because the discovery had resulted from intense intellectual effort and because he possessed a faculty for serious self-criticism. He surmised that this episode might represent progress toward further understanding—which, indeed, it did. The recognition that the fantasies of his patients represented what he later called "psychic reality" paved the way for the eventual discovery of infantile sexuality and the decisive importance of the first years of life for normal and abnormal development.

BREAKTHROUGH IN SELF-ANALYSIS

A few days later, at the end of September, Freud and Fliess met in Berlin. The weeks following this meeting brought a real "breakthrough" in Freud's self-analysis. Three letters written during the month of October, 1897 (L. 70, 71, 72) contain in essence many of the basic discoveries of psychoanalysis.

During this congress, Freud had not been able just to report; he also had to listen. However, it became increasingly apparent that Freud could not follow Fliess's new flight of ideas. He pleaded respectful ignorance, starting the first letter after his return as follows:

> One advantage of my visit to you is that, as I now know the present outline of your work as a whole, you can keep me informed of the details again. But you must not expect an answer to everything, and in the case of many of my answers you will not, I hope, fail to make allowances for my limitations on your subjects which are outside my sphere . . . [L. 70].

Was Fliess able to accept this plea of ignorance in a letter in which Freud had reported—as we shall see—a reconstruction referring directly to the "neurotic aspect" of his relationship with Fliess? The next paragraph expressed Freud's doubts more directly:

> I am still grateful to you each time for every little bit you unselfishly let me have; e.g., the remarks about the connection between infection and conception in mother and daughter seem to be highly important to me because these can be explained only by the stipulation of the germ plasm's immortality[21] and not by anything of the kind in the life of

[21] Here Freud was introducing an idea which he later pursued at great length in *Beyond the Pleasure Principle* (1920, pp. 44-61).

a phenotype. For they must be dependent on absolute time and not on the life-span. It then occurred to me that this might not be necessary after all; if the infection of the mother were given by falling within a time period according to the formula a. 28 + b. 23, and the conception of the daughter by a similar equation, then the difference between them must again result in a similar formula, without there necessarily being a special connection between infection on the one hand and conception on the other. Whether this is nonsense I cannot judge. For that I would have to know your "periodic disposition" [apparently a term coined by Fliess] [18].

This passage reveals the extent of the ambivalence conflict; profuse thanks for the sharing of information, awe at Fliess's flight of imagination; some doubts, which, however, did not extend to the observational data or to the "periodicity" hypothesis as such, only its application in a given set of circumstances is questioned.[22] As for Freud's alleged poor grasp of numbers, he was certainly going Fliess one better here in the "numbers game!"

Apparently Freud took it for granted that Fliess would accept his plea of ignorance concerning the latter's work, because he continued to describe in this and in his next letters the amazing results of his self-analysis. For example, he triumphantly reported a reconstruction of an event which had taken place when he was 2½ years old, and which his mother confirmed. At the end of this letter (October 15, 1897) he rememberd to whom he was writing and promised to investigate at a later date Fliess's hypothesis that repression was always initiated by the "male part" and directed against the "female" one.

Such a long introduction indicated also a quality which was so characteristic of Freud's correspondence. In view of the content of the main part of the letter it is not difficult to imagine how eager Freud was to tell Fliess what he had discovered. And yet Freud had the ability to restrain such eagerness and first to discuss Fliess's theories.

The reconstructions about which Freud reported were in the main the results of the interpretation of his dreams. He indicated in this letter that at certain points during the period he had known "where the next night of dreams would continue." Apparently, therefore, he did not send this letter until the following day, adding the dreams of that night.

[22] It is not easy to reconstruct from Freud's letters a precise formulation of Fliess's hypotheses establishing some time-period link between certain infections of the mother and conception in the daughter, but what interests us here are Freud's reactions.

Some additional factors are essential for an evaluation of these reconstructions. They must be correlated with the actuarial data reported by me in Chapter 1. A few remarks about early memories and their development are necessary. We know that normally most memories pertaining to events preceding the fifth year are covered by what Freud called "infantile amnesia." Usually certain isolated memory traces stand out, like tiny islands. It is not easy to determine whether such memories are really recollections of actual events or are "memories" of the family legend, kept alive and often embellished and distorted by parents or other older family members, and told to a child at a later age. Such spontaneous early memories are usually "screen memories," i.e., condensations of a series of memories which have been stored like a series of superimposed photographs. Freud learned only later that memories reconstructed in analysis were in most instances screen memories, related to each other by associative links.

Our understanding of "screen memories" is intimately connected with our understanding of the development and the functioning of memory. During the analysis of one of his patients, Freud arrived at the hypothesis that a memory of a percept and/or an experience may be laid down at a time when the infant cannot perceive the meaning of this experience. Such a memory trace can be "revived" at a later date through a similar perception or experience, at which time it can have a great and even traumatic impact. Freud came to this conclusion when faced with a dream of a patient which indicated that the patient had observed parental intercourse at the age of one and a half (Freud, 1918).[23]

There can be no doubt that a host of memory traces are laid down before the maturation of those structures which eventually make possible the acquisition of language. Preverbal thought, affects, and communication are now being widely studied through longitudinal observation of children.

Only a few actual observations have been recorded in confirmation of this observation of Freud's. One such observation recently published (see H. Schur, 1966) shows conclusively that a percept laid down at the age of 18 months, at a time when language development was limited and the concept of color and other abstractions were not yet within the repertoire of the child, was recalled and expressed exactly a year later in the framework of a higher level of abstraction

[23] See p. 129 ff. of this Chapter.

than that characterizing the original memory trace. The conclusion could only be that memory traces of early percepts eventually reflect on the impact of later experiences and learning.

I turn now to a comparison of Freud's reconstructions with the actuarial data, a scrutiny that indicates that the former were partly screen memories, which at one time or another were supplemented by information supplied by his environment, and that early percepts, which must have left memory traces, underwent transformations of the kind described above. In his paper on screen memories which contains some of the most subtle formulations about the intricate interplay of memory and fantasy, of true memories and their distortions, Freud (1899) indicates clearly that an early memory can also be used chiefly as a screen against a later event, in contrast to the general assumption that an earlier event is screened by a later memory.[24] In this paper Freud states:

> I have at my disposal a fair number of early memories of childhood which I can date with great certainty. For at the age of three I left the small place where I was born and moved to a large town; and all these memories of mine relate to my birthplace and therefore data from my second and third years. They are mostly short scenes, but they are very well preserved and furnished with every detail of sense-perception, in complete contrast to my memories of adult years, . . . which are entirely lacking in the visual element. From my third year onwards my recollections grow scantier and less clear; . . . and it is not, I believe, until my sixth or seventh year that the stream of my memories becomes continuous [p. 309].

Freud then distinguishes three types of memories pertaining to the first three years of life: (1) scenes described to him repeatedly by his parents; (2) scenes which had not been described to him (this type of memory figured mainly in his reconstructions); and (3) screen memories proper.[25]

> I was the child of people who were originally well-to-do and who, I fancy, lived comfortably enough in that little corner of the provinces. When I was about three, the branch of industry in which my father was concerned met with a catastrophe. He lost all his means and we

[24] See also Strachey's Introduction to this paper, in which he lists where in Freud's published writings indications to the facts described in this paper can be found.

[25] It is pertinent that Freud used the term *scene* to refer to fantasies of one of his patients in the unpublished part of a letter written to Fliess on May 4, 1896 (L. 45; and Schur, 1966a).

were forced to leave the place and move to a large town. Long and difficult years followed, of which, as it seems to me, nothing was worth remembering. I never felt really comfortable in the town. I believe now that I was never free from a longing for the beautiful woods near our home, in which (as one of my memories from those days tells me) I used to run off from my father, almost before I had learnt to walk [p. 312f.].

In view of the actuarial facts Freud's statement that his father was "well-to-do and lived comfortably enough" was an embellishment of the "golden past." Freud qualifies this statement by adding, "I fancy" (*"wie ich glaube"*).

The family's cramped living quarters, where two children were born after Freud, must have meant that during those three formative years Freud was subjected to perceptions of the kind he later described as traumatic. The situation and a comparison of Freud's reconstructions with the actuarial data also suggest that the timing of some of the memories recovered in Freud's self-analysis was inaccurate, and that these memories reflected the complex maturational development discussed above.

The following sets of memories were reported by Freud in his October letters to Fliess and then supplemented and elaborated upon mainly in *The Interpretation of Dreams* (1900) but also in other works (1899, 1901b):[26]

In the letter of October 3, 1897 (L. 70), Freud claimed that he had greeted the birth of his younger brother (Julius, who was born in 1857 and died on April 15, 1858, the same year in which Fliess was born) with "ill wishes and real infantile jealousy," and that Julius's death within a few months left "a germ of guilt" in him. This "memory" had far-reaching repercussions in Freud's life and will be discussed repeatedly throughout this book.

In the same letter Freud spoke of his playmate, his nephew and "companion in crime[27] between the ages of one and two," and his niece whom they "treated shockingly."[28] He then wrote: "My nephew and younger brother determined not only the neurotic side of all my friendships but also their depth." The nephew was John (born in 1854 or 1855) and the niece Pauline (born in 1856), both the chil-

---

[26] I shall indicate which of these memories are primarily the result of reconstruction in his self-analysis and which result from a combination of reconstruction and additional information.

[27] *"Untat"* in German is in this context better translated as "mischief."

[28] The German word *grausam* should be translated as "cruelly."

dren of Freud's half-brother Emanuel. Both of these memories were reconstructions.

Freud stated in the same letter that his "libido" toward his mother was aroused between the ages of two and two and a half, that "the occasion must have been the journey with her from Leipzig to Vienna, during which we spent a night together and I must have had the opportunity of seeing her *nudam*" (p. 219). This too was a reconstruction. Freud then linked his (mild) anxiety over travel with this incident.

A comparison of those reconstructed memories with the actuarial data immediately shows a discrepancy in timing. Freud's trip from Leipzig to Vienna occurred in 1860, when Freud was four years old or thereabouts. It is also highly unlikely that in view of the family's cramped living quarters Freud had not already been exposed much earlier to the nudity of his mother and to other visual and auditory sexual stimulation.

The error in the timing of the reconstruction represents, however, a very pertinent telescopic condensation of memories. On the one hand, the timing points to stimulations which must have occurred before the trip from Leipzig to Vienna. On the other hand, it is entirely plausible that the response of a nearly four-year-old boy had been different in quality and quantity from that of a boy aged two to two and a half. The dating of the memory of playing with John and Pauline, both of whom repeatedly came up in Freud's works (1899; 1900, pp. 424f., 483-486), was somewhat different from his reports in *The Interpretation of Dreams* (p. 424) that "until the end of my third year we had been inseparable."

A complex set of memories refers to a maid who took care of Freud in Freiberg. According to Freud's reconstruction she took him repeatedly to services in Catholic churches and spoke to him about heaven and hell, but she was also his instructress in sexual matters "who chided [him] with clumsiness." She allegedly also washed him in "reddish water" in which she had previously washed herself (see below), and encouraged him to steal money for her. At first Freud dated all these memories before the age of 2 (before his exposure to his mother's nudity).

For this memory concerning the maid Freud asked his mother for verification, about which he reported to Fliess in his next letter of October 15, 1897. She had told him that the maid in question had really been found to be a thief, that his saved-up coins were found in her possession. His half-brother Philipp had called the police and she was sent to prison.

Freud then suddenly became aware of a memory, which had been haunting him since his childhood:

> If the woman disappeared so suddenly, I said to myself, some impression of the event must have been left inside me. Where was it now? Then a scene occurred to me which for the last twenty-nine years has been turning up from time to time in my conscious memory without my understanding it. I was crying my heart out, because my mother was nowhere to be found. My brother Philipp (who is twenty years older than I) opened a cupboard for me, and when I found that mother was not there either I cried still more, until she came through the door, looking slim and beautiful. What can that mean? Why should my brother open the cupboard for me when he knew that my mother was not inside it and that opening it therefore could not quieten me? Now I suddenly understand. I must have begged him to open the cupboard. When I could not find my mother, I feared she must have vanished, like my nurse not long before. I must have heard that the old woman had been locked, or rather "boxed" up, because my brother Philipp . . . was fond of such humorous expressions, and still is to the present day. The fact that I turned to him shows that I was well aware of his part in my nurse's disappearance [L. 71].

Freud gave two versions of this memory and three interpretations. The comparison of these versions with each other and also with the actuarial facts is important on the one hand for a comprehension of the role of memories and their reconstruction, and on the other for an elucidation of the problem of death. The first version and a short interpretation are given in the same letter.

Freud returned to this memory, which he now classified as a screen memory, in *The Psychopathology of Everyday Life*. This second version includes additional material, and its interpretation is much more elaborate.

> When I began in my forty-third year to direct my interest to what was left of my memory of my own childhood there came to my mind a scene which had for a long while back (from the remotest past, as it seemed to me) come into consciousness from time to time, and which I had good evidence for assigning to a date before the end of my third year. I saw myself standing in front of a cupboard ['*Kasten*'] demanding something and screaming, while my half-brother, my senior by twenty years, held it open. Then suddenly my mother, looking beautiful and slim, walked into the room, as if she had come in from the

street. These were the words in which I described the scene, of which I had a plastic picture, but I did not know what more I could make of it. Whether my brother wanted to open or shut the cupboard—in my first translation of the picture I called it a 'wardrobe' ['*Schrank*']—why I was crying, and what the arrival of my mother had to do with it—all this was obscure to me. The explanation I was tempted to give myself was that what was in question was a memory of being teased by my elder brother and of my mother putting a stop to it. Such misunderstandings of a childhood scene which is preserved in the memory are by no means rare: a situation is recalled, but it is not clear what its central point is, and one does not know on which of its elements the psychical accent is to be placed. Analytic effort led me to take a quite unexpected view of the picture. I had missed my mother, and had come to suspect that she was shut up in this wardrobe or cupboard; and it was for that reason that I was demanding that my brother should open the cupboard. When he did what I asked and I had made certain that my mother was not in the cupboard, I began to scream. This is the moment that my memory has held fast; and it was followed at once by the appearance of my mother, which allayed my anxiety or longing. But how did the child get the idea of looking for his absent mother in the cupboard? Dreams which I had at the same time [as the analysis of this memory] contained obscure allusions to a nurse of whom I had other recollections, such as, for example, that she used to insist on my dutifully handing over to her the small coins I received as presents—a detail which can itself claim to have the value of a screen memory for later experiences. I accordingly resolved that this time I would make the problem of interpretation easier for myself and would ask my mother, who was by then grown old, about the nurse. I learned a variety of details, among them that this clever but dishonest person had carried out considerable thefts in the house during my mother's confinement and had been taken to court on a charge preferred by my half-brother. This information threw a flood of light on the childhood scene, and so enabled me to understand it. The sudden disappearance of the nurse had not been a matter of indifference to me: the reason why I had turned in particular to this brother, and had asked him where she was, was probably because I had noticed that he played a part in her disappearance; and he had answered in the elusive and punning fashion that was characteristic of him: 'She's "boxed up" ["*eingekastelt*"].' At the time, I understood this answer in a child's way [i.e., literally], but I stopped asking any more questions as there was nothing more to learn. When my mother left me a short while later, I suspected that my naughty brother had done the same thing to her that he had done to the nurse and I forced him to open the cupboard ['*Kasten*'] for me. I now understand, too, why in the translation of this visual childhood scene my mother's slimness was emphasized: it must have struck me as having just been restored to her. I am two and a half years older than the sister who was born at that time, and when I was three years old my half-brother and I ceased living in the same place [1901b, p. 49ff].

In a footnote added in 1924, Freud gave his final interpretation:

Anyone who is interested in the mental life of these years of childhood will find it easy to guess the deeper determinant of the demand made on the big brother. The child of not yet three had understood that the little sister who had recently arrived had grown inside his mother. He was very far from approving of this addition to the family, and was full of mistrust and anxiety that his mother's inside might conceal still more children. The wardrobe or cupboard was a symbol for him of his mother's inside. So he insisted on looking into this cupboard, and turned for this to his big brother, who (as is clear from other material) had taken his father's place as the child's rival. Besides the well-founded suspicion that this brother had had the lost nurse 'boxed up', there was a further suspicion against him—namely that he had in some way introduced the recently born baby into his mother's inside. The affect of disappointment when the cupboard was found to be empty derived, therefore, from the superficial motivation for the child's demand. As regards the *deeper* trend of thought, the affect was in the wrong place. On the other hand, his great satisfaction over his mother's slimness on her return can only be fully understood in the light of this deeper layer [p. 51f].

As I remarked earlier, Freud first placed the seduction by the maid and her stealing at a time when he was under two. However, according to his mother, these events occurred at the time of the delivery of her third child, Anna, on December 31, 1858, when Freud was past two and a half years. The impact of this birth was not reconstructed at this time, whereas he reconstructed his response to the birth and death of his brother Julius which had happened earlier. (Julius was born when Freud was approximately one and a half years old and he died when Freud was slightly less than two years old.) Freud also never mentioned the fact that shortly after the birth of Anna, Emanuel and Maria Freud's daughter Bertha was born on February 22, 1859. In view of the close relationship between the two families and the fact that they shared the maid (according to the actuarial proof, a register of maids working for Jewish families), this omission is significant. Only in a much later paper (1917a) did Freud consider the possibility that occasionally memories of rivalry and death wishes directed against a younger sibling, who died when the older sibling was still very young, are actually memories screening against feelings toward another sibling born shortly after the first sibling's death.

The affect which comes through most prominently in these re-constructions is the desperate fear of losing the mother, something now generally subsumed under the term "separation anxiety." Thus the disappearance of the "nurse" (who was actually a simple maid) and some very short separations from his mother were condensed in these memories. These events, moreover, occurred against the background of the appearance and disappearance of his brother and the appear-ance of his sister Anna and his niece Bertha. We must also keep in mind, with regard to the births of Anna and Bertha, that at that time all deliveries took place at home,[29] so that there was no long separa-tion, unless the little boy had been sent for a day or two to the home of his half-brother.

Let us also consider here a discrepancy between the first and the second interpretation made by Freud. In the letter written to Fliess on October 15, 1897, under the immediate impact of his dreams, his reconstruction, and the confrontation with his mother, Freud spoke about a memory which had been recurring "for the last twenty-nine years," that is, since he was 12 years old, whereas in 1901 he spoke about a "scene which had for a long while back (from the remotest past, as it seemed to me) come into consciousness" (p. 49).

We must remember that only a few months after these appearances and disappearances Freud's father and immediate family left Freiberg and after an indeterminate interval of travel through parts of Ger-many arrived in Vienna. At the same time the families of Emanuel and Philipp moved to Manchester, England; thus Freud's playmates as well as his home and the meadows and woods of the rural scene also disappeared. All these "disappearances" were probably condensed in this screen memory.

That children of this age should respond with anxiety to sudden changes in their environment is normal. In *The Interpretation of Dreams,* written in 1899, Freud discussed the fact that for children the concepts of death and disappearance are inseparable. We shall see that the consequences of deaths experienced early in life played a major role both in Freud's early development and in his later concep-tualizations (see Chapters 5 and 9).[30]

Freud's reconstructions referring to his "ugly" but clever nursemaid consisted of several sets: the reconstruction of her thievery and her

[29] Even Freud's six children were born at home.

[30] For a purely speculative assumption about an added determinant of this screen memory, see Chapter 5.

disappearance, which in turn became fused with other precipitating causes of his separation anxiety. I have already indicated that Freud's dating of this incident was erroneous. That this woman might have taken Freud and Emanuel's children to church and told them about God and hell (as Freud claimed in the same letter of October 3, 1897) sounds plausible.

Some other details of this reconstruction sound partly contradictory and partly reminiscent of the "deductions" conveyed to Freud by his hysterical patients as actual memories. We must remember that Freud had reported only two weeks earlier about his realization that his patients must have confused memories with fantasies. The realization of the basic importance of fantasies and their universal character was only gradually emerging in Freud's thinking. It is therefore entirely plausible that *he* was one of the first patients who provided him with material for this distinction.

In his October 3 letter Freud spoke of this *"Urheberin"*—translated in the *Origins* as the "primal originator [of neurosis]." What Freud meant to convey was that she was the "seductress" and not his father, as he had earlier been inclined to think in analogy to his hysteria patients. Freud said:

> I still have not got to the scenes which lie at the bottom of all this. If they emerge, and I succeed in resolving my hysteria, I shall have to thank the memory of the old woman who provided me at such an early age with the means for living and surviving. You see how the old liking breaks through again. I cannot give you any idea of the intellectual beauty of the work [L. 70].

Freud also claimed that this maid gave him "a high opinion of [his] own capacities."

During this time Freud's dreams were probably a daily continuation of his self-analysis. Many details about his reconstruction referring to this nurse were contained in a postscript dated October 4, where he wrote:

> She was my instructress in sexual matters, and chided me for being clumsy and not being able to do anything (that is always the way with neurotic impotence: anxiety over incapacity at school gets its sexual reinforcement in this way). . . . Also she washed me in reddish water in which she had previously washed herself (not very difficult to interpret; I find nothing of the kind in my chain of memories, and so I take it for a genuine rediscovery). . . .

A severe critic might say that all this was phantasy projected into the past instead of being determined by the past. The *experiementa crucis* would decide the matter against him. The reddish water seems a point of this kind. Where do all patients derive the horrible perverse details which are often as alien to their experience as to their knowledge? [L. 70].

Much less hypothetical comments apply to Freud's reconstruction about his nursemaid. Freud had dated the "seduction" by this woman as having happened before he was 2. While nursemaids frequently "seduce" infants by fondling and stimulating them in various ways, it is highly unlikely that this woman would have on the one hand given him a high opinion of his capacities and on the other have "chided" him for his clumsiness in sexual performance.

It is pertinent that in *The Interpretation of Dreams* Freud referred to this woman in a much more plausible context. In a discussion of a dream of his, he wrote:

> [These] dreams were based on a recollection of a nurse in whose charge I had been from some date during my early infancy till I was two and a half. I even retain an obscure conscious memory of her. According to what I was told not long ago by my mother, she was old and ugly, but very sharp and efficient. From what I can infer from my own dreams her treatment of me was not always excessive in its amiability and her words could be harsh if I failed to reach the required standard of cleanliness [p. 247f.].

We may speculate that this woman responded to the little boy's transgressions against cleanliness not only with harsh words but also with spanking.

In the first reconstruction Freud was still wavering between the acceptance of the early seduction theory and the concept of early fantasies. At the time when Freud wrote *The Interpretation of Dreams* he had apparently already reconsidered his early interpretation. What Freud produced in this interpretation was (most likely) another example of a screen memory projected backward. We know that later conflicts about sexual inadequacies (arising, for instance, when a little boy is comparing his genitals with those of his father) are linked with earlier failure in "toilet training."

The reconstruction of being washed with reddish water in which the woman had previously washed herself sounds even more like a displacement and condensation. Freud must have seen during his first years—even if we assume that he did not witness the delivery of his siblings—signs of menstrual bleeding in his environment.

Among the reconstructions of early memories was one of an accident which Freud had sustained allegedly between the ages of two and three years. It was an injury under the left side of his chin which required some stitches. Interpreting a dream of his, Freud concluded rightly that the physician who had attended to the injury had been blind in one eye. This was confirmed by Sajner (1968), who also unearthed the name of this physician, Dr. Josef Pur.[31]

It is also important that Freud first mentioned the concept of the ubiquitous occurrence of the oedipus complex in the same letter in which he reported the reconstruction of his injury and the memory of the one-eyed physician. This injury must have been a frightening experience and must have resulted in some bleeding and washing off of the blood.

For all these reasons, this reconstruction of being bathed in reddish water must have been a condensation[32] of many memories such as we encounter so frequently in dreams.

I have already indicated that Freud must have been exposed to nudity and to other visual and auditory stimulation during his early years in Freiberg. According to Freud, the observation of sexual activities of adults—particularly of parents—has a special place among the potentially traumatic events of early childhood. Freud arrived relatively early at the conclusion that such observations are not infrequent. Probably the first allusion to this fact can be found in a letter of May 30, 1893, where he writes:

> I believe I understand the anxiety neuroses of young people who must be regarded as virgins with no history of sexual abuse. I have analysed two such cases, and the cause was an apprehensive terror of sexuality, against a background of things they had seen or heard and only half-understood . . . [L. 12].

In the *Studies on Hysteria* Freud wrote:

> I had found often enough that in girls anxiety was a consequence of the horror by which a virginal mind is overcome when it is faced for the first time with the world of sexuality.

[31] The name of Josef was to play an important role in Freud's life.
[32] The concept of "condensation" is discussed further on in this Chapter.

[At this point Freud added the following footnote:] I will quote here the case in which I first recognized this causal connection. I was treating a young married woman who was suffering from a complicated neurosis and . . . was unwilling to admit that her illness arose from her married life. She objected that while she was still a girl she had had attacks of anxiety, ending in fainting fits. I remained firm. When we had come to know each other better she suddenly said to me one day: 'I'll tell you now how I came by my attacks of anxiety when I was a girl. At that time I used to sleep in a room next to my parents'; the door was left open and a night-light used to burn on the table. So more than once I saw my father get into bed with my mother and heard sounds that greatly excited me. It was then that my attacks came on' [1893-1895, p. 127].

In one of his attempts to link the etiology of neuroses to traumatic experiences and to certain ages, Freud called the period up to 4 years the period I*a* and used the term "sexual scene" for the traumatic experiences of this period (May 30, 1896, L. 46). The term "primal scene" appears first in a letter dated May 2, 1897 in the following context:

The aim seems to be to hark back to the primal scenes. This is achieved in some cases directly, but in others only in a roundabout way, *via* phantasies. For phantasies are psychical outworks constructed in order to bar the way to these memories [L. 61, Draft L].

Very pertinent is a later reference (October 3, 1898):

Biologically dream-life seems to me to proceed directly from the residue of the prehistoric stage of life (one to three years), which is the source of the unconscious and alone contains the aetiology of all the psychoneuroses; the stage which is normally obscured by an amnesia similar to hysteria [L. 84].

I believe that Freud's use of the term "prehistoric stage of life" for age 1 to 3 is of special significance.

Many references can be found in later works; for example, in the Dora case Freud referred to the auditory awareness of parental intercourse as the source of his patient's "hysterical" dyspnea. In two famous case histories, Little Hans and the Rat Man, Freud claimed that the observation of parental intercourse had played an important role in the genesis of the patients' neuroses. However, he never used the term "primal scene" in these papers.

In both papers, especially the latter, Freud discussed in great detail the nearly insuperable difficulty of distinguishing between "the facts upon which [these] tales of the prehistoric are based" and fantasies based partly on stories told by persons in the child's environment. Freud states that "people's childhood memories" are consolidated only at a later period, usually at the age of puberty; and that this involves a complicated process of remodeling analogous in every way to the process by which a nation constructs legends about its early history (1909b, p. 206ff.). However, in one of his very last writings, *Moses and Monotheism* (1939), Freud insisted that there was always some historical truth behind myths and legends (see Chapter 23).

The term "primal scene" denoting the observation of parental intercourse was finally established when Freud in his most famous case history of the Wolf Man concluded (1918) that such an observation had taken place when the patient was one and a half years old, and that it had played a central role in the development of his very severe neurosis. Freud acknowledged that at the age of one and a half a child could not yet recognize the full meaning of what he had observed; on the other hand, that this child had responded to that early observation, with all its implications, was shown in a dream he had later, at the age of four. It is difficult to convey in a few words all the convincing evidence which Freud adduced for this interpretation.

He assumed that his patient had in the interval between the observation and the dream gained some information (e.g., observing the copulation of dogs) which enabled him to understand the old percept and to experience it in its proper context. Freud's reasoning was complicated, however, by the following fact: the memories and associations of this particular patient left the possibility open that the "primal scene" had not occurred when he was 18 months old, but when he was only six months old. Freud was confronted now with the following questions: could there be in the infant something comparable to the "instinctive" knowledge of animals which operates at a time before the infant's mental apparatus has matured sufficiently?

Freud grappled throughout his life with this idea of "primal" fantasies, of phylogenetically inherited knowledge. He dealt with this idea not only in his 1918 paper but in such works as *Totem and Taboo* [1913b), *Introductory Lectures* (1916-1917), "The Dissolution of the Oedipus Complex" (1924b), and *Moses and Monotheism* (1939), to mention only the most important ones.

Freud's application of this concept to the impact of the primal scene can be seen from the following two passages:

I should myself be glad to know whether the primal scene in my present patient's case was a phantasy or a real experience. . . . These scenes of observing parental intercourse, of being seduced in childhood, and of being threatened with castration are unquestionably an inherited endowment, a phylogenetic heritage, but they may just as easily be acquired by personal experience. With my patient, his seduction by his older sister was an indisputable reality; why should not the same have been true of his observation of his parents' intercourse?

All that we find in the prehistory of neuroses is that a child catches hold of this phylogenetic experience where his own experience fails him. He fills in the gaps in individual truth with prehistoric truth; he replaces occurrences in his own life by occurrences in the life of his ancestors. I fully agree with Jung in recognizing the existence of this phylogenetic heritage; but I regard it as a methodological error to seize on a phylogenetic explanation before the ontogenetic possibilities have been exhausted. I cannot see any reason for obstinately disputing the importance of infantile prehistory while at the same time freely acknowledging the importance of ancestral prehistory. Nor can I overlook the fact that phylogenetic motives and productions themselves stand in need of elucidation, and that in quite a number of instances this is afforded by factors in the childhood of the individual. And, finally, I cannot feel surprised that what was originally produced by certain circumstances in prehistoric times and was then transmitted in the shape of a predisposition to its re-acquirement should, since the same circumstances persist, emerge once more as a concrete event in the experience of the individual [1918, p. 97].

If one considers the behaviour of the four-year-old child towards the reactivated primal scene, or even if one thinks of the far simpler reactions of the one-and-a-half-year-old child when the scene was actually experienced, it is hard to dismiss the view that some sort of hardly definable knowledge, something, as it were, preparatory to an understanding, was at work in the child at the time. We can form no conception of what this may have consisted in; we have nothing at our disposal but the single analogy—and it is an excellent one—of the far-reaching *instinctive* knowledge of animals [1918, p. 120].

In the light of the actuarial data presented above, the following question is pertinent: in the case of his patient Freud was dealing with a single experience. But what if a child were exposed to such observations not just once but over the course of many years?

Freud's assumptions about the inheritance of acquired characteristics are contrary to the findings of modern genetics.[33] Even if the most recent research on genetics in viruses should make such transmission at all plausible, this would not justify Freud's belief in the inheritance

[33] For a discussion, see L. Ritvo (1965) and Chapter 23.

of such complex mental processes as the oedipus complex, knowledge about intercourse, guilt about the murder of the father or the "primal horde," etc.

Could the time covered by infantile amnesia, the time before language is acquired, before the links between percepts and word representation are finally established—could this period be the substratum which Freud ascribed to the phylogenetic heritage? It is very pertinent in this context that Freud called the time "until about the end of the third year" the "prehistoric epoch" (L. 84; 1900, p. 245; 1909b, p. 207).

My discussion of Freud's early childhood has its focal point in his exposure to all the intimacies taking place between adults living in one room, in which three children were born, with birth, death, and sex impinging on a little boy's "mental apparatus," as Freud later called it. Judging from what we know about the mature Freud, that little boy must have been perceptive, curious, and eager to know and to understand everything around him. I shall come back later in my book to the potential impact of these early impressions and also to the question whether Freud "knew" about the existence of his father's second wife.

I turn once again to Freud's reconstructions during October, 1897. In the same letter (October 15) in which Freud reported about the verification of his reconstruction concerning the nursemaid, he also revealed the discovery of the oedipus complex and its ubiquity. He introduced the concept in one of the classic understatements ever made by a discoverer:

> If the analysis yields what I expect of it, I shall write it all out systematically and then lay it before you. So far I have found nothing completely new, but all the complications to which by now I am used. It is no easy matter. Being entirely honest with oneself is a good exercise. One single idea of general value has occurred to me. I have found love of the mother and jealousy of the father in my own case too, and now believe it to be a general phenomenon of early childhood . . . If that is the case, the gripping power of *Oedipus Rex,* in spite of all the rational objections to the inexorable fate that the story presupposes, becomes intelligible. . . . Every member of the audience was once a budding Oedipus in phantasy, and this dream-fulfilment played out in reality causes everyone to recoil in horror, with the full measure of repression which separates his infantile from his present state.
>
> The idea has passed through my head that the same thing may lie at the root of *Hamlet.* I am not thinking of Shakespeare's conscious

intentions, but supposing rather that he was impelled to write it by a
real event because his own unconscious understood that of his hero.
How can one explain . . . Hamlet's phrase "So conscience doth make
cowards of us all," and his hesitation to avenge his father by killing his
uncle, when he himself so casually sends his courtiers to their death. . . .
How better than by the torment roused in him by the obscure memory
that he himself had meditated the same deed against his father because
of passion for his mother—"use every man after his desert, and who
should 'scape whipping?" His conscience is his unconscious feeling of
guilt [L. 71].

Thus within two weeks, in two letters, Freud unveiled the sources
of the universal abhorrence of fratricide and parricide, the Cain and
the Oedipus complexes, in addition to the incestuous roots of the sexual fantasies of early childhood. He also recognized what he was to
conceptualize only after many years: that "conscience" is based on
unconscious feelings of guilt.

Fliess apparently did not immediately answer Freud's letter of
October 15. Was Fliess overwhelmed and shocked by the oedipal
theory? In subsequent letters no reference was made to Freud's interpretation of the two plays. Was it the doubts Freud had expressed in
his letter of October 3 or his "barren amusement" about Fliess's theories which had offended the latter? Or, more likely, was it Freud's
genetic explanation of the "neurotic" aspect of all his friendships?
Whatever the reason, Freud prodded Fliess about his silence on October 27, 1897:

You certainly do not have as an explanation for your silence that you
have been whirled back with elemental force into a time period when
reading and writing were a burdensome chore for you, as happened to
me on Sunday when I wanted to celebrate your not-yet-fortieth [39th]
birthday with a letter—but I hope it was something just as harmless
[L. 72].

We know from the later correspondence that for Fliess his 40th
birthday was the "supercritical" period. The birthday before this one
was therefore to be remembered, and Freud's "forgetting" of this
event was especially pertinent.

Freud then reported his newest discovery: the relationship between
resistance in analysis and repression in childhood. Resistance makes
the "noble" person "mean, untruthful, and defiant."

Four days later (on October 31, 1897), after receiving a letter from Fliess, Freud banished not only thoughts of retaliation, but also all the doubts he had expressed three weeks earlier! He wrote:

> I am so glad to have a letter from you again (the third since Berlin) that I banished all thoughts of retaliation. And that your work is shaping itself into a whole and that biological types are emerging, such as your parallel between birth and illness in adults, delights me and holds out the promise of much more in the very near future [19].

Freud noticed during this period, significantly enough, that "Under the influence of the analysis my cardiac symptoms [which he had not mentioned for more than a year] are now frequently replaced by gastrointestinal ones" (L. 73).

Actually, Freud's cardiac symptoms had more or less subsided in 1896, long before his self-analysis could have reached the types of deep-seated conflict that may lie at the root of cardiac symptoms which can be considered equivalents of severe neurotic anxiety, conversion hysteria, or, as Jones believed, "anxiety hysteria." This appears to corroborate my theory that Freud had suffered either a mild coronary thrombosis or, less likely, a myocarditis in 1894—in other words, that he had an organic illness, neither a "psychogenic" nor a "psychosomatic" one. His excessive smoking was probably a contributory factor. Of course, the symptoms of any organic illness, especially a prolonged one, can on the one hand be exacerbated by emotional stress, and on the other hand give rise to a variety of psychological consequences. This vicious circle is especially prevalent in cardiac disease.

With regard to Freud's gastrointestinal symptoms, there was later evidence that Freud had an "irritable colon," which is frequently the functional expression of a psychic conflict.[34] In later years Freud maintained that the appearance of "anal" material in analysis is frequently preceded or accompanied by functional or even structural gastrointestinal pathology. It is therefore possible (although such a hypothesis must remain purely speculative) that Freud's discovery of this very phase, about which he reported in the following two months, had something to do with the type of somatic symptoms he had during that period.

In his letter of November 14, 1897 Freud introduced his next momentous discovery—that of the maturational phases of infantile sexuality—with a parody of astrological formulas, which was in reality a

[34] For years he went to Karlsbad to take "the cure" and drink the Karlsbad water.

mockery of Fliess's periodicity hypotheses. It was as if Freud were saying: "You see—it is I who am reaching for the stars on the psychic side of this world, and they will not elude me; but you will never really come very close to them." Without being aware of it, Freud was preparing for the first open break. He was completely engrossed in his self-analysis, experienced painful periods when he had to wait for new material to emerge from his unconscious before he could crystallize his ideas. On such days, he stated, "it is very silent within me, awfully lonely. . . . I have to wait until things start stirring inside of me and I come to know about them."

No wonder that at such times, on a completely different level, the longing for Fliess welled up again. On such days Freud was even ready to acknowledge Fliess's time periods, e.g., on December 3, 1897:

> Last evening your dear wife . . . visited with us, bringing us the short-lived illusion of our all being happily together, and taking it away again with her departure [literally: disappearance]. Such interruptions of loneliness have a salutary effect by reminding us how difficult renunciation actually is, and how wrong one is to get used to it [20].

He continued this letter on December 5 with the statement: "A critical day prevented me from continuing." A few pages further, he exclaimed: "Since I have been studying the *Ucs.* I have become so interesting to myself."[35]

Freud and Fliess were planning to meet in Breslau some time in December of 1897. They had met in September, just after Freud's crucial discovery that his patients were often describing fantasies rather than true events. But Freud had much that was new to report by this time. Hence he was longing for this meeting. He wrote on December 12, 1897:

> Only someone who knows he is in possession of the truth can write as you do. I am therefore looking forward to Breslau with extreme curi-

[35] In contrast, Freud said more than 30 years later, in a letter written to I. Hollos, whose book *Hinter der gelben Mauer* dealt with the problems of psychosis and mental institutions: "In the course of time I have stopped finding myself interesting—something which is certainly analytically incorrect—and have therefore not gotten very far with an explanation of this attitude [his dislike for psychotics]. Can you understand me better than I do myself? Am I behaving in this instance as the physicians of yesterday did toward hysterics? Is this the consequence of an increasingly evident partiality for the primacy of the intellect, the expression of an animosity toward the id? If not, then what?" (For the complete letter and German text, see Schur, 1966a.)

osity and I shall listen with all ears. As for myself, I shall not bring anything along. I have gone through a desolate and foggy period and am now suffering quite painfully from [nasal] suppuration and occlusion; I hardly ever have any energy. If this does not improve, I shall ask you to cauterize me in Breslau [21].

Anyone who has undergone an analysis or conducted one knows the powerful resistance that is encountered when the earliest conflicts, centering around the deepest layers of ambivalence and incestuous wishes, are being unearthed. But to discover the ubiquitous existence of murderous wishes against one's parents and siblings, of incest and of bisexuality *for the first time* must have been an even more frightening, awe-inspiring experience. When in 1917 Freud compared the psychological revolution initiated by psychoanalysis with the astronomical revolution started by Copernicus and Galileo, and with the biological one begun by Darwin and Wallace, his words were aimed at the audience he was then addressing. However, he certainly knew what this revolution meant for him. At the time he made these discoveries he was well aware of the fact that he risked incurring the enmity and derision of nearly everyone who learned of his work. It must have been an awesome feeling to penetrate, like Schiller's "Diver," to depths where no one had ever been before.[36] It is not surprising, then, that from time to time Freud needed a certain amount of help, support, encouragement, and the right to complain. This "weakness" Freud learned to master, but as he was to write to another friend nearly thirty years later (see Chapter 15): "one gets tired in the process."

However, Freud's resilience is demonstrated in the same letter of December 12 that began so wearily:

It will be so invigorating for me to chat with you, about harmless and serious matters, after I have for months again harbored in my head,

---

[36] Es freue sich,
Wer da athmet im rosigsten Licht!
Da unten aber, ist's fürchterlich,
Und der Mensch versuche die Götter nicht,
Und begehre nimmer und nimmer zu schauen,
Was sie gnädig bedecken mit Nacht und Grauen.

Rejoice,
You who breathe in roseate light,
For down there it is fearful!
And man should not tempt the Gods,
Nor ever desire to see
What they mercifully cover with night and horror.

without emptying it, the most *meschugge*[37] matters, and otherwise do not speak with a sensible person. Another draught of punch with Lethe[38] [21].

In Greek mythology Mnemosyne and Lethe—Memory and Oblivion—were two springs found at the entrance to the netherworld. Freud's reference to a draught of punch with Lethe was thus an expression of his longing for some respite from the superhuman task he had undertaken. He had reached the entrance to the lower world, had drunk from the spring of Mnemosyne, and was now yearning for a taste of Lethe. But not for long. The inner equilibrium was quickly re-established. The next paragraph of this letter already shows challenging new ideas for later works:

Can you imagine what "endopsychic myths" are? They are the latest product of my mental labour. The dim inner perception of one's own psychical apparatus stimulates illusions, which are naturally projected outward, and characteristically into the future and a world beyond. Immortality, retribution, the world after death, are all reflections of our inner psyche . . . [L. 78].

This letter is characteristic of the mode in which Freud's ideas developed. A year earlier he had expressed thoughts in such a way that they seemed to be the outgrowth of a mood, of the process of mourning after the death of his father. Now he investigated the *origin* of such concepts as immortality, retribution, the "beyond," ideas that would then lie dormant, to be taken up again only years or even decades later, e.g., in "Delusions and Dreams in W. Jensen's 'Gradiva' " (1907a), "Creative Writers and Day-Dreaming" (1908), "The Theme of the Three Caskets" (1913a), *Totem and Taboo* (1913b), "Thoughts for the Times on War and Death" (1915d), "On Transience" (1916a), *Beyond the Pleasure Principle* (1920), and *The Future of an Illusion* (1927a). Until his last moment Freud wrestled with this problem of the "beyond," the meaning of death, the necessity to die and the wish to live, both as a theoretical psychological concept and as the individual fate of each human being.

In the next letter (December 22, 1897) Freud came back from "heaven to earth." The introduction was again written with a slightly ironic tone which somewhat belied the praise Freud was according to Fliess's speculations:

[37] A Yiddish word meaning crazy, frequently used colloquially.
[38] This expression appears quite frequently in Freud's letters.

I am in good spirits again, and keenly looking forward to Breslau— that is, to you and the fine new things you will have to tell me about life and its dependence on the world-process. I have always been curious about it, but so far I have never found anyone who could give me an answer. If there are now two people, one of whom can say what life is, and the other can say (nearly) what mind is, it is only right that they should see and talk to each other more often. I shall now quickly jot down a few novelties for you, so that I shall not have to talk and shall be able to listen undisturbed [L. 79].

The novelty was Freud's newly acquired insight that alcohol, morphine, and tobacco addictions were only substitutes for the "primary addiction"—masturbation. This recognition is characteristic of the unfailing honesty of Freud's introspection. Freud was never able to cure his own nicotine addiction. The somatic consequences of this failure were obvious. To what extent this addiction remained an obstacle to the solution of certain analytic problems is much more difficult to assess; Freud himself expressed some doubts in the same letter when he said:

The role of this addiction in hysteria is quite enormous, and perhaps it is here where my still unsurmounted great obstacle can be found. The doubt of course arises whether such an addiction is curable.

There is no doubt, however, that any attempt to stop smoking created a variety of severe "withdrawal" symptoms.[39]

COLLISION COURSE

The meeting in Breslau to which Freud was looking forward so expectantly brought to the fore certain insurmountable difficulties in the relationship between Fliess and Freud. During the period of his overestimation of Fliess, Freud's critical faculties were blunted. Assuming that this entire period, i.e., from 1893 to 1901, approximately, coincided with the period of Freud's self-analysis, we can distinguish several phases in this transferencelike relationship, though these are neither strictly delineated nor do they proceed on a linear course.

The first phase ended with the Irma dream (July 24, 1895). During that phase Fliess played the role of exalted judge and mentor, who, during the cardiac episode, also became the trusted physician and the

[39] For a striking example of Freud's attitude, see his letter to Ferenczi written on November 6, 1917 (Chapter 11).

representative of fate that would decide the length of Freud's remaining life span. The previously described Emma episode, which preceded the Irma dream, subjected the need for overvaluation of Fliess to severe strain, which had to be cloaked by such mechanisms as denial and displacement.

In the Irma dream the serious ambivalence of this relationship, which in a regular analysis would have been subjected to a searching investigation, remained hidden and disguised. However, Freud had by then acquired the tool of systematic dream analysis, which he was able to put to increasingly better use in understanding himself and his patients. Once he solved the problem of the dream, he knew that he was on the right path. Around the time of the Irma dream, his cardiac symptoms had also become less intense and thereafter, they subsided gradually.

Freud therefore very gradually became less dependent on Fliess's approval of his ideas, relatively less vulnerable to his own doubts and to disappointments over the progress of his patients. I do not wish to give the impression that such approval was a necessity, without which Freud would have been unable to proceed with his discoveries. Rather, I am describing this development mainly in terms of the progress of Freud's self-analysis, which was an essential element in the development of psychoanalysis, and also essential for the development of Freud's own attitude toward all aspects of living and dying.

With this increased security Freud's need to accept Fliess's own hypotheses also decreased. It was relatively easy for Freud to accept Fliess's "syndrome" of the "nasal reflex neurosis" because it was supported by at least a certain amount of clinical data, and seemed to offer evidence of some somatic compliance which Freud was on the lookout for before he discovered the maturational phase of infantile sexuality. But Fliess became more and more involved in "laws of periodicity" speculations that Freud could not follow without expressing doubts. Moreover, Freud became aware of Fliess's ambivalent acceptance of his own findings; on the one hand, Fliess appeared to believe in the "psychogenesis" of certain neurotic symptoms; on the other hand, he insisted that the manifestation of all symptoms and even of organic illness was precipitated by the periodicity factor. Freud's remark (in his letter of October 27): "You certainly do not have as an explanation for your silence that you have been whirled back . . . into a time period when reading and writing were a burdensome chore," was therefore a sign of open defiance which could not have escaped Fliess. Finally, Freud's complete honesty in confessing the origin of his sibling rivalry and its influence on all his friendships could not have failed to affect Fliess and precipitate some negative reaction.

Freud's increasing awareness of the importance of the first years of life, which were covered by amnesia; his growing mastery of dream interpretation, which had taught him the crucial importance of free association; and his reaction to the death of his father—all had led him, apparently in the spring of 1897, to begin his systematic self-analysis. This marked the end of the second phase of Freud's transferencelike relationship.

During its last phase the relationship continued on two different planes. This seems to have been the case with Fliess as well. Freud wrested the victory of discovering psychic reality from "defeat" when he recognized that his patients' fantasies rather than early seductions were the most frequent etiological factor of their hysteria; he uncovered the ubiquitous role of infantile sexuality and especially the oedipal conflict in normal and abnormal development. He now knew that he had solved one of the great riddles of nature. With this conviction he also achieved an inner independence. Simultaneously the critical part of him reasserted itself in relation to Fliess and the latter's hypotheses which increasingly appeared to be based on unverifiable speculations. It was especially painful for Freud to see that certain ideas which he had considered to be brilliant and fruitful had been destroyed by Fliess's tendency to rigid systematization. Nor is it surprising that the conflict between Freud and Fliess came into the open for the first time when Fliess turned the theory of man's inherent genetic *bisexuality* into a theory of *bilaterality*.[40] Bisexuality had evolutional, embryological, biological, and psychological connotations, whereas bilaterality arbitrarily and literally insisted on a feminine (left) and masculine (right) half in every human being.

With the progress of his self-analysis Freud began to realize that not only had he overvalued Fliess but that the latter was reaching a point of no return, while he himself was "reaching for the sky." Moreover, Fliess began to demand unconditional acceptance of his hypotheses from Freud, even if this meant relegating Freud's own findings about psychic determinism to secondary importance. Hence, it was inevitable that the relationship between Freud and Fliess headed

[40] Freud took issue with the bilaterality theory in Letters 80 and 81. See also Kris (1950, p. 241, n.).

toward a painful break, instead of terminating with a feeling of appreciation and mutual respect.

In the first letter after the Breslau meeting, Freud wanted to dwell on the positive aspects of the congress, but the unpublished parts of this letter indicate that he would have preferred to avoid the critical issue of bilaterality. He began the letter (December 29, 1897) by saying:

> Back home and in harness again, with the delicious aftertaste of our days in Breslau. Bi-bi [bisexuality-bilaterality] ringing in my ears, but I am still feeling too well for serious work [22].

Toward the end of this letter is an especially meaningful passage:

> I have not yet found the time to have a word with my feminine part.
> My nose is behaving itself and conveys its thanks [22].

But between these paragraphs Freud dealt with the problem more seriously:

> What I would wish now is plenty of material for a mercilessly severe test of the left-handedness theory. Needle and thread I already have. Incidentally, the question that is bound up with it is the first in a long time on which our hunches and inclinations have not taken the same path [L. 80].

Fliess probably reacted strongly to this, and in his next letter, written on January 4, 1898, Freud recognized the seriousness of their disagreement but demonstrated that his foremost preoccupation was with his own work. He said:

> I am sending you today No. 2 of the *Drekkologikal*[41] reports, a very interesting periodical, published by me for a single reader. No. 1, which I have retained, contains wild dreams which would hardly be of interest to you; they are part of my self-analysis which is still very much in the dark. I would appreciate your returning this to me for future examination, but by no means right away. As always, the first week after our talks was a very productive one for me. Then followed a few desolate days with rotten mood and pain, displaced from the head (or heart) to my legs. As of this morning complete clearing up [23].

[41] A witty neologism, partly deprecatory, partly indicative of the abundance of anal material then emerging in his self-analysis. The German word *Dreck* (mud, dirt, filth, feces) is written in Greek letters.

This statement is especially important because it clearly indicates that Freud attributed his somatic symptoms to his emotional state. Freud substantiated his doubts about Fliess's bilaterality theory only in the next paragraphs, leaving it open whether he would try to find further proof of the latter's hypotheses. However, the letter ends with a rather flowery sentence:

> On my side of the tunnel it is quite dark, but for you the sun and the stars are shining for this work as well [23].

Such remarks express the other side of Freud's relationship to Fliess. There was the magic of Fliess's personality which was still exerting its influence during their personal contacts. In addition Freud was now embarking on his biggest and most serious effort, the dream book, and could not at this point dispense with Fliess's help.

The opening sentences of Freud's next letter (January 16, 1898) sound like a mockery.

> I am sorry that this time our conditions have not remained on a parallel course. I have been well and gay. I hope by now, you, too.
> Enclosed No. 3 of DR. . . .[42] [24].

The postcongress elation, with its flood of new discoveries, could not last too long. The letdown that followed was accompanied by a diminution in Freud's defiance. In an unpublished letter of January 22, 1898 Freud commented on his mood as follows:

> This nasty habit of my organism [literally: my organization] suddenly to deprive me of all my mental resources is for me the hardest thing to bear in life [25].

After this, Freud somewhat changed his tone and informed Fliess that in the train coming back from Breslau he had already performed the unbuttoning experiment[43] and had found that Fliess was right. This "button business" (*Knopf-Geschichte*) kept coming up "out of the ground," etc.

In spite of Fliess's later claim that he had broken off the friendship at this point, the correspondence between the two men soon became more intimate again. Freud guessed from a letter of Fliess's that his wife was pregnant, and greeted this news with jubilation in an un-

---

[42] This abbreviation was to stand from now on for "Drekkology."
[43] Evidently to test Freud's latent left-handedness.

published letter of January 30, 1898. He promised "to listen most piously" at the next congress, "for it becomes more rewarding each time."

The manner in which transferences can blur critical judgment may be seen from the following sentences:

> The paths of symmetry and the numerical ratio of birth relationships are of course highly impressive. Once these single occurrences have been put together to form a structure, it will arouse much amazement in the pilgrims.
> The greatest of all fortunes, it sometimes seems to me, is either one's good humor [literally: mood] or a clear mind [literally: mental clarity] [26].

The explanation of all this came in the next letter, written on February 9, 1898:

> Apart from this, I am for no accountable reason in a splendid mood and have found my interest of the day. I am deep in the dream book[44] [27].

The dream completely dominated Freud's thinking for the next two years. This was clearly reflected in his letters to Fliess, in which he often alluded to dreams that subsequently appeared in *The Interpretation of Dreams*. A letter of March 15, 1898 is revealing for the interplay of a number of themes: Freud's self-analysis, the analysis of his own dreams, his need for Fliess as an audience and transference-like figure.

Freud began by reassuring Fliess that he did not underestimate the problem of bisexuality, "especially since that moment in the Breslau market place." He then continued with what sounds like a projection of his own wishes: "The idea occurred to me that you might like to read my dream study but are too discreet to ask." Indicating that he had reached another impasse, Freud outlined the parts of the book he had already written. Only at the end of the letter did it dawn on Freud that he might be imposing on Fliess, but he brushed this idea off quickly: "I hesitate to burden you during a time when you feel disinclined to work; I counter this with the consideration that this stuff, with its minimum of speculative content, will probably amuse you in a harmless sort of way" (L. 85).

---

[44] Freud was making a play on words here, calling the dream book his interest of the *day*.

On March 24, 1898 Freud begged Fliess: "You must not refuse the duties of [being] my first audience and supreme judge" (L. 86).

This need to have Fliess as an audience, critic, and "supreme judge" explains why the crisis in the relationship which occurred at the beginning of 1898 over the bilaterality problem not only did not result in an open break, but was followed by another, last upsurge of positive transferencelike manifestations, which continued until 1900. However, the negative side intermittently showed through in the letters and much more directly in some of Freud's dreams.

At this point, just when Freud needed Fliess so badly, their relationship was again exposed to external strains. Not only was Mrs. Fliess going through a rather stormy pregnancy, with severe physical symptoms the nature of which were not made apparent in the correspondence, but Fliess, too, felt poorly and had frequent "periodic" headaches. We have already seen that as far back as 1894 Freud did not tolerate Fliess's constant headaches too well and he responded no more sympathetically now, especially since Fliess's condition had killed their plans for an Easter congress. Instead, Freud and his brother Alexander went on a short trip to Istria, of which Freud gave a delightful description (L. 88), and which also played a role in his dreams of "The Castle by the Sea" (1900, pp. 463-466, 546-547).

Another incident, however, was much more serious. Fliess (1897) had published his book on the relationship between the nose and the female sexual organs in which most of his ideas on periodicity were already alluded to, including the statement:

> The wonderful accuracy with which the period of twenty-three, or, as the case may be, twenty-eight whole days is observed permits one to suspect a deeper connection between astronomical relations and the creation of organisms [quoted by Kris (1950, p. 7f.)].

A devastating critique of Fliess's book appeared in the *Wiener Klinische Rundschau* on whose editorial board Freud served, and whose editor-in-chief, Dr. Paschkis, was a friend of Freud. The review, signed "Ry.," was published in this issue of April 10, 1898 (just when Freud had left for his trip to Istria) and contained quotations from the book which vividly pointed up the absurdity of some of Fliess's claims and deductions.[45] When Freud learned about the review, he wrote a strong letter of protest to Paschkis. Receiving no satisfactory reply, he with-

---

[45] For a recent scathing evaluation of Fliess's theories, see the article entitled "Mathematical Games" by Martin Gardner in *Scientific American,* July, 1966.

drew from the editorial board as Dr. Oskar Rie, Freud's friend and Fliess's brother-in-law, eventually also did.

The manner in which this incident came up in the correspondence with Fliess is significant with regard to Freud's conflict. He wrote Fliess a long letter on April 14, 1898, the following portion of which was not included in L. 88:

> Enclosed is a letter which has the following history: In the last issue of the *Wiener Klinische Rundschau* one could read a review of your book by a certain "Ry.," a sample of that type of insolence which is characteristic of absolute ignorance.[46] I wrote Paschkis a harsh letter with a request for an explanation. Here is the loyal but sterile answer. I do not want to do anything further without having asked you. What do you plan to have done? There would be several possibilities for obtaining satisfaction [28].

Freud did not wait for Fliess's answer before writing again (April 27, 1898):

> It was awkward of me to want to wait until the affair with Paschkis was settled. It is settled now in that I have dissolved my affiliation with the *Klinische Rundschau* and have withdrawn my name from the collaborators listed on its cover. I intentionally did not send you the lousy review. I believe we can now let the whole affair rest [29].

This "affair" was mentioned only once more when Freud wrote that Dr. Rie had followed suit by withdrawing his name as well.

The amazing thing is that Freud himself was not aware of the absurdity of Fliess's hypotheses, and especially that of the clinical examples. To cite only one: Fliess claimed that the initial strabismus of infants disappeared in spurts during the "critical periods" due to maturation of the eye muscles. Infected tonsils could inhibit this periodical maturation of the eye muscles. However, the simple scraping of a diseased tonsil with a fingernail had allegedly cured the squint of a 2½-year-old child within a few days because the periodic strengthening of eye muscles had thus been restored.

However, we must keep in mind that Freud was deep in the dream book—a strange new world. Could he dare to be critical while he himself was exploring the unknown?

We have seen that in connection with the Irma dream Freud was not

---

[46] Only a few years later Freud himself had to face the most vitriolic attacks on his dream book, which he learned to ignore completely.

aware of the day residues directly referable to the Emma episode. The dream clearly expressed his desperate need to deny Fliess's culpability and his own disappointment in and hostile feelings toward his friend-analyst. Something similar happened after this episode, with the difference that Freud had progressed in his own development and no longer had the same kind of relationship with Fliess. Moreover, as Freud's objectivity increased, it was much more difficult for the dream work to distort his unconscious awareness—which, of course, he consciously denied—of the absurdity of Fliess's theories.

A dream which reflected Freud's doubts about the validity of Fliess's work was that of "Goethe's Attack on Herr M.," which Freud discussed first in *The Interpretation of Dreams* (1900, pp. 326f.; 448f.) and later in the shorter essay "On Dreams" (1901a, p. 662f.). Freud reported it as follows:

> One of my acquaintances, Herr M., had been attacked in an essay with an unjustifiable degree of violence, as we all thought—by no less a person than Goethe. Herr M. was naturally crushed by the attack. He complained of it bitterly to some company at table; his veneration for Goethe had not been affected, however, by this personal experience. I now tried to throw a little light on the chronological data, which seemed to me improbable. Goethe died in 1832. Since his attack on Herr M. must naturally have been made earlier than that, Herr M. must have been quite a young man at the time. It seemed to be a plausible notion that he was eighteen. I was not quite sure, however, what year we were actually in, so that my whole calculation melted into obscurity. Incidentally, the attack was contained in Goethe's well-known essay on 'Nature' [1901a, p. 662].

Freud's interpretation of the dream included the following points:

> The material of the dream was derived from three sources:
> (1) Herr M., whom I had got to know among some *company at table,* asked me one day to examine his elder brother, who was showing signs of [general paresis]. In the course of my conversation with the patient an awkward episode occurred, for he gave his brother away for no accountable reason by talking of his *youthful follies.* I had asked the patient the *year of his birth* (cf. the *year of* Goethe's *death* in the dream) and had made him carry out a number of calculations in order to test the weakness of his memory.
> (2) A medical journal, which bore my name among others on its title-page, had published a positively *'crushing'* criticism by a *youthful* reviewer of a book by my friend F. in Berlin. I took the editor to task over this; . . . but in my letter of resignation expressed a hope that *our*

personal relations would not be affected by the event. This was the true source of the dream. The unfavourable reception of my friend's work had made a profound impression on me. It contained, in my opinion, a fundamental biological discovery, which *is only now—many years later—beginning to find favour with the experts* [my italics].

(3) A woman patient of mine had given me an account a short time before of her brother's illness, and how he had broken out in a frenzy with cries of 'Nature! Nature!' The doctors believed that his exclamation came from his having read Goethe's striking essay on that subject . . . *it seemed to me more plausible* that his exclamation of the word 'Nature' should be taken in the sexual sense in which it is used by the less educated people here. . . .

Behind my own ego in the dream-content there lay concealed, in the first instance, my friend who had been so badly treated by the critic. *'I tried to throw a little light on the chronological data.'* My friend's book dealt with the *chronological data* of life and among other things showed that the length of *Goethe's* life was a multiple of a number of days that has a significance in biology. But this ego was compared with a paralytic: *'I was not quite sure what year we were in.'* Thus the dream made out that my friend was behaving like a paralytic, and in this respect it was a mass of absurdities. The dream-thoughts, however, were saying ironically: 'Naturally, it's *he* [my friend F.] who is the crazy fool and it's *you* [the critics] who are the men of genius and know better. Surely it couldn't be the *reverse?* There were plenty of examples of this *reversal* in the dream. . . .

I should like to lay it down that no dream is prompted by motives other than egoistic ones. In fact, the ego in the present dream does not stand only for my friend but for myself as well. I was identifying myself with him, because the fate of his discovery seemed to foreshadow the reception of my own findings. If I were to bring forward my theory emphasizing the part played by sexuality in the aetiology of psychoneurotic disorders (cf. the allusion to the eighteen-year-old patient's cry of 'Nature! Nature!'), I should come across the same criticisms; and I was already preparing to meet them with the same derision [1901a, p. 662ff.].

This dream must have occurred shortly after the critical review of Fliess's book had appeared, and it obviously deals with Fliess's "calculations." We may assume that Freud's associations at a certain point plainly side with dream thoughts such as these: "It's he [my friend F.] who's the crazy fool; it's he who's suffering from a general paresis and has gotten completely and hopelessly involved in his calculations." With an ingenious twist Freud tried to extricate himself by asserting that this was only an ironic expression of how absurd it was to make such an evaluation of Fliess. At a later date Freud himself would certainly have recognized that what was represented was Freud's conflict. One part of Freud was siding with the devastating critique, while another was denying it emphatically. Freud even told us why this was so by saying that he anticipated receiving the same kind of severe criticism of his own work and was preparing to meet it with the derision he was supposedly heaping on the heads of Fliess's critics. It is significant that even while he was writing the essay "On Dreams" in 1900, when the break with Fliess was actually already an accomplished fact, Freud still needed to cling to the fiction that Fliess's speculations about periodicity were valid. We shall see that he did not totally overcome this conviction for many decades, if indeed he ever did.

As for Freud's fears about the reception of his dream book, these proved to be only too realistic! The work was greeted with derision in some quarters and almost completely ignored in others.

In the dream of Goethe's attack on Herr M. we can discern Freud's dilemma. Was Fliess crazy or a genius? Were his speculations valid or the outgrowth of an obsessional, even paranoid system?

The dream work barely managed to disguise Freud's own evaluation of Fliess. The letter of May 1 exemplifies the manner in which Freud denied his doubts and negative feelings:

> What you say about the two hands of the life-clock again sounds so familiar and self-evident that it must be an unprecedented novelty and a marvelous piece of truth. May has come,[47] and so at the end of May I shall hear about it. I feel as if parched, some spring within me is drying up and all sensibilities are withering. I do not want to give you too detailed a description lest it sound too much like complaining. You will tell me whether it is old age[48] or just one of the many periodic fluctuations.
>
> I have the impression that you might already have determined the sex of your next child, so that this time "Paulinchen" may well become a reality[49] [30].

Again and again Freud reiterated his gratitude for having Fliess as an audience and critic:

> I am so immensely happy that you bestow on me the gift of an Other. . . . I cannot write entirely without an audience, but I do not at all mind writing only for you [31].

[47] "Der Mai ist gekommen" is the beginning of a German poem.
[48] This letter was written five days before Freud's 42nd birthday!
[49] The next child was in fact a daughter, who was called Pauline.

On June 9 Freud was obliged to report that his work on the dream book had hit a snag. He could not yet conceptualize fully what he called "the new psychology" of the dream. He wrote:

It is abominably difficult to set out the new psychology in so far as it relates to dreams, as it is necessarily fragmentary only, and all the obscure parts which I have so far neglected out of laziness are now demanding clarification. I need a lot of patience, cheerfulness and some good ideas. I am stuck over the relationship between the two systems of thinking; I must get down to them in earnest. For a time I shall be of no use for anything again. The tension of uncertainty results in a state of wretched discomfort, which one feels almost physically [L. 90].

In *The Interpretation of Dreams* Freud conceptualized what in this letter he called "the two systems of thinking" as the primary and secondary processes of mental functioning. These concepts were—and still are—fundamental to psychoanalytic theory.

In his investigations of hysterical symptoms Freud had already found out that in order to understand their meaning we cannot apply the regular logical criteria of cause and effect, but that symptom formation had a "logic" of its own. However, Freud was able to establish the multiple determinants and the genetic roots of symptoms only after he had begun to use the method of free associations in the treatment of his patients. Once he had adopted this method, Freud followed with dogged determination the rule that no association is irrelevant, even if it might seem so at first glance.

When Freud first became interested in dreams he started with the simple assumption that they were manifestations of mental functioning and therefore could be meaningful. When he later started to apply the method of free associations to *each* element of the manifest dream content, he was faced with a seemingly chaotic, bewildering array of material. He then had to find "method in the madness."

Following the thesis of the relevance of all associations Freud realized that what he called the "dream thoughts" or the "latent dream content" (in contrast to the manifest content of the dream, which is recalled, reported or written down immediately after the dream) encompassed a rich field of ideas, ranging from memories of the most recent past to long-forgotten fantasies, conflicts, and actual events of early childhood. There were always associative links between past and recent memories, but they were mostly loose and well disguised.

Freud used such concepts as "condensation" to illustrate the striking differences between the dream thoughts and the manifest dream content. He said:

> The dream-thoughts and the dream-content are presented to us like two versions of the same subject-matter in two different languages. Or, more properly, the dream-content seems like a transcript of the dream-thoughts into another mode of expression, whose characters and syntactic laws it is our business to discover by comparing the original and the translation. The dream-thoughts are immediately comprehensible, as soon as we have learnt them. The dream-content, on the other hand, is expressed as it were in a pictographic script, the characters of which have to be transposed individually into the language of the dream-thoughts [1900, p. 277].

The concept of condensation was meant to express more than this, however. It applied not only to the dream work but also, in one of its principal aspects, to that amazing process by which some, if not most, memory traces are stored in the "mental apparatus." The process might be compared to that of producing an "ultra-microfilm" which simultaneously would record its material in a certain code that defied all laws of Aristotelian logic, but would nonetheless follow certain "rules" so that it could be deciphered with the aid of clues furnished by free association (see Schur, 1966b, Ch. 7).

To chart one's way in this new world of thoughts was a near superhuman task, as was the attempt to formulate these new ideas in words that could convey their meaning.

Freud had learned that the flow of new creative ideas as well as of new material in his self-analysis could not come on command, that he had to accept painful waiting periods of varying lengths. It is not surprising that during such periods Freud developed physical symptoms which he observed with a slightly detached scientific interest, not lacking a certain irony directed both against himself and against Fliess.

In an unpublished part of L. 91 (June 20, 1898), Freud reported to Fliess some observations on his family pertaining to Fliess's "period" of 28, and added teasingly that his head and Fliess's head were after all two very different heads, even if both were labile—because his head now felt very good. He could, however, replace headache or cardiac symptoms with backache, which had the tendency of irradiation into various zones of the skin in common with his previous cardiac pain. Here Freud obviously recognized that such symptoms were what we would now call "psychosomatic," and did not take them seriously.

During the summer of 1898 Freud filled such a waiting period with reading the works of C. F. Meyer, the Swiss novelist, who was Fliess's favorite author. However, he rarely read merely for enjoyment, but looked to poets and writers for confirmation of his theories. Following his first reconstructions in October, 1897, he had referred to *Oedipus Rex* and *Hamlet*. Letter 91 (June 20, 1898) contained the first sample of analysis applied to a work of art. He also saw that some, if not all poets, writers, and painters revealed in their works of art a great deal about their own conflicts. In later years, as is well known, Freud examined many works of art from a psychoanalytic point of view.

The first work of C. F. Meyer which Freud analyzed was *Die Richterin* [*The Female Judge*]. In view of the complex family constellation in which Freud spent his early years in Freiberg (see Chapter 1), it is pertinent that the first problem which Freud singled out was the family romance.[50]

> All neurotics create a so-called family romance . . . ; on the one hand it serves the need for self-aggrandisement and on the other as a defence against incest. If your sister is not your mother's child, you are relieved of guilt. (The same applies if you yourself are the child of other parents.) Where does the material about adultery, illegitimacy, etc., needed to create these romances come from? [L. 91].

During this summer Freud read other works of C. F. Meyer and continued to comment on them. Freud focused on the incestuous aspect of the relationships depicted in these works, especially those between brother and sister. However, particularly in his historical novels, Meyer also described with extreme realism a host of cruel and gory acts of violence. Freud interpreted those acts mainly as the vicissitudes of rivalry and incestuous conflict. The discovery of aggression as one of the "instinctual drives" was still two decades away.

Death, guilt, and retribution were prominent features in all these novels. That Freud was deeply preoccupied with problems connected with these aspects became apparent from a series of "slips" (forgetting of names, misspelling, etc.), which were linked with this theme.[51]

In July, Freud met with Fliess for a few days. This time he listened

[50] Freud had coined this phrase to describe the frequent fantasies of the small child who often contends that an exalted figure is one of his parents, usually instead of his real father, or that he is the adopted (or found) child of a "king" or "hero."
[51] For a discussion see Schur (1968).

to new perspectives opened up to him by Fliess. In a letter written after this meeting on July 30, 1898 Fliess was accorded the title of "the Kepler of Biology."[52]

In the same letter Freud wrote, without any sign of concern, that anything reminiscent of science seemed like something in the distant past. But he also pointed to his faculty of turning everything to something desirable; he therefore considered this fact as a sign of his *innate resilience* ("die Elasticität meiner Natur"). After discussing his vacation plans, Freud added the following remarkable passage:

> Don't let yourself be deterred from writing to me about the ellipses,[53] although I am at present passing through such an unreasonable part of my own. For each should give what he has, without consideration for the other. I am doing it the same way. The lack of constraint that one feels constitutes the main attraction of the correspondence.
>
> I would so much like to give you what *you do not* have: a free head; but you know that this is not possible. The incompleteness in your findings does not bother me at all; you know, I do not reflect; I respond, enjoy, marvel, and am full of expectations. The carrying time[54] will soon be over. This is probably your consolation in regard to Ida's condition. Unfortunately the vacation too [will soon be over] [32].

This letter indicates another progress in Freud's self-analysis. He treated himself with the same objectivity that an analyst shows toward a patient who seemingly does not produce new, very important material. He did not lose his self-confidence, and spoke proudly of his inner resilience. Freud's emphasis on the unconstrained freedom of expression in his correspondence with Fliess explains his past and future frankness toward the latter.

In the same letter in which Freud called his friend the Kepler of Biology, he also expressed compassion and sadness, that he could not give Fliess something which the latter lacked: a "free head." While Freud was referring to Fliess's recurrent headaches which soon required further surgery, this phrase also had another meaning, that of keeping one's thinking clear.

In a letter written later during his vacation Freud reported that he at last understood a "little thing"!—the meaning of a parapraxis as well as the means of unraveling it by the method of free associations.

---

[52] It is possible that it was Fliess who put himself on a par with Kepler. This was claimed by the German gynecologist Riebold (1942), who mentioned this in a critical discussion of Fliess's work (see Kris, 1950, p. 8, n. 2).

[53] Freud and Fliess were obviously calling ellipses the periods of feeling below par.

[54] Referring to Fliess's wife's pregnancy.

Thus he discovered a new approach to "the Unconscious," which led to the *Psychopathology of Everyday Life*. The first parapraxis analyzed in this way involved the forgetting of the name of a German poet Julius Mosen. Julius was the name of Freud's brother who had died on April 15, 1858.

The period from June, 1898 to the end of the year was a time of self-analysis, of consolidation, but also of new discoveries (such as the psychic determination of parapraxes).

Freud's main interest remained centered on the dream book. The work on it proceeded in bursts of creativity that were interrupted by long intervals. On June 6, he had stated that he was stuck because of his difficulty to conceptualize "the psychology." Yet only two weeks later he reported that it was nearly completed, "composed as if in a dream" but "neither fit nor intended for publication." Nevertheless, only two weeks later, Freud sent Fliess a draft, which was "fully copied from the unconscious" (L. 92).

During the rest of the year there was very little progress. Freud had his moments of doubt. For example, on October 23, 1898, he wrote:

> The dream book rests unchangeably . . . the gap in the psychology as well as the other gap left by the thoroughly analyzed example[55] are both obstacles to finishing it that I cannot yet overcome. . . . If ascertaining the few points required to explain the neuroses involves so much work, time, and error, how can I ever hope to acquire an insight into the whole of mental activity, which was something I at one time proudly looked forward to achieving? [L. 99].

And yet another part of Freud was convinced of his inner resilience, as he had said in an earlier letter. A year later he expressed it with the words: *"Fluctuat nec mergitur* [it wavers but it shall not sink[56]]."

At the time Freud wrote this letter another crisis in his relationship with Fliess was developing. It manifested itself first in a dream, which represented both a landmark in his analysis and in his mastery of dream interpretation.

[55] This refers to a dream which Fliess had strongly urged Freud not to publish (see Schur, 1966a, pp. 73-76).

[56] My own translation. Strachey (Freud, 1914a) has translated it as "it is tossed by the waves but does not sink" (p. 1n.). See also Chapter 5, footnote 8.

5

DREAMS AND DEATH

The Interpretation of Dreams is for many reasons an important source of biographical information: Freud reported and interpreted in it his own dreams; he told us that it was an essential part of his self-analysis (1900, p. xxvi).

With the help of the Fliess correspondence, it has been possible to establish the dates of many of the dreams which Freud used in his book. We can trace the intricate interplay of successful dream interpretation, followed frequently after painful intervals by a burst of new memories leading to new insight, the comparison of new discoveries with the material produced by his patients, renewed, "deeper" interpretations of his own dreams, and so on. Freud indicated repeatedly in *The Interpretation of Dreams* that self-revelation must have its limits out of consideration for the privacy of others, and for this reason he did not publish all of his interpretations. We know from the Fliess correspondence how much more Freud was able to find in a dream in 1899 than in 1895. It is obvious, therefore, that by 1899 Freud's associations to his dreams could reach completely forgotten (repressed) memories of his childhood and link them with recent events, conflicts, and wishes, whereas at the time of his first systematic dream interpretation in 1895 he had not yet acquired the necessary tools for such penetrating interpretations.

At the time he wrote this book he was not yet aware of all the aspects of the growing ambivalence in his relationship with Fliess. However this ambivalence came up in dreams, where it could be "safely" expressed under various disguises, thus permitting Freud to remain unaware of the intensity of his conflict.[1]

I shall try to document in the course of this book that this lack of full awareness, this failure to "work through" these transferencelike, present-day conflicts, which in turn were rooted in his early infantile conflicts, were responsible for the persistent recurrence and the specific manifestations of Freud's obsessive preoccupation with the date of his death. The theme running through the dreams in question is that of "the guilt of the survivor."

I shall therefore interrupt the chronological narrative at this point in order to consider this group of dreams. Some of them will become more fully understandable, when we re-examine them in the light of the published and unpublished correspondence with Fliess.

In the fall of 1898, Freud had the following dream, known as the *non vixit* dream, of which he gave us a highly penetrating analysis. Freud reported the dream as follows:

> I had gone to Brücke's laboratory at night, and, in response to a gentle knock on the door, I opened it to (the late) Professor Fleischl, who came in with a number of strangers and, after exchanging a few words, sat down at his table. This was followed by a second dream. My friend Fl. [Fliess] had come to Vienna unobtrusively in July. I met him in the street in conversation with my (deceased) friend P., and went with them to some place where they sat opposite each other as though they were at a small table. I sat in front at its narrow end. Fl. spoke about his sister and said that in three quarters of an hour she was dead, and added some such words as 'that was the threshold.' As P. failed to understand him, Fl. turned to me and asked me how much I had told P. about his affairs. Whereupon, overcome by strange emotions, I tried to explain to Fl. that P. (could not understand anything at all, of course, because he) was not alive. But what I actually said—and I myself noticed the mistake—was 'NON VIXIT.' I then gave P. a piercing look. Under my gaze he turned pale; his form grew indistinct and his eyes a sickly blue—and finally he melted away. I was highly delighted at this and I now realized that Ernst Fleischl, too, had been no more than an apparition, a 'revenant' ["ghost"—literally, "one who returns"]; and it seemed to me quite possible that people of that kind only existed as long as one liked and could be got rid of if someone else wished it [1900, p. 421; italics omitted].

It is necessary to present in detail all we know about the background of the dream as well as most of Freud's associations and the

---

[1] See also my discussion of the Emma episode and its relation to the Irma dream (Chapter 3) and the Goethe dream (Chapter 4).

conclusions derived from them. Freud discussed this dream in two separate sections of *The Interpretation of Dreams,* the second part of the interpretation supplementing and expanding the first. We know from Freud's correspondence that the interpretation of the *non vixit* dream was completed only in the course of writing the dream book, most probably during the summer of 1899.

During his self-analysis and his preparation of the dream book Freud frequently used the following method, which he most likely used in the interpretation of the *non vixit* dream too:

> An observation which I have been able to make in the course of preparing this manuscript has shown me that dreams are no more forgotten than other mental acts. . . . I had kept records of a large number of my own dreams which for one reason or another I had not been able to interpret completely at the time or had left entirely uninterpreted. And now, between one and two years later, I have attempted to interpret some of them for the purpose of obtaining more material in illustration of my views. These attempts have been successful in every instance; indeed the interpretation may be said to have proceeded more easily after this long interval than it did at the time when the dream was a recent experience. A possible explanation of this is that in the meantime I have overcome some of the internal resistances which previously obstructed me. When making these subsequent interpretations I have compared the dream-thoughts that I elicited at the time of the dream with the present, usually far more copious, yield, and I have always found that the old ones are included among the new [1900, p. 521f.].

My discussion (see also Schur, 1969) will not follow precisely the sequence of Freud's presentation; rather, I shall follow the over-all outline of the dream and the dream work, interpolating whenever necessary additional pertinent material from Freud's correspondence.

Freud reported several sets of day residues, each set linked by associations with all others as well as with events of the past. The first was the unveiling of the memorial to Fleischl in the cloisters of the University of Vienna, which took place on October 16, 1898.

Ernst Fleischl von Marxow, one of the "revenants" of the dream, was an associate of the physiologist Ernst Brücke, in whose laboratory Freud had started his scientific career. Fleischl had all the qualities to make him an object of identification and admiration—and probably of some envy as well. Unusually brilliant, full of creative scientific ideas, handsome and charming, a member of a wealthy and influential aristocratic family, he was destined for a rapidly advancing academic career, which for many reasons Freud could never hope to match. Freud lacked the material resources for such a career because it took many years, sometimes even decades, for a *Privatdozent* or an Assistant or Associate Professor to earn a moderately satisfactory salary in a theoretical field such as physiology. As a Jew, Freud had little chance of ever reaching a rank higher than these.

In the course of an experiment, Fleischl sustained an injury to his hand and the wound became infected, necessitating the amputation of several fingers. He then developed amputation neuromata (causalgia), a condition known to cause unbearable pain. Several surgical interventions were unsuccessful, and Fleischl started to resort to morphine, to which he became addicted. Freud's studies on the anesthetic properties of cocaine had led him to believe that it was possible to cure morphine addiction by administering cocaine orally. Only much later did he become aware of the psychological factors underlying all addictions (see L. 79, December 22, 1897). Nor did he realize that cocaine, even when taken only by mouth, can also result in addiction. Initially the results with Fleischl seemed miraculous, and Freud was elated. Soon, however, Fleischl developed a cocaine addiction, the symptoms of which were even more disastrous than those of morphinism. To see the progressive physical and mental deterioration of this admired and beloved friend was extremely painful for Freud, not only because of the empathy with Fleischl but because of his guilt feelings over having recommended the cocaine in the first place. In Freud's betrothal letters we find vivid descriptions of the harrowing nightly vigils he spent with his friend, trying to allay the latter's suffering, until finally Fleischl died in 1891.

Adding to Freud's "guilt of the survivor" was the fact that he had given cocaine not only to Fleischl but, after his discovery of its stimulating effect, had taken it himself on many occasions—for example, during his stay in Paris. He had also prescribed it to his fiancée Martha and to his sister. However, neither they nor he had developed an addiction to cocaine. We can only speculate why Freud, who was addicted to nicotine, did not develop an addiction to cocaine.

It is obvious that Freud's guilt feelings were still with him at the time of the Irma dream in 1895, for the Fleischl theme was also prominent in that dream, whose main motif was "exculpation."

Freud's associations to the *non vixit* dream show an additional determinant for the guilt feelings which he felt in relation to Fleischl. The number of associate appointments to Brücke's laboratory was limited, and Freud was aware of occasional death wishes directed against Fleischl, whose life was in any event a constant torture.

Furthermore, we know that Fleischl, who was a man of some means, had most generously and tactfully lent Freud money at various times when Freud was literally destitute. Without this support Freud could never have managed to study in Paris with Charcot on the meager stipend that had been allotted.

Another "revenant" of the dream was Josef Paneth, whom Freud had annihilated with the gaze of his eyes, as he had once felt annihilated by the reproachful expression in the eyes of his teacher, Brücke. Freud tells us in his associations that Paneth, who took Freud's place as "demonstrator" [assistant instructor] in Brücke's Institute, had waited with a certain impatience for Fleischl's demise in order to obtain the latter's position. Actually, Paneth died a year earlier than Fleischl without ever attaining the post he had so coveted.

Paneth, one year younger than Freud, had been a friend for many years. In relation to this man, too, Freud felt a sense of obligation and guilt because Paneth, who, like Fleischl, had come of a wealthy family, had been even more generous to Freud than Fleischl. Aware of Freud's hopelessly long courtship, he had set aside a sum of money the interest on which had permitted Freud at least to visit his fiancée from time to time, while the principal had speeded up the marriage and helped the young couple to furnish their home.

Freud confessed in his associations that:

> Not unnaturally, a few years earlier, I myself had nourished a still livelier wish to fill a vacancy. Whenever there is rank and promotion the way lies open for wishes that call for suppression. Shakespeare's Prince Hal could not, even at his father's sick-bed, resist the temptation of trying on the crown. But, as was to be expected, the dream punished my friend, and not me, for this callous wish [p. 484].

In the second part of the interpretation Freud related what he considered to be the *main* "exciting cause" of the dream: an operation Fliess had just undergone and the first disquieting reports about his condition.[2]

> The dream-thoughts now informed me that I feared for my friend's life. His only sister, whom I had never known, had, as I was aware, died in

2 We are here reminded of an analogous situation when in September, 1894 Freud had gone on a pleasant vacation with his wife while Fliess was undergoing surgery. This had occasioned guilt feelings which he then expressed in a veiled way (see Chapter 3).

early youth after a very brief illness. (In the dream *Fl. spoke about his
sister and said that in three quarters of an hour she was dead.*) I must
have imagined that his constitution was not much more resistant than
his sister's and that, after getting some much worse news of him, I
should make the journey after all—and arrive *too late,* for which I
might never cease to reproach myself.

[Note 1:] It was this phantasy, forming part of the unconscious
dream-thoughts, which so insistently demanded *'Non vivit'* instead of
'Non vixit': 'You have come too late, he is no longer alive' [p. 481].

Fliess's sister, mentioned in this paragraph, was named Pauline. So
was Freud's niece, the sister of his nephew John, who played a very
important role in the associations to this dream. Freud had mentioned
this niece in the same letter to Fliess (October 3, 1897) in which he
reported the reconstruction of his memories about his nephew. He
wrote then: "We [John and Freud] seem occasionally to have treated
my niece, who was a year younger, shockingly" (L. 70).[3]

I have already referred to Freud's allusion to the possibility of there
being a new "Paulinchen" in the Fliess family (letter of May 1, 1898),
and the baby born to Fliess in the last week of August, 1898 was
named Pauline.

On October 9, 1898, in a letter written less than two weeks before
the *non vixit* dream, Freud said:

> The sense of enjoyment which shines through your letters is heart-
> warming and contagious. Note how soon Paulinchen will reveal herself
> to you as the reincarnation of your sister [see Schur, 1969].

Here is the revenant *theme of the* non vixit *dream!*

At this point some additional information is essential. Some time
after this letter, Fliess's letters must have indicated severe headaches,
which, as we know, were prone to evoke in Freud a mixture of concern and angry resentment.

What Freud did not indicate in his interpretation *was that on October 24 (a few days before the* non vixit *dream) Fliess had had his 40th
birthday.*

The year before Freud had forgotten to send Fliess his usual birthday wishes. At that time he did not yet know the meaning of such
parapraxes, but in the meantime he had discovered it. In 1898, Freud
did not forget to write, but sent a letter on October 23, a week after

---

[3] See also Freud's paper on "Screen Memories" (1899) and Chapter 4.

the unveiling of the Fleischl memorial. This letter showed little of Freud's usually elegant style.

My dear Wilhelm,

This letter is intended to reach you on that most significant date of all to you, and to bring you good wishes for happiness from me and mine across the distance between us. These wishes are—as they should be, according to their nature, though not according to human misuse—directed toward the future, and their substance is: keep and extend the possessions you now have and acquire new ones in children and knowledge; and, finally, be spared every vestige of suffering and illness beyond that which man urgently needs to harness his powers and for comparison with the good [things in life] [L. 99]. [A short unpublished paragraph of this letter reads as follows:] My sister Rosa gave birth to a girl on October 18.[4] Both are well [2].

Why was the 40th birthday such an important date for Fliess? Was it crucial *in* or *for* Fliess's life?

We know about Freud's preoccupation with dates at which he might die, a preoccupation which in contrast to his travel phobia never yielded completely to his self-analysis. It was first focused on the numbers 41 and 42, later even more strongly on the number 51. In 1899, he began to be preoccupied with the numbers 61 and 62, and in 1936 with the number 81½.

Fliess believed that he could ascertain the "critical" dates in the periodic cycles which predetermined birth, illness, and death. For him, his 40th birthday obviously represented such a "most critical" period, and we have here one additional reason for the assumption that Freud's preoccupation with such dates developed as a partial identification within the context of his relationship with Fliess.

As is characteristic of a fantastic hypothesis of this kind, however, it provided a magical means for the evasion of a fateful date, for example, by substituting a more or less severe illness for a fatal one. And so Fliess chose just this "period" for his surgery!

This letter also indicates that the "non vixit" dream must have occurred after October 23—because no mention was made in it of Fliess's operation. One week later, on October 30, Freud wrote again to Fliess:

After having sent off my last letter with the wishes for your happiness, I reproached myself for having deviated from the traditional formulation which seeks to abolish the very last vestige of anything that implies

[4] This event may represent another "day residue" of the *non vixit* dream.

suffering or illness. I wanted to sound rational and provide a place and positive function for that which in any event cannot be avoided. This was nonsense, since wishing will not become rational by means of such corrections. In my inattentive reading I overlooked your first intimation that you planned to let yourself in for new experimental torments, and I was therefore greatly surprised to hear the news of your operation so soon thereafter [3].

The self-reproaches about the manner in which Freud expressed his birthday wishes in the preceding letter, and the admission that he had "overlooked" the earlier intimation that Fliess was thinking of surgery, reflect Freud's barely veiled ambivalence.

In his associations to the dream Freud had indicated that he could not rush to his friend's bedside because he was at that time the "victim of a painful complaint which made movement of any kind a torture." However, the correspondence of August, 1899 contains a passage which indicates that Freud had made an error in claiming that his own painful illness (a large furuncle on the raphe scrotis) had coincided with Fliess's operation, an error picked up by Fliess at the time he was reading the galleys of the dream book—to Freud's great embarrassment. It was not until a week *after* the above-quoted letter, on November 6, that Freud wrote about a large furuncle on his scrotum which had to be lanced. Painful as this was, Freud did not interrupt his work with patients, the number of which was growing steadily. Reporting on his illness, he spoke of it as evidence of a "secret biological sympathy" between himself and Fliess which had led them both to submit to the surgeon's knife at the same time.

This error, which expressed Freud's wish to exculpate himself for his failure to rush to Fliess's bedside, was facilitated by the fact that this part of his interpretation was not composed until the summer of 1899, when the final version of *The Interpretation of Dreams* was written. Knowing that Freud could not have had the *non vixit* dream before he heard the details of Fliess's illness, which he acknowledged in the letter of October 30, and assuming that it took a few days for this furuncle (which also figured in one of Freud's dreams [1900, pp. 229-232]) to develop, we can now narrow down the date of the "non vixit" dream: it must have occurred close to October 30.

This date has a very special significance: the night after his father's funeral, on October 26, 1898, two years almost to the day before the *non vixit* dream, Freud had a further dream which he reported to Fliess:

I found myself in a shop where there was a notice up saying:

You are requested
to close the eyes.

I recognized the place as the barber's to which I go every day. On the day of the funeral I was kept waiting, and therefore arrived at the house of mourning rather late. The family were displeased with me, because I had arranged for the funeral to be quiet and simple, which they later agreed was the best thing. They also took my lateness in rather bad part. The phrase on the notice-board has a double meaning. It means "one should do one's duty towards the dead" in two senses—an apology, as though I had not done my duty and my conduct needed overlooking, and the actual duty itself. *The dream was thus an outlet for the feeling of self-reproach which a death generally leaves among the survivors* [my italics] [L. 50; see also Freud, 1900, p. 317f.].

In 1899 Freud had not yet discovered the significance of anniversary reactions, which manifest themselves not only in dreams but also in symptomatic actions on anniversaries of crucially important events of the past, particularly death anniversaries.

I return now to Freud's (1900) associations to the *non vixit* dream:

Along with the unfavourable reports during the few days after the operation, I was given a warning not to discuss the matter with anyone. I had felt offended by this because it implied an unnecessary distrust of my discretion. I was quite aware that these instructions had not emanated from my friend but were due to tactlessness or over-anxiety on the part of the intermediary, but I was very disagreeably affected by the veiled reproach because it was—not wholly without justification. As we all know, it is only reproaches which have something in them that 'stick'; it is only they that upset us. What I have in mind does not relate, it is true, to this friend, but to a much earlier period of my life. On that occasion I caused trouble between two friends (both of whom had chosen to honour me, too, with that name) by quite unnecessarily telling one of them, in the course of conversation, what the other had said about him. At that time, too, reproaches had been levelled at me, and they were still in my memory. One of the two friends concerned was Professor Fleischl; I may describe the other by his first name of 'Josef'—which was also that of P., my friend and opponent in the dream [p. 481f.].

The associations established many links between the Fleischl-Paneth themes and the Fliess theme, between the present, the not-too-distant past, and early childhood. The links were established by such elements as rivalry, "carrying tales," the name Pauline, and also by such problems as birth, illness, death, love, hate, and guilt.

The associations added new figures to the dream: Breuer—whose first name Josef was the same as that of Paneth, who also was an associate in the Brücke Institute, and who had played such an important role in Freud's life. Breuer's name, furthermore, brought back memories of times when Freud had really been indiscreet and therefore had created trouble between Breuer and Fleischl.

Various themes of his associations led Freud beyond the rivalries and conflicts of the Brücke period deep into his early childhood, to memories he had recovered during his self-analysis (cf. L. 70). He thought of his nephew John, one year his senior, the son of his oldest brother Emanuel. John had "disappeared" when his family had moved to Manchester, England, in 1859. He "reappeared," becoming a "revenant" (like the figures in the dreams) when he and his family visited Vienna in 1870; Freud was then 14.

In both chapters of the dream book which dealt with the *non vixit* dream, Freud returned to the John theme, elaborating on the reconstruction of this early childhood event (which he had reported to Fliess in L. 70). Freud and his nephew John were, according to Freud, inseparable until his third year. They loved and fought each other. Freud reported in both chapters, in nearly identical sentences, that his relationship with John influenced, in a decisive way, all his subsequent relationships with contemporaries:

All my friends have in a certain sense been re-incarnations of this first figure . . . : they have been *revenants*. My nephew himself re-appeared in my boyhood, and at that time we acted the parts of Caesar and Brutus together. My emotional life has always insisted that I should have an intimate friend and a hated enemy. I have always been able to provide myself afresh with both, and it has not infrequently happened that the ideal situation of childhood has been so completely reproduced that friend and enemy have come together in a single individual—though not, of course, both at once or with constant oscillations, as may have been the case in my early childhood.

. . . let us assume that a childhood memory arose, or was constructed in phantasy. . . . The two children had a dispute about some object. . . . They came to blows and might prevailed over right. On the evidence of the dream, I may myself have been aware that I was in the wrong (*'I myself noticed the mistake'*). However, this time I was the stronger and remained in possession of the field. The vanquished party hurried to his grandfather—my father—and complained about me, and I defended myself in the words which I know from my father's account: 'I hit him 'cos he hit me.' . . . From this point the dream-thoughts proceeded along some such lines as these: 'It serves you right if you had to make way for me. Why did you try to push *me* out of the way? I don't need you. I can easily find someone else to play with,' and so on. These thoughts now entered upon the paths which led to their representation in the dream [p. 483f.].

Freud not only described the circuitous route of his associations which led him to the theme of Julius Caesar and Brutus and to his relationship with John, but most vividly depicted his great effort to overcome certain inhibitions arising in the course of the interpretations.

He was groping for the source of the phrase *non vixit* in the dream. The high degree of clarity which the words possessed in the dream pointed to a visual impression. Freud remembered an inscription on the pedestal of the statue of the Emperor Josef II[5] which stood in front of the Imperial Library. The inscription read:

*Saluti publicae vixit
non diu sed totus.*
[For the well-being of his country he lived not long but wholly.][6]

Freud then had to trace the change in the manifest dream content from *non vixit*—he did not live—to *non vivit*—he is not alive.

There must have been some other element in the dream-thoughts which would help to make the transition possible. It then struck me as noticeable that in the scene in the dream there was a convergence of a hostile and an affectionate current of feeling towards my friend P., the former being on the surface and the latter concealed, but both of them being represented in the single phrase *Non vixit*. As he had deserved well of science I built him a memorial; but as he was guilty of an evil wish (which was expressed at the end of the dream) I annihilated him. I noticed that this last sentence had a quite special cadence, and I must have had some model in my mind. Where was an antithesis of this sort to be found, a juxtaposition like this of two opposite reactions towards a single person, both of them claiming to be completely justified and yet not incompatible? Only in one passage in literature— but a passage which makes a profound impression on the reader: in Brutus's speech of self-justification in Shakespeare's *Julius Caesar* [p. 423f.].

In this circuitous way Freud arrived at the association to Julius Caesar and his nephew John. Freud recognized that he "had been playing the part of Brutus in the dream" and continued:

[5] Josef II, the son of Maria Theresa, was one of the representatives of the "enlightenment" of the 18th century. This figure frequently came up in Freud's writings.
[6] For a slip in Freud's quotation of this inscription, see Freud (1900, p. 423, n. 1) and Wittels (1924, p. 100).

If only I could find one other piece of evidence in the content of the dream. . . . So far as I knew, my friend Fl. had never been in Vienna in July. But the month of July was named after Julius Caesar and might therefore very well represent the allusion I wanted to the intermediate thought of my playing the part of Brutus [p. 424].

It is the last sentence of this paragraph which is so pertinent for the following reasons:

(a) The second part of the interpretation of the *non vixit* dream started out with "the exciting cause of the dream," Fliess's illness and operation, and the warning not to be indiscreet. These themes led via the theme of Fliess's sister Pauline and the "telling of tales" directly to both the infantile constellation between Freud, John, and his niece, Pauline, and to the rivalry within the hierarchy of the Brücke Institute —which then included another Josef—Breuer.

(b) Fliess did not come to Vienna in July, but Freud and Fliess met in July somewhere near Salzburg (see Chapter 4).

(c) In Freud's interpretation, there was a most significant omission. I have indicated that Freud had recovered his memory about John in his self-analysis and reported it to Fliess on October 3, 1897 (L. 70). In the same letter, before mentioning John, Freud had commented: "I greeted my one-year-younger brother (who died within a few months) with evil wishes and genuine infantile jealousy, so that his death implanted a seed of self-reproach in me." Freud concluded: *"This nephew and this younger brother now determine the neurotic element, but also the intensity of all my friendships"* [my italics].

This was an amazing confession to make to Fliess, implying as it did that Freud's friendship with the latter contained neurotic elements. Only a *few weeks* after this reconstruction (October 27, 1897) Freud claimed that his self-analysis was a valid reason for "forgetting" to congratulate Fliess on his "not-yet-40th birthday"—October 24, exactly one year after the death of Freud's father.

What Freud did *not* mention in his analysis of the *non vixit* dream is his brother Julius, even though he associated Julius Caesar to the element in the manifest dream: "My friend Fl. came to Vienna in July." Inasmuch as Fliess was born in 1858, the year Julius died, Fliess was a "revenant" of Freud's younger brother, just as Fliess's daughter Pauline was a "revenant" of the latter's dead sister.

After having associated Julius Caesar, Brutus, and Prince Hal, Freud turned once more to his friend Josef Paneth, who was born in 1857, the same year as Freud's younger brother Julius.

'As he was ambitious, I slew him.' As he could not wait for the removal of another man, he was himself removed. These had been my
thoughts immediately after I attended the unveiling at the University of
the memorial—not to him but to the other man. Thus a part of the
satisfaction I felt in the dream was to be interpreted: 'A just punishment! It serves you right!'

At my friend's [P.'s] funeral, a young man had made what seemed
to be an inopportune remark to the effect that the speaker who had
delivered the funeral oration had implied that without this one man
the world would come to an end. He was expressing the honest feelings
of someone whose pain was being interfered with by an exaggeration
[p. 484f.].

Only now did Freud fully establish the link between these dream
thoughts and Fliess:

> . . . this remark . . . was the starting-point of the following dream-
> thoughts: 'It's quite true that no one's irreplaceable. How many people
> I've followed to the grave already! But I'm still alive. I've survived
> them all; I'm left in possession of the field.' A thought of this kind,
> occurring to me at a moment at which I was afraid I might not find my
> friend [Fl.] alive if I made the journey to him, could only be construed
> as meaning that I was delighted because I had once more survived
> someone, because it was *he* and not I who had died, because I was left
> in possession of the field, as I had been in the phantasied scene from
> my childhood. This satisfaction, infantile in origin, at being in posses-
> sion of the field constituted the major part of the affect that appeared
> in the dream. I was delighted to survive, and I gave expression to my
> delight with all the naïve egoism shown in the anecdote of the married
> couple one of whom said to the other: 'If one of us dies, I shall move
> to Paris.' So obvious was it to me that I should not be the one to die.
>
> It cannot be denied that to interpret and report one's dreams de-
> mands a high degree of self-discipline. One is bound to emerge as the
> only villain . . . the *revenants* were a series of re-incarnations of the
> friend of my childhood [i.e., of nephew John, *not* of his brother]. It was
> therefore also a source of satisfaction to me that I had always been
> able to find successive substitutes for that figure; and I felt I should
> be able to find a substitute for the friend whom I was now on the point
> of losing: no one was irreplaceable [p. 485].

Freud and John acted the roles of Brutus and Caesar on the occasion of John's visit to Vienna in 1870. The dialogue did not stem from
Shakespeare's play but from Schiller's *Die Räuber* (IV, 5). This Schiller tragedy centers mainly around the vicious sibling rivalry between
a younger brother, born deformed and ugly, and an older brother, a
born leader endowed with superior physical qualities, who gains the

affection of his father and wins the love of a cousin, a sister figure. The play ends with the death of all the main figures. The father, incarcerated in a dungeon by his vicious son, is rescued by the good son —who previously had been told that his father was dead. However, the father dies from exhaustion a short while later. The villainous son commits suicide when his brother returns to avenge his crimes, but not before being told by a priest that parricide and fratricide are the crimes which can never be forgiven. In the meantime the older son has become a robber captain in the style of Robin Hood. Knowing that he will have to pay for his crimes with his life, he kills his beloved cousin and commits suicide. All of these tragedies result from the murderous ambition and intrigue of the younger brother, driven by Fate (*Daimon*) to all his evil deeds.[7]

In the scene from *Die Räuber* (The Robbers) which Freud mentions, the poet leaves to the imagination of the reader whether "the good son" is singing a song (he is awake while his band is sleeping) or is watching an apparition: either way, the scene takes place after the battle of Philippi. Brutus is nearing the brink of the underworld when Caesar's ghost appears. In the dialogue that follows Caesar calls Brutus his son, who has become the greatest of all Romans by plunging his sword into his father's chest. Brutus replies that he knows only one man who would be equal to the great Caesar—he whom Caesar has called his son, and ends by saying, "Where Brutus lives, Caesar must die."

Thus, the father, Caesar and Brutus, and Schiller's play also were revenants.

After expressing his delight at having survived Fliess, Freud asked himself what had become of the dream censor. Why did it permit this "blatantly egoistic train of thought" to emerge without evoking severe unpleasure or anxiety? Freud tried to explain this as follows:

> I think that other, unobjectionable trains of thought in connection with the same people found simultaneous satisfaction and screened with *their* affect the affect which arose from the forbidden infantile source. In another stratum of my thoughts, during the ceremonial unveiling of the memorial, I had reflected thus: 'What a number of valued friends I have lost, some through death, some through a breach of our friendship! How fortunate that I have found a substitute for them and that I have gained one who means more to me than ever the others could,

---

[7] On the day of his first systematic dream interpretation, July 24, 1895, Freud had addressed Fliess: "Daimonie" ("You Demon").

and that, at a time of life when new friendships cannot easily be formed, I shall never lose his! My satisfaction at having found a substitute for these lost friends could be allowed to enter the dream without interference; but there slipped in, along with it, the hostile satisfaction derived from the infantile source. It is no doubt true that infantile affection served to reinforce my contemporary and justified affection. But infantile hatred, too, succeeded in getting itself represented [p. 486].

This explanation sounds as strained as the one Freud gave in interpreting the Goethe dream, when he tried to prove to himself that it was not Fliess who was "crazy," but the reviewer of the latter's book.

In the dream book Freud emphasized the crucial importance of infantile conflicts for our development. This, of course, was one of the basic discoveries of psychoanalysis. Freud was also able to show that virtually every dream expressed certain infantile wishes and the conflicts precipitated by them. Moreover, by studying the dream work, Freud had learned that recent events, trivial or important, pleasurable or conflictual, are utilized by the dream work to permit such repressed infantile wishes and fantasies (id derivatives) to gain expression in the manifest and especially in the latent content of the dream.

What he did not know at that time—and this applies to the Irma and to the *non vixit* dreams—was that recent, highly conflictual, partly unconscious thoughts and wishes can gain representation and expression via associations with old infantile material that may be less "egodystonic" than the more "superficial" current conflict. The dream work can operate genetically in two directions—from the present to the past and vice versa.

During the writing of the dream book, Freud was for many reasons deeply preoccupied with the reconstruction of early infantile material, which played an important part in his self-analysis, the treatment of his patients, and the development of his theoretical scaffolding.

For all these reasons, it was probably especially difficult for Freud to realize that occasionally *the emphasis on infantile material can be used successfully as a defense against recent conflicts, in particular those which arise in the transference relationship,* a phenomenon which manifests itself in every analysis.

The relationship of Prince Hal to his father, Henry IV, and that of Brutus to Caesar were both prime examples of the oedipal conflict. Yet Freud presented these examples in his associations as conflicts of rivalry and ambition.

The fact that the *non vixit* dream can also be seen as an "anniversary reaction" to Freud's father's death, as well as an elaboration on the "guilt of the survivor" dream which he had reported to Fliess two years earlier may explain the omission of the oedipal theme in Freud's interpretation. That Freud did not link the theme of intensive rivalry with his "Crime of Cain" is, however, much more pertinent.

If we are to understand fully the *non vixit* dream and the repercussions which the conflicts it manifested had in Freud's later life, we must understand this dream in the context of Freud's most complex relationship to Fliess. Freud's own remark, that his relationships to his nephew and younger brother determined both the neurotic elements and the intensity of all his adult friendships, makes evident that he was aware of the transferencelike elements in his relationship to Fliess.

I have singled out many remarks from Freud's letters which indicate that he was more than skeptical about Fliess's far-reaching speculations, and yet he felt obliged again and again to uphold the basic importance of Fliess's hypotheses, trying to reinforce in himself his trust and belief in Fliess by being critical of and mocking all those empty-headed professors who dared not accept Fliess's findings.

While Freud, during the writing of *The Interpretation of Dreams,* was as convinced as one can be about the basic truth of his own discoveries, they were so revolutionary that a grain of doubt must have remained, as well as a feeling of awe at having looked into an abyss which perhaps was forbidden to human eyes. Hence Freud needed Fliess and therefore had to silence his judgment and reason, relegating the hostile part of his ambivalence and doubt to parapraxes and dreams.

By comparing and contrasting the *non vixit* dream with the Goethe and Irma dreams, we can trace the growing conflict between Freud and Fliess.

In the Irma dream the hostility to Fliess was disguised by being displaced onto others. In the dream of Goethe's attack on Herr M., Freud's agreement with the devastating criticism of Fliess's work was disguised as a derisive attack on the critics themselves. The conflict in the *non vixit* dream went much further, or, to be more accurate, deeper. It was expressed in the most elementary terms: who will survive whom?

In 1896, Freud first referred to the universal guilt experienced by the survivors after the death of a parent. However, the guilt of the survivor also manifests itself after the death of siblings and peers. In the "non vixit" dream Freud was alluding not only to survival proper, but also to outlasting those who had been left professionally by the wayside.

In the manifest dream Freud "annihilated" Paneth and Fleischl, who were actually dead at the time; he declared that all his friends were reincarnations, "revenants," including Breuer. Freud never failed to acknowledge Breuer's role in the development of psychoanalysis. Breuer's attempts at a cathartic treatment of hysteria proved to be the catalyst which led to Freud's discoveries about the working of the mind.

Although Breuer was alive at the time of the dream, he, too, had been left by the wayside. He had followed the unfolding of Freud's ideas with a mixture of skepticism and awed admiration. He sometimes praised him highly, but frequently expressed underhand criticism of Freud to third parties.

We know some of the reasons why Breuer had to dissociate himself from Freud's later work (see Freud, 1914a, 1925b; Jones, Vol. 1; Pollock, 1968). From the unpublished letters to Fliess we learn much about the complexity and intensity of Freud's ambivalent relationship with Breuer (see Chapter 6). Thus Breuer was in a certain sense also someone whom Freud could include in his statement *non vixit* or *non vivit*.

It was an earmark of Freud's genius that he was able to turn a stimulus he received from others into the nucleus of a psychological revolution. Himself a source of inspiration for so many, he was on the receiving end with regard to certain people in his life. One of these was Breuer; another was Fliess.

Several questions can be asked at this point: Why did Freud have to "do away with" Fliess at this time? Why did he have to confess it all to Fliess, including his past indiscretion, thus leaving himself open to the attack which Fliess eventually launched against him (see Chapter 7)? Finally, how did Fliess take this "killing off"?

For a possible answer to these questions, all we can do is turn to Freud.

In September, 1899 Freud had finished the dream book. Although he found fault with his work, he knew that it was his *magnum opus*, that from then on the world would never again be the same. On his return to Vienna he wrote to Fliess: "And now for another year of this extraordinary life in which one's state of mind is the only thing that really matters. Mine is wavering, but . . . as it says on the coat of arms of our beloved Paris: 'Fluctuat nec mergitur' (L. 119).[8]

He sent Fliess another 60 galleys, and announced triumphantly: "The principal part of my interpretative achievements comes in this installment. The absurd dreams! It is astonishing how often you appear in them. In the *non vixit* dream I am delighted to have survived you. Isn't it awful to have to hint at such things?" (L. 119).

The writing of his book took precedence over every other consideration. Freud did not spare himself. In order to present his theories in an intelligible fashion he had to divulge some of the most intimate details of his life, which nowadays one would tell only to one's analyst. This included the hostile wishes and fantasies which an analyst is expected to accept without any resentment.

During all this time Freud's self-analysis was continuing. Within the framework of this unique analytic situation Freud needed to preserve the overvaluation of Fliess, his alter ego, his audience, and trusted physician. Yet in a still submerged part of himself, Freud knew that Fliess's theories were figments of imagination. Freud knew, moreover, that eventually he would have to realize the impossibility of coexistence between his own concepts of psychic determinism and Fliess's concept of cosmic determination of human events. Thus Freud was anticipating that Fliess, too, would soon be left by the wayside to become a "revenant." In the language of infantile wishes, Fliess would be killed off.

In Freud's dreams and in his triumph over having reached the climax of his achievement, his guilt feelings were muted. In his interpretation he was also able to deny the importance of his death wishes regarding Fliess, by using the device of "resistance downward,"[9] that is, in interpreting the *non vixit* dream, by establishing in his associations a link to his early infantile conflicts with his nephew John, while omitting any mention of his dead brother Julius, thus overlooking the importance of his current conflict.

The confession of past indiscretions, rivalries, and death wishes often serves as a device to mute guilt feelings, but they rarely remain muted for long. Moreover, we do not know how Fliess responded to Freud's confessions. We know only (from an unpublished letter written on November 30, 1898, approximately one month after the *non*

---

[8] Freud used this as a motto to "On the History of the Psycho-Analytic Movement" (1914a). See also Chapter 4, footnote 56.

[9] A term suggested in a personal communication by R. M. Loewenstein.

vixit dream) how Freud reacted to the episode of Fliess's operation, namely, with ambivalence. Freud reported the "phenomenon" of obviously feeling angry about Fliess's ill-health, and that he wanted to find fault with Fliess's surgery. However, he was looking forward to a meeting around Christmastime. He admitted apologetically that he had made a great deal of his furuncle to put a damper on his expression of sympathy and on Fliess's further discussion of his illness.

When Freud conceived of the dream book, he was interested primarily in the operation of the dream work and the infantile roots of the latent dream, being much less familiar with the ego aspects and the transference implications of dreams. While we know that day residues attach themselves to unconscious—chiefly infantile—material in order to gain mental representation, we cannot neglect the dynamic importance of current conflicts, even when these are expressed in connection with repressed fantasies (id derivatives.) Thus in 1899, when Freud was finishing *The Interpretation of Dreams,* he could gloss over his wish to survive Fliess which necessitated "killing him off" in fantasy. Nevertheless, such fantasies, especially if followed eventually by the rupture of a friendship, leave their traces in our mental life. One can re-experience the "guilt of the survivor," as Freud pointed out in connection with memories of his childhood fight with his nephew John, if one has "remained in possession of the field" later in life (1900, p. 483).

DEATH IN DREAMS

We dream about our chief conflicts, our wishes and fears about the people we love or hate, or the ones we love *and* hate; about our own life and death and those of others. It was left to Freud to discover that death wishes against parents and siblings were not the exception but the rule, and that they originate in early childhood. Giving examples in *The Interpretation of Dreams* of how death wishes against siblings show up in dreams, Freud wrote:

> In none of my woman patients . . . have I failed to come upon this dream of the death of a brother or sister. . . . I have only found a single exception: and it was easy to interpret this as a confirmation of the rule. On one occasion during an analytic session I was explaining this subject to a lady, since in view of her symptoms its discussion seemed to me relevant. To my astonishment she replied that she had never had such a dream. Another dream, however, occurred to her,

which ostensibly had no connection with the topic—a dream which she had first dreamt when she was four years old and at that time the youngest of the family, and which she had dreamt repeatedly since: *A whole crowd of children—all her brothers, sisters and cousins of both sexes—were romping in a field. Suddenly they all grew wings, flew away and disappeared.* She had no idea what this dream meant; but it is not hard to recognize that in its original form it had been a dream of the death of all her brothers and sisters, and had been only slightly influenced by the censorship. . . .

At this point someone will perhaps interrupt: 'Granted that children have hostile impulses towards their brothers and sisters, how can a child's mind reach such a pitch of depravity as to wish for the *death* of his rivals or of playmates stronger than himself, as though the death penalty were the only punishment for every crime?' Anyone who talks like this has failed to bear in mind that a child's idea of being 'dead' has nothing much in common with ours apart from the word. Children know nothing of the horrors of corruption, of freezing in the ice-cold grave, of the terrors of eternal nothingness—ideas which grown-up people find it so hard to tolerate, as is proved by the myths of a future life. The fear of death has no meaning to a child; hence it is that he will play with the dreadful word and use it as a threat against a playmate: 'If you do that again, you'll die, like Franz!' Meanwhile the poor mother gives a shudder and remembers, perhaps, that the greater half of the human race fail to survive their childhood years. It was actually possible for a child, who was over eight years old at the time, coming home from a visit to the Natural History Museum, to say to his mother: 'I'm so fond of you, Mummy: when you die I'll have you stuffed and I'll keep you in this room, so that I can see you *all* the time.' So little resemblance is there between a child's idea of being dead and our own!

[In 1909, Freud added the following footnote:] I was astonished to hear a highly intelligent boy of ten remark after the sudden death of his father: 'I know father's dead, but what I can't understand is why he doesn't come home to supper.'

To children, who, moreover, are spared the sight of the scenes of suffering which precede death, being 'dead' means approximately the same as being 'gone'—not troubling the survivors any longer. A child makes no distinction as to how this absence is brought about: whether it is due to a journey, to a dismissal, to an estrangement, or to death.

[Footnote added by Freud in 1919:] An observation made by a parent who had a knowledge of psycho-analysis caught the actual moment at which his highly intelligent four-year-old daughter perceived the distinction between being 'gone' and being 'dead.' The little girl had been troublesome at meal-time and noticed that one of the maids at the pension where they were staying was looking at her askance. 'I wish Josefine was dead,' was the child's comment to her father. 'Why dead?' enquired her father soothingly; 'wouldn't it do if she went away?'

'No,' replied the child; 'then she'd come back again.' The unbounded self-love (the narcissism of children regards any interference as an act of *lèse majesté;* and their feelings demand (like the Draconian code) that any such crime shall receive the one form of punishment which admits of no degrees [p. 253ff.].

The recognition that small children do not truly understand the meaning of death was the basis for Freud's eventual formulation that in our unconscious we know nothing about death in general and of our own death in particular.

I have indicated (in Chapters 1 and 4) that the sudden disappearance of people was an important factor during the first years of Freud's life. To recapitulate: the people who "disappeared" were his brother Julius, who died; his nursemaid, who was sent to prison; his playmates John and Pauline; his half brothers Emanuel and Philipp and Emanuel's wife Maria; the locksmith and his family; and, if Freud knew anything about her existence, his father's second wife, Rebecca. Added to all this was the disappearance of the countrylike environment, the locksmith's workshop, the meadows and the woods. The migration through foreign cities and the final quarters in a rather uninviting district of Vienna added to the impact of all these memories.

That his brother Julius had actually died intensified the linkage between the concepts disappearance and death.

The preceding passages quoted from *The Interpretation of Dreams* may give the impression that Freud might not have been aware of the later consequences of early death wishes against siblings and parents. Freud's reconstruction of his own childhood, which he had accomplished in 1897, proves that such an impression would be misleading.

What Freud implied is one of the many complexities of our mental life. Freud knew from his self-analysis and from the analysis of his patients, and principally from the interpretation of dreams, that completely contradictory thoughts can coexist in the mind. Thus small children may make seemingly callous remarks, openly express their death wishes against siblings, peers, or parents, because, as Freud said at *that* time, death has no meaning to them. However, with the development of conscience, such wishes, which usually are repressed, become the stimulus for the formation of various normal and abnormal defenses, and frequently result in guilt feelings.

Once the linkage between disappearance and death has been established in early childhood, it may in later life also extend to rivals or competitors (see my discussion of the *non vixit* dream).

The Interpretation of Dreams contains many of Freud's dreams showing his reactions to the death of various people, especially his own father. Other dreams of his deal with his own death and his fears about it. This theme was introduced in *The Interpretation of Dreams* through a dream which ended with the words: "I was then told I could go. But I could not find my hat and could not go after all" (p. 336). Pursuing a chain of associations to these sentences, Freud remembered a line from Schiller's drama *Fiesco* (III, 4): "Der Mohr hat seine *Schuldigkeit* getan, der Mohr *kann gehen*." "The Moor has done his *duty* [Freud used the vernacular quote here by writing *Schuldigkeit*— duty, rather than the author's word *Arbeit*—work]; the Moor *can go*." The quotation, like so many from the classics, had become an idiomatic expression meaning: "You have done your job; you are expendable; we don't need you any more." The figure of the Moor is pertinent here. Schiller's character was an ex-convict, used for some "dirty work" by rebels trying to unseat the government of Genoa. He was sent to the gallows by Fiesco, the leader of the revolution, because he had put the torch to some buildings after the victory. Freud identified the wish "to be recognized as an honest man and told I could go." (Compare the dream of Irma's injection with its theme of exculpation.) His associations to "the Moor" taught Freud how overdetermined the last sentences of the dream were. Freud's family legend had it that he was born with such a tangle of black hair that his mother declared he looked like a little Moor. Of the last words of the dream: "I could not go after all," Freud had this to say:

> The end of this dream also concealed a rejection of some melancholy thoughts about death: 'I am far from having done my duty, so I must not go yet.'—Birth and death[10] were dealt with in it, just as they had been in the dream of Goethe and the paralytic patient, which I had dreamt a short time before [p. 337 n.].

Freud was right in speaking of "melancholy thoughts about death." His association was not: "I do not yet have to die," but "I must not go yet." Dreams such as this one reflected the feelings of a man who was groaning under a superhuman burden, as he made clear in letters to Fliess where he compared himself to a "neoplasm" or to Jacob struggling with the angel. Four decades later Freud was forced to struggle with the same cruel dilemma: "How long must I continue to suffer

[10] See the motto of my book and Chapters 6 and 22.

such intolerable pain? When will I be permitted to accept 'sweet peace' or even to ask for it?"

The interpretation of such dreams revealed to Freud that birth and death could be represented in dreams by similar symbols (travel, ships, trains, sea, river, etc.), symbols that also appear in the myths, religious rites, and works of art of many civilizations. Freud's reference to his dream discussed earlier, about Goethe and the paralytic patient, and the link to the dream of Irma's injection and hence to the Emma episode, also indicate how intimately Freud's dreams were interwoven with his relationship to Fliess.[11]

The fact that the problem of death came up so frequently in Freud's dreams was not due to any "morbid" preoccupation with this subject. We must bear in mind that Freud's self-analysis and his work on *The Interpretation of Dreams* were greatly stimulated by his discovery of the decisive influence of early conflicts with parents and siblings, above all the oedipal conflict (see Chapter 4), both in normal and abnormal development; and that the death of Freud's father played a great catalytic role in the formation of his ideas. The death of his father was therefore a frequent theme in Freud's dreams and associations. In the process of interpreting such dreams Freud also recognized that concern about one's own death can be hidden in dreams about a beloved person who is already dead.

It is true that dreams of dead people whom the dreamer has loved raise difficult problems in dream-interpretation and that these cannot always be satisfactorily solved. The reason for this is to be found in the particularly strongly marked emotional ambivalence which dominates the dreamer's relation to the dead person. It very commonly happens that in dreams of this kind the dead person is treated to begin with as though he were alive, that he then suddenly turns out to be dead and that in a subsequent part of the dream he is alive once more. This has a confusing effect. It eventually occurred to me that this alternation between death and life is intended to represent *indifference* on the part of the dreamer. ('It's all the same to me whether he's alive or dead.') This indifference is, of course, not real but merely desired; it is intended to help the dreamer to repudiate his very intense and

[11] Freud's reference to the "paralytic patient," whose illness began with a frenzied cry "nature, nature," is reminiscent of Ibsen's tragedy *Ghosts,* which ends with the repeated utterance: "The sun, the sun" by the paresis-stricken young Oswald, a victim of congenital syphilis. At that time Ibsen's play was in the repertory of every German theatre, and the role of Oswald, with its dramatic last scene, was as eagerly sought by leading actors as that of Hamlet. Moreover, Goethe's last words were said to have been: "Mehr Licht" [More light].

often contradictory emotional attitudes and it thus becomes a dream-representation of his *ambivalence*.—In other dreams in which the dreamer associates with dead people, the following rule often helps to give us our bearings. If there is no mention in the dream of the fact that the dead men is dead, the dreamer is equating himself with him: he is dreaming of his own death. If, in the course of the dream, the dreamer suddenly says to himself in astonishment, 'why, he died ever so long ago,' he is repudiating this equation and is denying that the dream signifies his own death—But I willingly confess to a feeling that dream-interpretation is far from having revealed all the secrets of this character [p. 431].

While Freud already recognized after the death of his father that feelings of self-reproach were commonly experienced by survivors after the death of a beloved person, he had yet to discover the full importance and metapsychological implications of identification with the dead person in the process of mourning and in melancholia (see Freud, 1917a).

Always an avid reader, Freud became aware early in life that poets and writers depicted in their works of art our deepest problems. When he began to uncover the riddles of the unconscious, he read such works with a twofold purpose: on the one hand, he found in them verification of his own theories; on the other hand, believing that the genius of great artists gives them access to the most secret recesses of our minds, he also learned from them to crystallize some of his own germinating ideas, which he then formulated in the language of a scientist. The Fliess correspondence contains, for example, several analyses of works by C. F. Meyer. Freud's interpretations of his own dreams contain abundant associations to works of art in various languages by authors of many nationalities. A preoccupation with death and immortality is of course a common theme in literature, religion, and mythology.

The way in which such thoughts can be represented in the latent dream content is perhaps most pertinently demonstrated in Freud's analysis of his dream of dissecting his own pelvis. I shall deal with only those parts of the dream and Freud's interpretation of it which are pertinent to my theme.

At the beginning . . . there was a clear expression of astonishment at the subject which had cropped up. Old Brücke must have set me some task; *strangely enough,* it related to a dissection of the lower part of my own body, my pelvis and legs, which I saw before me as though in the dissecting-room, but without noticing their absence in myself and also without a trace of any *gruesome* [italics added] feeling. . . . I was then once more in possession of my legs and was making my way through the town. But (being tired) I took a cab. . . . Finally I was making a journey through a changing landscape with an Alpine guide who was carrying my belongings. Part of the way he carried me too, out of consideration for my tired legs. The ground was boggy; we went round the edge; people were sitting on the ground like Red Indians or gipsies—among them a girl. . . . At last we reached a small wooden house at the end of which was an open window. There the guide set me down and laid two wooden boards, which were standing ready, upon the window-sill, so as to bridge the chasm which had to be crossed over from the window. At that point I really became frightened about my legs, but instead of the expected crossing, I saw two grown-up men lying on wooden benches that were along the walls of the hut, and what seemed to be two children sleeping beside them. It was as though what was going to make the crossing possible was not the boards but the children. I awoke in a mental fright [p. 452f.].

Freud pointed out that it was impossible to follow up all the associations to such a complex and highly condensed manifest dream. While he discussed this dream as an example of "intellectual activities in dreams," e.g., the function of judgment, the main trend of his associations as he reported them was toward an explanation of the *absence* of the *gruesome* feeling which might have been expected from the dream's manifest content, and of the *fearful* affect with which he awoke from the dream.

The associations to the words "strangely enough" involved a conversation Freud had had about two strange books "full of hidden meaning," dealing with "the eternal feminine,"[12] the "immortality of

[12] This is an allusion to the death and salvation of Faust. Goethe's drama ends with the verses:

> Alles Vergängliche
> Ist nur ein Gleichnis;
> Das Unzulängliche,
> Hier wirds Ereignis;
> Das Unbeschreibliche,
> Hier ists getan;
> Das Ewig-weibliche
> Zieht uns hinan.
> [All that is transient
> Is but a symbol;
> Here imperfection
> Becomes actuality;
> The indescribable
> Here is fulfilled;
> The eternal feminine
> Draws us on high.]

The Faustian theme which turns up in Freud's discussion of this dream recurred in his life up to the very end.

our emotions"—H. Rider Haggard's *She* and *Heart of the World*. The conversation also dealt with Freud's own work, giving him a foretaste of the response it might arouse. His visitor had asked:

'Have you nothing of your own?'—'No, my own immortal works have not yet been written.'—'Well, when are we to expect these so-called ultimate explanations of yours which you've promised even *we* shall find readable?' she asked, with a touch of sarcasm. At that point I saw that someone else was admonishing me through her mouth and I was silent. I reflected on the amount of self-discipline it was costing me to offer the public even my book upon dreams—I should have to give away so much of my own private character in it.
> Dass Beste was du wissen kannst,
> Darfst du den Buben doch nicht sagen.[13]

. . . In both novels the guide is a woman: both are concerned with perilous journeys; while *She* describes an adventurous road that had scarcely ever been trodden before, leading into an undiscovered region. The tired feeling in my legs, according to a note which I find I made upon the dream, had been a real sensation during the day-time. It probably went along with a tired mood and a doubting thought: 'How much longer will my legs carry me?' The end of the adventure in *She* is that the guide, instead of finding immortality for herself and the others, perishes in the mysterious subterranean fire. A fear of that kind was unmistakably active in the dream-thoughts. The 'wooden house' was also, no doubt, a coffin, that is to say, the grave. But the dream-work achieved a masterpiece in its representation of this most un-wished-for of all thoughts by a wish-fulfillment. For I had already been in a grave once, but it was an excavated Etruscan grave near Orvieto,[14] a narrow chamber with two stone benches along its walls, on which the skeletons of two grown-up men were lying. The inside of the wooden house in the dream looked exactly like it, except that the stone was replaced by wood. The dream seems to have been saying: 'If you must rest in a grave, let it be the Etruscan one.' And, by making this replacement, it transformed the gloomiest of expectations into one that was highly desirable. Unluckily . . . a dream can turn into its opposite the *idea* accompanying an affect but not always the affect itself. Accord-

---

[13] "The best of what you know
You may not tell the boys!"
> Mephistopheles to Faust, Part I, Sc. 4.

See also Freud (L. 77 and 83), and Freud's address on the occasion of receiving the Goethe Prize (1930a).

[14] This experience was probably also part of the background to Freud's forgetting the name of the painter Luca Signorelli, whose altar pieces Freud had seen and admired on his visit to Orvieto (see Freud, 1901b, p. 13; Rosen, 1969; and this volume, Chapter 9).

ingly, I woke up in a *'mental fright,'* even after the successful emergence
of the idea that children may perhaps achieve what their father has
failed to—a fresh allusion to the strange novel in which a person's
identity is retained through a series of generations for over two thousand years [p. 453ff.; see also Chapter 8].

[Freud returned to this dream later in the book:] If we turn back to
the dream about the strange task set me by old Brücke of making a
dissection of my own pelvis, it will be recalled that in the dream itself
I missed the gruesome feeling [*'Grauen'*] appropriate to it. Now this
was a wish-fulfilment in more than one sense. The dissection meant the
self-analysis which I was carrying out, as it were, in the publication of
this present book about dreams—a process which had been so distressing to me in reality that I had postponed the printing of the finished
manuscript for more than a year. A wish then arose that I might get
over this feeling of distaste; hence it was that I had no gruesome feeling
[*'Grauen'*] in the dream. But I should also have been very glad to miss
growing grey—*'Grauen'* in the other sense of the word. I was already
growing quite grey, and the grey of my hair was another reminder that
I must not delay any longer. And, as we have seen, the thought that I
should have to leave it to my children to reach the goal of my difficult
journey forced its way through to representation at the end of the
dream [p. 477f.].

This dream and its interpretation depict the torment experienced
in his self-analysis, which, as Freud expressed it, left his "legs tired"
and his hair gray. The dream reveals a sense of urgency, of racing
against time to conquer the vast unknown. It also shows that Freud
felt he was working for posterity but expected only slander and derision in return.[15]

After a day of working with patients, followed by long hours of
creative work and writing, during which time he inevitably experienced
doubt about and awe at his discoveries, the content of Freud's dreams
was interwoven with day residues, old memories and fantasies, and
thoughts of death and "immortality." Freud labeled as "wish fulfillment" the dream element of finding himself in a beautiful Etruscan
grave rather than a wooden coffin, but such a transformation of what
Freud called "the gloomiest expectations into one that was highly
desirable" was actually only the dream work's "valiant" attempt at

---

[15] For a different interpretation of this dream, see Peto's paper (1969) which
appeared after the completion of this book. Peto argues that such "dismemberment"
dreams occurring in the final stages of analysis indicate the appearance of a crucial
conflict in the transference and give impetus to its resolution—an argument very
much in line with that developed in this Chapter.

denial, at creating a pleasant illusion, which, however, was not capable of preventing a painful affect from arising.[16]

This dream provides a graphic expression of the many ideas, including those on death, which were germinating in Freud during that period; among others he found that death in dreams can be represented through a variety of symbols connected with traveling (ships, trains, etc.).

The Fliess correspondence and many letters to family and friends give us vivid indications of Freud's intense enjoyment of traveling. During the period of his painful struggle, the trips he took, though often short and strenuous, were among Freud's greatest joys and an important source of physical and mental relaxation.

For years, partly because of inner causes, a trip to Rome remained an unattainable goal (for a discussion see 1900, pp. 193-196; Jones, Vol. 2, pp. 16-19). For Freud, who grew up on the fringe of poverty, in an atmosphere of utmost frugality, travel was to some extent a forbidden luxury because an extravagance of this kind had not been available to his father.

In the second edition of *The Interpretation of Dreams* (1909) Freud indicated that dreams about missing a train, when accompanied by anxiety, may actually be expressing a fear of dying while also serving in a roundabout way as a denial of death—the train has left without you; you won't depart. Freud commented that the difficulty in understanding these kinds of dreams stemmed from the fact that the anxiety was attached to what was ostensibly an expression of consolation, namely, the fact of "not departing."

Here, as in Freud's dream of dissecting his own pelvis, the attempt to deny the fear of death, or more specifically, *death itself*, had failed; hence the anxiety affect.[17]

Freud knew very well that anxiety dreams such as those involving the missing of a train were overdetermined. He himself suffered from a

---

[16] It was characteristic of the continuity of Freud's creative thinking that he took this same thought up nearly thirty years later in *The Future of an Illusion* (p. 30ff.). The theme that his children (later students) might perhaps achieve what he had failed to do was also a recurrent one in Freud's works and letters.

The concept of the "immortality" afforded by the germplasm was elaborated in *Beyond the Pleasure Principle* (1920). See also Freud's response to Fliess's speculations (Chapter 4).

[17] It was not until 1919 that Freud recognized the extent to which the ego may participate in the construction of dreams. Even then an understanding of this role of the ego encountered many obstacles. (For a more detailed discussion, see Chapter 12).

mild "train phobia," but this did not prevent him from traveling. The Fliess correspondence also reveals Freud's fearful preoccupation with the danger of a train accident when members of his family, or Fliess, went on a trip (e.g., L. 68).[18] He was not yet aware that fears were also an expression of ambivalence, of unconscious death wishes. In many letters to Fliess, Freud indicated the terrifying thoughts he had whenever he did not hear from the latter at regular intervals (e.g., letter of February 1, 1900, see Chapter 6).

A dream of Freud's in which his fear of death was intermingled with highly enjoyable memories of several trips is especially pertinent —the dream of the castle by the sea. From Freud's associations and the Fliess letters we can place this dream at the end of April, 1898. Freud was under intense strain at that time, attempting to put on paper the first draft of *The Interpretation of Dreams*. He was grappling in particular with the difficult section on psychology, which was to become Chapter VII. This task he had had to abandon temporarily. His relationship to Fliess was put under a severe strain by the publication of Fliess's book. Freud needed to preserve his positive feelings for Fliess in order to complete the dream book, as he clearly indicated in a number of letters.

An illness of Fliess's had prevented their meeting. Instead, as indicated previously, Freud took a highly enjoyable trip with his younger brother Alexander. The letter which Freud sent Fliess after this trip (on April 14, 1898) was remarkable for many reasons. It began with the following, somewhat gruffly humorous sentences:

> I think it a good rule in letter-writing to leave unmentioned things that the recipient knows already and to tell him something new instead. So I shall pass over the fact that I heard you had a bad time at Easter; you know that anyway. Instead I shall tell you about my Easter trip, which I undertook moodily but from which I returned refreshed [L. 88].

This was followed by a delightful lengthy description of the trip (which supplied the main theme of the above-mentioned dream of the castle), and ended with the unpleasant news (not included in the published version of the letter) of the "slanderous" criticism of Fliess's book.

So Fliess was sick, his discoveries had been declared to be the work

---

[18] Such a fearful preoccupation returned, for instance, as late as 1925 in the disguise of a parapraxis which Freud interpreted in a letter to Ferenczi (see Jones, Vol. 3, p. 111; and Chapter 15).

of an insane man, and Freud had had an enjoyable trip. Moreover, Freud was now on the verge of penetrating to a new level of understanding the mind, as he had done earlier by interpreting the Irma dream. He had therefore to "pay" for all this by identifying himself with a dead governor. With this background in mind, excerpts from the dream and from Freud's associations will be self-explanatory.

A castle by the sea; later it was no longer immediately on the sea, but on a narrow canal leading to the sea. The Governor was a Herr P. I was standing with him in a big reception room [reminiscent of the setting of the Irma dream]—with three windows. . . . I had been attached to the garrison as something in the nature of a volunteer naval officer. We feared the arrival of enemy warships, since we were in a state of war. Herr P. intended to leave, and gave me instructions as to what was to be done if the event that we feared took place. His invalid wife was with their children in the threatened castle. If the bombardment began, the great hall was to be evacuated. He breathed heavily and turned to go; I held him back and asked him how I was to communicate with him in case of necessity. He added something in reply, but immediately fell down dead. No doubt I had put an unnecessary strain upon him with my questions. After his death, which made no further impression on me, I wondered whether his widow would remain in the castle, whether I should report his death to the Higher Command and whether I should take over command of the castle as being next in order of rank. I was standing at the window, and observing the ships as they went past. They were merchant vessels rushing past rapidly through the dark water. . . . Then my brother was standing beside me and we were both looking out of the window at the canal. At the sight of one ship we were frightened and cried out: 'Here comes the warship!' But it turned out that it was only the same ships that I already knew returning. There now came a small ship, cut off short, in a comic fashion, in the middle. On its deck some curious cup-shaped or box-shaped objects were visible. We called out with one voice: 'That's the breakfast-ship!'

[After recounting the dream, Freud continued:] The rapid movements of the ships, the deep dark blue of the water and the brown smoke from the funnels—all of this combined to create a tense and sinister impression.

The localities in the dream were brought together from several trips of mine to the Adriatic (to Miramare, Duino, Venice and Aquileia). A short but enjoyable Easter trip which I had made to Aquileia with my brother a few weeks before the dream was still fresh in my memory. The dream also contained allusions to the *maritime war* between America and Spain and to anxieties to which it had given rise about the fate of my relatives in America. At two points in the dream affects were in question. At one point an affect that was to be anticipated was absent: attention was expressly drawn to the fact that the Governor's death made no impression on me. At another point, when I thought I saw the warship, I was *frightened* and felt all the sensations of fright in my sleep. In this well-constructed dream the affects were distributed in such a way that any striking contradiction was avoided. There was no reason why I should be frightened at the death of the Governor and it was quite reasonable that as Commandant of the Castle I should be frightened at the sight of the warship. The analysis showed, however, that Herr P. was only a substitute for my own self. (In the dream *I* was the substitute for *him*.) *I* was the Governor who suddenly died. The dream-thoughts dealt with the future of my family after my premature death. This was the only distressing one among the dream-thoughts; and it must have been from it that the fright was detached and brought into connection in the dream with the sight of the warship. On the other hand, the analysis showed that the region of the dream-thoughts from which the warship was taken was filled with the most cheerful recollections. It was a year earlier, in Venice, and we were standing one magically beautiful day at the windows of our room on the Riva degli Schiavoni and were looking across the blue lagoon on which that day there was more movement than usual. English ships were expected and were to be given a ceremonial reception. Suddenly my wife cried out gaily as a child: *"Here comes the English warship!"* In the dream I was frightened at these same words. . . . Here, then, in the process of changing the dream-thoughts into the manifest dream-content, I have transformed cheerfulness into fear. . . . This example proves . . . that the dream-work is at liberty to detach an affect from its connections in the dream-thoughts and introduce it at any other point it chooses in the manifest dream.

I take this opportunity of making a somewhat detailed analysis of the 'breakfast-ship,' the appearance of which in the dream brought such a nonsensical conclusion to a situation which had up to then been kept at a rational level. When subsequently I called the dream-object more precisely to mind, it struck me that it was black, . . . cut off short where it was broadest in the middle, it bore a great resemblance at that end to a class of objects which had attracted our interest in the museums in the Etruscan towns. These were rectangular trays of black pottery, with two handles, on which there stood things like coffee- or tea-cups, not altogether unlike one of our modern *breakfast-sets*. In response to our enquiries we learned that this was the *'toilette'* [toilet-set] of an Etruscan lady, with receptacles for cosmetics and powder on it, and we jokingly remarked that it would be a good idea to take one home with us for the lady of the house. The object in the dream meant, accordingly, a black 'toilette,' i.e. mourning dress, and made a direct reference to a death. The other end of the dream-object reminded me of the funeral boats in which in early times dead bodies were placed and committed to the sea for burial. This led on to the point which explained why the ships *returned* in the dream.

Still, auf gerettetem Boot, treibt in den Hafen der Greis [Safe on his
ship, the old man quietly sails into port].

It was the return after a shipwreck [*Schiffbruch,* literally 'ship-break']
—the breakfast-ship was broken off short in the middle. But what was
the origin of the name 'breakfast'-ship? It was here that the word
'English' came in, which was left over from the warships. The English
word 'breakfast' means 'breaking fast'. The 'breaking' related once
more to the shipwreck ['ship-break'] and the fasting was connected with
the black dress or *toilette.*

But it was only the *name* of the breakfast-ship that was newly constructed by the dream. The *thing* had existed and reminded me of one
of the most enjoyable parts of my last trip. Mistrusting the food that
would be provided at Aquileia, we had brought provisions with us from
Gorizia and had bought a bottle of excellent Istrian wine at Aquileia.
And while the little mail steamer made its way slowly through the
'*Canale delle Mee*' across the empty lagoon to Grado we, who were
the only passengers, ate our breakfast on deck in the highest spirits,
and we had rarely tasted a better one. This, then, was the 'breakfast-
ship,' and it was precisely behind this memory of the most cheerful
joie de vivre that the dream concealed the gloomiest thoughts of an
unknown and uncanny future [pp. 463-466].

In discussing the *non vixit* dream I spoke of Freud's deep-seated
conflict which might be characterized as the "guilt of the survivor" or
the problem of "revenants." The dream of the castle has a similar
theme: guilt over happiness and success which one part of the dreamer
feels has been gained at the expense of a beloved friend. "Who am I
to become a peer of Copernicus, Galileo, and Darwin when the man
whose theories I have so greatly admired, is regarded as a lunatic?
Shall I see Rome if my father never did, when Hannibal got no closer
than Lake Trasimene, when Moses saw the Promised Land only from
afar?"

A few years later, during another trip, this conflict flared up again
(see Chapter 7), manifesting itself in a series of symptoms the most
prominent of which was a renewal of the preoccupation with the
possible imminence of death on a particular date.

Freud first mentioned the ominous age of 51 in his letter of June
22, 1894 to Fliess, in connection with the death of the physicist Kundt.
As I have indicated in Chapter 2, Kundt actually died at the age of
54½ and not 51. The following dream and some of Freud's associations to it, as reported in *The Interpretation of Dreams,* are remarkable
in this context. The dream is reported in the chapter on "Absurd

Dreams," and its analysis is given in several parts. I shall first discuss the points pertinent to the significance of the number 51.

> I received a communication from the town council of my birthplace concerning the fees due for someone's maintenance in the hospital in the year *1851,* which had been necessitated by an attack he had had in my house. I was amused by this since, in the first place, I was not yet alive in *1851* and, in the second place, my father, to whom it might have related, was already dead. I went to him in the next room, where he was lying on his bed, and told him about it. To my surprise, he recollected that in *1851* he had once got drunk and had had to be locked up or detained. It was at a time at which he had been working for the firm of T————. 'So you used to drink as well?' I asked; 'did you get married soon after that?' I calculated that, of course, I was born in *1856,* which seemed to be the year which immediately followed the year in question [p. 435f.].

Freud first pointed out that the figure of his father, who in the manifest content of the dream had been the object of ridicule, had actually been "made into a man of straw, in order to screen someone else." In contrast to the procedure he had adopted in the interpretation of the *non vixit* dream, which had taken place earlier, Freud was here interpreting "upward," i.e., discussing primarily current and recent conflicts rather than a childhood one. His associations included the surprised and critical attitude of a senior colleague (Breuer) toward the fact that a patient of Freud's had begun his fifth year of treatment. Freud's reaction to this criticism was: "What were *four or five* years in comparison to a lifetime?" He went on to say:

> The most blatant and disturbing absurdity in the dream resides in its treatment of the date 1851, which seemed to me not to differ from 1856, *just as though a difference of five years was of no significance whatever.* But this last was precisely what the dream-thoughts sought to express. *Four or five years* was the length of time during which I enjoyed the support of the colleague whom I mentioned earlier in this analysis; but it was also the length of time during which I made my *fiancée* wait for our marriage; and it was also, by a chance coincidence which was eagerly exploited by the dream-thoughts, the length of time during which I made my patient of longest standing wait for a complete recovery. *'What are five years?'* asked the dream-thoughts; *'that's no time at all, so far as I'm concerned; it doesn't count.* I have time enough in front of me. And just as I succeeded in the end in *that,* though you would not believe it, so I shall achieve *this,* too.' Apart from this, however, the number 51 by itself, without the number of the century, was determined in another, and indeed, in an opposite sense; and this,

too, is why it appeared in the dream several times. 51 is the age which seems to be a particularly dangerous one to men; I have known colleagues who have died suddenly at that age, and amongst them one who, after long delays, had been appointed to a professorship only a few days before his death [p. 438f.].

Here the age 51 is again linked with the sudden death of a colleague at 51, and in the context of a confusion about a lapse of time which also showed up with regard to Kundt's age at his death. (However, we have no way of determining whether Freud actually ever knew Kundt's date of birth.)

Freud returned twice to the interpretation of this dream. In one passage he stated that the dream had been stimulated by a wish that his hypotheses concerning the etiology of neuroses should not prove to be absurd. The same wish applies, of course, to his dream theory. Freud showed that *he* had recognized the absurdity of the dream's mathematical content:

> . . . an algebraic equation . . . plus and minus signs, indices and radical signs, and as though someone were to copy out the equation without understanding it, taking over both the operational symbols and the numerals into his copy but mixing them all up together [p. 451].

But who used complex formulas of this kind?

In a later chapter of *The Interpretation of Dreams* Freud returned to the "absurd dream" and stated:

> In the apparently absurd dream which treated the difference between 51 and 56 as a negligible quantity, the number 51 was mentioned several times. Instead of regarding this as a matter of course or as something indifferent, we inferred from it that there was a *second* line of thought in the latent content of the dream leading to the number 51; and along this track we arrived at my fears of 51 years being the limit of my life, in glaring contrast to the dream's dominant train of thought which was lavish in its boasts of a long life. In the *'Non vixit'* dream there was an inconspicuous interpolation which I overlooked at first: *'As P. failed to understand him, Fl. asked me'*, etc. When the interpretation was held up, I went back to these words and it was they that led me on to the childhood phantasy which turned out to be an intermediate nodal point in the dream-thoughts [p. 513].

Here Freud was speaking openly of his fears in connection with age 51, and immediately returned to the *non vixit* dreams in which P. stood for Paneth and Fl. for Fliess.

Whereas in 1894 the deadline of 51 years had been linked to the death of Kundt, in September, 1896, Freud had stated: "I would so much like to hold out until that famous age limit of approximately 51."

By that time Fliess had arrived at his periodicity theory, with its formula of 28 and 23 as the female and male periods, and had "predicted" that the age of 51 (28 + 23) would be either the limit of Freud's life, or at least a critical period for him. At the height of Freud's cardiac episode even 40 or 42 to 43 had seemed a desirable age to attain, and 51 a far-fetched hope. With the gradual improvement in Freud's cardiac symptoms, 51 became a threat rather than a hope. Although Freud did not believe intellectually in Fliess's theories, they nonetheless retained a hold on him. He had many dreams concerned with complex calculations, and most of them also had some relation to birth and death (see, for example, the discussion of his dream of Goethe's attack on Herr M.).

While the numbers involved in the prospective (and dreaded) dates of his life's end were connected with Fliess's calculations, they were obviously overdetermined. They were probably related to Fliess's own "critical periods," coming one or two years later, for example, than these. I pointed out in connection with the *non vixit* dream that Fliess's "very critical" and "most important date" was his 40th birthday. Freud's "critical period" was accordingly, 41 to 42. The age of 51 (52) resulting from the combination of the two critical periods 28 + 23, was a continuation of the same theme, with 61 to 62 to follow.[19] I have already indicated the possible link between this speculation, with its one- to two-year divergence from Fliess's "critical" dates, and the dates of the birth and death of Freud's younger brother.

Freud always emphasized that every symptom has many determinants, which converge and contribute to its specific manifestations. This applies of course also to Freud's preoccupation with prospective dates of his death. The new information about the Freud family brought to light by Sajner (see Chapter 1) justifies a re-examination of this dream in search of such additional determinants.

Commenting on this dream Freud states:

> We should conclude from the preceding discussion that the insistence with which this dream exhibited its absurdities could only be taken as indicating the presence in the dream-thoughts of a particularly embittered and passionate polemic. We shall therefore be all the more astonished to observe that in this dream the polemic was carried on in the

[19] For the determinants of this "critical" age, see Chapter 7.

open and that my father was the explicit object of the ridicule. Open-
ness of this kind seems to contradict our assumptions as regards the
working of the censorship in connection with the dream-work [p. 436].

We can detect here a striking analogy to the *non vixit* dream in
which Freud also posed the question of what had happened to the
dream censor to permit such an open expression of pleasure in having
survived Fliess. He explained this in a roundabout way by attributing
to infantile affection the reinforcement of the "contemporary and justified affection" for Fliess, while assigning his death wishes against the
latter entirely to "infantile hatred" of his playmate and rival, his
nephew John.

Freud's explanation of the failure of the dream work to censor the
exposure of his father to ridicule in the dream under discussion was
much more complex and roundabout.

In the manifest content of this "absurd" dream the numbers 1851
and 1856 were most conspicuous. In his interpretation Freud changed
the actual time span of 5 years (between 1851 and 1856) to four or
five years. He linked this time span to the duration of his engagement
and to the length of the psychoanalytic treatment of one of his patients.
Freud then linked the "embittered and passionate" polemics in the
dream to Breuer's critical disapproval of the long duration of this
treatment and to his own disparaging remarks about his father. He
also established a link to the fact that his teacher, the neurologist
Meynert, who was for a while bitterly critical of Freud's concepts
about hysteria, and who also used to become intoxicated by consuming
chloroform, had confessed on his deathbed to Freud that he himself
was "one of the clearest cases of male hysteria."

How did Freud explain the role of his father in the dream? On the
one hand, Freud said:

> . . . the sentence '*I went to him in the next room*' . . . reproduced the
> circumstances in which I informed my father of my having become
> engaged to be married without consulting him. This sentence was there-
> fore reminding me of the admirable unselfishness displayed by the old
> man on that occasion [p. 437].

On the other hand, Freud saw in the dream and the dream work an
"instance of a process of judgement at work."

> In the absurd dream . . . I asked: '*Did you get married soon after that?*'
> *I calculated that, of course, I was born in 1856, which seemed to be the*

year which immediately followed the year in question. All of this was
clothed in the form of a set of logical conclusions. My father had married in 1851, immediately after his attack; I, of course, was the eldest
of the family, and had been born in 1856; Q.E.D. As we know, this
false conclusion was drawn in the interests of wish-fulfilment; and the
predominant dream-thought ran: *'Four or five years, that's no time at
all; it doesn't count.'* Every step in this set of logical conclusions, however alike in their content and their form, could be explained in another
way as having been determined by the dream-thoughts. It was the
patient, of whose long analysis my colleague had fallen foul, who had
decided to get married immediately the treatment was finished [p. 449f.].

Freud then compared the manner of his interview with his father
in the dream with a question asked of students at the University by
means of which the inquisitive professor might, from the first name of
the student's father "draw conclusions" (what was meant was the
Jewish extraction of a student):

Thus the *drawing of the conclusion* in the dream was no more than a
repetition of the *drawing of a conclusion* which appeared as a piece of
the dream-thoughts. [What follows is a complex and somewhat cryptic
statement:] Something new emerges from this. If a conclusion appears
in the content of the dream there is no question that it is derived from
the dream-thoughts; but it may either be present in these as a piece of
recollected material or it may link a series of dream-thoughts together in
a logical chain. In any case, however, a conclusion in a dream represents a conclusion in the dream-thoughts [p. 450].

Freud's associations repeatedly came back to the theme "four or
five years don't count." However, he did not give any direct associations to one element of the manifest dream: that the year of Freud's
birth, 1856, "seemed to be the year which immediately followed the
year in question"—1851. In actuality, Freud's birth occurred the year
after Jakob Freud's marriage to his third and last wife, Amalia (July
29, 1855).

We can date the approximate time Freud composed the interpretation of this dream for the dream book from a letter he wrote to Fliess
on August 1, 1899 (3 days after the anniversary of Freud's parents).
In this letter he indicated that "the gap made by the big dream which
you took out is to be filled by a small collection of dreams (innocent,
absurd dreams, calculating and speeches in dreams" (L. 113).

One more of Freud's associations should be mentioned before posing some questions. After discussing "an algebraic equation . . . plus

and minus signs, indices and radical signs, and as though someone were to copy out the equation without understanding it, taking over both the operational symbols and the numerals into his copy but mixing them all up together," Freud said:

> The two arguments [in the dream-content] could be traced back to the following material. It was distressing to me to think that some of the premises which underlay my psychological explanations of the psycho-neuroses were bound to excite scepticism and laughter when they were first met with. For instance, I had been driven to assume that impressions from the second year of life, and sometimes even from the first, left a lasting trace on the emotional life of those who were later to fall ill, and that these impressions . . . might constitute the first and deepest foundation for hysterical symptoms. Patients, to whom I explained this at some appropriate moment, used to parody this newly-gained knowledge by declaring that they were ready to look for recollections dating from a time *at which they were not yet alive* [p. 451f.].

In view of the fact that in 1852, the "year after 1851" Jakob Freud had been married to a woman other than Freud's mother, a number of questions seem justified, with the understanding that they express no more than a speculation: could it be that Freud really was asking his father whom he had married "soon after" 1851? Could the "conclusions" he was drawing and the repetitive search for the wish fulfillment that "four to five years don't matter" be an expression of the same theme? Could his association about his patients who used to parody his claim of the importance of early memories by saying that they were ready to look for recollections "dating from a time at which they were not yet alive" also refer to this unknown wife of his father, about whom he perhaps had learned during his "prehistoric" time in Freiberg? Finally, could this mysterious date 1851 also have contributed to Freud's preoccupation with the critical age of 51?

A final comment to the question of whether Freud was unconsciously aware of his father's second wife is purely speculative. Freud ended his report about his realization that his seduction theory of neurosogenesis was erroneous in the following way:

> To go on with my letter. . . . I might be feeling very unhappy. The hope of eternal fame was so beautiful, and so was that of certain wealth, complete independence, travel, and removing the children from the spheres of the worries which spoiled my own youth. All that depended on whether hysteria succeeded or not. Now I can be quiet and modest again and go on worrying and saving, and one of the stories from my

collection [of Jewish anecdotes] occurs to me: *"Rebecca, you can take off your wedding-gown, you're not a bride any longer!"* [L. 69, September 21, 1897; my italics].

This was written less than two weeks before the "reconstruction" letter of October third. The meaning of this Jewish joke is obvious: "You were once a proud bride, but you got into trouble, the wedding is off —take off your bridal gown.

Why just this joke at this time? Why a joke in which Freud identifies himself with a disgraced woman? And a joke, the punchline of which contains the name of this mysterious second wife of his father?

COMPLETION OF *The Interpretation of Dreams*

I shall now turn back from a consideration of Freud's dreams to the correspondence exchanged between Freud and Fliess during the last few years of their friendship. Throughout that period the conflict between the positive and negative aspects of this relationship grew in intensity. Freud's reluctance to accept Fliess's hypotheses, the resulting resentment on Fliess's part, Freud's progress in his self-analysis, and his deepening insight into the workings of the mind—all inevitably led to a painful break. But first *The Interpretation of Dreams* had to be completed.

Fliess had not been feeling well when Freud wrote on December 5, 1898:

> In view of your illness, I have also foregone, as you have noticed, the exchange of ideas with you into which such a great deal has gone; *another piece of resignation* [italics added]. Occasionally I longed for a strong and sweet drop of the juice of grapes—even if it can't be "Punch with Lethe"[20]—but I was ashamed to acquire a new vice [4].

But on December 20, Freud wrote:

> Rarely have three months of separation seemed to me to have been as long as these last ones [5].

The two men met at the end of December, 1898, this time in Vienna, where Fliess's parents-in-law and Mrs. Fliess's sister, the wife of Dr. Rie, lived. This meeting resulted in new insight; but it also stirred up painful feelings. This was mirrored in the first letter written by

[20] See the same allusion in the letter of December 12, 1897.

Freud after the meeting. He began the letter of January 3, 1899 by stating:

> So I am after all the first one who gives news of himself. After the falling of the meteor there is a ray of light that brightens the gloomy sky for a long time. For me it has not yet been extinguished. In this brightness I then suddenly caught sight of several things . . . [6].

After this poetic introduction Freud indicated that he had solved another part of the dream psychology, which he considered to be "universally valid" and which might thus provide the key to the understanding of other mental processes. Freud ended this letter (a day later) with the following words:

> Here I live in bad temper and darkness until you come; I get rid of all my grumbles, kindle my flickering light at your steady flame, feel well again, and after your departure I again have eyes to see and what I see is beautiful and good. Is this just because the term of the period had not yet been reached? Or couldn't one out of the many days available for all purposes fashion the dates by means of the mental influences that affect the one who is waiting? Must not some place be left for that, so that the [dynamic] force is not ruled out by the time factor? [L. 101].

This was a touching appeal to Fliess to leave a place for psychical determinism within his rigid system, which related all human events exclusively to a predetermined confluence of mysterious dates.

The appeal was to no avail. Fliess could not give up his system without giving up his belief in his own destiny, and evidently Freud could not yet part completely with the illusion of Fliess's greatness, certainly not at this crucial point.

In answer to an inquiry from Fliess which probably dealt with the problem of fear of death in patients suffering from an organic illness, Freud wrote on February 6, 1899:

> From your description poor S. reminds me of one of the most vexing aspects of our modern medicine [7]. The art of deceiving a patient is certainly not highly desirable. But what has the individual come to, how negligible must be the influence of the religion of science, which presumably has replaced the old religion, if one no longer dares disclose that this or that man now must die. . . . The Christian at least has the last sacraments administered to him a few hours beforehand. Shakespeare says: "Thou owest Nature [God] a death." I hope that when my time comes I shall find someone who will treat me with more respect and tell me when to be ready. My father knew it clearly, said nothing about it, and retained his beautiful composure to the end [L. 104].

It should not be difficult to imagine what these lines meant to me, reading them a decade after Freud's death. Years later, Freud insisted that he be kept fully informed about any phase of his own illness and at the end be permitted to die with dignity. His reference to his father's manner of meeting death and the memory of his father's shrinking steadily into pneumonia and that fateful date (see letter of September 29, 1896) were to be of great significance in Freud's own last years.

The letter written on February 19, 1899 contains some sentences that create an uncanny impression because of the particular choice of metaphor 24 years before that metaphor was to become a tragic reality.

> Well, the same thing is happening to you, so I do not need to feel ashamed. You, too, start letters on the 11th which you continue only on the 16th, and on the 16th you can write about nothing other than that one tremendously huge piece of work, entirely too hard for the powers of a poor human being, which has a hold on every stirring thought, and eventually sucks up all faculties and susceptibilities, a kind of neoplastic tissue which infiltrates into the human one and finally replaces it. My lot is almost better—or worse. Work and gainful professional activity coincide in my case. I have turned completely into a cancer. The neoplasm likes to drink wine in its latest stages of development. Today I am supposed to go to the theatre, but this is ridiculous —like trying to graft on top of the cancer. Nothing can adhere to it, and so from now on the duration of my life is that of the neoplasm [8].

Freud had often spoken of his drive to advance his work as an "inner tyrant" to which he was forced to submit. Now—and to my knowledge this was never repeated—he was calling it a neoplasm, which was eating away at whatever was still left of him as a human being. Why did Freud use this metaphor just at this time? In the same letter Freud spoke of a new discovery:

> A symptom arises where the repressed and the repressing thoughts can come together in the fulfillment of a wish. The wish fulfillment of the repressing thought is seen in the symptom, e.g., in the form of punishment, self-punishment, the final substitute for self-gratification—masturbation [L. 105].

Thus, Freud viewed masturbation not only as the "primary addiction" (L. 79), but also as the "original sin." Was Freud thinking about being punished for his own addiction to nicotine—which he called a derivative of the "primary addiction"? Was he thinking, on another level, that his "inner tyrant" was punishing him for his audacity in revealing the secrets of the mind? "Eritis sicut deus, scientes bonum et malum"[21] was followed by expulsion from Paradise! Was Freud—as he said in a later letter—begging "the angel to desist"?

I am not inclined to believe, as some do, that the unconscious "knows" about a future illness 24 years before it becomes manifest. Nor do I believe that Freud's cancer was a *direct* consequence of guilt feelings about this "original sin" or any other. I do believe, however, that on some level Freud never forgot this metaphor so that some of the expressions he used in letters written during the last year of his life take on new and tragic meaning. Freud eventually did "punish" himself: while he did not develop his cancer out of guilt, he contributed to its recurrences by persisting in his heavy smoking.

However, Freud did not groan too often under the pressure of his "tyrant." He could rightly state on March 5, 1899: "All this work has done a lot of good to my own mental life; I am obviously much more normal than I was four or five years ago" (L. 106).

It was not only Freud's mental state which had improved. On May 25, after reporting to Fliess about a migraine that had fit into a period $28 + \dfrac{28}{2}$, Freud wrote:

> Monday morning I climbed the Rax[22] with my brother-in-law H. as in the good old days; 3½ hours going up, 2½ coming down. Only, the Rax has gotten much higher since I climbed it the last time, at least 500 meters. My heart took it splendidly [9].

A few months later Freud was able to refer to "one of my finest attacks of travel phobia," with the implication that it was a thing of the distant past (L. 110). Freud was spending that summer near Berchtesgaden in an ideally situated villa, where he could take walks, collect mushrooms, and work on his dream book. He was feeling very fit, and complained only once: after writing for five hours (in longhand) he had a slight "writer's cramp" (L. 115).

All during that summer and early fall Freud kept sending Fliess the galleys of his dream book, asking for and receiving comments, criticism, and a great deal of encouragement. In turn, Freud wrote on June 27, 1899:

---

[21] A quotation from Goethe's *Faust* (Part I, Sc. 4).
[22] A mountain, about 2,000 m. high, not far from Vienna.

Many thanks for the undeserved rich letter. I am prepared to wait, and I have resignedly given up my usual complaints about the unalterable distance. I hope your path will lead you even farther and still deeper, and that as the new Kepler you will uncover for us the iron-clad rules of the biological machinery [10].

At first glance this letter impresses one by its exalted terms. However, the German words Freud used in the last sentence of this paragraph made me think of one of his favorite lines from Schiller's poem "Die Weltweisen" ("The World's Wise Men"). Freud also alluded to this poem in his paper on "Screen Memories," which he mentioned to Fliess in the previously quoted letter written on May 25th.

In this satirical poem Schiller pokes fun at metaphysics, poets, at Locke and Descartes, at moralists, priests and professors, declaring that it is Nature which watches over the continuity of events on this earth. The poem concludes with the following favorite lines of Freud:

> Einstweilen, bis den Bau der Welt
> Philosophie zusammenhält
> Erhält sie das Getriebe
> Durch Hunger und durch Liebe.
> Meanwhile, until philosophy maintains the
> working of the world, it [nature] maintains the
> machinery through hunger and through love
> [translated in prose].

In his paper Freud calls hunger and love "the two most powerful motive forces" (1899, p. 316; also n. 1). In using similar words in his letter, Freud essentially tells Fliess: "You may be the new Kepler of biology, but I believe that the instinctual forces, hunger and love, are the determinants of human actions." I am not assuming that Freud consciously expressed thoughts of this kind, but in view of the basically irreconcilable position of the two men the ambiguous meaning of such exalted praise seems to be beyond doubt.

An analyst writing a biographical study is in a peculiar position when he deals with a given piece of information. He knows some of the past as well as some of the future, and traces development in a particular way. I am taking the liberty of following Freud's example here—*"si licet parva comparare magnis"*—by using my own associations and tying them in with later events which will be discussed at length in the framework of the period in which they occurred.

A few pages back I spoke of the uncanny feeling aroused in me by Freud's letter of February 19, 1899 which contained the metaphor of his "cancer." In his letter of August 27, 1899 Freud reported to Fliess about his work on the final chapter—the all-important Chapter VII— of *The Interpretation of Dreams,* remarking: "Any attempt to make it better than it turns out to be by itself will give it something forced. So it will have 2,467 errors—which I shall leave."

At that time Freud was already aware of the meaning of parapraxes. *The Psychopathology of Everyday Life* (1901b) established the principle that nothing in our mental life was purely accidental. It was with this in mind that Freud added to the above letter the following postscript, which he then included unchanged in the *Psychopathology:*

'Let me hastily add a contribution to the psychopathology of everyday life. You will find that in the letter I put down the number 2467 as a bold, arbitrary estimate of the number of mistakes which will be found in the dream book. What I meant was some very big number; but that particular one emerged. However, nothing in the mind is arbitrary or undetermined. You will therefore rightly expect that the unconscious had hastened to determine the number which was left open by the consciousness. Now, immediately before, I had read in the newspaper that a General E. M. had retired from the post of Master of Ordnance. I should explain that I am interested in this man. While I was serving as a medical officer-cadet he came to the sick quarters one day (he was then a colonel) and said to the medical officer: "You must make me well in a week, because I have some work to do for which the Emperor is waiting." After that episode I decided to follow his career, and lo and behold! now he has reached the end of it, having become Master of Ordnance, and is already (1899) on the retired list. I wanted to work out how long he had taken over this. Assuming that it was 1882 that I saw him in hospital, it must have been seventeen years. I told my wife this and she remarked: "Oughtn't you to be on the retired list too, then?" "Heaven forbid!" I exclaimed. After this conversation I sat down to write to you. But the earlier train of thought went on in my mind, with good reason. I had miscalculated; I have a fixed point in my memory to prove it. I celebrated my majority, i.e. my twenty-fourth birthday, under military arrest (having been absent without leave). So that was in 1880, or nineteen years ago. That gives you the "24" in 2467. Now take my present age—43—add 24, and you have 67. In other words, in answer to the question whether *I* meant to retire too, my wish gave me another twenty-four years' work.[23] I was obviously annoyed at having failed to get very far myself during the period in which I have followed Colonel M.'s career; and yet I was celebrating a kind of triumph over his career being at an end, while I still have everything in front of me. So one can say with justice that not even the

[23] In other words, an additional length of time equal to that which had been required to reach his majority.

number 2467 which I threw out unthinkingly was without its determinants from the unconscious' [p. 242f.].

Freud reached the age of 67 in 1923—and it was in 1923 that he
developed cancer! Let me reiterate that I in no way believe that Freud
developed cancer at 67 because at 43 he wished for 24 more years of
productive work. However, Freud's behavior in 1923, just after the
detection of his cancer, was unusually fatalistic (see Chapter 13).
This uncharacteristic attitude of Freud's seemed difficult to explain at
the time. Could it have been a reverberation of that earlier wish, a
resigned acceptance of what he had asked for? Was he saying, in effect:
"Fate *did* grant me another 24 years, so who am I to complain?"

At this point we cannot fail to recognize a significant series of links
between several statements in Freud's letters and subsequent events
revolving around Freud's fatal illness. The relevant statements are
his allusion to the "shrinking" of his dying father; the definition of
masturbation as the "primal addiction"; the expression of the wish
not to be deceived when his time had come to die; the reference to
himself as a "neoplasm"; the explanation of symptom formation as a
compromise between gratification and the punishment for it, as in the
case of masturbation; and the expressed desire to reach the age of 67.
The connection is reinforced by another introspective unpublished
letter in which Freud spoke of his "frequently fatalistic conviction"
(letter of April 28, 1900; see Chapter 6 [6]).

While it might be merely hypothetical for me to link Freud's complex calculations pointing to his retirement at the age of 67 with his
fatalistic attitude when he actually reached the age of 67 in 1923, we
have an authoritative interpretation from Freud himself (in a letter
written in 1909) in which he linked, by means of a similar type of calculation, the age at which he might die with this obviously fateful year
of 1899.

Two weeks after expressing the expectation that *The Interpretation
of Dreams* would have 2,467 errors, on September 11, 1899 Freud
could report that the manuscript of the dream book had been sent to
the printer, and that he was already experiencing the beginning of the
letdown which inevitably followed supreme effort (L. 118). It is interesting that Freud's criticism of his own work expressed itself mainly
in a depreciation of the style in which the book was written, while the
depressive mood expressed itself—as was usual when he returned from
a vacation—in a condemnation of Vienna, a city where he could

neither obtain a professorship nor acquire a sufficient medical practice to free himself of financial worry. This had been a bad year financially, and Freud knew that his mood was generally influenced by meager income. He wrote to Fliess on September 21, 1899:

> You will see that my style will improve and my ideas be better when this town provides me with a prosperous living [L. 119].

Fliess must have hit the right chord in his answer, enabling Freud to understand better one of the deeper sources of the letdown following the completion of his work. (This is an example of Fliess's being more than just a sounding board. There must have been other such occasions as well.) On October 4, 1899, Freud replied:

> You describe very aptly the painful feeling of parting with something that has been your very own. It must have been that which made this work so distasteful to me. Now I like it, certainly not much, but a lot better. In my case it must have been even more painful because what separated itself was not ideational possessions but my very own feelings. There is still a long way to the book on hysteria.[24] At times like these no desire to work stirs in me.
>
> Life and illness have moved back in. However, the first victim— Ernst [Freud's youngest son]—has already recovered. The others are still well.
>
> My mood is holding up bravely. I shall let you know the date of my next breakdown for your calculations. They are really primary periodical fluctuations because two weeks of inactivity and a fifth to a quarter of my income would be sufficient as external etiology [11].

In this letter Freud expressed deep insight which contained more than just the seeds of concepts he developed later, such as separation anxiety, the importance of object loss for depression, and the reaction of mothers after delivery, ranging from mild sadness that the pregnancy is over (regardless of the joy in the new baby) to postpartum depression.[25]

---

[24] Freud was working on "Fragment of an Analysis of a Case of Hysteria" which was published only in 1905.

[25] In this connection, note Freud's unusual but meaningful formulation that his ideas and emotions were possessions [*Eigentum*] which had "separated themselves" from him—a wording that the translation of the letter could render only very inadequately.

6

DEATH OF A FRIENDSHIP

The date of the letter discussed at the end of the last chapter is important. Freud's father died in 1896, in the month of October. One year later, in October, 1897, Freud reported to Fliess his most revolutionary findings, based on the reconstruction of his childhood. He also forgot Fliess's 39th birthday. The following October, 1898, was Fliess's most critical time—his 40th birthday, his surgery, the *non vixit* dream. Finally, in October, 1899, Freud was preparing the first copy of his dream book as a present for Fliess's 41st birthday. Yet, the last paragraph of Freud's letter contains a very thinly veiled ironic debunking of Fliess's calculations.

We would, of course, like to know how Fliess reacted to such a letter. Freud himself was concerned about this. The delay in Fliess's response seemed ominous to him. Was it possible that some of the passages in the dream book had offended him? However, Freud soon learned that Fliess's little daughter Pauline had been seriously ill. Fliess, as evident in subsequent letters, apparently linked her illness to the influence of certain fateful periods, which he felt had also contributed to the death of his sister Pauline. Freud tried to reassure Fliess on realistic medical grounds, and reproached him for not sharing his worries. On November 9, 1899, Freud wrote:

> I have always behaved differently; for weeks I have been complaining to you whenever I had reason to, risking the danger of putting you off, yet expecting that you would not be put off, though I surely would rather tell you about good and hopeful things [1].

Freud learned eventually not to complain to Fliess!

199

Freud's nostalgia for the period of the heroic struggle before the completion of the dream book, a reaction which I have compared with a "postpartum" letdown, may explain his erroneous dating of the next two letters to Fliess. The first was dated September 12, 1899 and the subsequent one, September 19, 1899. Judging from the contents of these letters and a comparison of their dates with those on a "perpetual calendar," I would surmise that they were actually written on November 12 and 19, 1899.

Freud ended the correspondence of the year—and the century— with a poem, the only one contained in the Fliess letters and, to the best of my knowledge, one of the very few he ever wrote. It was written on the occasion of the birth of Fliess's second son, on the eve of the new century. The poem is an apotheosis of Fliess's hypotheses about conception and even the possibility of influencing the sex of the offspring. One is reminded of Freud's response to such amazing speculations of Fliess's as the mysterious link between infection in the mother and conception in the daughter (see Chapter 3). It is also possible that Freud was writing with tongue in cheek, and that his extravagant praise concealed some derision. However, as the poem progresses, we can detect a mood reminiscent of Freud's dream of dissecting his own pelvis (see Chapter 5), the associations to it which led to melancholy thoughts about death and a redeeming hope that his children might provide him with a certain measure of immortality, in part by continuing the work which he had only begun. In the poem, Freud expressed the same hope for Fliess and his newborn son.[1]

Is it strange that a man like Freud should permit himself this kind of "daydream" at the close of a century, and that he should express it with reference to Fliess in a poem which at the same time reflects his complex conflicts just as the friendship of the two men was reaching the point of no return?

New ideas and projects were now taking shape in Freud's mind, but they were subject to the same fitful progression as his earlier ideas. Freud was fully aware that there were new and different recesses of the mind which his understanding had not yet reached. Precisely for this reason, he needed to wait for new material to come from his chief patient—himself—and from his other patients, now very few in number. In these circumstances, Freud hesitated to write letters because he had decided not to complain. However, on February 1, 1900, he

[1] In view of the difficulties of translating this poem, it is reproduced here only in the original German; see [2].

wrote Fliess an amazing letter, published in part by Ernest Jones (Vol. 1, p. 348), who called it a "half-serious but very interesting description of himself." This letter was anything but "half-serious":

Dear Wilhelm:

My presentiment of something uncanny turned out to be right, after all. I think it is bad that the interval is so short.[2] But perhaps the two attacks belong together, and afterwards the well-being will persist. It is very sad; I too do not know more about it.

Martin took to bed with an acute onset of the illness on January 14 ($5 \times 28^2 – 10 \times 23$)[3] between 2 and 3 o'clock in the afternoon. He remained the only case and is well again. Thus the series of observations breaks off abruptly this time. Perhaps another time.

If we lived in the same city—this would have to be Berlin, though, and not Vienna—many things would have turned out differently, and I believe I would never have gotten into difficulties or would already have extricated myself. For this reason I have so often regretted our separation. Unfortunately, this doesn't change anything. Perhaps hard times are ahead of me and my cure. On the whole I have noticed quite often that you habitually overestimate me. The motivation for this mistake, though, disarms any reproach. For I am actually not at all a man of science, not an observer, not an experimenter, not a thinker. I am by temperament nothing but a *conquistador*,[4] an adventurer, if you want to translate this term—with all the inquisitiveness, daring, and tenacity characteristic of such a man. Such people are customarily valued only if they have been successful, have really discovered something; otherwise they are thrown by the wayside. And this is not altogether unjust. At the present time, however, luck has left me; I no longer find anything worthwhile.

A kind and perceptive, somewhat diffuse review of the dream book is in No. 17 of *The Nation,* written by J. J. David, a personal acquaint-

---

[2] This had to do with the periodic involutional illness of Fliess's mother.

[3] This calculation, inserted by Freud above the number 14, is formulated in terms of Fliess's "periodical" theories.

[4] In a letter written to Fliess on April 14, 1898, Freud used the term *conquistador* in a completely different context. On an Easter trip with his brother Alexander he visited a cavern with beautiful stalactite formations. This is how Freud described their guide:

He was the discoverer of the cave, and obviously a genius run to seed. He kept talking about his death, his conflicts with the priests, and his achievements in these subterranean realms. When he said he had already been in thirty-six "holes" in the Carso, I recognized him as a neurotic and his *conquistador* exploits as an erotic equivalent. He confirmed this a minute later, because when Alexander asked him how far one could penetrate into the caves, he answered: "It's like with a virgin; the farther the better" [L. 88].

The use of the same term in two completely different contexts is a beautiful example of what Freud called "sublimation" (albeit to different degrees)—the utilization and transformation of instinctual goals for intellectual and professional achievements.

ance of mine. I promised Löwenfeld to finish a brief extract from the book which is to appear as a separate number of the new *Grenzfragen des Nerven- und Seelenlebens*.[5]

I find science increasingly more difficult. In the evening, I would like something gladdening and refreshing. *But I am always alone* [italics added].

The Hohenzollern sample is amusing.[6] Of course, an ignoramus immediately has all sorts of questions which are deferred for an ideal congress. Why does lawful regularity bring out the difference? I hope that in your work I too would have had an entirely different share had I lived in Berlin. Thus we are getting estranged from each other through what is most our own.

I have just acquired Nietzsche[7] where I hope to find words for much that remains mute within me, but I have not yet opened the book. Too lazy for the time being.

Remember that I regularly work up the gloomiest expectations when your letters fail to arrive, and write soon to

Your

Sigm. [3]

Freud wrote this letter at the beginning of a new century which he had greeted earlier with a caustic remark:

The new century—the most interesting thing of which, for us, may be that it includes the dates of our deaths—has brought me nothing but a stupid review in the *Zeit*.[8] . . . It is highly unflattering, lacking in understanding to an unusual degree, and—worst of all—will be continued in the next number . . . [L. 127].

Freud felt hemmed in on all sides. He had always been disgusted by the prevailing prudishness and provincial atmosphere of Vienna, which overshadowed the high artistic, literary, and scientific achievements of a relatively small intelligentsia. The anti-Semitism and the prejudiced evaluation of his work stood in the way of his attaining the rank of professor, which at that time was extremely important for

[5] See "On Dreams" (1901a).

[6] Fliess was using the family trees of the Hohenzollern and the Hapsburg families for confirmation of his theories.

[7] This is one of the few occasions on which Freud mentions Nietzsche, who figured in Freud's correspondence with A. Zweig during the last years of his life (see Introduction and Chapter 22). Much has been written about the analogies between Freud's formulations and those of Nietzsche, especially with regard to the unconscious. Freud's statement in this letter establishes that he was not familiar—at least not thoroughly—with Nietzsche's work prior to this time, but by then Freud had already formulated his concepts about the working of the unconscious and had published them in *The Interpretation of Dreams*.

[8] A Vienna daily newspaper. See Kris's footnote 2 to L. 127.

building a private practice as a specialist and consultant. At moments when his ideas were not flowing freely or crystallizing clearly, Freud found himself "straining at the leash." While Freud had not expected ready acceptance of his dream book, he had not foreseen the peculiar combination of complete disregard ("killing by silence"), especially in professional circles, and malicious distortion and derision. As Strachey points out in his introduction to *The Interpretation of Dreams,* only 351 copies of the book were sold in the first six years following its publication.

Freud had a small number of valued friends; he loved his family; but he had broken off all contact with men of his profession,[9] although in reality there were no men of "his profession." His contact with Breuer had ended in bitter disappointment. Hence Freud's statement: "I am always alone"! And now he and his only audience, his "other," his treasured friend, were growing apart.

Freud was still willing to offer a painstaking mathematical formula about his son's illness, but it was not without deeper meaning that he remarked on the abruptness with which his observations had broken off. A host of conflicting emotions is expressed in the short paragraph in which Freud comments on Fliess's Hohenzollern sample. They range from detached amusement to the most succinct and even tragic expression of the pain of separation. Previously Freud used to claim ignorance and lack of understanding of complex mathematical formulas after a "congress." This time the "ignoramus" first offered a complex algebraic formula for an example of periodicity and pointed out a basic contradiction in Fliess's thinking: "why should lawful regularity also bring out the difference?" He suggested, very parenthetically, a congress, but this would have to be an ideal one. And then once more the big "if"—if only they had lived in the same city. And finally the painful ending: the estrangement literally means a tearing apart of the most intimate oneness.

When Freud referred to himself as a *conquistador,* he had in mind such men as Cortes who, with a handful of men, had conquered empires. Freud had "conquered" the problem of the dream virtually alone, except for the help of his friend and adopted analyst. But as a *conquistador* he had to proceed to further conquests. Was his luck leaving him because he was losing his friend?

Hence this was a letter written in dead earnest and not "half seri-

---

[9] He may have done so in part as a result of Fliess's "demand" (see Chapter 4).

ously." Freud ends this letter pleading with his friend: don't leave me to the gloomiest expectations, and write to me.

Thus it was necessary for Freud to pass through one more final crisis in his relationship with Fliess before he was able to carry the burden entirely alone, and be prepared for decades of struggle, of triumphs but also disappointments, and eventually suffering, illness, exile, and a long, cruel death.

Freud's conflictual feelings expressed themselves in various ways in the letters that followed the one just quoted. In the next letter, February 12, 1900, Freud explained that he was writing less frequently because he did not want to complain, but then tried to justify his complaints by pointing out the trials and difficulties he had experienced in his work, along with his financial worries, ending up by stating that he was "further from home than ever," while the vigor of youth was diminishing very noticeably.

The crisis I indicated above was described by Freud in two letters written on March 11 and 23, 1900 (cf. L. 130 and 131). These letters (particularly an unpublished portion of the first one) not only represented the turning point in the relationship between Freud and Fliess but give us additional insight into some aspects of the nature of the conflict. After expressing his pleasure about receiving a long letter from Fliess, Freud continued his letter of March 11:

> In view of my increasing lack of freedom and your constriction; in view of the unpalatable matter which always forces itself into my pen; with the prospect of being pushed still further apart from you and your family through the impending "Breuerization,"[10] it would be utterly senseless to attempt to deny the influence of such factors, and that of women in general, on our relationship as well. —In short, in view of all these considerations, I have made up my mind to restrict my demands on you. This was the reason for my prolonged silence, which I could present as waiting for an answer from you [4].

While the letter of February 1 had expressed the conflict in terms of an incompatibility of ideas, this passage, written after the receipt of a friendly letter from Fliess, expressed the conflict in terms of feeling excluded. Freud reiterated this theme in various ways throughout the

---

[10] "Verbreuerung"—a neologism meaning an increasing association with Breuer. What Freud had in mind was the forthcoming marriage of Breuer's daughter to a certain Dr. Schiff, who was either related to or was at least very close to Fliess and his wife's family. When the engagement became known, Freud called it a "political" one, and anticipated that now Fliess's theories would suddenly be fully accepted by Breuer and his circle, which apparently was actually the case.

remainder of that year. In contrast to this sad and even bitter passage, the rest of the letter was written with genuine serenity.

Freud's letter of March 23, 1900 marked the turning point in the relationship even more clearly. After thanking Fliess again for his interest in the dream book and for his effort to generate some interest in others, Freud wrote:

> In many a dark hour it has been a consolation to me to be able to leave this book behind me. True, the reception it has had so far has certainly not given me any pleasure. Understanding is meager, praise like acts of charity. To most people it is obviously distasteful. I have not yet seen a trace of anyone suspecting what is significant in it. I explain this by telling myself that I am fifteen to twenty years ahead of my time.[11] Then, of course, sets in the doubt [literally torment] that is regularly associated with forming a judgment *in propriis* [about oneself].
>
> There has never been a half-year period during which I so persistently and ardently longed to live in the same place as you and your family, as the one which has just passed. You know I have been going through a deep inner crisis, and if we met, you would see how it has aged me. I was therefore deeply affected when I heard of your proposal for a reunion at Eastertime. Anyone who did not understand the more subtle resolution of contradictions would think it incomprehensible that I am not hastening to assent to the proposal. In reality, it is more likely that I shall avoid you—not only because of my almost childish yearning for the spring and the greater beauties of nature, which I should willingly sacrifice for the gratification of having you near me for three days. There are still other, inner reasons, an accumulation of imponderables which weigh heavily on me. . . . Inwardly I am deeply impoverished. I have had to demolish all my castles in the air, and I have just plucked up some courage to start rebuilding them. During the catastrophic collapse you would have been invaluable to me; in the present stage, I should hardly be able to make myself intelligible to you. I conquered my depression with the aid of a special diet of intellectual matters and now, under the influence of the distraction, it is slowly healing. In your company, I should inevitably attempt to grasp everything consciously and describe it all to you; we should talk reason and science, and your beautiful and positive biological discoveries would arouse my innermost (impersonal) envy. The upshot would be that I should unburden my woes to you for the whole five days and come back all upset and dissatisfied for the summer, for which I shall probably need all my composure. No one can help me in the least with what oppresses me; it is

---

[11] Twenty years later Freud was preparing the sixth edition of *The Interpretation of Dreams,* which by then had been translated into many languages. In 1913, before the appearance of the fourth edition, the first English translation, by A. A. Brill, had been published, as well as a Russian version.

my cross, I must bear it; and heaven knows in the process of adaptation
my back has become noticeably bent [L. 131].

This letter needs no comment. It will remain an important human
document that goes beyond Freud's individual quest *per aspera ad
astra*.

And yet after writing these moving sentences, Freud made one
further gesture of reconciliation, but one which simultaneously expressed the full intensity of his ambivalence. He continued with the
following lines:

> During the summer or fall, no later, I shall see you, talk to you, and
> then explain to you all the riddles of Count Oerindur.[12] You will be-
> come convinced that it is merely complicated. . . . Then we shall also
> discuss the pros and cons of nasal therapy, preferably right on the
> object [5].

It was this summer meeting that brought about the final break.

At about this time, Freud came to the conclusion that the "endless"
duration of an analysis might be primarily an expression of transference phenomena. On April 16, 1900 he wrote to Fliess about a patient
who was concluding his analysis:

> I am beginning to see that the apparent endlessness of the treatment is
> something of an inherent feature and is connected with the transference.
> . . . I could have continued the treatment if I had wanted to, but it
> dawned on me that such prolongation is a compromise between illness
> and health which patients themselves desire, and that the physician
> must therefore not lend himself to it [L. 133].

An unpublished letter of April 28, 1900, began with the following
sentence:

[12] Count Oerindur was the hero of a drama entitled *Guilt* by the German poet
Müllner (1774-1829). Its first performance was in 1813. It contained the following
stanza:
> [Und] erklärt mir, Oerindur,
> Diesen Zwiespalt der Natur!
> Bald möcht' ich in Blut sein Leben
> Schwinden seh'n, bald—ihm vergeben.
> Can you explain, Oerindur,
> This contradiction of nature?
> One moment I would like to see his life disappear in blood,
> The next moment, to forgive him.

A condensed version of this stanza had become an idiomatic expression: "Please explain, Count Oerindur, this contradiction of Nature." What better expression of
ambivalence could one hope to find?

Well, do you agree now that Rome cannot be forced? I frequently have a fatalistic conviction of this kind which serves my inertia very well [6].

This "fatalism" was to play a crucial role 23 years later at the time of Freud's first cancer operation. We shall have occasion further on to examine the multiple determinants of that attitude (see Chapters 5, 11, and 13).

The letter of May 7, 1900, written on the day after Freud's 44th birthday, was in a sense a continuation of the March 23 letter:

Many thanks for your kind words. They are so flattering that I might almost believe some of them—if I were with you. However, I look at it a little differently. I would not object to the fact of splendid isolation if it did not extend too far and did not come between you and me as well. On the whole—except for one weak point: my fear of poverty—I have too much sense to complain, and at present I feel too well to want to do so; I am well aware of my blessings, and I know how little, if one takes the statistics of human misery into account, one has a right to claim. But there can be no substitute for the close contact with a friend which a particular—almost feminine—side of me demands,[13] and the inner voices to which I am accustomed to listen suggest a much more modest estimate of my work than that which you proclaim. . . . No critic . . . can see more acutely than I the disproportion between the problems and my solutions, and it will be fitting punishment for me that none of the unexplored provinces of the mind in which I have been the first mortal to set foot will ever bear my name or submit to my laws. When in the [course of the] battle my breath threatened to give up, I implored the angel to desist and since then he has done so. But I did not turn out to be the stronger, though since then I have been limping noticeably. Well, I really am already 44 years old, a rather shabby old Jew, as you will see for yourself in the summer or autumn. My family insisted on celebrating my birthday. My greatest consolation is that I have not stolen a march on them with regard to the whole future. They can experience and conquer, so far as they will have the power to do so. I leave them only a foothold; I have not lead them to a mountain peak from which they can climb no higher [L. 134].

This letter, too, had special significance, indicating the continuity of certain leitmotifs in Freud's life. As I mentioned before, Freud looked to great poets for ways of expressing and documenting some of his thoughts and theories. He often remarked that the great poets knew and gave expression to all the problems he was struggling so painfully to uncover. He enjoyed meeting, talking, and corresponding with such

[13] See letters of March 11 and August 7, 1901.

important writers of his day as Romain Rolland, Thomas Mann, Arnold Zweig, and Stefan Zweig, among others. He felt great admiration for Richard Beer-Hofmann, whose relatively few plays, poems, and short stories were considered to be masterpieces.[14] One of Beer-Hofmann's best known plays was *Jacob's Dream,* published in 1918, the main theme of which was Jacob's struggle with the Angel, depicted as a dream. In his struggle Jacob attempted to prevail upon the Angel not to bestow upon him a blessing which would make him the "chosen one," the first of a "chosen people." Finally, however, Jacob had to submit to his destiny and accept the blessing, which was to bring him a life of unending struggle.

I knew that Freud was particularly fond of this play, but I had not realized that he saw himself as having "struggled with the Angel," or that he had used this metaphor, along with those of the inner tyrant and the cancer, to describe the force of his drive toward making new discoveries decades before he had read *Jacob's Dream*[15] or met its author.

We also see in this letter a veiled allusion to Moses, who was to glimpse the Promised Land only from afar. It was this figure which was to occupy Freud's thinking during the last years of his life.

The last letters heralded the end of a period which was probably

[14] Beer-Hofmann was my patient at the time I was also treating Freud, and at the latter's suggestion I arranged in early 1930 to have him visit Freud. They met several times, both enjoying the meetings greatly.

[15] This play was translated into English by Ida Bension Wynn, with a brilliant introduction by Thornton Wilder, and published in the United States by the Press of the Jewish Publication Society of America, Philadelphia, 1946. It might be pertinent to quote here the following passage from Wilder's introduction, written in 1946 after 6,000,000 Jews, among them four sisters of Freud, had been exterminated by the Nazis: "The second myth [retold in *Jacob's Dream*] is that of God's message to Jacob at Bethel, the famous promise to the Jewish people:

'. . . and in thee and in thy seed shall all the families of the earth be blessed. And behold I am with thee and will keep thee withersoever thou goest, and will bring thee back into this land: for I will not leave thee, until I have done that which I have spoken to thee of.'

"Beer-Hofmann's interpretation of these words avoids none of the difficulty of understanding them in the light of the thousands of years of persecution; with prophetic power he describes the new trials which were to be visited on the Jewish people during the years following the writing of the play. There are few more impressive passages in modern literature than those in this work, wherein it is developed that suffering can be experienced as a 'distinction.' It is a doctrine which is not easy to express in words: those in comfort do not wish to hear it, and those under trial are wary of receiving facile consolations. Beer-Hofmann's statement irresistibly recalls three other passages on the subject: Milton's two sonnets on his blindness and the invocation to Light in *Paradise Lost;* Pascal's prayer on his illness; and the Baron von Huegel's letters on 'the uses of pain,' written to a friend dying of an incurable disease" (p. xv).

the most dramatic in Freud's life. It was during that time that all his great discoveries were made, at least in essence, or their foundations laid for later elaboration. I have already indicated that this foreshadowing was also true for certain events in Freud's life, in particular some of his attitudes and reactions to his illness and approaching death. I have already quoted from his letter of June 12, 1900, written in a triumphant and expansive mood from the villa Bellevue, where 5 years earlier he had "solved" the Irma dream (see Chapter 3; and Schur, 1966a). A somewhat later letter (July 10, 1900) offers an example of a theme then only touched upon but taken up decades later.

> The big problems are still unresolved. Everything is in flux and in twilight, an intellectual inferno, with layer beneath layer; in the darkest core one can glimpse the outlines of Lucifer-Amor [L. 138].

This "darkest core" was eventually (1920) to be formulated as the theory of dual instinctual drives—Eros and Thanatos.

There was still one more meeting between Freud and Fliess which took place at the end of July, 1900, a description of which was published by Fliess in 1906 (see Kris's footnote to L. 138). It is remarkable that not until a year later does a letter Freud wrote on August 7, 1901 gives us an idea of what precipitated the final break: it was the incompatibility of Freud's belief in psychic determinism with Fliess's rigid assumption that all psychopathology was regulated by the laws of periodicity, a view which led the latter to make the statement, "the thought-reader [Freud] reads only his own thoughts in those of others."

Up to this point—and even afterward—Freud's letters continued to reflect an ebb and flow in the relationship, the pain and nostalgia of his feelings. And while Fliess claimed in his 1906 statement that it was he who discontinued the correspondence, we can deduce easily from Freud's letters that this was not quite the case.

This phase of the Fliess episode would correspond in a "regular" analysis to its end phase, theoretically and technically a difficult and still incompletely understood process. We know that an important factor in this phase is the gradual dissolution of the transference relationship, a process which is subject to constant analysis and should not be disrupted by a personal conflict resulting from external events. In the absence of such a harmonious end phase, the persistence of unsolved conflicts is frequent and often long-lasting. The end of the relationship between Freud and Fliess was anything but harmonious. Because this phase was so important for many aspects of Freud's development, in particular his persistent preoccupation with possible death dates, and possibly also for some of his later theoretical formulations, I shall document this period somewhat further, using Freud's letters.

As we shall see (Chapters 7 and 9), Freud himself for many years subjected this relationship to a self-analysis. After the July, 1900 meeting, Freud went on a long trip and on his return wrote Fliess a very friendly eight-page letter, full of charming descriptions of his tour. It was as if nothing had changed.

A new topic now began to occupy a good part of their correspondence. The mother of Mrs. Fliess (and Mrs. Rie) was quite sick. Breuer was her physician, although Rie gave her a great deal of attention. Fliess did not agree with Breuer's treatment. Hence a good deal of Freud's ambivalence toward Fliess could now be expressed in terms of bitter criticism of Breuer. It was also something of a triumph for Freud that not only Fliess but Mrs. Fliess—heretofore greatly under Breuer's influence—now concurred in Freud's criticism, with the result that Mrs. Fliess seemed to be on much better terms with Freud than she had previously been.

October was the month of Fliess's birthday. For his 41st birthday (1899) Freud had presented him with the most precious gift he could bestow on anyone—the first copy of *The Interpretation of Dreams.* Now in 1900 he had not yet finished his new book, *The Psychopathology of Everyday Life,* and his birthday letter to Fliess was rather a subdued one.

October 23, 1900

Dear Wilhelm,

Just a heartfelt wish, a handshake of friendship across the distance Berlin-Vienna. No gift such as last year, when I was able to greet you with the "firstborn" of the dream book. May everything and everyone around you thrive and compensate you for the unavoidable decline of the older units.[16] Your work, as an organically growing creation, is also included in this wish.

> Most cordially,
> Your
> Sigm. [7]

---

[16] Freud was alluding here to the mental deterioration of Fliess's mother and the progressive illness of his mother-in-law.

Freud did not hear from Fliess for some weeks until the latter wrote to him again about his mother's condition. Freud replied on November 25, 1900:

> My hunch that your long silence was indicative of something bad was correct after all. I am used to this from past times, when it usually meant that you yourself were feeling *very* badly. Well, fortunately, this is not the case.
>
> I myself would not have waited so long to inquire if I had not promised myself at the beginning of this year's exchange of letters to refrain under any circumstances from complaining so much to you. You see how soon we then lose contact with each other. After all, you yourself write: "I haven't answered because I had nothing to report, at least nothing satisfactory." If we had to wait for that! So perhaps [we can find] a compromise: just a bit of complaining but writing more frequently.
>
> Your news distressed me greatly. So it does not recede but comes and goes periodically and probably adds something new during each phase of the advance. I believe it is always this way with paranoia. There is no other kind of cure for it than its subsidence with maintenance of the repression. Thus its periodic nature becomes a blessing. . . .
>
> In my work I am not precisely at a standstill; on a subterranean level it is probably proceeding quite well; but it is certainly not a time of harvest or of conscious mastery. There probably will be no more surprising discoveries. The conclusions have probably all been drawn. All that is missing is the organization and the detailed elaboration. I do not see any prospect of substantially shortening the duration of therapy, and it will hardly be possible to widen the scope of indications.
>
> It is entirely uncertain when I shall get to the presentation [of the material], if I shall do so at all, there must be no errors, no imprecisions [preliminary impressions]. Thus [I'll stick to] Horace's rule: *Nonum prematur in annum.* Moreover, who cares about all this? *Cui bono*[17] shall I undertake this work? I have resigned myself to living like a person speaking a foreign language or like Humboldt's parrot! Being the last of one's tribe—or the first and perhaps the only one—these are quite similar situations.
>
> . . . Let me hear more from you and accept cordial greetings from your
>
> Sigm. [8]

In asking *Cui bono* did Freud have in mind the loss of his friend, his only audience, his "alter [ego]"?

The pain of separation lingered, and so did the hope of maintaining

---

[17] A phrase frequently used in legal language. It means: "Who stands to gain?"

at least some aspects of their friendship. Freud started the new year (1901) by expressing this hope.

January 1, 1901

My dear,

I am tossing *The Psychopathology of Everyday Life* aside to answer you immediately, now that your last letter has finally broken the alarming silence. I could not make up my mind to press you once more for an answer when you had shown so clearly that writing was tedious for you and that you were not moved by any need for communication. I also gave myself the correct explanation for the otherwise inexplicable phenomenon, and therefore tolerated my deep isolation with relative calm. I could well imagine how your mother's illness must have affected you; all logic notwithstanding, because I know that for a long time now you have not lost anything through her; but just because of this you feel it even more intensely.

I am quite glad now that I did not go to Berlin at Christmas. . . .

I certainly cannot easily forget your wife's visit and the few quarter-hours of conversations we had. [It is therefore] all the more sad that I must found my hope of seeing her again on an "unfortunately."[18] I now ask you: should we wait to exchange letters until a time that brings neither of us anything difficult to bear? And would this not mean expecting too much and showing too little friendship? . . . [9].

In this letter Freud was still offering his friendship, but now it was he who was the helper and adviser, who provided understanding and solace. The roles were being reversed.

A few letters were concerned mainly with reports on discussions about Fliess's theories and findings which had been held in the Vienna medical societies, after Breuer's new son-in-law had given a lecture on Fliess's work, a development which Freud had predicted. Freud was still expressing derision and contempt for the Viennese medical community over their lack of acceptance of Fliess's hypotheses. He asked, in effect: if confirmation of the successful therapeutic results from treating the nose locally with cocaine under certain conditions was forthcoming only now, how many years would it take the medical world to recognize the importance of the series 28 and 23?

Freud also reported about his work on his new paper "Dreams and Hysteria," published only four years later as the famous Dora case (1905a). In the same letter he gave Fliess advice about his work, writing:

[18] Her visits to Vienna were connected with the expectation of her mother's death.

Do you not think that this would be the right moment to jot down on a few sheets of paper the additions you have made to your present subject—Head's zones, the effect of *herpes zoster,* and whatever else you may have—and have them published? Keeping your name before the public would, after all, be a way of assuring a certain amount of attention later on, for the big, biological things which are more important to you. People only follow authority, and authority is achieved only by doing things that they can grasp.

[The letter ended with a daydream:] In the midst of this mental and material depression I am haunted by the thought of spending Easter week in Rome this year. Not that there is any justification for it—I have achieved nothing so far, and in any event external circumstances will probably make it impossible. Let us hope for better times. My heartfelt wish is that you may soon have such times to report [L. 141].

By now Freud could quickly submit this daydream to analysis and on February 15, 1901 replied to a letter from Fliess:

My dear Wilhelm,
I shall no more get to Rome this Easter than you will. What you say explained the meaning of what would otherwise have remained an incomprehensible interpolation in my last letter. Behind it there was, of course, a reference to the promise you once gave me in happier times, to hold a congress with me on classical soil. I knew perfectly well that such a reference was out of place at that moment. I was merely escaping from the present into the most beautiful of my former fantasies, and it was clear which one. In the meantime the congresses themselves have become relics of the past; I am doing nothing new, and, as you point out, I have become completely estranged from what you are doing.

I can only still rejoice from a distance when you announce that you are at work on a book containing your great solutions and say that you are very satisfied with the way it is going. In that case, you are certainly right to postpone any more writing on the nasal relationship in favor of the broader synthesis [L. 142].

And yet when in March Freud found that there was a chance of a consultation in Berlin, he wrote a long letter to Fliess fantasizing about a "surprise visit." However, nothing came of it all.

There was a letter from Fliess on Freud's 45th birthday, but it obviously contained praise mixed with a bitter pill, judging by Freud's answer:

May 8, 1901
You may certainly take my birthday as an occasion for wishing me the prolongation of your energetic mood and the repetition of such refreshing interludes, and I shall unselfishly support the wish. Your letter lay

on the birthday table with other presents which gave me pleasure and were in part connected with you, although I had asked that the day be overlooked, as it falls in the wretched middle period; I am too young for a jubilee and much too old to be a birthday child. Your letter gave me by no means the least pleasure, except for the part about magic, which I object to as a superfluous plaster to lay your doubts about "thought-reading." I remain loyal to thought-reading and continue to doubt "magic." .

I seem to remember having heard somewhere that only necessity brings out one's best. I have therefore pulled myself together, as you wanted me to . . . and have come to terms with the circumstances. A basket of orchids gives the illusion of luxury and sunshine, a fragment of a Pompeiian wall with a centaur and a faun transports me to my longed-for Italy [L. 143].

On June 9, 1901 Freud wrote Fliess a letter of unusual beauty which may be considered his "farewell" letter:

Dear Wilhelm,

I am taking advantage of this strange Sunday to write to you once again. It is the first Sunday I have been completely free, with nothing to remind me that at other times I am a physician. My aged lady, whom I have been visiting twice a day at fixed hours, was taken to the country yesterday, and I have been looking at my watch every 15 minutes to see whether I am not keeping her waiting too long for her injection. *Thus we still feel the shackles even after they are removed, and do not really know how to enjoy our freedom* [italics added].

I will answer your questions: the place where we will spend the summer has not yet been decided. I think it will be somewhere near Salzburg. . . .

You have reminded me of that beautiful and difficult time when I had reason to believe that I was very close to the end of my life, and it was your confidence that kept me going. I certainly did not behave either very bravely or very wisely then. I was too young, my instincts still too hungry, my curiosity still too great to be able to remain indifferent. However, I have always lacked your optimism. It is certainly foolish to want to banish suffering and dying from the earth, as we do in our New Year's wishes, and it was not for this that we did away with our dear Lord God, only to shift both of these things from ourselves and our dear ones to strangers.

I am thus more humble now, and more ready to bear whatever may come. There is no doubt that not all wishes can be fulfilled. Many a thing for which I have striven ardently is today no longer possible; why shouldn't I have to bury some new hope each year? If you don't agree, this may be an attempt to soothe me, or it may be an appraisal led astray by friendship.

It is true that it is hard to tolerate complainers. This, too, I have learned to understand. I have been quite pleased with my mood for many weeks now . . . [10].

Although on first reading this letter might seem pessimistic, it is actually an indication of the great strides Freud had made in his ability to maintain his equilibrium without the props of illusion. In its serenity it is thus comparable to letters written much later in his life (cf. his letter of May 10, 1925 to Lou Andreas-Salomé, Chapter 17). His remarks about forgoing the need to believe in God and the magic omnipotence of our wishes are a prelude to *The Future of an Illusion*.

However, this letter also gives evidence of the price Freud had to pay for reaching this level of independence and tranquility.

It would have been less painful and more harmonious if this farewell letter had really marked the end of the relationship instead of the bitterness and disappointment which were to follow. However, the illnesses of the mothers of Fliess and Mrs. Fliess kept the correspondence going. On July 4, 1901 Freud wrote:

I am of course being kept well informed about the sad changes in Kaltenleutgeben.[19] We shall go there next week and also visit Königstein,[20] whose daughter is expecting her first baby there. "Birth and death," etc.[21]

Your mother must be in dreadful torment. From your allusions I imagine that your presentation of why some people die suddenly in their primes, while others keep disintegrating right to the very last, is very interesting. Strangely enough, we are dissatisfied with either course of events [11].

Fliess must have "explained" this difference by means of his all-encompassing hypotheses. Freud's dry remark brought the whole thing down to earth, as had the preceding quotation from *Faust*, which said plainly: in the face of the ultimate mysteries of birth and death, which constitute the essence of human existence, we must humbly confess our ignorance.

The next letter (August 7, 1901) not only brought the whole conflict out in the open, but also revealed many of its sources on different levels. Freud set the tone by saying: "First business, then something

---

[19] The summer home of Fliess's in-laws.

[20] Freud's old ophthalmologist friend who, with Koller, first utilized cocaine for eye surgery, at Freud's suggestion.

[21] An allusion to Goethe's *Faust*, Part I, Scene I. See the "motto" of this book and also a similar statement made by Freud to me in 1933 (Chapter 22).

serious, and at the end pleasure." Freud first discussed the unpleasant conflicts which had arisen between the Fliess and Rie families. Freud made no bones about his absolute confidence in and esteem for his old friend Rie, and then went on to say:

> There is no concealing the fact that we have drawn somewhat apart from each other. By this and that I can gauge the distance [L. 144].

The next, crucial paragraph was related to the fact that Fliess and his wife were deeply disappointed by Breuer's handling of the treatment of Fliess's mother and were apparently "writing him off."

> So, too, in the judgment of Breuer. I do no longer despise him. I have felt his strength. If he is dead as far as you two are concerned, he is still exerting his power posthumously. What else is your wife doing but working out, under a dark compulsion, the suggestion Breuer planted in her soul when he congratulated her on the fact that I was not living in Berlin and could not disrupt her marriage? [12]

In the following two paragraphs Freud expressed his pain about the loss of Fliess's friendship.

> And in this you, too, have reached the limit of your acumen, you take sides against me and tell me all that deprives my work of its value: "The thought-reader merely reads his own thoughts into other people."
> If that's what I am, just throw my *Everyday Life* unread into the wastepaper basket. It is full of references to you: manifest ones where you supplied the material, and concealed ones where the motivation leads backs to you. You also gave me the motto as a present.[22] Apart from any lasting value that its contents may have, you can take it as a testimonial to the role you have played in my life until now. After this announcement I can send you the book, as soon as it reaches me, without another word [L. 145].

Finally, an unpublished paragraph bore eloquent testimony to Freud's understanding of his own personality:

> As far as Breuer is concerned, you are certainly quite right in calling him *the* brother. However, I do not share your contempt for friendship

---

[22] The motto which appears on the title page of *The Psychopathology of Everyday Life* is from *Faust*, Part II, Act 5:

> Nun ist die Luft von solchem Spuk so voll,
> Dass niemand weiss, wie er ihn meiden soll.

> Now fills the air so many a haunting shape,
> That no one knows how best he may escape.
> (Bayard Taylor's translation)

between men, probably because I am to a high degree a party to it. As you well know, in my life a woman has never been a substitute for a comrade, a friend. If Breuer's masculine inclination were not so odd, so faint-hearted, so contradictory, as is everything emotional in him, he would be a beautiful example of the kinds of achievements to which the androphile current in man can be sublimated [12].

Thus this letter dealt with the inevitable clash on two levels. Fliess's intransigent views that human events are determined by cosmic factors were incompatible with Freud's belief in psychic determinism. Moreover, while Freud always stressed the importance of the biological substratum of everything mental, Fliess felt so threatened by the concept of psychic determinism that he had to deny all validity to Freud's interpretations and see in them only a projection of the latter's thoughts, explaining away Freud's therapeutic results by the "magic" of his personality.

The conflict on the second level derived from an even greater incompatibility. Freud had alluded in his letter of May 7, 1900 (L. 134) to the feminine quality of his need for a friend. Now he had recognized and was stating openly that intimacy and friendship between men could be the highly adaptive outcome of sublimated "androphile" tendencies in men or, to put it more simply, of the ubiquitous latent male homosexuality. The ability to recognize this specific aspect fully, resulted from self-analysis which, as seen from his correspondence, he continued at least until 1912 (see Chapter 9). What made it so painful and guilt-producing was the fact that Freud was actually telling Fliess, although he was speaking about Breuer: "You, too, have contempt for this type of friendship. Therefore you, too, will be left by the wayside." Here we see at work the incredible feat of Freud's self-analysis, for one of the most difficult accomplishments of a regular analysis is to show the analysand both the existence of latent homosexuality and its adaptive possibilities. Fliess, in turn, was doomed to come to grief over it.

Freud made one more attempt at reconciliation. In the same letter he offered Fliess the possibility of collaborating on a biological-psychological work dealing with human bisexuality. Of course, nothing came of this suggestion.

After taking this decisive step, Freud could permit himself the fulfillment of his old dream. In September, his ardent wish to see Rome was satisfied. Many such eagerly anticipated events end in disappointment, but Rome met most of Freud's expectations. His letters to his family contained vivid descriptions of his impressions and activities (see Jones, Vol. 2, p. 19f.). A letter to Fliess after his return to Vienna summarized the impact of the visit.

September 19, 1901

My dear Wilhelm,

I received your card a few hours before I left. I ought to write to you about Rome, but it is difficult. It was overwhelming for me, too, and the fulfillment of a long-cherished wish, as you well know. It was a little spoiled, as all such fulfillments are when one has waited for them too long, but nevertheless a high point in life. But, while I was completely undisturbed by ancient Rome (I could have worshipped the humble and mutilated remnant of the Temple of Minerva near the forum of Nerva), I did not succeed in freely enjoying the second Rome;[23] its [particular] tendency disturbed me and, being incapable of putting out of my mind my own misery and all the other misery which I know exists, I did not tolerate very well the lie of the salvation of mankind which rears its head to the skies [L. 146].

This passage once again expressed Freud's distaste for the "illusions" of redemption and immortality, inherent specifically in the Christian dogma. He returned to this theme in 1927 in *The Future of an Illusion*.

In this same letter Freud could now deal with the inevitable change in his relationship with Fliess, probably in answer to a series of arguments from the latter. In a serene, dispassionate way Freud wrote:

Your last letter was really beneficial. I can now understand the way you have been writing to me during the past year. It was at any rate the first time that you have ever said anything but the truth to me.

I know in myself that what you say about my attitude to your big work is unjust. I know how often I have thought about it with pride and trembling, and how distressed I have felt when I could not follow you in this or that conclusion. You know that I lack the slightest mathematical ability, and have no memory for numbers and measurements; perhaps it was that that gave you the impression that I did not appreciate what you told me. I do not believe that anything qualitative, any point of view which arose out of the calculations, was wasted on me. Perhaps you have been too quick to renounce me as a listener [*Mitwisserschaft*]. A friend who has the right to contradict, who because of his ignorance can never be dangerous, is not without value to one who explores such dark paths and associates with very few people, all of whom admire him uncritically and unconditionally.

[23] I.e., the Christian Rome.

The only thing that hurt me was another misunderstanding in your letter, when you connected my exclamation "But you're undermining the whole value of my work" with my therapy. . . . I was sorry to lose my "only audience", as our Nestroy[24] called it. For whom shall I write now? If as soon as an interpretation of mine makes you feel uncomfortable you are ready to conclude that the "thought-reader" perceives nothing in others but merely projects his own thoughts into them, you really are no longer my audience, and you must regard the whole technique as just as worthless as the others do.

I do not understand your answer about bisexuality. It is obviously very difficult to understand one another. I certainly had no intention of doing anything but get to grips, as my contribution to the theory of bisexuality, with the thesis that repression and the neuroses, and thus the independence of the unconscious, presuppose bisexuality.

You will have seen from the reference to you as the discoverer of the idea in the "Everyday life" that I have no intention of exaggerating my share in it. But some linking up with the general biological and anatomical aspects of bisexuality would be indispensable and, as nearly all my biological and anatomical knowledge comes from you, there is nothing for it but to ask your aid or leave the whole of the introductory matter to you. But I am not in the least hankering after appearing in print at the moment. Meanwhile, we must discuss it some time.

My cordial greetings, and I hope for good news of you and yours. Your
Sigm. [L. 146]

The letters of the last two years indicate, on the one hand, Freud's recognition that a break was unavoidable and, on the other hand, that this was extremely painful to him. The letter of June, 1901 clearly expresses Freud's deep gratitude for all that Fliess had done for him.

Freud's integrity did not permit him to pretend to accept theories which he could not believe. The measure of objectivity, which he achieved in his self-analysis, sharpened Freud's critical view of Fliess's hypotheses. And yet the last quoted letter of September 19, 1901 shows that Freud in the main insisted only on his right to contradict, while expressing his willingness to accept the "qualities" and points of view in Fliess's work.

A letter written only a day later was much more positive. Fliess had sent Freud the manuscript of a new book. Freud expressed his praise in such terms as "You have never before produced any piece [of work] of such clarity, conciseness, and depth of substance. And what a bless-

---

[24] Nestroy was a contemporary Austrian writer of popular comedies. For the meaning of this allusion, see Kris (1950, p. 342, n. 1).

ing that there is no doubt about the truth of it" [L. 147]. This was the last letter in which Freud referred to Fliess's work.

However, even as late as 1920 Freud again expressed admiration mixed with some doubt about Fliess's "grand" contribution (see Introduction).

Freud kept up the correspondence with Fliess until 1902. He still reported on projects and events in his life, and Fliess apparently did the same. There were still birthday letters and gifts with occasional references to their disagreements. A last, delightful letter described the success of an influential lady patient, who had used "connections" and donations to a museum to bring about Freud's appointment to a professorship (although he never attained the rank of full professor). The last communication was a one-line postcard from a trip to Italy, written on September 10, 1902.

The death of such a friendship was of necessity followed by a period of mourning.

In connection with the *non vixit* dream (Chapter 5), I discussed the role of the "guilt of the survivor" in the latent content of this dream, as well as in the complex relationship between Freud and Fliess. Knowing that Fliess considered his hypotheses to be at least as important and pioneering as Freud's discoveries, Freud felt both pained and guilty that he could not—in spite of all his positive statements—wholeheartedly accept Fliess's far-reaching speculations.

Freud felt guilt because he knew that in the end he could never repay Fliess for the help the latter had given him when he needed it most. He knew that Fliess, too, would be a "revenant." He probably foresaw that Fliess was heading for a truly critical period, without the benefit of a helping friend.

Freud very graphically expressed his feelings at this point by quoting in his essay "On Dreams," published in 1901 at about the same time as his "farewell" letter to Fliess, the following poem by Goethe:[25]

Wer nie sein Brot mit Tränen ass
Wer nie die kummervollen Nächte
Auf seinem Bette weinend sass,
Der kennt euch nicht, ihr himmlischen Mächte.

[25] Only a great poet could hope to offer an adequate verse translation of this poem. Carlyle's translation, included in Strachey's editorial notes to *Civilization and Its Discontents,* where Freud used the same quotation, fails to convey either the meaning or the feeling of the original. I have therefore not attempted a verse translation, but tried simply to convey the meaning of the poem.

Ihr führt ins Leben uns hinein
Ihr lasst den Armen schuldig werden
Dann überlässt ihr ihn der Pein
Denn alle Schuld rächt sich auf Erden.

[He who has never eaten his daily bread with tears,
Who has never spent nights filled with sorrow
Sitting and weeping on his bed
Cannot know you, Heavenly powers.[26]

You guide our entry into life,
You let poor man become guilt-laden,
Then to agony you abandon him.
For every sin is avenged upon this earth.]

What had been the lingering death of a friendship turned into a shocking final break in 1904 when Fliess accused Freud of not having sufficiently acknowledged the former's priority in the conceptualization of bisexuality, of not having carefully enough guarded the "secret" of Fliess's theories; in brief, he accused him of plagiarism.[27]

Freud had embarked upon the period of his life, discussed in the last five chapters, as a man who had just become a happy husband, but who had not yet found his real destiny. His extraordinary potential, his genius, had not yet found its pathway of expression and was still impeded by severe conflicts. When Freud discovered his goal, he could not begin to reach it without magnifying these conflicts to a dangerous level. Physical illness, ostracism, prejudice, the ever-present threat of want, and nearly complete isolation, all increased his turmoil. He had to learn to bear the torments of doubt, depression, and visions of death or incapacitation. And yet during this decade Freud founded a new science, initiating the second scientific revolution of the century. What started as a new method to treat psychoneuroses grew into a bold attempt to arrive at a general psychology. He opened the world of "the Unconscious" to our understanding, he unraveled the secret of the dream. The culmination of this work was the writing of *The Interpretation of Dreams*.

Freud's self-analysis, an achievement which can never be duplicated, became a most important research tool. It also enabled him to tolerate all the obstacles of this trying period, to overcome in large part the manifestations of his own conflicts—his travel phobia, his

[26] "Heavenly" expresses the awesome aspect of the forces which face man. "The heavens" represent fate and destiny.
[27] For a discussion of this, see Kris (1950, pp. 41; 324, n. 1), Jones (Vol. 1, p. 315). See also Chapter 7 in this book.

rare attacks of dread of dying, his gloomy predictions of early death, his doubts about ever finding or even approaching the answers to his many questions, and last, his occasional rather severe depressive moods.

In the same way, the self-analysis enabled Freud to overcome the crisis in his relationship to Fliess. Freud emerged from their relationship the stronger and richer man. Mature and vigorous, he was now ready to accept loneliness and to travel the next stretch entirely by himself.

Freud's tendency toward a strong letdown after intense creative efforts or following the publication of a major work persisted throughout his life, but this mood became rarer and much less severe. Such swings of moods were no more marked in him than in many highly creative people. What persisted throughout Freud's life was his preoccupation with certain dates at which he might die. Immediately after Fliess's unexpected attack in 1904, this preoccupation reached the intensity of an obsessive symptom. At that time, however, and on later occasions as well, Freud was able to recognize this preoccupation as a neurotic mechanism and subject it to successful analysis (see Chapter 7).

In sum, Freud has become a much wiser and more serene man, considerably better prepared to face whatever the remainder of his life might bring. Nonetheless, he felt that he had aged much during this period of struggle, and many of his letters to Fliess spoke of feeling old. (Photographs of this period do not quite bear out this description; nor did he look older than his age to me, when I first saw him in the fall of 1915.) Jones and others consider that Freud's many references to aging, both in the Fliess period and the decades that followed, fall into the same category as his obsessive preoccupation with the possible dates of his death, and hence are signs of an unresolved neurotic conflict. However, when we reflect on the letter to Fliess of May 7, 1900, where he referred to himself as "quite aged," a 44-year-old, "rather shabby Jew," limping after his encounter with the Angel, and on the "farewell" letter of June 9, 1901, where he remarked that it was hard to tolerate complainers, we must realize that while Freud had learned to refrain from complaining, he felt that each of the new steps he had to take drained him of some of his resources and sapped his strength. He therefore believed that every step toward wisdom could be acquired only at its special price. Yet Freud never gave up "wrestling with the angel."

Part II

TOWARD A SCIENTIFIC WELTANSCHAUUNG

7

"THE REVENANTS":
THE ACROPOLIS EPISODE

The turn of the century was heralded by changes in the scientific, intellectual and social attitudes of the Western world. Simultaneously with the publication of *The Interpretation of Dreams* a new phase began in Freud's life, and while the world took little notice of the psychological revolution, the following period was one of consolidation of advances that had been so breathtaking because Freud had started practically *de novo*. The next decade was also the period in which Freud emerged from his isolation and psychoanalysis rapidly gained worldwide attention. Freud acquired an increasing number of students, friends, and followers, and eventually also adversaries.

Many of Freud's works, although as we know from the Fliess correspondence, conceived in the previous period, were pursued and published in the next decade. To mention only the major works of this period: *The Psychopathology of Everyday Life* (1901b), *Three Essays on the Theory of Sexuality* (1905b), *Jokes and Their Relation to the Unconscious* (1905c), as well as three of Freud's most important case histories known as the Dora case (1905a), Little Hans (1909a), and Rat Man (1909b).

It is not surprising that Freud's self-analysis during this whole period was still related to his complex relationship with Fliess. It played a significant role after the attack by Fliess and it proved to be important later on, during the 1912 crisis of the fledgling International Psychoanalytic Association, a crisis that involved Freud's relationship with Jung. We are accustomed to consider the publication of *The Interpretation of Dreams* as coinciding with the end of the "Fliess period." However, a relationship of the kind which existed between Freud and Fliess does not end on a specific date. It continued well beyond the publication of the dream book, and had repercussions which manifested themselves long after the two men had broken off their correspondence, and no longer had contact with each other.

For the period that follows we do not have such excellent source material as the Fliess letters; therefore, we must rely on less explicit sources, which indicate that at intervals, in situations of particular stress, Freud found the old ghosts coming back, like the "revenants" of the "non vixit" dream. We learn of these episodes from letters written to various friends.

One such repercussion was Freud's recurrent preoccupation with possible death dates. Freud himself described the mechanism operative in manifestations of this kind: an old conflict which has neither been completely solved ("worked through") nor become intense enough to give rise to a well-circumscribed symptom remains "encapsulated" as if it were a foreign body, and from time to time becomes sufficiently active to call for some expression.

It is important to remember, however, that this preoccupation with "deadlines" was but one aspect of the manner in which Freud dealt with the complexities of death as a fact and as a concept in both his life and his writings. It is nonetheless of special interest to observe how an old conflict can maintain a life of its own and only gradually become integrated into a mature, serene, supremely autonomous ego attitude capable of withstanding unending trials and eventually the inevitable "moment of truth."

In his letter to Fliess of August 7, 1901, Freud said of the soon-to-be-published *Psychopathology of Everyday Life* that it was full of references to his friend, both obvious and hidden. The last chapter of this book, entitled "Determinism and Superstition," contains certain apparent contradictions. On the one hand, Freud stated, rightly, that he was not a "superstitious person"; on the other hand, he did acknowledge some "superstitions."

Freud ended a discussion of various examples of numbers seemingly chosen at random with the following statement:

> In analyses of this kind which I conduct on myself I find two things particularly striking: firstly, the positively somnambulistic certainty

with which I set off for my unknown goal and plunge into an arithmetical train of thought which arrives all at once at the desired number, and the speed with which the entire subsequent work is completed; and secondly, the fact that the numbers are so freely at the disposal of my unconscious thinking, whereas I am a bad reckoner and have the greatest difficulties in consciously noting dates, house numbers and such things. Moreover in these unconscious thought-operations with numbers I find I have a tendency to superstition, whose origin for long remained unknown to me [1901b, p. 249f.].

The above-quoted passage appears in the 1907 edition of *The Psychopathology of Everyday Life*. As Strachey points out in a footnote:

In 1901 and 1904, this sentence ended: '. . . whose origin is still unknown to me myself.' The [omitted] paragraph continued: 'I generally come upon speculations about the duration of my own life and the lives of those dear to me; and the fact that my friend in B[erlin] has made the periods of human life the subject of his calculations, which are based on biological units, must have acted as a determinant of this unconscious juggling. I am not now in agreement with one of the premises from which this work of his proceeds; from highly egoistic motives I should be very glad to carry my point against him, and yet I appear to be imitating his calculations in my own way.' [Strachey adds:] The whole of this passage was omitted, and the sentence preceding it was given its present form, from 1907 onwards. The references in the omitted passage are to . . . Fliess, and to the analysis of the number 2467 which (in 1901 and 1904) immediately preceded it. The hypothesis of Fliess's with which Freud had egoistic motives for disagreeing was no doubt that which predicted his death at the age of 51 in 1907—the year in which the passage was cancelled [p. 250n].

Here we have confirmation from Freud himself that although he was not a superstitious person, there was within him an encapsulated, "ego-alien" conflict manifesting itself as superstition.

It is noteworthy that the sentence omitted in the 1907 edition was still included in the edition of 1904, a year in which Freud's obsessive superstition reached the intensity of a symptom. This occurred under the following circumstances:

On July 20, 1904, Fliess wrote to Freud, asking whether the philosopher Otto Weininger had obtained his information about the concept of bisexuality from a student of Freud's, H. Swoboda. This concept played an important role in Weininger's book on *Sex and Character* (1902, 1906).

Freud's answer was not satisfactory to Fliess. On July 27, Freud received a second letter written on July 26, Martha Freud's birthday, a date very familiar to Fliess. In this letter Fliess accused Freud of misrepresentation, insisting that he had not sufficiently acknowledged Fliess's priority in the conceptualization of bisexuality or carefully enough guarded the "secret" of Fliess's theories. The breach of confidence allegedly occurred when Freud told his patient Hermann Swoboda about these theories, and Swoboda in turn spoke of them to the philosopher Otto Weininger, who made use of the information in his book. Freud's "confession" in the *non vixit* dream about being glad to outlive Fliess had thus come home to roost, as had the recurrent theme of indiscretion.[1]

In August, 1904, only a few weeks after Fliess's accusation, Freud set out on a short trip. As was so often the case, his traveling companion was his brother Alexander, 10 years his junior. Alexander had only a week's time, so the two men decided to travel via Trieste to the island of Corfu, and spend a few days there. An acquaintance of Alexander's in Trieste advised against this, and suggested that they take instead the boat then leaving for Athens, which would give them a few days in Greece and get them back in time to Trieste.

The initial reaction of the two travelers to this suggestion was a strange one, which Freud described and analyzed (many years later, in "A Disturbance of Memory on the Acropolis") as follows:

> As we walked away from this visit, we were both in remarkably depressed spirits. We discussed the plan that had been proposed, agreed that it was quite impracticable, and saw nothing but difficulties in the way of carrying it out; we assumed, moreover, that we should not be allowed to land in Greece without passports. We spent the hours that elapsed before the Lloyd offices opened in wandering about the town in a discontented and irresolute frame of mind. But when the time came, we went up to the counter and booked our passages for Athens as though it were a matter of course, . . . and indeed without having discussed with one another the reasons for our decision. Such behaviour . . . was most strange. Later on we recognized that we had accepted the suggestion that we should go to Athens instead of Corfu instantly and most readily. But, if so, why had we spent the interval before the offices opened in such a gloomy state and foreseen nothing but obstacles and difficulties? . . .

[1] See Kris (1950, p. 41); Jones (Vol. 1, p. 315); Pfenning (1906); and Chapter 8 of this book. See also Brome (1968), who discussed this and other episodes of Freud's life in a publication which appeared after the completion of my manuscript.

It is one of the cases of 'too good to be true'[2] that we come across so often. It is an example of the incredulity that arises so often when we are surprised by a piece of good news, when we hear we have won a prize, for instance . . . or when a girl learns that a man whom she has secretly loved has asked her parents for leave to pay his addresses to her.

When we have established the existence of a phenomenon, the next question is of course as to its cause. Incredulity of this kind is obviously an attempt to repudiate a piece of reality; but there is something strange about it. We should not be in the least astonished if an attempt of this kind were aimed at a piece of reality that threatened to bring unpleasure. . . . But why should such incredulity arise in something which, on the contrary, promises to bring a high degree of pleasure? Truly paradoxical behaviour! But I recollect that on a previous occasion I dealt with the similar case of the people who, as I put it, are 'wrecked by success' [1916b]. As a rule people fall ill as a result of frustration, of the non-fulfilment of some vital necessity or desire. But with these people the opposite is the case; they fall ill, or even go entirely to pieces, because an overwhelmingly powerful wish of theirs has been fulfilled. But the contrast between the two situations is not so great as it seems at first. What happens in the paradoxical case is merely that the place of the external frustration is taken by an internal one. The sufferer does not permit himself happiness: the internal frustration commands him to cling to the external one. But why? Because—so runs the answer in a number of cases—one cannot expect Fate to grant one anything so good. In fact, another instance of 'too good to be true', the expression of a pessimism of which a large portion seems to find a home in many of us. In another set of cases, just as in those who are wrecked by success, we find a sense of guilt or inferiority, which can be translated: 'I'm not worthy of such happiness, I don't deserve it.' But these two motives are essentially the same, for one is only a projection of the other. For, as has long been known, the Fate which we expect to treat us so badly is a materialization of our conscience, of the severe super-ego within us, itself a residue of the punitive agency of our childhood [1936, pp. 240, 242f.].

Freud and his brother took the suggested trip to Athens, where Freud's preoccupation with a specific death date reached such a peak that he experienced it as a disturbing symptom. On the same trip Freud also had what he called "a disturbance of memory," but which was actually a fleeting state of derealization in which he was assailed by a disbelief in the reality of what was before him and asked his brother if it were really true that they were on the Acropolis.[3]

[2] In English in the original.
[3] Freud (1919) himself supplied a vivid description of this unexpected adventure which apparently led him to experience his surroundings as "unreal" or "uncanny."

'And now, here we are in Athens, and standing on the Acropolis! We really *have* gone a long way!' So too, if I may compare such a small event with a greater one, Napoleon, during his coronation as Emperor in Notre Dame, turned to one of his brothers—it must no doubt have been the eldest one, Joseph—and remarked: 'What would *Monsieur notre Père* have said to this, if he could have been here to-day?'

But here we come upon the solution of the little problem of why it was that already at Trieste we interfered with our enjoyment of the voyage to Athens. It must be that a sense of *guilt* was attached to the satisfaction in having gone such a long way: there was something about it that was wrong, that from earliest times had been forbidden. It was something to do with a child's criticism of his father, with *the undervaluation which took the place of the overvaluation* [italics added] of earlier childhood. It seems as though the essence of success was to have got further than one's father, and as though to excel one's father was still something forbidden.

As an addition to this generally valid motive there was a special factor present in our particular case. The very theme of Athens and the Acropolis in itself contained evidence of the son's superiority. Our father had been in business, he had had no secondary education, and Athens could not have meant much to him. Thus what interfered with our enjoyment of the journey to Athens was a feeling of *filial piety*. And now you will no longer wonder that the recollection of this incident on the Acropolis should have troubled me so often since I myself have grown old and stand in need of forbearance and can travel no more [1936, p. 247f.].

Jones (Vol. 2, p. 23f.) has furnished a description of this trip based on Freud's letters to his family (actually mostly picture postcards) and impressions which Freud had reported to Marie Bonaparte, who was then in the habit of taking notes on her conversations with him. Jones of course referred to the "disturbance of memory," but he made no mention of Freud's preoccupation with death during this trip. What he did point out was that the trip had not been planned beforehand.

Nor did Freud mention, in this 1936 paper, his superstitious preoccupation with death in the course of that trip to Athens, but he discussed this in detail in a letter to Jung written on April 16, 1909, which was highly significant for more reasons than this one. The entire letter will be quoted here, although a portion of it will be discussed further in Chapter 9.

April 16, 1909

Dear Friend,

Thinking that you were already on your bicycle tour of Northern Italy, I wrote your wife a card from Venice, where I went for an Easter excursion in the vain expectation of providing myself with an early taste of spring and some relaxation.

It is remarkable that on the same evening on which I formally adopted you as my oldest son and anointed you successor and crown prince *in partibus infidelium*[4] you simultaneously divested me of my paternal dignity, a divestiture which you apparently enjoyed as much as I, in contrast, did your investiture. Now I am afraid of falling back into the role of father for you by speaking of my reaction to the "Poltergeist." Nevertheless I must do so because it is different from what you might think. Now I do not deny that your communications and experiment made a strong impression on me. I decided after you left to make some observations, and here are the results. In my first room there is a constant cracking on the spot where the two heavy Egyptian steles rest on the oak boards of the bookcases. So this one is too transparent. In the second one where we heard it, there is very seldom any cracking. At first I would have considered it as evidence if the noise, which was heard so frequently in your presence, never made itself heard again after your departure. However, it has since recurred repeatedly, but never in connection with my thoughts and never when I was preoccupied with you or with this special problem of yours (not now either, I might add as a further challenge). However, the observations soon lost their value for other reasons. My belief, or at least my readiness to believe, disappeared along with the magic of your personal presence. Once again it seems to me quite unlikely, for some kind of inner motives, that anything of this nature should occur. The piece of furniture appears before me stripped of its spirits just as god-forsaken nature appeared before the poet after the departure of the Greek gods.

Thus I again put on the horn-rimmed paternal glasses and warn the dear son to keep a cool head and rather not understand something than make such great sacrifices for the sake of understanding. I also shake my wise head over the psychosynthesis and think: "Yes, that's the way they are, the young ones; they really enjoy only those things where they do not have to take us along; where we, with our short breath and weary legs, cannot follow."

And now I shall exercise the privilege of my years to turn loquacious and tell you about another thing between heaven and earth which cannot be understood. A few years ago I discovered in myself the conviction that I would die between the ages of 61 and 62, which at that time seemed to be a long way off. (Now there are only 8 more years.)[5] I then went with my brother [Alexander][6] to Greece, and it was abso-

---

[4] The term goes back to the seventh century and stems from ecclesiastical law. It refers to a priest on whom an honorary title but not the functions of a bishop has been bestowed.

[5] This letter was written about three weeks before Freud's 53rd birthday, and 15 years after his most severe heart attack in 1894.

[6] As he had also done during the Fliess period.

lutely uncanny how the numbers 61 or 60, in conjunction with 1 or 2, kept cropping up under all kinds of circumstances involving the naming of countable objects, especially in connection with means of transportation, all of which I conscientiously noted down. Being in low spirits, I hoped to breathe again when in our Athens hotel a room on the first floor was assigned to us; there could be no 61. Well, at least I got room 31 (with fatalistic license, after all, half of 61-62), and this more intelligent and nimble number proved to be more persistent in its persecution than the first one. From the time of my return *until quite recently* the number 31, usually in close association with a 2, remained faithful to me. But since I also have regions in my system in which I am merely avid for knowledge and not at all superstitious, I have in the meantime attempted the analysis of this conviction, and here it is. It started in the year 1899. Two events coincided at that time; first, I wrote *The Interpretation of Dreams* (which was published *pre*dated 1900); and secondly, I was assigned a new telephone number, which I have to this day—14362.[7] It is easy to establish a link between these two facts; in the year 1899, when I wrote *The Interpretation of Dreams,* I was *43* years old. What then was more natural than that the other numbers should signify the end of my life, namely, 61 or 62. Suddenly there was method in the madness. The superstition that I would die between 61-62 turned out to be the equivalent to the conviction that with *The Interpretation of Dreams* I had completed my life work, needed to produce no more, and could die in peace. You will admit that with this knowledge it no longer sounds so nonsensical. Incidentally, the hidden influence of Fliess plays a part in this; the superstition erupted in the year of his attack[8] [on me]. Here you will once again find confirmation of the *specifically Jewish nature of my mysticism.*[9] Otherwise, I am inclined to say only that adventures such as the one with the number 61 can be explained by two factors. The first is an enormously heightened alertness on the part of the Unconscious, which sees Helen in every woman;[10] the second is the undeniable existence of a "compliance of chance," which plays the same role in

---

[7] See my remarks about Freud's interpretation of the number 2467 in his letter to Fliess of August 27, 1899 (Chapter 5).

[8] I.e., 1904. Actually it had manifested itself much earlier as a latent, encapsulated superstition (see also Chapters 3, 4, and 5).

[9] See also Chapter 1.

[10] An allusion to *Faust,* Part I, Scene 6. Mephistopheles gives Faust a magic potion, saying:

> Du siehst mit diesem Trank im Leibe
> Bald Helenen in jedem Weibe
> [With this potion in your body
> You will soon see Helen in every woman.]

This has become an idiomatic expression indicating that, obsessed by a preconceived idea, one can find confirmation for it in every environmental situation that provides some semiplausible associative link.

the formation of delusions as somatic compliance in hysterical symptoms and linguistic compliance in puns.

I therefore shall be able to hear about your further investigations of the spook-complex with the interest one has in a lovely illusion which one does not share oneself.[11]

Your

Freud [1]

This letter can be enjoyed simply from an aesthetic point of view as an admirable example of Freud's art as a letter writer, an art which is so difficult to convey in translation. In addition, this letter has a very special meaning. Here Freud himself provides us with a unique opportunity to apply "the genetic point of view" to an important developmental aspect of his life. It provides the "missing link" between events extending over a period of four decades from 1896, the date of his father's death, to 1936, the date of the publication of the Acropolis paper.

I pointed out previously that Freud was not a superstitious person, which did not exclude his having superstitious traits. In the same way, Freud cannot be characterized as an obsessional neurotic, but his preoccupation with the prospective date of his death had the character of an obsessive trait. While Freud records some details of his self-analysis, we have no way of knowing whether he found it necessary to tell Jung everything.

Fortunately, we are not left entirely to speculation. I pointed out earlier in this chapter that the development of Freud's relationship to Fliess was reflected in the changes Freud made in the text of *The Psychopathology of Everyday Life* between 1901 and 1907. Similarly, a careful correlation of the content of Freud's letter to Jung with some of Freud's pertinent writings between 1901 and 1909 may throw additional light on the whole episode.

From the passages of the *Psychopathology of Everyday Life* and Strachey's footnotes quoted earlier in this chapter, we learned that in *1904,* the year of Fliess's attack on Freud, and of the episode during the trip to Greece, Freud linked his superstitions with Fliess's calculations, *which he was imitating in spite of the fact that he was then already in disagreement with Fliess's premises.*

---

[11] We shall see that Freud's attitude toward "occult" phenomena was to go through many complex phases in the ensuing decades of his life.

In Freud's interleaved copy of the 1904 (second) edition, the following remarks were found after the 2,467 example (see Chapter 5):

> Rage, anger and consequently a murderous impulse is the source of superstition in obsessional neurotics: a sadistic component, which is attached to love and is therefore directed against the loved person and repressed precisely because of this link and because of its intensity.— *My own superstition has its roots in suppressed ambition (immortality) and in my case takes the place of that anxiety about death which springs from the normal uncertainty of life* . . . [1901b, p. 260, n. 3; italics added].

In addition to his insight into the ego-alien nature of his superstition, Freud reveals that his superstition was not only the expression of his ambivalence, but also served as defense against the normal, inescapable fear of death.

These notes go much closer to the core of his conflict than the previously quoted additions of 1907. However, in the same year Freud added another passage to *The Psychopathology of Everyday Life:*

> Anyone who has had the opportunity of studying the hidden mental impulses of human beings by means of psycho-analysis can also say something new about the *quality* of the unconscious motives that find expression in superstition. It can be recognized most clearly in neurotics suffering from obsessional thinking or obsessional states—people who are often of high intelligence—that superstition derives from suppressed hostile and cruel impulses. Superstition is in large part the expectation of trouble; and a person who has harboured frequent evil wishes [*Unheilserwartung* in the original] against others, but has been brought up to be good and has therefore repressed such wishes into the unconscious, will be especially ready to expect punishment for his unconscious wickedness in the form of trouble [*Unheil* in the original] threatening him from without [1901b, p. 260].

The *Standard Edition* translation of this passage contains two pertinent inaccuracies. In the second sentence the correct translation would be: "the often very intelligent *nervous people* [in the original, *die Nervösen*, in contrast to *Neurotiker*, which would be the German word for "neurotics"] who are *affected by* (or *subject to*) [in the original, *behafteten* rather than *leiden*, which would be the German word for "suffering from"]. . . ." The second inaccuracy is the use of the word "trouble" for the German *Unheil*, which should be translated as "disaster."[12] It is certainly not too speculative to apply this interpretation

---

[12] See Chapter 10, footnote 5.

—with certain modifications—to Freud's own obsessive superstitious preoccupations.

In the same year Freud published a short paper about "Obsessive Actions and Religious Practices" in which he made a similar distinction between "nervous people" (translated as "sufferers from nervous affections") and people who suffer from obsessive thinking, obsessive ideas, obsessive impulses and the like. Taken together, these form a particular clinical entity, to which the name of 'obsessional neurosis' [*'Zwangsneurose'*] is customarily applied" (1907b, p. 117). Freud emphasized subsequently that not only the obsessional neurosis but other morbid mental phenomena might have the same obsessive (compulsive) character.

In this paper Freud said that "the sufferer from compulsions and prohibitions behaves as if he were dominated by a sense of guilt, of which, however, he knows nothing, so that we must call it *an unconscious sense of guilt*" (p. 123; italics added).

This was the first time Freud used this term in a published paper. It played a very important part in Freud's later writings, although the significance of unconscious guilt had been implied earlier. He had used it in the letter to Fliess in which he first reported the "discovery" of the oedipus complex. Applying it to the tragic story of Hamlet, he had said:

> How better than by the torment roused in him by the obscure memory that he himself had meditated the same deed against his father because of passion for his mother—"use every man after his desert, and who should 'scape whipping?" *His conscience is his unconscious feeling of guilt* [L. 71].

In his 1907 paper Freud linked the guilt mainly to the repression of forbidden sexual impulses. We know, however, that as early as 1897 Freud had discovered the "oedipal" conflict and the ubiquity of the rivalry with the father, leading to murderous wishes. Freud had also reconstructed in his self-analysis his own "murderous wishes" against his younger brother (L. 70) and had described in *The Interpretation of Dreams* the ever-present hostile aspects of sibling rivalry (see Chapter 5).

He indicated specifically that a little child, whose younger sibling had died, might after the birth of the next sibling harbor the wish that the same fate should meet this new competitor. Freud also indicated, however, that the degree of this hostility could be explained on the one hand by the completely egoistic attitude of small children and on the other by the fact that death was a concept which had no real meaning to young children.

However, in 1914, Freud added the following footnote: "Deaths that are experienced in this way in childhood may quickly be forgotten in the family; but psycho-analytic research shows that they have a very important influence on subsequent neuroses" (1900, p. 252). This statement had a direct bearing on Freud's own life; his younger brother had died in 1858 only to be replaced after a few months by a sister born on December 31, 1858.

All these examples demonstrate—anew—that Freud only very gradually recognized the full impact of aggression in the instinctual life of man. The discovery of incestuous wishes toward the mother and hostility toward the father as the superior rival was probably by itself a shattering experience, yet the recognition that the harboring of murderous wishes was an ubiquitous psychological experience, to some extent independent of the oedipal rivalry, and that it extended toward siblings, was even more unacceptable.

Only a few months after the publication of the paper on "Obsessional Acts and Religious Practices," Freud began the treatment of a case of obsessional neurosis, which he published in 1909 under the title "Notes upon a Case of Obsessional Neurosis," probably the most fascinating and important psychoanalytic case history ever published.

This patient had—among many other severe symptoms—what he called "trains of thought" about the death of his father which he brought up in some of his first sessions. When in his sixth(!) session the patient told Freud that "his father's death could never have been an object of his desire but only of his fear" (1909b, p. 179f.), Freud provided him with the interpretation that, according to psychoanalytic theory, every fear corresponded to a former (unconscious) wish.

The following passages from this paper are pertinent:

> [The patient] wondered how he could possibly have had such a wish, considering that he loved his father more than any one else in the world; there could be no doubt that he would have renounced all his own prospects of happiness if by so doing he could have saved his father's life.—I answered that it was precisely such intense love as his that was the necessary precondition of the repressed hatred. In the case of people to whom he felt indifferent he would certainly have no difficulty in maintaining side by side inclinations to a moderate liking and

to an equally moderate dislike. . . . [To this Freud added in parenthesis:] Shakespeare makes Brutus speak in a similar way of Julius Caesar: 'As Caesar loved me, I weep for him; as he was fortunate, I rejoice at it; as he was valiant, I honour him; but, as he was ambitious, I slew him.' But these words already strike us as rather strange, and for the very reason that we had imagined Brutus's feelings for Caesar as something deeper [1909b, p. 180].

It was this association which played such an important role in the *non vixit* dream and led to the memory that Freud once played the role of Brutus (see Chapter 5).

In the next session Freud engaged his patient in a long discussion about the infantile origin of evil, murderous thoughts and wishes. The patient responded during this session with quotations from Nietzsche's *Beyond Good and Evil* about the conflict between "Memory" and "Pride" involved in the memory of having committed a criminal act. Freud ended the report of this session with the following passage:

> He went on to adduce the fact of his illness having become so enormously intensified since his father's death; and I said I agreed with him in so far as I regarded his sorrow at his father's death as the chief source of the *intensity* of his illness. His sorrow had found, as it were, a pathological expression in his illness. Whereas, I told him, a normal period of mourning would last from one to two years, a pathological one like this would last indefinitely [1909b, p. 186].

I have quoted these passages for many reasons. In the correspondence with Fliess, Freud frequently indicated how intimately his self-analysis and his findings about patients were interconnected.

In the self-analysis of this period, Freud was still particularly involved in the working through of his own guilt rooted in the ubiquitous oedipal and Cain conflicts.[13]

Another passage of this 1909 paper is especially important for our topic. After a lengthy discussion of his patient's attitude toward super-

---

[13] Another reason for quoting these passages is the fact that at that time Freud still assumed that intellectual "understanding" and "conviction" alone could lead to the solution of our innermost conflicts. It took Freud many years of often disappointing experience to realize that understanding and insight were processes taking place on many levels, that resistances required a long period of "working through." He also learned that in the analysis of obsessional neurotics, as in that of people with obsessional character traits, intellectualization was frequently the most stubborn form of resistance. He learned, further, that the transference phenomena were the most important vehicles for the "working through" of such resistances.

stition and death, in which he connected it to the infantile sense of omnipotence and the inherently ambivalent feelings of such patients toward loved objects, Freud said:

> . . . the behavior of other obsessional neurotics does not differ greatly from that of our present patient, even though it has not been their fate to come face to face with the phenomenon of death at such an early age. Their thoughts are unceasingly occupied with other people's length of life and possibility of death; their superstitious propensities have had no other contact to begin with, and have perhaps no other source whatever [1909b, p. 236].

We know of course that this behavior is not restricted to obsessional neurotics, but can appear in varying degrees in obsessive preoccupations of the kind manifested by Freud.

The material presented and discussed in this chapter brings into clear relief how intimately interwoven were certain events in Freud's life, scientific work, discoveries, and self-analysis. In *The Interpretation of Dreams,* Freud used his own dreams [and] conflicts to illustrate the working of the mind. Once we correlate the content of such passages as that quoted in this chapter with the 1904 episode, the letter to Jung of 1909, and the Acropolis paper of 1936, we recognize how frequently Freud addressed himself directly to his own problems. We can see, moreover, to what extent the progress of his work and of his self-analysis were reflected in the vicissitudes of his relationship to Fliess. I shall summarize the passages quoted which are most pertinent to the topic of this book:

The additions, changes, or omissions which Freud made in his three editions of *The Psychopathology of Everyday Life*[14] illustrate clearly his growing awareness that his preoccupation with numbers and his "tendency to superstition" were on the one hand linked to speculation about the duration of his own life and the lives of the ones dear to him, and on the other hand to Fliess's number "juggling" which he was imitating, although he did not agree with one of the premises from which this work of Fliess's proceeded. In 1907, some of these passages were either omitted or changed. For instance, in the first edition Freud analysed his seemingly arbitrary use of the number 2,467 which had

---

[14] The footnotes in which James Strachey singled out and commented upon the importance of these changes are one of the many examples of the unique historical and didactic value of his editorial work on *The Standard Edition* of Freud's work.

first appeared in a letter to Fliess of August 27, 1899 (see L. 116, and Chapter 5 in this volume).

Freud's interleaved copy of the 1904 edition of *The Psychopathology of Everyday Life* contains remarks distinguishing Freud's superstition, which he linked to suppressed ambition (immortality), from "anxiety about death which springs from the normal uncertainty of life." It was not until 1926, with *Inhibitions, Symptoms, and Anxiety*, that Freud made a clear distinction between normal anxiety and neurotic anxiety which manifests itself only as an exaggeration of a normal response to real danger or as a displacement to situations which are not dangerous per se.

These remarks are pertinent for the following reasons: in 1904 Freud linked his superstitions only to his "suppressed ambition" (immortality), while from the previously quoted paragraphs and changes it was obvious that in 1907 Freud linked these superstitions also to what he later would have called an identification with Fliess.

Freud did not elaborate on the source of what he called the ambition for immortality nor on the mechanisms of its suppression. *The Interpretation of Dreams* contains several scattered remarks to the effect that children, for example, have no exact concept of death and that adults express their wish for immortality in their attitude toward their children. Only in later works did Freud subject this concept to a much more detailed discussion.

Even more pertinent is Freud's remark that this "superstition" (we might say the superstitious preoccupation with death) was replacing the "normal anxiety" about death. This is one of the very few passages where Freud spoke about a fear of death which springs from the "normal uncertainty of life." It is perhaps not accidental that he spoke of these uncertainties at a time when he had recovered completely from his cardiac episode and therefore could more safely relegate to the realm of superstition the thought that he would not live beyond the age of 51, the year in which he published *The Psychopathology of Everyday Life*.

Only from 1907 on did Freud compare superstition with manifestations of "obsessional states," obsessional thinking and actions, symptoms of obsessive-compulsive neurosis, and religious practices.

The most far-reaching generalization was the one made in the 1907 edition of *The Psychopathology of Everyday Life:* "Superstition derives from suppressed hostile and cruel impulses." In most other instances the suppressed hostile wishes are linked to rivalry with the father in the oedipal situation and with siblings. At that time Freud saw repression of forbidden sexual impulses as the main source of unconscious guilt.

In other passages quoted, Freud also stated that the intensity of symptoms and guilt feelings was indicative of the intensity of both positive and negative feelings to an object.

Finally, Freud pointed out that people whose fate it has been to come face to face with death at an early age are predestined to a preoccupation with the length of life and the prospect of death. The length of the mourning period also depends on all these factors.

We know from Freud's own accounts how important the deaths of his brother and his father were in his life. All we need to add is that a state of severe mourning is initiated not only by the actual death of a beloved person but also by the loss of an object with whom an intimate relationship has been broken off.

We may ask: why did Freud show a preoccupation with his own death rather than that of *other* people?

As pointed out in the discussion of several letters to Fliess, Freud was frequently quite concerned when Fliess or others were traveling and he either did not receive regular messages from them or read in the newspaper about train accidents. But such thoughts never had a persistent, obsessive quality.

We have only to add here some of the explanations which Freud used to such advantage concerning the obsessional thoughts of his patients: one was that behind fears we often find a wish, and that in the final obsessional thought some important links are missing. Thanks to Freud we know that behind *obsessive* thoughts and the concern with other people's death there frequently lies a hostile wish. But we also know that such wishes are unacceptable to us, especially when they are directed toward persons we love; therefore, if these hostile wishes occur in a person who has a strong conscience, they may be turned into a superstitious preoccupation with the person's own death.

The eruption of such phenomena can be observed in many different intense relationships, for example, in the state of infatuation, or in the conflicts of some women after the birth of a child.

In the psychoanalytic situation such conflictual wishes and fears are frequently expressed in the transference phenomena, and only a thorough analysis of such phenomena in both their positive and negative aspects can resolve the conflicts after the link with their infantile prototype has been established. It is our experience that "working through" is greatly impeded by an overly intense transference relationship. It is for this very reason that Freud eventually realized the necessity of an optimal distance between analyst and analysand.

The extreme opposite of an optimal distance made the break between Freud and Fliess so painful. The acute eruption of Freud's obsessive preoccupation with the date of his death in the year of Fliess's violent attack on him can therefore be easily understood.

Furthermore, Freud had emerged by then as one of the most important men of his time, while his formerly admired, beloved, overvalued, self-chosen analyst-friend not only had turned into an attacker but had also been left by the wayside.

The "guilt of the survivor" was the link between the then current conflicts, which arose from the still unsolved ambivalence conflict, and the "guilt of the survivor," which had followed the deaths of Freud's father and brother.

In his letter to Jung, written in 1909, Freud made a vague allusion to the "hidden influence of Fliess." We are entitled to assume that during the episode in 1904, and at the time of the second edition of *The Psychopathology of Everyday Life* (which was also published in 1904), Freud was not yet aware of *all* the implications of this "hidden influence." In the analysis of his number superstition which Freud submitted to Jung in this letter one essential factor was missing: the element of guilt. Without the element of guilt there seems to be no reason why Freud should have felt he had only a limited life-span left to him after the publication of *The Interpretation of Dreams*.

In his 1936 Acropolis paper Freud limited himself to discussing the experience of derealization, omitting the symptom which he had described in the 1909 letter to Jung. Moreover, in analyzing the derealization, he restricted himself to the infantile root of this phenomenon, which he characterized as "filial piety" and guilt over outstripping his father.

In addition to the factor of the "guilt of the survivor," there was probably also another mechanism operating in this episode and in the continuous resurgence of an obsessive preoccupation with dates in general, as well as in some of Freud's speculative formulations.

In "Mourning and Melancholia" (1917a) Freud described the tendency to incorporate certain characteristics of the lost object as part of the process of mourning. Freud certainly went through a painful mourning period after losing Fliess, especially under the circumstances in which this loss occurred. Obviously Freud was greatly influenced by Fliess's "number game," incorporating and to some extent identifying with certain of the latter's ideas. Freud himself confirmed this assumption by saying in his *Psychopathology of Everyday Life* up to 1904 that he was still imitating Fliess's calculations in spite of the fact that he no longer agreed with them. I mentioned earlier in this Chapter that in 1920, in *Beyond the Pleasure Principle,* Freud referred again to the "grand conceptions of Wilhelm Fliess."

Freud's remarks about the significance of normal and pathological mourning are equally applicable to Freud's own response. Moreover, the same mechanism was operative, in a mitigated way, in Freud's later relationships, especially that with Jung.

8

IMMORTALITY

The years 1906 and 1907 were significant in many respects.

In 1906, Fliess published his attack on Freud, Swoboda, and Weininger (see Chapter 7). We may assume that the form of the attack and its unmistakably paranoid character contributed to the "working through" process required for the dissolution of Freud's special relationship to Fliess, but it also must have heightened Freud's feelings of sadness and disappointment and deepened his largely unconscious guilt.

In 1906, furthermore, Freud began his correspondence with Jung, who, along with his chief, Bleuler, professor of psychiatry in Zürich, had begun two years earlier to put out a series of publications strongly influenced by Freud's work. Thus started a relationship which involved some, but by no means all, of the elements of Freud's relationship to Fliess. There was a certain amount of overvaluation along with exaggerated hopes for a "son" and "spiritual heir," but there was never any mistake as to which of the two was the teacher, the leader.

1907 was a year of expanding recognition for psychoanalysis, a year when Freud met not only Jung but Abraham and Ferenczi, who became his friends and close collaborators. Jung was accompanied on his first visit to Vienna by Ludwig Binswanger, who struck up a friendship with Freud that was characterized by great mutual respect, cordiality, and a certain intimacy, despite the fact that Binswanger was 25 years younger than Freud and that in later years he shifted his theoretical work in a direction which is now called existentialism. Freud maintained a steady correspondence with him to the end of his life. Binswanger wrote one of the most moving biographical essays on Freud, including Freud's letters to him, some of which are most pertinent to my topic.

In 1906 Freud also celebrated his 50th birthday when an incident occurred, described by Jones as follows:

> In 1906, on the occasion of his fiftieth birthday, the little group of adherents in Vienna presented him with a medallion . . . having on the obverse his side-portrait in bas-relief and on the reverse a Greek design of Oedipus answering the Sphinx. Around it is a line from Sophocles' *Oedipus Tyrannus* . . . ["Who divined the famed riddle and was a man most mighty."] . . .
>
> At the presentation of the medallion there was a curious incident. When Freud read the inscription he became pale and agitated and in a strangled voice demanded to know who had thought of it. He behaved as if he had encountered a *revenant,* and so he had. After Federn told him it was he who had chosen the inscription Freud disclosed that as a young student at the University of Vienna he used to stroll around the great arcaded court inspecting the busts of former professors of the institution. He then had the phantasy, not merely of seeing his own bust there in the future, which would not have been anything remarkable in an ambitious student, but of it actually being inscribed with the *identical* words he now saw on the medallion [Vol. 2, p. 13f.].

Freud disliked such celebrations where arbitrarily chosen dates—decade, or later half-decade marks—were made occasions for special attention. Nonetheless he viewed as a special feat one's having wrested another few years away from death or from "inexorable Ananke," as he would later call it, while at the same time having overcome the "burden of existence" and the "exigencies of life."

While Freud expressed the idea that he had aged prematurely in numerous letters written between 1900 and 1902, his appearance and the tempo of his activities would seem to belie it. We have only to read Jones's description of each vacation trip to see that Freud was by this time a vigorous and healthy man. And although after 1904 he repeatedly expressed his resentment about aging, he did so with some exaggeration but apparently without any obsessive preoccupation with dying after the acute upsurge of that year. This held true even in 1907 when Freud reached the "fateful" and "critical" age of 28 + 23.

GRADIVA

I now turn to Freud's works during this period. One of these was an essay entitled "Delusions and Dreams in Jensen's *Gradiva*" (1907a), which Freud wrote during his vacation in 1906 and in which he touched on the problem of death and immortality.[1]

The particular attraction of this work lies in the special method Freud used in presenting his ideas. Following the example of the author of *Gradiva,* he allowed the main figures of the work to present through dreams and a delusion of the "hero" certain special aspects of "immortality" and of the parallel between the history of mankind and the history of the individual.

In its bare outlines and without following it as it unfolds, the "plot" dealt with a young archaeologist, Norbert Hanold, whose childhood playmate had been a girl across the street. The two had been very close until their early teens, when the boy began to withdraw more and more from "the world" and immerse himself completely in his studies. He "forgot" his childhood sweetheart to the point of not recognizing her at a party, much to her chagrin. The only child of a scientist father, motherless since infancy, the girl had never lost her attachment to the young man. One day the young archaeologist came across a Greek relief of a female figure (or one of its Roman copies) which probably represented one of the "Horae, the goddesses of vegetation, and the deities of the fertilizing dew who are allied to them" (1907a, p. 95). He "fell in love" with the statue, especially with her graceful feet, depicted as partly lifted in a walking position. He therefore named her Gradiva, "the girl who steps along," which then became "the girl with the graceful gait." He fantasied that she had lived in Pompeii and died there during the eruption of Mt. Vesuvius in 79 A.D. He mourned and loved her, so that driven by an "invincible compulsion" he found himself going to Pompeii to find the imprint of her feet in the petrified ashes. Or perhaps he would find Gradiva herself.

In Pompeii he met a young girl who had an uncanny likeness to Gradiva; she recognized him immediately and led him gradually toward the unraveling of the mystery. She was his childhood sweetheart Zoe—"Life"—whose image had lived on in his unconscious and instigated his peculiar delusional states. Freud, again following the author's lead, was also able to trace the unfolding of the young man's symptom and its solution through a series of dreams. A few passages from Freud's essay where he quoted Jensen will best convey the spirit of this theme:

[1] See also Chapter 5.

She also learned that he had given her portrait on the relief the name of 'Gradiva,' and told him her real name, 'Zoe.' 'The name suits you beautifully, but it sounds to me like a bitter mockery, for Zoe means life.' 'One must bow to the inevitable,' was her reply, 'and I have long grown used to being dead.' Promising to be at the same place again at the mid-day hour next day, she bade him farewell after once more asking him for the sprig of asphodel: 'to those who are more fortunate people give roses in the spring; but to me it is right that you should give the flower of forgetfulness.' No doubt melancholy suited some one who had been so long dead and had returned to life again for a few short hours [p. 21].

Later, she said:

'I was thin air for you, and you . . . you were as dull, as dried-up, and as tongue-tied as a stuffed cockatoo, and at the same time as grandiose as an—*archaeopteryx*—yes, that's right, that's what they call the ante-diluvian bird-monstrosity they've dug up. Only there was one thing I hadn't suspected: that there was an equally grandiose phantasy lodged in your head of looking on me too, here in Pompeii, as something that had been dug up and come to life again' [p. 32].

And still further:

'You mean,' said the girl, 'the fact of someone having to die so as to come alive; but no doubt that must be so for archaeologists.' Evidently she had not forgiven him yet for the roundabout path by way of archaeology which he had followed from their childhood friendship to the new relation that was forming.

'No, I mean your name . . . Because "Bertgang" means the same as "Gradiva" and describes someone "who steps along brilliantly" [p. 37].

He proposed that he and his Zoe should come for their honeymoon to Italy and Pompeii. . . . Zoe's reply to the plan . . . suggested by 'her childhood friend who had also in a sense been dug out of the ruins again' was that she did not feel quite alive enough yet to make a geo-graphical decision of that sort [p. 39].

It was Jung, supposedly, who had called Freud's attention to this book. Freud was always fascinated by the fact that writers or poets "knew" in their fantasies about the working of the "unconscious," and especially in the early phases of his work he found in literature wel-come confirmations of his findings. This was also one of the reasons why Freud turned more and more to the study of mythology and anthropology, to which he had always been attracted.

But there were probably other reasons why Freud found this book of Jensen's so appealing (see Jones and also L. J. Friedman, 1966).[2] Freud was always intensely interested in archaeology. In a letter written to Stefan Zweig on February 2, 1931 (see Freud, 1960a) he remarked that he had read more books on archaeology than on psychology. The new excavations in Crete were most exciting events to him and it was deeply frustrating that Fate would not permit him to see their results. He used to show me wistfully any new book that came out about the excavations. Freud was also a collector of antiquities, calling this activity an addiction second in intensity only to his nicotine addiction. With his propensity for metaphor he was wont to compare the psychoanalytic process to the excavation of hidden structures and linked this image specifically with Pompeii by describing the "unconscious" as virtually immortal and unchanged by the passage of time except as it was made accessible through analysis to the forces of the ego, reason, and the secondary process. Only then could the old "fixated" conflicts and complexes crumble, as did the buildings of Pompeii when exposed to wind, sun, and rain after the removal of the lava covering that had preserved them unchanged for 2,000 years. Next to seeing Rome, visiting Pompeii was one of Freud's ardent wishes.[3]

In addition, Freud and Jensen had several leitmotifs in common. Freud also drew analogies between ontogenesis and phylogenesis, comparing the development of each man with the development of mankind. The victory of life and love over the forces of destruction and madness runs throughout Freud's work. And finally, they shared the theme of the revenants. Jensen referred to Zoe, appearing like an apparition of "Gradiva" amidst the ruins of Pompeii, as a *rediviva*.

> When they reached the Herculanean Gate . . . Norbert Hanold paused and asked the girl to go ahead of him. She understood him 'and pulling up her dress a little with her left hand, Zoe Bertgang, Gradiva *rediviva* walked past, held in his eyes, which seemed to gaze as though in a dream; so, with her quietly tripping gait, she stepped through the sun-

[2] Friedman (1966) tried to establish a link between the figure of the young archaeologist, with his repressed relationship to his childhood sweetheart, and Freud's screen memory of his own early childhood, on the assumption that Freud must have identified *himself* to a certain extent with the hero of Jensen's story. It is obvious that Freud was interested in the book primarily because it reproduced in a poetic way the complex process of the repression of childhood memories, of symptom formation influenced by the displaced upsurge of disguised sexualized fantasy, and the "cure" through a combination of love, reconstruction, and catharsis.

[3] See also Chapter 4, section entitled, *"Todesangst*—the Tilgner Episode."

light over the stepping-stones to the other side of the street' [1907a, p. 39f.].[4]

This is reminiscent of the *non vixit* dream whose leitmotif was "revenants" and survival, and of Freud's associations to that dream which included the birth of a daughter to Fliess several weeks prior to the dream. As we have seen, the child was named Pauline after a sister of Fliess's whose early death following a short illness had been a major traumatic event of Fliess's childhood. The infant Pauline was thus a *rediviva*. According to the *Minutes of the Vienna Psychoanalytic Society* (see Nunberg and Federn, Vol. 1, p. 266), Freud mentioned during a discussion of this and other works of Jensen's that the latter must have been attached to a little girl in his own youth. According to Jones, Jensen confirmed in a letter to Freud that his first love had been a childhood playmate who had died of T.B. at the age of 18, and that many years later he became very fond of another girl who reminded him of the first one.

In his "Gradiva" essay, Freud reported that one day there appeared in his consulting room a girl who reminded him so strongly of a previous patient of his, then dead for several years, that for a moment, despite all his efforts, he could not help identifying the visitor as the dead girl. Only one thought came to mind: "So it's true after all that the dead can come back to life." The young woman before him was the sister of the deceased girl. Another *rediviva*—and a sister at that!

In this work, based on an artist's use of dreams and delusions, Freud permitted himself to deal with the problem of death and immortality in a manner more poetic than scientific. Immortality was seen in the continuity of "Zoe," life, arising out of the ashes. It is this immortality, exemplified by evolution, which is represented in the genetic principle that everything arises out of something which existed prior to it. It is a concept of immortality without mystic or religious connotations.

---

[4] The following episode which had occurred in 1882 was described by Freud in one of his betrothal letters and quoted by Jones as follows: "You don't seem to know how observant I am. Do you remember how in our walk with Minna along the *Beethovengang* you kept going aside to pull up your stockings? It is bold of me to mention it, but I hope you don't mind." There had to be an apology for even a milder allusion. Contrasting her with the robust woman of 2,000 years ago, he remarked that the foot of the Venus di Milo would cover two of hers. "Forgive the comparison, but the antique lady has no hands" (Jones, Vol. 1, p. 128).

Could the memory of this episode including the name *Beethovengang* (so similar to Bertgang) and the comparison between Martha's foot and that of the Venus di Milo have been an added determinant for Freud's interest in the Gradiva story?

9

DISCIPLES AND FRIENDS—
REVIVAL OF OLD CONFLICTS

JUNG

On May 26, 1907, Freud wrote Jung:

Dear Colleague,
Many thanks for your praise of the "Gradiva"! You won't believe
how few people are capable of doing just that; it is actually the first time
that I have heard a friendly word about it. . . . This time I knew my
little work deserved praise; *it was written during sunny days and I derived great pleasure from doing it* [L. 124*; italics added].[1]

Freud himself acknowledged how much it meant to him to have the
importance of his work recognized by such prominent men as Bleuler
and Jung. It is true that Freud was to a certain extent proud of his
isolation, of the fact that he had created a new science single-handedly.
But he was human enough to want his discoveries to become universally known, tested, and, if proven true, accepted. He was fully aware
that all he could do by himself was to open doors and show the way;
psychoanalysis would need scores of co-workers to continue its development. He was also fully aware that psychoanalysis was applicable
in various ways to all disciplines dealing with human behavior.

[1] Freud's relationship to Jung has been described in detail by Freud himself in his
autobiographical writings, by Jones (Vol. 2), and recently in the autobiography of
Jung (1961) who presents his own version of the relationship. Freud also carried
on an extensive correspondence with Jung which I have had the privilege of reading.
In the context of this study, I shall touch only on very specific aspects of this relationship.

People who had imagination and a wide range of interests always appealed to Freud, and Jung certainly had these qualifications. He also had the attraction of novelty, being different in every respect from the academic and professional circles which were Freud's milieu.

Although some of the elements of the earlier relationship with Fliess showed up in this new relationship with Jung, Freud was wary. Some of his letters dating from these years show us that Freud's self-analysis, especially as it involved his relationship to Fliess, was still going on. Its progress was reflected not only in Freud's development as a scientist, but in every other aspect of his life—including his death.

The importance of the letter of May 26, 1907 lies not only in its contents, pointing to "sunny days" but in its date as well. It was written shortly after Freud's 51st birthday. While what we would now call the "autonomous, nonconflictual ego" of Freud knew that the "critical periods" worked out by Fliess were meaningless, there lingered in him a residue of the obsessive superstition that 51 was in fact a "critical" age. It is apparent from Freud's correspondence that these "critical" phases were believed to extend over a period of months both preceding and following the actual birthday.[2] Hence it is important that Freud should speak of "sunny days" at this time. The beginnings of international recognition, the financial security which he had now attained at least temporarily, and perhaps also the satisfaction he felt in having passed the fateful "deadline" undoubtedly contributed to those "sunny days." Freud must also have overcome the pain he had felt at Fliess's attack on him in 1906, feelings which he expressed with unusual vehemence in a letter of January 12, 1906 to Karl Kraus, a Viennese writer and journalist (L. 122*).

The letter which Freud wrote to Jung on April 16, 1909 has been quoted in connection with Freud's obsessive-superstitious preoccupation with the date of his own death, and as a link between the *non vixit* dream, which manifested the intensity of his ambivalence toward Fliess, and his derealization on the Acropolis (see Chapter 7).

But this same letter is important for many other reasons. Freud ostensibly described the intensification into a symptom of his superstitious preoccupation with death dates during his 1904 Athens trip in order to show Jung that one must analyze one's "superstitions," which is how he classified Jung's telepathic experiments. But Freud admitted

[2] See Freud's letters in 1918 (Chapter 11).

that he was deeply impressed by Jung's "communications" and experiments. We know from Jung's description of the episode referred to in Freud's letter of April 16, 1909 that Jung had revealed to Freud the extent of his mystical preoccupations and convictions (see Jung, 1961, p. 159f.).

Curious to know Freud's general attitude toward "precognition and parapsychology," Jung claimed he raised the question with Freud, who allegedly characterized these concepts as "nonsense" out of his "materialistic prejudice." While Freud was developing his arguments, Jung had "a peculiar sensation" as though his diaphragm were made of iron which was starting to get red-hot—"a red-hot diaphragm vault." At the same moment there was such a crash in the bookcase standing beside them[3] that both men became terribly frightened. Jung claimed that this was a "catalytic exteriorization phenomenon." When Freud protested against this "explanation," Jung predicted that another crash would follow shortly, and in fact it did. Jung never knew why he felt so sure of his prediction. As Freud looked horrified at all this, Jung (rightly) inferred that Freud had been left with feelings of distrust, and Jung himself felt that he had done something harmful to Freud.[4] Jung claimed that he never spoke further to Freud about the matter. I would suspect, however, that Freud was more horrified at Jung's utterances than at the cracking sounds in his bookcase!

We know that Freud, despite his skepticism and insistence on scientific scrutiny, was reluctant to reject *a priori* as mere fantasy even those phenomena which seemed to be nothing else, and was ready to assume that there were "more things in Heaven and earth . . . than are dreamt of in [your] philosophy" [Shakespeare: *Hamlet,* I.5].

We have already seen in the Fliess correspondence an acknowledgment by Freud of possible "heavenly influences" on human affairs (letter of October 8, 1896; see Chapter 4).

In the 1907 edition of the last chapter of *The Psychopathology of Everyday Life* Freud discussed the problem of "extrasensory perception," indicating his basically open-minded attitude on this issue.

Though we admit that these remarks of ours in no way exhaust the psychology of superstition, we shall at least have to touch on the question of whether we are to deny entirely that superstition has any real

---

3 According to Freud's description in his letter, this bookcase was in the next room.

4 A critical evaluation of Jung's description of this incident is beyond the scope of this study.

roots; whether there are definitely no such things as true presentiments, prophetic dreams, telepathic experiences, manifestations of supernatural forces and the like. I am far from meaning to pass so sweeping a condemnation of these phenomena, of which so many detailed observations have been made even by men of outstanding intellect, and which it would be best to make the subject of further investigations. We may even hope that some portion of these observations will then be explained by our growing recognition of unconscious mental processes, without necessitating radical alterations in the views we hold to-day. If the existence of still other phenomena—those, for example, claimed by spiritualists—were to be established, we should merely set about modifying our 'laws' in the way demanded by the new discovery, without being shaken in our belief in the coherence of things in the world.

In the compass of these discussions the only answer I can give to the questions raised here is a subjective one—that is, one in accordance with my personal experience. To my regret I must confess that I am one of those unworthy people in whose presence spirits suspend their activity and the supernatural vanishes away, so that I have never been in a position to experience anything myself which might arouse a belief in the miraculous. Like every human being, I have had presentiments and experienced trouble, but the two failed to coincide with one another, so that nothing followed the presentiments, and the trouble came upon me unannounced. During the days when I was living alone in a foreign city—I was a young man at the time—I quite often heard my name suddenly called by an unmistakable and beloved voice; I then noted down the exact moment of the hallucination and made anxious enquiries of those at home about what had happened at that time. Nothing had happened. To balance this, there was a later occasion when I went on working with my patients without any disturbance or foreboding while one of my children was in danger of bleeding to death. Nor have I ever been able to regard any of the presentiments reported to me by patients as veridical. [Added in 1924:] I must however confess that in the last few years I have had a few remarkable experiences which might easily have been explained on the hypothesis of telepathic thought-transference [1901b, p. 260ff.].

This attitude of Freud's was understandable: he himself had discovered things which had been scorned as wild fantasies by the academic world. It thus behooved him to think twice before branding other opinions as the outgrowth of wild imagination.

In this period there were occasional signs of Freud's fatalistic preoccupation. In the aforementioned letter to Jung of May 26, 1907 Freud tried to prepare the latter for the harsh opposition he would encounter, but also encouraged Jung not to be distressed by claims that analysis furnished no proof of the correctness of its hypotheses.

But just let five to ten years go by and analysis . . . which is inconclusive at the moment, will have become conclusive without anything about it having changed. The only thing to do is to go ahead and work, not waste too much energy on refutations, and let the fertility of our ideas have its effect on the sterility of those we are fighting against. . . .

And yet, don't worry, everything will turn out all right. *You will live to see it, even if I don't.* We aren't the first who have had to wait for the world to understand their language [L. 124*; italics added].[5]

Taken in conjunction with his advice to "wait five or ten years" the next-to-last sentence of this letter contains a hint that Freud did not expect to live beyond his next "deadline" (61-62).

In his next letter to Jung (August 18, 1907) Freud expressed in even stronger terms that their work should be looked upon *sub specie aeternitatis,* i.e., from a historical, developmental point of view (see also Chapter 15).

It is immaterial whether or not one is understood by official representatives at the moment. Among the masses who anonymously hide behind them, there are enough people who *want* to understand and who, as I have often seen happen, will suddenly step forth. After all, one works primarily for the annals of history. . . . [L. 125*].

More details were given about this theme in the next letter (September 2, 1907). This probably marked the high point of Freud's attempts to encourage and help Jung by opening up the vista of an important cause and offering the younger man his friendship.

Whether you have been or will be lucky or unlucky I don't know; but I would like to be with you at just this time to enjoy the sensation of being no longer isolated, and to tell you, in case you need some encouragement, of my many years of honorable but painful isolation which started after I had had my first glimpse into the new world; of my closest friends' lack of interest and understanding; of the anxious periods when I myself believed I had been mistaken and wondered how I could still turn to advantage a bungled life for the sake of my family; of the gradually growing conviction that kept clinging to the interpretation of dreams as to a rock in a stormy sea, and of the calm assurance that finally took possession of me and bade me wait till a voice from the unknown answered mine. That voice was yours; I also realize now that Bleuler can be traced back to you. Let me thank you for this, and don't lose confidence that you will live to see and enjoy victory.

Luckily I don't as yet have to claim your sympathy for my suffering

[5] See also Freud's letter of November 25, 1900 to Fliess where he compared himself to Humboldt's parrot (Chapter 6).

condition. I am celebrating my entrance into the climacteric age with a dyspepsia (following influenza) which proved rather stubborn but which, during these beautiful weeks of tranquility, has receded except for some very slight reminders [L. 126*].

When Jung received Freud's letter of April 16, 1909 (quoted in Chapter 7), he did not answer it for many weeks and finally wrote that he would give serious consideration to Freud's "admonition," adding that everyone after all wished to discover something essentially new.

However, Jung's "experiments," and even more so his explanations, far exceeded general claims to the validity of extrasensory perception. As a result, Freud felt obliged to warn himself: "Beware of this brilliant young man; you have just chosen him as your successor, but he is already after your crown like Henry IV. Also—remember Fliess!"

This letter to Jung probably marked the beginning of the end of Freud's relationship with him. Although their association continued for 3 more years, Jung's response to Freud's letter did not augur well for the continuation of their relationship. But Freud was still far from convinced that a break between them was inevitable.

Cordiality was quickly restored between Freud and Jung, and the two men undertook a joint trip to the United States that same year. This was a period when all the future analysts such as Jung, Ferenczi, and others, were pouring out their secrets and problems to Freud, and he was "analyzing" them during trips, walks, through correspondence, etc. It took Freud many years to learn the importance of a regular training analysis, and to recognize that the procedure he had utilized at the beginning with what he thought were basically healthy people had often increased the intensity of their unresolved conflicts. We know from Jones that Jung used to talk with Freud for hours on end.

I have already mentioned the continuous "analysis" which Freud carried on with his pupil-colleagues during meetings and joint travels. At this early stage of the development of psychoanalysis this was the only way in which Freud could share his experiences with his pupils and try to elucidate their conflicts. Occasionally Freud recounted dreams of his own, as he apparently did during the crossing to America, and submitted them to joint interpretation. This was probably more than others—especially Jung—could tolerate.

Freud's trip to the United States, which he made in order to deliver a series of lectures at Clark University in Worcester, Mass., has been described by himself in his *Autobiography* and in great detail by Jones

(Vol. 2, Ch. 2). Both during and after the trip Freud suffered from gastrointestinal symptoms. According to Jones, he also had an attack of appendicitis[6] and prostatic discomfort (frequency) while in the United States.

Freud grumbled for some years afterward about the dyspepsia which he had presumably acquired from American cooking, and he several times "took the cure" at Karlsbad.[7]

FERENCZI

The Second International Congress, held in Nuremberg (the first had taken place in Salzburg in 1908) led Freud to write to Ferenczi on April 3, 1910:

> With the Nuremberg *Reichstag* closes the childhood of our movement. I hope now for a rich and happy time of youth [see Jones, Vol. 2, p. 71].

In September, 1910 Freud took Ferenczi along on a trip to Sicily where they saw not only Palermo and Syracuse but the wonderful Greek temples in Segesta, Girgenti, and Selinunte.

When Freud traveled, especially in Italy, he was eager to soak in all the beauty of the landscape, but especially of the works of art. He was indefatigable in his quest to take advantage of opportunities which were denied to him during the years of utter frugality.

When he took a companion along, he wanted somebody who would keep up with his tempo and to some extent also share his interests, and spare him undue demands. With the growth of the International Psychoanalytic Association, Freud had to see an increasing number of visitors from various countries during his summer vacations. Some of his close friends were also his disciples. They eagerly sought his advice in the handling of their patients and his guidance in their research. During this period when personal analysis was not yet a prerequisite to becoming an analyst and when Freud was the only training analyst,

---

[6] Jones mentions a "definite, though mild attack of appendicitis," citing as a reference a letter by Freud to Ferenczi of January 2, 1910, and also speaks of a "recurrence of his old appendicular pain" (Vol. 2, p. 59f.). During the time Freud was under my care, there was no evidence of any past appendicitis.

[7] This "cure," which consisted of drinking considerable amounts of mildly laxative, warm Karlsbad water pumped directly from natural springs, was at that time a standard prescription for a variety of gastrointestinal and biliary symptoms. Karlsbad also had beautiful woods, good hotels, and excellent food—comforts provided by all European spas in those decades.

they also made use of their correspondence as a substitute for personal analysis.

Jones, who throughout his Freud biography was quite critical of Ferenczi, specifically when he discussed Ferenczi's behavior on this trip to Sicily, described his own visit with the Freud family, then vacationing on the Dutch coast prior to Freud's trip, as follows: "I spent a few days with them . . . and had many interesting talks with Freud. *I poured out a stream of questions* which he answered most patiently" [italics added].

Freud showed utmost patience on other occasions as well. When I perused his correspondence in preparation for this book, I was amazed again and again that Freud always found the time to answer every letter within a few days, and dealt not only with scientific questions, but with the host of personal problems presented to him.

But on a vacation trip which represented not just a period of rest, but a time to give his inquisitive mind new food for creative thoughts in many areas Freud needed some protection. He could not silence his dreams and escape his self-analysis, but neither could he fulfill every demand of his travel companion.

Ferenczi, during their trip, apparently could not adjust fully to this piece of reality. A letter by Freud of October 6, 1910, was probably written in answer to an apologetic letter from Ferenczi after his return to Budapest.

October 6, 1910

Dear Friend,

　　It is remarkable how much more clearly you can express yourself in writing than in speaking. Naturally I knew very much or most of what you write and now need to give you only a few explanations. Why I didn't give you a scolding and so opened the way to a mutual understanding? Quite true, it was weak of me. I am not the psychoanalytical superman that you construed in your imagination, nor have I overcome the counter-transference. I couldn't treat you in that way, any more than I could have my three sons because I am too fond of them and should feel sorry for them.

　　You not only noticed, but also understood, that I *no longer* have any need to uncover my personality completely, and you correctly traced this back to the traumatic reason for it. Since Fliess's case, with *the overcoming of which you recently saw me occupied, that need has been extinguished. A part of homosexual cathexis has been withdrawn and made use of to enlarge my own ego.* I have succeeded where the paranoiac fails [italics added].

　　Moreover, you should know that I was less well, and suffered more

from my intestinal trouble, than I was willing to admit. I often said to
myself that whoever is not master of his Konrad[8] should not set out on
travels. That is where the frankness should have begun, but you did
not seem to me stable enough to avoid becoming over-anxious about
me.

As for the unpleasantness you caused me, including a certain passive
resistance, it will undergo the same change as memories of travels in
general: one refines them, the small disturbances vanish and what was
beautiful remains for one's intellectual pleasure.

That you surmised I had great secrets, and were very curious about
them, was plain to see and also easy to recognize as infantile. Just as I
told you *everything* on scientific matters I concealed very little of a
personal nature; the incident of the *Nationalgeschenk*[9] was, I think, indiscreet enough. My dreams at that time were concerned, as I hinted to
you, entirely with the Fliess affair, which in the nature of things would
be hard to arouse your sympathy.

So when you look at it more closely you will find that we haven't so
much to settle between us as perhaps you thought at first.

I would rather turn your attention to the present . . . [quoted in
Jones, Vol. 2, p. 83f.].

This letter is characteristic of Freud's utter frankness. As he himself
remarked, he liked Ferenczi too much to treat him other than he would
have treated one of his three sons. And the same frankness extended
to his own innermost problems. For this reason, this letter is an important document. It gives us another intimate glimpse into the working of Freud's self-analysis. The manner in which the letter was written
shows us on the one hand that even in 1910, six years after the 1904
episode, his self-analysis was still concerned with the Fliess affair,
which he himself called "traumatic" in the letter. On the other hand,
the letter clearly suggests Freud's growing mastery of his conflicts.

In his correspondence with Fliess, Freud had spoken frankly about
"a certain, almost feminine side" of his personality which had made
him seek Fliess's friendship; he had expressed his disappointment that
Breuer lacked the potential for understanding "what achievements can
result from the sublimation of the androphile current in man" (see
Chapter 6). In this letter Freud did not hesitate to refer to the "homosexual cathexis" of his relationship to Fliess.

8 The name Konrad was first used by the Swiss writer Spitteler to personify his
body in his 1904 novel *Imago*. *Imago* then became the name of a journal dealing
with what is now called applied psychoanalysis.
Especially in his correspondence with Abraham, Freud used to refer to his "Konrad" whenever he was suffering from gastrointestinal symptoms.
9 A jocular allusion to Freud's fondness for acquiring antiquities.

While we cannot tell with any degree of certainty why during this trip Freud was once again intensely preoccupied with Fliess, we may gain some understanding by carefully looking at the scientific problems which occupied Freud's mind at that time.

In the spring of 1910 Freud had finished a study of Leonardo da Vinci. As early as October 9, 1898, Freud had mentioned in a letter to Fliess that perhaps the most famous left-handed individual was Leonardo, who is not known to have had any love affairs (L. 98). The genesis of a particular type of homosexuality plays an important part in this study.

We also learn from Strachey's introduction to Freud's "Psycho-Analytic Notes on an Autobiographical Account of a Case of Paranoia" (1911c) that Freud read Schreber's memoirs during the summer of 1910, and "is known to have talked of them, and of the whole question of paranoia, during his Sicilian tour with Ferenczi in September of that year" (p. 3). The connection between repressed homosexuality and paranoia is one of the main themes of Freud's study of the Schreber case.[10]

Thus we have once again an example of the intricate interplay between Freud's discoveries and his self-analysis. It is therefore not surprising that at this point the problem of homosexuality and along with it his relationship to Fliess once more had to be worked through, particularly, if we must consider the possibility that Freud's relationship to Jung contributed to the revival of the old conflict. However, Freud stated that he had succeeded in enlarging his ego where the paranoiac fails. Such "enlarging of the ego" was essential not only for the progress of his science, but also for his ability to overcome inner conflicts and fears.

As usual, letters to a variety of correspondents provided him, among other things, with an outlet for a certain amount of complaining, and also occasionally revealed his intimate thoughts on illness, aging, and death. It is apparent from the letters of this period that Freud felt no fear of death but rather an utter dislike of aging, especially if this entailed a loss or even a decline of his creative powers.

---

[10] After completion of this manuscript, I received from Dr. M. Balint a transcript of Freud's October 6, 1910 letter to Ferenczi quoted above. Freud ends with the following paragraph:

> I surely have not yet written that I have worked through the Schreber [Memoirs] once, that I found the core of our paranoia hypotheses corroborated, as well as all sorts of material lending itself to solid interpretation [1].

PFISTER

One of his correspondents was the Swiss clergyman-analyst Oskar Pfister, a true idealist for whom Freud developed a great liking, as evidenced in such passages as the following from his letter of August 16, 1909:

> I do not know what promises you left behind with my children, because I keep hearing things like next year I'm going with Dr. Pfister, I'm going climbing with him, and so on and so forth. I dare not mention your 10,000-foot climb with your son, because it would rouse my boys' blackest envy; they would wish they had a father like you, who could still climb with them instead of being tormented by his Konrad and picking strawberries in the woods down below. . . .
> [With regard to his work and productivity:]
> Fortunately I am no longer so necessary and can gradually shrink into an ornament; perhaps there is a bit of providence in that.

In his letter to Pfister of March 6, 1910, written before the Nuremberg Congress, Freud revealed an attitude toward aging and death to which he held for the rest of his life. At the point of writing this letter Freud had completed the case histories of Little Hans and the Rat Man as well as a series of shorter papers, prepared a new edition of the *Three Essays on the Theory of Sexuality,* and started his essay on Leonardo da Vinci, all the while preparing for the Congress and recovering from his trip to the United States. It is thus not surprising that he should write:

> I cannot face with comfort the idea of life without work; work and the free play of the imagination are for me the same thing, I take no pleasure in anything else. That would be a recipe for happiness but for the appalling thought that productivity is entirely dependent on a sensitive disposition. What would one do when ideas failed or words refused to come? It is impossible not to shudder at the thought. Hence, in spite of all the acceptance of fate which is appropriate to an honest man, I have one quite secret prayer: that I may be spared any wasting away and crippling of my ability to work because of physical deterioration.
> In the words of King Macbeth, let us die in harness.[11]

---

[11] This quotation is not quite accurate. Macbeth's statement in a hopeless situation, where he faced overwhelmingly superior armed forces, was: "At least we'll die with harness on our backs." This was an expression of desperate defiance, not of hope for uninterrupted productivity, as in Freud's case.

We shall see how cruelly fate was to deny this secret wish to be spared ("shrinking" as his father had done).

A DISTURBING EPISODE

During the winter of 1910-1911 an incident occurred which caused Freud to have some disquieting symptoms for several weeks: severe headaches, difficulties in concentration, a feeling of confusion. Freud had reported some of his complaints to Jung, who considered them to be "psychogenic." On February 17, 1911 Freud was able to report:

> Dear Friend,
> I see that you don't believe me and think of me as a cyclothymic who with the passing of time is suddenly inclined to see the world through rose-colored glasses. So I must give you further details. During the day no smell of gas was perceptible because with the spigot closed no gas could escape. At night, however, between 10 P.M. and 1 A.M. when I sat near the light on the writing desk, gas escaped from a loose connection between the metal gaspipe and the rubber tubing to which the flue of the lamp was attached. When a test was made at this spot a flame shot up. I didn't smell anything because I sat enveloped by cigar smoke while the gas was slowly infiltrating into the atmosphere. I am still very proud that I didn't attribute to neurosis the peculiar headaches which set in or became intensified only during work at night and the annoying trouble I had with my memory so that I constantly had to ask myself who said this and when did that happen, etc. However, I must admit that I had resigned myself to an arteriosclerotic condition. Now that specter has vanished without any trace. The headache slowly disappeared within 3 days after the rubber tubing was changed [2].

Freud's description of this potentially dangerous episode shows clearly how his scientific curiosity prevailed even in such circumstances.

BINSWANGER

The Binswanger correspondence provides an important source of information for the years 1911 and 1912, during which time Freud was constantly thinking about "the cause," as he called psychoanalysis. In line with the Moses theme, his concern was with his successor. Among his Viennese students there was no one he could visualize in this role; hence the importance of Jung. Binswanger (1956) quotes a pertinent passage from a letter which Freud wrote to him on March 14, 1911:

When the empire I founded is orphaned, no one but Jung must inherit
the whole thing. As you see, my politics incessantly pursues this aim. . . .

In letters to Binswanger Freud occasionally permitted himself to
voice some complaints. Binswanger, in turn, was given comfort when
illness or death struck, and a sharing of his happiness when new life
had come into being. Two letters to Binswanger reflect Freud's reactions to the polarities of death and birth. The first was Freud's response
to Binswanger's letter announcing the death of his father on December
6, 1910:

> The few grave words in which you announce to me your father's death
> say more than long speeches would. We, who are further removed
> from him, will envy him for the end of his fruitless sufferings and the
> fine quick death; what this death means to the son, we do not try to
> divine from our respectful distance. As to whether he was happy, we
> know that he was successful in his work and that he has left behind
> children like you: this is not little. I beg you in the name of my wife
> and children to convey our sympathy to your entire family. A cordial
> handshake to yourself.

When shortly thereafter Binswanger notified Freud of the birth of
his daughter (he already had a son), Freud wrote (January 30, 1911):

> Only extreme pressure of time can excuse these belated good wishes
> on the occasion of the birth of your daughter. Now you are a father in
> every sense of the word, and you have twice experienced the most re-
> markable thing there is in life. May she prosper and give joy to her
> charming mother and yourself.

Nothing better expresses the impact of Freud's letters on Binswanger
than the comments of this rather shy, "sober" scientist who was not
given to expansive emotionalism.

> As I have said, I do not intend to write a commentary on each of
> Freud's letters for I am convinced that the human figure that bears the
> name of Freud has often been criticized for his allegedly cold rational-
> ism. I should like to call the reader's attention to the above passage. It
> shows that he had a warm heart, that he took a lively interest in our
> general human lot—the *condition humaine* with its "remarkable
> things," such as births or deaths—and that his wonder at the riddles of
> human existence did not prevent him from sharing his friends' joys
> and sorrows [p. 28].

Freud did not hesitate to express the doubts which occasionally beset him. On May 28, 1911 he wrote to Binswanger:

It is certainly a friend's business to dispel the gloomy thoughts that creep up on an aging man. Nor shall I complain. Indeed, most often I too believe that I have begun something that will occupy the minds of men for a long time; sometimes, I am assailed by dissatisfaction with its extension and deepening, and there come slight doubts as to the future. The truth is, *there is nothing for which man's capabilities are less suited than psychoanalysis.*

Freud was also fully aware that it was his destiny to "disturb the peace[12] of this world" (letter to Binswanger of September 10, 1911). In a Christmas (1911) letter to Binswanger, he wrote that the latter might live to see the day when psychoanalysis would be accepted and acknowledged, and that he would then be proud to have been numbered among the rebels in his youth. To which Freud then added: "Don't worry about me; I can not at all wish to live to *such an old age.*"

Binswanger underwent surgery in 1912 for what turned out to be a highly malignant tumor. The patient dryly remarked that the average survival rate after such surgery was 1 to 3 years. Fortunately, the tumor had been detected early, and Binswanger survived for over 50 years more!

It was only to Freud that Binswanger confided the facts of his illness, and he rightly never forgot Freud's response to this confidence. Freud felt honored by the trust of a strong and valuable man who in a moment of severe stress had stretched out his hand to an older friend. Freud's answer (April 14, 1912) to Binswanger's letter is an example of what K. R. Eissler, in reviewing Freud's published letters, called "Mankind at Its Best" (1964).

I, an old man, who will have no right to complain if his life ends in a few years (and I have decided not to complain) am particularly pained when one of my flowering young men—one of those who were supposed to continue my own life—tells me that he has become uncertain of his life. I have gradually composed myself and recalled that despite the present doubts you still have every chance, and that you have only been reminded more forcefully of the uncertainty which keeps all of us in suspense, and which we so readily forget. Now you won't forget it, and life, as you write, will have for you a special and enhanced charm. Moreover, we shall hope for what our present knowledge permits us to think of without any self-deception. Naturally I shall keep the secret, in accordance with your wishes. But it is natural that I should desire to

[12] In Hebbel's *Gyges und sein Ring* (V. 1), which Freud quotes, the word is not "peace," but "sleep."

see you as soon as I can do so without inconveniencing you. How about Whitsun? You will write to me whether this is all right with you. I am glad to learn that you are at present more interested in your project than before, and now I will hasten to answer all your other questions, which testify to your interest in everything that goes on in our circle.

There was no exaggerated expression of hope but rather a restatement of the attitude Freud had first expressed in a letter to his daughter Mathilda,[13] namely, that life gains rather than loses in value when one is aware of its limits; that one may hope without harboring illusions, an attitude toward death of serene acceptance Freud was to express even more eloquently in his essay "On Transience" (1916a).

Freud then turned to a discussion of their work, adding probably in response to a letter of Binswanger's:

I have always thought that self-reliance and natural self-confidence are the indispensable conditions of that which appears to us to be greatness if it has led to success. I also think that a distinction must be made between greatness of achievement and greatness of personality [p. 40].

Freud visited Binswanger a few weeks later in Kreuzlingen. The whole episode of Binswanger's illness and Freud's reactions to it had both long-range and immediate reverberations. In 1919 Freud lost a devoted patient and friend, Anton von Freund, from the same type of malignancy as Binswanger's and this tragedy found him in a very vulnerable mood. When, in 1923, Freud's friends and physicians discovered his malignancy, they did not reveal the truth to him, failing to duplicate the frankness, trust, and respect that Freud and Binswanger had shown each other in the latter's crisis.

The immediate reverberations of the Binswanger episode had to do with the mounting crisis in Freud's relationship to Jung, the details of which have been described at length by Jones. What interests us in the context of this study is the critical situation which developed in November, 1912, when Freud had come to realize that the scientific differences between him and Jung had carried them beyond any possibility of fruitful collaboration.

---

[13] You have, my poor child, seen death break into the family for the first time, or heard about it, and perhaps shuddered at the idea that for none of us can life be made any safer. This is something all we old people know, which is why life for us has such a special value. We refuse to allow the inevitable end to interfere with our happy activities. So you, who are still so young, may as well confess that you really have no reason to be downhearted. I am very pleased to hear that the sun in Meran is doing you good . . . [L. 137*].

Jung did not know why Freud had gone to visit Binswanger in Kreuzlingen (which is not far from Zürich), and he felt jealous and slighted because Freud had not visited him during the same trip or at least arranged for a meeting. Actually, as it turned out later, Freud had notified Jung in time, but the latter had been out of town and had not checked the date of arrival of Freud's letter. Jung kept referring in his increasingly irritable correspondence to the "Kreuzlingen gesture."

Freud wrote Binswanger on July 29, 1912 that he was trying to separate scientific from personal problems with Jung in an effort to avoid a break, but that he was in any case not really pained by Jung's behavior.

> I am completely indifferent. Warned by earlier experiences, and proud of my elasticity, I withdrew my libido from him months ago, at the first signs, and I miss nothing now. Also, this time things are easier for me, for I can redistribute the quantity of libido that has been set free in new places, such as with you, Ferenczi, Rank, Sachs, Abraham, Jones, Brill, and others.

The first words indicate how clearly Freud recognized a certain similarity in his relationships to Jung and Fliess. But they also show that he had been forewarned, so that the later relationship was by no means a repetition of the earlier one.

FAINTING SPELLS AND THEIR MEANING

Freud did not feel well later that summer, and for the first time since his cardiac episode he mentioned his heart in letters to Binswanger and Jones. On September 22, 1912 Freud wrote to Binswanger from Rome:

> One line of your letter tempted me to telegraph to Constance: I too am in Italy! Come here to the Hotel Eden, Via Ludovisi. The fact that I didn't telegraph was only partly due to the consideration that my company would mean to you an effort and not a rest; the stronger motive was that I felt in very poor health myself. I have a few weeks of misery behind me, with the diagnosis unclear as usual. If one may judge *ex juvantibus*,[14] after Karlsbad I was suddenly unable to tolerate my customary smoking and the drinking that was added to it in the

[14] A common term indicating that the diagnosis was being deduced from the therapy which had helped the illness; in Freud's case, abstinence from wine and nicotine which had brought about or coincided with a subsiding of his symptoms.

Tyrol. And so I suppose the heart rebelled; everyone will now construe psychic influence to account for this, only I beg you not to accuse Jung too much. Enough, I am recovering here after all kinds of relapses, and I think now, after almost renouncing the Roman red wine, that I am on the way to my former state of health. I am very happy in Rome, in fact each time I am here, this time particularly so. . . . With regard to Jung I am willing to take any step leading to an outward reconciliation, but inwardly nothing will change any more. . . .

It is probable that a combination of factors precipitated Freud's indisposition: he may have overdone the "cure" in Karlsbad; he had interrupted his vacation to rush to Vienna because his eldest daughter Mathilde had again fallen ill; while he had not taken his growing disenchantment with Jung too hard, he may have underestimated the disappointment he felt and the extent of his concern for the future development of "the cause." Moreover, Jung's defection had stirred up painful old conflicts.

It was Jones who suggested that the causes of Freud's symptoms might be "psychogenic," his anxiety about his daughter and about his "mental child"—psychoanalysis—combining to give him trouble. Freud answered Jones on the same day as he wrote to Binswanger.

What you construed about the *Verdichtung* [condensation] of the two daughters sounds so ingenious that I dare not contradict it, the more so as it gave you the occasion for promises which touch my ear as music might another man. Of course there is a great difficulty, if not impossibility, in recognizing actual psychical processes in one's own person. To me the physical side must be more evident, the sudden intolerance of the heart muscle for tobacco and it seems even more for wine. My last improvement here is due to a great restriction of the delicious Roman wine I was indulging in. . . . We will shake hands in a few days [Jones, Vol 2, p. 96].

Actually, both Jones's interpretation and Freud's answer were oversimplifications. The overdetermination of such somatic symptoms is much more complex.

An actual "crisis" with Jung occurred later that year when Freud met with Jung, Jones, Abraham, and some other colleagues to discuss organizational and editorial matters. Freud talked privately with Jung and confronted him with his peculiar "slip" (ignoring the date of Freud's letter) which had led to his denunciation of the so-called "Kreuzlingen gesture." Jung became defensive and apologetic. At the luncheon which followed, Freud pursued his criticism and suddenly "fell on the floor in a dead faint," as Jones reported. Jung carried him to a couch where his first words upon regaining consciousness, according to Jones (Vol. 1, p. 317), were: "How sweet it must be to die!" ("Es muss süss sein zu sterben" in the German translation of Jone's biography [1960].)

Freud himself commented freely on the meaning of this incident in his correspondence with Ferenczi, Jones, and Binswanger. In considering "meaning" we must distinguish between the *cause* of such a somatic response as fainting and the *meaning* it assumes.

A "resomatization"[15] of this kind usually has complex multiple determinants; the somatic equivalents of intense affective reactions, related at times to conscious, but often at the given moment to unconscious events, combine with various physiological factors. I have previously mentioned a certain propensity on Freud's part to respond with "vasovagal reflex reactions" (see Chapter 2).

Freud's comments on this incident complement each other, indicating on the one hand that he was submitting it to the scrutiny of self-analysis and on the other that he never neglected the aspect of overdetermination—including specific somatic factors.

Freud reported this incident to Ferenczi, who was not present during the Munich meeting, two days after it happened, on November 26, 1912:

> Jung said good-bye around 5 [P.M.] with the following words: you will find me fully on the side of the cause. We stayed together until the time of leavetaking. Unfortunately I had not had a good day. Tired from a week [of work] and a sleepless night on the train, I had an anxiety attack at the table, similar to the one I had had at the Essighaus[16] in Bremen. I tried to get up and fainted for a moment. I got up

---

[15] "Desomatization" and "resomatization" are terms suggested by me (1953, 1955) for the conceptualization of the following processes: On the one hand, I assume a parallel development and mutual interdependence between secondary processes, the maturation of the motor apparatus, the development of the central nervous system, and the stabilization of homeostatic processes. This results in an increasing *desomatization* of reactions to certain excitations. The development tends toward maximal use of integrated automatization of muscle action, replacement of action by thought, and reduction of vegetative discharge phenomena. The desirable result is mastery of excitations with a minimum consumption of energy. This desomatization is an essential part of our maturation. Any disturbance of this development represents a danger to the economy of our existence. On the other hand, I assume that in states of "regression" of certain ego functions this developmental path can be reversed, which may result in a "resomatization" of responses. This implies that affective responses may be accompanied by a great variety of somatic symptoms. These concepts have proved to be fruitful for our understanding of psychosomatic phenomena.

[16] The name of a restaurant.

by myself, however, and felt nauseous for some time; in the evening, the nausea gave way to headache and yawning. . . .

I slept splendidly during the night on the trip to Vienna, and I arrived here completely well [3].

As I indicated previously, the problem of "taking one's father's place" played a role in the meetings of Freud and Jung. Just before they boarded the ship in Bremen for the transatlantic voyage, Freud and Ferenczi persuaded Jung to relinquish his strict abstinence from alcohol and take some wine at lunch. Freud then pointed out to Jung (according to Jones, Vol. 2, p. 146) the operation of certain unconscious death wishes on his part against Freud, to which Jung strongly objected (see also Jung, 1961, p. 160f.). During this discussion Freud suddenly fainted.

Ferenczi, in his answer of November 28, made the following comment on the fainting episode:

I don't know how this idea came to me, the fact remains, however, that during those days I wondered whether the indisposition you had in Bremen might not repeat itself in Munich. (At that time in Bremen we interpreted it as reaction to Jung's apostasy from anti-alcoholism.)[17] [4].

To Jones Freud wrote on December 8, 1912:

I cannot forget that six and four years ago I suffered from a very similar though not as intense symptom in the *same* room of the Park Hotel. I saw Munich first when I visited Fliess during his illness and this town seems to have acquired a strong connection with my relation to that man. There is some piece of unruly homosexual feeling at the root of the matter. When Jung in his last letter again hinted at my "neurosis," I could find no better expedient than proposing that every analyst should attend to his own neurosis more than to the other's. After all I think we have to be kind and patient with Jung and, as old Oliver said, keep our powder dry [Jones, Vol. 1, p. 317].

A day later, on December 9, Freud wrote another letter to Ferenczi:

I have fully regained my capacity to work, have analytically settled the dizzy spell in Munich, and even started [work] on the long-prevented third point of agreement.[18] All these attacks point to the significance of very early experiences with death (in my case a brother who died very

---

[17] Jung, like his teacher Bleuler, was an ardent anti-alcoholic.

[18] *Übereinstimmung* was the title of the first publication of *Totem and Taboo* ("Über einige Übereinstimmungen im Seelenleben der Wilden und der Neurotiker" ["Some Points of Agreement between the Mental Lives of Savages and Neurotics"]).

young, when I was a little over one year old).[19] The war atmosphere[20] dominates our daily life; my practice has not yet been affected, but it could happen to me that I would simultaneously have three sons on the war front [5].

He wrote to Binswanger on January 1, 1913, pointing out the multiple determinants of this episode:

My fainting attack in Munich was surely provoked by psychogenic elements, which received strong somatic reinforcements (a week of troubles, a sleepless night, the equivalent of a migraine, the day's tasks). I had had several such attacks; in each case there were similar contributory causes, often a bit of alcohol for which I have no tolerance. Among the psychic elements there is the fact that I had had a quite similar seizure in the same place in Munich, on two previous occasions, four and six years ago. With careful scrutiny, it seems scarcely possible to maintain that my attacks are due to a more serious cause, for instance, a weak heart. Repressed feelings, this time directed against Jung, as previously against a predecessor of his, naturally play the main part.

There are contradictions in the various accounts. For instance, Jones, who was an eye-witness to the scene, wrote that Freud "fell suddenly on the floor in a dead faint." Freud himself wrote in the first letter to Ferenczi about an anxiety attack with an attempt to rise followed by fainting. The apparent contradiction is probably due to the fact that Freud's description is based on his *memory* of a subjective experience. Slight amnesia for the actual sequence of feelings and physical manifestations is very frequent in fainting spells. An element of anxiety in fainting is nearly universal. It is, however, extremely difficult to distinguish between anxiety as the precipitating cause of such a somatic phenomenon, the anxiety as response to the manifold sensations with which one is flooded before one loses consciousness, and the anxiety which follows this sudden loss of control on so many levels. It would therefore be an oversimplification to attribute this incident to anxiety alone. Freud's later analysis of the precipitating factors is much more revealing. Naturally, this analysis took some time, whereas the first letter was written the day after Freud's return to Vienna.[21]

When Freud wrote to Jones he obviously had already worked on

[19] Actually Freud was nearly two years old at that time (see Chapter 6).
[20] Refers to one of the frequent crises during the Balkan war.
[21] The meeting took place on a Sunday. Freud returned to work on Monday, and wrote the letter to Ferenczi on Tuesday.

the analysis of this incident, which he attributed to his relationship with Fliess and to "some piece of unruly homosexual feeling at the root of the matter." Freud also indicated that he had visited Fliess in Munich during the latter's illness (in 1894; see Chapter 2)[22] and that Munich had acquired in his mind a strong connection with Fliess.[23]

One passage that is almost identical in the letters to Jones and Binswanger remains puzzling: Freud states that he had similar symptoms at the same place six and four years before. Apparently, he had had an attack resembling fainting during his visit to Fliess in Munich, which had occurred in 1894 (16 years before this episode). We have no indication that Freud was in Munich either in 1904 or 1906. Being thoroughly familiar with his yearly travels, we must assume that this could not have happened. I have not seen the original German letters, but it is not likely that Jones and Binswanger, who were familiar with Freud's handwriting, should both have misread this passage in an identical way, and we must therefore assume that it was Freud who twice made the same slip.

Freud's letter to Ferenczi written the following day is the most pertinent of the three. Should we assume that Freud's self-analysis had "penetrated" to a deeper layer during this 24-hour interval? Or was Freud willing to tell Ferenczi more because their relationship was a more intimate one?

Freud's letter to Binswanger reflects the "distance" which Freud had achieved in the meantime. He now called the episode his "fainting attack," and considered its multiple somatic and psychic determinants. Jones's interpretation of these attacks (Vol. 2, p. 146f.), which in some respects coincided with Ferenczi's, was influenced by his observations, by conversations with Freud, and by the letters written to him and to Ferenczi.

Several common denominators emerge from these various sources: The fainting spells of 1909 and 1912 had both occurred in the pres-

---

[22] We know that Freud had had another fainting spell which also related to Fliess: in 1895, when he witnessed his patient Emma's hemorrhage resulting from Fliess's blunder in leaving the iodoform gauze in her nasal cavity (see Chapter 3).

[23] Pertinent in this connection is a comparison of two interpretations which Freud used for his forgetting of the name "Monaco." In the 1907 edition of *The Psychopathology of Everyday Life* he described how he could arrive at the recovery of a forgotten name by the method of free association. He did not explain what caused him to forget this name. In the *Introductory Lectures* Freud supplemented this interpretation as follows: "Monaco is also the Italian name for Munich; and it was that town which exerted the inhibiting influence" (1916-1917, p. 111). (See also Chapter 5, footnote 14).

ence of Jung. On both occasions Freud had drunk some wine. On both occasions certain problems pertaining to death and death wishes had been discussed—in 1909, in connection with the discovery of some prehistoric human skeletons; in 1912, in connection with Abraham's essay on the Egyptian Pharaoh Amenhotep.[24] Jones emphasizes that on both occasions Freud had "won a little victory" over Jung. In 1909, Freud and Ferenczi had "seduced" Jung into giving up his strict tee-totaling attitude, which later contributed to difficulties between Jung and Bleuler, for whom alcohol continued to be anathema. In 1912, Freud had taken Jung to task for his misinterpretation of Freud's visit to Binswanger, and Jung had recanted—at least temporarily.

Jones, after reporting Freud's first words on regaining consciousness, commented that this was "another indication that the idea of dying had some esoteric meaning for him." In the next paragraph Jones expressed his doubt whether all the memories connected with the incident were completely correct. We should assume that Jones quoted Freud's words from notes taken at that time. However, the term "esoteric" seems somewhat "esoteric" in this context. Freud was in a state of fatigue and severe tension. He hated controversies, which did not stay within the framework of a scientific discussion. Seen from the standpoint of his own analysis, his deepest conflicts had been stirred up. A fainting spell occurring at such a moment simply takes one away from it all. (This does not imply that one faints *because one wants* to be away from it all!) As far as death is concerned, Freud was not alone among those who, while not wanting to die (as he said in a letter "either immediately or completely" [see Chapter 2]), preferred a sudden death. Furthermore, many people who have had a severe accident or an acute, severe illness occasionally have the feeling: "Is this all there is to dying?" A remark of this kind might be another indication of the underlying conflict about death wishes and guilt.

Jones interpreted occurrence of both fainting spells after the achievement of a small victory as evidence that Freud was paying a price for that victory. Similarly he viewed Freud's own analysis of the episode which pointed to the death of his brother Julius, as paying for "the success of defeating an opponent."

Jones rightly links the psychic components of the fainting episode

---

[24] Abraham had tried to trace the revolution of this monarch, one of the first founders of monotheism, to his hostility to his father. Jung, who also discussed Freud's fainting spells in his autobiography (1961, p. 160f.), was, by his own admission, deeply disturbed by this assumption.

with Freud's derealization on the Acropolis, but without knowing, or at least without mentioning, the facts revealed in Freud's 1909 letter to Jung, and referring only to the gratification of the forbidden wish to excel one's father.

In my discussion of Freud's *non vixit* dream I emphasized the part played by the "guilt of the survivor," a concept first referred to by Freud after the death of his father. I have related this guilt to Freud's relationship to Fliess, Breuer, and Fleischl, which in a sense repeated itself with Jung who also was about to be "left by the wayside." In discussing Freud's interpretation of that dream, I pointed out how Freud's conflict with Fliess had become enmeshed for many reasons—including Fliess's having been born the year Julius had died—with his much older guilt feelings toward this jealously received younger sibling, but that nowhere in his analysis of the dream did Freud mention this fact.

In summary, the background information and most of all Freud's own analysis indicate the overdetermination of these fainting spells. Freud's conflict around his latent homosexuality played a large role in his relationship with Fliess and a much smaller one in that with Jung, and was one of many determinants which contributed to the whole episode, of which the fainting spell was just a culminating manifestation.

Freud's relationship with Fliess was characterized by deep ambivalence, accentuated both by the intensity of his positive feelings and by the vicious attack with which Fliess had definitely ended the relationship. This intense ambivalence linked Freud's conflict with Fliess, and to a much lesser degree his relationship with Jung, to the deepest layer of early ambivalence conflicts. While all the precipitating factors contributed to the acute episode, the deep ambivalence conflict carried more weight in determining such manifestations as the fainting spell and also the recurrent preoccupation with prospective death dates.[25]

A final, somewhat sarcastic but humorous aspect of Freud's reaction was evident in another letter to Binswanger (December 16, 1912):

> I am resigned to being declared a candidate for eternity on the basis of my attack in Munich. Recently Stekel wrote that my behavior was already showing the 'hypocritical streak.' All of them can hardly wait for it, but I can answer them as Mark Twain[26] did under similar cir-

[25] See Freud's letter to Ferenczi of December 9, 1912 (this chapter).

[26] Mark Twain was one of Freud's favorite writers. He not only read Twain's books, but loved to attend the author's readings from his own work.

cumstances: 'Reports of my death grossly exaggerated.' Rather, I am at work—at last—on the third of my *Übereinstimmungen* for *Imago,* which should pave the way for the fourth, to which I am very much looking forward. . . .[27]

While Jung "repented" in Munich, this incident marked for all practical purposes the end of their collaboration. At the end of the 1913 International Psycho-Analytical Congress in Munich, Jung was re-elected president, with many abstentions. When Jung noted that Jones was among the dissidents, he remarked to the latter: "I thought you were a Christian [i.e. a non-Jew]." Jones's comment (Vol. 2, p. 102f.), "It sounded an irrelevant remark, but presumably it had some meaning," proved to be an understatement in view of Jung's stand during the Hitler period. In 1914, Jung withdrew from the International Psycho-Analytical Association and went his own way. While Freud was disappointed and concerned about the effects of this defection on the psychoanalytic movement, he was not depressed, and soon was again completely engulfed in his work.

[27] The reference is to Parts III and IV of *Totem and Taboo.*

10

THE THEME OF DEATH ELABORATED IN THREE WORKS

"Great Is the Diana of the Ephesians"

Three of Freud's works of this period—two minor, one major—are pertinent to our topic. The first, one of the shortest ever published by Freud, bore the title "Great Is Diana of the Ephesians" (1911a), the name of a poem by Goethe. The material is derived from a chapter on Ephesus in F. Sartiaux's *Villes mortes d'Asie mineure* (Paris, 1911), which Freud came upon in the course of his extensive reading in connection with *Totem and Taboo*. This paper is indicative of Freud's interest in archaeology, but it must have other determinants as well.

One of the main themes is similar to one dealt with in the *Gradiva* paper—the continuity of history over a period of centuries or even millennia; the rising of new monuments on the ruins or ashes of the old; an "immortality" that does not run counter to scientific thinking.

In early antiquity, many temples were dedicated to the goddess Artemis-Diana. The temple in Ephesus became a center for pilgrims because of the miracles attributed to the goddess and her priests. Freud compared "the commercial metropolis of Ephesus" to "a modern Lourdes."

With the advent of Christianity, the apostles John, author of the Apocalypse, and Paul became linked with Ephesus. Legend had it that the Virgin Mary went with John to Ephesus after the Crucifixion. As early as the fourth century A.D., a basilica honoring Mary existed in Ephesus. Freud remarked:

273

Now once again the city had its great goddess, and, apart from her name, there was little change [p. 343].

If the little paper on the Diana of Ephesus was something of a day-dream put to paper, the next paper to be discussed here was of quite a different order. It represents such an important step in Freud's treatment of the problem of death from a scientific-psychological point of view that I shall discuss it in detail.

"THE THEME OF THE THREE CASKETS"

In "The Theme of the Three Caskets" (1913a) Freud met the theme of death head-on, perhaps for the first time. We know that during the most intense period of his self-analysis Freud discovered in the Oedipus legend the expression of one of the deepest and most basic conflicts in human existence. In the years 1911 and 1912 he was deeply involved in studying all aspects of mythology. In 1912, furthermore, he was in the midst of his conflict with Jung and was again intensively engaged in his self-analysis.

The conception of the paper on the "Three Caskets" took shape, according to Freud's correspondence, in the space of a few days in June, 1912, just after Freud's visit to Binswanger in Kreuzlingen when his young friend in the prime of life was facing a dim prognosis after surgery. Binswanger's crisis had in turn been preceded by an illness of Freud's mother, who was then 77 years old.

The paper starts with a consideration of the three caskets in Shakespeare's *The Merchant of Venice,* where the suitor who chooses the third, or leaden casket, wins the bride. Freud traced the casket theme through the mythology of various cultures. Since the common symbolic meaning of a casket was a woman in all of them, Freud believed the theme to be a choice among three women. This also was the theme of *King Lear,* where the choice was made among three daughters, the old king discovering too late how he had erred in disowning Cordelia because he had not recognized her unassuming, unspoken love. Freud then enumerated many myths and fairy tales involving a man's choice among three women, such as Aphrodite, chosen by Paris, Cinderella, chosen by the Prince, and Psyche, revered as Aphrodite in human form, the youngest and fairest of three sisters. In each case the third woman was the chosen one. Freud observed:

In all the stories the three women, of whom the third is the most ex-cellent one, must surely be regarded as in some way alike if they are represented as sisters. (. . . Lear's choice is between three *daughters;* this may mean nothing more than that he has to be represented as an old man. An old man cannot very well choose between three women in any other way. Thus they become his daughters.)

But who are these three sisters and why must the choice fall on the third? . . . We have once already made use of an application of psychoanalytic technique, when we explained the three caskets symbolically as three women. If we have the courage to proceed in the same way, we shall be setting foot on a path which will lead us first to something unexpected and incomprehensible, but which will perhaps, by a devious route, bring us to our goal [p. 293f.].

The conclusion which Freud drew from these examples is certainly an unexpected one. The common quality which he found in the objects of these choices was their silence, their lack of eloquence. Bassanio remarks in choosing the leaden casket: "Thy paleness moves me more than eloquence." Cordelia, "inconspicuous like lead," remains dumb; she "loves and is silent" (*King Lear,* I, 1). Even Aphrodite in the libretto of Offenbach's *La Belle Hélène* remains silent, dumb.

Freud then cited an example of an analysand's dream.

More than ten years ago a highly intelligent man told me a dream which he wanted to use as evidence of the telepathic nature of dreams. In it he saw an absent friend from whom he had received no news for a very long time, and reproached him energetically for his silence. The friend made no reply. It afterwards turned out that he had met his death by suicide at about the time of the dream. Let us leave the problem of telepathy on one side: there seems, however, not to be any doubt that here the dumbness in the dream represented death. Hiding and being unfindable—a thing which confronts the prince in the fairy tale of Cinderella three times, is another unmistakable symbol of death in dreams; so, too, is a marked pallor, of which the 'paleness' of the lead in one reading of Shakespeare's text is a reminder [p. 295].

This dream was followed by several examples from Grimm's fairy tales in which dumbness symbolized death. Freud then made explicit the conclusion to which all the foregoing had brought him:

These indications would lead us to conclude that the third one of the sisters between whom the choice is made is a dead woman. But she may be something else as well—namely, Death itself, the Goddess of Death. Thanks to a displacement . . . the qualities that a deity imparts to men are ascribed to the deity himself. Such a displacement will surprise us least of all in relation to the Goddess of Death, since in modern versions and representations . . . Death itself is nothing other than a dead man.

But if the third of the sisters is the Goddess of Death, the sisters are known to us. They are the Fates, the Moerae, the Parcae or the Norns, the third of whom is called Atropos, the inexorable [p. 296].

There followed a discussion of the relationship between *Moira* (destiny),[1] the Horae, and the Norns of German mythology. All three, Freud pointed out, referred to the concepts of season and time.

It was inevitable . . . that a deeper view should come to be taken of the essential nature of these deities, and that their essence should be transposed on to the regularity with which the seasons change. The Horae thus became the guardians of natural law and of the divine Order which causes the same thing to recur in Nature in an unalterable sequence.

This discovery of Nature reacted on the conception of human life. The nature-myth changed into a human myth: the weather-goddesses became goddesses of Fate. But this aspect of the Horae found expression only in the Moerae, who watch over the necessary ordering of human life as inexorably as do the Horae over the regular order of nature. The ineluctable severity of Law and its relation to death and dissolution, which had been avoided in the charming figures of the Horae, were now stamped upon the Moerae, *as though men had only perceived the full seriousness of natural law when they had to submit their own selves to it* [p. 297f.; italics added].[2]

Freud then tried to account for an apparent contradiction between his conclusion that the third, chosen sister was "the Goddess of Death, Death itself" and the fact that in the judgment of Paris she was the Goddess of Love, in *The Merchant of Venice* the fairest and wisest of women, in *King Lear* the only loyal daughter.

. . . there are motive forces in mental life which bring about replacement by the opposite in the form of what is known as reaction-formation; and it is precisely in the revelation of such hidden forces as these that we look for the reward of this enquiry. The Moerae were created as a result of a discovery that warned man that he too is a part of nature and therefore subject to the immutable law of death. Something in man was bound to struggle against this subjection, for it is only with extreme unwillingness that he gives up his claim to an exceptional position. Man, as we know, makes use of his imaginative activity in order to satisfy the wishes that reality does not satisfy. So his imagination rebelled against the recognition of the truth embodied in the myth of the Moerae, and constructed instead the myth derived from it, in which the Goddess of

[1] It is interesting that in Yiddish *Moira* means fear rather than destiny.
[2] See also Chapter 12.

Death was replaced by the Goddess of Love and by what was equivalent
to her in human shape. The third of the sisters was no longer Death;
she was the fairest, best, most desirable and most lovable of women.
. . . The Goddess of Love herself, who now took the place of the Goddess of Death, had once been identical with her. Even the Greek Aphrodite had not wholly relinquished her connection with the underworld,
although she had long surrendered her chthonic role to other divine
figures, to Persephone, or to the tri-form Artemis-Hecate. The great
Mother-goddesses of the oriental peoples, however, all seem to have
been both creators and destroyers—both goddesses of life and fertility
and goddesses of death. Thus the replacement by a wishful opposite in
our theme harks back to a primaeval identity.

[The feature of choice in the myth of the three sisters involves the
same reversal.] Choice stands in the place of necessity, of destiny. *In
this way man overcomes death, which he has recognized intellectually.*
No greater triumph of wish-fulfilment is conceivable. A choice is made
where in reality there is obedience to a compulsion; and what is chosen
is not a figure of terror, but the fairest and most desirable of women
[p. 299; italics added].³

Freud ended this paper, which is so revealing of how myths and
works of art deal with mankind's ultimate problem, by applying his
interpretation to *King Lear*—and probably to himself as well.

But Lear is not only an old man: he is a dying man. In this way the
extraordinary premise of the division of his inheritance loses all its
strangeness. But the doomed man is not willing to renounce the love of
women; he insists on hearing how much he is loved. Let us now recall
the moving final scene, one of the culminating points of tragedy in modern drama. Lear carries Cordelia's dead body on to the stage. Cordelia
is Death. If we reverse the situation it becomes intelligible and familiar
to us. She is the Death-goddess who, like the Valkyrie in German
mythology, carries away the dead hero from the battlefield. Eternal
wisdom, clothed in the primaeval myth, bids the old man renounce love,
choose death and make friends with the necessity of dying.

The dramatist brings us nearer to the ancient theme by representing
the man who makes the choice between the three sisters as aged and
dying. The regressive revision which he has thus applied to the myth,
distorted as it was by wishful transformation, allows us enough glimpses
of its original meaning to enable us perhaps to reach as well a superficial allegorical interpretation of the three female figures in the theme.
We might argue that what is represented here are the three inevitable
relations that a man has with a woman—the woman who bears him,
the woman who is his mate and the woman who destroys him; or that
they are the three forms taken by the figures of the mother in the course

³ See also Chapter 11.

of a man's life—the mother herself, the beloved one who is chosen after her pattern, and lastly the Mother Earth who receives him once more. But it is in vain that an old man yearns for the love of woman as he had it first from his mother; the third of the Fates alone, the silent Goddess of Death, will take him into her arms [p. 301].

All of Freud's later life—including his death—is embodied in these few pages. Freud's serenity finds expression in his masterful and parsimonious style and in his ability to capture in a few sentences the tragedy and beauty of a masterpiece such as *King Lear,* and combine it with myth, fairy tale, and psychological insight to illuminate man's methods of coping with the problem of death.

Against this background all the turmoil and strife of individual rivalry and ambition, which perforce preoccupied Freud at this time, pale into insignificance; and yet problems of this kind affected him because he was human and therefore vulnerable.

Does this explain Freud's rueful comment on awaking from his fainting spell in November, 1912: "How sweet it must be to die"? "Peace, sweet peace, come, oh come into my breast" said Goethe (*Wanderer's Nachtlied*). Freud, too, felt this utter lassitude on that occasion, and was to express Goethe's words as an ardent wish more than 27 years later, when he had nearly reached the end of his resources.

Totem and Taboo

Freud elaborated on many of the thoughts expressed in this essay in his discussion of animism in *Totem and Taboo* (1913b).[4]

He held that "animism itself is not yet a religion but contains the foundations on which religions are later built," and that myths too are based on animistic premises. He pointed out that primitive man did not arrive at his first systematic view of the universe by "pure speculative curiosity," but out of a need and wish to control the world around him. The wish was accorded magical power, which could achieve its effects by a multitude of symbolic acts. Magic and sorcery helped primitive man deny his basic vulnerability in an environment filled with danger. The mode of thought governing magic is an animistic one. Freud called it the "principle of the omnipotence of thought." This was a term he had "adopted" from his previously mentioned patient, the Rat Man (1909b), as Freud related:

---

[4] Originally published as a series of essays under the title "Some Points of Agreement between the Mental Lives of Savages and Neurotics" (1912-1913).

He had coined the phrase as an explanation of all the strange and uncanny events by which he . . . seemed to be pursued. If he thought of someone, he would be sure to meet that very person immediately afterwards, as though by magic. If he suddenly asked after the health of an acquaintance whom he had not seen for a long time, he would hear that he had just died, so that it would look as though a telepathic message had arrived from him. If . . . he swore at some stranger, he might be sure that the man would die soon afterwards, so that he would feel responsible for his death. In the course of the treatment he himself was able to tell me . . . by what contrivances he himself had helped to strengthen his own superstitious beliefs. All obsessional neurotics are superstitious in this way, usually against their better judgement. [Footnote:] We appear to attribute an 'uncanny' quality to impressions that seek to confirm the omnipotence of thoughts and the animistic mode of thinking in general, after we have reached a stage at which, in our *judgement,* we have abandoned such beliefs [1913b, p. 86].

Freud next formulated one of his basic discoveries—the difference between "psychic reality" and "reality proper," and this distinction permitted him to build a bridge between the mental processes of neurotics—especially obsessional ones—and the "magic" thinking of primitive man.

The primary obsessive acts of these neurotics are of an entirely magical character. If they are not charms, they are at all events counter-charms, designed to ward off the expectations of disaster[5] with which the neurosis usually starts. Whenever I have succeeded in penetrating the mystery, I have found that the expected disaster was death. Schopenhauer has said that the problem of death stands at the outset of every philosophy; and we have already seen that the origin of the belief in souls and in demons, which is the essence of animism, goes back to the impression which is made upon men by death [p. 87].

We may add the following remarks here. In superstitious thinking or in obsessional actions, the aim, as Freud illustrated so convincingly in his case history of the Rat Man, is also the "undoing" of a wish, which on the unconscious level has been equated with a deed. However, this frequently is not enough. Such thoughts and actions often have a self-punitive effect. All of this held true for the totemistic and taboo rituals of primitive man.

When Freud spoke of the meaning of "neurotic superstitions" he undoubtedly knew full well that he was also speaking of himself, since his self-analysis was never far from his thinking and writing.

[5] Here the German word *Unheil* is correctly translated as "disaster" (see Chapter 7).

In his paper on the Rat Man and other papers dealing with obsessional symptoms, Freud also described the defense mechanism of "isolation," by means of which certain memories and affects are effectively separated from the rest of a person's mental life and thus maintain an existence of their own. Intellectual understanding alone is not sufficient to "dissolve" these foreign structures. Only incessant "working through" can achieve this. This explains why certain obsessional "superstitions" can persist for decades in a man like Freud, to flare up under specific stress situations.

In *Totem and Taboo* Freud traced the evolution of attitudes toward death in human civilization—toward individual death and death in general—to death as the ultimate expression of human helplessness.

Freud not only compared the magic thinking of primitive man with the thought processes of neurotics; he also investigated the evolution of man's views of the universe and the ontogenetic development of such views. The animistic phase is followed in both cases first by a religious and then by a scientific one.

> At the animistic stage men ascribe omnipotence to *themselves*. At the religious stage they transfer it to the gods. . . . The scientific view of the universe no longer affords any room for human omnipotence; men have acknowledged their smallness and submitted resignedly to death and to the other necessities of nature. None the less some of the primitive belief in omnipotence still survives in men's faith in the power of the human mind, which grapples with the laws of reality [p. 88].

During the time when Freud wrote the last two chapters of *Totem and Taboo* he was also preoccupied with the concept of narcissism. Primitive man's belief in the omnipotence of thought, which permitted him to retain an unshakable confidence in his ability to control the environment, seemed to Freud to have a parallel in the narcissistic phase of development in children and in the narcissistic components of certain types of neurosis. This narcissistic element permits both primitive man and small children to disregard their basic helplessness.[6] Freud summarized the parallel as follows:

> If we may regard the existence among primitive races of the omnipotence of thoughts as evidence in favour of narcissism, we are encour-

[6] Freud quotes the work of a contemporary writer, Marett, in this connection: " 'It is almost an axiom with writers on this subject, that a sort of Solipsism or Berkleianism (as Professor Sully terms it as he finds it in the Child), operates in the savage to make him refuse to recognize death as a fact.' "

aged to attempt a comparison between the phases in the development
of men's view of the universe and the stages of an individual's libidinal
development. The animistic phase would correspond to narcissism both
chronologically and in its content; the religious phase would correspond
to the stage of object-choice of which the characteristic is a child's
attachment to his parents; while the scientific phase would have an exact
counterpart in the stage at which an individual has reached maturity,
has renounced the pleasure principle, adjusted himself to reality and
turned to the external world for the object of his desires [p. 90].

Freud also used the concept of projection, which is so pathog-
nomonic for paranoia, to explain the origin of "spirits" and "demons,"
which he regarded as the projection of man's emotional impulses.
Freud assumed that the "firstborn" spirits were evil spirits linked with
death's impact on survivors and the emotional conflict generated
thereby. Freud concluded this discussion with the following passage:

If the survivors' position in relation to the dead was really what first
caused primitive man to reflect, and compelled him to hand over some
of his omnipotence to the spirits and to sacrifice some of his freedom
of action, then these cultural products would constitute a first acknowledgment of *Ananke* [Necessity], which opposes human narcissism.
Primitive man would thus be submitting to the supremacy of death with
the same gesture with which he seemed to be denying it [p. 93].

Thus we can see how in Freud's view the impact of death, its uncanny aspect, the dim realization of its inevitability, the guilt associated with unconscious or conscious wishes against the dead person
became one of the pivotal points in the development of mankind.

In the last chapter of *Totem and Taboo* Freud made his boldest
claim: that totemism in its various manifestations, the development of
sacrificial ritual and feasts, and the subsequent transition from the
totem meal and sacrifice to religion can be traced back not only to
conflicting ambivalent wishes but to the original parricidal act, the
sons' murder of the leader of the primal horde (as this term was de-
fined by Darwin).

Within the framework of this study I am not concerned with the
validity of this bold hypothesis, which has raised nearly as much controversy, especially among anthropologists, as Freud's views about the
importance of sexuality in normal and abnormal development. I am
concerned chiefly with the fact that Freud assigned to the "oedipus
complex," i.e., to the wish, and more important the deed, of parricide,

with all its consequences, a role of equal importance in the development of both the individual and mankind.[7]

In the first chapters of *Totem and Taboo* Freud dealt with the development of the religious phase in the evolution of man's views of the universe. In the last chapter he discussed the development of religious thought mainly from the viewpoint of the glorification of the murdered father, the submission to God-the-Father, the attempts to deny the primal sin or expiate it through sacrifice, as Christ did in giving his own life to redeem "the company of brothers" (p. 153) and all mankind from original sin.[8]

Totem and Taboo was among the works which remained very important to Freud, for in writing it he had permitted himself to engage in bold and wide-ranging speculation, and to apply psychoanalytic thinking to many humanistic problems which had held his interest from the time of his youth. His fascination with the genetic principle, which he was extending here from the "development of the mental apparatus" (1900) to the genesis of culture and religion, found full expression in *Totem and Taboo*. He returned to this same line of thought in his last major work, *Moses and Monotheism*.

We may speculate about one additional factor that possibly contributed to the last chapter of *Totem and Taboo*. Freud himself felt like the father of the "primal horde" when he looked at some of his "sons." As he remarked in a letter (December 12, 1912) to Binswanger: "All of them [Stekel and Jung in particular] can hardly wait for it [i.e., his death]." On the one hand, Freud was seeking a "son," a "successor" to whom he could entrust the future of psychoanalysis with full confidence; on the other hand, he was forced to recognize that the instinctual sources of his pupils' rebelliousness, "the need to find something really new on one's own" (see Chapter 9), were strong, that the oedipal conflict was operative in everyone, including himself as he had discovered through his own analysis. For his pupils, self-

---

[7] In Freud's discussion, the murderous wishes and the actual killing of the father were seen as the primal sin. However, Freud realized even then that fratricide was inevitably the next crime and sin. Only later, as we shall see (Chapter 14), when Freud formulated the dual instinct theory and thus postulated a conflict between libido and aggression, was the whole concept of ambivalence given a much wider meaning.

[8] The theme of the development of religious thought during the early history of mankind was later expanded in *The Future of an Illusion* (1927a), in which Freud examined the reasons for the persistence of religious belief in mankind's and in the individual's history to date (see Chapter 17).

analysis, combined with occasional discussions with Freud and other colleagues, was not sufficient to eliminate their conflicts.[9]

After the completion of *Totem and Taboo* Freud went through a period of letdown even more pronounced than usual. The last part of the book in particular had raised doubts in him. He sent the galley proofs to the members of the "Committee"—Abraham, Ferenczi, Jones, Rank, and Sachs—asking for their opinions. He was prepared, as he wrote Ferenczi, for a "storm of indignation" similar to the one evoked by *The Interpretation of Dreams,* but he wanted to gauge at least the reactions of his closest associates.

Jones, who at that time was "in analysis"[10] with Ferenczi in Budapest, joined with the latter in interpreting Freud's letdown reaction. They claimed that his original elation represented the excitement of killing and eating the father, and that his doubts were the reaction to this fantasied deed. Freud's response only partly supports this interpretation, as Jones relates:

> When I saw him [Freud] a few days later on a visit to Vienna and asked him why the man who wrote *The Interpretation of Dreams* could now have such doubts he wisely replied: "Then I described the wish to kill one's father, and now I have been describing the actual killing; after all it is a big step from a wish to a deed [Vol. 2, p. 354].

The interpretations of Ferenczi and Jones were couched—in accordance with the state of psychoanalytic thinking at that time—mainly in "id" or instinctual terms. They underestimated the elation that arises from a supreme intellectual effort, the "ego" aspect of pleasure and gratification. However, Freud's response remains valid. Voicing the hypothesis that the "oedipal myth" has its roots not only in a wish but in a deed was bound to be a frightening experience.

[9] For these reasons, a training analysis was eventually postulated as an integral part of psychoanalytic training.

Of all the first generation analysts, none of whom had undergone a training analysis, with the exception of Jones (see below), probably only Abraham and Eitingon were able to master their individual conflicts, and of the two, only Abraham had the intellectual endowment to become a "carrier of the torch"; but he was to die at a very young age.

[10] Jones was the first of Freud's inner circle to undergo an "analysis," which, of necessity, was experimental in nature. It consisted of one or two hours daily on the couch, followed by endless discussions in the evening at one or another of Budapest's coffee houses. The whole process lasted only a few months. The recognition that a training analysis had to follow the same "ground rules" as a therapeutic analysis came only after decades of trial and error.

Totem and Taboo ends with the sentences:

> Primitive men . . . are *uninhibited:* thought passes directly into action. With them it is rather the deed that is a substitute for the thought. And that is why, without laying claim to any finality of judgement, I think that in the case before us it may safely be assumed that 'in the beginning was the Deed.' [Note:] 'Im Anfang war die Tat' (Goethe, *Faust,* Part I, Scene 3) [p. 161].

Although Freud had achieved another supreme victory of the intellect, he also had had to recognize and give utterance to the helplessness inherent in man's existence when he is face to face with the powers of nature of *Ananke*.

11

WORLD WAR I

Freud was soon to live through a period where "deed," evil deed, would become nearly universal, when all the raw power of destruction would be unleashed and reason and intellect muted; World War I was not far off.

Ever since 1908, the Austro-Hungarian empire had been going through a series of crises involving the Balkans, during which war had several times been imminent. The growing imperialism and militarism of Germany were running on a collision course with the interests of the Western powers, while Austro-Hungarian policy clashed with the pan-Slavic tendencies of Russia and with the mounting nationalism of the Balkan countries and also of the constituent provinces of the Austro-Hungarian empire. I remember from my own childhood that war was "in the air" several times prior to 1914, and yet not many people in Europe anticipated the catastrophe which eventually threw that continent into chaos.

Freud read the daily papers and was fully aware of what was going on in the world, but the "cause"—psychoanalysis—filled his life. Several passages in an extremely revealing letter written by Freud on July 8, 1915 to the American neuropsychiatrist James J. Putnam clearly express this attitude. Putnam had sent Freud his book *On Human Motives,* which took the idealistic view that something akin to a drive for ethical betterment was an integral part of human endowment. Freud's reaction, which he was to express later in such works as *The Future of an Illusion* (1927a) and the *New Introductory Lectures* (1933b), was that any progress which might be expected from the

285

human race would come from a progressive sublimation of the instinctual drives once the conditions for such sublimation were as clearly understood as was the process of repression. This concept was to be summed up in Freud's famous dictum: "Where id was, there ego shall be."

Within the context of his discussion with Putnam, Freud also made some unusually frank statements about himself. He acknowledged first that he had of necessity limited himself to a certain *Einseitigkeit* (one-sidedness) in order to uncover the hidden things which had escaped the understanding of others before him.[1] He then stated:

> I think I ought to tell you that I have always been dissatisfied with my intellectual endowment and that I know precisely in what respects, but that I consider myself a very moral human being who can subscribe to Th. Vischer's excellent maxim: "What is moral is self-evident." I believe that when it comes to a sense of justice and consideration for others, to the dislike of making others suffer or taking advantage of them, I can measure myself with the best people I have known. I have never done anything mean or malicious, nor have I felt any temptation to do so, with the result that I am not in the least proud of it. . . .
>
> The emphasis placed on moral laws in public life often makes me feel uncomfortable. What I have seen of religious-ethical conversions has not been very attractive. . . .
>
> On one point, however, I see that I can agree with you. When I ask myself why I have always aspired to behave honorably, to spare others and to be kind wherever possible, and why I didn't cease doing so when I realized that in this way one comes to harm and becomes an anvil because other people are brutal and unreliable, then indeed I have no answer. Sensible this certainly was not. In my youth I didn't feel any special ethical aspirations, nor does the conclusion that I am better than others give me any recognizable satisfaction! You are perhaps the first person to whom I have boasted in this fashion. So one could cite just my case as a proof of your assertion that such an urge toward the ideal forms a considerable part of our inheritance. If only more of this precious inheritance could be found in other human beings! I secretly believe that if one had the means of studying the sublimation of instincts as thoroughly as their repression, one might find quite natural psychological explanations which would render your humanitarian assumption unnecessary. But as I have said before, I know nothing about this. . . .
>
> Everything else you say about psychoanalysis I can subscribe to without sacrificing anything. For the time being psychoanalysis is compatible with various *Weltanschauungen*. But has it yet spoken its last

[1] A similar formulation can be found in an early letter to Jung of December 19, 1909 (see Schur, 1966b).

word? For my part I have never been concerned with any comprehensive synthesis, but invariably with certainty alone. And it is worth sacrificing everything to the latter [L. 169*].

Freud had many interests. He was equally at home in archaeology and literature. He was an exemplary *pater familias* and devoted friend, ready at all times for personal sacrifice. Yet in a sense his quest for answers to the unknown remained his overriding motive force. For all these reasons he could not mobilize sufficient interest or acumen to evaluate the brewing crisis which threatened to overwhelm Europe and much of the rest of the world.

Freud's correspondence in 1914 prior to the outbreak of war was filled with references to the conclusion of the Jung crisis, the reorganization of the International Psycho-Analytical Association, his various publications, and other aspects of his work.

A Brief Paradoxical Reaction

In the spring of 1914 Freud did not feel well. He was fatigued and had an upper-respiratory infection. He decided to go south for a few days. On May 7, 1914 he wrote to Abraham (see Freud/Abraham, 1965):

I am still unwell and without energy for work. . . .
I still have no idea what we shall be doing in the summer. . . .
I hope your children have now fully recovered, and that you and your wife are as well as is appropriate to your youth and harmony.
I was fifty-eight yesterday.

The same month we hear for the first time (since the "neoplasm" letter of the Fliess period) the ominous word "cancer." On May 13—one week after his 58th birthday—Freud wrote to Abraham:

My last bout of intestinal trouble caused my *"Leibarzt"*[2] to take the precaution of carrying out a rectoscopy, after which he congratulated me so warmly that I concluded that he had regarded a carcinoma as highly probable.
So this time it is nothing, and I must struggle on.

[2] *Leibarzt* was the term which royalty used to designate their personal physician. In this case Freud was also making a pun, since the word *Leib* means abdomen. In later years he used to speak of me as his *Leibarzt*. The physician referred to in this letter was Dr. Walter Zweig, lecturer in gastrointestinal diseases at the University of Vienna.

The last words "So this time it is nothing and I must struggle on" exemplifies a manner of speaking, or rather writing, which Freud used not infrequently. It was probably an indication of simply being tired of the incessant struggle. Perhaps it was also a hidden expression of his old superstition, as if Freud were substituting for the assertion, "I am expecting to die soon, or at a certain age," its apparent reversal, "So I must continue to struggle on; my time has not yet come."

The letter to Abraham continued:

> It is true that it is my personal wish to see you as our definite president. . . . Your suggestion that I should become honorary president does not appeal to me; in the first place there is a flavour of retirement about it, and in the second the present bad and crisis-ridden times do not seem to me to be appropriate for anything honorary. But I must not refrain from heartily thanking you for the friendly idea. In quiet, successful times I should gladly have accepted. For the time being the institution of a president and vice-president seems to me to be indispensable, and the sharing of the two functions between you and Jones at brief (two-yearly) intervals advisable. . . .
>
> What really upsets me is my lack of desire or incapacity for work, which has persisted since Easter. This week I at last finished the proofs of the first third of the 'History of the Psycho-Analytic Movement,' the part in which there was practically nothing to alter. I have only added a motto, *fluctuat nec mergitur*,[3] . . .
>
> Do not take amiss the low level of morale in this letter and accept the most cordial greetings. . . .

Such a letter frequently sufficed to restore Freud's normal "level of morale."

He was now making various preparations for the summer and for the next psychoanalytic congress, which was to take place in September in Dresden. He spoke about publishing his paper "On the History of the Psychoanalytic Movement," in which he was highly critical of Adler and even more so of Jung, whom he called "the bombshell." Ironically, Freud wrote Abraham on June 25, 1914, three days before the assassination of the Austrian Archduke Franz-Ferdinand in Sarajevo, which was the prelude to World War I, that "the bombshell has now burst." The entire correspondence with Abraham over the next few weeks dealt only with organizational and personal matters, and not with the crisis which was assuming ever greater proportions.

---

[3] Freud also used this quotation in his letters to Fliess (L. 119 and 143).

Freud went to Karlsbad to take the "cure" and allowed his daughter Anna to go to England on July 18!

A discussion of the events of those next weeks may not at first glance appear pertinent to the main theme of this book. As we shall see, however, the war and all its consequences had a strong impact on Freud's scientific formulations and his personal attitudes toward the integral problems of life and death.

On July 23, 1914 Austria submitted an ultimatum to Serbia, and on July 29, the Austro-Hungarian army mounted an attack on Serbia.

Freud's letter of July 26 to Abraham showed that the former, like so many others, did not see the handwriting on the wall.

Dear Friend,
Simultaneously with the declaration of war, which transformed our peaceful spa, your letter arrived, at last bringing the liberating news. So we are at last rid of them, the brutal, sanctimonious Jung and his disciples. I must now thank you for the vast amount of trouble, the exceptional clear-sightedness, with which you supported me and our common cause. All my life I have been looking for friends who would not exploit and then betray me, and now, not far from its natural end, I hope I have found them.

I can now satisfy your recently expressed wish and tell you what my subject is; it is aspects of psycho-analytic technique. Please put me in somewhere when the people have warmed up.

It will not be difficult to comment on the motivation of the Swiss refusal with regard to the programme of the International Psycho-Analytical Association.

It is of course impossible to foresee whether conditions will now permit us to hold the congress. If the war remains localised in the Balkans, it will be all right. But the Russians are unpredictable.

However, for the first time in thirty years I feel myself to be an Austrian and feel like giving this not very hopeful Empire another chance. Morale everywhere is excellent. Also the liberating effect of courageous action and the secure prop of Germany contribute a great deal to this. The most genuine symptomatic actions are to be seen in everyone.

I wish you undisturbed enjoyment of your well-earned holiday.

The last paragraph of the letter is most surprising: on the one hand, it must be understood in terms of an overwhelming response to a mass reaction; on the other hand, it bears witness to a factor which at that time created conflict in a majority of the liberal public in general, and the Jewish population in particular. There was no great love for Germany as represented by Kaiser Wilhelm II and the aggressively militant General Staff. There was, on the contrary, widespread admiration for the English brand of democracy. But this was counter-balanced by a profound and widespread repugnance for Russian absolutism as well as hatred for the brutal anti-Semitism which had found expression in the pogroms of the first decade of the century. These had been incited by propaganda about the "ritual murder" of gentile children by the Jews.[4]

Freud soon expressed this dilemma by saying: "I should be for it [the war] with all my heart if I did not know England to be on the wrong side" (August 2, 1914).

Vanishing Illusions: "Thoughts for the Times on War and Death"

Freud's "patriotic" mood began to evaporate quickly. England declared war "on the wrong side." Freud's eldest son Martin enlisted in the army and was to be in the thick of battle for many years to come. Anna was caught in England, but reached Vienna eventually with the staff of the Austrian Embassy in London.

Although Freud was back in Vienna himself, he was not yet able to settle down to work. Quotations from the classics were always at hand to express his attitudes. In a letter to Abraham of August 25, he wrote:

Was sind Hoffnungen,
was sind Entwürfe,
die der Mensch, der vergängliche macht![5]
Or something of the sort. . . . But perhaps *et haec olim meminisse juvabit,*[6] in the words of Virgil.

---

[4] The Jews were accused of using the blood of their victims to make their *matzoth,* the ritually prescribed unleavened bread eaten during the Passover holidays. (A famous trial involving a Jew accused of such a ritual murder is the main topic of the recent novel, *The Fixer,* by Bernard Malamud.) An early childhood memory of mine is linked to one of the worst of these pogroms which took place in Kishineff in 1905. At that time I was living in Stanislau, Galicia, about 60 miles from the Russian border. My father, in cooperation with some Jewish philanthropic agencies in Europe and the United States, had organized a local receiving station for the refugees who were streaming over the border. They were given "first aid," screened, and helped to emigrate. It was then that a strong wave of Jewish immigrants reached the United States. I still remember the pathetic figures passing through our home, their faces showing the horror of the Cossack assaults. Compared with the mass extermination of Jews during World War II, this was, of course, an "innocent" episode! But the mortal terror of the individuals involved was no less at that time. Freud was of course very familiar with these events.

[5] "What are the hopes, what are the plans, made by frail and transient man?" A quotation from Schiller's *Braut von Messina.*

[6] "And even this one day, it may be useful to remember."

There were more factors conducive to a subdued mood. In November, 1914, Freud received word that his half-brother Emanuel, whom he had always loved, had died in a train accident in England. Freud's practice was minimal and he was becoming concerned over his lack of financial security.

During the previous few years, after his isolation had ended, he had been accustomed to a steady exchange of letters with students, many of whom had become his friends. Most of these were now in the army, and contact with them was difficult. It was even more difficult to keep in touch with those who were now in enemy territory. Besides his ongoing correspondence with Abraham and Ferenczi, Freud began an exchange of letters with Lou Andreas-Salomé, a poet and writer who had many friends among the great. She had become interested in psychoanalysis a few years prior to this and had gained a grasp of its most intricate problems which amazed Freud and earned his deep respect. She provided one more proof for Freud that certain poets and artists "knew" intuitively what he had had to unearth with painful effort. She spent a year in Vienna, and published a beautiful book on her experience with Freud: *In der Schule bei Freud* (1958) (*The Freud Journal of Lou Andreas-Salomé*).[7] Freud wrote to her on November 14, 1914, shortly after he had learned about the death of Emanuel:

> How are you these days that are difficult for all of us? Did you expect this and did you imagine it that way? Do you still believe that all the big brothers are so good? A comforting word from you is expected.

Freud commented on her answer in a letter to Abraham (December 11, 1914):

> Lou Salomé has written a touching reply to a letter of mine. Her optimism is too deeply rooted to be shaken. As you know, she had six big brothers, all of whom were kind to her.

Freud's reply to her letter, written on November 25, 1914, portended many of his future writings:

> What you write gives me the courage to come in as a second voice. I do not doubt that mankind will recover even from this war, but I know

---

[7] In 1966, the correspondence between Freud and Lou Andreas-Salomé was published in German. Unless otherwise identified, the letters quoted are from this collection (see Freud/Andreas-Salomé, 1966), and the translation is my own.

for certain that I and my contemporaries will never again see a joyous world. It is too hideous. And the saddest thing of all is that it is precisely what psychoanalysis has led us to expect of man and his behavior. Because of this attitude to people, I have never been able to agree with your blithe optimism. My secret conclusion was: since we can view the current highest civilization only as afflicted by a gigantic hypocrisy, we are organically unfit for this civilization. We have to abdicate, and the Great Unknown, he or it, lurking behind Fate, will one day repeat such an experiment with another race.

Running parallel to this pessimistic mood and perhaps resulting from a valiant effort to counteract it was an upsurge of scientific productivity unequaled since *The Interpretation of Dreams*. Within a few months, Freud wrote, or at least drafted, not only a series of twelve essays on metapsychology,[8] of which eleven were already written by July, 1915, but also a paper that has particular significance for my topic: "Thoughts for the Times on War and Death."[9]

Freud's changed attitude toward the war was also reflected in a letter to the Dutch writer and "psychopathologist" Frederik van Eeden, which was fittingly added by Strachey as an Appendix to Freud's paper on war.[10]

---

[8] Unfortunately, seven of these manuscripts were never published and were probably burned by Freud. We do not know when or why. From his correspondence we know only that they dealt with a wide range of topics such as consciousness, the choice of neurosis, and probably also the pleasure-unpleasure principle. It is likely that some, if not most, of the ideas expressed in these works were included in Freud's later writings; for example, his preoccupation with the pleasure-unpleasure principle during that period was probably given its later formulation in *Beyond the Pleasure Principle*.

There were several other occasions when Freud destroyed drafts, letters, and manuscripts. He did so after his case of smallpox in 1885 (see Chapter 1). He may also have destroyed all letters written to him by Fliess (see Schur, 1965). Before leaving Vienna in 1938, Freud burned or threw away many "unnecessary" sheets. Marie Bonaparte, who was present at one of these "housecleanings," saw Freud throw some sheets of paper into a wastebasket. She persuaded Paula Fichtl, the devoted housekeeper who had been with the Freud family since 1928 and who emigrated with them to London, to fish the bundle out of the basket. The papers were eventually shipped to London, where I found them when I was preparing this study in 1963. The Freud family has subsequently donated them to the Freud Archives.

[9] In his introduction to the essay "Thoughts for the Times on War and Death," Strachey mentioned that part of it "seems to have been first read by Freud at a meeting, early in April, 1915, of the B'nai B'rith, the Jewish Club in Vienna to which he belonged for a large part of his life" (1915d, p. 274). A nearly complete version of this lecture was among the manuscripts found by me in the Freud library. It is being prepared for publication.

[10] It is always striking how Freud adapted his style of letter writing to fit his correspondent. The letter to van Eeden is "clinical," "analytic," while his letters to Lou Andreas-Salomé most of the time had a certain poetic quality.

December 28, 1914

Dear Dr. van Eeden,

I venture, under the impact of war, to remind you of two theses which have been put forward by psycho-analysis and which have undoubtedly contributed to its unpopularity.

Psycho-analysis has inferred from the dreams and parapraxes of healthy people, as well as from the symptoms of neurotics, that the primitive, savage and evil impulses of mankind have not vanished in any of its individual members, but persist, although in a repressed state, in the unconscious. . . . It has further taught us that our intellect is a feeble . . . thing, a plaything and tool of our instincts[11] and affects. . . .

If you will now observe what is happening in this war—the cruelties and injustices for which the most civilized nations are responsible, the different way in which they judge their own lies and wrong-doings and those of their enemies, and the general lack of insight which prevails— you will have to admit that psycho-analysis has been right in both its theses.

It may not have been entirely original in this; many thinkers and students of mankind have made similar assertions. But our science has worked out both of them in detail and has employed them to throw light on many psychological puzzles.

I hope we shall meet again in happier times.

Yours very sincerely,

Sigm. Freud

The war with its wanton destruction, cruelty, and hatred, as well as the calumnies and lies for which these provided a fertile breeding ground, had shattered many illusions. Freud was the analyst again. He realized painfully that his own objectivity might have been influenced by propaganda. The time had come for him to do away with all illusions.

The opening sentences of the essay plunged him *in medias res.*[12]

In the confusion of wartime in which we are caught up, relying as we must on one-sided information, standing too close to the great changes that have already taken place or are beginning to . . . we are at a loss as to the value of the judgements which we form. We cannot but feel that no event has ever destroyed so much that is precious in the common possessions of humanity, confused so many of the clearest intelligences, or so thoroughly debased what is highest.

[11] "Instinctual drive" is a more accurate translation of the German *Trieb* than "instincts," which implies an innate behavior pattern rather than a tendency or motivating force.

[12] It required considerable courage to publish this essay at a time of overheated patriotism and rampant censorship. Was it evidence of a certain enlightenment or only an example of characteristic Austrian "muddling-through" that this essay escaped censorship and was published in 1915?

Then followed a discussion of two factors which were responsible for the distress: the disillusionment which war itself evoked, and the altered attitude toward death which its destructiveness forced upon those involved in it. Freud was opposed to illusions and denial and he had no illusions about the value of life. But he said once in so many words: "Life is not all that wonderful, but still, it is all we have." He hated destruction and he loved *logos*. Hence he hated war.

How significant these first pages are to us in these war-filled times! How prophetic they sound to us who lived through World War II and who are now living in the shadow of the atom bomb. For these reasons I shall quote extensively from this essay.

> When I speak of disillusionment, everyone will know at once what I mean. One need not be a sentimentalist; one may perceive the biological and psychological necessity for suffering in . . . human life, and yet condemn war . . . and long for the cessation of all wars. We have told ourselves . . . that wars can never cease so long as nations live under such widely differing conditions, so long as the value of individual life is so variously assessed among them. . . . But we permitted ourselves to have other hopes. We had expected the . . . nations . . . upon whom the leadership of the human species has fallen . . . to succeed in discovering another way of settling misunderstandings and conflicts of interest. Within each of these nations high norms of moral conduct were laid down for the individual. . . . He was . . . forbidden to make use of . . . the practice of lying and deception in the competition with his fellow-men. The civilized states regarded these moral standards as the basis of their existence. . . . It was to be assumed, therefore, that the state itself would respect them. . . .
>
> Relying on this unity among the civilized peoples, countless men and women have exchanged their native home for a foreign one. . . . anyone could create for himself out of all . . . attractions of these civilized countries a new and wider fatherland. . . .
>
> From among the great thinkers, writers and artists of all nations he had chosen those to whom he considered he owed the best of what he had been able to achieve in enjoyment and understanding of life, and he had venerated them along with the immortal ancients as well as with the familiar masters of his own tongue [pp. 275-278].

Freud also reminded his readers that they were cherishing an illusion if they believed that wars, though possibly inevitable, could be conducted by rules of international law.

> [The] war in which we had refused to believe broke out, and it brought —disillusionment. Not only is it more bloody and more destructive than any war of other days, because of the enormously increased perfection

of weapons of attack and defence; it is at least as cruel . . . as implacable as any that has preceded it. It disregards all the restrictions known as International Law. . . . It tramples in blind fury on all that comes in its way, as though there were to be no future and no peace among men after it is over. It cuts all the common bonds between the contending peoples, and threatens to leave a legacy of embitterment that will make any renewal of those bonds impossible for a long time to come. . . .[13]

A belligerent state permits itself every such misdeed, every such act of violence, as would disgrace the individual. It makes use against the enemy . . . of deliberate lying and deception. . . . The state exacts the utmost degree of obedience and sacrifice from its citizens, but at the same time it treats them like children by an excess of secrecy and a censorship upon news and expressions of opinion which leaves the spirits of those whose intellects it thus suppresses defenceless against every unfavourable turn of events and every sinister rumour [p. 278f.].

Freud then showed us that all his pessimism and complete disillusionment ultimately served a scientific purpose. It was his conviction that the destruction of illusions, even if these spared us unpleasurable feelings, should be welcomed. "We must not complain, then, if . . . they come into collision with some portion of reality, and are shattered against it" (p. 280).

Among these illusions were the beliefs that man was born "virtuous and noble"[14] and that education and civilized environment could eradicate all evil human tendencies.

Freud reminded us that there is no such thing as "eradicating evil," that the deepest essence of human nature, the elementary instinctual impulses common to all men, always aim at satisfaction of primal needs. These impulses are only "good" or "bad" in relation to the

[13] For all his "disillusionment" Freud could not have envisioned Auschwitz and Hiroshima, or conceived of the possibility that four of his own sisters would die in extermination camps.

[14] Freud obviously had in mind here a frequently quoted poem by Goethe: "Das Göttliche" ("The Godly"):

Edel sei der Mensch
Hilfreich und gut!
Denn das allein
Unterscheidet ihn
Von allen Wesen
Die wir kennen.
Noble be man
Helpful and good!
For only this
Distinguishes him
From all creatures
That we know.
Lyrische und Epische Dichtungen, Vol. I.

standards of the environment. What the human community condemns as evil can be transformed by internal and external factors. The internal factor is essentially love in the widest sense of this term: out of the need to be loved we learn to sacrifice many of our "evil," egotistic strivings. The external factors can be summarized as the pressures of civilization. With this Freud introduced a concept which he later elaborated upon in *Civilization and Its Discontents*. In 1915, he stated:

> Civilization has been attained through the renunciation of instinctual satisfaction, and it demands the same renunciation from each newcomer in turn. Throughout an individual's life there is a constant replacement of external by internal compulsion [p. 282].

Freud's uncompromising conclusion is that anyone who is compelled to act in accordance with precepts which contradict his instinctual inclinations is "psychologically speaking" a hypocrite, and living beyond his means, that there are many more cultural hypocrites than truly civilized men. Freud then offers some hope for the future of mankind when he states that the maintenance of civilization, even on a dubious basis, offers the prospect of paving the way in each new generation for a more radical transformation of instinctual drives, which could become the basis for a more stable civilization. Having arrived at this realization, Freud can dispense with the grave disillusionment about the total abrogation of moral restraints by individual citizens and nations.

In what follows Freud offers ideas pertaining to group psychology. He acknowledged the fact that the educative influence of external factors on morality, often highly effective in individuals, is, under certain conditions, barely discernible in such groups as nations and states, especially during a state of war.

We must remember that in 1915 Freud had not yet conceptualized aggression as one of the two basic instinctual drives nor the superego as one of the structures of the mental apparatus. However, this whole discussion already anticipates his subsequent formulations in *Beyond the Pleasure Principle* (1920) and *The Ego and the Id* (1923).

Freud's discussion of one type of disillusionment served chiefly as an introduction to his analysis of the cause of "the sense of estrangement in this once lovely and congenial world"—the change in man's attitude toward death.

In *The Interpretation of Dreams* Freud had described the inability of children to understand the meaning of death. In *Totem and Taboo* he had discussed the inability of primitive man to conceive of, understand, and accept death. Now he pointed out that modern man was only seemingly prepared to believe that death was a necessary outcome of life, that everyone "owed nature a death."[15] In short, that death was natural, undeniable, and unavoidable.

> In reality, however, we were accustomed to behave as if it were otherwise. . . . It is indeed impossible to imagine our own death; and whenever we attempt to do so we can perceive that we are in fact still present as spectators. Hence . . . no one believes in his own death, or, to put the same thing in another way, that in the unconscious every one of us is convinced of his own immortality.
>
> When it comes to someone else's death, . . . [our] habit is to lay stress on the fortuitous causation of the death—accident, disease, infection, advanced age; in this way we betray an effort to reduce death from a necessity to a chance event. A number of simultaneous deaths strikes us as something extremely terrible. . . . Towards the actual person who has died we adopt a special attitude—something almost like admiration for someone who has accomplished a very difficult task. . . .
>
> The complement to this . . . conventional attitude towards death is provided by our complete collapse when death has struck down someone whom we love. . . .
>
> But this attitude of ours towards death has a powerful effect on all lives. Life is impoverished, it loses in interest, when the highest stake in the game of living, life itself, may not be risked. . . .
>
> It is evident that war is bound to sweep away this conventional treatment of death. Death will no longer be denied; we are forced to believe in it. People really die: and no longer one by one, but many, often tens of thousands, in a single day. And death is no longer a chance event. To be sure, it still seems a matter of chance whether a bullet hits this man or that; but a second bullet may well hit the survivor; and the accumulation of deaths puts an end to the impression of chance. Life has, indeed, become interesting again; it has recovered its full content [p. 289ff.].

We might add here that our attitude toward death is somewhat different where the old are concerned. We may experience grief and mourn for them, but we despair and revolt if death strikes the young, especially if these are our children. When Freud spoke of "the second bullet" he may have had in mind his oldest son Martin, who several times during the war suffered minor injuries, and once had a Russian

---

[15] Freud once again misquoted this line from Shakespeare's *Henry IV*, Act V, Sc. 1, substituting the word "nature" for "God," just as he had done in his letter to Fliess of February 6, 1899 (see Chapter 5).

bullet pierce his cap when he raised his head over the top of his trench.

Freud then repeated and elaborated some of his earlier formulations in *Totem and Taboo*. He assumed that for primitive man his own death was as unimaginable as it is for any of us today. But even primitive man must have experienced pain when he saw someone die who belonged to him—his wife, his child—for, as Freud put it: "Love cannot be much younger than the lust to kill."

Freud assumed that the law of ambivalence of feeling which extends to those whom we love most had an even greater validity in primitive man. He disputed the assumption of philosophers that the experience of death forced primitive man to reflection:

> What released the spirit of enquiry in man was not the intellectual enigma, and not every death, but the conflict of feeling at the death of loved yet alien and hated persons. Of this conflict of feeling psychology was the first offspring. Man could no longer keep death at a distance, for he had tasted it in his pain about the dead; but he was nevertheless unwilling to acknowledge it, for he could not conceive of himself as dead. So he devised a compromise: he conceded the fact of his own death as well, but denied it the significance of annihilation—a significance which he had had no motive for denying where the death of his enemy was concerned. It was beside the dead body of someone he loved that he invented spirits, and his sense of guilt at the satisfaction mingled with his sorrow turned these new-born spirits into evil demons that had to be dreaded. . . . His persisting memory of the dead became the basis for assuming other forms of existence and gave him the conception of a life continuing after apparent death [p. 293f.].

Freud then described two kinds of denial of death. On the one hand, religion succeeded in representing afterlife as the truly desirable existence, attainable only for the virtuous ones. On the other hand, life was extended backward into the past and led to the belief of transmigration of souls and reincarnation. The doctrine of the soul, the belief in immortality, the sense of guilt and the earliest ethical commandments also had their origin in the response to the dead body of the loved objects.

The most important prohibition: "Thou shalt not kill" was gradually extended from the loved ones to men in general. The extension of this commandment to the enemy is lost in times of war. The killer becomes the hero—he does not even have to go through the complex rituals of primitive man, who has to atone even for the killing of his enemies.

Turning to the unconscious in our mental life, Freud asked:

> What . . . is the attitude of our unconscious towards the problem of death? The answer must be: almost exactly the same as that of primaeval man. In this respect, as in many others, the man of prehistoric times survives unchanged in our unconscious. Our unconscious, then, does not believe in its own death; it behaves as if it were immortal. What we call our 'unconscious'—the deepest strata of our minds, made up of instinctual impulses—knows nothing that is negative, and no negation; in it contradictories coincide. For that reason it does not know its own death, for to that we can give only a negative content. Thus there is nothing instinctual in us which responds to a belief in death. This may even be the secret of heroism [p. 296].

Freud then expressed a thought which he elaborated in much later works, namely, that the fear of death "which dominates us oftener than we know" (p. 297) is usually the outcome of a sense of guilt.

Freud ended this essay with the exhortation:

> To tolerate life remains, after all, the first duty of all living beings. Illusion becomes valueless if it makes this harder for us. . . .
>
> We recall the old saying: *Si vis pacem, para bellum.* If you want to preserve peace, arm for war.
>
> It would be in keeping with the times to alter it: *Si vis vitam, para mortem.* If you want to endure life, prepare yourself for death [p. 299f.].

Although Freud was able to express fully the illusions, or rather the delusions, which we all harbor about death, he did not stop there, for this would have meant hopeless pessimism, an attitude of which Freud has been falsely accused. He subjected these illusions to an analytic appraisal in both a serene and scientific manner. The outpouring of papers which took place during the winter and spring of 1915 undoubtedly helped enormously to combat the "low" moods. His correspondence during these times of crisis, disillusionment, and feverish creative activity shows occasional signs of letdown and suffering.

In letters to Ferenczi and Abraham, Freud had reported on the very satisfactory progress of his work. For example, on December 21, 1914 he wrote to Abraham:

> The only thing that is going well is my work, which at intervals produces respectable novelties and conclusions. I recently discovered a characteristic of both systems, the conscious (cs) and the unconscious (ucs), which makes both almost intelligible and, I think, provides a

simple solution of the problem of the relationship of dementia praecox to reality.

Only a few weeks later, on January 25, 1915, he again wrote to Abraham:

Dear Friend,
Such a long time has passed since your last meagre and unpleasing postcard that I must write to you again.
First about myself. Physically I am well again and in good spirits, but am not working and have dropped everything on which I had started, including some things that were very promising. I still think it is a long polar night, and that one must wait for the sun to rise again. Whether this feeling is part of a progressive development or only the consequence of *an organic periodicity* that now reveals itself in the deprivation of so much is a question it will be possible to answer only retrospectively [italics added].

Was Freud harking back here to the Fliess period in speaking of "organic periodicity"?

However, soon thereafter he wrote within a short time most of the papers published in 1915. In 1914 he had written complainingly to Abraham the day after his 58th birthday. In 1915 he wrote two days before his 59th birthday, reporting on the completion of the five (published) papers on metapsychology, adding:

I think that on the whole it will represent an advance. The manner and level will be that of the seventh chapter of the *Interpretation of Dreams*.
I finished the paper on melancholia a quarter of an hour ago. I shall have it typed and send you a copy. You must let me have your comments. . . .
[He ended this letter by saying:] We have all shown unexpected adaptability in getting used to the war, with the result that we too can say we are well. The biggest surprise to me is my ability not to miss my practice and earnings. I fail to see that I shall ever again get used to a working day of six or eight hours—I had grown accustomed to ten. Is one's elasticity equally great in both directions? We like to quote an advertisement that is very common here and says . . . you quickly get used to the pleasant taste. By the time you read this I shall be fifty-nine years old, which should perhaps give me a right to comfort, but I have no way of staking my claim to it. So C.C.,[16] and let us leave something over the next generation.

[16] C.C. stands for "Coraggio, Casimiro," a "code" phrase which Freud and Abraham used in their correspondence to stand for something like "take heart."

Freud significantly signed this letter "Ihr alter Freud" ("Your old Freud"). This is probably the only time he used such a closing with Abraham, indicating in this way that he was feeling his age. This meaning is not conveyed by the English translation included in the published Freud-Abraham correspondence, which reads "Yours as ever."

On July 3, 1915 Freud wrote that he had reached the half-way point for 11 of the 12 metapsychological papers. He announced his summer plans: first, Karlsbad once again, and from there to Berchtesgaden where he had already spent several summers and would spend several more. There would be:

> an interruption in August for a visit to Ischl on the occasion of my mother's eightieth birthday. (My father reached the age of 81½ and my eldest brother[17] the same age, so there's a gloomy prospect.) Of course in these times all plans are rather uncertain. *Was sind Hoffnungen, was sind Entwürfe, die der Mensch, der vergängliche baut?*[18]

This is a remarkable paragraph which expresses in a condensed way some contradictions: Freud characterized his genetically determined expectations of living as long as his father as a "gloomy prospect." He had yet to reach the age of 62, the "critical" date which had been preoccupying him since 1899, but already the next "critical age" was looming up beyond the more immediate one—that of his father and stepbrother, which he might be permitted to reach but not surpass.

Freud must have felt, however, that he had other prospects than these "gloomy" ones, for in the sentence that followed, which spoke of the uncertainty of plans and expectations (both for the summer and for his life), he quoted the very lines he had used in his letter of August 25, 1914. In this condensed way he was expressing the feeling (which he was to repeat only a few months before his death) that while he might often be tired of the struggle, especially during the agonies of his illness, he basically loved life and wanted to preserve it up to the point where it could no longer be called life.

ON TRANSIENCE

Freud expressed his basic love of life in a little essay which approached the problem of life and death in a manner very different

17 Emanuel, who died in November 1914.
18 See footnote 5 of this Chapter.

from the scientific discussion in "Thoughts for the Times on War and Death." The title of this essay, "On Transience" (1916a), illustrates again the degree to which Freud expressed the same thoughts (or pre-occupations) in his letters and his works. In the rather pessimistic letter just mentioned, Freud had quoted Schiller on transient man and he now used the same word for the title of one of his most superb papers. Written at the invitation of the Berlin Goethe Society for a commemorative volume entitled *Das Land Goethes* (*The Land of Goethe*), which included contributions from leading German poets, writers, and artists,[19] the essay is set down in a style eminently appropriate to the occasion and gives clear evidence of the qualities for which, as a writer, Freud was awarded the Goethe prize in 1930. Freud described a conversation that had occurred during a "summer walk through a smiling countryside" in the company of "a taciturn friend and of a young but already famous poet."[20] The poet could admire but not enjoy the beauty of the scene around him because the beauty would vanish when winter came. Not only this scene but everything the poet loved was shorn of its value for him by virtue of the transience which spelled its doom.

While this poet was reacting with despondency, others, as Freud pointed out, react with rebellion or denial:

> No! It is impossible that all this loveliness of Nature and Art, of the world of our sensations and of the world outside, will really fade away into nothing. . . . Somehow or other this loveliness must be able to persist and to escape all the powers of destruction.
>
> But this demand for immortality is a product of our wishes too unmistakable to lay claim to reality: what is painful may none the less be true. I could not see my way to dispute the transience of all things, nor could I insist upon an exception in favour of what is beautiful and perfect. But I did dispute the pessimistic poet's view that the transience of what is beautiful involves any loss in its worth.
>
> On the contrary, an increase! Transience value is scarcity value in time. Limitation in the possibility of an enjoyment raises the value of the enjoyment. . . . A flower that blossoms only for a single night does not seem to us on that account less lovely. Nor can I understand any

[19] Freud may thus have unwittingly lent himself to a German propaganda effort intended to counteract Allied accusations and the derogatory name "huns" by presenting Germany as the "Land of Goethe." It was left to psychoanalysis to show how one nation could be the country of both barbarians and Goethe.

[20] Herbert Lehmann, in a recent publication (1966), offers convincing evidence that the taciturn friend was Lou Andreas-Salomé, and the poet, her friend and lover Rainer Maria Rilke.

better why the beauty and perfection of a work of art or of an intellectual achievement should lose its worth because of its temporal limitation. A time may indeed come when the pictures and statues which we admire to-day will crumble to dust, or a race of men may follow us who no longer understand the works of our poets and thinkers, or a geological epoch may even arrive when all animate life upon the earth ceases; but since the value of all this beauty and perfection is determined only by its significance for our own emotional lives, it has no need to survive us and is therefore independent of absolute duration [1916a, p. 305f.].

Freud then tried to understand and explain why the considerations which appeared "incontestable" to him made no impression on his companions. He proffered an explanation which he elaborated in one of the metapsychological papers written in the same year—"Mourning and Melancholia." All this beauty, he thought, was giving "these two sensitive minds" a foretaste of mourning, against which they were revolting. Mourning a loved person we have lost or even an inanimate object which has become part of us is a difficult and painful process which may take a long time and the end of which is inconceivable at the moment of the loss.

Freud compared this little episode, which had taken place the summer before the outbreak of the war (1913), with the situation current in 1915.

[War] destroyed not only the beauty of the countrysides through which it passed and the works of art which it met with on its path but it also shattered our pride in the achievements of our civilization, our admiration for many philosophers and artists and our hopes of a final triumph over the differences between nations and races. It tarnished the lofty impartiality of our science, it revealed our instincts in all their nakedness and let loose the evil spirits within us which we thought had been tamed for ever by centuries of continuous education by the noblest minds. . . .

But have those . . . possessions, which we have now lost, really ceased to have any worth for us because they have proved so perishable and so unresistant? To many of us this seems to be so, but once more wrongly, in my view. I believe that those who think thus . . . are simply in a state of mourning for what is lost. Mourning, as we know, however painful it may be, comes to a spontaneous end. When it has renounced everything that has been lost, then . . . our libido is once more free (in so far as we are still young and active) to replace the lost objects by fresh ones equally or still more precious. It is to be hoped that the same will be true of the losses caused by this war. When once the mourning is over, it will be found that our high opinion of the riches of civilization has lost nothing from our discovery of their fragility. We shall build up again all that war has destroyed, and perhaps on firmer ground and more lastingly than before [p. 307].

These words reveal the serenity which Freud had achieved at that time, his ability to see present and future beauty amidst ruins, to recognize value which went beyond one's personal existence. He made but one reservation, and that parenthetically—"in so far as we are young and active." The emphasis here was on "active," and this referred to mental activity, creativity. This serenity was the result of an unceasing battle which had been going on since the beginning of his self-analysis. As with every victory it was won at a cost. Nor could such serenity remain a permanent, unshakable, "uncontestable" acquisition. It had to be continually rewon in the unceasing struggles of life.

Mourning and Melancholia

All five essays on metapsychology were written in 1915. They represent in many ways an elaboration of the formulations presented in Chapter VII of *The Interpretation of Dreams*. Almost every psychoanalytic investigation requires a careful study of these papers.

The last of the metapsychological papers "Mourning and Melancholia" was published in 1917, although it had been written in 1915. As was the case with most of Freud's works, the concept formulated in this paper had been foreshadowed in his earlier writings. As early as 1895, in draft G (1950, L. 21), Freud had expressed many similar ideas. Several of its ideas were also sketched in the paper "On Transience."

Freud's analysis of the mourning process is to a certain extent a continuation of his discussion of this problem in the Rat Man (1909b; see Chapter 7). In the present paper Freud illustrates the great complexity of the normal mourning process in the context of object relations and points out the similarities and differences between mourning and the illness melancholia. As we have learned, the development of Freud's scientific concepts nearly always took the following course: a study of the individual, including himself, led to the recognition of certain ubiquitous phenomena, such as the dream work, infantile sexuality, and the oedipal conflict. In addition Freud drew upon data from mass phenomena, history, and anthropology for the understanding of the individual.

We see this development when we compare the essays "Thoughts for the Times on War and Death" and "Mourning and Melancholia." The first essay takes as its point of departure the observation and analysis of the impact of war and its wanton killing of millions of people on our thoughts about death. In the second essay Freud discusses the normal and abnormal response of the individual to the loss of an object, whether the loss be caused by death or the disruption of a relationship. Study of a normal reaction enables us to gain better understanding of a pathological process; in turn, pathology can contribute to our understanding of normal development.

Our psychological understanding of suicide derives to a great extent from this paper. Moreoever, mourning and melancholia contribute greatly to our understanding of the concept of identification, which plays such an important role in normal and abnormal development. Such concepts as aggression, ambivalence, and guilt were elucidated here several years before Freud formulated his dual instinct theory and the structural point of view, which considers mental functioning in terms of the id, ego, and superego (1920, 1923).

THE *Introductory Lectures*

Freud, who used to lecture on various aspects of psychoanalysis at the University of Vienna and at private gatherings of the Vienna Psychoanalytic Society (see Nunberg and Federn, 1962-1967; Andreas-Salomé, 1958; and others) decided in the fall of 1915 to begin bringing psychoanalysis up to date through a systematic exposition of its hypotheses and findings. This he did during the academic years 1915-1916 and 1916-1917, in the form of the famous *Introductory Lectures*.

We may ask what precipitated or contributed to all the creative activity of this year. Such questions are very difficult to answer, particularly because we know so little about creativity. I can only hazard some conjectures. Freud himself mentioned in one of the letters of this period that his mode of creative work had changed. We know from the Fliess correspondence that Freud had had to wait at that time for ideas to come to him, especially at the height of his self-analysis. Now he was "going to meet them halfway."

Jones attributes this upsurge of productivity mainly to the pressure of age, to the race against time. There were other factors, too, however. Through all of Freud's work we can trace the gradual fruition of ideas continually tested against empirical facts as they were furnished by the ongoing analyses of his own patients and supplemented by the experiences (including the trials and errors) of his students and even of dissenters. Because Freud had the unique faculty of listening to everyone with the free-floating attention requisite for the analytic session, he could turn casual hints and remarks into new concepts. Thus, whatever ideas were formulated in the metapsychological papers had already been half prepared, and were merely awaiting final expression.

There was an external factor as well: throughout the preceding years Freud had spent 10 hours daily with his patients (until 1924 he also saw patients on Saturdays and Sundays). His practice fell off during the first years of the war, and there were no meetings, congresses, or discussions, and less correspondence. Thus Freud simply had more time.

When considering the atmosphere in which Freud created the *Introductory Lectures* I must presume that there was still another strong motivating factor. Although Freud repeatedly proclaimed that he had no *Weltanschauung,* he actually did have one; he later characterized it as "scientific." He believed in the power of the intellect, in truth and reason; and he also believed that his creation, psychoanalysis, would help strengthen these forces. At a time when the world was in shambles or, as he put it in the essay on transience, when war had "shattered our pride in the achievement of our civilization, . . . tarnished the lofty impartiality of our science, . . . let loose the evil spirits within us which we thought were tamed," he wanted to proclaim that there was still one voice of reason which could help to rebuild all that war had destroyed, "perhaps on firmer ground and more lastingly than before."

In discussing the *Introductory Lectures* I must dwell a little on reminiscences. I attended every one of these lectures. I was not really able to integrate the lectures at that time. My friend and classmate Otto Fenichel was probably better able to do this. But I can still see Freud entering the "Small Lecture Hall" of the Psychiatric Institute. I remember hearing his voice for the first time, as yet unmarred by the later mutilating surgery. I see him before me in fur coat and top hat when winter came.

Freud spoke without a single note, yet whatever he said was later published practically verbatim. I remember his unique ability to anticipate possible objections or doubts that might arise at given points of his presentation, and how surprised and occasionally proud I felt if these proved to be my own objections too!

It was a mixed audience; people attended the lectures for a variety of reasons. Freud had already achieved fame, but he was still a controversial figure. Some came expecting to hear "shocking" views about sex. Some—but very few—disappeared after the first lectures. But the rest listened in hushed silence and with undivided attention every Saturday from 7-9 P.M.

The passage which has stayed most vividly in my memory—I should say in my ears and before my eyes—was the one with which he closed the 18th lecture:

> But in thus emphasizing the unconscious in mental life we have conjured up the most evil spirits of criticism against psycho-analysis. Do not be surprised at this, and do not suppose that the resistance to us rests only on the understandable difficulty of the unconscious or the relative inaccessibility of the experiences which provide evidence of it. Its source, I think, lies deeper. In the course of centuries the *naïve* self-love of men has had to submit to two major blows at the hands of science. The first was when they learnt that our earth was not the centre of the universe but only a tiny fragment of a cosmic system of scarcely imaginable vastness. This is associated in our minds with the name of Copernicus, though something similar had already been asserted by Alexandrian science. The second blow fell when biological research destroyed man's supposedly privileged place in creation and proved his descent from the animal kingdom and his ineradicable animal nature. This revaluation has been accomplished in our own days by Darwin, Wallace and their predecessors, though not without the most violent contemporary opposition. But human megalomania will have suffered its third and most wounding blow from the psychological research of the present time which seeks to prove to the ego that it is not even master in its own house, but must content itself with scanty information of what is going on unconsciously in its mind. We psychoanalysts were not the first and not the only ones to utter this call to introspection; but it seems to be our fate to give it its most forcible expression and to support it with empirical material which affects every individual. Hence arises the general revolt against our science, the disregard of all considerations of academic civility and the releasing of the opposition from every restraint of impartial logic. And beyond all this we have yet to disturb the peace of this world in still another way, as you will shortly hear [p. 284f.].

This declaration, that the astronomical and biological phases of the scientific revolution were now being followed by the psychological phase, was made with that inimitable combination of serenity, conviction, strength, pride, and humility which is unforgettable to anyone who has known Freud. The reference in the last sentence to "disturbing the peace of the world in another way" was connected with the themes of the two subsequent lectures in the series—resistance, repression, and infantile sexuality—but Freud knew, of course, that his declaration meant the end of many other illusions as well.

Freud republished some of these paragraphs in a short paper (1917b) in which he also included some remarks about Schopenhauer's concept of the power of the will. He sent the proofs of this paper to Abraham, who was then stationed in Allenstein in East Prussia. Abraham wrote on March 18, 1917:

> [The] paper which you sent me in proof gave me special pleasure, because of its train of thought and particularly as a personal document.
> . . . When you have completed your next paper, you might be tempted to come to this furthest north-eastern corner of Germany, if I tell you that your colleague Copernicus lived in Allenstein for many years. The interesting Templars' castle still contains some mementoes of him.

And Freud answered on March 25, 1917:

> Dear Friend,
> You are right to point out that the list in my last paper is bound to create the impression that I claim a place side by side with Copernicus and Darwin. However, I did not wish to relinquish an interesting idea just because of that semblance, and therefore at any rate put Schopenhauer in the foreground [Freud/Abraham, 1965 p. 249].

When, as Freud remarked, one makes discoveries which disturb the peace of the world, one cannot help disturbing one's own peace. To maintain serenity without the help of illusions, to sustain the supremacy of the ego in the face of what looked like the complete breakdown of Western civilization, was difficult at times even for Freud.

The war raged on, uglier every day. Victory was becoming an illusion, too, it seemed. Freud was approaching his 60th birthday. Before his 59th he had signed his letter to Abraham "Your Old Freud." Three days after that birthday he had written to Eitingon with a "Fliessian" preoccupation with numbers: "Nebenbei war es einer der *ungradesten* Geburstage, die man haben kann. Es ist ein Trost, dass es *vielleicht* nicht mehr so lange dauern kann, als es schon gedauert hat." ("By the way, this was one of the *oddest* birthdays one can have. It is a comfort that *perhaps* it [life] can no longer last as long as it has already lasted.")

Freud's 60th was celebrated by his students, in spite of the war. He grumbled in his letters about the festivities, writing Abraham on May 8, 1916:

> I have received so many flowers from Vienna that I have lost all claim to further funeral wreaths, and Hitschmann[21] sent me an 'undelivered' speech which was so moving and laudatory that when the time comes I shall be entitled to ask to be buried without a funeral oration.

Freud thanked Hitschmann graciously, but asked:

> No doubt I have meant to be and to do everything you say about me, but will it be possible in soberer hours to maintain that I succeeded? [L. 171*].

He complained to Eitingon about having entered "das Greisenalter" (senescence).

Life in Austria was becoming more and more difficult. By 1917, food had become quite scarce and of miserable quality. I remember the bread made mostly of cornmeal which crumbled in the hand and looked like sawdust. Meat, which Freud liked best, was hard to obtain. Heating was a serious problem.

The Russian Revolution was being hailed as a great event. However, the Kerenski government and the German government, which under the influence of its General Staff still believed in victory, failed to arrive at terms for a reasonable peace, and this ruined the opportunity to shorten the war and perhaps changed the subsequent course of history.

With the initial high hopes that the Russian Revolution would embark on a course leading toward progressive liberal democracy, many Austrian liberals lost any motivation for desiring a victory of the Central Powers. Freud expressed this point of view frankly—with utter disregard of German censorship and despite a previous warning from Abraham—in a letter written to the latter on December 10, 1917:

> Dear Friend,
> I am using the leisure of a Sunday to reply to your letter of the 2nd of this month (and I am so cold as I do so that I wrote 'the 7th' instead of the '12th' by mistake). . . .
> I am at daggers drawn with writing, as with many other things. Included among them is your dear German fatherland. I can hardly imagine myself ever going there again, even when it again becomes

[21] Dr. Edward Hitschmann, one of Freud's earliest students, born in Vienna, 1871; died in Boston in 1957.

physically possible. In the struggle between the Entente and the Quadruple Alliance I have definitely adopted the viewpoint of Heine's Donna Bianca in the disputation at Toledo:

Doch es will mich schier bedünken. . . . [22]

The only thing that gives me any pleasure is the capture of Jerusalem and the British experiment with the chosen people.[23]

A letter to Ferenczi written somewhat earlier (November 6, 1917) is pertinent from several points of view:

> Yesterday I smoked my last cigar and since then have been bad-tempered and tired. Palpitation appeared and a worsening of a painful swelling in the palate which I have noticed since the straitened days [cancer?]. Then a patient brought me fifty cigars, I lit one, became cheerful, and the affection of the palate rapidly went down. I should not have believed it had it not been so striking. Quite à la Groddeck [quoted in Jones, Vol. 2, p. 192].

Freud unfortunately linked the swelling to enforced abstinence, its disappearance to the end of that frustration-tension common to every addiction. Jones's comment on this episode is somewhat vague and misleading:

> That was six years before the real cancer attacked him there, and one knows that surgeons speak of a "pre-cancerous stage." The connection with smoking is unmistakable.

Freud *was* suffering from leukoplakias which developed as the consequence of cigar smoking. These may represent a precancerous condition, and did so in Freud's case. Freud eventually developed a malignancy, but we have no way of knowing whether it was on the same spot as this "painful swelling." Some palpitation may be experienced in a state of abstinence. However, a leukoplakia would not have developed because of abstinence and then disappeared with the resumption of smoking. Such a "belief" fit into Freud's rationalizations about smoking, the one important area where he could not establish the "supremacy of the ego." Freud's exclamation "Ganz Groddeck" expressed this clearly. But more about this later.

I mentioned before that Freud, with his preference for *Logos,* in-

---

[22] "But I rather suspect . . ." (the quotation from Heine that Freud leaves incomplete continues: *"Dass der Rabbi und der Mönch/Dass sie alle beide stinken* [that both the rabbi and the monk stink alike].")

[23] The reference is to the Balfour declaration.

sisted on a slow, careful empirical approach. He expressed this view-point most distinctly in a letter to Lou Andreas-Salomé on July 13, 1917.

> Most esteemed Lady,[24]
> I have to disappoint you. I am not going to say "yes" or "no," nor shall I deal out question marks, but I shall do what I have always done with your comments: enjoy them and let them have their effect on me. It is quite evident that you anticipate and complement me each time, how you try in a visionary way to complete my fragments, build them into a structure. I am under the impression that this is true to a special degree since I began employing the concept of the narcissistic libido. Without this, I feel you too might have slipped away from me to the system-builders, to Jung, or rather to Adler. But through the ego-libido you have observed how I work, step by step, without the inner need for completion, continually under the pressure of the problems immediately on hand and taking infinite pains not to be diverted from the path. It seems that in this way I have gained your confidence.
> If I should be in the position to continue building up this theory, you may perhaps recognize with satisfaction several new things as having been anticipated or even announced by yourself. But in spite of advancing age I am not in a hurry [L. 177*].

And yet Freud was also taken in by people of imagination, and was ready to "give them rope" for quite some time. We know to what extent this had happened with Fliess. Every now and then Freud reiterated his opinion that there was some measure of truth in Fliess's periodicity theory. He did so, for example, in a letter of August 4, 1916 to Josef Popper-Lynkeus, the writer-philosopher-sociologist to whom Freud gave credit for having discovered before he did that the distortion in dreams was due to censorship. Freud thanked Popper-Lynkeus for having sent him an 18th-century thesis on dreams, and added:

> The all but hundred-year-old dissertation by Dr. Heinrich Straus is indeed very remarkable. It contains several things with which a former friend of mine, W. Fliess of Berlin, used to be very much preoccupied. By his own observation the latter revived many of the assertions about the rhythm of vital phenomena, and added the considerable discovery

---

[24] He addressed her as *Verehrteste Frau,* which the published translation gives as "Dear Frau Lou." This does not convey the meaning of the German. Freud addressed Lou Andreas-Salomé this way for a number of years. Later it became *Liebste Lou* ("Dearest Lou").

For a recently published study of Lou Andreas-Salomé, see Binion (1968), who, in my opinion, completely misinterprets Freud's relationship to Lou Andreas-Salomé.

that two such rhythms exist, a masculine one of 23 days and a feminine one of 28, and even after that friendship came to an end I retained some faith in this idea [L. 174*].

Freud had been caught up by Jung's imagination, and now the work of Georg Groddeck was impressing him greatly. Groddeck might be called one of the "fathers" of "psychosomatic" medicine (see Grossman and Grossman, 1965). He published a series of observations on fantastic-sounding cures of severe organic illnesses, cures which were a combination of psycho- and physiotherapy. He believed in the unlimited influence of unconscious thoughts on somatic processes, including malignancies. It was Groddeck who coined the name *id,* which Freud then adopted when he formulated the structural point of view.

When some years later Mrs. Groddeck, Swedish by birth, was translating *The Psychopathology of Everyday Life* into Swedish, she encountered Freud's interpretation of his remark that he had made 2,467 mistakes in *The Interpretation of Dreams* (see Chapter 7). She showed this to her husband, who was convinced that it was Freud's "id" which had produced his malignancy 24 years after the event, in line with Freud's interpretation of the number in question. From then on Groddeck ardently wished Freud would come to his private hospital in Baden-Baden for treatment.

Freud encouraged Groddeck in his work and spoke of him with great enthusiasm to friends. Ferenczi, who initially was very skeptical about Groddeck, became his friend and patient in 1921, when Groddeck treated him for toxic goiter.

When Groddeck published a novel entitled *The Soul-Seeker,* Freud was amused at the moral indignation which it provoked, especially in Switzerland. He wrote to Eitingon: ". . . otherwise, I shall stick to my opinion that it is a delicacy, although, to be sure, caviar to the general [masses], the work of a mind on par with that of Rabelais" [2].

In spite—or perhaps because—of the fact that the world looked so gloomy at that time, Freud occasionally let his imagination run far afield, as he did, for example, with the outline of a study on the application of psychoanalysis to the neo-Lamarckian theory of the inheritance of acquired characteristics.[25] He wrote to Abraham on November 11, 1917 concerning his ideas on this subject, and also called Abraham's attention to Groddeck's work.

[25] Freud adhered stubbornly to this belief throughout his life (see L. Ritvo, 1965; and Schur and Ritvo, 1970).

Have I really not told you anything about the Lamarck idea? It arose between Ferenczi and me, but neither of us has the time or spirit to tackle it at present. The idea is to put Lamarck entirely on our ground and to show that the 'necessity' that according to him creates and transforms organs is nothing but the power of unconscious ideas over one's own body, of which we see remnants in hysteria, in short the 'omnipotence of thoughts'. This would actually supply a psycho-analytic explanation of adaptation; it would put the coping stone on psycho-analysis. There would be two linked principles of progressive change, adaptation of one's own body and subsequent transformation of the external world (autoplasticity and heteroplasticity), etc.

I am not sure either whether I have drawn your attention to a book by Groddeck in Baden-Baden (*Psychologische Bedingtheit und psychoanalytische Behandlung organischer Leiden,* S. Hirzel, 1917). . . .[26]

Here we can detect in some way "the return of the repressed"—the belief in the omnipotence of thought, which must be overcome in every individual because it clashes with the reality principle, and which is relegated to the "unconscious" of our phylogenetic ancestors. This would have to be a global biological unconscious found in all living matter.[27]

In contrast to such lofty ideas, Freud expressed the "other side of the coin" in a letter written to Ferenczi only a few days later:

I have been working very hard, feel worn out and am beginning to find the world repellently loathsome. The superstition that my life is due to finish in February 1918 often seems to me quite a friendly idea. Sometimes I have to fight hard to regain ascendancy over myself [quoted in Jones, Vol. 2, p. 194].

Here the superstition which had plagued Freud since 1899, and which had come to a head again in 1904 during the trip to Athens, was showing up once more. In February, 1918 Freud would be 61 years and nine months old. According to Fliess's calculations, one's date of death was predetermined at impregnation and hence fixed at birth. Ferenczi must have protested against this idea, for Freud answered on December 16, 1917:

When I read your letter I looked down on your optimism with a smile. You seem to believe in an 'eternal recurrence of the same' and want to

---

[26] Freud wrote a similar letter around this time to an unidentified American. It will be published in due course by Dr. Samuel Gutman, who has brought its existence to my attention.

[27] In *Inhibitions, Symptoms and Anxiety* Freud also offered some evolutional speculations about the reasons for the development of the "latency period" in man.

overlook the unmistakable direction of fate. There is really nothing
strange in a man of my years noticing the unavoidable gradual decay
of his person. I hope you will soon be able to convince yourself that
it doesn't mean I am in a bad mood. I work splendidly the whole day
with nine ninnys, and I can hardly control my appetite, but I no longer
enjoy the good sleep I used to [*ibid.*].

The winter of 1918 was even more dismal than the previous one.
Few people in Austria doubted the outcome of the war, and the continuation of the slaughter, including the last big German offensive on
the western front in March, 1917, was seen only as a senseless delay-
ing of the inevitable. We knew in Austria that the new American army
was arriving in Europe.

Very often Freud's ups and downs were reflected in a single letter
during this period; for example, one to Abraham on January 18, 1918:

> Your equable temperament and indestructible vitality stand up well to
> my alterations between cheerfulness and resignation. . . . [Pötzl] is
> soon to go to Prague as successor to Pick; this too will be no drawback
> to us.
>
> The Dutch are now doing things in earnest. We recently received
> from them a pile of reviews of Dutch papers and polemical writings,
> and a quite admirably clear and definite rebuttal of Jung's latest prod-
> uct on the psychology of the unconscious process (1917). A new local
> group is about to be formed at Warsaw. . . .
>
> I am reading about Darwinism without any real aim, like someone
> with plenty of time in front of him, which may be appropriate in view of
> the paper shortage. The practice is still very busy, and also interesting.
> Successes have been good. One of my sons (Ernst) is at present nearer
> to you than to me. He should be visiting his sister at Schwerin today.
> We receive occasional news of the other two, none of it bad. If the war
> lasts long enough, it will kill off everybody any way.

Nevertheless Freud was heartened by various publications dealing
with the application of psychoanalysis to war neuroses. He was also
putting the final touches on his last and perhaps most brilliant case
history "From the History of an Infantile Neurosis."

THE SECOND DEADLINE PASSES

On May 19, 1918 Abraham wrote Freud that his mother was gravely ill. Freud answered on May 29:

> My mother will be eighty-three this year, and is now rather shaky.
> Sometimes I think I shall feel a little freer when she dies, because the

idea of her having to be told of my death is something from which one shrinks back.

So I really have reached sixty-two. . . . My prevailing mood is powerless embitterment, or embitterment at my powerlessness.[28]

This letter is pertinent for many reasons. Freud had passed another of his ominous "deadlines." His next one was 81½, the age at which his father and older brother had died. His mother had already passed this age. The terrifying thought that his mother might have to be told of his death came back to haunt Freud five years later.

Freud showed his resilience a few months after this when, against all hope, another Congress, the fifth, was held in Budapest, attended, besides the Austrian and German contingents, by only two Dutch analysts who represented the neutral countries and thus made the Congress "international." The arrangements were facilitated by Anton von Freund, a rich Hungarian industrialist and doctor of philosophy. Freund, whom Freud later spoke of in his correspondence as "Toni," was approximately as old as Binswanger. He had been stricken by the same type of malignancy as the latter (see Freud's letter to Binswanger in Chapter 9), and after his surgery developed symptoms of neurotic anxiety for which he underwent an analysis with Freud that proved most helpful. He became enthusiastic about psychoanalysis, and being doubtful about the prognosis of his illness—in which he unfortunately proved to be right—decided to use part of his fortune to provide financial help to psychoanalytic publications, institutes, teaching clinics, etc. Freud, who became very fond of him and held him in very high esteem, was for once quite optimistic about the future.

The Congress held in the second half of September, 1918 was in every respect a great success. The festive spirit which pervaded it was in marked contrast to the country's expectation of the imminent collapse of the Central Powers. Freud was happy to see Abraham after so many years. He was also relieved that his sons were not involved in actual fighting at this time. After the Congress Freud wrote Ferenczi a glowing letter:

Do you remember the prophetic words I uttered before the first Congress in Salzburg, when I said that we expected great things from you?

I am reveling in satisfaction, my heart is light since I know that my problem child, my life's work, is protected by your interest and that

[28] Freud subsequently expressed similar feelings in his letters to Arnold Zweig after Hitler came to power.

of others, and its future taken care of. I shall be able to see better times approaching, even if I do so from a distance [L. 183*].

To Abraham he wrote on August 27, 1918:

The reception in Budapest by my new friends [von Freund and his family] was charming, the mountain air of the Tatras did the rest, and so for a time I can venture to join again in
der Erde Lust, der Erde Leid zu tragen.[29]

A few weeks later the war ended, and with it the Austro-Hungarian empire. For a few months there was no news from Freud's oldest son Martin, who, during the final chaotic retreat, had been captured by the Italian army.

Freud was of course relieved to see the end of the war. He shed no tears over the defeat of the Austro-Hungarian empire. His sympathies, especially after the Russian Revolution, had shifted more and more toward the Western Powers.

Freud and Jones tried to re-establish personal contact as soon as possible. The news about the "cause" was all favorable. The psychoanalytic movement had spread during the war, especially in England and the United States. However, the first direct letter from Jones also brought the news about the tragic death of his young (first) wife.

THE DEATH OF ANTON VON FREUND

The war had ended, but not the misery and want rampant in Austria. The winter of 1919 was gloomy indeed. Food was extremely scarce.[30] During the war Freud occasionally obtained some food from Ferenczi and von Freund. The galloping inflation ate up all of Freud's savings, and all the glowing hopes for a foundation to be established by von Freund dwindled away as the value of the Hungarian and Austrian currencies declined. Freud, like most of the inhabitants of Vienna, could hardly heat his office. The flu pandemic was now raging, and eventually took more lives than the war. Martha Freud came down with bronchopneumonia in March, 1919. Anton von Freund developed abdominal symptoms, which eventually proved to be caused by

---

[29] "Bearing the world's pleasure and the world's pain." A quotation from Goethe's *Faust,* Part I.

[30] I remember how I saved food from my hospital meals to bring home to my family, and my delight over the cans of American corned beef and cocoa which were served occasionally at special eating places for students.

abdominal metastases from his earlier malignancy. Toni came to Vienna and Freud had to watch the slow, agonizing death from cancer of a man who was fully aware of his fate.

To see this happen to someone so much younger than he, full of hope and promise, gave Freud a sense of that tormented helplessness which he had recently described to Abraham (see letter of May 29, 1918). All of Freud's letters about von Freund's illness and death vividly expressed his reactions to this tragic situation. When Abraham asked whether von Freund was aware of his condition, Freud replied (on December 15, 1919):

> Freund knows everything; he has, for instance, directed that the ring he wears is to be restored to me after his death. He has also sensed that it is intended for Eitingon.[31]

On January 21, 1920, Freud wrote to Eitingon:

> T. F. died yesterday, peacefully delivered from his incurable illness. For our cause a great loss, for me a keenly [felt] pain, but one which I have been able to assimilate during the past months. He bore his

---

[31] Von Freund had been appointed by Freud to membership on the "Committee," organized in 1912, at the suggestion of Jones, following the defection of Adler and Stekel from the first Psychoanalytic Society organized in Vienna. Anticipating the growing tension between Freud and Jung, Jones had proposed the formation of a small group of absolutely trustworthy analysts to act as a kind of "inner" committee with whom Freud could unhesitatingly discuss the organizational problems of the developing International Psycho-Analytical Association. Jones indicates that only one definite obligation was placed upon the members, namely: none would publicly renounce such basic tenets of psychoanalytic theory as repression, the unconscious, infantile sexuality, etc., without first discussing such an action with the other members. Jones confesses that "The whole idea of such a group had of course its prehistory in my mind: stories of Charlemagne's paladins from boyhood and many secret societies from literature" (Vol. 2, p. 152). Freud had responded to the proposal not only with enthusiasm but with great relief, although he admitted to Jones in a letter of August 1, 1912 that there might be a "boyish and perhaps romantic element" in the idea.

In two letters Freud wrote to Eitingon on October 22, and November 23, 1919, his remarks on the subjects were more meaningful. Eitingon was utterly devoted to Freud, who knew that he could rely on the former completely. Freud's letters to Eitingon therefore had an especially warm quality. In these two letters Freud commented that the "Committee" had freed him from concern over the future of the "cause," so that he could now calmly follow his path to the end. Freud also explained that this feeling of concern stemmed from the time when psychoanalysis had depended upon him alone. Since the formation of the "Committee" he felt more carefree about how long he might still have to live (see in this connection my discussion of *Beyond the Pleasure Principle* in Chapter 12).

Von Freund had been named a member probably not only because of his merits but as a gesture of friendship in the face of his extreme suffering. The ring referred to was one worn by all members of the "Committee."

hopelessness with heroic and clear awareness and was no disgrace for psychoanalysis.[32]

When he received your letter, in which you welcomed him as a member of the Committee, he cried and said: "I know, he will be my successor," pointing to the Committee ring which he had received from me. With his usual acuteness he guessed correctly that I had intended this ring, which has a particularly interesting stone, for you and therefore had not tried to find another one for you. Some time later he actually took the ring off and gave instructions to have it returned to me after his death [1].

Only a few days after von Freund's death, Freud's daughter Sophie, who had fallen ill on the day of von Freund's funeral, died at the age of 27 from fulminant influenza pneumonia, the biggest killer at the time.[33]

Soon after this Jones's father died, also from a malignancy. Freud wrote to him on February 12, 1920:

So your father has not to hold out until he got devoured piecemeal by his cancer as poor Freund was. What good fortune. Yet you will soon find out what it means to you. I was about your age when my father died (43)[34] and it revolutionized my soul. Can you remember a time so full of death as this?

I have dwelled on the von Freund episode for several reasons. Besides the deep empathy which Freud had evidenced when Binswanger had developed his malignancy a few years earlier and Freud had helped his friend keep up his moral fiber, Freud himself had twice had a "cancer scare," once in 1914 and again in 1917. It was only 3 years after von Freund's death that Freud himself developed a malignancy, and we may assume that the specter of Toni's suffering was constantly before him. Moreover, the Freund episode was among the important events which formed the environmental background for one of Freud's most controversial works, and one which is especially pertinent for our topic—*Beyond the Pleasure Principle*. It is to this work that I now turn my attention.

[32] This passage shows that in Freud's estimation facing suffering and death with "heroic" awareness was an obligation for one who, through analysis, should have learned to master his fear in the face of this supreme test.

[33] I shall deal with Freud's reaction to Sophie's death in another context (Chapter 12).

[34] Jones calls our attention to a slip made by Freud in this letter: he states that both he and Freud were 41 when their fathers died. Jones attributes this slip to the fact that Freud was 43 when he wrote *The Interpretation of Dreams* (Vol. 3, p. 20). Actually Freud was not quite 40 and a half when his father died; so Jones, too, made a slip.

12

BEYOND THE PLEASURE PRINCIPLE: THE DEATH INSTINCT AND THE REPETITION COMPULSION

In the preceding chapter, I discussed Freud's work written during World War I. But the effect of the war years did not stop with the fighting. The senseless destruction of life and human values confirmed Freud's recognition of the importance of aggression in mental life. The concept of turning aggression against the self, foreshadowed in *Totem and Taboo*, was clearly described in "Mourning and Melancholia." It is likely that such a keen psychologist as Freud in the course of his continuing self-analysis had recognized the strictness of his own superego and his preoccupation with death as signs of aggression turned against himself.

The obscure symptomatology of the war neuroses, especially the post-traumatic dream, called for an explanation. Freud recognized the wish for self-punishment as an important motivating force behind unpleasant and frightening dreams and also the importance of the ego in general in dream formation. In 1919 he incorporated these insights into a revised edition of *The Interpretation of Dreams*. In other words, Freud was already thinking more and more in terms of the structural point of view, which, as he formulated it in *The Ego and the Id* (1923), "divided" the mental apparatus into three "provinces": id, ego, and superego.

319

Last, Freud was confronted with a disturbing phenomenon in the treatment of his patients, especially in that of such severe cases as, e.g., the Wolf Man. This case had required what at that time was considered a very long analysis, lasting over a numbers of years. Freud had come to recognize that instead of _remembering_ the past, the patient had been obliged to repeat it to some extent in the transference situation. Freud realized that many patients again and again reenacted a series of highly unpleasant experiences both in and outside of the analytic situation. Freud believed that all such experiences were repeated under the _pressure of a compulsion_ (1920, p. 21).

These observations required new conceptualizations. In _Beyond the Pleasure Principle_, Freud (1920) set out to do just that. However, in this work we encounter not only new ideas, but also a departure from Freud's usual method of approaching his topic, i.e., the inductive reasoning that in Freud's case almost always was solidly grounded on observed phenomena here gives way to speculation.

Beyond the Pleasure Principle

Like all of Freud's works, _Beyond the Pleasure Principle_[1] encompassed many ideas which had been germinating for decades. Only with the recovery and publication of the Fliess correspondence have we been able to detect the similarity between many of Freud's later formulations and those already contained in the "Project" (1895), which formed part of this correspondence.

Freud's application of Fechner's constancy principle, which already played an important role in the "Project," was a vital part of his theory of the functioning of the mental apparatus. He conceptualized it in Chapter VII of _The Interpretation of Dreams_ (1900) and later in "Formulations on the Two Principles of Mental Functioning" (1911b) and the metapsychological papers of 1915 to 1917. We know of Freud's preoccupation with problems of evolution and his study of Darwin and Lamarck, his application of Haeckel's ontogenetic principle ("ontogeny recapitulates phylogeny") to psychoanalysis, especially to the development of the mental apparatus. He had also made ambitious speculative attempts to apply psychoanalytic principles to the theory of evolution.

Beyond the Pleasure Principle contains what Freud called "often

[1] For a more extensive discussion of this work, see Schur (1966b). Some parts of this chapter, especially the first one, are addressed mainly to readers familiar with psychoanalytic theory.

far-fetched speculations" (p. 24). In permitting his mind to range far and wide, Freud brought up some extremely challenging ideas which led eventually to the formulation of the structural point of view, the dual instinctual drive theory, and the concept of a stimulus barrier. But it also led him to the introduction of the theory of a death instinct and the concept of the repetition compulsion as a superordinated regulatory mechanism of mental functioning, hypotheses which have been haunting psychoanalytic theory since 1920.

A discussion of the actual merits of Freud's concept of the death instinct viewed as a cosmic phenomenon would be completely outside the scope of this study. What is pertinent to our theme is the *unusual* method of reasoning by which Freud arrived at these concepts. This suggests that this essay, probably more than most of Freud's other writings since the dream book, had multiple determinants in his inner life. The point at which Freud departed from his empirical, tightly reasoned discussion is closely linked with his use of the concept "pleasure principle" within the context of his speculations.

When the concepts unpleasure and pleasure and the unpleasure and pleasure principles[2] were introduced in Chapter VII of *The Interpretation of Dreams,* they were set forth in "economic" terms. Any accumulation of tension was equated with unpleasure and any diminution of tension with pleasure. This formulation was modeled after Fechner's constancy principle. In biological terms this principle was believed to guarantee the organism a certain equilibrium, although Freud recognized that complete freedom from excitation was a fiction. In psychological terms, Freud formulated the pleasure-unpleasure principle as follows: the mental apparatus strives to avoid undue tension. This can be achieved either by the avoidance of too intense, "painful" stimuli, which impinge on the mental apparatus from without; or by the gratification of certain tension producing (inner) needs, which, once they have gained mental representation, may be called instinctual drives.

Freud tried to base his "far-fetched speculations" in *Beyond the Pleasure Principle* on a series of empirical observations. The question is whether his constructs were as valid as his observations and necessary for their explanation.[3]

[2] In a recently published monograph (1966b), I suggested that a distinction between an unpleasure principle and a pleasure principle is advisable for many reasons.
[3] The evaluation which now follows is framed in the terminology which Freud used only after he had introduced the structural point of view (1923).

After restating that it is the endeavor of the mental apparatus "to keep the quantity of excitation as low as possible, or at least constant," Freud added an important restriction:

> Strictly speaking it is incorrect to talk of the dominance of the pleasure principle. . . . If such a dominance existed, the immense majority of our mental processes would have to be accompanied by pleasure . . . , whereas universal experience completely contradicts any such conclusion. The most that can be said, therefore, is that there exists in the mind a strong *tendency* towards the pleasure principle [p. 9].

This restriction of a regulatory principle to a "tendency" has validity of course. However, we see in the above-quoted paragraph one fundamental difficulty: Freud's original formulation of the unpleasure-pleasure regulatory principles, as I have already indicated, was expressed on the one hand in biological (neurophysiological) terms, and on the other—to the extent that he used a metapsychological framework—primarily in "economic" terms. Yet, in that part of *Beyond the Pleasure Principle* in which Freud tried to prove his main concepts, he used the terms pleasure and unpleasure chiefly to stand for an *experience* or an *affect*. The unpleasure-pleasure *principles* deal with the accumulation and avoidance of tension and with the seeking of stimuli and objects for discharge of tension. The *affects* pleasure and unpleasure—like all affects—are complex ego responses having many genetically determined hierarchical layers, and dependent on the state of all three psychic structures and their relationship to the environment. This difference has been overlooked frequently, unfortunately, even by Freud.

Freud wrote that, although the transition from the pleasure principle to the reality principle could be understood as an *inhibition* of the pleasure principle, and *breaches* in the pleasure principle could be explained by maturation and development of the "mental apparatus" leading to conflict, and hence to experience of unpleasure instead of pleasure, there were some phenomena which were evidence of a principle *beyond* the pleasure principle. These were posttraumatic dreams in which the patient repeats a traumatic situation; certain games of children, especially the reel and peek-a-boo games; the compulsion of patients to repeat painful experiences of the past; and the phenomenon Freud called "fate neurosis" in which people's behavior led them from one tragedy to another giving one the impression they were "being pursued by a malignant fate or possessed by some 'daemonic' power" (p. 21).

The example of the posttraumatic dreams, however, formed the main pillar of his thesis. He considered it impossible to explain such dreams by any wish fulfillment, and therefore assumed that they arose beyond the pleasure principle in obedience to the repetition compulsion. The following explanation led finally to a new theory of "instincts."

> But how is the predicate of being 'instinctual' related to the compulsion to repeat? . . . we cannot escape a suspicion that we have come upon the track of a universal attribute of instincts and perhaps of organic life in general. . . . *It seems, then, that an instinct is an urge inherent in organic life to restore an earlier state of things* which the living entity has been obliged to abandon under the pressure of external disturbing forces [p. 36].

Once Freud had taken this step, the logical inference was:

> It would be in contradiction to the conservative nature of the instincts if the goal of life were a state of things which had never yet been attained. On the contrary, it must be an *old* state of things, . . . from which the living entity has at one time . . . departed and to which it is striving to return. . . . If we are to take it as a truth that knows no exception that everything living dies for *internal* reasons—becomes inorganic once again—then we shall be compelled to say that *'the aim of all life is death'* and that . . . *'inanimate things existed before* living ones' [p. 38].

It was then also logical for Freud to say that all that the organism wishes is to die only in its own fashion and to regard as "paradoxical . . . that the living organism struggles most energetically against events (dangers, in fact) which might help it to attain its life's aim [death] rapidly" (p. 39).

Freud's new definition of an instinct was repeated in identical form in connection with the regulatory principles:

> The dominating tendency of mental life . . . is the effort to reduce, to keep constant or to remove internal tension due to stimuli (the 'Nirvana principle' . . .)—a tendency which finds expression in the pleasure principle, and our recognition of that fact is one of our strongest reasons for believing in the existence of death instincts [p. 55f.].

He then added that the repetition compulsion had first put him on the track of the death instinct. Thus, the constancy-Nirvana-pleasure and repetition-compulsion principles are then taken as proof of the death-instinct concept, which in turn is used as an explanation for these same principles—a classical example of circular reasoning.

I have had to outline Freud's "speculations" before disputing both the necessity to explain certain behavioral phenomena as being *beyond* the pleasure-unpleasure principles and the necessity to establish the repetition compulsion as an overriding regulatory principle of mental functioning.

All the examples offered by Freud as proof of the existence of some "daemonic" power—posttraumatic dreams, children's play, the behavior of patients in the psychoanalytic situation and in the fate neurosis—have one common denominator: the repetitiveness of all physiological functioning and of behavior. Freud himself emphasized throughout his work that unconscious wishes have this character of indestructibility in common with all other mental acts which are truly unconscious, and he described the "compulsion to repeat" as characteristic of the operation of the instinctual drives.

Freud stated again and again that infantile instinctual demands which have not found gratification press for discharge. This assumption about the incessant recurrence of unfulfilled wishes is one of the cornerstones of Freud's theory of dream[4] and neurotic symptom formation. Yet, though he recognized the tendency to repetitiveness as characteristic of instinctual demands, he seemed to have been puzzled by other similar characteristics of behavior which now, in structural terms, we would call repetitive aspects of ego and superego functioning.

Freud used the attribute "daemonic" to describe the motivational forces which repeatedly lead to behavior that results in frustration, unhappiness and often tragedy. Caught in a teleological approach, Freud was concerned here with the *consequences* and not the forces at work, deducing his theory of these forces from their consequences.

When we seek *causes* for the fact that on a hot, humid night the air in wooded areas adjacent to stagnant water is filled with myriads of tiny insects which, attracted by light, pass through every screen, we find them in the insects' species-specific response pattern to certain stimuli. When the next morning we find screens and windowpanes covered with masses of dead insects, we may be awed by the backfiring of certain behavior patterns which, nevertheless, must have developed in the course of evolution because they had a high survival value. However, the fact that such patterns, instead of serving survival, end in the destruction of the phenotype does not denote the presence of an instinct whose *aim* it would be to achieve this fatal goal. Such

---

[4] Modern dream psychology confirms this assumption for the most part.

events are terrible and awe-inspiring, but even when they occur in human tragedies we need not characterize them as "daemonic." It is evident that for Freud the attribute "daemonic" was a necessary stepping-stone toward the formulation of the death instinct theory and the repetition compulsion as superordinated principles of mental functioning. We cannot escape the conclusion that Freud had already arrived at his hypothesis of the "death instinct" and was using various aspects of "unpleasurable" repetitiveness to confirm it, while at the same time using this hypothesis to explain the phenomenon he had observed.

Among the examples which Freud viewed as contradictory to the pleasure-unpleasure principle, the one he considered to be the most valid was the post-traumatic dream, which has "the characteristic of bringing the patient back into the situation of his accident, a situation from which he wakes up in another fright" (p. 13). Freud emphasized that the causation of traumatic neurosis is linked with the factor of surprise, the lack of preparedness for danger. This element also applies to neuroses following car and train accidents. However, during World War II, traumatic neuroses, often with acute psychosislike states, were also frequently observed in soldiers after prolonged harrowing experiences which were characterized by a mounting crescendo of danger rather than by the suddenness of the trauma. Furthermore, traumatic neuroses can be produced by traumatization extending over a long period of time as we have so tragically seen in the survivors of the extermination camps of Nazi Germany. All of these categories have in common: the repetitive dreams, the contents of which are endless variations of the traumatic situation, including the events preceding the actual trauma.

Freud offers two interpretations of posttraumatic dreams. First he considered that "these dreams (endeavor) to master the stimulus retroactively, by developing the anxiety, whose omission was the cause of the traumatic neurosis" (p. 32). Second, they are therefore not under the dominance of the pleasure (-unpleasure) principle, but under the dominance of the repetition compulsion, which in turn expresses the urge of all instinctual drives to restore an earlier—inorganic—state of things.

I propose that an alternative explanation, derived from Freud's work before and after *Beyond the Pleasure Principle* and clinical observations which contradict those Freud had available at that time, can be framed in the context of the pleasure-unpleasure principle.

Namely, the repetition of traumatic events in dreams represents—apart from the gratification of various derivatives (e.g., passive, homosexual, and masochistic wishes) and superego demands (e.g., "guilt of the survivor")—the ego's unconscious wish to undo the traumatic situation. This cannot be achieved without reliving the latter in endless variations. The resulting anxiety is an ego response to danger, no different from the outcome of other anxiety-producing dreams, in which the wish represents a forbidden instinctual (sexual and/or aggressive) demand. The other examples Freud cited to support his hypotheses can be explained along similar lines.

If Freud's interpretation of the post-traumatic dream as being beyond the pleasure principle is not valid, then his hypothesis about the repetition compulsion as a superordinated regulatory principle beyond the pleasure principle, instinct as an "urge inherent in organic life to restore an earlier state of things" (i.e., inorganic state), and finally the death instinct concept, are all deprived of what Freud considered to be the cornerstone of his reasoning.[5] Before I venture some ideas as to *why* Freud formulated these concepts and *why* in doing so, he did not evidence his usual lucidity and logic, I will note another speculative theme in the book and Freud's attitude toward his new ideas.

Near the end of *Beyond the Pleasure Principle,* after commenting upon how little science, following "sober Darwinian lines," had thus far been able to tell us about the origin and evolution of sexuality, Freud remarked:

> In quite a different region, it is true, we *do* meet with such a hypothesis; but it is of so fantastic a kind—a myth rather than a scientific explanation—that I should not venture to produce it here, were it not that it fulfils precisely the one condition whose fulfilment we desire. For it traces the origin of an instinct to *a need to restore an earlier state of things.*
>
> What I have in mind is, of course, the theory which Plato puts into the mouth of Aristophanes in the *Symposium,* and which deals not only with the *origin* of the sexual instinct but also with the most important of its variations in relation to its object. "The original human nature was not like the present, but different. In the first place, the sexes were originally three in number, not two as they are now; there was man,

---

[5] I would like to emphasize that Freud's concepts of the death instinct, the repetition compulsion, and "beyond the pleasure principle" are logically inseparable, although this is not recognized by many authors who disagree with Freud's death-instinct concept but accept his formulations about the repetition compulsion as a superordinated regulatory principle beyond the pleasure principle, thus accepting also the reasoning by which Freud arrived at this hypothesis.

woman, and the union of the two. . . ." Everything about these primaeval men was double: they had four hands and four feet, two faces, two privy parts, and so on. Eventually Zeus decided to cut these men in two, "like a sorb-apple which is halved for pickling." After the division had been made, "the two parts of man, each desiring his other half, came together, and threw their arms about one another eager to grow into one."

Shall we follow the hint given us by the poet-philosopher, and venture upon the hypothesis that living substance at the time of its coming to life was torn apart into small particles, which have ever since endeavoured to reunite through the sexual instincts? that these instincts, in which the chemical affinity of inanimate matter persisted, gradually succeeded, as they developed through the kingdom of the protista, in overcoming the difficulties put in the way of that endeavour by an environment charged with dangerous stimuli—stimuli which compelled them to form a protective cortical layer? that these splintered fragments of living substance in this way attained a multicellular condition and finally transferred the instinct for reuniting, in the most highly concentrated form, to the germ-cells? [pp. 57-58].

At his most boldly speculative here, Freud was following up the trend of thought he had indicated to Abraham in his letter of November 11, 1917, where he had hinted about attempting to combine the concepts of evolution and psychoanalysis. This speculation was now being applied not to Thanatos, the death instinct, but to Eros, the uniting, synthesizing force which counteracted the "natural," "instinctive" tendency toward dissolution. This was Eros the "mischief-maker," as Freud was to call it in *The Ego and the Id*.

Freud was thus attributing omnipotence to the sexual instinctual drives as these developed through evolution. Expressed in modern evolutional terms based on observed animal behavior, the mating instinct has developed in evolution in such a way that it enables the animal "to overcome the difficulties put in the way of that endeavour by an environment charged with dangerous stimuli" (for a discussion, see, for example, Lorenz [1963]).

In dealing with this subject, Freud had reached the limit of his speculations, if we except the last chapter, which he seems to have added later.[6] With admirable frankness and self-criticism, Freud remarked:

[6] We know from Freud's correspondence that *Beyond the Pleasure Principle* was written with many interruptions. It was begun in March, 1919, and the first draft was completed in May. He started to work on it again during the winter of 1920 and finished the book after making several revisions in July, 1920.

But here, I think, the moment has come for breaking off.

Not, however, without the addition of a few words of critical reflection. It may be asked whether and how far I am myself convinced of the truth of the hypotheses that have been set out in these pages. My answer would be that I am not convinced myself and that I do not seek to persuade other people to believe in them. Or, more precisely, that I do not know how far I believe in them. There is no reason, as it seems to me, why the emotional factor of conviction should enter into this question at all. It is surely possible to throw oneself into a line of thought and to follow it wherever it leads out of simple scientific curiosity, or, if the reader prefers, as an *advocatus diaboli,* who is not on that account himself sold to the devil. I do not dispute the fact that the third step in the theory of the instincts, which I have taken here, cannot lay claim to the same degree of certainty as the two earlier ones—the extension of the concept of sexuality and the hypothesis of narcissism. These two innovations were a direct translation of observation into theory and were no more open to sources of error than is inevitable in all such cases. It is true that my assertion of the regressive character of instincts also rests upon observed material—namely on the facts of the compulsion to repeat. It may be, however, that I have over-estimated their significance. And in any case it is impossible to pursue an idea of this kind except by repeatedly combining factual material with what is purely speculative and thus diverging widely from empirical observation. The more frequently this is done in the course of constructing a theory, the more untrustworthy, as we know, must be the final result. But the degree of uncertainty is not assignable. One may have made a lucky hit or one may have gone shamefully astray. . . . Unfortunately, however, people are seldom impartial where ultimate things, the great problems of science and life, are concerned. Each of us is governed in such cases by deep-rooted internal prejudices, into whose hands our speculation unwittingly plays. Since we have such good grounds for being distrustful, our attitude towards the results of our own deliberations cannot well be other than one of cool benevolence [p. 58f.].

However, later in life Freud stood by his concepts of the death instinct and the repetition compulsion, although, as we shall see, he did not always apply them in the same context.

TRAGIC EVENTS IN FREUD'S LIFE

At this point it is pertinent to consider Freud's life situation in 1919-1920. Some authors have hypothesized that *Beyond the Pleasure Principle* was written under the impact of the death of Freud's daughter Sophie. This appears to have been an unfounded speculation (see Wittels, 1924; Ekstein, 1949; Friedman, 1966). Freud himself anticipated—or was told—that such an assumption might be made, and he wrote to Eitingon on July 18, 1920:

> The "Beyond" is finally finished. You will be able to certify that it was half finished when Sophie was alive and flourishing [1].

However, the term "death instinct" seems to have made its first appearance in letters to Eitingon of February 12 and February 20, 1920, shortly after the deaths of Anton von Freund and Sophie. Also, throughout the writing of *Beyond the Pleasure Principle,* Freud was under the influence of the prolonged death struggle of Anton von Freund. How the two events—the illness and death of von Freund and the death of Sophie—merged in their impact on Freud can be gauged from a letter to Binswanger of March 14, 1920:

> On receiving your admonitory postcard yesterday I asked myself: Is it possible that I have left your amiable, interesting letter of Jan. 7 unanswered: Yes, so it is, and this is accounted for by the sad events of this month. First I had day by day to watch the gradual failing of a dear friend, whose name you will learn from an obituary notice in the Zeitschrift, 1920, No. 1. You will easily understand why it was particularly to *you* that I could not write, when I tell you that for a year and a half the thought of what had happened to you filled me with hope for him. He had undergone the same operation as you, but was not spared the recurrence. We buried him on January 22. The same night we received a disquieting telegram from our son-in-law Halberstadt in Hamburg. My daughter Sophie, aged 26, mother of two boys, was stricken with the grippe; on January 25 she died, after a four days' illness. At that time our railroads were shut down, and we could not even go there. Now my deeply distressed wife is preparing for the trip, but the new unrest in Germany makes it doubtful that this intention can be carried out. Since then a heavy oppression has been weighing on all of us, which also affects my capacity for work. Neither of us has got over the monstrous fact of children dying before their parents. Next summer—this will answer your friendly invitation—we want to be together somewhere with the two orphans and the inconsolable husband whom we have loved like a son for seven years. If this is possible! You are not unfamiliar with all the other difficulties of the situation. I have a great deal of work, but there is no way to avert impoverishment.

Letters written to Jones on January 26, and February 8, 1920 also referred to both deaths. In the first letter Freud wrote:

> Poor or happy Toni Freund was buried last Thursday, 22nd of this month. Sorry to hear your father is on the list now [Jones's father was

dying], but we all must and I wonder when my turn will come. Yesterday I lived through an experience which makes me wish it should not last a long time [Jones, Vol. 3, p. 19].

[In the second:] You know of the misfortune that has befallen me. It is depressing indeed, a loss to be forgotten. . . . Now I may well be declining in power of thought and expression, why not? Everyone is liable to decay in the course of time and I have had my full measure of effort, perhaps even of success. But I rejoice in your and other friends' performances as if they were my own [unpublished letter, written in English].

Freud tried to regain his equilibrium. In his letters to Ferenczi and Eitingon he used such expressions as *"La séance continue,"* "blunt necessity," "mute *submission"* (my italics), a state most difficult for Freud to tolerate. Other letters also reflected Freud's attempt to regain control of his reactions to Sophie's death. Freud wrote to Pfister on January 27, 1920:

On the same afternoon we received the news that our dear Sophie in Hamburg had been snatched away by influenzal pneumonia, snatched away from glowing health, from her busy life as a capable mother and loving wife, in four or five days, as if she had never been. We had been worried about her for two days, but were still hopeful. From a distance it is so difficult to judge. *The distance still remains.* We could not, as we wished to, go to her at once when the first alarming news came, because there were no trains, not even a children's train.[7] *The undisguised brutality of our time weighs heavily on us.* Our poor Sunday child is to be cremated to-morrow. Not till the day after to-morrow will our daughter Mathilde and her husband, thanks to an unexpected concatenation of circumstances, be able to set off for Hamburg in an Entente train. At least our son-in-law was not alone. Two of our sons who were in Berlin are already with him, and our friend Eitingon has gone with them.

Sophie leaves behind two boys, one aged six and the other thirteen months, and an inconsolable husband who will have to pay dearly for the happiness of these seven years. The happiness was only between them, not in external circumstances, which were war and war service, being wounded and losing their money, but they remained brave and cheerful.

I do as much work as I can, and am grateful for the distraction. The loss of a child seems to be a grave blow to one's narcissism; as for mourning, that will no doubt come later [italics added].

---

[7] Children from starving Austria were sent abroad by an international children's aid association.

To Ferenczi he wrote on February 4, 1920:

Dear Friend,
Please don't worry about me. Apart from feeling rather more tired I am the same. The death, painful as it is, does not affect my attitude toward life. For years I was prepared for the loss of our sons; now it is our daughter; as a confirmed unbeliever I have no one to accuse and realize that there is no place where I could lodge a complaint. "The unvaried, still returning hour of duty"[8] and "the dear lovely habit of living"[9] will do their bit toward letting everything go on as before. Deep down I sense a bitter, irreparable narcissistic injury [L. 187].

Within a few months after the deaths of Sophie and Anton von Freund, Freud had obviously regained his equilibrium. He wrote to Eitingon on May 27, 1920:

I am now correcting and completing "Beyond," that is, of the pleasure principle, and am once again in a productive phase. *Fractus si illabatur orbis impavidum, ferient ruinae.*[10] All merely [a matter of] mood, as long as it lasts [2].

At the beginning of this chapter I discussed the conceptual and empirical precursors of Freud's *Beyond the Pleasure Principle*. Post-war Vienna was utterly gloomy, accentuated for Freud by worry about his sons and by the painful necessity of seeing his young patient-friend "shrink" to death, followed only a few days later by the loss of his daughter Sophie.

We must bear in mind, too, that Freud, although able again and again to muster his resilience and regain inner mastery, was exhausted by those years, by the tremendous creative activity carried on under trying circumstances. He had passed his second "deadline" but at times felt quite old (cf. his letter of December 16, 1917, to Ferenczi in which he remarked: "There is really nothing strange in a man of my years noticing the gradual decay of his person").

There is a passage in the *Beyond the Pleasure Principle* which might indicate that the formulation of the death-instinct concept ful-

---

[8] A quotation from Schiller's *Piccolomini*.
[9] A quotation from Goethe's *Egmont*.
[10] A quotation from an Ode by Horace: "If the sky should fall in pieces, the ruins will not daunt it." (*Horace Odes*, Book III, Ode 3.) The correct quotation is:

Si fractus illabatur orbis,
impavidum ferient ruinae.

filled an important function in Freud's inner struggle with the problem of death:

> Perhaps we have adopted the belief [that all living substance dies from internal causes] because there is some comfort in it. If we are to die ourselves, and first to lose in death those who are dearest to us, it is easier to submit to a remorseless law of nature, to the sublime *Ananke* [Necessity], than to a chance which might perhaps have been escaped. It may be, however, that this belief in the internal necessity of dying is only another of those illusions which we have created *"um die Schwere des Daseins zu ertragen"* [p. 45].[11]

Here Freud was repeating thoughts he had previously expressed in "Thoughts for the Times on War and Death" and *Totem and Taboo*. Could there have been more than just *comfort* in what Freud called "the belief" *(Glaube)*, a word which he did not use frequently for his concepts? The most potent driving force in Freud the scientist was his wish to know. Could it be that uncovering a "death instinct" permitted Freud literally to *live* with the reality of death, especially with the further aid of his simultaneous *creation* of Eros through the sheer omnipotence of thought?

We are reminded at this point of Freud's paper on the "Theme of the Three Caskets," specifically of the Moerae who watch "inexorably" over "the regular order of nature." Freud stated then that men only perceived the full seriousness of natural law when they had to submit their own selves to it, and that man tried to overcome death after having recognized it intellectually (see Chapter 10).

Therefore, the formulation of the death-instinct concept—paradoxical as this may seem—may not only have steeled Freud for the 16-year ordeal of his cancer, but prepared him for his belief in the supremacy of the ego, of the intellect, of *Logos,* the only force with which he could face *Ananke*.[12] It paved the way for the *Future of an Illusion* and for the formulation of a "scientific *Weltanschauung.*" He wrote to Pfister on April 6, 1922:

> Complete objectivity requires a person who takes less pleasure in life than you do; you insist on finding something edifying in it. True, it is

---

[11] "To bear the burden of existence," a quotation from Schiller's *Die Braut von Messina*, I, 8.

[12] Friedman (1966) independently arrived at the conclusion that this passage may be very significant for what it indicates of Freud's frame of mind when he wrote the book.

only in old age that one is converted to the grim heavenly pair *Logos kai Ananke.*

This "conversion" can only be a painful, gradual process. We may thus modify Freud's statement of 1913 and say that in recognizing death intellectually man can hope to overcome not *death,* but his *fear* of it.

"THE UNCANNY"

In his correspondence Freud mentioned that he had written an essay on "The Uncanny" ("Das Unheimliche") before starting work on *Beyond the Pleasure Principle.* The concept of a "repetition compulsion" powerful enough to override the pleasure principle was first introduced in "The Uncanny." There are a number of clues in this essay pointing to factors that might have influenced his conception of the death instinct and the repetition compulsion.[13]

The adjective "daemonic" which he applied to the examples he used to illustrate his formulations makes an early appearance in this paper and is related to the central theme. In the philological section of the paper Freud indicated that while the English translations of the German word *unheimlich* are "uncomfortable, uneasy, gloomy, dismal, uncanny, ghastly; (of a house) haunted; (of a man) a repulsive fellow" (1919, p. 221), of which "uncanny" is the closest in meaning to the German in the examples cited by him, the Arabic and Hebrew equivalents for "uncanny" mean the same thing as "daemonic," "gruesome."

Freud introduced this paper as a study on "aesthetics," meaning by this not just a theory of beauty but a theory of the quality of feelings, one of these being uncanniness. He used various works of literature as his point of departure (in *Beyond the Pleasure Principle* he introduced such works only to give additional support to his speculations). E. T. A. Hoffmann was a master of tales dealing with the fantastic and the supernatural. Freud selected his story "The Sand-Man" as an example of the uncanny,[14] pointing out that the feeling of uncanniness evoked in the reader by this writer and others who had mastered the technique depended on their leaving the reader in doubt for some time whether

---

13 We have, of course, no way of knowing whether Freud added some passages to the final draft of this paper *after* he had completed the first draft of *Beyond the Pleasure Principle.*

14 This story contains the model of the character of Olympia used by Offenbach in his opera *Tales of Hoffmann.*

the situation was a realistic one or a supernatural one, as in fairy tales.[15] Freud then traced the uncanny quality to a series of themes.

He called attention to the mysterious presentation in which early childhood (screen) memories of the hero are interwoven with scenes which are either fantasies or distortions of experience, involving undisguised castration threats displaced to gouging out of eyes and loss of arms, and eventually the threat of death itself.

Another theme is that of two father figures representing a split of the "father-imago" into the good, protecting father and the cruel, uncanny, castrating one who interferes with love and eventually, in the form of the "Sand-Man," brings about the death of the main figure of the tale. Moreover—and this Freud did not emphasize—the "Sand-Man" not only brings about death but actually represents the "daemonic" power of death which lures its victim to self-destruction after he has nearly strangled his beloved bride-to-be. Thus Death—Thanatos—defeats and kills love.

Freud then introduced other elements of the uncanny from Hoffmann's work, in particular a book called *Die Elixiere des Teufels (The Devil's Elixir)*. He selected from this "devilish" story themes of uncanniness which, like the castration fear in "The Sand-Man," can also be traced to infantile sources. Freud said:

These themes are all concerned with the phenomenon of the 'double'. . . . Thus we have characters who are to be considered identical because they look alike. This relation is accentuated by mental processes leaping from one of these characters to another—by what we should call telepathy[16]—, so that the one possesses knowledge, feelings and experience in common with the other. Or . . . the subject identifies

---

[15] While Hoffmann was probably influenced by Grimm's fairy tales, E. A. Poe was probably influenced by Hoffmann (see Bonaparte, 1933). Another masterful example of the technique involved in this type of story is Thomas Mann's *Mario and the Magician*.

[16] Freud's open-minded attitude toward telepathy has some parallels to his superstitions about dying at "critical" dates. Jones devoted a whole chapter in Vol. 3 of his biography to Freud's ideas on this subject. We have seen how Freud had accepted elements of Fliess's "number games" and how after the break in their friendship these ideas were intensified to an obsessive superstition. I assume that the mechanism of identification has to be considered as an important determinant here, an identification which was intensified by the mourning process. Both Jung and Ferenczi were interested in the occult and tried to convince Freud of its validity. His acceptance was far less than it had been with Fliess's ideas, but he did try to remain open to argument. After the break with Jung a similar identification with the lost object may have operated to maintain his interest in these phenomena, even though as in his paper on "Dreams and Telepathy" he admitted that whenever he was tempted to posit a "telepathic" factor, he was soon able to disprove its existence.

himself with someone else, so that he is in doubt as to which his self is, or substitutes the extraneous self for his own. In other words, there is a doubling, dividing and interchanging of the self. And finally there is the *constant recurrence of the same thing*—the repetition of the same features or character-traits or vicissitudes, of the same crimes, or even the same names through several consecutive generations [p. 234; italics added].

Freud used a similar phrase in inverted commas in *Beyond the Pleasure Principle* when he discussed the "fate neurosis." This phrase "the constant recurrence of the same thing" seems to have been taken from Nietzsche's *Also Sprach Zarathustra* (see Strachey's footnote on p. 234). Freud then discussed this phenomenon of the "double," following the main lines of Otto Rank's presentation in his paper "Der Doppelgänger" (1914). This phenomenon was traced back to reflections in mirrors, shadows, guardian spirits, to the belief in the soul and the fear of death. The double, which originally served to deny death by providing for immortality—in the grave images of the Egyptians, for example—then frequently became the uncanny harbinger of death. The double thus becomes "a thing of terror, just as, after the collapse of their religion, the gods turned into demons" (p. 236).

Anticipating the question why a continued repetition of the same thing should be regarded as a source of uncanny feeling, Freud gave two specific examples in addition to general descriptions of "uncanny" situations such as losing one's way in a fog or a dark forest and wandering in circles only to arrive over and over again at the same spot.

From what I have observed, this phenomenon does undoubtedly . . . arouse an uncany feeling, which, furthermore, recalls the sense of helplessness experienced in some dream-states. As I was walking, one hot summer afternoon, through the deserted streets of a provincial town in Italy which was unknown to me, I found myself in a quarter of whose character I could not long remain in doubt. Nothing but painted women were to be seen at the windows of the small houses, and I hastened to leave the narrow street at the next turning. But after having wandered about for a time without enquiring my way, I suddenly found myself back in the same street, where my presence was now beginning to excite attention. I hurried away once more, only to arrive by another *détour* at the same place yet a third time. Now, however, a feeling overcame me which I can only describe as uncanny, and I was glad enough to find myself back at the piazza I had left a short while before, without any further voyages of discovery [p. 236f.].

The second example was cited without indication that it had been an actual occurrence in Freud's life, but the incident is familiar to us from the earlier discussion of Freud's trip to Greece and his letter to Jung of April 16, 1909. Freud said:

> If we take another class of things, it is easy to see that there, too, it is only this factor of involuntary repetition which surrounds what would otherwise be innocent enough with an uncanny atmosphere, and forces upon us the idea of something fateful and inescapable when otherwise we should have spoken only of 'chance.' For instance, we naturally attach no importance to the event when we hand in an overcoat and get a cloakroom ticket with the number, let us say, 62; or when we find that our cabin on a ship bears that number. But the impression is altered if two such events, each in itself indifferent, happen close to-gether—if we come across the number 62 several times in a single day, or if we begin to notice that everything which has a number—addresses, hotel rooms, compartments in railway trains—invariably has the same one, or at all events one which contains the same figures. We do feel this to be uncanny. And unless a man is utterly hardened and proof against the lure of superstition, he will be tempted to ascribe a secret meaning to this obstinate recurrence of a number; he will take it, per-haps, as an indication of the span of life allotted to him [p. 237f.].

The importance of this example in this context is of course self-evident. Not quite a year before writing this paper Freud had passed his 62-year "deadline"!

In the next paragraph Freud directly connected these episodes and their origin to the crucial controversial formulations of *Beyond the Pleasure Principle,* saying:

> How exactly we can trace back to infantile psychology the uncanny effect of such similar recurrences is a question I can only lightly touch on in these pages; and I must refer the reader instead to another work [*Beyond the Pleasure Principle*], already completed, in which this has been gone into in detail, but in a different connection. For it is possible to recognize the dominance in the unconscious mind of a 'compulsion to repeat' proceeding from the instinctual impulses and probably in-herent in the very nature of the instincts—a compulsion powerful enough to overrule the pleasure principle, lending to certain aspects of the mind their daemonic character, and still very clearly expressed in the impulses of small children; a compulsion, too, which is responsible for a part of the course taken by the analyses of neurotic patients. All these considerations prepare us for the discovery that whatever reminds us of this inner 'compulsion to repeat' is perceived as uncanny [p. 238].

But the uncanniness of repetitiousness was not the only experience described by Hoffmann that was familiar to Freud. We know of at least two experiences of his seeing his "double." Jones mentioned that on a trip to Naples Freud met in the train somebody who looked like his double and asked his brother Alexander: "Does this signify *Vedere Napoli e poi morire?*" (Vol. 2, p. 21).

A letter written to Arthur Schnitzler,[17] the famous Viennese poet and writer, on the occasion of his 60th birthday is more important in this context because of its contents and also because it was written on May 14, 1922.[18] Freud wrote:

> But I will make a confession which for my sake I must ask you to keep to yourself and share with neither friends nor strangers. I have tormented myself with the question why in all these years I have never attempted to make your acquaintance and to have a talk with you (ignoring the possibility, of course, that you might not have welcomed my overture).
>
> The answer contains the confession which strikes me as too intimate. I think I have avoided you from a kind of reluctance to meet my double. Not that I am easily inclined to identify myself with another, or that I mean to overlook the difference in talent that separates me from you, but whenever I get deeply absorbed in your beautiful creations I invariably seem to find beneath their poetic surface the very presuppositions, interests, and conclusions which I know to be my own. Your determinism as well as your skepticism—what people call pessimism—your preoccupation with the truths of the unconscious and of the instinctual drives in man, your dissection of the cultural conventions of our society, the dwelling of your thoughts on the polarity of love and death; all this moves me with an *uncanny* [my italics] feeling of familiarity. (In a small book entitled *Beyond the Pleasure Principle,* published in 1920, I tried to reveal Eros and the death instinct as the motivating powers whose interplay dominates all the riddles of life.) [L. 197*].

Here is an unmistakable link between Freud's own feeling of having a "double," the paper on "The Uncanny," and *Beyond the Pleasure Principle.*

In a preceding paragraph of this letter Freud had written of one

---

[17] Schnitzler had a medical degree; his brother Julius was a prominent surgeon and friend of the Freud family, who also was a frequent partner of Freud's in their regular Saturday afternoon card games.

[18] The fact that Schnitzler was born in the same month as Freud may have intensified the latter feeling of having a double.

further source of the feeling of uncanniness—the element of the "omnipotence of thoughts."[19]

> Had I retained a remnant of belief in the "omnipotence of thoughts," I would not hesitate today to send you the warmest and heartiest good wishes for the years that await you. I shall leave this foolish gesture to the vast number of your contemporaries who will remember you on May 15.

In "The Uncanny" Freud cited examples from the analyses of obsessive neurotics (principally from that of the Rat Man, which was an endless source of information) of superstitions such as the "evil eye," etc. The common denominator of all the examples was that they actually represented the "return of the repressed"; the uncanny is something which "ought to have remained hidden but has come to light" (1919, p. 241). According to Freud, the feeling of uncanniness is experienced to the highest degree in relation to death and dead bodies.

> We might indeed have begun our investigation with this example, perhaps the most striking of all, of something uncanny, but we refrained from doing so because the uncanny in it is too much intermixed with what is purely gruesome. . . . There is scarcely any other matter, however, upon which our thoughts and feelings have changed so little since the very earliest times, and in which discarded forms have been so completely preserved under a thin disguise, as our relation to death. Two things account for our conservatism: the strength of our original emotional reaction to death and the insufficiency of our scientific knowledge about it. Biology has not yet been able to decide whether death is the inevitable fate of every living being or whether it is only a regular

---

[19] Freud very frequently included a remark about not believing in the omnipotence of thoughts in letters of congratulations. He did so in a letter to me on the occasion of my wedding in 1930:

Berlin-Tegel
June 28, 1930

Dear Dr. Schur:

I shall not be in Vienna when you get married, so I am writing to you today, a few days before the event, to wish you all the happiness you have the right to expect in your married life. Mindful of the rare kindness and conscientiousness that you have shown in caring for the remains of my physical self, I should like to endow my wishes with the power to enforce their fulfillment.

This is hardly the occasion to bother you with medical reports. I only want to say that I do not forget how often your diagnoses have turned out to be correct in my case, and that for this reason I am a docile patient, even if it is not easy for me.

In warm remembrance,
Yours faithfully,
Freud

but yet perhaps avoidable event in life. It is true that the statement 'All men are mortal' is paraded in text-books of logic as an example of a general proposition; but no human being really grasps it, and our unconscious has as little use now as it ever had for the idea of its own mortality. Religions continue to dispute the importance of the undeniable fact of individual death and to postulate a life after death. . . . In our great cities, placards announce lectures that undertake to tell us how to get into touch with the souls of the departed; and . . . not a few of the most . . . penetrating minds among our men of science have come to the conclusion, especially towards the close of their own lives, that a contact of this kind is not impossible. Since almost all of us still think as savages do on this topic, it is no matter for surprise that the primitive fear of the dead is still so strong within us and always ready to come to the surface on any provocation. . . . Considering our unchanged attitude towards death, we might . . . enquire what has become of the repression, which is the necessary condition of a primitive feeling recurring in the shape of something uncanny. But repression is there, too. All supposedly educated people have ceased to believe officially that the dead can become visible as spirits . . . ; their emotional attitude towards their dead, moreover, once a highly ambiguous and ambivalent one, has been toned down in the higher strata of the mind into an unambiguous feeling of piety [p. 241ff.].

And yet Freud had introduced this essay with the statement:

The writer of the present contribution, indeed, must himself plead guilty to a special obtuseness in the matter, where extreme delicacy of perception would be more in place. It is long since he has experienced or heard of anything which has given him an uncanny impression. And he must start by translating himself into that state of feeling, by awakening in himself the possibility of experiencing it [p. 220].

Unconscious Death Wishes and the Death Instinct

In the light of the examples which followed, such a strong affirmation would seem to indicate that this study of Freud's, too, was part of his unceasing struggle to gain mastery over phenomena which had an aspect of uncanniness, especially if these were connected with the problem of death.

We have seen in the essay on "The Uncanny" how Freud related his superstition about dying at the age of 62 to the compulsion to repeat and its "daemonic" effect on mental functioning. In my earlier discussion of this symptom, as it was presented in Freud's letter to Jung of April 16, 1909, I showed how this obsessive superstition, like any symptom, was a complex compromise formation. It was linked to

Freud's highly ambivalent relationship to Fliess, a relationship not dissimilar to what he described in *Beyond the Pleasure Principle* as a transference phenomenon. It was also linked to the complex ambivalence manifestations of the Irma and "non vixit" dreams, and the day residues behind them revealed in the Fliess correspondence. These in turn were traceable to his infantile conflicts around the death of his younger brother Julius. I showed that Freud himself connected his conflicts about Fliess to those about Julius in his analysis of the fainting spell in Munich in 1912.

However, there is another piece of evidence concerning Freud's sibling rivalry. In 1917 Freud wrote a paper on "A Childhood Recollection from *Dichtung und Wahrheit*" (the title of Goethe's autobiography), in which he interpreted Goethe's earliest childhood memory, a "mischievous prank in which he had thrown a good part of the family's crockery," as a screen memory representing Goethe's sibling rivalry. Freud never intimated that this paper had any autobiographical significance, but this aspect is unmistakable, and I am sure that Freud was fully aware of it.

Goethe had been born on August 28, 1749, his younger sister Cornelia a little over 15 months later, about the same interval as that separating the birth of Freud and of his brother Julius. The next four children of the Goethe family died either in childhood or early infancy. The brother born when Goethe was three and a quarter years old died when Goethe was nine and a half. Freud quoted from a contemporary biographical account by Bettina Brentano the fact that Goethe "shed no tears at the death of his younger brother." We find in Freud's paper the following passage:

> Goethe's next youngest sister, Cornelia Frederica Christiana, was born on December 7, 1750, when he was fifteen months old. This slight difference in age almost excludes the possibility of her having been an object of jealousy. It is known that, when their passions awake, children never develop such violent reactions against the brothers and sisters they find already in existence, but direct their hostility against the newcomers. Nor is the scene we are endeavouring to interpret reconcilable with Goethe's tender age at the time of, or shortly after, Cornelia's birth [1917c, p. 151].

Freud was the oldest child born to his father's third wife, Amalie. Next came Julius who died at the age of 8 months, and then sister Anna, born on December 31, 1858 when Freud was nearly 2 years and 8 months old. His mother's pregnancy and the events around the time of sister Anna's birth came up in the most ingenious of Freud's reconstructions during his self-analysis, reported both in the Fliess correspondence (L. 70 and 71), in *The Interpretation of Dreams* (1900, p. 247f.) and in *The Psychopathology of Everyday Life* (1901b, p. 49ff.). Like Goethe, Freud showed the greatest hostility to this "newcomer." As a matter of fact, Anna remained for Freud the least liked of his sisters.[20]

It is therefore entirely plausible that Freud's memories of jealousy concerning Julius and his guilt feelings over his brother's death were a displacement backward (genetically speaking) of his jealous feelings toward Anna. This displacement may have been facilitated by his conflicts with Fliess, who was born on October 24, 1858—only about two months before Anna.

Not counting Julius, Freud had six siblings born after him, as did Goethe. The autobiographical aspect of Freud's paper on Goethe becomes even more obvious in its closing paragraph:

> I have, however, already remarked elsewhere that if a man has been his mother's undisputed darling he retains throughout life the triumphant feeling, the confidence in success, which not seldom brings actual success along with it. And Goethe might well have given some such heading to his autobiography as: 'My strength has its roots in my relation to my mother' [1917c, p. 156].

This statement certainly applies to Freud as well as to the subject of the essay.

We know from the letter to Jung that Freud's obsessive superstition reached its peak during the time Fliess was openly accusing Freud of indiscretion and plagiarism. The former accusation was one of the elements of both the Irma and the *non vixit* dreams, and had its infantile roots in Freud's "telling on" his nephew John. The letter to Jung also contained the first indication of the future break with Jung. In later years, the superstition recurred only when the "critical" period was close or, as during the war, in times of extreme stress.

In using Freud's formula for explaining obsessional superstitions, I indicated that there was a wish to die behind Freud's own superstition, stemming from aggression turned against the self. In terms of wishes, his superstition meant that because he wanted Fliess, Fleischl, his father, his brother Julius, his sister Anna, and anyone else he hated

---

[20] Anna (Bernays) died in New York at the age of 97. All of Freud's other sisters died in Nazi concentration camps.

to die, that he would die. Expressed differently, in defensive terms, it meant that it was not true that he wanted all those people to die; he himself wanted to die. Let us recall at this point the words which, according to Jones, Freud uttered on awakening from his fainting spell in 1912: "How sweet it must be to die." Most of us experience at moments of despair or extreme mental fatigue, pain, and grief a conscious or unconscious *wish* to see the "end of it all." During the war years, when his sons were in mortal danger, or later, when his young friend was dying and Freud permitted himself to utter pessimistic thoughts in his letters, there were probably moments when he asked himself: "How much longer must I bear this cross?" These were fleeting moments. In the next letter after a complaining one, or even in the same letter, Freud's resilience, his wish to carry on, to live, would come through again. This resilience lasted for another 20 years, of which 16 were marked by deep misery and suffering.

Is it not probable, then, that the recurrent wish to die hidden behind Freud's superstition coincided with his wish for "peace, sweet peace," and that he should experience this death wish as "uncanny," "daemonic"? Freud believed that "wishes" could be traced principally to derivatives of instinctual drives. Was it not logical, then, on some deep level to attempt to trace death wishes to an instinctual drive more powerful than any other? Instead of saying: "Death is daemonic, uncanny," is it not equally "logical" under the circumstances to theorize that there is a *death instinct* which seeks a return to the inorganic, a superordinated regulatory principle, a repetition compulsion which is "beyond" the pleasure principle? And is it not "logical,"[21] too, that we should have to counteract this "daemonic" power either by Eros, as Freud suggested in *Beyond the Pleasure Principle,* or by Logos, as he believed later; in other words, by using the same forces with which we try to subdue the other "irrational" forces of the id?

Freud's formulations of the death instinct and the repetition compulsion were in part determined by an unceasing attempt to "work through" his obsessive superstitions and to come to terms with the problem of death by treating it as a scientific problem. If this is so, then we might understand that the reasoning by means of which Freud arrived at this concept did not reach his usual unfailing level of logic and power of conviction. The "logic" of unconscious conflicts can be expressed in a work of art—and many passages of *Beyond the Pleasure*

---

[21] I refer in all these instances to the "logic" of the unconscious.

Principle are written with admirable grace and mastery of the German language—but this unconscious logic interferes with the "sober" logic of scientific inquiry.

POSTSCRIPT

By the time *Beyond the Pleasure Principle* was completed in the summer of 1920, Freud was able to turn his attention in a new direction. That summer, he completed a draft of *Group Psychology and the Analysis of the Ego,* the second major work of this period.

In May, 1921, Freud would turn 65, and for this birthday, too, a celebration was being prepared. In March, 1921, Freud seems to have suffered from some cardiac symptoms, which always came closest to representing danger for him. This, combined with his approaching 65th birthday and the letdown he felt after completing *Group Psychology,* brought on one of his depressive reactions, though a short-lived one. Two letters to Eitingon reflect both his upsurge of pessimism and his ironic attitude toward himself. On March 27, 1921 he wrote:

> For *Beyond* I have been sufficiently punished. It is very popular, is bringing me lots of letters and expressions of praise. I must have done something very stupid there [3].

On March 29, he wrote:

> In view of the difficulty of evaluating one's own organic condition, I naturally do not know whether I should now call upon the friends of the Committee to accustom themselves to the thought of continuing the work without my participation. Right now or a little later, this is really the whole question [4].

Two days after the dreaded celebration of his 65th birthday he wrote to Ferenczi:

> On March 13 of this year I quite suddenly took a step into real old age. Since then the thought of death has not left me, and sometimes I have the impression that seven of my internal organs are fighting to have the honor of bringing my life to an end [quoted by Jones, Vol. 3, p. 79].

These letters, especially the last, are characteristic of Freud's struggle with the problem of aging and death, the core of his occasional depressive moods. Puzzled by this image of the competing "seven organs," I carefully studied the correspondence of this period and even enlisted the aid of Anna Freud in searching for its origin. It suddenly occurred to me that Freud was paraphrasing, with the self-irony that is often so therapeutically effective, the Greek pentameter which means: "Seven cities are competing for the honor of being the birthplace of Homer: Smyrna, Rhodos, Kolophon, Salamis, Thios, Argos, Athens." This quotation had come into idiomatic usage among the well-educated people of Freud's time. His letters and works are full of such quotations. To say simply *"Hepta Poleis"* ("Seven Cities") meant that a number of people were competing for something or were expressing conflicting ideas.

The letter to Ferenczi continued:

> There was no proper occasion for it [i.e., the "step into real old age"], except that Oliver said good-by on that day when leaving for Roumania. Still I have not succumbed to this hypochondria, but view it quite coolly, rather as I do the speculations in *Beyond the Pleasure Principle*.

If *Beyond the Pleasure Principle* was an effort to "work through" the obsessive superstitions and to come to terms with the problem of death, this letter would appear to indicate that the "therapy" was successful. There was a faint hint of superstition in that the thoughts of death followed his son's departure just before the "Ides of March." But we can clearly see the cool detachment with which Freud viewed these thoughts, a detachment which he also extended to "the speculation in *Beyond the Pleasure Principle*."

Part III

ILLNESS AND DEATH

13

1923–THE CANCER SURGERY

During the second half of 1922 Freud devoted himself to a major work in which he was trying to conceptualize a new theory about the three "provinces" of the mind: the id, the ego, and the superego, and to integrate this with his new theory of the instinctual drives formulated in *Beyond the Pleasure Principle*. He also attempted to formulate his views on the psychological meaning of the fear of death in metapsychological terms. The book was published in April, 1923, that fateful month when Freud's cancer was discovered.

The events leading to Freud's first surgery, the operation itself, and its aftermath in the months that followed have been described in detail by Ernest Jones (Vol. 3, pp. 89-94), Felix Deutsch (1956), and especially by H. Pichler who kept notes on Freud's treatment between the years 1923 and 1938 and had many personal communications with me. Freud himself spoke briefly about the events at our first meetings, and many of his letters supply us with additional information and insight.

Moreover, many aspects of these tragic months became understandable to me in the light of Freud's attitudes and behavior during the time he was under my care (1928-1939). Much later I gained further comprehension from a study of the Fliess correspondence, which, unfortunately, was not known to me at that time.

I shall attempt to piece the facts together from all the available sources of information. If the report that follows seems lacking in "detached objectivity," this is due to the facts of the situation and not

347

to the feelings aroused by them, although I cannot deny the existence
of such feelings.

We know that Freud was not only a heavy cigar smoker, but, in his
own terms, addicted to nicotine or at least to cigar smoking. He was
aware that nicotine was potentially harmful, but only during his most
severe cardiac episode could he give up his cigars for any length of
time. He knew, too, that he had some tendency to leukoplakia, a
frequent consequence of heavy cigar smoking, but dreaded the prospect of being told to abstain from tobacco. Contrary to Deutsch's
report, Freud was much more prone to consider cardiac symptoms as
a danger, warranting a temporary reduction in smoking, than any
other pathological condition. I have previously referred to the episode
of November, 1917, when Freud developed a worrisome lesion on his
palate, and reported to Ferenczi that this lesion had worsened when
his supply of cigars gave out but miraculously disappeared with the
appearance of a new supply.

On April 25, 1923, Freud wrote to Jones:

> I detected two months ago a leucoplastic growth on my jaw and palate
> [on the] right side, which I had removed on the 20th. I am not yet
> back at work and cannot swallow. I was assured of the benignity of the
> matter, but, as you know, nobody can guarantee its behaviour if it is
> permitted to grow further. My own diagnosis had been epithelioma,
> but was not accepted. Smoking is blamed as the etiology of this tissue
> rebellion [Vol. 3, p. 89].

Initially Freud took no steps to have the growth examined, nor
did he mention it to a doctor, friend, or member of the family. At that
time, as during the early months of his cardiac episode, Freud had no
physician whom he consulted regularly. His friend Otto Rie, his family
pediatrician, was his trusted advisor, and he also had many physician
friends, among them the cardiologist Ludwig Braun and the surgeon
Julius Schnitzler, who was a brilliant and very experienced diagnos-
tician. Felix Deutsch, who at that time was practicing internal medicine but was already analytically oriented, was consulted occasionally
by Freud when he needed a physician.

Freud's letters of this fateful period may give us some inkling of his
frame of mind.

Abraham, knowing of Freud's vital interest in archaeology, and
being himself especially interested in Egyptian art and history, had
sent Freud some newspaper clippings about the discovery of the tomb
of Tutankhamen. Freud answered on March 4, 1923:

I return the newspaper cuttings with thanks. Some of them I have had from other sources. My chief feeling is of annoyance at not being able to be there, and . . . at the prospect of descending to the Styx without having sailed on the Nile. . . .

A charming letter from Romain Rolland recently arrived here like a breath of fresh air; he mentions incidentally that he was interested in analysis twenty years ago.

Abraham, the faithful "optimist," tried to reassure Freud with a story about an uncle who had celebrated his golden wedding anniversary at the age of 75 by traveling with his wife to Egypt, where he even rode on a camel in the desert.

How ironic this letter must have sounded to Freud, who was undoubtedly preoccupied with what to do about his lesion. He answered on April 8, 1923:

Every letter of yours bears the mark of the lively and successful Berlin constellation and of your own optimism. May it be long preserved.

It is extraordinary how much you still overrate me, both materially and physically. Though I am still eight years short of your uncle's age at the time of his camel ride in the desert, I cannot imitate, but only envy him. I am neither rich nor well enough. You must gradually get used to the idea of my mortality and frailty.

Another very significant letter written on the same day as the first one to Abraham gives us an example of Freud's uniqueness of style, which took on a particular quality in letters to writers and poets—in this case to the French novelist Romain Rolland—and translated the "sober" psychoanalytic theory of the conflict between the life and death instincts into language which revealed its applicability to all mankind.

Let us imagine Freud, sitting late one evening in his inner sanctum, at the desk where he had composed most of his works, writing the letters to Abraham and Rolland after a full day of work with patients, facing alone the harbinger of what might turn out to be a mortal illness, and then retiring for a night of uninterrupted sound sleep, followed by "just another day"! He wrote to Rolland:

Dear Sir:
That I have been allowed to exchange a greeting with you will remain a happy memory to the end of my days. Because for us your name has been associated with the most precious of beautiful illusions, that of love extended to all mankind.

I, of course, belong to a race which in the Middle Ages was held responsible for all epidemics and which today is blamed for the disintegration of the Austrian Empire and the German defeat. Such experiences have a sobering effect and are not conducive to make one believe in illusions. A great part of my life's work (I am ten years older than you) has been spent [trying to] destroy illusions of my own and those of mankind. But if this one hope cannot be at least partly realized, if in the course of evolution we don't learn to divert our [instincts] from destroying our own kind, if we continue to hate one another for minor differences and kill each other for petty gain, if we go on exploiting the great progress made in the control of natural resources for our mutual destruction, what kind of future lies in store for us? It is surely hard enough to ensure the perpetuation of our species in the conflict between our instinctual nature and the demands made upon us by civilization.

My writings cannot be what yours are: comfort and refreshment for the reader. But if I may believe that they have aroused your interest, I shall permit myself to send you a small book which is sure to be unknown to you: *Group Psychology and the Analysis of the Ego,* published in 1921. Not that I consider this work to be particularly successful, but it shows a way from the analysis of the individual to an understanding of society.

Sincerely yours,
Freud [L. 200*]

Some time around the second week in April, Freud finally went to consult one of his friends, the dermatologist Maxim Steiner, who was also among the earliest members of the Viennese Psychoanalytic Society. The mucous membrane of the mouth was a "borderline" region "shared" by E.N.T. specialists, oral surgeons, and dermatologists.

Now began a tragic chain of deceptions which was to have far-reaching consequences.

Steiner obviously recognized the lesion for what it was, because he advised an excision, but told Freud only that it was a leukoplakia. According to Deutsch's account, Steiner also told Freud to give up smoking, a medically sound but untimely piece of advice. Judging from my later experience, this advice was much more threatening and unacceptable to Freud than surgery.

Freud had rightly suspected that he had an epithelioma, as indicated in his letter to Jones. When Deutsch visited Freud that same week to discuss some private matters, Freud took him aside as he was about to leave and asked Detusch to look at his mouth, remarking: "Be prepared to see something you won't like." Freud must have known by then the variety of reactions that his illness would provoke in different people, especially his pupils.

"At the very first glance," Deutsch saw that he was dealing with an advanced cancer. He obviously (and admittedly) was shocked at what he saw, took a second look, and pronounced it a "bad leukoplakia" due to smoking, advising an excision. Freud told Deutsch of Steiner's similar diagnosis and advice, and confessed his distress that the latter had told him to give up smoking. For all intents and purposes, this was consciously at least, Freud's main concern.

Freud then mentioned his misgivings over having the excision done by the surgeon who eventually did perform it—Professor Marcus Hajek—because he knew the man personally and was aware of his ambivalent attitude. No decision was made about the choice of a surgeon, and the matter was left in Freud's hands.

The days that followed had the quality of a grotesque nightmare. Deutsch kept urging Freud—over the telephone—not to delay the consultation with the surgeon. Freud obviously took this urging for what it was, an indication of the diagnosis which both Steiner and Deutsch really had in mind. He then did arrange to have an excision performed by the very man about whom he had voiced reservations. Professor Hajek had earned his rank for valuable research on the pathology of the sinuses and had written some important textbooks, but he was generally known to be a somewhat mediocre surgeon[1] rather than "the most outstanding surgeon in his field" (Deutsch, 1956). He certainly was not qualified to operate on a malignancy involving the resection of the maxilla. A procedure of that kind was even then the domain of surgeons. During World War I the Vienna Surgical Clinic had established a special department of oral surgery directed by Hans Pichler, who later performed the radical operation on Freud that was necessary. Nor was Hajek Freud's friend. He was the brother-in-law of the surgeon Julius Schnitzler.

The excision was done not at a private hospital, but in the outpatient department of the hospital headed by Hajek, where the facilities were as deficient as those in the outpatient wards of the older New York City hospitals. This hospital had no private wards. Freud's family had not been informed of the procedure. Deutsch accompanied Freud to the hospital, but did not remain with him during the operation.

We drove to the hospital together with the understanding that he would be at his home immediately after the operation. But he lost more blood

---

[1] I had occasion as a student and practicing internist to witness several operations performed by him.

than it was foreseen and as an emergency he had to rest on a cot in a tiny room on a ward of the hospital, since no other room was available, with another patient who, by tragicomic coincidence, I might say, was an imbecile dwarf [Deutsch, 1956, p. 280].

As Deutsch indicates, the operation did not go entirely smoothly. There was a good deal of bleeding, which apparently was not adequately controlled. Afterward Freud was neither properly admitted to the ward nor transferred to the quite luxurious Löw Sanatorium, a private hospital one block away from the clinic (to which Freud had brought his patient Emma after her hemorrhage; see Chapter 3).

Only then was the family notified of the operation and requested to bring a few things to the hospital, as Freud might have to stay the night there.

Upon their arrival at the hospital, "Frau Professor" Freud and Anna found Freud sitting on a kitchen chair, covered with blood. There was no nurse or physician in attendance. What follows now is the description pieced together by Jones from information supplied by Deutsch, Freud, and Anna Freud:

The ward sister sent the two ladies home at lunch time, when visitors were not allowed, and assured them the patient would be all right. When they returned an hour or two later they learned that he had had an attack of profuse bleeding, and to get help had rung the bell, which was, however, out of order; he himself could neither speak nor call out. The friendly dwarf, however, had rushed for help, and after some difficulty the bleeding was stopped; perhaps his action saved Freud's life. Anna then refused to leave again and spent the night sitting by her father's side. He was weak from loss of blood, was half-drugged from the medicines, and was in great pain. During the night she and the nurse became alarmed at his condition and sent for the house surgeon, who, however, refused to get out of bed. The next morning Hajek demonstrated the case to a crowd of students, and later in the day Freud was allowed to go home [Vol. 3, p. 90f.].

Many questions come to mind concerning the attitude and behavior of Deutsch, Hajek, and, above all, Freud himself in connection with this utterly unbelievable story. The first question which occurred to me after my initial meeting with Freud, during which, probably with this experience in mind, he laid down the basic "rules" of our relationship, was this: why did Deutsch withhold the truth from Freud?

In his article Deutsch explained that he had done so on this day and for quite some time thereafter because "Freud had been insufficiently prepared in the beginning to face a reality as he saw it," whereas after the ordeal of the first surgery, with its aftereffects and the follow-up treatment, Freud "could see the term 'cancer' in another light." However, in a communication to Jones, Deutsch reported that Freud had asked him "for help" in disappearing from the world with decency if he were doomed to die in suffering, and that Freud had spoken of his old mother who would find the news of his death very hard to bear. Deutsch was apparently under the impression that Freud was thinking of suicide. If Deutsch really believed this—and I would like to emphasize here that Deutsch was a senior colleague and friend of mine for whom I had high esteem—this was one time when he did not know his patient. To put the record straight on this matter is one of the main reasons for going into such detail here.

In Freud's letter to Abraham of May 29, 1918, Freud remarked, in reply to Abraham's report of his mother's illness, that he would "feel a little freer" when his own mother had died because the idea that she might have to be told of his death was terrifying to him.

As early as 1899, Freud had written to Fliess, at a time when the latter's mother and pregnant wife both were ill:

[How] uncanny when the mothers are shaky, the only ones who still stand between us and redemption [1].

This is one of the many examples that foreshadows Freud's later attitudes and tendencies. Freud repeatedly expressed similar thoughts about his mother until her death. Afterward he reiterated them with regard to his own family. What he meant, as we shall see clearly from letters to be quoted further on (e.g., Chapter 24), was that among the painful aspects of facing death were the prospects of being separated forever from one's loved ones and the anticipation of the pain of the survivors. Freud certainly had not forgotten the pain he had recently experienced on losing Sophie, Anton von Freund, his niece, many of his friends, and most of all his beloved grandson Heinele. If Freud was stressing his duty to continue living, he could not have been considering suicide, and certainly not out of a fear of suffering. It is likely that the prospect of having to abstain from smoking, which usually led to a diminution of his creativity, represented a greater threat than the anticipation of suffering. The thought of suicide never entered his mind, not even during the worst agonies of the following years, as a most poignant incident in the spring of 1938 demonstrates (see Chapter

26). Basically he wanted to prolong *life* to the bitter end; he asked only for the assurance that his *dying* would not be needlessly prolonged. He had expressed this attitude in a letter (February 6, 1899) to Fliess, when he said, "the art of deceiving patients is certainly not a very necessary one. . . . I hope that when my time comes I shall find someone who will treat me with more respect and tell me when to be ready" (see Chapter 5). The man who, after the death of Anton von Freund, had written of the latter that he had been fully aware of his fate and had behaved in a manner which had not brought dishonor to psychoanalysis was a man who wanted to hear the truth, and who would not have destroyed himself upon hearing it.

Freud's reaction upon finally being told the truth—and this was still some time off—confirmed this fully.

Even Deutsch's apprehension about Freud's lack of preparedness leaves many questions unanswered. Why didn't Deutsch share his responsibility with a member of Freud's family or with Rie or with Schnitzler? Why didn't he himself suggest a consultant? Why did he think of Pichler only months later?

Only one explanation seems possible, an all too human and understandable one in a man who admired Freud and was awed by him. The inner obstacles to revealing the truth were the same as I had to overcome later when I was given the task of watching over this most revered man.

It was Deutsch who could not "face reality" when he saw the ugly lesion in Freud's mouth and was assailed by the horrifying conviction that this was not a leukoplakia but an epithelioma.

Hajek's behavior is more difficult to explain. Jones has rightly characterized it as "cavalier." That he satisfied himself with a local excision which, as he must have known, could not have arrested the spread of the malignancy, can be explained only by the assumption that he had given up the case as hopeless, and was therefore just going through the motions of taking palliative measures. That Hajek performed the not-so-small excision on an ambulatory basis and then left Freud without proper medical and nursing care after his hemorrhage would have been inexcusable in any case, even if the patient had not been someone who had achieved world fame and was, moreover, a friend of his brother-in-law's.

In view of the powerful hold that resistance to psychoanalysis and its findings has on the behavior of many people, we can assume that the very fact that the patient was Freud, the discoverer of psychoanalysis, actually contributed to the course of events during and after that first surgery.

Freud's operation took place on April 20, 1923, just prior to his 67th birthday. The birthday was celebrated, as Freud remarked in a letter to Lou Andreas-Salomé, as if he were "the star of an operetta."

Freud's letters of May 10, 1923 are significant. One was to Lou Andreas-Salomé, the other to Abraham; both were "thank-you" notes for birthday wishes. In both Freud mentioned that he could smoke again. The two letters indicate that even then Freud was aware, though perhaps not completely, of the nature of the growth in his mouth. He wrote to Lou Andreas-Salomé: "Even after the operation they declare the prognosis to be good." And to Abraham he wrote:

> I can again chew, work and smoke, and I shall try your optimistic slogan: *many happy returns of the day and none of the new growth.*[2]

A letter (unpublished) written to Jones on May 18, 1923, was even more pessimistic:

> The day before I got your dear wife's letter I heard about your operation and was rather struck by this coming in series. I expect a permanent improvement of your health to result from your experience as a patient, whereas incomplete recovery is all I am entitled to expect from mine.

In addition to the attitude, and behavior of Deutsch and Hajek, however, we must also give consideration to Freud's own behavior during this period. In attempting to understand this we must make a distinction between Freud's attitude prior to surgery and his behavior during the weeks that followed it because of an external event which occurred in that interval.

That Freud did not tell his family about his symptoms and the forthcoming surgery was understandable in the light of his great considerateness for his loved ones. We remember that during the cardiac episode Freud had not told his wife of his worries. His daughter Anna was still young in 1923, and he certainly wanted to spare her worry and concern.

But why didn't Freud ask Schnitzler or his devoted old friend Oskar Rie for advice about the choice of a surgeon? One reason may have been Freud's exemplary loyalty. He evidenced this toward his pupils

2 These words in English in the original.

(only reluctantly and painfully recognizing that some did not return this loyalty), toward his friends, and later toward his doctors. This quality, among many others, helped Professor Pichler and me greatly during the last 10 years of Freud's life.

The most important question about Freud's behavior is why he waited two months before doing anything about his lesion. There was, of course, his reluctance to face the expected, dreaded verdict: "Give up smoking." But there must have been more to the matter than this.

When I was preparing the draft of my Freud Lecture in 1964 I wrote on this point: "One factor was a certain element of what might be called fatalism. Freud himself might have called this the working of the death instinct. I would characterize it as a certain, fortunately temporary, submission to *Ananke*." Only after I had carefully re-studied the published and unpublished Fliess correspondence did I realize that the "2,467 errors" in *The Interpretation of Dreams*, of which Freud had half jokingly spoken in his letter to Fliess of August 27, 1899, and the determinants of which he had subsequently an-alyzed in *The Psychopathology of Everyday Life*, could now, in 1923, be having their effect on the events of his life, *24* years later, when he had reached the age of *67!* I am referring to the fact (see Chapter 5) that 67 was interpreted by Freud, in analyzing this seemingly random number, as the age at which he would be ready to "retire"; 67 also was the age of his older brother Emmanuel in 1899. Emmanuel died at 81 and a half in 1914—nine years before Freud's surgery, and 81 and a half also was the age at which Freud's father had died (see Chapter 4).

In another letter to Fliess Freud had spoken about his "fatalistic conviction" (Chapter 5). Hence Freud's 67th year—24 years after he had completed *The Interpretation of Dreams*, had recognized a break with Fliess as unavoidable, and had expressed "the guilt of the sur-vivor" in his analysis of the *non vixit* dream—could have been linked in his unconscious with his retirement, and felt to be a "critical date" more dangerous than the ones he was consciously aware of. This may well have contributed to his fatalism in dealing with his lesion.[3]

The question might be raised whether such "fatalistic" behavior was not the expression of an unconscious "death wish" and therefore the sign of an inclination to suicide. If so, would this not disprove my

---

[3] I have mentioned that Groddeck went much further than this: he assumed that Freud's "id" "created" the cancer in 1923 because he had had these associations in 1899 (Chapter 5).

claim that Freud never contemplated suicide after finally being told that he was suffering from cancer? Here we must remind ourselves of the great difference between actually considering or committing suicide and having an unconscious wish that manifests itself in a "fatalistic" mood and behavior which can certainly be called imprudent and can result in self-destructive behavior.

The pathology report of the excised specimen indicated a malignant epithelioma. After the excision Hajek referred Freud to Dr. Guido Holzknecht, chairman of the Radiology Department of the Vienna Medical School, for a few X-ray treatments. He was also turned over to one of Hajek's assistants for local radium applications. Two facts are pertinent here: first, radiotherapy for this type of malignancy is usually unsuccessful. This was later stated by the experts Professors Rigaud and Lacassagne, directors of the Institut Curie in Paris. Second, radium treatment, outside of Paris and especially in Vienna, was carried out somewhat haphazardly. The radiation Freud received only caused tissue damage and violent pain. As yet neither Freud nor anyone else had been told the truth.

However, as I have indicated, Freud suspected the truth all along. He was anything but a fool and must have known why X-ray and radium treatments were being given. In a letter to Deutsch written from Lavarone in southern Tyrol, where he was spending the summer, he spoke of his "dear neoplasm." Denial of death and mortal illness is an adaptive defense. While Freud did not want to use this defense, it was forced upon him. That he resented this, and was even eventually ashamed of it, may be seen from a letter to Deutsch:

> I could always adapt myself to any kind of reality, even endure an uncertainty due to a reality—but being left alone with my subjective insecurity, without the fulcrum or pillar of the *Ananke,* the inexorable, unavoidable necessity, I had to fall prey to the miserable cowardice of a human being and had to become an unworthy spectacle for others [Deutsch, 1956, p. 282].

This letter would also appear to confirm my assumptions about Freud's inner motivations for formulating the death-instinct theory. In *Beyond the Pleasure Principle* Freud states that "it is easier to submit to a remorseless law of nature, the sublime Ananke, than to . . . chance. . . ."

Freud's fatalism on his own behalf was suddenly deepened by the saddest blow which had ever befallen him. Nothing can describe the event better than Freud's own letters. On June 11, 1923 he wrote to two close Hungarian friends, Katá and Lajos Levy:[4]

> About my operation and affliction there is nothing to say that you yourselves couldn't know or expect. The uncertainty that hovers over a man of sixty-seven has now found its material expression. I don't take it very hard; one will defend oneself for a while with the help of modern medicine and then remember Bernard Shaw's warning:
> Don't try to live for ever, you will not succeed.
>
> *(The Doctor's Dilemma)*
> But now there is something else. We brought here from Hamburg Sophie's younger son, Heinele, now aged 4½. My eldest daughter Mathilde and her husband have almost adopted him and have fallen in love with him to an extent that couldn't be foreseen. He was indeed an enchanting little fellow, and I myself was aware of never having loved a human being, certainly never a child, so much. Unfortunately he was very weak, never entirely free of a temperature, one of those children whose mental development grows at the expense of its physical strength. We thought that in Hamburg he lacked the proper kind of care or medical supervision.
> This child became ill again two weeks ago, temperature between 102 and 104, headaches, no clear local symptoms, for a long time no diagnosis, and finally the slow but sure realization that he has a miliary tuberculosis, in fact that the child is lost. He is now lying in a coma with paresis, occasionally wakes up, and then he is so completely his own self that it is hard to believe. . . . After each waking and going to sleep one loses him all over again; the doctors say it can last a week, perhaps longer, and recovery is not desirable, fortunately not likely. His father arrived yesterday.
> I find this loss very hard to bear. I don't think I have ever experienced such grief; perhaps my own sickness contributes to the shock. I work out of sheer necessity; fundamentally everything has lost its meaning for me [L. 203*].[5]

Heinele died on June 19, 1923, six days after this letter was written. What a tragic coincidence that both grandfather and grandchild should have had an oral operation at approximately the same time![6]

---

[4] Katá Levy was a psychoanalyst. Dr. Lajos Levy was an internist who, especially during the interval between 1923 and 1928, when I became Freud's physician, frequently visited Freud in Vienna and advised him on medical matters. He and I translated Pichler's notes on Freud's illness, some of which were published by Jones as Appendix II of Volume 3 of his biography of Freud.

[5] It is uncanny how Thomas Mann's beautiful description in *Dr. Faustus* of the elfin child *Echo* and of his death from meningitis parallels Freud's description of Heinele.

[6] Heinele had undergone a tonsillectomy.

That this enchanting, elfish little boy, who had won everyone's heart, should have died from tubercular meningitis within a few days was *Ananke* at its cruelest. In a letter to Ferenczi written on July 18, Freud declared that he was suffering from "the first depression in my life." Afterward he remarked repeatedly that this event had killed something in him, so that he was never able to form new attachments. Some three years later Freud had occasion to express this attitude once again when tragedy struck Binswanger. In 1926, the latter's eight-year-old son, who somewhat resembled Heinele in personality, also died of tubercular meningitis. Binswanger informed Freud about his heavy loss in a letter of great delicacy which bore eloquent testimony to the fact that differences in scientific points of view were no hindrance to Freud's friendships. Both Freud's letter and part of Binswanger's warrant quoting here.

Binswanger wrote to Freud:

At a time when my life was most gravely threatened you stood by me in a way that, aside from all other ties, binds me to you for ever. Now my life is no longer threatened; however, one of my children, a lovely eight-year-old boy, who showed promise of developing into an energetic personality, died suddenly after a fourteen days' illness, amidst great suffering. He succumbed to a tubercular meningitis. He was our fifth child, and we were particularly attached to him because of his delicacy of spirit. I could not bring myself to inform you about the death of my boy by way of a printed announcement, nor could I write to you directly, particularly to you. Now it is done. I know that you went through a similar experience, and it is perhaps still harder to lose a grown child.[7] My wife, who had given this child, from the first days of his life, an especially great amount of her motherly love and care, and who was particularly fond of him, did not make the blow I suffered more difficult to endure, but helped me, through her absolute submission to the inevitable.

Also with regard to the remaining children the sense of triumphant security has now gone, and our sharpened awareness naturally finds things to worry us here and there.

I expect no letter from you, dear Herr Professor, but a line from you would give me and my wife more pleasure than anything else. In cordial devotion, ever yours, L. B.

P.S. I have not dictated this letter, but written it by hand; however, I am having it copied for you.[8]

---

[7] Binswanger did not know about the Heinele tragedy.
[8] Binswanger had a handwriting that was so difficult to decipher that Freud often asked him to type his letters.

Freud replied at once, on October 15, 1926:

> Even though you don't expect it, I must write to you—not a note of superfluous sympathy, but—in fact I am writing out of an inner urge, because your letter has awakened a memory in me—absurd—for after all, this memory has never been asleep. Correct—I lost a beloved daughter when she was twenty-seven, but I bore this remarkably well. That was in 1920, when we were crushed and miserable, after years of war, during which we had steeled ourselves against hearing that we had lost a son or even three sons. Thus we had been resigned to fate in advance. But two years later I brought the younger child of this daughter, a little boy of three or four, to Vienna, where my childless oldest daughter took him into her home, and this child died—on June 23—from an acute miliary tuberculosis. He was far advanced intellectually, so much so that the consulting specialist based his diagnosis on this fact when the nature of the disease was still uncertain. To me this child had taken the place of all my children and other grandchildren, and since then, since Heinele's death, I don't care for my grandchildren any more, but find no joy in life either. This is also the secret of my indifference—it was called courage—toward the danger to my own life. In fact my case is similar to your own in that I have suffered no recurrence either. I hope this similarity between us will not extend to the other thing. You are young enough to surmount your loss; as for me, I don't have to any more.
>
> If you come to Vienna on September 27 and I am still alive, I won't be in Vienna, but in the Semmering, as in recent years. Then come up there.

Here Freud was speaking the language of his old depression, grief, and mourning, revived through the loss which his friend had suffered. It is hard for me and for anyone who knew Freud closely during the subsequent years of his life to take these statements at face value. Freud never ceased to love. He did form new attachments, and old attachments grew in intensity. Freud would not have survived without them. He remained intensely fond of his grandchildren, and I remember the utter tenderness with which he took leave of his granddaughter Eva[9] in August, 1939, knowing full well that he would never see her again. Nor was his fondness for children limited to his own. Thus it was not only Freud's ego strength which helped him eventually regain his often unbelievable resilience. His strength was fed constantly by his ability to love and to give.

Throughout this period the deception was still going on. Freud was permitted to leave for his regular long summer vacation, although he

[9] She was the daughter of his son Oliver (see Chapter 26).

was feeling much discomfort. The radium reaction had not yet subsided and probably the neoplasm, too, was giving trouble. He wrote to Deutsch and described his symptoms, adding a remark to the effect that as a result of his indifference to such trifles as science, the mourning process would have to carry on in the dark. This indicated that initially Freud's grief and mourning after the death of Heinele and the reaction to his cancer merged into each other.

Deutsch went to Lavarone to see Freud during his vacation and the entire Committee also met there. Deutsch realized at that point that a second, radical operation would be necessary. He told the truth to the members of the Committee (Abraham, Eitingon, Ferenczi, Jones, Rank, and Sachs), but not to Anna Freud or Freud himself. The Committee "decided" to let Freud carry out his plans to spend two weeks with Anna in Rome, as he had decided to do right after his April operation. Deutsch returned to Vienna and made the arrangements for the second operation. Only during the last year of Freud's life did Jones tell him about this "decision" of the Committee in Lavarone. According to Jones (Vol. 3, p. 93), Freud asked, with blazing eyes: "Mit welchem Recht?" ("With what right?")

"Allowing" Freud to see Rome once more and to show it to Anna was the most humane and constructive action of all those months, despite the fact that during the train trip from Verona to Rome Freud suddenly bled profusely from the mouth.

Only upon his return from Rome was Freud told the truth, which he faced with complete composure, as evidenced by a letter to Eitingon written on September 26, 1923, the day he had been seen for the first time by Professor Hans Pichler.

> Today I can satisfy your need to have news from me. It has been decided that I must undergo a second operation, a partial resection of the maxilla, because my dear neoplasm has reappeared there. The operation will be performed by Professor Pichler, the greatest expert in these matters, who is also preparing the prosthesis that will be needed afterward. He promises that within 4-5 weeks I shall be able to eat and talk satisfactorily, so that for the time being I have postponed the beginning of my practice until November 1 [2].

Pichler was the ideal choice for Freud's case. During World War I he had become the chief of a newly formed department of oral surgery at the University hospital, where he operated on scores of severely injured soldiers, using heroic procedures that had never been attempted before with excellent results. As it turned out, he had to devise a new approach for Freud, too. He was the type of surgeon who did not shy away from radical surgery when necessary, something which was not common at that time. Yet Pichler was an extremely kind and humane person. Although he certainly had no inkling of Freud's place in the history of science, he not only treated him for 15 years with the utmost respect, tact, and courtesy, but he exerted every possible influence on the authorities to protect Freud following Hitler's invasion of Austria.

After I became Freud's physician in 1928, Pichler extended the same courteous treatment to me, and a closer, more amiable cooperation between us could not be imagined. Pichler was, fortunately, an "obsessive" man in the best, sublimated sense of the word. Throughout the 15 years that he treated Freud, he kept notes on every single visit and surgical intervention. At the end of World War II Pichler and I resumed our correspondence, and after his death in 1949[10] his son graciously permitted Pichler's secretary to type out his complete set of notes and send them to me.

When Pichler first examined Freud he found that, in addition to a large crateriform ulcerated recurrence on the right soft palate, the tumor had spread toward the cheek and the lower jaw. There was also some shrinkage from the first surgery. The consequences of the perfunctory nature of the first operation were far-reaching for Freud's later life. Much more extensive surgery was now needed involving a procedure which Pichler had to try out first on a corpse to test its feasibility!

Pichler made complex preparations, including several different models for the prosthesis of both the maxilla and the mandible to allow for whatever surgery might be required.

On October 4, 1923, under local anesthesia, the external carotid artery was ligated and an extensive dissection of the submaxillary and jugular glands was performed to prevent a spread of the cancer. Fortunately, the enlarged glands revealed no malignancy. Only on October 12, again under local anesthesia, did Pichler perform the radical surgery, consisting of a resection of the major part of the right maxilla, a considerable part of the mandible, the right soft palate, and the buccal (cheek) and lingual (tongue) mucous membranes.[11]

[10] An obituary by me appeared in *The Bulletin of the American Psychoanalytic Association* (1949).

[11] In view of Fliess's hypothesis that Freud suffered from a chronic sinus infection, it is remarkable that the maxillary (largest) sinus showed only some polyps but otherwise no pathology!

Finally, he replaced with skin grafts those parts of the removed mucous membranes which could not be sutured, and put the prosthesis in place. Freud, who had received some unaccustomed sedation in addition to the local anesthetic, slept through most of the operation, which lasted for several hours. After the operation his pulse rate was 64!

Pichler's notes about this surgery ended with the words: "The only mistake is that perhaps more of the internal pterygoid muscle should have been removed." Pichler certainly had a strict "superego" and left himself no loopholes!

I must remind the reader that this was the time before antibiotics and intravenous feedings. Fluids were supplied by rectum; feeding was done by nasal tube.

For two days Freud had high fever, but was able to go home on October 28. Pichler carefully watched the spot where he thought that he had not removed enough tissue. On November 7 he noticed a slightly ulcerated spot under a tiny necrotic part of the graft, and took a biopsy. On November 12, he received the report that there was still malignant tissue in the area. Now both Pichler and Freud proved their mettle. Most surgeons would have given up at this point. Pichler told Freud the truth, suggested immediate further surgery, and Freud agreed. The operation was performed the same afternoon, again under local anesthesia plus some sedation. There was a further resection of the mandible and the soft tissues, with considerable blood loss. Only now was Pichler satisfied that he had performed radical surgery—and rightly so. There were no further serious complications, but Freud again received a series of "prophylactic" X-ray treatments.[12]

Only a *homo surgicus* could have performed this type of surgery at that time. The surgery as such was entirely successful. Freud did not die of a recurrence or a metastasis of the original cancer. However, the extensive surgery made a really satisfactory prosthesis im-

---

[12] He also underwent another type of surgical procedure. Freud had mentioned in *Beyond the Pleasure Principle* and other papers the work of the endocrinologist Steinach who was one of the first to discover the function of the interstitial cells of the testicles, which produce the male sex hormone. He arrived at the hypothesis that the ligation of the spermatic ducts resulted in a relative hypertrophy of the sex hormone-producing cells, thus bringing about a "rejuvenation" of the subject. Effective injectable sex hormones were not yet available at that time. Because cancer formation was considered to be in part a result of the aging process, the duct ligation procedure, which had been named "Steinach's rejuvenation operation," was believed to be helpful in preventing a recurrence of disease. I was not able to find out who had advised Freud to undergo the ligation at that time until Freud told me that it was he himself who had favored it, and that it had been performed (it is a minor procedure) on November 17, 1923.

possible, and the loss of the greater part of the buccal mucous membrane could not be made good completely by grafting. The result was a life of endless torture. Eating, smoking, talking could be carried on only with great effort and pain. If the prosthesis was just right for proper occlusion and separation between the oral and nasal cavities, this resulted in sores, pressure upon the mandibular joint, and often intolerable pain. If some of the prosthesis was removed, speech, eating, and smoking became much more difficult. This was really existing between Scylla and Charybdis. Thus started the incessant attempts to improve the prosthesis or to build a new one. The prosthesis could be taken out only for cleaning purposes—to avoid shrinkage. To take it out and reinsert it required an intricate technique.[13]

But all this was only the beginning. Freud could not overcome his addiction and give up smoking, which caused a constant irritation of the area and provided the stimulus for the formation of new leukoplakias. It soon became evident that these had a tendency to grow and proliferate. Thus, in 1926, there began an endless cycle of leukoplakia, proliferation, precancerous lesions. Each of them had to be treated surgically, by excision, electrocoagulation, or a combination of both. This happened more than 30 times. Only in 1936 was one of these lesions again malignant, and only in 1939 was such a lesion so situated that it could no longer be reached surgically. Frequently the attempt was made to cover the operative site with skin grafts. For the most part local anesthesia was used. The procedure often lasted over an hour, but only more extensive surgery was done in a hospital. After each intervention the prosthesis had to remain in place for several days; cleaning was possible only by irrigation. The first insertions and removals were usually a special ordeal, and generally could be done only by Pichler himself.

Pain and discomfort were not the only trials. Those who are not familiar with German cannot experience the beauty of Freud's style, his mastery of language. The only international award Freud received

---

[13] Jones mentions that the prosthesis "was labeled 'the monster' " (p. 95). Actually it was never called that during Freud's lifetime, although it certainly was monstrous. I gave it this name in the essay (entitled "The Last Chapter") which I sent to Jones for publication as the final chapter of Volume 3 of his book.

Concerning the prosthesis, I must add that while Pichler was a superb surgeon and an excellent physician, his art as a dental technician may not have been quite the equal of his surgical skill. In later years, two other specialists were asked to try their hand at creating a prosthesis. Perhaps, given an opportunity to be in constant attendance, they could have produced a more efficient and less troublesome instrument.

was the Goethe prize, awarded for literary achievement. He was more frequently proposed for a Nobel prize in literature than in medicine. But to listen to Freud's delivery of the spoken word was an equally unique experience. Anyone who met him before his surgery was impressed by it. His manner of speaking blended with the content of what he said and with his facial expression and his eyes. A good deal of this was still left after the surgery, but what had been an easy, natural flow had become a painful effort, interrupted by movements which looked like mannerisms but in reality served to make some readjustments of the prosthesis to relieve the pressure.

We must bear in mind, too, that all this took place over a period of 16 years which brought with it not only the natural process of aging but the political crisis that culminated in the rise of Nazism, the invasion of Austria (making an "exodus" necessary for Freud), and, finally, World War II. Only in the light of all this can we evaluate Freud's attitude toward life, illness, and death during this era.

Our attitude toward death depends in part on how much we savor life and on our capacity to tolerate life, if need be, out of a sense of duty to ourselves, our families, a cause, a group. Expressed in psychoanalytic, structural terms, it depends on the ability to achieve some instinctual gratification, on the ego's ability to tolerate frustration, on the faculty for sublimation, on the kind of superego one has, on the ability to establish intrasystemic and intersystemic harmony. Prolonged illness and suffering—which means not only prolongation of life but prolonged dying—must reflect themselves in a gradual shift in the balance of all these factors.

Freud's physical state, which varied only from severe discomfort to real torment, persisted more or less constantly over the next 16 years. Pain and discomfort were of course more intense during the first year after the radical surgery until the wound was finally covered by a combination of newly formed mucous membrane and scar tissue, the prosthesis was gradually adjusted to the remaining anatomical structures, and Freud adjusted to the prosthesis. It took a long time for him to learn how to take it out and put it in again. I vividly remember what a complex maneuver this occasionally required even after years of use.

Freud also had to learn gradually how to eat, smoke, and talk. The prosthesis had to fit as tightly as possible in order to take the nasal pitch out of his speech and to allow the proper suction for his cigar smoking. This, however, made for more pressure and pain.

The second radical surgery took place on November 12, 1923. There were sixteen entries in Pichler's notes for the remainder of 1923 and 74 in 1924! Each of the visits, fittings, etc., took a long time.

Freud avoided visitors during the first months because speaking was so painful. He dictated a few short notes to Anna, but soon began to write them himself. After the first radical surgery he had not failed to write to his mother, then over 88 years old.

On January 2, 1924, Freud resumed his practice, seeing six patients daily. In later years, after most of the surgical procedures except the major ones, he resumed seeing patients within a day or two.

14

DEATH AS A METAPSYCHOLOGICAL PROBLEM

A few weeks after Freud resumed his work in January, 1924, he completed a paper on "The Economic Problem of Masochism," which he had begun *after* his second radical operation. This paper is in part a continuation of *Beyond the Pleasure Principle* and *The Ego and the Id*. The latter book had been published immediately before Freud's cancer surgery. It contains Freud's most concerted effort to present the fear of dying in metapsychological terms.

In *The Ego and the Id* Freud said:

The high-sounding phrase, 'every fear is ultimately the fear of death',[1] has hardly any meaning, and at any rate cannot be justified. It seems to me, on the contrary, perfectly correct to distinguish the fear of death from dread of an object (realistic anxiety) and from neurotic libidinal anxiety. It presents a difficult problem to psycho-analysis, for death is an abstract concept with a negative content for which no unconscious correlative can be found. It would seem that the mechanism of the fear of death can only be that the ego relinquishes its narcissistic libidinal cathexis in a very large measure—that is, that it gives up itself, just as it gives up some *external* object in other cases in which it feels anxiety. I believe that the fear of death is something that occurs between the ego and the super-ego.

We know that the fear of death makes its appearance under two conditions (which, moreover, are entirely analogous to situations in which other kinds of anxiety develop), namely, as a reaction to an

[1] A phrase used by Stekel in 1908.

367

external danger and as an internal process, as for instance in melancholia. Once again a neurotic manifestation may help us to understand a normal one.

The fear of death in melancholia only admits of one explanation: that the ego gives itself up because it feels itself hated and persecuted by the super-ego, instead of loved. To the ego, therefore, living means the same as being loved—being loved by the super-ego, which here again appears as the representative of the id. The super-ego fulfils the same function of protecting and saving that was fulfilled in earlier days by the father[2] and later by Providence or Destiny. But, when the ego finds itself in an excessive real danger which it believes itself unable to overcome by its own strength, it is bound to draw the same conclusion. It sees itself deserted by all protecting forces and lets itself die. Here, moreover, is once again the same situation as that which underlay the first great anxiety-state of birth and the infantile anxiety of longing— the anxiety due to separation from the protecting mother.[3]

These considerations make it possible to regard the fear of death, like the fear of conscience, as a development of the fear of castration. The great significance which the sense of guilt has in the neuroses makes it conceivable that common neurotic anxiety is reinforced in severe cases by the generating of anxiety between the ego and the super-ego (fear of castration, of conscience, of death).

The id, to which we finally come back, has no means of showing the ego either love or hate. It cannot say what it wants; it has achieved no unified will. Eros and the death instinct struggle within it; we have seen

[2] Freud had just begun to recognize the preponderant role of the mother and the early infant-mother relationship. At this point the father was still referred to as the protector and savior of the young child.

[3] Here the role of the mother is acknowledged.

It is pertinent that as early as 1883 Freud had singled out abandonment as the worst evil which could befall anyone. At that time Freud was in high spirits because he had just perfected a new staining process to facilitate microscopic examination of the C.N.S., which was to prove of great value and lead to the discovery of the neurone as the functional unit of that system. Thus he wrote to his fiancée Martha on October 25, 1883: "I have succeeded in doing something I have been trying to do over and over again for many years. When I look back at the time since I first began to tackle this problem, I realize that my life has after all progressed. I have longed so often for a sweet girl who might be everything to me, and now I have her. The same men whom I have admired from afar because I thought them inaccessible, I now meet on equal terms and they show me their friendship. I have remained in good health and done nothing dishonorable; even though I have remained poor, those things which mean something to me have become available, and I feel safe *from the worst fate, that of being abandoned*" [L. 27*].

Thus, it is not surprising that a book which Freud read in December, 1938—*Der Kaiser, die Weisen, und der Tod (The Emperor, the Sages and Death)*—when he knew full well that his own death was not far off, should have made such a deep impression on him, for the book ends on an uncanny note with the death of the main figure who finds himself utterly abandoned one frozen night, the last inhabitant of a world devoid of all other living creatures (see Chapter 27).

with what weapons the one group of instincts defends itself against the other. It would be possible to picture the id as under the domination of the mute but powerful death instincts, which desire to be at peace and (prompted by the pleasure principle) to put Eros, the mischief-maker, to rest; but perhaps that might be to undervalue the part played by Eros [p. 57ff.].[4]

These formulations are highly condensed, but we can distinguish in them the following progression:

Freud was repeating a formulation which he had first presented in *The Interpretation of Dreams* and later in most of his theoretical discussions of the problem of death: death is actually something "unknown to the unconscious" (in *The Ego and the Id* he called it a "negative concept"). Thus he acknowledged that death presented a knotty problem for psychoanalysis, since it was difficult to understand death in psychological terms.

Freud then distinguished a fear of death from both realistic anxiety (of an external object) and "neurotic libidinal anxiety" (which at this stage in his theorizing meant anxiety arising from sexual frustration). He therefore approached the problem of death with the help of the theoretical concepts he had developed over the previous 10 years. Here we can see how the metapsychological points of view are interrelated with the concepts of narcissism and the conflict between Thanatos and Eros—the death instinct and libido.

There followed what sounded like a tentative formulation: fear of death arises when the ego "relinquishes" its narcissistic libidinal cathexes and therefore "gives itself up." The fear of death is something that "occurs between the ego and the super-ego." This explanation was probably too general, and Freud had to resort to an empirical approach which was so often helpful to him. He compared a normal with a neurotic mechanism, reminding himself that fear of death occurred either as a reaction to external danger or as an internal process, e.g., in melancholia. In the latter situation, the fear of death, Freud believed, could be explained only by the concept that the ego felt itself "hated and persecuted" by the superego, which meant that living had become equated with being loved.

The superego was then described in genetic terms as the successor to the parents, Providence, and Destiny. Under conditions of excessive real (external) danger (which later, in *Inhibitions, Symptoms and*

---

[4] It is interesting that here, too, Freud warns against the underestimation of Eros.

Anxiety, would be characterized as a "traumatic situation") the ego again "sees itself deserted and lets itself die." Freud then introduced a hierarchy of danger situations, which foreshadowed his more system-atic genetic formulations in *Inhibitions, Symptoms and Anxiety* (writ-ten in 1925 and published in 1926): separation from the protecting mother; fear of castration; fear of conscience (*Gewissensangst;* see Strachey's note [1926a, p. 128]); and, finally, fear of death.

The last paragraph of the passage from *The Ego and the Id* quoted above may explain some of the difficulty which Freud encountered in dealing with this theme. Behind all these formulations loomed the death-instinct concept. How Freud's need to utilize this concept de-tracted from his usual lucidity of expression can be seen from the two paragraphs which preceded the ones referred to above:

> Towards the two classes of instincts the ego's attitude is not impartial. Through its work of identification and sublimation it gives the death instincts in the id assistance in gaining control over the libido, but in so doing it runs the risk of becoming the object of the death instincts and of itself perishing. In order to be able to help in this way it has had itself to become filled with libido; it thus itself becomes the representa-tive of Eros and thenceforward desires to live and to be loved.
>
> But since the ego's work of sublimation results in a defusion of the instincts and a liberation of the aggressive instincts in the super-ego, its struggle against the libido exposes it to the danger of maltreatment and death. In suffering under the attacks of the super-ego or perhaps even succumbing to them, the ego is meeting with a fate like that of the protista which are destroyed by the products of decomposition that they themselves have created. From the economic point of view the morality that functions in the super-ego seems to be a similar product of decomposition [1923, p. 56f.]

Freud had presented the death-instinct concept in *Beyond the Pleasure Principle* as a daring hypothesis, even using the term "specu-lation." The passages from *The Ego and the Id* quoted above show that 3 years later Freud treated the death-instinct concept as an in-tegral part of his theory of instinctual drives. The formulation quoted earlier: "The mute but powerful death instincts . . . desire to put Eros, the mischief-maker, to rest; but perhaps that might be to undervaluate the part played by Eros" illustrates that Freud was using a dualistic instinct theory in which Eros was considered to be the preserver of life, "protecting" it against the drive to return to the inorganic state.

In his paper on "The Economic Problem of Masochism" Freud elaborated on his dual instinct theory, and also added to his formulations concerning the regulatory principles of mental functioning which he had begun in *Beyond the Pleasure Principle* (see Chapter 12). He accepted the term "nirvana principle," suggested by the English analyst Barbara Low for the tendency of the mental apparatus to reduce "to nothing, or at least of keeping as low as possible, the sums of excitation which flow in upon it" (1924a, p. 159).

Freud then tried to reconcile his previous formulations about the pleasure-unpleasure principles with the death-instinct theory and his new formulation of the dual instinct theory, as well as with the experiential aspects of pleasure and unpleasure. To do this Freud resorted to the following chain of reasoning:

> [He stated:] . . . we have unhesitatingly identified the pleasure-unpleasure principle with this Nirvana principle. Every unpleasure ought thus to coincide with a heightening, and every pleasure with a lowering, of mental tension due to stimulus; the Nirvana principle (and the pleasure principle which is supposedly identical with it) would be entirely in the service of the death instincts, whose aim is to conduct the restlessness of life into the stability of the inorganic state, and it would have the function of giving warnings against the demands of the life instincts— the libido—which try to disturb the intended course of life [1924a, p. 159f.].

Freud now acknowledged that this biological hypothesis could not be reconciled with certain facts. For example, in the state of sexual excitation an increase of stimulation is *experienced* as pleasurable. Freud thus recognized the necessity to distinguish between what he considered regulatory principles of mental functioning (the pleasure-unpleasure principle, or the newly conceptualized Nirvana principle) and the affects pleasure and unpleasure (see Chapter 12).

> [Freud thus reached the conclusion that] we must perceive that the Nirvana principle, belonging as it does to the death instinct, has undergone a modification in living organisms through which it has become the pleasure principle; and we shall henceforward avoid regarding the two principles as one. It is not difficult . . . to guess what power was the source of the modification. It can only be the life instinct, the libido, which has thus, alongside of the death instinct, seized upon a share in the regulation of the processes of life. In this way we obtain a small but interesting set of connections. The *Nirvana* principle expresses the trend of the death instinct; the *pleasure* principle represents the demands of the libido [p. 160]. . . .
> We are without any physiological understanding of the ways and means by which this taming of the death-instinct by the libido may be

effected. So far as the psycho-analytic field of ideas is concerned, we can only assume that a very extensive fusion and amalgamation, in varying proportions, of the two classes of instincts takes place, so that we never have to deal with pure life instincts or pure death instincts but only with mixtures of them in different amounts. Corresponding to a fusion of instincts of this kind, there may, as a result of certain influences, be a *de*fusion of them. How large the portions of the death instincts are which refuse to be tamed in this way by being bound to admixtures of libido we cannot at present guess [p. 164].

There is only a short reference to the fear of death in "The Economic Problem of Masochism":

To the imagos they [the parents] leave behind there are then linked the influences of teachers and authorities, self-chosen models and publicly recognized heroes, whose figures need no longer be introjected by an ego which has become more resistant. The last figure in the series that began with the parents is the dark power of Destiny which only the fewest of us are able to look upon as impersonal. There is little to be said against the Dutch writer Multatuli[5] when he replaces the *Moira* [Destiny] of the Greeks by the divine pair *Logos* and *Ananke* [Reason and Necessity]; but all who transfer the guidance of the world to Providence, to God, or to God and Nature, arouse a suspicion that they still look upon these ultimate and remotest powers as a parental couple, in a mythological sense, and believe themselves linked to them by libidinal ties. In *The Ego and the Id* . . . I made an attempt to derive mankind's realistic fear of death, too, from the same parental view of fate. It seems very hard to free oneself from it [p. 168].

The fear of death is thus related to the difficulty inherent in replacing the personal *Moira* (Fate, Destiny) by Reason and Necessity in one's inner world. Freud had already stated in 1922, in a letter to Pfister, that only in old age did man become converted to that "grim pair"—Logos and Ananke.

Freud's formulations about the fear of death in *The Ego and the Id* and "The Economic Problem of Masochism" contain many ambiguities. Some of these are evident in passages where Freud indulged more than usual in anthropomorphic metaphors. Using melancholy as an example, Freud said that the fear of death arises if the ego "gives itself up" and "lets itself die" when it feels unloved or even hated by the superego and unprotected from internal or external danger. In part these thoughts are reminiscent of Freud's discussion in "Mourning

---

[5] E. D. Dekker (1820-1887), or "Multatuli," had long been a favorite of Freud's. His work heads the list of "ten good books" which Freud (1907c) sent in reply to a questionnaire.

and Melancholia." But this state of the ego would provide an explanation for a lack of *will to live,* for fatalism, even for suicide in cases of severe depression. It does not explain the *fear* of death except in terms of the dual instinct theory, which would hold that the ego, when depleted of libido, "feels" itself defenseless against the force of the death instinct.

This complex example indicates the great importance of the danger-hierarchy concept introduced in *Inhibitions, Symptoms and Anxiety,* for our understanding of *all* situations in which anxiety[6] arises (the fear of death being only one example of anxiety). Another formulation, and one which would also make the introduction of the death-instinct concept superfluous, would be: The ego experiences as dangerous being exposed to overwhelming external threats and being "hated," "unloved," "abandoned" either by love objects or by their internalized representatives in the superego. It also experiences as dangerous the reaction of "letting itself die," which *can become a wish to die.* Such a wish to die would then be one source of a fear of death.

I might add that for anyone who suffered as Freud did while he was writing the "Masochism" paper, the wish to die and not suffer any longer could be in a precarious balance with the wish to live and carry on the struggle. It is generally known that the wish to live plays an important role in the course of any serious illness. There is a fundamental difference, however, between the well-documented concept of a conscious or unconscious *wish* to live or die and the concept of an *instinct* which strives to restore an inorganic state, counteracted only by Eros.

In discussing the death-instinct concept (Chapter 12) I hypothesized that Freud arrived at this concept not only because of his basic adherence to dualistic formulations, but because conceptualizing the wish to die in biological terms enabled him to deal better with his own fear of death.

Those parts of the "Masochism" paper which are based primarily on the death-instinct concept are ambiguous. However, we find in the same paper, and even within the same paragraph, formulations which have pertinence far beyond the framework of psychoanalysis proper. Freud asserted that:

---

[6] It is pertinent that Freud did not use the word *Furcht* (fear) in all these passages, but *Angst* (anxiety), which encompasses all shades of this affect from the (often unconscious) awareness of danger to the panic experienced in a traumatic situation (see Schur, 1953).

In (multicellular) organisms the libido meets the instinct of death, or destruction, which is dominant in them and which seeks to disintegrate the cellular organism and to conduct each separate unicellular organism [composing it] into a state of inorganic stability (relative though this may be). The libido has the task of making the destroying instinct innocuous, and it fulfils the task by diverting that instinct to a great extent outwards—soon with the help of a special organic system, the muscular apparatus—towards objects in the external world. The instinct is then called the destructive instinct, the instinct for mastery, or the will to power. A portion of the instinct is placed directly in the service of the sexual function, where it has an important part to play. This is sadism proper [p. 163].

Divorced from the death-instinct theory, the concept of the destructive instinct—or, as it is much more commonly called, the instinct of aggression, with all its vicissitudes—is indispensable for psychoanalysis, the psychology of man and animals, sociology, criminology, and education, to name only some of its areas of application. Equally indispensable are such concepts as "aggression turned outward" and aggression "turned against the self." No study of crime, suicide, or psychosomatic disorders can easily dispense with these concepts. Just as fruitful as these was Freud's discussion of "moral masochism," which helps us understand so many dark areas of human behavior.

The next work of this period in which Freud explicitly discussed the fear of death was *Inhibitions, Symptoms and Anxiety* (see Chapter 15). One of the many important aspects of this work was the conceptual distinction made between the affective response of anxiety in its various manifestations and the precipitating cause, the danger situation. Freud then formulated a genetic hierarchy of danger situations which follow the lines of human development. Throughout *Inhibitions, Symptoms and Anxiety* the death-instinct theory is used mainly in terms of the destructive (aggressive) instinctual drive and its vicissitudes. The fear of death is dealt with principally in terms of the danger concept and of its importance in neurosogenesis.

If anxiety is a reaction of the ego to danger, we shall be tempted to regard the traumatic neuroses, which so often follow upon a narrow escape from death, as a direct result of a fear of death (or fear *for* life) and to dismiss from our minds the question of castration and the dependent relationships of the ego. Most of those who observed the traumatic neuroses that occurred during the last war took this line, and triumphantly announced that proof was now forthcoming that a threat to the instinct of self-preservation could by itself produce a neurosis without any admixture of sexual factors and without requiring any of the complicated hypotheses of psycho-analysis. . . . In view of all that we know about the structure of the comparatively simple neuroses of everyday life, it would seem highly improbable that a neurosis could come into being merely because of the objective presence of danger, without any participation of the deeper levels of the mental apparatus. But the unconscious seems to contain nothing that could give any content to our concept of the annihilation of life. Castration can be pictured on the basis of the daily experience of the faeces being sep- arated from the body or on the basis of losing the mother's breast at weaning. But nothing resembling death can ever have been experi- enced; or if it has, as in fainting, it has left no observable traces behind. I am therefore inclined to adhere to the view that the fear of death should be regarded as analogous to the fear of castration and that the situation to which the ego is reacting is one of being abandoned by the protecting super-ego—the powers of destiny—so that it has no longer any safeguard against all the dangers that surround it [1926a, p. 129f.].

The main difference—we might say progress—in this formulation, as compared with the ones presented in *The Ego and the Id* and "The Economic Problem of Masochism," is that the feeling of being un- loved, abandoned is not *equated* with the fear of death. Death is repre- sented as one of the many danger situations to which we respond in the course of our development.

And yet here, too, Freud returned to his previous claim that the unconscious contained nothing resembling our concept of annihilation of life.

One explanation for this repeated formulation is that all these meta- psychological explanations can be applied to neurotic anxiety, mean- ing not a neurotic exaggeration of realistic anxiety but an anxiety based on *unconscious* infantile conflicts.

But even if it should be true that "death is an abstract concept with a negative content for which no unconscious correlative can be found," may we not say that even something which has no such correlative can become the content of *danger* to which the ego then responds with anxiety? Must Freud's metapsychological explanation be restricted to neurotic anxiety? The hierarchical development of the danger concept depends not only on instinctual development but on ego development as well. What Freud implied was that every type of anxiety had to follow certain prototypes. Yet, what may change is the content of danger to which one responds with anxiety. The appraisal of death certainly lends itself most readily to being connected with all previous traumatic situations. The constant denial of death which we all practice seems to be evidence in favor of this assumption. As some of our loved ones, more especially our peers, begin to die, the reality of death draws closer and denial becomes harder. Moreover, whenever we actually see people die and observe the uncanny change from life to death, or when we see the dead buried, death becomes more real to us. As Freud said in "Thoughts for the Times on War and Death," "people really die, not only some but all, each of us in our turn."

What Freud called the core of the danger situation is the feeling of helplessness. This certainly applies to our attitude toward death. The fact that it is unfathomable as an experience makes the helplessness supreme.

It was only in the last sentence of the above-quoted passage from *Inhibitions, Symptoms and Anxiety* that Freud provided a simpler explanation of the fear of death as a reaction to a danger situation in which there is no longer any safeguard against the powers of destiny. Freud usually equated the latter with *Ananke (Moira)*. Here, instead, this term was applied to the "protective superego." Freud may have been expressing the notion that one part of the superego—the heir of the protective parent—guaranteed the ego the possibility of immortality, of denying death, an illusion which Freud would shortly feel obliged to shatter in more direct terms.

15

ADJUSTMENT TO PAIN
AND ILLNESS

As mentioned before, Freud resumed his work routine of seeing six patients daily at the beginning of 1924. And he continued to write. During this year he also had to devote much time and energy to organizational matters, some of them unpleasant, such as the defection of Otto Rank who for years had been one of the closest collaborators. (For a detailed discussion of this episode, see Jones, Vol. 3, pp. 44-77, 93.) Throughout this period he submitted with utmost patience to the endless attempts to change and to improve his prosthesis. In his daily life he not only retained the greatest self-control and dignity, but acquired a serenity which had an impact on everyone. Once again all this was achieved at a price.

Freud was forced to change his way of life in many respects. He could no longer attend meetings of the Vienna Psychoanalytic Society, although later on he was able to institute monthly gatherings of the members in his own home. He tried to see as few people as possible because of the strain imposed by speaking. For several years he did not travel.

I shall quote only a few samples from the years of "adjustment," 1924 and 1925, to illustrate some of these points. He wrote to Eitingon on March 22, 1924:

> I cannot look forward to your visit with the same pleasure as heretofore because I foresee that it will bring you disappointments. You belong to those who refuse to believe that I am no longer the same man. In reality,

however I am tired and in need of rest, can scarcely get through my six hours of analytic work, and cannot think of doing anything else. The right thing to do would be to give up all work and obligations and wait in a quiet corner for the natural end. . . . I am also constantly tortured by something. . . . It sounds like such a simple thing to replace a piece of the jaw by a prosthesis and put everything in order. But the prosthesis is never quite right, and the attempts to improve it are not yet over. The lower right part of my face (especially the nose and earlobe) is severely hypesthetic, the right ear has been put out of action due to the deformation and occlusion of the [Eustachian] tube. I do not hear anything on this side but a constant murmur, and am greatly disturbed if I have to listen to a few people at a small gathering. My speech has become intelligible, is adequate for ordinary use, and will presumably improve still further. I am of course able to chew and swallow, but my [way of] eating does not permit any onlookers. I am writing you all this, first, so that you will know about it, and secondly, so that you need not ask about my condition when you are here [1].

The last sentence is pertinent. Freud not only wanted to spare others the necessity of asking about his condition; he himself did not want to be asked about it. Thus he was very appreciative if his friends did not inquire in their letters about his health. Pfister was one of these friends. Freud wrote to him on January 4, 1924:

Your cordial New Year's letter celebrating the fifteen-year jubilee of our friendship gave me great pleasure. You have the gift of throwing a rosy sheen over the everyday life one takes part in so colourlessly. I also thank you for saying so little about my illness, which during the past few months has been taking up much too much space in our lives.

And again on February 26, 1924:

You are the only one of my friends who does not mention my illness in your letters, but I assume you will be glad to hear that I am getting on with my work and expect further improvement from the treatment, which is not yet over.

The following passage in a letter to Abraham written on March 31, 1924 is revealing:

As a result of a possibly influenzal nasal catarrh at the beginning of this month,[1] my health has progressively deteriorated so much that last

---

[1] Because of the open communication between the oral and nasal cavities, every cold lasted longer and frequently led to an infection of the sinuses and right ear. It also made speaking, eating, and smoking more troublesome.

Saturday and Sunday for the first time in my medical career I had to stop work over the weekend [italics added].

Freud always saw most of his patients daily.

Many of Freud's letters written before birthdays indicated that these were often periods of precarious equilibrium. Before his 68th birthday he wrote to Abraham on May 4, 1924:

> You must make a real effort to put yourself in my position if you are not to feel ill-disposed towards me. Though apparently on the way to recovery, there is deep inside me a pessimistic belief in the closeness of the end of my life, nourished by the never-ceasing petty torments and discomforts of the scar, a kind of senile depression centred on the conflict between irrational pleasure in life and intelligent resignation. Accompanying this there is a need for rest and a disinclination to human contacts, neither of which are satisfied, because I cannot avoid working for six or seven hours a day. If I am mistaken and this is only a passing phase, I shall be the first to confirm the fact and again put my shoulder to the wheel. If my forebodings are correct, I shall not fail, if sufficient time remains, to ask you quickly to come and see me.
>
> The idea that my sixty-eighth birthday the day after tomorrow might be my last must have occurred to others, because the city of Vienna has hastened to grant me on that day the freedom of the city, which is normally not given until the recipient's seventieth birthday. I have been informed that at mid-day on the sixth Professor Tandler,[2] representing the burgomaster, and Dr. Friedjung,[3] the children's specialist and a member of the council, who is one of our people, are to pay me a ceremonial visit.

The letters written to Lou Andreas-Salomé were among the most beautiful. He wrote to her on May 13, 1924, after receiving her congratulations for his 68th birthday:

> I have admired your art more than ever this time. Here is a person who, instead of working hard into old age . . . and then dying without preliminaries, contracts a horrible disease in middle age, has to be treated and operated on, squanders his hard-earned bit of money, generates and enjoys discontent, and then crawls about for an indefinite time as an invalid. In *Erewhon* (I trust you know Samuel Butler's brilliant phantasy) such an individual would certainly be punished and locked up. And you can still praise me for bearing my suffering so well. Actually, it isn't quite like this; although I have weathered the awful realities

[2] Julius Tandler, Professor of Anatomy in Vienna, and Commissioner of Health of the City of Vienna.
[3] Dr. Josef K. Friedjung, a member of the Vienna Psychoanalytic Society.

fairly well, it is the possibilities that I find hard to bear; I cannot get accustomed to life under sentence.

It is now six months since my operation and the attitude of my surgeon, who allows me to travel far afield in summer, ought to lull me into something like security—so far as such a feeling is admissible, considering the *di doman non c'è certezza*[4] which affects us all. But it has no effect on me; perhaps partly because the extent to which the prosthesis has restored both functions of the mouth is a very modest one. In the beginning it promised to be more successful, but the promise was not fulfilled.

Six hours of psychoanalysis, this is all I have retained of my capacity for work; everything else, especially social contact, I keep at bay. (Of course Romain Rolland, who has announced himself for tomorrow, I cannot refuse. . . .)

Well, I have written this off my chest because we both seem to be prevented from meeting. The number of things one has to renounce! And instead one is overwhelmed with honors (such as the Freedom of the City of Vienna), for which one would never have lifted a finger [L. 208*].

A letter to Abraham written on August 22, 1924 is pertinent for quite different reasons: Abraham was not only a most astute psychoanalytic clinician, but also the author of many clinical papers, some of which are still considered classics. He was also interested in what is now called applied psychoanalysis—e.g., the meaning of myths, etc. At that time Abraham was interested in the meaning of the number seven in old myths and superstitions of many ancient cultures. He discussed this in the course of a visit paid to Freud in August, 1924, the last time the two men were ever to meet.

It may well be significant that Abraham had frequent professional contacts with Fliess, who was to treat him during the last phase of his mortal illness one year later. Thus Abraham's interest in the number seven may have been influenced—as Freud's letter (August 22, 1924) seems to imply—by Fliess's "number game."

Dear Friend,
In re 7
    I am putting at your disposal an idea the value of which I cannot judge myself because of ignorance.
    I should like to take a historical view and believe that the significance of the number 7 originated in a period when men counted in sixes. (Here ignorance sets in.) In that case seven would not be the last of a

----

[4] Last line of the poem "Il Trionfo di Bacco e di Arianna," by Lorenzo de Medici (1449-1492): "Of tomorrow there is no certainty."

series as it is now in the week, but the first of a second series and, like first things, subject to taboo. The fact that the initial number of the third series, that is to say, 13, is the unluckiest of all numbers would fit in with this.

The origin of my idea was a remark in a history of Assyria that 19 was also one of the suspect numbers, which the author explains with reference to the length of the month by the equation $30 + 19 = 49$, or 7×7. However, $19 = 13 + 6$, the beginning of a fourth series of sixes.

This system of sixes would thus be pre-astronomical. One should now investigate what is known of such a system, of which enough traces remain (dozen, gross, division of the circle into 360 degrees).

Moreover, it is notable how many prime numbers appear in this series:

1

7

13

19

25 is an exception, but is followed by

31

37

43

49 which is again 7×7

The craziest things can be done with numbers, so be careful.

Cordially yours,

Freud

Note the warning at the end!

Freud's scientific curiosity had remained very much alive. He was still *"novarum rerum cupidus."*

The last letter of 1924 to be quoted here was written to Eitingon on August 2 from the Semmering, where Freud was spending the summer:

Please come, and bring your wife if she cares to. I am very comfortable here, feel rested, and no longer shy away from people. But do not expect to find me "symptom-free."[5] Is that at all possible in my situation? Eating, drinking, and talking are still tasks requiring a conscious effort on my part. There are so very many misleading sensations, they change their locality and quality to such an extent, that there remains sufficient ground for vague apprehensiveness, and they are so taxing that only a fraction of my interest is left for the impressions of daily life. Thus, it would be best if you never asked me how I felt. I myself would not remain silent about a decisive change, which is not likely to occur in a few weeks [2].

[5] A hope Eitingon must have expressed in a letter.

This was one of the few occasions on which Freud permitted himself to express in writing how much the uncomfortable bodily sensations with which he was being flooded preoccupied him and interfered with his well-being.

During the year 1925 the battle with the prosthesis continued. A few comfortable days would alternate with many miserable weeks. There were 69 entries in Pichler's notes and one surgical intervention because of an apical abscess. Freud saw patients, continued with his writing, and at times worked at the old feverish pace. Some letters again illustrate Freud's struggles, the first, to Eitingon on April 1, 1925:

> Tiring times are behind me; constant work to improve my prosthesis (how much more I would like to miswrite: "hypothesis"!), the "appropriate misery of restoration," the absorption of all freely mobile energy in organ cathexis, necessitated by the unbelievable variety of paresthesias. Today we have come so far as to eliminate the gross difficulties; the more subtle ones are still enough to make me feel ill-humored. Surrounded and watched over by three tender females, I do not have much freedom to complain, but much opportunity to practice the necessary self-control. *However, one gets tired in the process* [italics added] [3].

The self-control was necessary for the benefit not only of the three loving women (Martha, Minna, and Anna), but also of Freud's patients. Every analyst who has suffered a serious illness knows how difficult the situation becomes, especially when a patient is alternating between cruel fantasies and the suppression or repression of any awareness of the analyst's illness, owing to anxiety and guilt. We see here at work again "the unvarying call of duty," which had sustained Freud after Sophie's death. This was manifested, for example, in one of Freud's numerous letters to Marie Bonaparte in which he apologized to her in a deeply moving way for having allowed his preoccupation with his cancer to keep him from recognizing a certain transference phenomenon in her analysis.

Jones (Vol. 3, p. 153) reports an incident mentioned to him by Eva Rosenfeld, at the time a patient and student of Freud's.[6] In 1930, Freud was spending his summer vacation in Grundlsee, a beautiful spot in the Austrian Alps. As usual, he had a few patients and trainees with him, among them Eva Rosenfeld, to whom another student, Dr. Ruth Mack-Brunswick, confided her fears about Freud's condition. In

[6] Now an analyst practicing in London.

the course of her next session Mrs. Rosenfeld tried to withhold this from Freud, who sensed that she was hiding something. After she had "confessed" to him what she had been holding back, Freud admonished her: "We have only one aim and only one loyalty, to psychoanalysis. If you break this rule you injure something much more important than any consideration you owe to me." When I visited Freud in Grundlsee and was able to reassure everyone that this time, at least, their concern was unfounded, Mrs. Rosenfeld told me about this incident. How often Freud had to endure such "free associations" from his patients during those years!

In May, 1925, Lou Andreas-Salomé wrote to Freud on the occasion of his 69th birthday. Here is his answer:

> Sunday afternoon and quiet! This morning with the help of Anna and the typewriter I dealt with my correspondence, which had accumulated as a result of my superannuated imprudence, and [now] I can thank you and have a talk with you.
>
> First of all let me thank your dear old gentleman [her husband] for the charming lines he wrote to someone unknown to him. May he keep well as long as he himself wants to.
>
> As for me, I no longer want to ardently enough. A crust of indifference is slowly creeping up around me; a fact I state without complaining. It is a natural development, a way of beginning to be inorganic. The "detachment of old age," I think it is called. It must be connected with the decisive crisis in the relationship of the two instincts stipulated by me. The change taking place is perhaps not very conspicuous; everything is as interesting as it was before; neither are the qualities very different; but some kind of resonance is lacking; unmusical as I am, I imagine the difference to be something like using the pedal or not. The never-ceasing tangible pressure of a vast number of unpleasant sensations must have accelerated this otherwise perhaps premature condition, this tendency to experience everything *sub specie aeternitatis*.
>
> Otherwise existence is still bearable. I even think I have discovered something of fundamental importance for our work, which I am going to keep to myself for a while. It is a discovery of which one ought almost to be ashamed, for one should have divined these connections from the beginning and not after thirty years. One more proof of the fallability of human nature[7] . . . [L. 214*].

This is perhaps the most succinct example of Freud's self-observation, a highly subtle, controlled, and yet very human description of the

[7] In the original German: "überall mit Wasser gekocht" (they cook with water everywhere) an idiomatic, colloquial expression meaning: there are no exceptions, i.e., everyone is fallible.

gradual transition from the organic to the inorganic, from life to death.
I have already pointed out how differently Freud "spoke" in his letters
to different recipients. This is quite apparent when we compare this
letter with the previously quoted one to Eitingon, written only five
weeks earlier, in which he also discussed the impact of painful sensations. Without knowing the addressee, we could have surmised that
this was a letter written to Lou Andreas-Salomé, from whom he expected a very special "resonance." This letter marked Freud's progress
in the mastery of his suffering, and indicated at the same time that
there would ultimately be a change in the balance between the ability
to "enjoy it all," even if ever so slightly, the amount of suffering to be
withstood, and the feeling, "What more can be demanded of me?"
However, when he wrote this letter, Freud was still far from having
reached that point.

The last passage of the letter referred to *Inhibitions, Symptoms and
Anxiety,* in which Freud overhauled so many of his basic concepts
concerning symptom formation and the role of anxiety in normal and
abnormal development. The composition of *Inhibitions, Symptoms
and Anxiety* gives evidence of the feeling: "I still have important work
to do, but I must hurry. I must fight against the inexorable Chronos.
I must do this before the resonance becomes even more muted."

Those who accuse Freud of rigidity, of dogmatism, of an inability
to change his mind, have never read or tried to understand this book.
Let us reconsider for a moment Freud's explanation of the fear of
death which he saw as the ego's *fear* of being abandoned by the protecting superego. Freud's letter indicates that he had reached the
phase of overcoming the fear. But what may have remained was
Freud, like all of us, asking *Ananke:* "Why do you require all this
of me?" This question was to be asked by Freud in various ways during the years to come.

Other letters show how ready Freud was, whenever the flood of
painful sensations subsided or at least ebbed for a while, to open himself up to the many big and little things which enabled him to "enjoy
it all" again.

Before Freud left for his summer vacation in 1925, Pichler cauter-
ized a very painful area, which after a severe initial reaction brought
Freud considerable relief. For the first time since his surgery, Freud
was able to enjoy a period of relative well-being. When he described
his condition in a letter to Abraham, written on June 9, he was not
aware of the fact that the latter had been stricken by the mortal illness

to which he succumbed only a few months later. Abraham's letter informing Freud about his illness (written on June 7) had apparently not yet reached Freud, who wrote on July 21, 1925:

> The energetic intervention with which my doctor took leave of me three weeks ago has changed the character of my complaints thoroughly for the better. All the paresthesias that tyrannically forced themselves upon my attention have disappeared, and have left behind an individual free to complain, if he feels like it, about his awkward speech and never-ending nasal catarrh. So life is admittedly tolerable, but after this spoiling and weaning[8] process what will regular work taste like in October?
>
> I have written a few short papers, but they are not meant very seriously. Perhaps if I am willing to admit their parentage, I shall tell you about them later.

Many writers and scientists take such an attitude toward their work. It was in no way a pose or self-belittlement on Freud's part, although throughout his life he took a special pride only in a few of his works, above all *The Interpretation of Dreams.*

One explanation for the negative reaction which Freud experienced toward a completed work can be found in his method of writing. We know from the Fliess letters and later correspondence, as well as from his own descriptions, that most of his works—even the very complex ones such as the "Project," the final version of Chapter VII of *The Interpretation of Dreams,* and his papers on metapsychology—were written in days or weeks of feverish activity. Such periods must be followed by a certain state of depletion, which may manifest itself only in a swing of mood but may also be reminiscent of mild states of depression. We know that Freud was given to such fluctuations. If we consider what obstacles must have been presented by the normal aging process combined with intolerable physical suffering, it becomes even more amazing that Freud's creativity should have persisted nearly to the end, and even more understandable that he should have had to combat a depressive reaction in the intervals between new spurts of creativity. We can also anticipate that the final ebbing of his creativity was to prove more difficult for him to bear than any amount of suffering.

---

[8] *Entwöhnung und Verwöhnung,* a play on words. *Entwöhnung* means literally both weaning and abstinence, but also "becoming unused to"—here to pain. For abstinence from smoking Freud always used the word *Abstinenz. Verwöhnen* means "being spoiled."

16

FREUD ENTERS THE BIBLICAL AGE

In the fall of 1925, tragedy struck where Freud least expected it. He had repeatedly warned the members of the Committee, his closest friends and followers, to be ready for the time when he would no longer be around. Rank's defection after Freud's surgery, related probably to the impact of Freud's illness, made him wish even more strongly that the other members would close ranks.

It was with Ferenczi that Freud was perhaps most intimate, and in later years with Eitingon, too. But it was Abraham who was the soundest of the members. His objectivity and sober evaluation of people and situations were most reliable. It was Abraham, along with Jones, who first recognized the inevitability of a break with Jung and the neurotic conflicts of Rank; who for all his unfailing loyalty never hesitated to stand up for his opinions; who was both an imaginative researcher and an excellent organizer.

And now Abraham succumbed, after a relatively short illness. This illness, which had been diagnosed as a lung abscess following an injury to the pharynx from a fishbone, required repeated surgery. After the first acute phase, the news seemed reassuring and Abraham was apparently recovering in Switzerland. He was even able, in September, to attend the Psycho-Analytical Congress held in Homburg. He reported about this congress in a long letter written on September 8, 1925. However, this letter contained a passage which threw a cloud over the last phase of the close relationship between the two men.

I mentioned earlier that Fliess, with whom Abraham had become acquainted when he began to practice in Berlin, took care of the latter during the last phase of his illness. Fliess seems to have exerted his magnetic influence on Abraham, as some of the latter's last letters indicate. The letter of September 8, 1925, concluded with the following paragraph:

> On the whole, therefore, I am satisfied with the Congress. . . . I really had some exhausting days. All the people who only wanted to speak to me for 'half a minute' exacted such an amount of talking from me that I found it a very great strain and I shall need several days to get my breathing right again. I shall in any case have to undergo some treatment for my nose and throat from Fliess. If this letter were not already unduly long, I would tell you how my illness has most strikingly confirmed all Fliess's views on periodicity.

This from Abraham, the sober scientist!

In his answer to this letter Freud did not respond to the remarks concerning Fliess.

The next letter from Abraham did not convey any reason for undue alarm. He wrote (on October 19, 1925):

> You may be interested to hear that Fliess, who heard about your illness two years ago, has repeatedly asked after your health with the warmest interest. As far as I am concerned, I must repeat here once again that I owe him the utmost gratitude.

That Fliess had either retained, or more likely regained, his interest in psychoanalysis, was reading Freud's publications and referring patients for psychoanalytic treatment, has also been confirmed by others.[1]

Freud brushed this message off and wrote in one of the *Rundbriefe* (a circular letter written on October 20, 1925 to the members of the Committee): "This expression of sympathy after twenty years leaves me rather cold" (Jones, Vol. 3, p. 116).

During the last months of Abraham's life, Freud's relationship to him was slightly strained by an unfortunate episode. At that time Freud had just refused to collaborate on a film project proposed by the American producer Samuel Goldwyn, but he offered no active opposition to Abraham's cooperation in the production of a "popular scientific film" to be made by the educational unit of a German film com-

---

[1] Among them, Dr. Marianne Kris, a niece of Mrs. Fliess. Fliess's son Robert became a prominent psychoanalyst.

pany (see Abraham letter of June 7, 1925). The production of this film led to a controversy between Abraham and some of the other analysts, who were either involved in the project or were suggesting alternate ones (for details see Jones, Vol. 3, p. 114f.). Freud spoke in the circular letter quoted above of Abraham's "harshness" in handling this affair.

Abraham responded to these comments in the last letter he wrote to Freud, where he reminded the latter of previous occasions on which his judgment of "personalities" had proven to be correct (e.g., the split with Jung and Rank). In spite of his expression of genuine concern about Abraham's health, Freud's answer could not conceal his mixed feelings in the statement: "You are not necessarily always right."

When I read about this episode in Jones's biography, which indicated that the correspondence with Abraham had ended on this note, I could not reconcile such a fact with my knowledge of Freud's feelings for Abraham, his concern and supreme gentleness in situations where his younger friends were seriously ill. Only when I read the last letters exchanged between Freud and Abraham did it occur to me that the somewhat angry remarks in Freud's last letter may have been a displaced response to Abraham's repeated comments about Fliess in preceding letters. Abraham had obviously expected some response to these comments, but none had been forthcoming except Freud's rather sarcastic remark in the circular letter. Freud had apparently never forgotten—nor quite forgiven Fliess.

That Abraham, whom Freud admired for his sharp intellect and the qualities of character he expected from a scientist, fell under the spell of Fliess did not "sit well" with Freud.

At the time of his last letter to Abraham (November 5, 1925) Freud probably already suspected that Abraham's illness was a serious one. From letters written by Freud after Abraham's death, we may conclude that Abraham died from a bronchogenic carcinoma. Freud himself did not want to be fooled, and he probably expected from people like Abraham an attitude toward the inevitable of the kind he had praised so highly in Anton von Freund. Freud therefore could not quite condone the signs of euphoria Abraham was showing in response to Fliess's influence.[2]

---

[2] See also Freud's letter to Eitingon (March 10, 1926) quoted below, and his letter to Fliess of February 2, 1899 (Chapter 5).

In October, 1925 Abraham was still writing optimistic letters, but shortly afterward he began to fail rapidly, and died on Christmas Day.

Freud experienced Abraham's death as an "unfairness of fate," since it was the much older of the two cancer-stricken men who had survived (see Glover's introduction to Freud/Abraham, 1965). Freud wrote to Jones on December 30, 1925:

> Who would have thought when we met that time in the Harz mountains that he would be the first to leave this unreasonable life!—We must continue to work and stand together. As a human being no one can replace this loss, but for psychoanalysis no one is allowed to be irreplaceable. I shall soon drop out, the others not till much later, I hope, but our work, compared to whose importance we are all insignificant, must continue [L. 216*].

Freud wrote a short obituary on Abraham for the first 1926 number of the *Internationale Zeitschrift*. When he found that the subsequent number was to be devoted to his forthcoming 70th birthday, he wrote, in a very characteristic manner, to the journal's editor, Sandor Rado, asking that the birthday number be postponed, and the next issue be devoted instead to commemorations of Abraham, which Rado had intended to print at the end of the year:

> One cannot celebrate any festival until one has performed the duty of mourning [Jones, Vol. 3, p. 120].

Freud's letter to Jones concerning Abraham's death revealed one of the motivations for both the obligation and the wish to live and to carry on: the "cause," the work to be continued on the edifice he had erected. The other motive was the necessity to continue to provide for his large family, not only children and grandchildren but sisters, their children, etc.

Freud's inner struggle was intensified in 1926, the year he turned 70. To get a perspective on what Freud referred to as the constant flux of painful sensations, I consulted Pichler's notes for 1926, a "typical" year with no major surgical procedures, just the unceasing attempt to achieve a bare minimum of comfort. There were 48 office visits, one biopsy, two cauterizations, and constant experiments with three different prostheses involving attempts to preserve the few remaining teeth.

In the third week of February, 1926, *Inhibitions, Symptoms and Anxiety* was published, in which Freud formulated the concept of "signal anxiety" as an immediate response to a conscious or unconscious awareness of danger. In the same week a new "danger signal" flashed for Freud. On several occasions he felt anginal pain after effort (without anxiety and, in contrast to his 1894 cardiac episode, without dyspnea). Freud's cardiologist friend Ludwig Braun diagnosed angina pectoris[3] and ordered a rest cure.

At that time Freud had reason to hope that his cancer would not recur in the near future.[4] Cancer had always meant danger for him in some unforeseeable future, whereas cardiac symptoms represented a more immediate danger. Therefore he was willing to subject himself to at least temporary abstinence from nicotine. After some hesitation he also agreed to spend a few weeks in the Cottage Sanatorium, a luxurious private hospital located in one of the outlying districts of Vienna.

A long letter to Eitingon written on March 10, 1926, reflected both Freud's reaction to the new danger situation and his aversion to the prospect of participating in the various festivities which were being planned for his 70th birthday.

Because most of this letter has been quoted by Jones (Vol. 3, p. 120f.) I shall refer only to its most pertinent points.

> [Freud expected to meet with the Committee on the occasion of his birthday, especially since this might prove to be the last such meeting.] I say that without railing against fate, without making any effort at resignation, but as a calm matter of fact, though I know how hard it is to persuade other people of that outlook.
>
> [He then informed Eitingon that the diagnosis was a myocarditis.[5]] The number of my various bodily troubles makes me wonder how long I shall be able to continue my professional work, especially since renouncing the sweet habit of smoking has resulted in a great diminution of my intellectual interests. . . . The only real dread I have is of a long invalidism with no possibility of working. . . .
>
> [He was not protesting, he asserted, because] the affection of the heart opens up a prospect of a not too delayed and not too miserable exit. . . . Do not make the mistake of thinking I am depressed. I regard it as a triumph to retain a clear judgment in all circumstances, not like poor Abraham to let oneself be deceived by a euphoria.

[3] Electrocardiograms were not yet done regularly.

[4] See his letter to Binswanger (October 15, 1926) quoted in Chapter 13.

[5] Any myocardial damage, even of vascular origin, was then sometimes loosely referred to as "myocarditis." It is possible, however, that Freud was using the same term as he had done in the cardiac episode of the 1890's, because Braun (whom I knew well) was a very precise man and always complied with Freud's demand for correct information.

The last sentence is characteristic of the posture which Freud was able to assume in the face of danger. It also shows how serious was his insistence on being told the full truth. We are reminded here of the 1910 letter to Pfister with its concluding remark: "In the words of King Macbeth, let us die in harness."

Only two weeks later Freud had recovered, and wrote to Eitingon on March 28, 1926:

> Now that I have started to write about the most intimate matters, I see that I must continue and report that the time I spent at my "Riviera"[6] did me a lot of good as far as looks, weight, and subjective feelings are concerned. The heart sensations are not quite gone but have become minimal. I can take long walks without pain, and I am now disposed to look upon the condition as an episode, as my cunning internist Braun has tried to convince me. With this, according to the well-known universal human pattern, the "worries" too are receding into the background [1].

By this time Freud began to write to Marie Bonaparte. In 1925, she had asked to be analyzed by Freud. He accepted her as a patient; eventually she became an analyst herself, and also a devoted friend. Freud corresponded with her to the end of his life. It is from his letters to her, among others, that we learn the details of Freud's various bouts of illness, his struggles against the temptation to smoke the excellent cigars she had sent him, etc.

Freud returned home from the sanatorium early in April, 1926. He was still working on a reduced schedule, but his heart symptoms had disappeared. A letter written to Marie Bonaparte on April 27, only nine days before the dreaded 70th birthday, showed clearly Freud's sustained receptivity to beauty, especially the beauty of nature. He wrote:

> I must continue my morning drives in the Viennese spring, and find it truly beautiful. What a pity that one has to become old and sick to make this discovery. How fortunate that you did not have to wait so long in your garden.[7]
>
> By the way, do you know the little spring poem by our Uhland? It expresses better than anything else the mood of spring. I do not have it quite completely and securely in my memory, but I want to quote what I remember of it:

---

[6] Freud's nickname for the Cottage Sanatorium.
[7] In St. Cloud, near Paris.

> The world grows lovelier each day,
> We do not know what still may come;
> The flowering will not end,
> The farthest, deepest valley is abloom.
> Now, dear heart, forget your torment,
> Now everything, everything must change.
> I'm still being very virtuous[8] [2].

Ten years later, as we shall see, Freud quoted the same poem in a letter to Arnold Zweig, but without the hopeful ending.

The tone of this letter indicates that the will to live and the ability to "enjoy it all" were still there, given a minimum of physical comfort. Freud's 70th birthday brought recognition from all parts of the globe. Freud sent Marie Bonaparte a detailed, witty descripton of the celebration on May 10, 1926. A characteristic passage follows:

> I got all kinds of flattering things to hear and read. It was concluded by a celebration of the Jewish Lodge to which I have belonged for 29 years. My doctor, Prof. Ludwig Braun, made a speech there of a kind which cast a spell over the whole audience, including my family. I had asked to be excused from attending. It would have been embarrassing and in poor taste. As a rule when I am attacked I can defend myself; but when I am praised, I am helpless [L. 221*].

It was embarrassing, he commented, to be exposed on a "praise pillory" (*"Lobespranger,"* a word combination of Freud's creation). Despite his misgivings and protestations, Freud was really gratified by the tribute, which he summarized in the following statement:

> General impression: the world has acquired a certain respect for my work. *But so far analysis has been accepted only by analysts* [L. 221*].

The brilliant and moving speech by Braun was published in the *Mitteilungen* of the B'nai Brith Lodge. Freud wrote its members a letter (on May 6, 1926) reminding them of how he had come to join their organization. In a few sentences Freud was able to depict that unyielding inner strength which permitted him to master all obstacles, past and still to come.

> It happened that in the years after 1895 two strong impressions coincided to produce the same effect on me. On the one hand I had gained the first insight into the depths of human instinct, had seen many things

---

[8] Meaning: abstinence from smoking.

which were sobering, at first even frightening; on the other hand the disclosure of my unpopular discoveries led to my losing most of my personal relationships at that time; I felt as though outlawed, shunned by all. This isolation aroused in me the longing for a circle of excellent men with high ideals who would accept me in friendship despite my temerity. Your Lodge was described to me as the place where I could find such men. . . .

And before long there followed the realization that it was only to my Jewish nature that I owed the two qualities that have become indispensable to me throughout my difficult life. Because I was a Jew I found myself free of many prejudices which restrict others in the use of the intellect: as a Jew I was prepared to be in the opposition and to renounce agreement with the "compact [solid] majority."[9]

So I became one of you, took part in your humanitarian and national interests, made friends among you . . . at a time when no one in Europe would listen to me and I had no pupils in Vienna, you offered me your sympathetic attention. You were my first audience. . . . I can assure you that during the years I have belonged to you, you have meant much to me and done much for me [L. 220*].

---

[9] A quotation from Ibsen's *An Enemy of the People.*

17

THE FUTURE WITHOUT
ILLUSIONS

Freud had now passed into the "patriarchal age." At the celebration, he addressed all his "sons" and warned them that they would
henceforth have to be on their own. (Actually, on the day after the
celebration, Freud had seven and a half hours of discussion and con-
ferences with the various analysts who had gathered for the occasion!)
Despite this warning, however, Freud not only continued to be actively
interested in the ongoing development of psychoanalysis as a science,
but all his "sons" went on asking for his advice and help with regard to
scientific, organizational, and even personal problems.

This address of Freud's heralded a shift in his main interest. After
writing his brilliant essay, *The Question of Lay Analysis,* in which he
succeeded in presenting a most lucid and yet completely nontechnical
outline of psychoanalysis, he could turn again to other problems.
Freud spoke repeatedly of this shift of interest. In the Postscript to the
Lay Analysis he wrote:

> After forty-one years of medical activity, my self-knowledge tells me
> that I have never really been a doctor in the proper sense. I became a
> doctor through being compelled to deviate from my original purpose;
> and the triumph of my life lies in my having, after a long and round-
> about journey, found my way back to my earliest path. I have no
> knowledge of having had any craving in my early childhood to help
> suffering humanity. My innate sadistic disposition was not a very strong
> one, so that I had no need to develop this one of its derivatives. Nor
> did I ever play the 'doctor game'; my infantile curiosity evidently chose

394

other paths. *In my youth I felt an overpowering need to understand something of the riddles of the world in which we live* and perhaps even to contribute something to their solution [1926b, p. 253; my italics].

In the 1935 Postscript to his *Autobiographical Study* (1925b) Freud said:

Two themes run through these pages: the story of my life and the history of psycho-analysis. They are intimately interwoven. This *Autobiographical Study* shows how psycho-analysis came to be the whole content of my life and rightly assumes that no personal experiences of mine are of any interest in comparison to my relations with that science.

Shortly before I wrote this study it seemed as though my life would soon be brought to an end by the recurrence of a malignant disease; but surgical skill saved me in 1923 and I was able to continue my life and my work, though no longer in freedom from pain. In the period of more than ten years that has passed since then, I have never ceased my analytic work nor my writing. . . . But I myself find that a significant change has come about. Threads which in the course of my development had become intertangled have now begun to separate; interests which I had acquired in the later part of my life have receded, while the older and original ones become prominent once more. It is true that in this last decade I have carried out some important pieces of analytic work, such as the revision of the problem of anxiety in my book *Inhibitions, Symptoms and Anxiety* (1926a) or the simple explanation of sexual 'fetishism' which I was able to make a year later. . . . Nevertheless it would be true to say that, since I put forward my hypothesis of the existence of two classes of instinct (Eros and the death instinct) and since I proposed a division of the mental personality into an ego, a super-ego, and an id (1923), I have made no further decisive contributions to psycho-analysis: what I have written on the subject since then has been either unessential or would soon have been supplied by someone else. This circumstance is connected with an alteration in myself, with what might be described as a phase of regressive development. My interest, after making a lifelong *détour* through the natural sciences, medicine, and psychotherapy, returned to the cultural problems which had fascinated me long before, when I was a youth scarcely old enough for thinking [1925b, p. 71f.].

This was how Freud described his inner development from which emerged *The Future of an Illusion* (1927a) and *Civilization and Its Discontents* (1930b).

There was no significant change in his daily life, which still involved an unending struggle to build a satisfactory prosthesis. The Pichler notes show 77 entries for the year 1927 (including one surgical intervention, and an electrocoagulation of a small leukoplakia). A new "complication" arose out of the government's imposition of currency restrictions: it was forbidden to import cigars into Austria, while the Austrian cigars had become much worse. So Eitingon, the tireless Paladin, had to find both new sources of supply in Germany and new ways to get them into Austria.

The following letter is characteristic for this period:

> . . . secondly, I want to thank you for again sending me those good cigars—150 of them, since the first sample. It has been a good many years since I have had anything so pleasant and soothing to smoke. And since it is not my intention to forgo this source of gratification for the short remainder of my life, please take any future opportunity you may have to send me additional supplies.
>
> . . . My new prosthesis is being delayed again and again, nor do I have any guarantee that it will fit much better; in the meantime I am living very uncomfortably [1].

In the early spring there was another recurrence of his anginal pain and two more weeks at the Cottage Sanatorium. This meant another futile attempt at abstinence. Freud wrote to Eitingon on April 14, 1927:

> Many thanks for sending me new cigars, the cost of which, I hope, Ernst is settling each time.[1] Of course I am being asked to smoke less. My new prosthesis, which in some respects is better, is in other respects a disappointment after all [2].

That Freud never failed to subject his own feelings and reactions to analysis is evident from the following entry of Pichler's: "The patient has made interesting self-observations about the ingratitude of patients and about the revolt against dependency" (May 12, 1927).

On June 6, Freud wrote again to Eitingon:

> So you, too, are among the visionaries! That "nearly" [Eitingon had obviously reassured Freud that the prosthesis was "nearly" perfect] has its source in a not-yet abandoned illusion that Pichler will succeed in removing the last trouble spot and that I shall then be able to associate with people without thinking more about the spot on my jaw than about the person. But the last spot is always only the next-to-last, and in the meantime something new comes up, as now, for instance, a periostitis by which a tooth is making it known that it no longer feels like helping to carry the burden. And so this illusion takes the path of all the others [3].

---

[1] Ernst Freud lived in Berlin.

This letter, with the attitude it reveals about illusions, shows very clearly the parallel between Freud's life and his work. During this same spring of 1927 Freud began to write *The Future of an Illusion*, which he finished in November of that year. Taking up where he had left off in *Totem and Taboo* and "Thoughts for the Times on War and Death," Freud brought to its logical conclusion the "manifesto of the psychological revolution" proclaimed in the *Introductory Lectures*. The formulations found in *The Future of an Illusion* reflect Freud's whole development during the preceding decade.

I shall quote some of the most pertinent passages of the book which deal with "what is perhaps the most important item in the psychical inventory of a civilization. This consists in its religious ideas in the widest sense—in other words (which will be justified later) in its illusions" (1927a, p. 14). It was Freud's thesis that the principal task of civilization, its *raison d'être*, was to defend us against nature—the elements, diseases, and "the painful riddle of death."

> With these forces nature rises up against us, majestic, cruel and inexorable; she brings to our mind once more our weakness and helplessness, which we thought to escape through the work of civilization. . . .
> [Life is as hard to bear for the individual as for mankind in general.] We know already how the individual reacts to the injuries which civilization and other men inflict on him: he develops a corresponding degree of resistance to the regulations of civilization and of hostility to it. But how does he defend himself against the superior powers of nature, of Fate, which threaten him as they threaten all the rest?
> [To achieve this] life and the universe must be robbed of their terrors [nature must be humanized]. Impersonal forces and destinies cannot be approached; they remain eternally remote. But if the elements have passions that rage as they do in our own souls, if death itself is not something spontaneous but the violent act of an evil Will, . . . then we can breathe freely, can feel at home in the uncanny and can deal by psychical means with our senseless anxiety. . . .
> [This process is the repetition of an infantile prototype:] For once before one has found oneself in a similar state of helplessness: as a small child, in relation to one's parents. One has reason to fear them, . . . and yet one was sure of [their] protection against the dangers one knew. . . . Here, too, wishing played its part, as it does in dream-life. The sleeper may be seized with a presentiment of death, which threatens to place him in the grave. But the dream-work knows how to select a condition that will turn even that dreaded event into a wish-fulfilment: the dreamer sees himself in an ancient Etruscan grave which he has climbed down into, happy to find his archaeological interests satisfied [p. 16f.].

Freud here gave an example of the continuity of his creative activity by referring to one of his own dreams which he had discussed in *The Interpretation of Dreams,* and which at the time had helped him *deny* his fear of death (see Chapter 5). Now he was trying to deal with this fear in a different manner.

Mankind endows the forces of nature with the characteristics of a father, Freud asserted, and turns them into gods, assigning to them three tasks:

> . . . they must exorcize the terrors of nature, they must reconcile men to the cruelty of Fate, particularly as it is shown in death, and they must compensate them for the sufferings and privations which a civilized life in common has imposed on them. . . .
>
> As regards the apportioning of destinies, an unpleasant suspicion persisted that the perplexity and helplessness of the human race could not be remedied. It was here that the gods were most apt to fail. . . . The notion dawned on the most gifted people of antiquity that Moira [Fate] stood above the gods. . . . And the more autonomous nature became, . . . the more earnestly were all expectations directed to the third function of the gods—the more did morality become their true domain. It now became the task of the gods . . . to attend to the sufferings which men inflict on one another in their life together and to watch over the fulfilment of the precepts of civilization, which men obey so imperfectly. . . .
>
> And thus a store of ideas is created, born from man's need to make his helplessness tolerable. . . . It can clearly be seen that the possession of these ideas protects him in two directions—against the dangers of nature and Fate, and against the injuries that threaten him from human society itself. Here is the gist of the matter. Life in this world serves a higher purpose. . . . Over each one of us there watches a benevolent Providence. . . . Death itself is not extinction, is not a return to inorganic lifelessness, but the beginning of a new kind of existence which lies on the path of development to something higher. . . . Life after death, which continues life on earth just as the invisible part of the spectrum joins on to the visible part, brings us all the perfection that we may perhaps have missed here [p. 18f.].

In *Totem and Taboo,* Freud had tried to trace and explain the development of civilization and of religion. In *The Future of an Illusion,* after repeating and developing these concepts in an extremely condensed way, Freud asked some crucial questions:

> . . . what are these ideas in the light of psychology? . . . And, to take a further timid step, what is their real worth?

Freud was at his best as teacher and writer when he was presenting his thesis in the form of a dialogue with an imaginary student or opponent. He used this method in the *Introductory Lectures, The Question of Lay Analysis,* and in the last two chapters of *The Future of an Illusion.* It is likely, judging from his correspondence with Pfister, that the latter stood for the imagined discussant. After first articulating the objections of his opponents, Freud continued his inquiry by starting out with the following definition:

> Religious ideas are teachings and assertions about facts and conditions of external (or internal) reality which tell one something one has not discovered for oneself and which lay claim to one's belief [p. 25].

Freud cited many examples of facts which every school insisted its students accept as true, but not without attempting to supply adequate proofs to support this designation.

> They are put forward as the epitomized result of a longer process of thought based on observation and certainly also on inferences. If anyone wants to go through this process himself instead of accepting its result, they show him how to set about it [p. 26].

In connection with the teachings of religion, Freud saw three kinds of "proof" adduced in support of their credibility: first, our ancestors believed them; secondly, "we possess proofs which have been handed down to us from those same primaeval times; and thirdly, it is forbidden to raise the question of their authentication at all."

> We ought to believe because our forefathers believed. But these ancestors of ours were far more ignorant than we are. They believed in things we could not possibly accept to-day. . . . The proofs they have left us are set down in writings which themselves bear every mark of untrustworthiness. They are full of contradictions, revisions and falsifications. . . .
>
> Thus we arrive at the singular conclusion that of all the information provided by our cultural assets it is precisely the elements . . . which have the task of solving the riddles of the universe and of reconciling us to the sufferings of life . . . that are the least well authenticated of any. . . .
>
> And let no one suppose that what I have said about the impossibility of proving the truth of religious doctrines contains anything new. It has been felt . . . by the ancestors who bequeathed us this legacy. Many of them probably nourished the same doubts as ours, but the pressure imposed on them was too strong for them to have dared to utter them. And since then countless people have been tormented by similar doubts, . . . many brilliant intellects have broken down over this

conflict, and many characters have been impaired by the compromises with which they have tried to find a way out of it [p. 26f.].

The question Freud was raising once again was this: whence comes the inner force of religious doctrines, and to what do they owe their efficacy, "independent as they are of recognition by reason"? Freud's answer to this question was:

> [These doctrines] are not precipitates of experience or end-results of thinking: they are illusions, fulfilments of the oldest, strongest and most urgent wishes of mankind. The secret of their strength lies in the strength of those wishes . . . the benevolent rule of a divine Providence allays our fear of the dangers of life; . . . the prolongation of earthly existence in a future life provides the local and temporal framework in which these wish-fulfilments shall take place. . . . It is an enormous relief to the individual psyche if the conflicts of its childhood . . . which it has never wholly overcome . . . are removed from it and brought to a solution which is universally accepted [p. 30].

> To assess the truth-value of religious doctrines does not lie within the scope of the present enquiry. It is enough for us that we have recognized them as being . . . illusions. . . . We know approximately at what periods . . . religious doctrines were created. If in addition we discover the motives which led to this, our attitude to the problem of religion will undergo a marked displacement. We shall tell ourselves that it would be very nice if there were a God who created the world and was a benevolent Providence, and if there were a moral order in the universe and an after-life; but it is a very striking fact that all this is exactly as we are bound to wish it to be. And it would be more remarkable still if our wretched, ignorant and downtrodden ancestors had succeeded in solving all these difficult riddles of the universe [p. 33].

Freud then disposed of other objections raised by his "discussant": e.g., this paper might be dangerous, it might disrupt morality, promote lawlessness, etc. He even discarded as unimportant the possibility that his book might harm the reputation of psychoanalysis, saying:

> The most that can happen is that the translation and distribution of this book will be forbidden in one country or another—and precisely, of course, in a country that is convinced of the high standard of its culture [p. 36].

Special attention was given to the question [p. 47]:

> Since men are so little accessible to reasonable arguments and are so entirely governed by their instinctual wishes, why should one set out to deprive them of an instinctual satisfaction and replace it by reasonable

arguments? [Freud answered by posing another question:] It is true that men are like this; but have you asked yourself whether they *must* be like this, whether their innermost nature necessitates it?

[Freud thought not. He acknowledged:] It is certainly senseless to begin by trying to do away with religion by force and at a single blow. Above all, because it would be hopeless. The believer will not let his belief be torn from him, either by arguments or by prohibitions. And even if this did succeed with some it would be cruelty.

[However, this does not imply that men *must* have the consolation of religion in order to function as human beings:] I must contradict you when you . . . argue that men . . . without the consolation of the religious illusion . . . could not bear the troubles of life and the cruelties of reality. That is true, certainly, of the men into whom you have instilled the sweet—or bitter-sweet—poison from childhood onwards. But what of the other men, who have been sensibly brought up? Perhaps those who do not suffer from the neurosis will need no intoxicant to deaden it. They will, it is true, find themselves in a difficult situation. They will have to admit . . . their insignificance in the machinery of the universe; they can no longer be the centre of creation, . . . the object of tender care on the part of a beneficent Providence. They will be in the same position as a child who has left the parental house where he was so warm and comfortable. . . . Men cannot remain children for ever; they must in the end go out into 'hostile life'. We may call this *'education to reality'*. Need I confess to you that the sole purpose of my book is to point out the necessity for this forward step?

You are afraid, probably, that they will not stand up to the hard test? Well, let us at least hope they will. It is something . . . to know that one is thrown upon one's own resources. . . . And men are not entirely without assistance. Their scientific knowledge has taught them much since the days of the Deluge, and it will increase their power still further. And, as for the great necessities of Fate, against which there is no help, they will learn to endure them with resignation. Of what use to them is the mirage of wide acres in the moon, whose harvest no one has ever yet seen? As honest smallholders on this earth they will know how to cultivate their plot in such a way that it supports them. By withdrawing their expectations from the other world and concentrating all their liberated energies into their life on earth, they will probably succeed in achieving a state of things in which life will become tolerable for everyone and civilization no longer oppressive to anyone. Then, with one of our fellow-unbelievers, they will be able to say without regret:

> Den Himmel überlassen wir
> Den Engeln und den Spatzen [p. 49f.].[2]

[2] Strachey inserted the following note: " 'We leave Heaven to the angels and the sparrows.' From Heine's poem *Deutschland* (Caput 1). The word which is here translated 'fellow-unbelievers'—in German *'Unglaubensgenossen'*—was applied by Heine himself to Spinoza."

This sounds like the last word to be said on the subject, but Freud gives his opponent one more chance, assigning to him the following argument:

> We seem to have exchanged roles: you emerge as an enthusiast . . . carried away by illusions, and I stand for the claims of reason, the rights of scepticism. What you have been expounding . . . I may call illusions, because they betray clearly enough the influence of your wishes. You pin your hope on the possibility that generations which have not experienced the influence of religious doctrines in early childhood will easily attain the desired primacy of the intelligence over the life of the instincts. This is surely an illusion: in this decisive respect human nature is hardly likely to change. . . . If you want to expel religion from our European civilization, you can only do it by means of another system of doctrines: and such a system would from the outset take over all the psychological characteristics of religion—the same sanctity, rigidity and intolerance, the same prohibition of thought [p. 51].
>
> [Nonetheless, it is Freud, the author, who has the final say:] You will not find me inaccessible to your criticism. I know how difficult it is to avoid illusions; perhaps the hopes I have confessed to are of an illusory nature, too. . . . Take my attempt for what it is. . . . These discoveries derived from individual psychology may be insufficient, their application to the human race unjustified, and this optimism unfounded. I grant you all these uncertainties. But . . . we may insist as often as we like that man's intellect is powerless in comparison with his instinctual life, and we may be right in this. Nevertheless, there is something peculiar about this weakness. The voice of the intellect is a soft one, but it does not rest till it has gained a hearing. Finally, after a countless succession of rebuffs, it succeeds. This is one of the few points on which one may be optimistic about the future of mankind, but it is in itself a point of no small importance. And from it one can derive yet other hopes. The primacy of the intellect lies, it is true, in a distant, distant future, but probably not in an *infinitely* distant one [p. 53].
>
> Science has many open enemies, and many more secret ones. . . . She is reproached for the smallness of the amount she has taught us and for the incomparably greater field she has left in obscurity. But, in this, people forget how young she is, how difficult her beginnings were and how infinitesimally small is the period of time since the human intellect has been strong enough for the tasks she sets. . . .
>
> No, our science is no illusion. But an illusion it would be to suppose that what science cannot give us we can get elsewhere [p. 55f.].

Thus, *The Future of an Illusion* ends on a triumphant note—the conviction that Logos, the primacy of the intellect, will prevail.

For the next two years Freud continued his discussion of the last two chapters of *The Future of an Illusion* in his correspondence with Pfister. His genuine tact and hesitancy to hurt the feelings of a friend are revealed in the letter (October 16, 1927) in which Freud prepared Pfister for the publication of *The Future of an Illusion:*

> In the next few weeks a pamphlet of mine will be appearing which has a great deal to do with you. I had been wanting to write it for a long time, and postponed it out of regard for you, but the impulse became too strong. The subject-matter—as you will easily guess—is my completely negative attitude to religion, in any form and however attenuated, and, though there can be nothing new to you in this, I feared, and still fear, that such a public profession of my attitude will be painful to you. When you have read it you must let me know what measure of toleration and understanding you are able to preserve for the hopeless pagan.
>
> Always your cordially devoted
Freud

Pfister's reaction was not unexpected. Nothing could change his love and loyalty for Freud, but he answered in the style which Freud had attributed to his "discussant" in the last two chapters of his book. Pfister also called on Nietzsche for support, saying that the latter had already expressed Freud's position in the words (November 24, 1927):

> The reader will have realised my purport; namely that there is always a metaphysical belief on which our belief in science rests—that we observers of to-day, atheists and anti-metaphysicians as we are, still draw our fire from the blaze lit by a belief thousands of years old, the Christian belief, which was also that of Plato, that God is truth and that the truth is divine. . . . But supposing that this grew less and less believable and nothing divine was left, save error, blindness, lies?

A year later Freud again wrote to Pfister (on November 25, 1928):

> In your otherwise delightful letter I am somewhat bewildered by one point, namely, your finding something surprising and remarkable in the attitude of the *International Journal* (editors and publisher) on the subject of the *Illusion*. There is by no means any merit in such tolerance.
>
> In both works which have recently reached me from the publishing house, one of which contains a reprint of your *Discussion,* I note with satisfaction what a long way we are able to travel together in analysis. The sudden hiatus, not in analytic but in scientific thinking, which occurs as soon as the subject of God and Christ is touched on, I accept

as one of the logically untenable but psychologically only too intelligible irrationalities of life. In general I attach no value to the 'imitation of Christ'. In contrast to utterances as psychologically profound as 'Thy sins are forgiven thee; arise and walk', there are a large number of others which are conditioned exclusively by the time, psychologically impossible, useless for our lives. Besides, the above statement calls for analysis. If the sick man had asked: 'How knowest thou that my sins are forgiven?' the answer could only have been: 'I, the Son of God, forgive thee'. In other words, a call for unlimited transference. And now, just suppose I said to a patient: 'I, Professor Sigmund Freud, forgive thee thy sins'. What a fool I should make of myself. . . .

I do not know if you have detected the secret link between the *Lay Analysis* and the *Illusion*. In the former I wish to protect analysis from the doctors and in the latter from the priests. I should like to hand it over to a profession which does not yet exist, a profession of *lay* curers of souls who need not be doctors and should not be priests.

During the summer of 1927, when Freud was working on *The Future of an Illusion,* he was also preoccupied with the work and personality of Fyodor Dostoevsky. A letter to Marie Bonaparte written on August 5, 1927, exemplifies the manner in which both life and work were reflected in Freud's correspondence. Marie Bonaparte's daughter was seriously ill at that point, and Freud wrote her:

It was really rotten news to hear that the little one had a relapse. I hope she will get over the whole thing. My old prejudice that illness is superfluous—the necessity of dying I do accept—grows stronger all the time.

[The passage following this one dealt with another problem which Marie Bonaparte had raised:] It is the old problem that is raised in a grandiose manner in Dostoevsky's "Grand Inquisitor," namely, whether mankind is able to profit from its freedom or whether a superior absolutism is most beneficial for it—the problem, yes, but where is the solution? Where do we find the guarantee of the superiority? [4]

Here Freud was grappling with the problems which he had raised in *The Future of an Illusion.* In its first chapters he had discussed the fact that civilization, represented by certain authorities, had to impose a number of moral and ethical standards on the individual to enable him to suppress his instinctual urges. But Freud's "discussant" also raised the question: Will the individual be able to live without the illusion you are taking away from him? Aren't you harboring an illusion by thinking that he can? Freud answered the first question in the affirmative, but with a qualification—that all this, if it took place, would do so in the distant future. We may presume that Freud himself had achieved this stage of the dominance of "Logos," the ego. But what about the majority of mankind?

It is likely that the title of Freud's essay had a double meaning. *He* was sure that religious doctrines were illusions; that he had to proclaim this to be so because it was the truth; that *he* did not require such illusions. As for the rest, he hoped that the eventual primacy of the intellect would not prove to be equally illusory, although it might seem so now.

The events of the next years did not shake Freud's own convictions, his ability to live without illusion and denial, but they taxed to the utmost his belief in the future victory of Logos and Reason.

Following the publication of *The Future of an Illusion* came a letdown in Freud's productivity. There was the usual misery with his prosthesis. Pichler tried building one new one after another, having tried out five by the spring of 1928. Freud occasionally could not tolerate wearing the lower one at night, but leaving it out would in the long run have caused shrinkage and more difficulty. Pichler saw Freud for the last time that year on June 15, 1928, the 49th visit in five and a half months!

Freud then began to consider going to Berlin to have the oral surgeon, Professor Schroeder, construct a new prosthesis. Freud had been extremely reluctant to take this step, an attitude which he expressed clearly in a letter of July 1, 1928, to Jones:

> Pichler's efforts to provide me with a better prosthesis have caused me a great deal of suffering during this past year, and the outcome is quite unsatisfactory. So I have finally given in to pressure from all sides to turn to someone else. This has not been easy for me because basically it is after all a defection from a man to whom I already owe a four-year prolongation of my life. But it could not go on like this. Last week Prof. Schroeder of Berlin sent his assistants here to examine me and then left me with the promise that in about four weeks he would make me something better. It was agreed that I should go to him in Berlin in September [5].

Pichler, who had realized that he could make no headway, behaved like the perfect gentleman he always was. When Freud eventually had to return to Pichler, the latter treated him with the same devotion as before.

Schroeder's prosthesis brought Freud considerable temporary relief, one of its advantages being that it was less bulky. While Freud could report a "70 per cent improvement," he was quite exhausted and could only gradually resume his psychoanalytic practice.

That the spirit of the *Illusion* had not been broken, however, is evident from the letters to Pfister quoted previously.

Twice during the year 1928 death touched those around Freud. During the winter Jones lost a little girl who had been particularly brilliant. Freud tried to comfort him as best he could. On March 11, he wrote:

> My painful sympathy draws on my own experience. I recognize that the potion you had to take in one drain was set before me in two doses. To be sure, Sophie was a beloved daughter, but not a child. Only when three years later, in June of 1923, little Heinele died did I become weary of life for good. There is a very peculiar point of agreement between him and your little one. He, too, was of superior intelligence and indescribable spiritual grace, and he repeatedly said that he would die soon! How do these children come to know these things?
>
> You and your dear wife are of course young enough to regain your attachment to life [6].

On May 3, he wrote to Jones again:

> You allude to the fact that within a few days I shall be 72 years old. . . .
>
> You know that I have gotten an agreement that until my 75th birthday the others will not be celebrated, and you can easily surmise the expectation hiding behind this. I nevertheless assume that on that day the Verlag will present to me Volume XI of my *Gesammelte Schriften*. And that I am quite prepared to put up with.
>
> "Young" and "old" now appear to me to be the greatest opposites of which human psychic life is capable, and an understanding between the representatives of each is impossible. . . . Should I be permitted to grace this earth for some time longer, I confidently expect to learn that you both have overcome the cruel blow like young people. [7]

18

FREUD BECOMES MY PATIENT

Toward the end of 1928, one of Freud's previously mentioned analysand-students, Marie Bonaparte, became acutely ill in Vienna, where she had come to resume her analysis which frequently had to be interrupted because of her manifold private and social responsibilities. During several weeks of hospitalization, she was under my professional care. Her illness, at a time when she was in analysis, established a contact between Freud and myself.

Since his parting with Felix Deutsch in 1923, Freud had been without a personal physician. Pichler had been taking care of his surgical problems. In addition, Freud occasionally consulted his old friend Ludwig Braun, the cardiologist, while another friend, the internist Dr. Lajos Levy of Budapest, would occasionally come for a visit. Finally, there was the old stalwart friend of the family and pediatrician to Freud's children, Dr. Oskar Rie, who could give general advice. Freud's reluctance to engage a personal physician was based not only on his memory of 1923, but on his realization of the potential impact of ambivalence on any human relationship, especially on the delicate one between a physician and a towering father figure such as he was. Freud's family and friends realized that this was not a satisfactory state of affairs.

Marie Bonaparte did everything she could to persuade Freud to employ me as his personal physician. In my favor were the facts that I had attended Freud's "Introductory Lectures" and that I belonged to what was at that time an extremely rare breed—a psychoanalytically oriented internist. There were at least two reasons, however, which might have made for some reluctance on Freud's part: my age (I was not yet 32) and the fact that at that time I had not quite finished my personal analysis, which might give rise to difficulties similar to those Freud had previously encountered with Deutsch. Nevertheless, he decided to "try me out."

I have never forgotten our first meeting. Since the "Introductory Lectures," I had been under the spell of Freud not only as a person but as a towering intellectual figure. At heart, I was already an analyst, even though I had, for various reasons, devoted myself to internal medicine. I was an avid reader of all of Freud's writings, and had many friends among what was to become the second generation of analysts. I had started my personal analysis in 1925, and, by this time, could hope to be able to retain the measure of objectivity essential for such an assignment.

At our first meeting, I was admitted to the "inner sanctum"—Freud's study. Biographical studies of Freud abound in accounts of such first meetings. The most poetic are probably the descriptions of H. D. (Hilda Doolittle) in her *Tribute to Freud* (1956) and of Lou Andreas-Salomé in her *Freud Journal* (1958). I shall therefore restrict myself to a few facts.

There was nothing patronizing in this meeting of the sage master with a young doctor more than 40 years his junior. While I could not miss the searching quality of those wonderfully expressive eyes, he put me immediately at ease by acknowledging his appreciation of the way I had handled the treatment of Marie Bonaparte. In the shortest possible time, he showed his readiness to establish a patient-doctor relationship based on mutual respect and confidence. Before telling me his history or his present complaints, he wanted a basic understanding on the conditions for such a relationship. Mentioning only in a rather general way "some unfortunate experiences with your predecessors," he expressed the expectation that he would always be told the truth and nothing but the truth. My response must have reassured him that I meant to keep such a promise. He then added, looking searchingly at me: "Versprechen Sie mir auch noch: Wenn es mal so weit ist, werden Sie mich nicht unnötig quälen lassen." ["Promise me one more thing: that when the time comes, you won't let me suffer unnecessarily."] All this was said with the utmost simplicity, without a trace of pathos, but also with complete determination. We shook hands at this point.

Freud ended the interview with the statement that he did not wish

to be given professional courtesy but wanted to be charged a normal fee.

Freud really meant what he said. It was customary in Vienna to
submit a bill at the end of the year. Freud asked for my bill at that
time, but did not consider it adequate. He wrote me the following
letter:

January 10, 1930

My dear Doctor Schur:
I am in a quandary as to how to react to the bill you sent me for the
past year. If I submitted it to a professional medical organization, you
would probably be called upon to account for an unprofessional disregard of medical accomplishment. I feel that you have backed away
from the contract upon which our formal relations are based. I do not
want to pay this bill and suggest you send me a more appropriate
one.

With cordial devotion

Your

Freud [1]

The same held true with Pichler, whose first note contains the following statement:

> Case History
> Professor Freud
> 1923
> 9.26   Consultation with Professor Hajek
>   . . . .
> Patient makes it a condition that he not be treated as a col-
> league, but be charged [a fee].

After I had passed the test, we arranged for subsequent visits at
which I would take Freud's history and examine him. Because of the
difficulty he had in talking, this was done in several meetings. Freud
of course gave me a detailed history of his various surgeries and his
battle with the prosthesis. He told me about his anginal symptoms of
1926 and his occasional extrasystoles. We agreed that I would obtain
any additional information I needed from his cardiologist, Braun. He
spoke very little about the old cardiac episode. At that time I had no
reason to assume that he had already had serious cardiac symptoms
over a period of several years, nor did Braun.

Freud also informed me of his occasional gastrointestinal symptoms, for which he repeatedly went to Karlsbad. They were typical of

an irritable, spastic colon. He also told me that in the past he had had occasional urinary frequency, which had subsided during the last years.

Freud's condition, apart from his oral cavity, was amazingly good. He had disciplined himself to keep up good nutrition in spite of his great difficulty in chewing and swallowing. His heart showed no consequences of his anginal episodes. There was no marked enlargement of the heart and the aorta. Despite his heavy smoking, he had no chronic bronchitis or pulmonary emphysema.

It took me quite some time to familiarize myself with the distorted anatomy of what was now an oral-nasal cavity. His mouth contained a large amount of scar tissue next to somewhat more normal-looking epithelial lining. I could not detect any conspicuous leukoplakias at that time. There was a great deal of partly purulent secretion, apparently coming mainly from the right maxillary sinus. There were many spots that were tender to the slightest touch, and it was obvious how painful the manipulation of the prosthesis was. And this was the "good" time of the improved prosthesis!

I inquired, of course, about his habits, and could not avoid discussing his smoking. I could recognize immediately that this was an area where, as Freud himself had realized, he could not establish the "dominance of the ego."

I have discussed at length (Chapter 2) Freud's attempts at abstinence during the severe cardiac episode of 1893-1895. He was not successful then, nor was he later. It is significant, however, that Freud submitted to abstinence for a while after periods of anginal pain or recurrent migraine, frequent extrasystoles or abdominal pain attributable to an irritable colon. Here he grudgingly had to admit to himself and others the immediate success of abstinence and thus the causal connection with his symptoms. In a letter to Eitingon written on May 1, 1930 Freud indicated this clearly:

> It is correct that cardiac and intestinal symptoms have forced me to go to a sanatorium, that is to say, to submit to a physician [i.e., me] who absolutely insisted on it. Here I have made a quick and satisfactory recovery, not through any therapeutic magic, but by an act of painful autonomy.[1] For 6 days now I have not smoked a single cigar, and it

---

[1] This is an allusion to a paper in which Ferenczi compared certain psychosomatic symptoms to the action of lizards who bite off their own tails when damaged (see Schur, 1955).

cannot be denied that I owe my well-being to this renunciation. *But it is sad* [2, italics added].

Such periods of abstinence did not last long. Sometimes when Freud had similar symptoms, he would tell me: "I know what you're going to say—don't smoke." After a few days of abstinence he would greet me with a disarming and touching gesture: "Well, I've started again." He once wrote me a letter during his summer vacation (September 9, 1930) saying that he was feeling better, and adding:

My condition is on the whole satisfactory; no cardiac symptoms. On the debit side: one cigar daily; since yesterday, two [3].

Freud knew full well that smoking was an irritant to his mucous membrane, but would never agree to give up smoking because of this, although he was advised to do so in no uncertain terms. The pathologist J. Erdheim, who examined most of the numerous excisions, repeatedly emphasized the link between nicotine and Freud's lesions. One report read:

Specially noticeable this time is the widespread inflammation which covers the whole of the mucous membrane and is the consequence of excessive smoking. There is every evidence that the inflammation develops first and that the typical leukoplakia appears as its sequel. Further, both pieces contain places where the leukoplakia shows intensified proliferation of the epithelium, i.e., a precancerous stage; both pieces also contain places where stratifying globules are beginning to develop. But there is no significant growth into the depth; the underlying connective tissue is callous, scarred, and enough has been removed to ensure the radical removal of the local proliferation of epithelium.

Erdheim added a remark to this report, saying: "The patient should be strongly advised to give up smoking." When I showed such reports to Freud, he shrugged his shoulders.

Reading the correspondence with Fliess and Eitingon, I gained a vivid confirmation of the intensity of Freud's craving for nicotine. Many letters to Eitingon are filled with requests for certain brands of cigars or complaints about others. I asked myself repeatedly whether I was entitled, or even obliged, to insist more strongly on the enforcement of abstinence. Perhaps a personal physician with the objective detachment of Pichler would have done so. I could not, and in retrospect I realize that I should not regret this fact. It is questionable in any event whether such an attempt would have been successful.

Freud did not take any barbiturates or opiates. We may speculate as to why Freud, who during the 1890s had used cocaine for several years, never developed an addiction to it, as did his friend Fleischl, but stuck to his cigars. One possible answer is that Freud neither needed nor desired the temporary euphoric effect of cocaine, which stimulates what we call "primary process" thinking, while nicotine stimulated his attention span and secondary process thinking. Proneness to addiction involving cocaine, morphine, heroin, etc., is generally rooted in a different constellation of psychic forces than that connected with nicotine addiction—despite their common denominator (masturbation) which Freud ascribed to all addictions in his letter to Fliess of December 22, 1897. Only much later did smoking assume the added function of tension relief, when other instinctual gratifications were not accessible and he was flooded by painful stimulation. Freud told me repeatedly that he could do no creative work without smoking. And when was Freud not occupied with creative work?

The following letters to Eitingon indicate this clearly. On June 1, 1931 he wrote:

> Your question about the cigars induces me to confess that I am smoking again. Considering my age and the amount of discomfort which I have to bear day after day, abstinence and the prospect [of preventing new lesions] which it involves do not seem justified to me [4].

And on July 13, 1931:

> Thank you very much for your supplies. Annoyed that the discomfort will not give way, I am again sinning more, and [my supply] was quite low [5].

Nicotine probably helped Freud tolerate pain and frustration and maintain his equilibrium. It may also have been essential for continuous sublimation.

The letters quoted above and the one of July 25, which follows, were written to Eitingon after Freud's 75th birthday, which provided him with a rationalization for "indulging" himself:

> The embargo on traveling will certainly also make it more difficult to keep me supplied with things to smoke. Since I have adopted the principle that after 75 one should not deprive oneself, my provisions are shrinking rapidly [6].

However, these letters also show that Freud still harbored some guilt feelings.[2] I shall document further on how the wish—and the obligation—to live gradually gained the upper hand.

Freud was otherwise a model patient. He hardly ever complained to me verbally; only an occasional tortured look, a pleading gesture indicated his suffering. Over the course of the years we developed a nonverbal form of communication in which he could convey to me how he felt and I could let him know what I thought about his condition. Any words on my part were then only additional explanations. Without ever being demonstrative about it, Freud never failed to show his considerateness and generosity and genuine interest in anyone (like myself) whom he had accepted as a member of his extended family. This ability to love, to give, to feel stayed with him to the end.

With the exception of his nicotine addiction, Freud was able to retain in his daily life not only the utmost self-control, but a serenity and dignity which had an impact on everyone—later even on the Gestapo and party officials with whom he had to deal during the Nazi occupation. Nor did his behavior have anything of the stereotyped in it. He retained up to the last moments the wonderful flexibility which permitted him to communicate with people of all walks of life.

A few "minor" facts were very significant to me as a measure of this truly beautiful, controlled behavior. He of course hated the monstrous prosthesis, but only once did he ever drop it during the complex cleaning procedures. He had an 8-day clock on his desk and never once forgot to wind it, right to the very end. We know that Freud had a photographic memory and that he made very few changes in his manuscripts. I have read thousands of his original letters, many of them written during the last decade of his life. Only very rarely was there a crossed-out word or a parapraxis.[3]

Never did I hear an angry or impatient word directed against anyone around him, and for the last few weeks of his life I lived in his home!

---

[2] While the nicotine addiction thus had an important adaptive function in Freud's life, we may speculate that, along with his constant oral frustrations during the last 16 years of his life, the addiction may have prevented Freud from penetrating even more deeply into the importance of the "oral phase" for normal and abnormal development.

During the Fliess period Freud himself had recognized that his addiction might prove to be a permanent obstacle to his work (see L. 79 and my discussion in Chapters 3 and 4).

[3] I have indicated some of these in the preceding chapters.

The only general sedative which Freud accepted up to the very end was an occasional aspirin or a Pyramidon for migraine. Only before and immediately after minor surgical procedures did he get any opiates. Freud was fortunately also able to retain his ability to sleep restfully. Until the last stages of his illness he could fall asleep quickly and sleep through the night with hardly any interruptions, except at those times when very severe pain woke him up.

After most of the surgical procedures, except the major ones, he resumed seeing patients within a day or two. One incident is remarkable as an indication of Freud's tolerance for pain, and also of the fact that others—Pichler, for example—came to take this for granted. One of the procedures carried out under local anesthesia took an especially long time. The anesthetic in all that scar tissue was not working too well. Freud started to moan, and then said simply: "Ich kann nicht mehr weiter." ["I cannot take any more."] Pichler's notes on the procedure report this statement, and end: "I am curious to know why." I shall report later on the only two occasions on which I saw Freud come close to losing his composure.

At first my function was to watch over Freud's general health and to invent some means of alleviating his suffering without medication. Between June, 1928 and November, 1929 Freud did not see Pichler. After he had gone to Berlin to have Schroeder build the new prosthesis, he had no one to take care of the minor day-to-day adjustments. I suggested that my own dentist and friend, Dr. Joseph Weinmann[4] go with Freud to Berlin the next time, so that while Schroeder was attempting to improve the prosthesis Weinmann could learn from the latter the handling of small changes. It was Weinmann who later on (in 1931) suggested to Freud that he try insufflations of Orthoform—a novocain derivative in powdered form used for local application to painful sores.[5] Here was the old "friend" cocaine back again! Since it was not absorbed and therefore had no systemic effect, this was one type of medication Freud could accept. He could also obtain some relief by careful treatment of the nose and sinuses.

After a time I got to know "intimately" every spot in Freud's

---

[4] Later a professor of dentistry in Chicago. He died in 1960.

[5] It was characteristic of Pichler's unassuming generosity that he remarked in his notes following one of the surgical procedures: "April 27, 1931: Yesterday and during the night attacks of very severe pain. April 28: The attacks of pain respond almost immediately to insufflations of Orthoform, a procedure suggested by Dr. Weinmann."

mouth; it became my function to detect the formation of any new lesion at the earliest possible moment, and to alert Pichler.

In 1929, in spite of his suffering, Freud greatly enjoyed his stay in Schneewinkel near Berchtesgarden, where I visited him in August. (This was the same place where, 30 years earlier, he had finished *The Interpretation of Dreams*.) Freud and his family were perfect hosts. What impressed me most, however, was Freud's enthusiastic appreciation of nature, of flowers, a meadow, the view of the mountains. It was obvious that all the suffering did not substantially impair his capacity for such enjoyment.

19

CIVILIZATION
AND ITS DISCONTENTS

During his stay in Schneewinkel Freud wrote *Civilization and Its Discontents*. His attitude toward this, as toward most of his works once they were written, as well as the place which writing held in his mental economy, were illustrated by a letter to Lou Andreas-Salomé of July 28, 1929:

> Dearest Lou:
> You will have guessed with your usual perspicacity why I have taken so long to answer you. Anna has already told you that I am writing something, and today I wrote the last sentence, which—as far as is possible here without a library—finishes the work. It deals with civilization, guilt feelings, happiness, and similar lofty matters, and it strikes me, no doubt rightly, as quite superfluous in contrast to earlier works, which after all always derived from some inner urge. But what else should I do? One cannot smoke and play cards the whole day; I no longer walk very much, and most of what there is to read does not interest me any more. I wrote, and the time passed quite pleasantly that way. I have discovered the most banal truths in the course of writing this work [L. 243*].

I have already mentioned that Freud referred to this book in the Postscript of his *Autobiographical Study*, where he said that he pursued the same train of thought and interest as in *The Future of an Illusion*. This is true inasmuch as Freud approached certain psychological problems in *Civilization and Its Discontents* as they affected all mankind, and in turn explained certain historical, sociological, and cultural phenomena from the vantage point of psychoanalysis as a

416

general and developmental psychology. Freud's statement to the effect that his interests had returned to the cultural problems which had fascinated him many years earlier certainly applies to this work too. We can, however, detect other determinants as well. Freud wrote this book 10 years after *Beyond the Pleasure Principle,* six, and five years, respectively, after *The Ego and the Id* and "The Economic Problem of Masochism." He had by now applied and tested the structural and dual instinct theories in his private laboratory—the analyses of his patients. He had come to recognize the vicissitudes of the aggressive instinctual drive, its relation to the superego, and the frequently insuperable difficulties it imposed on the course of an analysis. *Civilization and Its Discontents* supplies his most succinct presentation of the intricate relationship between the destructive instinctual drive, the superego, and character and symptom formation, as well as the potential application of this knowledge to education, to social problems, and to history. However, if we compare *The Future of an Illusion* with *Civilization and Its Discontents,* we are struck by the contrast in tone between the two: the former's triumphant battle cry, opposing the ego to *Ananke,* to illusions, weakness, and stupidity, is replaced in the latter by an undercurrent of deep pessimism. We can only speculate about the factors that may have contributed to this change. The Western world around Freud looked bleak. Although he was willing —despite his deeply ingrained moral and aesthetic dislike of violence[1] —to give the Communist Revolution the benefit of the doubt, he saw in time that the course it was taking was determined by the same inexorable instinctual forces that Marxist philosophy had tried to reduce to economic principles.[2]

In Germany, Nazism was growing rapidly, representing everything that negated Logos and Eros. An economic crisis was enveloping the Western world, and Freud again saw his financial security threatened only a short time after the disastrous inflation which had followed World War I.

But mainly there was his suffering, which was draining his resources, drawing attention to painful bodily sensations, depleting his capacity to enjoy life. All of these things may have contributed to the underlying pessimistic tone of *Civilization and Its Discontents.* There

[1] An attitude he was to express clearly in a 1932 letter to Albert Einstein (see Chapter 21).
[2] See Chapter 21 concerning Freud's treatment of this subject within the framework of his *New Introductory Lectures.*

was now in Freud's attitude a skepticism about the future development of the human race. This comes through clearly in the following
letter to Pfister which in many respects contradicts the conviction expressed in *The Future of an Illusion* that: "The primacy of the intellect lies . . . in a distant future, but probably not in an *infinitely*
distant one."

                                              Vienna, February 7, 1930
Dear Dr. Pfister,
Outside it is raining and so I have an hour's time in which to answer
your kind letter of yesterday without delay.

Not all the news that you give about yourself is good, but what right
have we to expect that everything should be favorable? At any rate I
am glad that you write about yourself and your work, your hopes and
disappointments. Physical distance easily causes people to drift apart
if they do not hear from each other and do not experience things together. There is something especially precious about personal relations
which shared work and interests cannot completely replace; and we
two, at this moment when we have become aware of the ultimate,
fundamental differences between our basic attitudes toward life, have a
particular reason—and, I hope, inclination—to foster such relations.

You are right in saying that my mental powers have not dwindled
with my surplus years (over seventy). Though they show the influence
of age plainly enough. There are three ways of disintegration among
which nature takes her choice in individual cases—simultaneous destruction of mind and body, premature mental decay accompanied by
physical preservation, and survival of mental life accompanied by physical decline; and in my case it is the third and most merciful of these
which has set in. Very well, then, I shall take advantage of this favorable circumstance to counter your brief and forbearing criticism with
an even briefer modest defense.

I shall deal with only one point. If I doubt man's destiny to climb
by way of civilization to a state of greater perfection, if I see in its life
a continual struggle between Eros and the death instinct, the outcome
of which seems to me to be indeterminable, I believe that in coming to
those conclusions I have not been influenced by any of my own constitutional factors or acquired emotional attitudes. I am neither a self-
tormentor nor a malicious mischief-maker [*Bosnickel*]. I would love to
grant myself and others something good, and I should find it much
more beautiful and consoling if we could count on such a rosy future.
But this seems to me to be yet another instance of illusion (wish fulfilment) in conflict with truth. The question is not what belief is more
pleasing or more comfortable or more advantageous to life, but of what
may approximate more closely to the puzzling reality which after all
exists outside of us. The death instinct is not a requirement of my
heart; it seems to me to be only an inevitable assumption on both bio-

logical and psychological grounds. The rest follows from that. Thus to me my pessimism seems a conclusion, while the optimism of my opponents seems an *a priori* assumption. I might also say that I have concluded a marriage of reason with my gloomy theories, while others live with theirs in a love-match. I hope they will gain greater happiness from this than I.

Of course it is readily conceivable that I may be mistaken on all three points, the independence of my theories from my disposition, my estimate of my arguments for these theories, and their content. You know that the more magnificent the prospect, the lesser the certainty, and also the greater the passion—in which we do not wish to be involved—with which men take sides.

I can imagine that several million years ago in the Triassic age all the great -odons and -therias were very proud of the development of the Saurian race and looked forward to heaven knows what magnificent future for themselves. And then, with the exception of the wretched crocodile, they all died out. You will object: 'Well, but those Saurians thought nothing of the sort! They thought of nothing but filling their bellies. But man is equipped with mind which entitles him to think about his future and believe in it.' Now, there is certainly something special about mind, so little is known about it and its relationship to nature. I personally have a vast respect for mind, but has nature? Mind is only a small part of nature, the rest of which seems to be able to get along very well without it. Will it really allow itself to be influenced to any great extent by regard for mind?

Enviable he who can feel more confident about that than I.[3]

With cordial greetings,
Your
Freud [my translation]

---

[3] Freud's recognition of the fact of evolution and his humble realization that mind, however special it may be, is only an infinitesimal part of nature cannot be disputed, but they do not justify any exalted optimism about the human race. Thinking of Freud's juxtaposition of the psychological, biological, and astronomical revolutions in his *Introductory Lectures on Psycho-Analysis* (see Chapter 11), we may also add that we cannot be optimistic about the future of our planet.

But within the narrow confines of our existence, we are still preoccupied with the working of the human mind and our immediate environment. I will therefore enter into the discussion between Pfister and Freud: Freud claimed in his letter that the death instinct was not a requirement of his heart and then stated "the rest follows from that." Taking death as an established fact, Freud ascribed his pessimism to a *conclusion* based on that fact, while he attributed the optimism of his opponent to an *a priori* assumption.

In my discussion of the manner in which Freud had arrived at the concepts of the death instinct and repetition compulsion (Chapter 12), I tried to show that it was Freud who arrived at these concepts via reasoning dictated by an *a priori* assumption. Freud was right, however, to be pessimistic, because man is mortal and the life of our planet is limited.

Sub specie aeternitatis. Therefore no discussion is truly meaningful, and yet in terms of our transient existence we are dealing with phenotypes and their vicissitudes. And within this framework we must also simply say: What a beautiful letter!

An important part of Freud's discussion in *Civilization and Its Discontents* was devoted to the nearly inevitable development of guilt in the face of the equally inevitable supremacy of instinctual demands, both aggressive and erotic:

> If civilization is a necessary course of development from the family to humanity as a whole, then—as a result of the inborn conflict arising from ambivalence, of the eternal struggle between the trends of love and death—there is inextricably bound up with it an increase of the sense of guilt, which will perhaps reach heights that the individual finds hard to tolerate. One is reminded of the great poet's moving arraignment of the 'Heavenly Powers':
>> Ihr führt in's Leben uns hinein.
>> Ihr lasst den Armen schuldig werden,
>> Dann überlasst Ihr ihn der Pein
>> Denn jede Schuld rächt sich auf Erden.[4]
>
> And we may well heave a sigh of relief at the thought that it is nevertheless vouchsafed to a few to salvage without effort from the whirlpool of their own feelings the deepest truths, towards which the rest of us have to find our way through tormenting uncertainty and with restless groping [1930b, p. 133].

How uncanny that 30 years after the publication of *The Interpretation of Dreams* these verses, which Freud associated then to a dream discussed both in this book and in his essay "On Dreams," should appear in this new context!

And yet Freud changed his original title of this book from *Unglück* [*Unhappiness*] *in der Kultur* to *Das Unbehagen* [*Discomfort, Discontent*] *in der Kultur*. And while he voiced his doubts, pointed to the difficulties, dismantled the mirages built by illusions, he still had faith in the one force which, apart from Logos, keeps our existence going— Eros. The book ends with the following lines:

> The fateful question for the human species seems to me to be whether and to what extent their cultural development will succeed in mastering the disturbance of their communal life by the human instinct of aggression and self-destruction. It may be that in this respect precisely the present time deserves a special interest. Men have gained control over the forces of nature to such an extent that with their help they would have no difficulty in exterminating one another to the last man. They know this, and hence comes a large part of their current unrest, their unhappiness and their mood of anxiety. And now it is to be expected that the other of the two 'Heavenly Powers,' eternal Eros, will make an

[4] For a translation of this previously quoted poem by Goethe, see Chapter 6.

effort to assert himself in the struggle with his equally immortal adversary [p. 145].

After the menace of Nazism had become ever more apparent, Freud added a further sentence in 1931:

But who can foresee with what success and with what result?

One wonders what Freud would have added after Hiroshima!

Freud had stated earlier in this book, when enumerating the various ways in which man strives for happiness, that "the way of life which makes love the centre of everything, which looks for all satisfaction in loving and being loved," comes perhaps "nearer to this goal [of achieving happiness] than any other method" [p. 82]. But he added:

The weak side of this technique of living is easy to see; otherwise no human being would have thought of abandoning this path to happiness for any other. It is that we are never so defenceless against suffering as when we love, never so helplessly unhappy as when we have lost our loved object or its love.

A few months earlier (April 11-12, 1929) Freud had expressed similar thoughts about the loss of a beloved object in a letter to Binswanger, after the latter had written about the death of his oldest son under tragic circumstances:

We know that the acute grief we feel after such a loss will come to an end, but we shall remain inconsolable, and never find a substitute. Everything that comes to take its place, even if it were to fill it completely, nevertheless remains something different. And this is really as it should be. It is the only way of perpetuating the love which we do not wish to renounce.

20

THE VIGIL FOR NEW LESIONS –
THE STRUGGLE WITH
THE PROSTHESIS

In the late summer of 1929 Freud again went to Berlin to have Schroeder work on his prosthesis. This resulted in some improvement, but Freud returned quite exhausted.

In November, 1929 Freud went to see Pichler because one spot looked suspicious to us. Pichler recognized it as a harmless area where the mucous membrane of the nose had spread toward the remnants of the palate, covering the scar tissue. Pichler received him graciously, and Freud was greatly relieved to know that he could turn to Pichler in times of need. Pichler's note about this visit gives us a measure of his objectivity.

November 23, 1929: Patient arrived with Dr. Weinmann who attends him now, cleans prosthesis, etc., and with prosthesis made by Schroeder in Berlin. Upper teeth are joined to form compact bridge; soldered distally to this are oblique slanting sides of wide range onto which prosthesis is slipped. Prosthesis leaves left posterior half of palate uncovered, closes merely as sort of obturator. Actual clod of prosthesis seems of smaller dimensions. At present functions rather well, was still better in beginning; now variable. Only objection is risk that all pillars of upper bridge may loosen simultaneously some time and then the catastrophe would be great. Patient called because Weinmann and apparently also Schroeder regard one spot as suspicious. This is an area which was marked down for some reason several years ago where mucous membrane of nose encroaches downward on palate. Nothing pathological. Perhaps swelling due to present bad coryza.

In April, 1930 Freud had an episode of cardiac and abdominal symptoms which responded favorably within a few days to abstinence from nicotine. Freud acknowledged this grudgingly, but did not keep up his abstinence for more than about three weeks, although not because of any writing he was doing (see letters to Eitingon in Chapter 18). Later in 1930 he went back to Berlin and underwent three months of torture in an attempt to get more lasting relief from a new prosthesis built by Schroeder.

The American diplomat William C. Bullitt, who had participated in the Paris Peace Conference after World War I and was the first American Ambassador to Moscow (later Ambassador to Paris as well, where, as we shall see, he played a very active role in getting Freud out of Vienna in 1938), was in Berlin in 1929 studying German archives on the Paris Peace Conference. He had met with Freud several times and visited him at the sanatorium where Freud stayed whenever he came to Berlin. The two men discussed a joint venture— a historical-psychoanalytic study of Woodrow Wilson.[1] Bullitt was "furious" that Freud had not given up smoking, and offered himself as an example of one who had succeeded in doing so (personal communication). He accomplished as little as all the rest of us.

Freud recovered in Grundlsee, where I visited him in September, shortly after he had received the notification that he had been awarded the Goethe Prize. Freud could not travel to Frankfurt to deliver his address of acceptance personally, so Anna Freud read the speech on his behalf. This address is important to any biographer of Freud because of his remarks concerning the biographical investigation of "great men" (see Introduction).

In the same summer Freud's mother died at the age of 95 from gangrene of the leg, after weeks of severe suffering. Whatever Freud's early relationship to his mother had been, during her last years it was, at least outwardly, one of cordial filial duty. I had never met her, and Freud had spoken of her very little. There was no obvious grief upon her death, although in a letter to Jones Freud wrote:

> I will not disguise the fact that my reaction to this event has because of special circumstances been a curious one. Assuredly, there is no saying

[1] Eventually published under the title *Thomas Woodrow Wilson: A Psychological Study* (1967). See Chapter 26 for further details.

what effects such an experience may produce in deeper layers, but on the surface I can detect only two things: an increase in personal freedom, since it was always a terrifying thought that she might come to hear of my death; and secondly, the satisfaction that at last she has achieved the deliverance for which she had earned a right after such a long life. No grief otherwise, such as my ten-years-younger brother is painfully experiencing. I was not at the funeral; again Anna represented me as at Frankfort. . . . This great event has affected me in a curious manner. No pain, no grief, which is probably to be explained by the circumstances, the great age and the end of the pity we had felt at her helplessness. With that a feeling of liberation, of release, which I think I can understand. I was not allowed to die as long as she was alive, and now I may. Somehow the values of life have notably changed in the deeper layers [Vol. 3, p. 152].

It was to this specific attitude of Freud's that I referred in discussing Freud's remarks to Deutsch in 1923 and Deutsch's interpretation of them.

In October, 1930, we noticed for the first time since I had been his physician that one leukoplakia had started to grow and change in appearance. We consulted with Pichler, who remained in charge from then on until 1939. It looked to Pichler like a precancerous lesion, and he recommended surgery. Thus started again the endless agony of surgical interventions, a fight for every ounce of comfort, the constant vigil to detect any small changes.

In the first surgical interventions that followed, Pichler tried to cover the defect with autoskin transplants. This made it even more imperative for Freud to keep the prosthesis in day and night, which caused unbearable pain and discomfort. We also learned how poorly Freud tolerated sedation, so that eventually the local application of Orthoform was to be of special value. After this surgery Freud developed small bronchopneumonic foci, which caused us no little concern.

This operation was soon followed by another on February 7, 1931. Early in April, I discovered a new lesion in the same area, which looked even more threatening. Pichler examined it on April 14 and advised immediate surgery. This is Pichler's note, an illustration of his cool, reasoned, and firm approach:

April 14, 1931: New appearance of a tumor further frontally corresponding to the scar fold protruding into mouth. Tumor is soft, irregular, partly dark colored, no longer wholly villous or velvety, has wrinkles and folds and can be shifted on underlying base. Supposedly grown fast and much. Because the excision and cauterization by diathermy supposedly caused two months of persistent pain, advice: excision and grafting. Patient to celebrate his 75th birthday soon, has had coryza. Would like postponement. I advise against such long postponement. I believe soft tumor still precancerous but am against waiting (in view of fast growth, which I have not pointed out to patient). [Pichler had not pointed it out, but I had.] Asked [by Freud] whether it would not be feasible to let it go and risk the development of a malignancy [this was the first time Freud pleaded with Pichler] I advised against it. To the question whether radium or X-ray [instead] I suggested consultation with Prof. Holzknecht who presently is in the sanatorium for a surgery of his hand. Telephone discussion with Dr. Schur.

This episode showed how the balance between the wish to live and the wish to be permitted to die underwent intense strain. The following letters to Eitingon show this conflict clearly, although the last one indicates that the reluctance to go on did not last too long.

April 12, 1931

Since the last operation and the last upper respiratory infection a persistent deterioration in the conditions surrounding the prosthesis and a marked decline[2] in the level of my general condition have established themselves, which make the notions of any festivities [his 75th birthday] even more hateful to me. I am closing to save you further samples of my mood [1].

The letter of April 16, 1931 starts with a critical remark about someone who might profit by his death, followed by the parenthetical remark: "By the way, no motive for me to speed my demise." The letter goes on:

At present I am not satisfied with myself. In view of a new uncertainty and threat I have forfeited my superior indifference, but will regain it soon, certainly as soon as the situation is clarified. Since last fall, as you know, I have had two minor operations in the area of my oral cavity; the first, because a part of the old scar looked suspicious; the microscopic examination supposedly proved its complete innocence. Soon afterward there appeared at the edge of the new scar a polyplike growth which led Pichler to insist on its immediate removal (February 7). To this day, I have not gotten over the changes following upon the healing process of this last procedure, but since then I have not had a single bearable day. Now, a few days after the second operation, the mucuous membrane formed a mighty fold, which the surgeon dislikes

2 See footnote to note 1 for this chapter in the Appendix.

again.[3] His attitude is: "This is certainly not malignant, but it can become so; and why not remove the still harmless precancerous stage?" My two *Leibärzte*[4] and I myself answer: "Because there is no assurance that such folds or proliferations will not form after the new operation as well—or even as a result of it; whereas there is every assurance that its consequence will be months-long misery.[5] However, it is difficult to argue with an authority like Pichler. We have resorted to considering radium therapy as an alternative, and because there is no one in Vienna whom we can trust to have sufficient experience with it, Dr. Schur came up with the idea of inviting Professor Rigaud of Paris,[6] who has the reputation of being the best authority in this field, to give an expert opinion. The negotiations with him—he is at the moment in Locarno—are being carried on through the Princess [Marie Bonaparte], who is a friend of his. He is now expected to agree and arrive here shortly. He is to decide whether these papillary growths [notice: it is no longer a fold; the denial did not last long!] have a pathogenic significance, whether and how they can be treated with radium, and what risks this would entail. [Freud had also forgotten the misery he had endured from the 1923 radium treatments.] Perhaps nothing will come of all this and I shall have to submit to the knife again. In any case you will understand if in the next weeks I shall be neither in the mood nor in the condition to participate in the festivities [2].

The last sentence is in a sense a repetition of Freud's warning uttered before his 70th birthday.

On April 21, 1931 Freud wrote once again to Eitingon:

The Frenchman (Rigaud) wants to have nothing to do with me. Unless there is unquestionably malignant tissue, radium should not be used. Afterward we still had a conference with the X-ray man Holzknecht. I must submit to Pichler without reservation. The operation will take place Thursday or Friday. I am now completely adjusted to Pichler.

Reality testing had prevailed. The equilibrium had been re-established. However, Freud granted himself a compensation at the end of the letter:

---

[3] This is one of the rare falsifications of Freud's memory. Pichler had not even seen him between February 13, when nothing was noticed, and April 14. The lesion we had seen was more than a mere fold.

[4] The second *Leibarzt* mentioned in this letter was Dr. Ruth Mack-Brunswick, who was greatly concerned—as were all of us—about the long aftereffects of surgical interventions.

[5] In this letter Freud uses a device normally reserved for his scientific writings—the dialogue in which Freud attributes some of his own thoughts to an opponent.

[6] Professor Rigaud was director of the Institut Curie in Paris.

About the cigars, I still want to report that the small ones—Pearl— proved to be very satisfactory. My supply is no longer very large. If the man from Berchtesgaden [where Eitingon could always find some satisfactory brand] cannot deliver the Soberanos, I am willing to accept the rather good Reina-Cabana which were once offered as a substitute [3].[7]

Freud still wanted to hear the opinion of Holzknecht, the X-ray specialist who had given him postoperative radiation treatments in 1923.

Holzknecht was the chief of the X-ray Institute of the University of Vienna (Allgemeines Krankenhaus). He was one of the pioneers of modern radiology. He was also a former patient of Freud's, as he readily admitted. Holzknecht was a victim of his science. He had developed an X-ray-induced skin cancer on his right hand, and had had to undergo successive amputations: finger—hand—arm. At that time he was again in the hospital. The cancer had spread to the axilla after the enucleation of his right arm. He knew that he was doomed, and in fact died a few months later. I went with Freud to see him. It was an unforgettable scene. The much younger Holzknecht, the former patient turned doctor; both men afflicted with the same ailment; both knowing the truth and facing up to it.

Holzknecht advised against radiation in favor of surgery. When they parted Freud said: "Sie sind zu bewundern wie Sie Ihr Schicksal tragen." ("You are to be admired for the way you bear your lot.") Holzknecht replied: "Sie wissen, dass ich das nur Ihnen zu verdanken habe." ("You know that I have only you to thank for this.") All this without any emotionality.

After Holzknecht's verdict Freud readily submitted to surgery. The operation took place on April 23, 1931. This time Pichler used scopolamine and Eucodal (a codeine derivative) as preoperative sedation. Freud was partly asleep during the operation and quite restless afterwards. He suffered badly and had repeated attacks of violent pain. Nevertheless, he did not want too much sedation, and I dreaded it too. It made his respiration shallow, and with all the necrotic material in his oral cavity, respiratory complications were only too likely.

---

[7] When I started my career as Freud's physician he always used to offer me—an inveterate nonsmoker—a cigar. Too bashful to refuse, I would puff away at it bravely. Freud must soon have noticed this. He once looked at me searchingly and asked with amusement: "Tell me, Schur, are you a cigar smoker?" When I admitted that I was not, he answered: 'And you smoke my precious cigars?"

All of us—but Freud most of all—were relieved when he reacted favorably to local insufflations with Orthoform. While this became his main relief for years to come, it later became apparent that the drug had a drying effect which gave rise to a peculiar crust formation leading to small hyperkeratotic lesions that had a tendency to proliferate like the leukoplakias and produce precancerous lesions. It therefore had to be used sparingly, and the crusts required special attention and treatment.

In spite of all precautions, Freud developed a small pulmonary focus on April 30. Yet again he responded well to treatment, although this was still the pre-antibiotic era. Pulmonary complications were treated with "Transpulmin" injections containing quinine, eucalyptus, and camphor; oxygen and, if necessary, cardiac stimulants were used. By May 4 he was home again, two days before his birthday.

Fortunately the histology again showed no malignancy. Erdheim's report about this specimen, dated April 24, 1931, was a masterpiece of pathological examination. It gave an excellent description of the typical lesion, stressing its precancerous character, and emphasizing the nicotine etiology. Rigaud, who received the specimen and Erdheim's report, was greatly impressed. Freud, however, shrugged at the "nicotine sentence" of Erdheim.

There was no birthday celebration this time. There were gifts, of course (among them a beautiful little Vishnu statue from the Indian Psychoanalytic Society), flowers, telegrams, etc. Freud enjoyed some of it, but when I visited him that day I found him terribly tired. This surgery had robbed him of a certain security, or at least hope, harbored for eight years, that he had been cured of his cancer. The change in his outlook was reflected in two letters written on May 10, 1931, one to Arnold Zweig[8] and the other to Marie Bonaparte. To Zweig:

> I wanted to reproach you—and would like to do so even now—for getting yourself involved in unnecessary diseases of various organs and functions, as your letter hints darkly, but I did remember in good time that I am not the right person to make such a criticism. On April 24, I had to undergo another operation for an exuberant growth basically similar to the one eight years ago. In the process I have lost a good part of my working capital of energy, and am today, after all the trials of this period, without strength, incapable of struggling, and inhibited

[8] A selection of the correspondence between Freud and Arnold Zweig was published in 1968.

in my speech—in no respect is there any enjoyable remnant of reality left. Well-meaning friends advise me to choose some other way out of life than just having recurrences on this spot. I agree, but somehow seem to have no influence on future events.

Tomorrow I shall venture to make a first attempt to sneak back to work. One session in the morning, one in the afternoon. To live for one's health and preserving it like a national treasure is otherwise hard to bear.

To Marie Bonaparte, he wrote:

Today you must be satisfied with a rather short thank-you note. I am still quite below par, and this time I have certainly taken a huge step out of the circle of life.

[He then thanked her for the beautiful Greek vase she had given him, and added, alluding to her great-grandfather, Lucien Bonaparte:]

I was very happy with it, and in other respects as well I feel approximately like a great-grandfather, and I can even muster some regrets that none of the beautiful urns will accompany me to my grave [4].[9]

And yet despite the weariness, both of these letters were written in longhand, and show in the handwriting, the mastery of language, and the self-ironical style Freud's unchanged capacity for expressing the most subtle variations of mood.

I have gone into a rather detailed description of the events of these few months because they illustrate on the one hand Freud's struggle against the unremitting progress of *Ananke*—represented by his cruel illness—and, on the other hand, his indomitable courage. Freud himself was aware that this quality was one of his greatest assets. He expressed this opinion in a letter to Stefan Zweig of February 17, 1931 in which he commented on the latter's biographical study on him (see also Introduction).

Another attempt was made to build a new prosthesis. This time Dr. Kazanijan, a renowned American oral surgeon, teaching at Harvard University Dental School, came to Vienna and worked for three weeks on Freud—in August—in Pichler's office, Pichler again graciously permitting someone else to try his hand. It was hot, the treatments took many hours daily; Freud resented the big financial sacrifice. The result brought only temporary relief, and was worth neither the strain, the disappointment, nor the expense.

[9] Actually, Freud's ashes were placed in this very urn after his cremation in 1939.

On September 17, 1931 Oskar Rie died. He was one of Freud's oldest friends and virtually the only one left from preanalytic days. Freud wrote to Marie Bonaparte the following day:

My friend Dr. Oskar Rie died yesterday; 45 years ago, when as a newly married man (1886) I announced the opening of my office for the treatment of the nervous ·disorders of children, he came to me first as an intern and then as an assistant. Afterward he became the physician of our children and our friend, with whom we shared everything for a generation and a half. One of his daughters, Marianne [Kris], became an analyst, as you know; the other married the analyst [Dr. Hermann] Nunberg, so that the ties became possibly even closer. It is an inevitable lot to see one's old friends die; Enough if one is not condemned to outlive the young ones.

Pichler is working every day on my three prostheses, and has improved them to the point where I can smoke with all of them and speak with two of them. None of them is entirely satisfactory yet. With them it is like with the pursuit of happiness—you think you already have it in your grasp[10] and it is always gone again [5].

By 1931 the depression in Central Europe was reaching disastrous proportions, with much more tragic political consequences than was the case in the United States. Unemployment was rising, and along with it the Nazi party. Eitingon, whose family fortune had been lost in the American depression, was no longer able to support the Berlin Institute. Simmel emigrated to the United States after being obliged to close his sanatorium, which, apart from the one in Kreuzlingen directed by Binswanger, was the only one giving psychoanalytically oriented therapy to hospitalized patients.

The Verlag was in jeopardy, and Freud later regretted that he had spent so much money on Kazanijan's prosthesis instead of using it for the support of the Verlag.

Added to this was the peculiar change in Ferenczi's behavior and the sudden radical, even weird, changes in his psychoanalytic technique. This was painful for Freud, who always called Ferenczi his Paladin, and considered his contribution to the development of psychoanalysis a very important one. In a letter published by Jones (Vol. 3, p. 163ff.), written on December 13, 1931, Freud expressed in most convincing terms his objections to Ferenczi's innovations, pointing out the dangers inherent in them. Freud was painfully aware

---

[10] See footnote to note 5 for this chapter in the Appendix.

that fate had not spared Ferenczi the one thing Freud dreaded most—a blunting or deterioration of his mental powers simultaneously with, or prior to, physical "shrinking." His deep affection for Ferenczi never wavered, as shown by letters written to others before and after Ferenczi's death in May, 1933, and by the obituary he wrote at that time. Not until quite late was it discovered that Ferenczi, who had previously suffered from exophthalmic goiter, had developed a pernicious anemia. This was diagnosed only after he had already developed a central nervous system pathology, which is quite typical for this illness.[11]

All of this added to the strain on Freud's inner equilibrium. The letters he wrote during the last months of 1931 reflect better than anything else his ongoing struggle, but also his resilience. On October 27, 1931 he wrote to Eitingon:

> Pichler is still working constantly on my prostheses and hopefully will be able to make me something more bearable. In the series of greater and lesser troubles of my old age there is—I was about to say "naturally"—no letup. Your shipments [of cigars] I have received gratefully. I have room for still more. "I won't be plucked of my feathers," Lord Bacon said in a situation calling for renunciation [6].

On November 15, 1931 Freud again wrote to Eitingon:

> If I must talk about myself, I had more than a simple stomach upset; it was a severe stomach rebellion—origin unknown—in the course of which an intestinal cramp lasting over an hour even forced me suddenly to interrupt an analytic hour, something which until then had been necessary only once in my life. I have not recovered completely even today, but I am very well prepared for the fact that if it is not this it will be something else.[12]
>
> For once I am free of internal complaints and those with the prosthesis have been reduced to their usual proportions. The strange variations in the feeling tone of life, which go along independent of well-being or illness, are something one can take note of only reverently [7].

11 It was my contention, which I communicated to Jones after reading the first proofs of Volume 3 of his biography of Freud, that Ferenczi's behavioral changes, including his actions with patients (mentioned, for example, in the letter from Freud to Ferenczi referred to above) had been precipitated by organic changes. Only later, when I had occasion to read Freud's correspondence with Jones, did I learn that Freud had expressed a similar opinion in a letter of May 29, 1933, written after Ferenczi's death.

12 In such instances Freud responded promptly to belladonna, one medication he accepted readily because it had no central nervous system sedative action.

He wrote to Marie Bonaparte on November 29:

I heard via Ruth [Mack-Brunswick] that illness broke out [literally: broke into] in your home, and since I have received no letter from you for a long time, I beg you to send me a message soon, hopefully with the news that everything is all right again.

This month has been a miserable time. I have been ill constantly— with the prosthesis or other things, on top of which we had a scare over the life-threatening melaena neonatorum [intestinal hemorrhage of the newborn] of Marianne Kris's baby, but the child was saved by a blood transfusion [8].[13]

This letter demonstrates that Freud's suffering never diminished his interest in and concern for his friends and their children.

On December 10 he wrote to Arnold Zweig rather dispiritedly:

Not much can be said about myself; little that would be worthwhile reporting. The feeling tone of life is getting weaker in a peculiar way.

In contrast he wrote to Eitingon only a few days later (December 14):

I am smoking again with more gusto, and anxiously see the last two Berchtesgaden boxes approach depletion. And during your absence? [Eitingon was about to go abroad] [9].

It became increasingly apparent that Freud's attitude toward death was influenced by his attitude toward the positive aspects of life. The two main factors that had a bearing on this attitude, especially from 1931 on, were the suffering induced by the slow but steady progress of Freud's illness and the ominous historical events that were shaping up in Western Europe.

With regard to his illness, we find 92 entries in Pichler's notes for 1932! I shall describe only the more pertinent facts—including five operations—from my own notes.

On March 7, 1932 Freud had another operation. Pichler's notes describe clearly the increasing difficulties encountered in closing the wound, either by suture or by a plastic procedure. Again it was a leukoplakia.

During the ensuing months Freud was in poor health, struggling constantly for a few days of less discomfort. Freud spent the summer

---

[13] Transfusions were not yet the routine procedure they are nowadays.

of 1932 in Pötzleinsdorf. He enjoyed the beautiful old house ("Mauth-nervilla"), the garden, the view of the Wienerwald. July was a better month, but two more "small" operations were performed on July 29 and August 16.

In September we observed how, within a few days, under our very eyes, a smooth area turned into a suspicious-looking lesion. This time a larger surgical intervention was required (on October 6). Erdheim's report again stressed the precancerous character of the growth and the strong inflammatory component caused by nicotine. This was the fourth operation within seven months! I therefore confronted Freud with Erdheim's report and urged him even more emphatically than before to stop smoking. Freud shrugged his shoulders, making a typical gesture with his hand, and dismissed the suggestion. As I mentioned previously, he would again and again submit to restrictions on his smoking when he was having trouble with his heart, but never on account of the danger of a lesion in the mouth developing into a new malignancy. "Heart" represented immediate danger to him; the mouth lesions and their connection with nicotine were disregarded.

In early November, 1932 Freud had his usual cold—this time a more severe upper respiratory infection with otitis media of the right ear. He felt quite miserable. It was raining constantly. When I visited him he showed me pictures of Crete and Rhodes, and told me of having daydreams about the sunny Mediterranean, the Greek temples of Sicily, etc. Another excision had to be postponed until he had recovered from the infection. This was finally done on December 8. Erdheim's report was again "leukoplakia."

Thus the year ended on a sad note.

21

THE SCIENTIFIC
WELTANSCHAUUNG

The year 1932 added severe environmental stresses to Freud's life. There was the necessity to intervene in the reorganization of the Verlag, including its financial structure (despite the fact that on his 70th birthday Freud had expressed the wish to stay out of the organizational affairs of psychoanalysis). The worsening health and increasingly controversial therapeutic experiments of Ferenczi also were causing him great concern.

Most serious of all, however, was the deterioration of the political situation in Germany. Freud, who had always thought of himself as Jewish (see letter to B'nai Brith of 1926 [Chapter 16], nevertheless had grown up under the strong influence of German culture. We know how much he was affected by Goethe's work *On Nature* in the choice of his vocation. For a long time Freud could not believe that the country of Goethe and Kant could be swallowed up by the antithesis of Logos. Now he could no longer fail to see the handwriting on the wall. Many analysts were starting to leave Berlin, along with numerous other people, but two of Freud's sons were still living in Germany. The political situation in Austria also was close to the breaking point.

It might therefore be expected that the combination of personal suffering and the precariousness of the political situation would be reflected in Freud's attitude and mood. It is true that Freud occasionally greeted me with a gesture of resignation. He showed disgust over the constant fight with his prosthesis, and sometimes he would look at me in a searching, pleading way. He expressed his worry about the situation in Germany. Yet during this year Freud's letters frequently showed a particular serenity. His correspondence was carried on with undiminished frequency. The letters to Eitingon and Jones were largely about personal, professional, and scientific matters. The correspondence with Marie Bonaparte was as intensive as ever, and that with Arnold Zweig grew steadily in intimacy. A letter written to Zweig on May 8, 1932 showed most clearly the range of Freud's interests and the scale of his emotions at that time.

> You are right, I have just celebrated my birthday and at this moment I am laboriously defending myself against the obligations ensuing from it. But to return to you: how strange this tragic and fantastic country you have just visited must have appeared to you! To think that this strip of our native earth is associated with no other progress, no discovery or invention—the Phoenicians are said to have invented glass and the alphabet (both doubtful!), the island of Crete is said to have given us Minoan art, Pergamon reminds us of parchment, Magnesia of the magnet, and so on *ad infinitum*—but Palestine has produced nothing but religions, sacred frenzies, presumptuous attempts to conquer the outer world of appearances by the inner world of wishful thinking. And *we* hail from there (although one of us considers himself a German also, the other doesn't), our ancestors lived there perhaps for half, perhaps for a whole, millennium (but this is also perhaps), and it is impossible to say how much of the life in that country we carry as heritage in our blood and nerves (as is mistakenly said). Oh, life could be very interesting if only one knew and understood more about such things! But the only things we can be sure of are our feelings of the moment! Among them my warm feelings for you and your work! [L. 264*].

We could ask for no better demonstration of the fact that Freud's great asset of being *novarum rerum cupidus* was still fully operative. We might say that in Faustian terms he was still reaching for ever more knowledge.[1]

---

[1] Faust's wager with Mephistopheles stems from his recognition that once he has renounced his search for knowledge, he has renounced life as well.

Faust: Werd ich zum Augenblicke sagen:
　　　Verweile doch! du bist so schön!
　　　Dann magst du mich in Fesseln schlagen,
　　　Dann will ich gern zu Grunde gehn!
　　　Dann mag die Totenglocke schallen,
　　　Dann bist du deines Dienstes frei,
　　　Die Uhr mag stehn, der Zeiger fallen,
　　　Es sei die Zeit für mich vorbei!

This same eagerness was displayed by Freud when he showed me more pictures of the new excavations in Crete, remarking wistfully how much he would love to see them and also to revisit the Greek temples of southern Sicily. In another letter to Arnold Zweig Freud expressed his great concern about him, for, like Einstein, who had already left Germany, Zweig was then the subject of violent attacks in the Nazi press and was constantly being threatened by anonymous letters.

In the spring of 1932, Freud had begun to write his *New Introductory Lectures,* which brought the conceptual framework of psychoanalysis up to date. They were written with the same lucidity and mastery of style as the "old" *Introductory Lectures.*

In its over-all attitude, this book showed a revival of the enthusiasm for Logos which had been so evident in *The Future of an Illusion.* Lecture XXXI ended with Freud's famous statement: "Where id was, there ego shall be." To which he added: "It is a work of culture [reclamation work]—not unlike the draining of the Zuyder Zee." This was a direct allusion to *Faust,* who dies after having reclaimed land from the destructive forces of the ocean, and with this last deed achieves salvation through love—Eros.

Most important for the topic of this book is the last lecture: "The Question of a Weltanschauung."[2] Freud was not generally inclined to proclaim his "credo" (which was, of course, also a "non credo"). Several factors undoubtedly contributed to his doing so now. The most important one probably was the rapidly growing threat of an upheaval in Germany. Perhaps Freud wished, as he had done once before with the first *Introductory Lectures,* to tell present and future generations that in those times of unreason there was one voice, more articulate and convincing than most, which still spoke on behalf of Logos, objectivity, science. This he could not do without reaffirming in even stronger terms than before his formulations about religion

---

If to the instant I should say:
Oh, stay awhile, you are so fair!
Put me in chains that very day,
I readily will perish then.
Then let the death bell toll its knell,
You shall be free, your duty done,
The clock may stop, the hand may fall
Time shall be at an end for me!
Faust, Part I, Scene 4

[2] The German word *Weltanschauung,* as Freud indicated at the very beginning of that chapter, is untranslatable.

previously expressed in *The Future of an Illusion*. In this context Freud also reaffirmed his frequently stated opinion of philosophy (1933b, p. 160f.):

> Of the three powers which may dispute the basic position of science, religion alone is to be taken seriously as an enemy. Art is almost always harmless and beneficent; it does not seek to be anything but an illusion. . . . Philosophy is not opposed to science, it behaves like a science and works in part by the same methods; it departs from it, however, by clinging to the illusion of being able to present a picture of the universe which . . . is coherent, though one which is bound to collapse with every fresh advance in our knowledge. It goes astray in its method by over-estimating the epistemological value of our logical operations and by not accepting other sources of knowledge such as intuition.

After having for years watched from a distance, as an interested but somewhat bewildered observer, the experiment represented by the Russian Revolution, Freud was now obliged to recognize in it—apart from its insensitivity "to the suffering of anyone who stands between them [the leaders] and their goal"—a puzzling development:

> Theoretical Marxism, as realized in Russian Bolshevism, has acquired the energy and the self-contained and exclusive character of a *Weltanschauung*, but at the same time an uncanny likeness to what it is fighting against. Though originally . . . built . . . upon science and technology, it has created a prohibition of thought which is just as ruthless as was that of religion in the past. Any critical examination of Marxist theory is forbidden, doubts of its correctness are punished in the same way as heresy was once punished by the Catholic Church. The writings of Marx have taken the place of the Bible . . . , though they would seem to be no more free from contradictions . . . than those older sacred books [p. 179f.].

Once again Freud resorted to his Socratic method of conducting an argument:

> So the struggle is not at an end. The supporters of the religious *Weltanschauung* act upon the ancient dictum: the best defence is attack. 'What', they ask, 'is this science which presumes to disparage our religion— . . . which has brought . . . consolation to millions of people over . . . thousands of years? What has it accomplished so far? What can we expect from it in the future? On its own admission it is incapable of bringing consolation and exaltation. Let us leave them on one side then. . . . But what about its theories? Can it tell us how the universe came about and what fate lies before it? Can it . . . show us where we

are to look for the unexplained phenomena of life or how the forces of the mind are able to act upon inert matter? . . . But . . . it collects observations of uniformities in the course of events which it dignifies with the name of laws and submits to its risky interpretations. . . . Everything it teaches is only provisionally true; what is praised today as the highest wisdom will be rejected to-morrow and replaced by something else. . . . The latest error is then described as the truth. And for this truth we are to sacrifice our highest good!'

. . . the reproaches against science for not having yet solved the problems of the universe are exaggerated in an unjust . . . manner; it has truly not had time enough yet for these great achievements. Science is . . . a human activity which developed late. Let us bear in mind . . . that only some three hundred years have passed since Kepler discovered the laws of planetary movement, that the life of Newton, who analysed light into the colours of the spectrum and laid down the theory of gravitation, ended in 1727 . . . and that Lavoisier discovered oxygen shortly before the French Revolution. The life of an individual is very short in comparison with the duration of human evolution; I may be a very old man to-day [Freud was then 76], but nevertheless I was already alive when Darwin published his book on the origin of species. In the same year as that, 1859, Pierre Curie, the discoverer of radium, was born. And if you go . . . to the beginnings of exact science among the Greeks, to Archimedes, to Aristarchus of Samos (about 250 B.C.) who was the fore-runner of Copernicus, or even to the first beginnings of astronomy among the Babylonians, you will only have covered a small fraction of the length of time which anthropologists require for the evolution of man from an ape-like ancestral form, and which certainly comprises more than a hundred thousand years. And we must not forget that the last century has brought . . . such a great acceleration of scientific advance that we have every reason to view the future of science with confidence. . . .

And what, finally, is the aim of these passionate disparagements of science? In spite of its present incompleteness and of the difficulties attaching to it, it remains indispensable to us and nothing can take its place. It is capable of undreamt-of improvements, whereas the religious *Weltanschauung* is not. This is complete in all essential respects; if it was a mistake, it must remain one for ever. No belittlement of science can in any way alter the fact that it is attempting to take account of our dependence on the real external world, while religion is an illusion and it derives its strength from its readiness to fit in with our instinctual wishful impulses [pp. 172-175].

Freud's statement that "a sweeping alteration of the social order has little prospect of success until new discoveries have increased our control over the forces of Nature and so made easier the satisfaction of our needs" (p. 181) may sound like a truly prophetic prediction of the atomic age. Freud was of course familiar with some of the research which was being carried on under the influence of Einstein's theories, as shown by an exchange of letters between Freud and Marie Bonaparte (see Schur, 1965). She reported on October 20, 1932:

> I have made the acquaintance here [in Copenhagen] of Niels Bohr, who, as you must know, is one of the outstanding physicists of our time. However, I cannot accept one of the points of his theories which he explained to us: namely, the "free will" of the atom. The atom is now to be excluded from determinism. I was pleased to hear him say that Einstein had objected to him: "I can't imagine God throwing dice." Planck (the quantum theory man) also seems to have objections, saying that it may be due to a lack of knowledge of all the factors that we have no idea which way an atom wishes to go.
>
> I came away with the impression that "free will" is trying to find a refuge in these atomic speculations. And metaphysics, which developed so beautifully out of the physics of the ancient Greeks, is coming full circle in this way. Modern physicists are simultaneously eternal metaphysicians.[3] The oedipus complex is less hypothetical.

Freud answered on October 22, 1932, after he had finished his *New Introductory Lectures*. His comments were brief but meaningful:

> What you tell me about the great physicists is really very remarkable. It is here that the breakdown of today's *Weltanschauung* is actually taking place. We can only wait and see.

In the summer of 1932, before completing the *New Introductory Lectures,* Freud had exchanged letters with Albert Einstein dealing with the question: "Why War?" (1933a) Freud again expressed his view about the gradual development of culture, its causes and consequences. He spoke especially about the many reasons why, on the one hand, war was so difficult to avoid, and why, on the other hand, some people were so strongly opposed to it. He was not entirely without hope that wars might be preventable.

> Why do you and I and so many other people rebel so violently against war? . . . The answer to my question will be that we react to war in this way because everyone has a right to his own life, because war puts an end to human lives that are full of hope, because it brings individual

---

[3] Marie Bonaparte, and perhaps also Niels Bohr, did not fully predict the eventual extension of "determinism" to the particles of the atom. The imputation of having "metaphysical" tendencies might better—although mistakenly—have been directed at Planck.

men into humiliating situations, because it compels them against their will to murder other men, . . . owing to the perfection of instruments of destruction a future war might involve the extermination of one or perhaps both of the antagonists. All this is true, and so incontestably true that one can only feel astonished that the waging of war has not yet been unanimously repudiated. . . . It is my opinion that the main reason why we rebel against war is that we cannot help doing so. We are pacifists because we are obliged to be for organic reasons. . . . For incalculable ages mankind has been passing through a process of evolution of culture. (Some people . . . prefer to use the term 'civilization'.) We owe to that process the best of what we have become, as well as a good part of what we suffer from. . . . It may perhaps be leading to the extinction of the human race, for in more than one way it impairs the sexual function; uncultivated races and backward strata of the population are already multiplying more rapidly than the cultivated ones. The process is perhaps comparable to the domestication of certain species of animals and it is undoubtedly accompanied by physical alterations. . . . The *psychical* modifications that go along with the process of civilization are striking and unambiguous. They consist in a progressive displacement of instinctual aims and a restriction of instinctual impulses. . . . Of the psychological characteristics of civilization two appear to be the most important: a strengthening of the intellect, which is beginning to govern instinctual life, and an internalization of the aggressive impulses, with all its consequent advantages and perils. Now war is in crassest opposition to the psychical attitude imposed on us by the process of civilization, and for that reason we are bound to rebel against it; we simply cannot any longer put up with it. This is not merely an intellectual and emotional repudiation; we pacifists have a *constitutional* intolerance of war, an idiosyncrasy magnified . . . to the highest degree.

And how long shall we have to wait before the rest of mankind become pacifists too? There is no telling. But it may not be Utopian to hope that these two factors, the cultural attitude and the justified dread of the consequences of a future war, may result within a measurable time in putting an end to the waging of war. By what paths or by what side-tracks this will come about we cannot guess. But one thing we *can* say: whatever fosters the growth of civilization works at the same time against war [p. 213ff.].

Our mythological theory of instincts makes it easy for us to find a formula for *indirect* methods of combating war. If willingness to engage in war is an effect of the destructive instinct, the most obvious plan will be to bring Eros, its antagonist, into play against it. Anything that encourages the growth of emotional ties between men must operate against war. These ties may be of two kinds. In the first place they may be relations resembling those towards a loved object, though without having a sexual aim. There is no need for psycho-analysis to be ashamed to speak of love in this connection, for religion itself uses the same words: 'Thou shalt love thy neighbour as thyself.' This, however, is more easily said than done. The second kind of emotional tie is by means of identification. Whatever leads men to share important interests produces this community of feeling, these identifications. And the structure of human society is to a large extent based on them [p. 212].

It is possible that the progress in the revolution of the physical sciences to which Freud had referred in his remarks to Marie Bonaparte was a motivating factor for the inclusion in the *New Introductory Lectures* of its most controversial chapter, "Dreams and the Occult," in which he presented essentially the same material as in the two previously discussed papers on this topic (see Chapter 12). In this chapter, however, Freud expressed with even firmer conviction his belief in telepathic phenomena. His exploratory attitude had been eloquently expressed in the letter of May 8 to Arnold Zweig, in which he had exclaimed: "Oh, life could be so very interesting if only we knew and understood more. . . ." Freud still wanted to know, to understand, to discover, and as long as there was the possibility of doing so, his will to live affirmed itself.[4]

----

[4] One area of investigation closely related to Freud's hypotheses is the matter of whether dreams can be influenced by extrasensory perception. Recently attempts have been made to work out an "objective" methodology for proving or disproving such hypotheses (see, for example, Ullman, 1965).

22

HITLER GERMANY
AND AUSTRIAN FASCISM

The completion of the *New Introductory Lectures* was followed by
a letdown. Freud announced its publication in a gloomy letter written
to Arnold Zweig on November 27, 1932:

> In a few days you will receive my latest opus—perhaps really the last
> one—a supplement to the *Introductory Lectures*. Since a bout of flu
> accompanied by otitis my condition has declined considerably.

The year 1933 started on a similar note. Freud wrote to Eitingon on
January 5, after having received a message that the latter's father had
died after surgery:

> With your father, a strange thing happened to me at the time you re-
> ported a disturbance during his postoperative recovery; I lost my con-
> fidence, began to develop an expectation, which later, when you
> informed me of his recovery, found expression in the thought: "At
> least a little time has been gained." You may remember that part of my
> letter! Well, too little time was gained. I had a dim notion that we are
> indeed all sentenced to die, the old people among us being on par-
> ticularly short probation [1].

During the first few months, Freud's health was not too bad. Even
the prosthesis, though requiring constant adjustments, occasionally
was less troublesome. Every suspicious spot in Freud's mouth had to
be watched carefully, but at least there was no surgical intervention

442

until May 16, and this was a minor one. However, there were 23 visits to Pichler during that period.

January, 1933 brought Hitler to power in Germany, and with his advent the years of escalating terror began. Freud felt the impact of the first wave. His sons had to leave Germany with their families. It soon became obvious that the Psychoanalytic Society and Training Institute would have to stop functioning. All Jewish analysts had to flee. His children would now have to find a new means of existence, and the analysts a place to which they could emigrate. Freud was deeply concerned about the fate of Arnold Zweig, who for various reasons had returned to Germany for a time after bringing his family to safety.

The impact of Hitler on the Austrians was, of course, overwhelming. Many of us were convinced that Austria would not be able to withstand the spread of Nazism. I tried from that moment on to convince Freud that sooner or later he—and all of us—would have to think of leaving Vienna. Freud received many invitations to settle elsewhere, first from Marie Bonaparte and then from Pfister and Binswanger, among others. All of these he turned down with thanks.

For complex reasons Freud refused for quite some time to anticipate the inescapably mounting horror which eventually led to World War II and the extermination camps.

This refusal was reflected in a series of letters to Marie Bonaparte. On March 16, 1933 he wrote:

> How fortunate that you are able to be so immersed in your work that you do not have to take any notice of all the loathsome things around you. In our circles there is quite a lot of trepidation. People fear that the nationalistic excesses in Germany may spread to our little country. I have even been advised to flee to Switzerland or France. That is nonsense; I do not believe there is any danger here, and if it does come I am firmly determined to await it here. If they should kill me—fine; it is one kind of death like any other. But this probably is only cheap boasting [Jones, Vol. 3, p. 175].

The last sentence shows the immediate insight of which Freud was capable when he caught himself saying something which was perhaps not quite genuine. His attitude may have stemmed from a combination of defiance and a certain horror of emigration, with all that this would imply. Although Freud finally did emigrate, he waited till the very last moment, when it was nearly too late.

The next letter, written on March 26, 1933, was curiously optimistic. Freud thanked Marie Bonaparte for her invitation to St. Cloud, but declined to make use of it. He believed that the brutalities in Germany were diminishing under the pressure of the adverse reactions from France and the United States. Freud predicted, however, that the small but painful torments would continue, and that in fact the systematic oppression of the Jews, which would deprive them of all positions, had only just begun. The persecution of the Jews and the suppression of intellectual freedom were the only aspects of the Hitler program which could be carried out, he thought. All the rest was "weakness and utopianism."

The last letter in this series, written on April 8, 1933, sounds incredible coming from Freud. He thought that the Nazi movement might spread to Austria, but without the excesses of the German movement, since the Austrians were not quite as brutal as the Germans (he forgot that Hitler was an Austrian)! He reminded Marie Bonaparte, obviously in an attempt to reassure himself, that the minority laws laid down in the Treaties of Versailles and St. Germain (with Germany and Austria, respectively) forbade an *Anschluss* between Austria and Germany.

It would seem that Freud, who had uncovered the force of the aggressive drive in the individual, could not believe that this force could be unleashed in an entire nation. We must remind ourselves, however, that it also took Freud a long time to recognize the growing hostility of such co-workers as Jung and Rank. He had avoided such a recognition through the defense mechanism of denial, which was operating in this case as well.

Freud shared the general incredulity of the Western world with regard to the utter ruthlessness of the Nazi plans. A letter to Arnold Zweig written during that same period (March 21, 1933) was a sad one:

> These difficult times make me despondent. . . . About myself I do not need to worry. As my pessimistic and ten-year-younger brother recently said, our old age is our greatest asset [2].

Freud's 77th birthday found him not only in a depressed mood, but suffering from a sudden attack of severe dizziness of a vestibular type, which had started shortly before I came to visit him. In a letter to Marie Bonaparte (May 9, 1933) Freud described this day and his mood:

I would gladly have been with you in Corsica [where the great granddaughter of Lucien Bonaparte, the brother of Napoleon, had been visiting for the first time]. I would have shared in your enjoyment of the beautiful landscape and the warm reception. . . .

My birthday was strenuous, overabundant in flowers, letters, and telegrams. I had restrained most people from sending presents, but not you. Your camel has already been proudly placed next to the other "chinoiseries"[1] . . . here in my room. . . . On that morning I had an attack of dizziness which nearly knocked me over, with no disturbance of consciousness. Dr. Schur, who by chance came in right afterward, did not make much of it. His diagnosis asserted that the dizziness was of a vestibular type and caused by nicotine. Since then I have been restricted to three cigars, but I really have not felt well since, whether due to abstinence or to something else. . . .

Are both of your children still in Denmark? Unfortunately, Denmark is no longer the only country where something is rotten [3].

At that time my wife was expecting our first child, by then a few days overdue. Freud was certainly feeling miserable that day when I arrived, yet he greeted me with the question: "Noch nichts?" ("Nothing yet?") After I examined him and was able to reassure him about the cause of his attack, he urged me to leave at once, saying: "Gehen Sie jetzt; Sie gehören jetzt zu Ihrer Frau." ("Go now, you should be with your wife.") Then he looked at me, yet not really at me, and remarked in a deeply meditative tone while holding on to my hand: "So gehen Sie von einem alten Mann, der noch nicht sterben will, zu einem Kind, das noch nicht auf die Welt kommen will." ("So you go from an old man who does not yet want to die to a child who does not yet want to come into the world.")

I was deeply touched then by the poignancy of this simple sentence with its recognition of the oneness of life and death. Many years later, after reading an unpublished letter to Fliess (see Chapter 6), in which Freud spoke of visiting first the pregnant daughter of an old friend and then Fliess's dying mother, commenting, " 'birth and grave' etc.," a quotation from Goethe's *Faust,* I recognized the continuity in Freud's thinking and what he called "the immortality of the unconscious." This is why I chose these lines as the "motto" of my book. Freud gave evidence of the same uncanny continuity during the last days of his life (see Chapter 27).

Freud added a postscript to the letter to Marie Bonaparte quoted

[1] Freud had recently become particularly interested in ancient Chinese art. This camel remained one of his prized possessions.

above: "Schur ist, seitdem ich an diesem Brief schreibe, Vater geworden." ("Schur became a father while I was writing this letter.")

This little episode—his greeting and parting remarks to me, the
letter to Marie Bonaparte and its postscript—showed Freud's undiminished interest in the lives of those to whom he felt close, and
more particularly his interest in children—his 1926 letter to Binswanger notwithstanding. It showed his ability to place an interest in
others before his own needs, an utterly genuine attitude which had
nothing in it of a polite gesture.

A similar sentiment was expressed in a letter to Jones, whose wife
had given birth to a baby at the same time as mine:

> In all the familiar uncertainty of life one may envy parents the joy and
> hopes which soon center round the new human creature, whereas with
> old people one must be glad when the scales are nearly balanced be-
> tween the inevitable need of final rest and the wish to enjoy for a while
> longer the love and friendship of those near to one. I believe I have
> discovered that the longing for ultimate rest is not something elementary
> and primary,[2] but an expression of the need to be rid of the feeling of
> inadequacy which affects age, especially in the smallest details of life
> [Vol. 3, p. 180].

On May 11, 1933, two days after the birthday letter to Marie Bonaparte was written, the newspapers reported the great bonfire in Berlin
on which the books of all Jewish and many non-Jewish but anti-Nazi
authors had been burned. Goebbels had ended the ceremony with a
speech, while the burning of each author's or group of author's books
was preceded by a declaration from a special announcer (all students
and S. A. men). The announcement preceding the burning of Freud's
books proclaimed: "Against the soul-destroying overestimation of the
sex life—and on behalf of the nobility of the human soul—I offer to
the flames the writings of one Sigmund Freud!" A Viennese newspaper
carried an account of the event and Marie Bonaparte kept a copy of it.

A similar ceremony had taken place in Frankfurt where, only three
years earlier, Freud had received the Goethe Prize. An editorial comment on the newspaper report stated: "Goethe reports in *Dichtung und
Wahrheit* [Goethe's biography] about the first book-burning he witnessed as a youngster. Even in his old age he could not help shudder-

---

[2] This is at variance with the death instinct theory! In this letter Freud speaks as
the analyst who expresses his feelings. He does not need his death instinct concept
to explain them.

ing at the memory. He would not have dreamed that such barbarism would be repeated a century after his death."

Freud was thus forced to start believing that the country of Goethe and Kant might be starting on a downward path to the abyss.

On June 6, 1933 Freud wrote to Marie Bonaparte:

> I cannot think of writing anything new. No mood, no topic, no audience, too many worries. You yourself described the political situation exhaustively. It seems to me that not even during the war lies and clichés were as unrestrictedly rampant. The world is becoming a huge prison, the worst cell being Germany . . .
> [Since I] myself no longer have much vital energy, the whole world seems to me doomed to destruction. I am gladdened by the thought that you are still living as on an Island of the Blessed [4].

The medical aspects of the rest of this year were summed up in my notes as follows:

On May 16, another "small" electrocoagulation. The following summer was poor. It was hot, he did not tolerate the heat too well, had occasional slight anginal symptoms; the crust formation was bothersome; he had a great deal of pain.

On September 5, Pichler performed a rather minor electrocoagulation. Immediately upon returning to his summer home, which was within walking distance of my own house, Freud went into a mild shock with tachycardia and slight precordial pain. It looked like a coronary insufficiency, probably due to some adrenalin in the local anesthesia. A coronary thrombosis could not initially be excluded, however.

Freud recovered quickly from the shock. Blood pressure and pulse were normal that evening. After a few days he developed a slight temperature and some pulmonary congestion. Since laboratory tests and electrocardiograms did not suggest a coronary thrombosis, I did not insist on prolonged bed rest.[3] Pichler agreed that in the future we should refrain from using adrenalin, which meant that local anesthesia, which was already not too effective because of the extensive scar tissue, would henceforth be even less so. We therefore decided that while we would watch even more closely than before, if this was possible, for suspicious spots we would wait with future surgery as long as this seemed safe.

During this episode, Freud repeatedly—although somewhat reluc-

---

[3] At that time coronary thrombosis was treated by six weeks of complete bed rest.

tantly—discussed his past cardiac history. He mentioned the similarity of symptoms to those he was now exhibiting, speaking of *"Herzjagen,"*[4] the slight pain, the hypersensitivity to nicotine. Not a word was said about Fliess. He asked me how he could have been so active and enjoyed such good cardiac functioning in later years if he had had any lesions in his '40s. He also compared his present symptoms with the anginal pain he had had in 1926.

During this last episode, and for some weeks thereafter, Freud refrained from smoking. His heart, blood pressure, circulation remained normal. He had a better month as far as his mouth was concerned, but suffered badly under the regimen of abstinence. When he started to work again, he eventually resumed smoking.

In November, along with his usual autumn cold, he had a diffuse inflammation of the lining of the oral cavity and of the sinuses, with severe pain in the mandibular joint, and with difficulty in eating, talking, smoking. Shortwave treatments brought some relief.

Some of Freud's letters reflected his mood. He wrote to Arnold Zweig on August 18, 1933:

> What is happening with me? I am submitting to nature, which is letting me age faster in the last three months than in the previous three years. Everything around me is gloomy, stifling to the point of choking. Fury is mounting and gnawing away at the core. If only one could do something liberating! . . .
>
> The women of the house are holding up better. They are indeed the more stable element. The male is—for good biological reasons—more frail [5].

To the best of my knowledge Freud had never before verbalized this idea. That he did so on this occasion can perhaps be explained by the fact that the letter was written on his mother's birthday, three years after her death.

On October 25 he wrote again:

> I can work again, but I cannot climb any stairs yet, and am therefore confined to the house.[5] I think this time I have acquired a claim to an acute cardiac death. The chances are not too bad. It was a coronary thrombosis,[6] but nonetheless I am still alive. As I am not smoking I will

---

[4] The literal translation would be "galloping heart." It was the same symptom which in his letters to Fliess during the early cardiac episode he had described as "delirium cordis."

[5] Freud lived on the second floor, and the house had no elevator.

[6] Freud had wrongly assumed that the more serious diagnosis was the correct one. Did he think of his cardiac episode (1893-1896)?

hardly write anything but letters. It reminds me of that cantor—he'll live but he won't be able to sing.[7]

To Marie Bonaparte he wrote on December 7, 1933:

Today is Martin's [birthday]. No children around here any more. And I myself have already exceeded my years, am outside the stream of life! . . .

My existence has again been restricted one further step. At the moment it is no great loss that I cannot leave the house; it is bitter cold and nasty outside. Whether I am writing anything? No, and I do not think I shall either. I am smoking one, small "denerved" cigar daily.[8]

From Bullitt no direct news.[9] Our book will never see the light of day [6].

In January, 1934 several areas looked slightly suspicious. In view of the previous episode, and also because of the rather inflammatory character of the lesions, we were reluctant to subject Freud to new surgery. While Rigaud had advised against radium therapy for a neoplasm, it was decided to use small amounts of radiation as an "anti-inflammatory" treatment. There was also a small wart on the upper lip requiring some attention. After a few attempts with X-ray treatment (handled by Dr. Eisler), radium was applied by Dr. Fuhs, the radium specialist of the Allgemeines Krankenhaus. Freud had a number of unpleasant reactions—migraine, epistaxis, and also some

[7] We know how often Freud liked to use a joke—especially a Jewish joke—to illustrate a situation. He used this method in his treatment as well. The last sentence of this letter refers to the delightful story about two poor Jews in desperate need of money just before the High Holy Days. While they were debating various possibilities of acquiring some, one of them came up with the idea of recommending his friend as cantor to a congregation which needed one for the coming holidays. When his friend protested that he had never done any singing, the first one reassured him by saying: "You leave everything to me. You walk out, and with the first prayer you suddenly faint." The friend agreed and proceeded according to plan. The congregation, witnessing the "faint," believed the man had died. However, when the friend shook him, the "cantor" opened his eyes but did not utter a sound. Whereupon the other man announced solemnly to the congregation: "He'll live, but he won't be able to sing." Freud used to point out that when a patient could recognize the humorous aspect of a situation, accept a joke or make one himself about it, this indicated a shift toward the dominance of the ego. That Freud could end this letter with a joke indicated that he had been able, this time at least, to master his depressive mood in spite of all the odds against him.

[8] Immediately after expressing the pessimistic thought that he would never write another book, Freud mentioned his enforced nicotine abstinence. This illustrates once again how dependent Freud was on the stimulating effect of tobacco for his creative work.

[9] Referring to their joint biography of Woodrow Wilson; see Chapter 26.

local reaction. Occasionally these were accompanied by slight anginal pain. Pichler was skeptical about the connection between this reaction and the radium treatment. I believed Freud, however, who felt that there was some connection, and suggested that he consult with Dr. W. Schloss, a radium expert who had been trained at the Institut Curie in Paris. Dr. Schloss explained that the metal in the prosthesis could have produced secondary radiation and therefore a stronger reaction than had been anticipated. The radium was now applied with a specially constructed prosthesis. This brought definite relief and fewer reactions. Against all expectations even small wartlike lesions and structures suggesting papilloma responded favorably. We could now avoid surgery for a whole year. Out of the temporary radium prothesis a new prosthesis was built, as the old "Kazanijan" one was no longer working.

During that time Freud's general condition was also better. He was receiving injections of a male hormone at regular intervals mainly for its anabolic action. (The androgen extracts available at that time were already somewhat effective, although not yet as standardized as they are now.) Whatever their pharmacological effect, he responded quite well to them.

This was to be the only year without surgical intervention!

Two events of that year made it difficult to maintain any complacency about the future of Austria. On February 14, 1934 civil war broke out—confined mostly to Vienna—after the Social Democratic party had decided to take a last stand against the gradual shifting to a fascistic government. The fighting was quite bloody, but the uprising was crushed, and from that time on Austria was ruled by a somewhat modified fascist-type administration.

Once again Freud was urged to leave the country, and for the first time he conceded that he might have to do so. This in itself was proof of a slight upward curve in his "vital energies." He expressed this change in three letters written during one week:

To Marie Bonaparte on February 19, 1934:

Once more my sincere thanks for your repeated invitations. It is of course invaluable to know that there exists a beautiful place where one would be welcomed gladly until a new home has been found. . . .

The future is unpredictable. . . . If the Nazis come here, and bring with them the same lawlessness as in Germany, then of course one must leave [7].

On the following day he wrote to his son Ernst, who was already living in England:

> The future is uncertain; either an Austrian fascism or the swastika. In the latter event we will have to leave [L. 273*].

His letter of February 25 to Arnold Zweig is in many ways the most revealing one:

> Dear Master Arnold,
> Keep working steadily on the *Education Before Verdun*.[10] Pack into it all the sarcasm, cruelty, and feelings of superiority which these times have awakened in you, because first of all I am burning to read the book—preferably in a shady garden with Wolf and Jofi [Freud's wolf-hound and chow] on the lawn next to me—and I really cannot know how much time I have left. And secondly, because I feel that the people who are the potential readers are already withdrawing their interest from the last war to be prepared for the unbelievably bewildering events of the immediate future. So you must not be too late.
> Our piece of civil war was far from pretty. You could not go out on the street without a pass, no electricity for a day, and the prospect that the water might be shut off was very uncomfortable. Now everything has quieted down, the quiet of tension, one would assume, as if one were waiting in a hotel room for the second boot to be thrown against the wall. Things cannot remain this way. Something must happen, whether it be that the Nazis come, or our home-baked fascism gets ready to take over, or, as some people now assume, Otto von Habsburg is in the offing. A story comes to mind which I remember only vaguely: "The Lady and the Tiger," in which a poor prisoner is waiting in the circus to find out whether the beast will be let loose against him or whether the lady will enter and free him from his punishment by choosing him as her husband. The point is that the story ends without our finding out who comes through the door—the lady or the tiger. This can only mean that for the prisoner it would be tantamount to the same thing, and therefore not worth telling.
> You anticipate rightly that we want to sit it out here resignedly. After all, where would I turn in my dependency and physical helplessness? And foreign lands are so unhospitable everywhere. Only if a Hitler type governor really comes to rule in Vienna, I must of course go, no difference where. My attitude toward the two warring parties [Austrian fascism and the swastika] I can describe only by quoting Shakespeare's Mercutio: "A plague on both your houses" [*Romeo and Juliet*].
> That the Nazis are now in possession of your beautiful library pains

---

[10] The second big novel by A. Zweig on the theme of World War I. The first was *Sergeant Grischa*. Both have appeared in English translation.

us all very much. My daughter Anna had the following idea: whether you do not feel an urgent desire which brooks no delay to own at least and immediately, as a replacement for everything else, an edition of my collected works, which you seem to hold in such high esteem? If you own up to such a wish, when and where can the Verlag send the 11 volumes?

Little comment is needed on this letter. This is once again Freud at his best, that same Freud who declared after Heinele's death that he could never form any new attachments! The will to live, to fight, to love is as strong as ever. And yet, the thought "How much more time do I have?" is always lurking in the background.

The two letters to Arnold Zweig which follow below are also pertinent in this context. Zweig had sent Freud the manuscript of a book entitled *Bilanz (Balance)*. Freud had found some errors in it, which he pointed out in a letter of April 3, 1934:

> April 3, 1934
>
> Dear Master Arnold,
> The old story goes: when the 10,000 [soldiers] under Xenophon finally reached the coast after a long period of wandering through Asia Minor, and got their first glimpse of the sea, deeply moved they broke out into the cry: Thalassa, Thalassa.[11] Whereupon Xenophon, who stood nearby, remarked: "One can also say Thalatta."

Freud was telling this story jokingly, to illustrate how a highly charged emotional reaction could be ironically tuned down by means of a semantic correction. He used the story as an introduction to the correction of certain errors which Zweig had made in his manuscript:

> On page 232 of your *Balance,* please correct the words "subconscious" to "unconscious," and on page 234 Ferency to Ferenczi.
> Most cordially,
> Your
> Freud
> P.S. Oh! Also *Edward* Jones to *Ernest* J.
>
> April 4, 1934
> A postscript to my letter of yesterday: Immediately after mailing it I realized that I had made an error, namely that I had spelled Thalassa with two l's. From all indications, it must have been a parapraxis [I] made despite my better knowledge. I very quickly understood its mo-

---

[11] Both Thalassa and Thalatta mean the sea but the words represent different dialects. Here as well as in the Postscript, these words were written in Greek in the original letters.

tivation. I had felt annoyed about the little errors in your essay—always very sensitive in such small matters.

(Ferency, Edward Jones, subconscious)! Instead of saying so outright, I quoted the anecdote about Xenophon. But love intervened and said that you were probably not responsible for these little transgressions; it is not as easy for you to make corrections as it is for others.[12] The *"sub*conscious" could have been due to your secretary's mishearing, and altogether I do not like to criticize you. You therefore should have a compensation, and the best one is that I myself give you a bit of misinformation which you could detect and point out to me. That's how Thallatta[13] came about and this is its explanation. Aside from this I have always been proud of the rich residues of Greek in my memory (Sophocles' chorus songs, passages from Homer).

Cordially

Your

Freud

There are many significant facets to this letter, but I shall single out only a few pertaining to Freud's memory, range of interests, and mastery of expression. Freud accused himself of a symptomatic act (a "Freudian slip"), which in fact he did not make. But this accusation contained within itself a symptomatic act of a different kind—a "forgetting" instead of a misspelling. In fact, the second letter also contains a "slip" which Freud did not notice—writing *Thallatta* for *Thallassa*. Freud's interpretation of the errors made by both Zweig and himself showed great tact and a reluctance to hurt Zweig's feelings through harsh criticism. Perhaps, too, Freud had been testing his memory of ancient quotations and was a bit ashamed of his boasting. The witty application of the Xenophon quote, his attentive reading of a long manuscript sent to him by Zweig (of which he did not approve because it praised him excessively, he thought) belied any unwillingness to continue the fight because of personal suffering and the gloominess of the world.

---

[12] Zweig suffered from a severe impairment of vision and had great difficulty reading.

[13] Freud, who had *not* made a parapraxis in the first letter by using two l's in Thalassa, as he had thought, was now making one instead by writing the word Thallatta!

23

MOSES AND MONOTHEISM

Neither at that nor at any other time of his life did Freud retire to an ivory tower of analytic work or writing about ancient history. Rather, he had a wonderful capacity to confine his very vital interest in current events to that part of his "ego interests" which would not interfere with his creative and professional life. Various letters from that period show that the depressive state of 1933 was passing, but they indicate too what was still missing. On May 2, 1934, after Freud had moved to his summer home, he wrote to Marie Bonaparte:[1]

My dear Marie,
We have moved and are now settled down at XIX., Strassergasse 47, and I can begin to repay my debts of letters. First to you. It is beautiful here, like a fairy tale. Without knowing your St. Cloud [an estate of Marie Bonaparte's near Paris], I would compete with it. [Freud then expressed a certain dread of his approaching birthday, the 78th, mentioning the attack of dizziness he had had on his 77th birthday. He continued:]
I am not writing anything. For this one does need a certain measure of physical well-being which I can no longer muster up, and also a friendlier attitude toward the world than it is possible to have at this time. It is of little help to know just how unimportant one's own condition is to the state of the world; one remains the slave of one's feelings, and the only thing one can accomplish is to keep feelings of disgust to oneself [1].

Despite these feelings, however, and his remark that he was in no frame of mind to work on anything, Freud had actually found the

[1] Even the handwriting of this letter was different from previous ones.

454

topic for his next—and last—major opus, which was to occupy him for years to come. The stormy occurrences of that summer of 1934 could only postpone his beginning it.

These occurrences were the "Roehm purge" of June, 1934, which raised false hopes for a speedy downfall of the Hitler regime (Freud and Zweig exchanged excited letters about this prospect), followed in July by the Nazi uprising in Vienna, which culminated in the murder of Chancellor Dollfuss and a temporary victory of the Austrian government. This gave rise to some hope that Austria might after all be able to retain a measure of independence.

During the rest of the summer of 1934, Freud, after having done a prodigious amount of reading on the subject, developed the outline of *Moses and Monotheism.* That he must have been preoccupied with its main theme for some time is evident from a remark in the letter to Zweig of August 18, 1933. Commenting on "our great leader Moses," Freud stated: "Perhaps he was really an Egyptian." The first two of the three essays that make up this book were first published in 1937, in *Imago,* under the title "Moses an Egyptian."

This is not the place to discuss the validity of the theories advanced in this *tour de force,* nor am I qualified to do so.[2] However, the upsurge of vitality and creativity which led to the writing of *Moses and Monotheism* was in turn fed by that activity, so that in his last years Freud was able to produce a number of important papers on the theory and practice of psychoanalysis.

In a long letter to Arnold Zweig of September 30, 1934 [L. 276*], Freud outlined the book and discussed the reasons for his reluctance to publish it—a feeling that the theory was not too well substantiated and fears about the reaction of Austria's Catholic regime, which was now the last bulwark against a Nazi takeover of the country.

Freud's mood, as he worked on the book, was reflected in such letters as the following one to Arnold Zweig, written on December 16, 1934:

As to the Moses, leave me in peace.[3] That this, probably final, attempt to create something has failed depresses me sufficiently. Not that I have

[2] I am in possession of a remarkable manuscript written by a German Biblical scholar who was killed in a German concentration camp, a Dr. Cohen. Working with different, mainly Biblical sources, he arrived at not only similar but even more far-reaching conclusions than Freud's. I hope that this work will be published in the near future.

[3] Zweig, fascinated by the idea of the *Moses,* was constantly feeding Freud historical material.

broken away from it. The man, and what I wanted to make of him, haunts me incessantly. But it isn't possible. The external dangers and the inner misgivings do not permit any other outcome to this attempt. I believe my memory for recent events is no longer quite reliable. That in a previous letter I wrote to you in detail about Moses being an Egyptian is not the essential issue, though it is the point of departure for this work. Nor is it the inner difficulty, because this point is as good as certain. Rather, it is the fact that I was forced to place an alarmingly grandiose image on feet of clay, so that any fool can topple it over.

With regard to my health, I am going through bad times. They're giving me radium in the mouth, and I react to this devilish stuff with the most dreadful symptoms. One often thinks: "Le jeu ne vaut pas la chandelle" ["The game isn't worth the candle"]. One feels bad. Resolutions are of little help against the immediate, unequivocal sensation.

Nothing can better exemplify Freud's capacity for introspection and insight than his words (to Arnold Zweig on February 13, 1935), written in a rather gloomy mood. Freud had received the manuscript of a poem from Zweig and an enthusiastic description of early spring in Palestine. Freud answered:

The description of spring made me sad, envious. *There is still so much capacity for enjoyment within me;* thus I feel discontent with the enforced resignation. Grim winter reigns in Vienna; I haven't left the house for months.[4] I also find it difficult to assume the role of the hero suffering for the sake of humanity, which your friendship has offered me. My mood is bad; very little is to my liking; my self-criticism has become much more severe. In someone else my diagnosis would be *senile depression.* I see a cloud of disaster closing in on the world, even on my own small one [italics added].

It was at this point, after an interval of a year and a half, that I noticed the development of a lesion which looked more suspicious than any of the previous ones. Pichler did an extensive electrocoagulation on March 23, 1935, under local anesthesia (containing, on my insistence, no admixture of adrenalin). Erdheim's report was even more ominous this time: "Proliferating leukoplakia, probably still in a precancerous stage." An additional electrocoagulation was therefore performed on April 30. This was followed by severe local pain and great difficulty in inserting the prosthesis. On his 79th birthday Freud was unable to insert it at all. Anna Freud and I tried to help him, and he kept at it to the point of exhaustion. Finally, we took him to

---

[4] During those months Pichler visited Freud with me at the Berggasse.

Pichler's office. A new prosthesis had to be started that day. This was one of the very few occasions on which Freud felt somewhat desperate. Yet he soon regained control and in Pichler's office was again his composed, patient, polite self.

The construction and adjustment of the new prosthesis took more than two months. Moreover, between April 30 and July 9, 26 visits with Pichler were needed! There was now a new sequence of pathological tissue formation: the formation of a crust, leading to hyperkeratosis and eventually to small, wartlike papillomata, which, as the next surgery showed, were as treacherous as those developing out of leukoplakias.

Pichler operated again on August 19, 1935. Erdheim described in a detailed report a papilloma which was growing definitely into the deeper layers, and the line of excision was done just under the deepest level of penetration. Erdheim's report ended: "There is no suspicion of malignant deep penetration, also no trace of abnormal cell formation of the epithelium, so that the diagnosis papilloma is equivocal. There certainly is no Ca.; however, such papillomata have to be considered precursors of Ca. if they are not removed surgically."[5]

All such reports were regularly shown to Freud. It is certain that everyone around Freud, including me and even Pichler, showed greater strain from this constant threat and unremitting vigil than Freud, who was fully preoccupied with compiling evidence for his hypotheses about Moses, as his continuing intensive correspondence with Arnold Zweig demonstrates.

Spring was rather cold that year, and Freud had daydreams of spending it in Palestine, on Mt. Carmel, where Arnold Zweig had his home. On March 14, 1935, he wrote to the latter: *"If* I come to Haifa, I'll certainly bring the *Moses* along for you."[6]

In a letter written on May 2, 1935, four days before his 79th birthday, Freud had referred to his idea of enjoying spring with Zweig as a mere fantasy.

The growing political crisis in Europe, underlined by the impotence of the League of Nations in the Abyssinian crisis, increased Freud's general pessimism about the future prospect of Austria. In the letter to Arnold Zweig of May 12, 1934 which I quoted earlier, Freud had

---

[5] This was the only surgical intervention not performed in my presence. I was on vacation, and a senior friend, Dr. Popper, substituted for me.

[6] The word "if" was italicized by Freud. He did so to express even better the subtle irony: I can as little expect to visit you in Haifa as to complete the *Moses.*

spoken of his pent-up fury about the events in Germany and his inability to do anything about them. This feeling was heightened by reports published in a weekly entitled *Das Tagebuch,* put out by a German journalist, Leopold Schwarzschild, who had fled to France (before eventually emigrating to New York). Both Freud and I subscribed to this publication, which printed detailed and accurate stories on Germany, including the first authentic description of the concentration camps (which had not yet become extermination camps). Schwarzschild's purpose was to warn the Western powers about Germany's feverish rearmament, the formation of the Luftwaffe, etc. He was listened to as little as Cassandra.

With this in mind, Freud wrote to Thomas Mann on June 6, 1935 on the occasion of the latter's 60th birthday, speaking to a man whose voice could still be heard and heeded:

> . . . in the name of countless numbers of your contemporaries I wish to express the confidence that you will never do or say anything—an author's words, after all, are deeds—that is cowardly or base, and that even at a time which blurs judgment you will choose the right way and show it to others [L. 280*].

During the year 1935 Arnold Zweig finally finished his *Erziehung vor Verdun,* which Freud had been eagerly awaiting. He received it in September and wrote to Zweig:

September 23, 1935

Dear Master Arnold,
Master, indeed! . . .

It's like a long-awaited liberation. At last the truth, the grim, definitive truth, which we really cannot do without. One does not understand the Germany of today if one does not know about "Verdun" (and what it stands for). . . .

But in the characterization of the numerous persons you prove your downright unbelievable mastery. To depict a person like Lieutenant Kroysink, how does one do that? By what means does one conjure up a Sister Claire and make her come alive? How do you arrive at the sketch of the bird-faced crown prince, likable in spite of everything? It would be interesting one day to question you about the "day residues" that went into this creation. But Vienna must not become German before you come to visit me.

With most cordial greetings and the expression of my most eager admiration.

Your old
Freud

This letter gives evidence of Freud's undiminished enthusiasm for literary production, his desire for the truth, and his eternal curiosity about the sources of artistic creativity, which he also hoped to explore by analytic means.[7]

After receiving Zweig's heartfelt thanks for this letter, Freud wrote to him again on October 14:

> Dear Master Arnold,
> It really is wonderful that one can give a strong man so much pleasure with a few words. And they were in no way a friendly gift, but merely an attempt to repay a debt. In addition to myself, my daughter and my son [Martin], there is in my close proximity still another person who appreciates your work and—I would say—who is groaning under it. This is my doctor, Max Schur, a very able physician, [who is] so deeply indignant about what is going on in Germany that he will not prescribe any German drugs.[8] I have to tell him about you again and again.[9]

Freud then commented on England's appeasement of Mussolini in the Abyssinian crisis. He foresaw that Hitler would be the *tertius gaudens,* and that Austria—including the Austrian Jews—would have to pay the price. The letter ended:

> In a few days we shall move back to our town apartment. It has been a glorious autumn. My condition is somewhat better. War or war tension may choke off all our analytic work in Vienna [2].

Toward the end of 1935 Freud was asked to write a contribution for a volume honoring Romain Rolland on his 70th birthday (January 29, 1936). A letter to Arnold Zweig gives us an important clue to Freud's motivation for choosing the topic he did: "A Disturbance of Memory on the Acropolis." Undoubtedly there was simple nostalgia:

---

[7] Arnold Zweig had long "analytic" conversations with Freud during his frequent visits. The last ones took place in London in 1938.

[8] In conjunction with the chief of my department (Dr. Julius Bauer, now in Los Angeles) I had organized a boycott of German drugs. We had drawn up a list of products—mainly Swiss, Austrian, and French—which were equivalent to the commonly used German drugs. For this reason we were *personae non gratae* with the Nazi cell in our hospital. We were certainly on a blacklist and destined for a concentration camp. What probably saved us was the fact that Bauer was the physician of a relative of Goering's, and I may have been saved, too, by the same people who eventually let Freud go. More about this later.

[9] I met Arnold Zweig in London in 1938, when he consulted me. I resumed a correspondence with him in the summer of 1963, which eventually led, in 1968, to the publication of the correspondence between Freud and him. Zweig graciously agreed to my using his letters, for which I am deeply indebted to him. He died a few weeks after their publication.

"How young I was at that time, and how wonderful it was to travel to Athens! What enthralling descriptions of Greece I've been getting from Marie Bonaparte," etc. There were certainly other determinants as well. Freud wrote to Zweig on January 20, 1936:

> I have been greatly importuned to contribute something written to Romain Rolland's 70th birthday, and I have finally yielded. I accomplished a short analysis of an "experience of derealization" which overcame me in 1904 on the Acropolis in Athens. It is something quite intimate which has hardly anything to do with R. R. (except that he is exactly the same age as my brother with whom I traveled to Athens at that time). However, put together the two old proverbs about the rascal who gives away more than he has and the beautiful girl who doesn't give more and you know my situation.

The letter to Zweig provides a link between the Rolland paper and Freud's obsessive preoccupation with the date of his death during his trip to Athens in 1904, which he had described in his 1909 letter to Jung. At a certain point the letter to Zweig begins to resemble free associations; Freud started a word, crossed it out, and continued with the remark that this analysis was "something quite intimate" and had little to do with Romain Rolland except for the fact that the latter and Freud's brother Alexander were the same age. This meant that both were "younger brothers," as were Jung (born in 1875), Fliess (who died at 70), and of course Freud's brother Julius. Moreover, Freud was getting closer to his 80th birthday, and his apprehension about this very "critical term" was to show up soon.

The last sentence of the letter quoted above is tantalizingly unclear. The "rascal" is obviously engaged in some kind of deception. The "beautiful girl" leaves one in doubt. Did she really give everything she had? What did Freud want to convey to Zweig? Did he mean to say only that this paper was all he could produce at that moment, or were the play on words and the few hints he gave in the letter a conscious or unconscious indication that he was not divulging all he knew about the incident on the Acropolis and was thus apparently giving away more in the paper than he actually was?

In the next letter to Arnold Zweig, written on February 21, 1936, Freud wrote:

> To have you here in Vienna-Grinzing[10] will be a great pleasure.—We shall forget all misery and criticism and fantasize about Moses. It need

[10] The suburb where Freud's summer home was located.

not be just at the time of my [80th] birthday; any other time is probably better. How I shall get out of all the tiring efforts that will be expected of me I do not yet know, but I shall certainly not participate. And what nonsense to try to make up for the ill-treatments of a long life by having celebrations on such a critical[11] date? No, we rather remain enemies.[12]

Old ghosts were obviously stirring as the new year approached. The numbers and their "magic" were coming back: 80 = 40 x 2 and 40 was Fliess's "critical" age. What accounted for the resurgence of the repressed but not extinguished past? Freud said in the *Moses* book which he was then working on:

> The memory-trace of . . . early experience has been preserved . . . , but in a special psychological condition. . . . What is forgotten is not extinguished but only 'repressed'; its memory-traces are present in all their freshness, but isolated by 'anticathexes'. . . . It may . . . be that certain portions of the repressed, having evaded the process [of repression], remain accessible to memory and occasionally emerge into consciousness. . . .
> The repressed retains its upward urge, its effort to force its way to consciousness. It achieves its aim . . . if the instinctual elements attaching to the repressed receive a special reinforcement . . . and . . . if at any time in recent experience impressions or experiences occur which resemble the repressed so closely that they are able to awaken it. In the last case the recent experience is reinforced by the latent energy of the repressed, and the repressed comes into operation behind the recent experience and with its help. In none of these . . . alternatives does what has hitherto been repressed enter consciousness smoothly and unaltered; it must always put up with distortions which testify to the influence of the resistance (not entirely overcome) arising from the anticathexis, or to the modifying influence of the recent experience or to both [1939, p. 94f.].

We shall see shortly how strongly Freud objected to the festivities that were being planned far ahead of time for his 80th birthday, when realistically he could not even be certain that he would live to see the day.

Surgery had been necessary more frequently in 1935, and Freud was aware of the contents of the pathology reports. Also, he was

---

11 I translated "bedenklichen Termin" as "critical date" because Freud had previously used these words in this connection.

12 Freud was referring here to the well-wishers among the official and scientific circles who had treated him with scorn and calumny during the early decades of his discoveries.

gradually approaching the age at which his father and older brother Emanuel had died—81½[13]—which he had long considered a "critical" date, and to which he referred again in a letter to Arnold Zweig, written on June 17, 1936 (see Chapter 24). Could there have been a special reinforcement of the repressed? Could the writing of the *Moses* book have contributed to this?

After he had completed *Totem and Taboo,* which dealt with the murder and eating of the father by the primal horde, Freud had felt a greater than usual letdown. In the "Acropolis" paper Freud's final interpretation was linked to the sense of guilt at having come such a long way and surpassed his father. There was even a comparison with Napoleon's coronation. I have added to this interpretation the aspect of the "guilt of the survivor" with regard to Fliess and Freud's brother, Julius, that is, the Cain complex in addition to the Oedipus complex.

Now came the essays on *Moses,* which dealt not with the murder of an anonymous, primeval father of a primal horde, but of Moses, whom Freud called "The Great Man," the man who had "created the Jews," who had renounced immortality entirely and done away with "magical abuses," who stood for the primacy of the intellect, the supremacy of the ego over raw instinctual drives. As Freud put it: "a triumph of intellectuality over sensuality or, strictly speaking, an instinctual renunciation, with all its necessary psychological consequences" (1939, p. 113).

Could Freud's old guilt also have been reinforced by the legend of Joseph's conflict with his brothers, which he mentioned in *Moses and Monotheism?*

> It might be thought that they [i.e., other nations, such as the Greeks] reacted as though they too believed in the superiority which the people of Israel claimed for themselves. If one is the declared favourite of the dreaded father [and in Freud's case, of the mother as well], one need

---

[13] Freud repeatedly referred to the fact that his father died at 81½. This would be correct, if the latter had been born, as he claimed, on April 1, 1815. The family calendar, however, gives his birth date as December 18, 1815, a date also accepted by Jones (Vol. I, p. 2).

In an unpublished letter to Fliess of August 1, 1898, Freud wrote that his father always claimed to have been born on April 1, 1815, the same day as Bismarck. Freud believed that this date came about as the result of the change to the Gregorian calendar. But there is a large discrepancy between April 1 and December 18 (the Gregorian and lunar calendar dates meet every 19 years and the differences are never greater than a few weeks). Whatever it was, the date of April 1 was obviously chosen arbitrarily. This did not interfere, however, with Freud's choice of 81½ as his next "critical age."

not be surprised at the jealousy of one's brothers and sisters, and the Jewish legend of Joseph and his brethren shows very well where this jealousy can lead [p. 106].

According to Freud's view, the problem of guilt over the "original sin," the unnamable, forgotten, repressed fact of parricide, was at the root of the vicissitudes of the Moses tradition. Acceptance of the concept of this original sin encountered greater resistance than the fact which constituted the subject matter of monotheism, namely, the fact of the existence of the primal father.

The term "original sin" was coined by the Apostle Paul. Freud said of this: "With the original sin death came into the world. In fact this crime deserving death had been the murder of the primal father who was later deified" (p. 86).

Paul thus could, according to Freud, deny the actual killing of God the father under the delusional claim that "we are freed from all guilt, since one of us sacrificed his life to absolve us." While Christian dogma ascribed the primal sin to the inherent sinfulness of men, which includes the "sin of the flesh," Freud stated that a crime which had to be atoned for by the sacrifice on the cross could only have been murder.

The guilt over the presumed murder of Moses, which led to a weakening of his teachings during the next few generations, smoldered, according to Freud, among the Jews like "a dull malaise."

Thereupon there arose from among the midst of the people an unending succession of men who were not linked to Moses in their origin but were enthralled by the great and mighty tradition which had grown up little by little in obscurity: and it was these men, the Prophets, who tirelessly preached the old Mosaic doctrine . . . the doctrines with which they re-established the old faith became the permanent content of the Jewish religion. It is honour enough to the Jewish people that they could preserve such a tradition and produce men who gave it a voice—even though the initiative to it came from outside [p. 51].

And evidence of the presence of a peculiar psychical aptitude in . . . the Jewish people is revealed by the fact that they were able to produce so many individuals prepared to take on the burdens of the religion of Moses in return for the reward of being the chosen people [p. 111].

The poor Jewish people, who with their habitual stubbornness continued to disavow the father's murder [of Moses], atoned heavily for it in the course of time. They were constantly met with the reproach 'You killed our God!' And this reproach is true, if it is correctly translated. If it is brought into relation with the history of religions, it runs: 'You will not *admit* that you murdered God (the primal picture of God, the primal father, and his later reincarnations).' There should be an addition declaring: 'We did the same thing, to be sure, but we have *admitted* it and since then we have been absolved' [p. 90].

There was no place in the framework of the religion of Moses for a direct expression of the murderous hatred of the father. All that could come to light was a mighty reaction against it—a sense of guilt on account of that hostility, a bad conscience for having sinned against God and for not ceasing to sin. This sense of guilt . . . had yet another . . . motivation. . . . Things were going badly for the people; the hopes resting on the favour of God failed in fulfilment; it was not easy to maintain the illusion, . . . of being God's chosen people. . . . a sense of guilt on account of their own sinfulness offered a welcome means of exculpating God: they deserved no better than to be punished by him since they had not obeyed his commandments. And, driven by the need to satisfy this sense of guilt, . . . they must make those command-ments grow even stricter . . . and even more trivial . . . they imposed more and more new instinctual renunciations on themselves and in that way reached—in doctrine and precept, at least—ethical heights which had remained inaccessible to the other peoples of antiquity. Many Jews regard this attainment of ethical heights as the second main characteristic and the second great achievement of their religion. The way in which it was connected with the first one—the idea of a single God—should be plain from our remarks. These ethical ideas cannot, however, disavow their origin from the sense of guilt felt on account of a suppressed hostility to God. They possess the characteristic . . . of obsessional neurotic reaction-formations; we can guess, too, that they serve the secret purposes of punishment [p. 134f.].

It is worth noticing how the new religion [Christianity] dealt with the ancient ambivalence in the relation to the father. Its main content was . . . reconciliation with God the Father, atonement for the crime com-mitted against him; but . . . the son, who had taken the atonement on himself, became a god himself beside the father and, actually, in place of the father. Christianity, having arisen out of a father-religion, be-came a son-religion. It has not escaped the fate of having to get rid of the father.

Only a portion of the Jewish people accepted the new doctrine. Those who refused to are still called Jews to-day. Owing to this cleav-age, they have become even more sharply divided from other peoples than before. . . . They were obliged to hear the new religious com-munity . . . reproach them with having murdered God. In full, this reproach would run as follows: 'They will not accept it as true that they murdered God, whereas we admit it and have been cleansed of that guilt.' It is easy therefore to see how much truth lies behind this re-proach. . . . In a certain sense, they have in that way taken a tragic load of guilt on themselves; they have been made to pay heavy penance for it [p. 136].

Thus *Moses* is replete with the old motif "Denn alle Schuld rächt sich auf Erden" ["For every sin is atoned for on this earth]" (see Chapter 6).

But the Jews also had their compensation;

> Moses . . . conveyed to the Jews an exalted sense of being a chosen people. The dematerialization of God brought a . . . valuable contribution to their secret treasure. The Jews retained their inclination to intellectual interests. The nation's political misfortune taught it to value at its true worth the one possession that remained to it—its literature. Immediately after the destruction of the Temple in Jerusalem by Titus, the Rabbi Jochanan ben Zakkai asked permission to open the first Torah school in Jabneh. From that time on, the Holy Writ and intellectual concern with it were what held the scattered people together. . . .
>
> The pre-eminence given to intellectual labours throughout some two thousand years in the life of the Jewish people has, of course, had its effect. It has helped to check the brutality and the tendency to violence which are apt to appear where the development of muscular strength is the popular ideal. Harmony in the cultivation of intellectual and physical activity, such as was achieved by the Greek people, was denied to the Jews. In this dichotomy their decision was at least in favour of the worthier alternative [p. 115].

It seems legitimate to assume that the temporary "return of the repressed" which led to the resurgence of an old conflict and led Freud to write his paper on "A Disturbance of Memory on the Acropolis," also reactivated his awareness and even slight fear of an approaching "critical" date. All this was to some extent connected with *Moses*. In turn, the whole concept of this book, over and above its scientific aspect, was part and parcel of Freud's unending search for answers to the basic questions of life and death—whence do we come and where do we go?

Throughout Freud's life Moses was one of the figures with whom he identified strongly. On every trip to Rome he spent hours in fascinated contemplation of Michelangelo's statue of Moses in the church of San Pietro in Vincoli, as he described in his paper "The Moses of Michelangelo" (1914b), first published anonymously in *Imago:*

> How often have I mounted the steep steps from the unlovely Corso Cavour to the lonely piazza where the deserted church stands, and have essayed to support the angry scorn of the hero's glance! Sometimes I have crept cautiously out of the half-gloom of the interior as though I myself belonged to the mob upon whom his eye is turned—

the mob which can hold fast no conviction, which has neither faith nor patience, and which rejoices when it has regained its illusory idols [p. 213].

In his study of this most cherished work of art, about which he was to write:[14] "My feeling for this piece of work is like that towards a loved child," Freud attempted to reinterpret the Biblical figure of Moses, arriving at the conclusion that:

> Michelangelo has placed a different Moses on the tomb of the Pope, one superior to the historical or traditional Moses. He has modified the theme of the broken Tables; he does not let Moses break them in his wrath, but makes him be influenced by the danger that they will be broken and makes him calm that wrath, or at any rate prevent it from becoming an act. In this way he has added something new and more than human to the figure of Moses; so that the giant frame with its tremendous physical power becomes only a concrete expression of the highest mental achievement that is possible in a man, that of struggling successfully against an inward passion for the sake of a cause to which he has devoted himself [p. 233].

We know that Freud began to read the Old Testament at the age of seven. We know from the Fliess correspondence that throughout the first decade of their friendship, especially during the cardiac episode, the question "Will I live long enough to see the Promised Land?" was paramount in Freud's thoughts. The nature of this Promised Land, as of many which beckon from afar, was elusive; it changed its name as it was approached, being now a solution to the riddle of the dream, now the key to the causes of neurosis, and so on.

Later Freud was like the "prophet in the desert" who was speaking for future generations. In *Moses* we find many transparent parallels to Freud's life and work. To mention only a few passages:

> We confess the belief . . . that the idea of a single god, as well as the rejection of magically effective ceremonial and the stress upon ethical demands made in his name, were in fact Mosaic doctrines . . . which, after a long interval had elapsed, . . . eventually became permanently established. How are we to explain a delayed effect of this kind and where do we meet with a similar phenomenon?
>
> It occurs to us at once that such things are not infrequently to be found . . . [and] come about in a number of ways which are understandable with greater or lesser ease. Let us take, for instance, the his-

---

[14] In a letter to Edoardo Weiss, written on April 17, 1933, on the occasion of the publication of the paper in an Italian translation (quoted in Jones, Vol. 2, p. 367).

tory of a new scientific theory, such as Darwin's theory of evolution. At
first it met with embittered rejection and was violently disputed for
decades; but it took no longer than a generation for it to be recognized
as a great step forward towards truth. Darwin himself achieved the
honour of a grave or cenotaph in Westminster Abbey. . . . The new
truth awoke emotional resistances; . . . the struggle of opinions took up
a certain length of time; from the first there were adherents and opponents; the number as well as the weight of the former kept on increasing till at last they gained the upper hand; during the whole time
of the struggle the subject with which it was concerned was never forgotten. We are scarcely surprised that the whole course of events took
a considerable length of time [p. 66f.].

More than 20 years earlier Freud had drawn the parallel between
the biological revolution initiated by Darwin and the psychological
revolution initiated by himself. A further parallel may be found in the
passages previously quoted in which Freud pointed to the triumph of
intellectuality over sensuality, the pre-eminence of intellectual achievements, and the mastery gained over brutality and violence as the
achievements brought about by the teachings of "The Great Man"
whose greatness was determined "by mental qualities," by "psychical
and intellectual distinctions."

When Freud was faced with defection and revolt among his pupils,
especially on the part of Rank, who reacted in this way to Freud's
illness, Freud frequently pointed out in conversations and letters the
parallel that existed between the sons of the primal horde and some
of his own followers who were awaiting the death of the "primal
father."

The Promised Land which Freud wanted to see now was the completed *Moses,* and this time he was facing not only a race against time
(old age and cancer), but also against uncontrollable external forces
and inner resistances. Most of this was spoken of in Freud's letters,
and now, as we have seen, it was chiefly to Arnold Zweig that Freud
was confiding his plans, hopes, fantasies, doubts, and disappointments.
I have already singled out Freud's letter to Zweig of May 8, 1932, in
which he showed a burning thirst for more knowledge, this time about
Palestine which had created "religions, sacred frenzies, attempts to
conquer the outer world of appearances [*Scheinwelt*]: by means of the
inner world of wishful thinking [*Wunschwelt*]," stressing also his own
indefinable ties to this part of his ancestors' past. This would appear
to be one of the first indications of an intensive involvement with the
Moses theme.

In this 1932 letter Freud had emphasized that—in contrast to Zweig—he had never considered himself German but rather Jewish, although he was never religious. He was also strongly opposed to any nationalistic or chauvinistic leanings. Zweig was torn between his wish to stay in Germany and to escape the obvious danger. As a writer he was further tied to his mother country by the language in which he wrote. Zweig had periodically been in analysis, and Freud, who had repeatedly advised him to leave Germany, had pointed out (in a letter of August 18, 1933) that some of Zweig's conflicts found expression in his ambivalent attitude toward being Jewish. This led to a remark which gave the first hint of the direction in which Freud's thinking was then heading. He continued: "One defends oneself in every way against the fear of castration. Here a piece of opposition to one's own Jewishness may still be hiding cunningly. Our great master Moses was, after all, a strong anti-Semite and made no secret of it. *Perhaps he really was an Egyptian*" [3] [italics added].

In speaking of the "anti-Semitism" of Moses Freud obviously had in mind the wrath which Moses unleashed against the Jews who had turned to worshiping the Golden Calf while Moses was receiving the Ten Commandments on Mt. Sinai. As we have seen in the passage quoted earlier, it was this scene which was at the core of Freud's essay on Michelangelo's Moses. "The Great Man" who was far ahead of his time became one of the main themes of Freud's book and of his own life.

It is obvious that the take-over of Germany by the Nazis, and the threat of a similar situation in Austria, contributed to Freud's interest in the Moses legend, but I, unlike Jones, believe that this was only one of the determining factors. The *Moses* book was a logical continuation of *Totem and Taboo, The Future of an Illusion,* and *Civilization and Its Discontents,* as well as part of Freud's own *final* confrontation with the "primal sin," his final step toward full serenity and the acceptance of peace in Faustian terms.

The paper on "A Disturbance of Memory on the Acropolis" was another of the episodes in this protracted struggle.

From a letter written to Arnold Zweig on September 30, 1934 we learn that Freud had then finished the first draft of his book and was considering calling it[15] *"The Man Moses: A Historical Novel* (With greater right than your novel about Nietzsche)." He ex-

---

[15] See my Introduction.

pressed doubts about the validity of his historical conclusions and voiced the fear that the publication of the last—and principal—part of the book might jeopardize the position of psychoanalysis in Austria. This fear was again expressed in a prefatory note to Part III of *Moses,* written at a time when Freud was uncertain whether he would be able to publish this section (after the first two parts had already been published in 1937). Freud had ended the second essay with the following statement:

> What the real nature of a tradition resides in, and what its special power rests on, how impossible it is to dispute the personal influence upon world-history of individual great men, what sacrilege one commits against the splendid diversity of human life if one recognizes only those motives which arise from material needs, from what sources some ideas (and particularly religious ones) derive their power to subject both men and peoples to their yoke—to study all this in the special case of Jewish history would be an alluring task. To continue my work on such lines as these would be to find a link with the statements I put forward twenty-five years ago in *Totem and Taboo* [1912-1913]. But I no longer feel that I have the strength to do so [p. 52f.].

In the prefatory note to Part III he said:

> With the audacity of one who has little or nothing to lose, I propose for a second time to break a well-grounded intention and to add to my two essays on Moses in *Imago* the final portion which I have held back. I ended the last essay with an assertion that I knew my strength would not be enough for this. By that I meant, of course, the weakening of creative powers which goes along with old age. [Footnote: I do not share the opinion of my contemporary Bernard Shaw, that human beings would only achieve anything good if they could live to be three hundred years old. A prolongation of life would achieve nothing unless many other fundamental changes were to be made in the conditions of life.] . . .
>
> We are living here in a Catholic country under the protection of that Church, uncertain how long that protection will hold out. But so long as it lasts, we naturally hesitate to do anything that would be bound to arouse the Church's hostility. This is not cowardice, but prudence. The new enemy, to whom we want to avoid being of service, is more dangerous than the old one with whom we have already learnt to come to terms. The psycho-analytic researches which we carry on are in any case viewed with suspicious attention by Catholicism. I will not maintain that this is unjustly so. If our work leads us to a conclusion which reduces religion to a neurosis of humanity and explains its enormous power in the same way as a neurotic compulsion in our individual

patients, we may be sure of drawing the resentment of our ruling powers down upon us. Not that I should have anything to say that would be new or that I did not say clearly a quarter of a century ago: but it has been forgotten in the meantime and it could not be without effect if I repeated it to-day and illustrated it from an example which offers a standard for all religious foundations. It would probably lead to our being prohibited from practising psycho-analysis. Such violent methods of suppression are, indeed, by no means alien to the Church; the fact is rather that it feels it as an invasion of its privileges if someone else makes use of those methods. But psycho-analysis, which in the course of my long life has gone everywhere, still possesses no home that could be more valuable for it than the city in which it was born and grew up.

I do not think but I *know* that I shall let myself be deterred by this second obstacle, by the external danger, from publishing the last portion of my study on Moses [p. 54f.].

In the letter to Zweig, Freud was more explicit. His fear was centered around the person of a certain Pater Schmidt, who had great influence on the Austrian Catholic hierarchy and apparently on the Pope as well. Schmidt was interested in anthropology, and was highly critical of Freud's thinking in such works as *Totem and Taboo*.

It would be idle to speculate on the validity of Freud's fears. One has the impression, however, that they may have represented an external reinforcement of Freud's inner doubts (see letter to Arnold Zweig, December 16, 1934).

In his letter to Zweig of February 13, 1935 Freud had said simply:

My own *Moses* cannot be helped. If you come to Vienna again one day, you are welcome to read this manuscript which has been put aside to confirm my opinion.

Yet on May 2, 1935 Freud had written to Zweig:

Moses will not let go of my imagination. I picture myself reading it out loud to you when you come to Vienna, despite my defective speech.

Zweig, Eitingon, and others were continually feeding Freud with information for his book. Late in 1935 Zweig reported to Freud that a "reliable source" had apparently received word from a certain Professor Smith of the Rockefeller Museum in Luxor that, in the course of a recent excavation, a clay tablet had been unearthed bearing the names of the students of the Temple of Re-Aton in Heliopolis, among them Moses and Aaron. Freud demonstrated his critical judgment and knowledge in the same letter to Arnold Zweig (January 20, 1936) in which he reported on his paper for the Romain Rolland volume:

> Dear Master Arnold,
> Just received your information; am pleased that you show so much interest in this subject. It would seem, then, that the assertions of your "poet" ["Dichter"] do not all come out of thin air, but rest on solid ground in certain places. Luxor exists, so do Rockefeller grants, and even a Professor Smith. But one point which occurred to me only later, and which devalues all expectations, is the following: If such a list of the students of the Sun-Temple of On (?) was found in Amarna, it could not possibly be on clay tablets in cuneiform script. It would have to be a papyrus with hieroglyphics. Cuneiform writing was used only in correspondence sent abroad. Thus, this call holds little hope of awakening my Moses from the sleep which is his destiny.

Here we see disappointment mingled with the gratification of a thorough researcher who cannot be fooled, all of which Freud depicted with a delightful, gentle irony.

These letters reflect the ups and downs through which Freud was going during those years when the *Moses* book had become part of his life and struggles, blending with all his other interests, his health, and his human relations.

One further aspect of the *Moses* book calls for special discussion here: never had Freud insisted with greater conviction and more emphasis on the inheritance of acquired characteristics in the form of "inherited tradition," the "survival of memory traces in the archaic heritage," the assertion that "men have always known that they once possessed a primal father and killed him" (p. 99ff.).

Freud knew full well that his position was "made more difficult by the present attitude of biological science, which refuses to hear of inheritance of acquired characters by succeeding generations." Freud's method of reasoning in this context was an unusual one. He said:

> If we assume the survival of these memory-traces in the archaic heritage, we have bridged the gulf between individual and group psychology: we can deal with peoples as we do with an individual neurotic. Granted that at the time we have no stronger evidence for the presence of memory-traces in the archaic heritage than the residual phenomena of the work of analysis which call for a phylogenetic derivation, yet this evidence seems to us strong enough to postulate that such is the fact. If it is not so, we shall not advance a step further along the path we entered on, either in analysis or in group psychology. The audacity cannot be avoided

And by this assumption we are effecting something else. We are diminishing the gulf which earlier periods of human arrogance had torn too wide apart between mankind and the animals. If any explanation is to be found of what are called the instincts of animals, which allow them to behave from the first in a new situation in life as though it were an old and familiar one—if any explanation at all is to be found of this instinctive life of animals, it can only be that they bring the experiences of their species with them into their own new existence—that is, that they have preserved memories of what was experienced by their ancestors. The position in the human animal would not at bottom be different. His own archaic heritage corresponds to the instincts of animals even though it is different in its compass and contents [p. 100].

In other words, he was claiming that because this hypothesis supplied a bridge between individual and group psychology and provided an explanation for the genesis of monotheism, it was a valid one.

Why did Freud not heed his own reasoning when he said:

The immediate and most certain answer is that it consists in certain [innate] dispositions such as are characteristic of all living organisms: in the capacity and tendency, that is, to enter particular lines of development and to react in a particular manner to certain excitations, impressions and stimuli. Since experience shows that there are distinctions in this respect between individuals of the human species, the archaic heritage must include these distinctions; they represent what we recognize as the *constitutional* factor in the individual. Now, since all human beings, at all events in their early days, have approximately the same experiences, they react to them, too, in a similar manner; a doubt was therefore able to arise whether we should not include these reactions, along with their individual distinctions, in the archaic heritage. This doubt should be put on one side: our knowledge of the archaic heritage is not enlarged by the fact of this similarity [p. 98].

In his own clinical experience Freud had seen again and again that virtually no human being failed to encounter in the course of his development the kind of situation which generated typical oedipal conflicts. Moreover, once he had discovered the importance of aggression and the inevitable ambivalence conflicts, Freud knew that every child had occasional murderous impulses not only toward his father but toward his mother and siblings as well; that guilt feelings arose not just from deeds but from thoughts, too, since on the level of psychic reality a thought may equal a deed. Freud himself raised—and rejected—two possible objections to these claims:

First, under what conditions does a memory of this kind enter the archaic heritage? And, secondly, in what circumstances can it become active—that is, can it advance to consciousness from its unconscious state in the id, even though in an altered and distorted shape? The answer to the first question is easy to formulate: the memory enters the archaic heritage if the event was important enough, or repeated often enough, or both. In the case of parricide both conditions are fulfilled. On the second question there is this to be said. A whole number of influences may be concerned, not all of which are necessarily known. A spontaneous development is also conceivable, on the analogy of what happens in some neuroses. What is certainly of decisive importance, however, is the awakening of the forgotten memory-trace by a recent real repetition of the event. The murder of Moses was a repetition of this kind and, later, the supposed judicial murder of Christ: so that these events come into the foreground as causes. It seems as though the genesis of monotheism could not do without these occurrences [p. 101].

Again we might ask why Freud needed this additional explanation of the archaic heritage? Murder, including parricide, was certainly rampant and already regarded as "sinful" in most cultures of the time of Moses. The crucifixion of Christ was immediately taken up into the oral and written tradition. It is true that the murder of Moses, if it ever occurred, may have been repressed, but Freud himself had supplied ample and convincing examples of the longevity of traditions which had extended and been embellished over generations. Hypothesizing the existence of such a repressed and revived memory did not necessarily entail the assumption of an archaic heritage. Yet Freud stubbornly adhered to this assumption. Jones was not alone in trying to convince him of its fallaciousness. At least one of the editors of *Imago*, Ernst Kris, tried to dissuade Freud from making such a claim, but to no avail.[16]

Nor does Freud's comparison of this archaic heritage with animal instincts stand up under scrutiny. What the adherents to the "instinct" concept call "instinctive behavior patterns" are species-typical responses to certain stimuli, the propensity to which is transmitted by the genetic code (see Schur, 1966b; Schur and Ritvo, 1970a). However, we cannot equate the "memory" of the genetic code, which guarantees such things as the maintenance of an optimal pH level in the blood and tissues, with memories of historical events.

We are reminded here of the type of reasoning which characterized *Beyond the Pleasure Principle*. There is a significant difference between the clear-thinking Freud who could invalidate immediately the "proof" of the genuineness of some inscription on a clay tablet and the

16 Personal communication.

Freud who made such *ex cathedra* statements as: "I have no hesitation in declaring that men have always known that they once possessed a primal father and killed him."

We must suspect that in this book, as in *Beyond the Pleasure Principle,* some of Freud's formulations arose out of inner conflicts, the existence of which he continually referred to throughout the period during which he was writing the *Moses* book. We can only speculate here as to why these particular formulations were chosen and, following Freud's example, ask *"Cui bono?"*—what psychic agency profits thereby? The only answer would seem to be that if man's guilt feelings about parricide were a response to an archaic heritage dating back to primeval times when parricide was still frequent, this would mean that a great distance existed between the feelings and the deed. We would then be able to say: "It is those long-gone ancestors who did the deed. We are merely repeating some fantasies in an attenuated way." This would be a different method of coming to terms with the "primal sin" from the one attributed by Freud to the Apostle Paul. It would be another aspect of Freud's struggle to come to terms with his own "primal sin."[17]

In his last work, the posthumously published *An Outline of Psycho-Analysis* (1940), Freud was more careful in his use of the concept of an "archaic heritage." Only in a footnote to his discussion of the castration complex did Freud come back to it by saying:

> The possibility cannot be excluded that a phylogenetic memory-trace may contribute to the extraordinarily terrifying effect of the threat—a memory-trace from the prehistory of the primal family, when the jealous father actually robbed his son of his genitals if the latter became troublesome to him as a rival with a woman [p. 190].

My discussion of Freud's dilemma concerning the "archaic heritage" was written before I learned about the recent publication by Sajner (see Chapter 1). I left it unchanged, because Freud evidenced in these passages of the *Moses* book more than in any of his previous discussions of this and similar concepts the intensity of his inner con-

---

[17] An ingenious speculation about Freud's adherence to the concept of the transmission of acquired characteristics has been offered by J. D. Benjamin (1961). Freud was always impressed by the role of experiential factors in normal and abnormal development. On the one hand he thus made formulations and assumptions about the universality of certain innate givens, while on the other he displaced to a certain extent the role of highly specific experience from the ontogenetic to the phylogenetic domain. If the innate *also* was a precipitate of the historical experiential, then the distinction between innate and experiential became less crucial.

flict. I have expressed earlier in the book my assumption that Freud's stubborn adherence to the hypotheses of the inheritance of acquired characteristics, of the "primal fantasies," as he called them in *Introductory Lectures* (1916-1917) and in "From the History of an Infantile Neurosis" (1918), and of archaic heritage were all rooted in his own "prehistoric" times: his first 3 years in Freiberg, where he lived in a one-room apartment and where he and two of his siblings were born. Being unable to reconstruct these events completely, he had to create maximum distance. And yet he did it with a maximum of ingenuity, which makes one regret not to be able to follow him in this flight of imagination.

In pointing out flaws of this kind in Freud's thinking, I am of course not questioning his genius. It is not impossible that one day he may prove to have been right in the matter of the transmission of acquired characteristics, which do not, of course, include mutations. Since 1951 the geneticist Roger I. Williams has been interested in individual differences between animals with very similar genetic background. Modern genetic thought holds that inherited traits are bound in DNA, and that this structure exists only within the nucleus of the cell.

Recent work, especially by Williams and Storrs (1968) suggests that heredity may be affected by cytoplastic components other than DNA. This would apply to animals with highly differentiated cells, and suggest that genetic transmission in complex living structures *may* be different from the presently accepted model, which has been established on single cell living structures. What bearing such findings may have on the transmission of acquired characteristics is for the time being a moot question.

Another line of research in genetics is concerned with "neutral mutations" and "genetic drift." It seems that such genetic changes as are manifested on the molecular level of various proteins are more frequent than had previously been assumed. Little is known about the causation of such changes and their consequences (King and Jakes, 1969). But such transmissible characteristics could not include specific memories, such as castration or the murder of the primal father.

24

FREUD'S EIGHTIETH BIRTHDAY

Around Christmas of 1935 I observed a wartlike lesion which had grown quite fast and worried me greatly. It was extensively coagulated on January 16, 1936. In his letter to Arnold Zweig (January 20, 1936) Freud remarked:

> As a consequence of a "small" surgical procedure performed recently on my mouth I can now neither chew nor speak properly. *I can wait until it gets better* [italics added].

My own and Pichler's notes show how much was summed up in this simple sentence. For weeks Freud had pain and could not keep the lower prosthesis in. The following note of Pichler's is very revealing both of Freud's suffering and the attitude of this *homo surgicus,* who was kind and gentle but of an unflinching thoroughness without which he could not have done all he did.

> January 24: Patient felt relatively well for 1-2 days, as always after surgery. Then a more severe lockjaw set in which has now subsided. Unfortunately he had taken the lower prosthesis out and now cannot get it back in. An attempt made after prolonged stretching nearly succeeded. Therefore took the prosthesis along to file it down. The wound is covered by secretion; it is actually larger than expected, which suggests thorough coagulation. Removed a necrotic piece of tissue. Reminder: Under all circumstances the lower prosthesis must be put in as soon as it is at all possible; otherwise patient must come immediately to the office.

In February of 1936 we noticed a leukoplakia about which Pichler wrote on February 20: "This doesn't look good. It will have to be removed." But there were also crust formations and keratotic lesions which Pichler treated first with ointments and cauterization with trichloracetic acid before he operated on the leukoplakia on March 10. Pichler's entry about this operation ended: "It was probably sufficient to have destroyed the entire mucous membrane. The delineation is not quite sharp, however, and it is possible that something was left at the edge." After this we ardently hoped for some quiet weeks, especially around Freud's 80th birthday. He had been having some cardiac symptoms since the previous surgery, which finally subsided after he refrained from smoking for several weeks.

Freud was of course well aware of the preparations being made for his 80th birthday. Jones, who at that time was president of the International Psycho-Analytical Association, had suggested a *Festschrift,* which would have had to be planned a year in advance. Freud got wind of this and protested energetically. The correspondence between Freud and Jones (Vol. 3, p. 200f.) is very revealing of Freud's attitude toward such festivities. It showed, moreover, that he did not wish to be reminded a year ahead of time about this "ominous" date.

At first Freud suggested as a compromise an album of pictures of all the members of the International Psycho-Analytical Association, but then rejected this idea too. He settled the question, at least as far as the Association was concerned, in the following letter written to Jones on July 21, 1935:

So let us bury the *Gedenkbuch* or *Sammelband,* etc. I turn to my own suggestion of an album and confess that now it pleases me just as little; indeed it fundamentally displeases me. Leaving aside the two objections that it would mean a deal of trouble and bring me no guarantee that I live to the date, now I am taking umbrage at the aesthetic monstrosity of 400 pictures of mostly ugly people of whom I don't at all know the half and of whom a good number do not want to know anything of me. No, the times are not suited to a festival, *'intra Iliacos muros nec extra.'* The only possible thing seems to me to renounce any action in common. Whoever feels that he must congratulate me let him do so, and who does not need not fear my vengeance.

There is still another argument. What is the secret meaning of this celebrating the big round numbers of one's life? Surely a measure of triumph over the transitoriness of life, which, as we never forget, is ready to devour us. Then one rejoices with a sort of communal feeling that we are not made of such frail stuff as to prevent one of us victoriously resisting the hostile effects of life for 60, 70 or even 80 years.

That one can understand and agree with, but the celebration evidently has sense only when the survivor can in spite of all wounds and scars join in as a hale fellow; it loses this sense when he is an invalid with whom there is no question of conviviality. And since the latter is my case and I bear my fate by myself I should prefer my 80th birthday to be treated as my private affair—by my friends.

Freud knew, however, that he could not prevent other celebrations of this occasion, and he felt the whole thing to be a "lästige Drohung" —"an annoying threat"—as he put it in a letter to Marie Bonaparte (March 11, 1936), written only a day after the quite extensive surgery of March 10th. In it Freud assured Marie Bonaparte that he was feeling and working well.

There followed weeks of intense pain, and even more gloom, certainly not the mood for a forthcoming celebration. The only thing Freud was looking forward to with pleasure was the opening of the new building which was to house the Psychoanalytic Institute and the Verlag.

An especially characteristic letter of this period was one written to Marie Bonaparte on March 26, 1936. Freud committed what he considered a "noteworthy blunder" by making an error in addressing the envelope, which he noticed and corrected,[1] and by having to cross out a word in the text. In reply to her question whether she should come to Vienna for the birthday celebration, he wrote:

> Whether you should come here for May 6th? I would certainly be very pleased; but it would only be an act of piety. We wouldn't get anything out of it. I assume that many will come, Eitingon, Jones, Laforgue, Landauer, among others. Everyone will expect something from me, and I shall not be capable of doing it. Lately there has been a distinct decline in my general condition. Yesterday I had a severe migraine, quite unusual for me,[2] and today I am still doing all kinds of confused things, as you will have noticed from the letter and the address. I am more irritable and more sensitive to bad news than I normally am. Yesterday Minna was operated on for bilateral glaucoma; she kept it a secret to the last minute. We hope for good results.
>
> From Leipzig comes the news that the Gestapo has confiscated a large proportion of the psychoanalytic books in stock at Volkmar's, almost a catastrophe for the poor Verlag [1].

[1] The address on the envelope read: Paris XVI, 6 rue Adolphe-Yvon, which Freud corrected to: rue Yvon-Adolphe. Because Freud referred to this error in his letter, Marie Bonaparte kept the envelope.

[2] Freud was forgetting for the moment the important role which his migraine headaches had played during the Fliess period.

Such was the prelude to the celebration! The constant delicate balancing between the ability to enjoy it all and the desire for peace.

Congratulations began coming in early, one of the earliest being a letter from Albert Einstein, which Freud answered immediately on May 3, 1936 (see L. 283*).

I went to see him early in the morning on his birthday. It was a beautiful spring day, the house was full of flowers—the orchids and gardenias he especially loved—as well as letters and telegrams from all over the world. A scroll bearing an address written by Thomas Mann and Stefan Zweig had arrived, its list of signers reading like a *Who's Who* of the literary, artistic, and scientific worlds. Thomas Mann had also sent a handwritten manuscript of the speech he was going to deliver in tribute to Freud on May 8. Freud opened it eagerly, but we discovered that Mann's handwriting was illegible. We tried to decipher the first few sentences, but had to give up.

After all his protestations, Freud enjoyed the whole affair! He was in great form, charming and gracious. We tried, of course, to keep the number of visitors to a minimum, and to see to it that no one stayed too long.

For the first time Freud had to resort to printed "Thank you" notes to answer the flood of birthday congratulations. However, he did not fail to add to very many of them a few individual words. My wife and I had brought our little boy—then three years old—to visit Freud and present him with some flowers on behalf of himself and his six-month-old sister. Freud sent each of the children a "thank you" card, adding: "Touched by so much courtesy at such a tender age." That Freud could derive pleasure from young and old and express it so easily in a brief sentence kept the balance on the side of living.

To some people Freud sent first a note of thanks and then a special letter. One of the most beautiful of these was written to a former woman patient, who was among the foremost American avant-garde poets. She published under the name H. D. (Hilda Doolittle).[3] Freud's letter to her was in response to her birthday wishes and a beautiful bouquet of white gardenias.

---

[3] In 1956, on the occasion of the centenary of Freud's birth, she wrote a most poetic and moving book entitled *Tribute to Freud,* including several of Freud's letters to her. After its publication, I carried on a correspondence with her in which she graciously continued the "free associations" which had provided the style and content of her book. We planned to meet (she spent her last years in Switzerland), but her untimely death intervened before we could do so.

May 24, 1936

Dear H. D.,

All your white cattle [gardenias] safely arrived, lived, and adorned the room up to yesterday.

I had imagined I had become insensitive to praise and blame. Reading your kind lines and getting aware of how I enjoyed them, I first thought I had been mistaken about my firmness. Yet on second thought I concluded I was not. What you gave me, was not praise, was affection, and I need not be ashamed of my satisfaction.

Life at my age is not easy, but spring is beautiful and so is love.

Yours affectionately,
Freud

Two addresses in honor of Freud were arranged by the *Akademischer Verein für Medizinische Psychologie,* an organization formed by a group of intelligent young doctors, mainly psychiatrists. The first was given by Freud's old friend Ludwig Binswanger, but the main event was Thomas Mann's speech. This was more than an address in honor of a single person. At that time the atmosphere in Vienna had become unbearably tense; demonstrations, bomb explosions were daily occurrences. The general topic of conversation in Vienna was "When will it happen? When and where should we emigrate?" On my way to the lecture hall I passed a group of marching Brown Shirts. Thomas Mann's address was thus a tribute not only to Freud but to the power of the spirit, to the rights of the individual, to the *wissenschaftliche Weltanschauung*—a ringing challenge to the forces of unreason and evil. Mann, who usually was rather detached and distant as a reader or speaker, rose to the occasion in the delivery of his address as well as in its content. It was a deeply moving experience for everyone present, giving us the feeling, which was rare in those days, that all was not yet lost.

I regretted that Freud could not hear the speech. At the reception which followed, I approached Mann and explained to him why Freud could not be present. I asked whether he would be willing to read the speech to Freud personally. Mann accepted gladly.

This meeting, which took place in Freud's summer residence on June 14, 1936, was an unforgettable experience for me. As it was I who had brought about the meeting, my wife and I were invited to be present, along with Freud's family and Mrs. Mann.

With obvious emotion Mann read the speech, which in the meantime he had given in several other places, all, of course, outside Germany. Freud, who never liked to listen to praise of himself, was this time profoundly impressed. (He commented on it soon afterward to Arnold Zweig and Marie Bonaparte.) It was to him a summary of his life's work, a vindication for the years of calumny and misunderstanding he had endured, and a confirmation that it really had been worthwhile to have lived that long.

At tea and afterward, Freud and Mann engaged in a long and fascinating conversation, mainly about Joseph and Moses (Mann was then writing his *Joseph* tetralogy, and Freud, of course, was preoccupied with his *Moses*). Freud and Mann were poles apart in looks, behavior, and even attire. Freud, the Jew who had absorbed the good aspects of Viennese culture and civilization, and Mann, the typical North German, in some ways as stiff as the collar he was wearing, could speak the same language. For Freud it was no surprise that this vindication should have come from a man of letters. After the meeting he spoke about Mann, expressing not for the first time the realization that poets knew intuitively so many things which he had had to learn the hard way.[4]

Freud harbored no illusions that psychoanalysis had achieved general acceptance at that time. He was fully aware, as shown by his letters, that the University of Vienna and the Minister of Education had only grudgingly acknowledged his 80th birthday. He wrote to Arnold Zweig on May 31, 1936:

> The Minister of Education sent a formal message of polite congratulation, whereupon the newspapers were forbidden on pain of confiscation to publish this act of sympathy within the country. In addition foreign and domestic newspapers printed numerous articles expressing repudiation and hatred. Thus one could declare with satisfaction that sincerity has yet not disappeared completely from the world.
>
> For me this date naturally marks no epoch; I am the same as I was before [L. 285*].

In another letter (June 17, 1936) to Arnold Zweig, Freud expressed satisfaction about the fact that Zweig had abandoned the idea of writing a biography of him, and also turned down the suggestion that he write an autobiography, adding: "I am well aware of my privileged destiny as innovator." He then went on:

---

[4] Freud expressed a similar appreciation of Arthur Schnitzler, Richard Beer-Hoffman, Stefan Zweig, and more particularly of Arnold Zweig when we talked about them later in London. This was one of the reasons why Stefan Zweig, who was then living in London, was asked to speak at Freud's funeral.

Thomas Mann, who has delivered his lecture about me five or six times in various places, was kind enough to repeat it for me personally on Sunday the 14th at my summer home in Grinzing. It was a great pleasure for me and [those of] mine who were present. A noble *goy!*[5] It's nice to know that these, too, exist. One is apt to doubt it sometimes.

I can understand, but for reasons of principle do not like to hear about, the postponement of your trip to Europe. My father and brother Emanuel lived *only* to the age of 81 and a half [italics added].

This was the first mention of a new "critical" age since Freud had referred to it in a letter to Abraham in 1915 ("Both my father and half-brother lived to be 81, so my prospect is gloomy.") (See Chapter 3.) I have already discussed the fact that even Freud himself did not know exactly when his father was born (see Chapter 23). Furthermore, the word "only" is meaningful, as is the fact that his brother died not from natural causes but in a railway accident.

It is noteworthy that Freud was no longer speaking of such "deadlines" as an obsessive superstitious idea, or the expression of a partly unconscious conflict. It was no longer a question of guilt about living longer than father or brother. Rather, the struggle was between the wish to live and the wish "not to survive oneself," as Freud had put it decades earlier in a letter to Fliess in connection with the death of the surgeon Billroth (see Chapter 2). He expressed such thoughts in a letter to Stefan Zweig on May 18, 1936:

The beautiful address which you and Thomas Mann composed together and Mann's speech in Vienna were the two events which almost reconcile me to having grown so old. For, although I have been exceptionally happy in my home, with my wife and children . . ., I nevertheless cannot reconcile myself to the wretchedness and helplessness of old age, and look forward with a kind of longing to the transition into nonexistence. Whatever happens, I am unable to spare my loved ones the pain of separation [L. 284*].

He repeated the same ideas even more eloquently later on. It is therefore understandable that Freud should have reacted with complete composure to the turn which his illness took shortly after the above letter to Stefan Zweig.

[5] The Yiddish word for Gentile. In the published correspondence between Freud and Zweig the last two lines were omitted. Freud wrote: "Ein edler Goi! Schön dass es auch das giebt. Man könnte manchmal zweifeln." Freud had in mind, of course, the German *goyim*. That he had no prejudice against non-Jews is evident from his correspondence with Pfister, Binswanger, Marie Bonaparte, Lou Andreas-Salomé, Romain Rolland, Jones, and many others; and from his relationship with Pichler.

25

CANCER STRIKES AGAIN

It had been a beautiful spring and Freud was enjoying the lovely garden. For a few weeks his condition was quite bearable. Then early in July, 1936, I observed the quite rapid development of an ugly-looking lesion close to the area operated on in March. We called Pichler, and he, too, was alarmed. He operated the following day (July 14). On July 16, we got the report from Erdheim that this time it was definitely a malignancy. Pichler and Erdheim studied all the slides of the excised specimen for hours. Because in one area the malignant tissue reached close to the edge, Pichler decided on another operation, for which he was prepared to use general anesthesia if necessary. This took place on July 18. Pichler had hoped that an electrocoagulation would be sufficient. He therefore began the operation under local and regional block anesthesia, but had to stop several times because Freud's pain was unbearable. Finally nitrous oxide was administered as a general anesthetic. Pichler had to remove another part of the underlying bone and extensively coagulate all the surrounding tissue.

Freud was brought home only 2 days after the surgery. There was not as much pain as we had feared, but much weakness and great fatigue. Pichler's note read:

July 20, 1936: Visit to Grinzing. No pain but bad mood [small wonder!]. Discomfort in talking. Several weak spells. Must rest for two more days.
July 27: Patient is complaining of poor smoking and speech, which will be corrected [by adjustment of the prosthesis].

Freud then had two comparatively comfortable months. During Pichler's vacation the latter's assistant, Dr. Berg, took care of Freud's mouth. He was a simple, stout, cheerful man, with unusually gentle and skillful hands, who managed to clean a wound or remove necrotic material without causing pain.

I, of course, kept my promise and told Freud the truth—that this time, 13 years after the first malignancy, the diagnosis was once again cancer. Freud received the information without any visible emotion. Nonetheless he reacted with no less pessimism than Pichler and myself. This had again been radical surgery. We could be as sure as it was reasonable to be under the circumstances that *this* lesion had been removed. The frightening factor was that now each new lesion had a tendency to grow fast and be potentially malignant. Our vigil had to be even more strict.

The recurrence of the cancer meant to Freud giving up one more illusion. In 1926 he had still been able to write to Binswanger that he shared the latter's fate because the neoplasm had not recurred (see Chapter 13). Now this hope was gone. With it had also gone the hope that *Ananke* would spare him the misery of a slow and painful end through a sudden cardiac death.

The political situation in Austria was deteriorating steadily, while the appeasement policy of the Western powers was becoming ever more apparent.

And yet that summer Freud was not depressed. He sustained his interest in *Moses* while recovering from the cancer surgery. Marie Bonaparte kept sending him fascinating reports about her visit to South America, including a trip up the Amazon River. He was somewhat wistful about all this, and also slightly amused and glad that she could still live on a sheltered island and be full of youthful curiosity. He showed me some of her descriptions, saying that in a sense she was following the voyage of the "Beagle."

On October 27, Freud had a severe nosebleed requiring a 24-hour packing of the nose. As usual, he had a bad winter cold. November and December are months of rain and sleet in Vienna, and a visit to Pichler on November 25 was Freud's only outing. In addition, the *Moses* book had run into some difficulties. The following exchange of letters with Marie Bonaparte is most revealing of Freud's mood. Freud wrote on December 1, 1936:

> For the last few days I have been suffering from the spread of my chronic catarrh to the trachea and the bronchi. Actually nothing serious, but with every illness new signs of the deterioration of old age push themselves forward. One can acknowledge this as unavoidable

and cannot demand an ounce of sympathy for it. 81½ was the limit of life which my father and brother reached. I am still lacking one more year until then.

P.S. If you are omnipotent, make the museum [in Athens, where she was staying] give you one of the Korxi, for me! [1].

Marie Bonaparte, somewhat perturbed, answered this letter on December 4, "scolding" Freud mildly for "superstitiousness," and even quoting analytic examples of identification with the father. She added:

Why shouldn't you live any longer? And remain productive? You also carry the heredity of your mother, who did so.[1]

Freud answered on December 6:

. . . if you, at the youthful age of fifty-four, can't help thinking so often of death, are you surprised that at 80½ I keep brooding on whether I shall reach the age of my father and brother, or even that of my mother, tortured as I am by the conflict between the desire for rest, the dread of renewed suffering (which a prolongation of life would bring with it) and the anticipation of sorrow at being separated from everything to which I am still attached? [L. 288*].

Marie Bonaparte made the following notation for herself at the bottom of this letter:

Notebook V, October 22, 1925
M.: How beautiful everything is that you say, but how sad!
Fr.: Why sad? That's what life is. It is precisely the eternal transitoriness which makes life so beautiful.[2]

Five days later, Freud had further surgery. It was after the first hour of this operation that Freud so surprised Pichler by protesting, "Ich kann nicht mehr weiter" (see Chapter 18). Since the adrenalin had been omitted, the local anesthesia had not taken full effect and had not lasted long enough, as the procedure was lengthy. Yet this was one of the few occasions when Freud reached the limit of his endurance. Only a man "without nerves" could have proceeded, as Pichler did, under such circumstances. His notes on the episode read:

---

[1] Freud's mother died at the age of 95.
[2] Freud had expressed similar thoughts in his 1916 essay "On Transience" (see Chapter 11).

December 12, 1936: . . . At the beginning patient had no pain whatsoever, but toward the end he said that he could not stand any more, although it is hard to tell just why.

This, incidentally, was the last specimen examined by Erdheim, who died shortly thereafter.

The operation was followed by two miserable weeks. Freud could not eat, smoke, or open his mouth. Short-wave treatments given at home with a portable machine (at that time a big innovation) brought some relief. Yet on December 21, 1936, Freud wrote to Marie Bonaparte, in answer to one of her letters containing an interpretation of something which had occurred in her analysis:

Superb! It must have been just the way you understood it. My comprehension was paralyzed by my preoccupation with the cancer.

At the end of 1936, Freud received news from Marie Bonaparte which was completely unexpected and deeply disturbing. The exchange of letters between them demonstrates Freud's discretion, sensitivity to encroachments on his privacy, and a combination of personal humility and insight into the probable historical development of psychoanalysis. Marie Bonaparte wrote on December 30, 1936:

Today a Mr. Stahl from Berlin came to see me. He has obtained from Fliess's widow your letters and manuscripts belonging to Fliess's estate. At first the widow wanted to deposit the whole thing in the National Library of Prussia, but as your works have been burned in Germany, she gave up the idea and sold the manuscripts in question to this Mr. Stahl, a writer and art dealer, who makes a very favorable personal impression. He apparently has had offers from America for this collection of your writings, but before letting these valuable documents go to America, he approached me, and I decided to buy them all from him. He even reduced the price so that it could all stay in Europe and in my hands—12,000 francs [$480] all told for 250 letters from you (several from Breuer) and a large number of very long theoretical drafts in your hand. . . .

Freud's answer of January 3, 1937 was an exercise in self-discipline. He first wrote a long paragraph discussing Marie Bonaparte's health, and then reported about his own health and the aftereffects of the last surgery, remarking: "In order to find all of this bearable, one must remind oneself constantly that one really has no right to be living any longer." Only then did he turn to the subject of the letters.

The matter of the correspondence with Fliess has stirred me deeply. After his death the widow requested the return of his letters to me and I agreed without question, but was unable to find them. I don't know till this very day whether I destroyed them, or only hid them ingeniously. . . . Our correspondence was of the most intimate nature, as you can surmise. It would have been most painful to have it fall into the hands of strangers. It is therefore an extraordinary labor of love that you have gotten hold of them and removed them from danger. I only regret the expense you've incurred. May I offer to share half of it with you? I would have had to acquire the letters myself if the man had approached me directly. I don't want any of them to become known to so-called posterity. . . .

Marie Bonaparte told me at our last meeting in St. Tropez in the summer of 1961 how extremely difficult it had been for her to act against the wishes of her beloved teacher-father, but she had been absolutely determined to save this material for posterity. How right she was!

Accordingly, she wrote Freud on January 7, presenting her (and our) case in the most brilliant and frank way.

Mr. Stahl has just delivered to me the first part of the Fliess papers: scientific essays scattered through your letters, which he has collected separately. The rest, the letters themselves, of which there are about 200 to 250, are still in Germany, and he will ask someone to bring them to Paris in a few weeks.

The letters and manuscripts have been offered to me on condition that I not sell them, either directly or indirectly, to the Freud family, for fear that this material, which is so important for the history of psychoanalysis, will be destroyed. This would not be a decisive reason for me not to discuss the matter with you. But you will not be surprised, as you know my ideas and feelings on the subject, that I *personally* have an immense aversion to any destruction of your letters and manuscripts.

Perhaps you yourself . . . do not perceive your full greatness. You belong to the history of human thought, like Plato, shall we say, or Goethe. What a loss it would have been for us, their poor posterity, if Goethe's conversations with Eckermann had been destroyed, or the *Dialogues* of Plato. . . .

In your letters there could be nothing . . ., if I know you, that could lower your stature. And you yourself . . . have written a beautiful paper opposing the idealization at any cost of great men, mankind's great father figures. Furthermore, if I predict correctly, some of the history of psychoanalysis, that unique new science which is your creation, and which is more important than even Plato's theory of ideas, would be lost if all of the material were destroyed because of a few personal remarks contained in these letters.

My idea was the following: to acquire the letters and thereby prevent them from being published by just anyone, and to keep them for years, e.g., in some government library—say Geneva, where one needs to be less afraid of the dangers of wars and revolutions—with the proviso that they not be looked at for 80 or 100 years after your death. Who could be hurt then, even among your family, by what they contain?

Moreover, I don't know what they contain. I shall not read any of your letters, if you so desire. I looked at just one of them today, which went along with one of the essays; there was nothing compromising in it.

Do you really recall what they contained after so many years? You have even forgotten whether you destroyed or hid the letters from Fliess—the rupture of your friendship must have been that painful.

. . . Besides, I do not yet have the letters. I shall receive them only in a few weeks.

If you would like, I can stop off in Vienna for a day or two on my way to Greece at the beginning of March, to discuss this matter with you.

I . . . revere you, and have therefore written to you in this way.

Freud answered on January 10, 1937, first speaking about his beloved chow Jofi, who had to undergo abdominal surgery for ovarian cysts (she died two days afterward). He then continued:

It is disappointing that my letters to Fliess are not yet in your hands, but are still in Berlin. . . . I cannot easily accept your opinion and the comparisons you draw. I just tell myself that after 80 or 100 years interest in this correspondence will be notably less marked than in our own time.

Naturally it's all right with me if you don't read the letters either, but you should not assume that they contain no more than a good deal of indiscretion. In view of the intimate nature of our relationship, these letters cover all kinds of things, factual as well as personal topics; and the factual ones, which indicate all the presentiments and blind alleys of the budding psychoanalysis, are also quite personal in this case [e.g., Freud's self-analysis]. There are also not a few mentions of intimate processes and relationships; things like the reproaches through which the friendship went to pieces are especially distressing in retrospect [2]. For these reasons, it would be so desirable for me to know that the material was in your hands.

With this deeply moving letter Freud tacitly accepted the whole idea of preserving the Fliess correspondence.[3]

[3] For the original letters quoted above, see Schur (1965).

During the first three months of 1937 Freud had less pain in his mouth, but he had a prolonged cold, and early in February considerable anginal pain.

On February 5, 1937, Lou Andreas-Salomé died at the age of 76. Freud had greatly admired her for her rare combination of intellect and creative imagination. He was deeply perturbed on learning of her death through a letter from Lou Andreas-Salomé's friend Ernst Pfeiffer, who was also her literary executor and later edited the exchange of correspondence between her and Freud. In a letter to Arnold Zweig, Freud commented how much he had liked Lou Andreas-Salomé as a friend, remarking that she was the same age as his wife.

With each death in his circle of friends and acquaintances Freud felt more and more as if his turn had been missed. He wrote the obituary for Lou Andreas-Salomé in the *International Journal of Psycho-Analysis*, and was still in a somewhat depressed mood when, on April 2, he wrote to Arnold Zweig, who had informed him that he was planning to leave Palestine for good:

> I may therefore count on seeing you again in late summer or early fall. As you already know, my hereditary claim on life is up in November [i.e., the age of 81 and a half]. I am ready to accept guarantees until then, but I really would not like to delay any longer because everything around me is getting darker, more threatening, and the awareness of my own helplessness [is becoming] more obtrusive. Therefore I would not like to let myself hope for a later visit of yours to Europe. So don't put it off. . . .
>
> The fear that the aging process will bring about a loss of important parts of the still intact personality is a factor which makes my wish [to see you] more urgent.

The last sentence again reveals that it is not the old superstition, the fear of death, which was operant now, but the old wish to "die in harness." It was probably no accident that the rest of the letter was devoted, among other things, to a discussion of various Shakespearean tragedies, in particular *Macbeth*.[4]

---

[4] It was one of Freud's stubbornly held beliefs that Shakespeare had not been the author of the plays attributed to him, but that these had been written by another, possibly the Earl of Oxford. He could never convince Jones of this and, having tried his luck with Arnold Zweig, was somewhat annoyed that the latter, too, held out against this hypothesis. Freud expressed in the same letter the following strange reasoning: "that Shakespeare takes everything secondhand—Hamlet's neurosis, Lear's psychosis, Macbeth's defiance and the character of his lady, Othello's jealousy, etc., that is for me an inconceivable notion."

Freud could, with good reason, speak of his still intact personality. During the early part of 1937 he had written a paper entitled "Analysis Terminable and Interminable," which was an extremely important contribution to both the theory and practice of psychoanalysis.

In April of that year I noted on the site of the last surgery a small, peculiar, pedunculated growth which was developing fast and looked very suspicious. Pichler operated on April 19, once again under general anesthesia (using intravenous Evipal, an equivalent of sodium pentothal). He did a thorough job and the pathology report showed no sign of malignancy. But there were again a few weeks of suffering, and another birthday marred by pain.

This explains two short,[5] rather sad letters written on the same day —May 16, 1937. In that to Marie Bonaparte, Freud expressed his thanks for the two beautiful vases she had sent, the best of this kind he had ever owned, and one of which he had fastened over the analytic chair in his summer home. He then added:

A wonderful spring has come upon us. The garden has never been so beautiful. Unfortunately, the persistent pain interferes with my enjoyment. . . . It is already 3½ weeks since the operation. Therefore I am writing no more [3].

To Arnold Zweig he wrote:

Things have turned beautiful in the garden, finally. One cannot help remembering the words of the poem about spring:
The world grows lovelier each day,
We do not know what still may come.
But then a contradiction arises: one knows that not much more will come.

Freud had quoted the entire stanza of this same poem in a letter to Marie Bonaparte of April 27, 1926 (see Chapter 16). Now in writing to Zweig he omitted the rest of the stanza.

Yet on May 27 he sent Marie Bonaparte one of his most succinct and lucid formulations about the vicissitudes of the aggressive drive, its relation to sublimation, and its repression. In June "Analysis Terminable and Interminable" was published; on August 13 he announced to Marie Bonaparte that the second part of the *Moses* book had been completed. Freud then had one of his best summers, interrupted only

---

[5] It was very rare for Freud to write only a one-page letter to either Marie Bonaparte or Arnold Zweig.

by two attacks of otitis, due to the direct spread of an infection from the neighborhood of the Eustachian tube, the pharyngeal opening of which was quite close to the field of the last surgery.

He spent the summer working on the last part of *Moses,* seeing patients, relatively unperturbed by the increasing turmoil of public affairs.

The letter to Marie Bonaparte had, like many of his other letters, a particular—though perhaps not fully conscious—aim. By giving him an outlet for the expression of certain pessimistic, or more accurately, realistic thoughts, it enabled him to turn back to work, enjoyment, wit. After announcing the completion of *Moses,* Part II (followed by a period of letdown, as always after creative activity), Freud continued:

> To the writer immortality evidently means being loved by any number of anonymous people. Well, I know I won't mourn your death, for you will survive me by years, and over mine I hope you will quickly console yourself and let me live in your friendly memory—the only form of limited immortality I recognize.
>
> The moment a man questions the meaning and value of life, he is sick, since objectively neither has any existence; by asking this question one is merely admitting to a store of unsatisfied libido to which something else must have happened, a kind of fermentation leading to sadness and depression. I am afraid these explanations of mine are not very wonderful. Perhaps because I am too pessimistic. I have an advertisement floating about in my head which I consider the boldest and most successful piece of American publicity: "Why live, if you can be buried for ten dollars?"
>
> Lün[6] has taken refuge with me after having been given a bath. If I understand her right, she wants me to thank you warmly for the greeting. Does Topsy realize she is being translated?[7]
>
> Write again soon [L. 290*].

During the fall of 1937, Freud's general condition—except for his usual November cold—remained good. In a note of November 26, Pichler remarked: "This month will mark 14 years since the operation." Around this time (December 1) Freud for the first and only time damaged the prosthesis by dropping it! He felt embarrassed about this "slip," and I remarked that I had often wondered why it had not happened before.

By now Freud could not be oblivious to the steady deterioration of the political situation in Vienna. All of us around him, all the members

---

6 Another of Freud's chows.

7 Marie Bonaparte's book *Topsy,* translated into German by Sigmund and Anna Freud, was published by Allert de Lange, Amsterdam, 1939, under the title *Topsy, der goldhaarige Chow.*

of the Psychoanalytic Society and most of our patients were living in a state of foreboding and uncertainty. In some letters Freud referred to this situation. He wrote to Stefan Zweig on November 17, 1937:[8]

> . . . The immediate future looks grim, for psychoanalysis as well. In any case I am not likely to experience anything enjoyable during the weeks and months I may still have to live.
>
> I have started complaining quite against my will. What I wanted was to come closer to you in a human way rather than be admired like a rock against which the waves break in vain. But even if my defiance remains silent, it remains defiance nevertheless and—*impavidum ferient ruinae* [L. 292*]

On December 20, 1937, Freud wrote to Arnold Zweig devoting the first page and a half to Zweig's problems, expressing satisfaction that the latter's eyes had improved, evaluating his latest book, etc., after which he continued:

> For your sake I can hardly regret that you did not choose Vienna as your new home. The government here is different, but the people are the same as their brethren in the Reich—all united in their worship of anti-Semitism. Our throat is being squeezed ever more tightly, although for the time being we are not being choked completely.

The year 1938 started poorly. Freud had severe pain, could not open his mouth, and developed an ulcer which quickly changed into a highly suspicious lesion. I saw it first when I visited on New Year's Day. Although it looked like a pressure sore, I alerted Pichler who, after watching it for some days, became convinced that it was again a malignancy. On this assumption he operated under general anesthesia, encountering special technical difficulties. The lesion was so far inside the oral-nasal cavity that access was extremely difficult. Pichler had to find an especially long handle for the coagulation needle. Even after a very thorough coagulation, Pichler was not completely confident that he had done a sufficiently radical job. Moreover, the tumor was embedded in hard scar tissue which made excision especially difficult. The lesions were getting dangerously close to the base of the orbita.

Freud asked Pichler to remove an old atheroma from under the left mandibula because it had recently grown, bothering him when he attended to his beard, and because it looked ugly.

---

[8] Erroneously dated in the *Letters* as October 17.

Freud went home after two days, and immediately thereafter we got the pathology report: cancerous tissue once again, a year and a half after the last malignancy. This time Pichler was hesitant about telling Freud the truth because no additional surgery was required, but I felt bound by my promise and passed on the report. Freud received the news, as he had in 1936, without any visible emotion.

Freud spent many weeks in misery before the necrotic tissue sloughed off. We spent a long time every day rinsing the wound to clean it. Freud submitted to all this with his usual grace and patience.

For several weeks Pichler was in doubt about whether additional extensive electrocoagulation would be necessary. As it turned out, all that remained to be done was a small excision of a wartlike leukoplakia on February 19.

We knew now that Freud was living on borrowed time, and so did he. He spent several more miserable weeks, during which the storm continued to brew all around us. And yet he was able to write a witty and delightful letter to Marie Bonaparte on January 27, 1938, five days after the surgery and three days after he had learned about the recurrence of the malignancy (see Schur, 1965).

Marie Bonaparte had written him on hearing about the operation, reporting on the progress of her paper "Problems of Time in Life, Dream, and Death," speaking about her own cardiac symptoms, and ending with the following paragraph:

> So much for me. But I want to hear about *you* soon, and learn that we will still be able to have long conversations on this earth, before we go to the hereafter in the Elysian fields.

Freud answered:

> Your kind letter, received today, put me into a mood which requires immediate expression. Well, I've been imagining how I would greet you on the Elysian Fields, after learning of your arrival. It's fine that you've finally gotten here. You let me wait so long, and I didn't get to read your last big opus about time. I'm already quite curious to learn what you've found out about it. Because, as you can readily imagine, conditions for acquiring experience about this strange aspect of our mental functioning are particularly unfavorable in this place. Altogether you'll have to tell me a great deal about analysis. . . .
> You will probably tell me that I look well, and I hope I shall be able to return the compliment. Staying in this place has a good effect on the appearance. Perhaps you will even notice that I've actually been beau-

tified. Wasn't I disfigured by a sebaceous cyst, an atheroma, which you never mentioned, probably out of tact? I had that ornament removed during my last—I mean of course next-to-last-operation. But enough about myself. A hearty welcome once again.

Yours among the blessed,[9]

Freud

---

[9] The translation of the original closing "Ihrem seligen," used by Freud, illustrates the great difficulties facing any translator. The German word *selig* means "blessed, happy, blissful," but is used specifically in speaking of a deceased person to indicate special respect, particularly among tradition-minded Jews, to whom an expression such as "your dead father," rather than "your *seliger* father," implies a certain disrespect for the dead.

26

THE NAZI INVASION–EXODUS

In February, 1938, Hitler summoned Schuschnigg, the Austrian Chancellor, to Berchtesgaden and faced him, literally, with an ultimatum. No one could doubt that the end of Austria was only a matter of weeks away. (I personally was so convinced of this that I applied for a United States visa a few days later.) I repeatedly implored Freud to leave the country. Once he promised to think it over—and then refused. On March 11, the Germans marched in.

I was making afternoon rounds at my hospital when the news of Schuschnigg's resignation reached me. I called home and then drove to the Berggasse. The streets were packed with marching stormtroopers. A number of friends were gathered at Freud's home, and we all tried to convince Freud to leave. The following day he gave in, but by then it was too late, and we had to wait for "legal permission."

The events of the next few weeks before Freud was able to leave Vienna, on June 4, have been vividly described by Jones (Vol. 3, p. 318ff.). Risking duplication of material available from this and other sources, I shall add some details.

It is hard to describe our state of mind during that period. A great deal has been written about the cruelties and the concentration and extermination camps. But less is known about the condition of suddenly being outside the protection of common law. Not to be afraid of a knock on the door would have been abnormal. Friends and relatives were disappearing. The Gestapo had moved in and established its headquarters, and the first news about torture was beginning to circulate.

Freud's home was invaded several times by roaming S.A. gangs looking mainly for loot. More serious was the search by Gestapo agents. Things like a signed photograph of Einstein—one of the prime enemies of the Fatherland—the latter's exchange of letters with Freud, Freud's membership in the B'nai Brith Lodge, which was considered to be affiliated with the Freemasons, constituted highly incriminating evidence at that time.

It is certain that for quite some time the future was in doubt, and that Freud and his family, the analysts who had remained, my family and I, were all in grave danger. In the midst of all this, Freud remained calm, full of dignity, and in complete self-control.

While there were of course many rumors abroad, the following seems to be factual. Within the Nazi hierarchy there were apparently several different factions with different opinions about what should be done with us. The Himmler-Goebbels faction, which believed in the paralyzing effect of terror, wanted to throw the whole group into prison. Goering, under the influence of his psychiatrist cousin, was in favor of moderation. The German Foreign Office was still concerned about the outcry which would probably arise in the entire Western world if anything should happen to the 82-year-old master. This attitude—which eventually prevailed—was greatly influenced by interventions from many quarters. In the fall of 1964 the late Ambassador William C. Bullitt gave me the following personal account: he had been extremely skeptical of Austria's ability to withstand the pressure of Nazism. While he was still United States ambassador to Moscow he had arranged for the appointment of a Mr. Wiley as consul-general in Vienna, with the special "assignment" of keeping a watchful eye and, within diplomatic limits, a protecting hand on Freud and his family. Upon the occupation of Austria, Bullitt immediately called Wiley and requested that he "show his presence." He then called on the German Ambassador in Paris, Count Wilczeck, an aristocrat of the old diplomatic service, to whom he pointed out in the strongest terms the consequences in the United States of any insult to Freud. He also insisted that Wilczeck transmit this information immediately to Berlin. Finally, he telephoned Washington and asked President Roosevelt to give full support to his intervention.[1]

---

[1] The question of the Wilson book also came up for discussion at my meeting with Mr. Bullitt. I knew of the existence of a manuscript because Freud had indicated his interest in this work to me. He also had expressed his disappointment about the delay in its completion in his letter written to Marie Bonaparte on December 7, 1933

Marie Bonaparte and Jones immediately went to Vienna, and their mere presence had an effect, too.

Mr. Wiley did his utmost. That same evening he called on Freud, and later the following procedure was established: the analyst, Mrs. Dorothy Burlingham, lived in the same house as Freud. A housephone connected the two apartments. As soon as any trouble (searching, looting, etc.) started, she called the American Embassy and within a few minutes an American official would "just drop in."

Pichler, although an old member of the "National Party of Greater Germany" (which, since World War I, had favored the unification of Germany and Austria), was completely divorced from the Nazi mentality, and could not have behaved better. He came to the house repeatedly whenever he was notified of trouble, and used every bit of his behind-the-scenes influence. O. Pötzl, the successor to Wagner-Jauregg as Chairman of the Department of Psychiatry at the University of Vienna, and an inactive member of the Vienna Psychoanalytic Society, did the same.

However, there were more ominous developments. Events occurred so quickly that, apparently, a copy of Freud's will, indicating that he had money abroad—a hideous crime—had been left at the Verlag. Freud's eldest son, Martin, tried to destroy it, along with some other documents, and was caught and held for hours at bayonet point. He

---

(Chapter 22). Jones had occasion to look at the manuscript during his stay in New York in 1956 (Vol. 3, p. 151).

Mr. Bullitt asked for my opinion about the publication of the book. My answer was that as a member of the Board of Directors of the Sigmund Freud Archives, which is vitally interested in the preservation of all material pertinent to our understanding of Freud (manuscripts, letters, interviews with persons who knew Freud, etc.), but also because I was engaged in writing a biographical study of Freud, I was in the first place concerned with the preservation of the manuscript. I emphasized this point because Mr. Bullitt told me that only one copy of this manuscript existed. I also conveyed to Mr. Bullitt my assumption that he probably had extensive notes on his many discussions with Freud about Wilson as well as many letters. Mr. Bullitt told me, however, that when he had to leave Paris in a hurry during the war, all these notes and letters were burned due to the carelessness of a valet.

I therefore suggested that Mr. Bullitt send a copy of the manuscript to Mr. Ernst Freud, who was in charge of the Sigmund Freud Copyrights, and expressed my belief that Miss Anna Freud would be willing to help him in the final formulation of the psychoanalytic aspects of the book. I suggested that any publication should be done by a university press. Upon Mr. Bullitt's request for more specific advice, I suggested that the Rutgers University Press, would be an excellent choice. Mr. Bullitt did send a copy to Mr. Ernst and Miss Anna Freud, but unfortunately did not see fit to accept any help from Miss Freud. After reading the manuscript, Miss Freud felt that only the Introduction showed unmistakably the character of Freud's style and thinking. I shared this opinion, as did others (see Erikson, 1967; and R. S. Stewart, 1967).

had reason to suspect that the "Nazi Commissar" of the Verlag had gotten wind of the matter.

One day Anna Freud was summoned to the Gestapo, from where many—indeed most—people never returned, being whisked away to a concentration camp. Martin expected the same summons at any moment. Both came to my home and informed me of the situation. At their request—they feared torture, and not without reason—I supplied them with a sufficient amount of Veronal, a strong barbiturate, and promised to take care of Freud as long as possible (this is the only thing we never told Freud). That was the worst day. I went to the Berggasse and stayed with Freud. The hours were endless. It was the only time I ever saw Freud deeply worried. He paced the floor, smoking incessantly. I tried to reassure him as well as I could. Finally, late in the evening, Anna Freud returned. Freud, who was rarely demonstrative in his affection, showed his feelings to some extent that evening. This danger was over. Martin was never called in. I have never inquired of Anna what actually happened at the Gestapo.[2]

Only later did we find out that at least part of our anxiety had been unfounded. The Nazi Commissar Sauerwald knew about the incriminating will but had kept the secret.[3]

[2] According to Jones, Mr. Wiley intervened on that occasion too; and so, apparently, did Mussolini. Dr. Edoardo Weiss, an Italian analyst who knew Il Duce, has stated that the Italian Ambassador in Vienna was instructed to intervene on Freud's behalf (see Jones, Vol. 3, p. 221ff.).

[3] While the following does not belong to the topic indicated in the title of this study, this might be the place to report about the "Dr. Sauerwald Episode," because it may have played an important part in Freud's destiny.

After the *Anschluss* every enterprise was assigned its "Nazi-Kommissar." Frequently it was a former employee or someone familiar with the particular business or industry. That Sauerwald, a Ph.D. in chemistry, became Commissar of the Psychoanalytischer Verlag is a peculiar twist of fate. At the beginning he behaved as a "tough brute" should; he was full of hatred and scorn. He castigated Drs. Hartmann and Sterba, as Gentiles, for having become mixed up with the "jüdische Schweinereien." But little by little things began to change. First, he was bored with his "job" and therefore began to read Freud's works, in the beginning because he was curious about psychoanalysis, but soon because he was interested and impressed. Second, he was even more impressed by Freud as a person. As a result, he became extremely helpful and used all his considerable influence with the Nazis to facilitate the emigration of Freud, his family, and his immediate group. He cooperated constantly with Freud's "Nazi" lawyer (Nazi in name only), Dr. Indra. Toward the end we learned that Sauerwald had actually found the evidence of Freud's account abroad, but had hidden it at considerable risk to his own safety. When one time the Gestapo people had been slightly disrespectful to Freud, he apologized to Anna, saying: "What can you expect? These Prussians don't know who Freud is." (The old antagonism between Prussia and Austria had never died out completely. It can be likened to that between the Yankees and the Confederates.) Later he personally supervised the packing of

It was not until quite recently that Anna Freud told me the following story and authorized me to publish it. When things were at their worst and escape seemed hopeless, Anna asked Freud: "Wouldn't it be better if we all killed ourselves?" To which Freud replied with his characteristic mixture of irony and indignation: "Why? Because they would like us to?" Such was his fortitude and defiance. And this was the man of whom it had been feared in 1923 that he might commit suicide when he was told he had cancer. While Freud was still in Vienna, but at a moment when the prospect for emigration had improved, he wrote to his son Ernst on May 12, a few days after his 82nd birthday (which this time really could not be celebrated):

> Two prospects keep me going in these grim times: to rejoin you all and —to die in freedom.

Freud's belongings, including his books and art collection, and after Freud's departure took care of Freud's old sisters, visiting them frequently (only after he was drafted into the German army were they sent to various extermination camps).

One day in 1939, Dr. Sauerwald appeared in London, none of us knew why; perhaps it was on some government or spying mission. He visited Alexander Freud (Freud's younger brother) to find out how Freud was. Alexander asked him point-blank about the motivation for his attitude, which was in such contrast to the general behavior of a Nazi. Sauerwald told him the following amazing story: he had been employed by the Viennese police as an expert on explosives. But he was also the manufacturer of explosives for the Nazi underground in Austria. After each explosion, he received for testing the explosives made by himself! He thus had an excellent reputation for fast and accurate analyses.

When asked by Alexander Freud how his Nazi *Weltanschauung* could be reconciled with his consideration for Freud and his family, he gave as an explanation a rationalization which was typical of many of the "good" Nazis: "The Führer, who of course knows best, realizes that the *Vaterland* is in a state of siege. The Jews, due to their internationalist leanings and their tendency toward individualistic behavior, cannot form a reliable element of the population. Thus they have to be eliminated. This might be deplorable, but the end justifies the means. This does not mean, however, that an individual should not be permitted to alleviate individual hardship in selected cases."

Jones reports that Sauerwald had studied chemistry under a Professor Herzig, an old friend of Freud's, and accorded to the latter the respect he felt for his old teacher. This in itself would not have explained Sauerwald's shift in behavior and his growing intention to be helpful. I have always assumed that he was one of those Nazis "by conviction" who gradually developed some guilt feelings and tried to come to terms with their conscience by being "decent" whenever circumstances permitted. This would have been a factor apart from the great impression that Freud himself had made.

During the war Sauerwald was wounded, contracted tuberculosis, and was brought to trial by the Austrian government as a war criminal. Marie Bonaparte and Anna Freud signed affidavits attesting to his helpfulness, which helped bring about his acquittal.

This was one of those weird incidents where "fate" may have saved Freud and all those around him, including myself and my family.

This letter was also written with a historical perspective, reflected in the next sentence:

> I sometimes compare myself with the old Jacob who in his old age was taken by his children to Egypt. . . . It is to be hoped that the result will not be the same, an exodus from Egypt. It is high time that Ahasuerus came to rest somewhere [L. 297*].[4]

We might point out another model for Freud which was also applicable to this situation. In the *Moses* book, Freud remarked: "Immediately after the destruction of the Temple in Jerusalem by Titus, the Rabbi Joachanan ben Zakkai asked permission to open the first Torah school in Jabneh" (1939, p. 115). Added to Freud's wish to live and die in freedom was the hope of establishing a new center for psychoanalysis in London.

A final motivation for emigrating, which Freud mentioned later, in 1939, was the wish to finish the third part of *Moses* and to have it published, something which would have met with innumerable obstacles in Austria.

During all these weeks Freud, of course, did not leave his home, as it was not safe to walk the streets of Vienna. He continued to see whatever patients were left, worked on Part III of *Moses*, and prepared for emigration by weeding out piles of correspondence and manuscripts. Freud's physical condition, including that of his mouth, was not bad. There were no new lesions, and only the crust formations were bothersome and needed constant attention. We tried not to disturb his daily routine. Pichler came as often as he could. He made no notes between February 19, 1938 (the date of the last surgical procedure) and June 2, when he wrote: "The last examination before leaving for England." The examination revealed no suspicious areas. This improvement in Freud's condition helped us convince him that his emigration was "worthwhile."

---

[4] Freud's father's name was Jakob, and the figure of Joseph had always fascinated Freud. He had discussed the subject at length with Thomas Mann in connection with the latter's *Joseph* tetralogy. Joseph was not only the interpreter of dreams. The Bible tells us that he was the firstborn son of Jacob and Rachel. It was Rachel, Leah's younger sister, whom Jacob really loved, for whom he was ready to serve her father for seven years. Rachel could not bear any children until "God remembered her . . . and opened her womb" (Genesis 30). Joseph remained Jacob's favorite son, envied by all his brothers.

We know that Freud grew up with "the Book." The analogy of his father's young wife, being her firstborn son, and the Biblical story lent themselves perfectly for identification, especially after Sigmund himself became the interpreter of dreams.

The last chapter in Vienna was the "ransom story." The Nazis demanded of every emigrant having a certain amount of money 20 per cent of his assets as a "tax" for fleeing the country (*Reichsfluchtsteuer*). However, they fixed the date of January 1, 1938, as the basis for their assessment, while in the meantime they had confiscated most of their victims' assets. As Freud's bank accounts, the Verlag, etc., had been confiscated, he no longer had the cash to pay this tax. Of course, no one could admit that he had money abroad. Thus Marie Bonaparte paid the tax for him, and Freud insisted on repaying the "loan" as soon as he got to Paris.

We all had to go through the same nightmarish procedure of shuttling from one office to the other to obtain the necessary papers. Fortunately, Freud's lawyer and Sauerwald helped all of us in these matters.

It had been decided that I should accompany Freud to England, along with my family, and to remain his "Leibarzt."[5] It was Ernest Jones who made this possible by arranging for the necessary permits, and I have not forgotten how deeply indebted I am to him. We made detailed plans for the trip. Freud and his family were a little worried; after all, he had not left Vienna for eight years. I was optimistic on this score, and was confident that he would have no untoward reactions. It was amazing, by the way, how well not only Freud but many

---

[5] Freud prepared the following list for submission to the British Consulate in Vienna for the necessary British visas:

Prof. Dr. Freud		Wien, IX Berggasse, 19
1. Prof. Sigm. Freud	82 J.	Prof. Sigm. Freud, 82
2. Seine Frau Martha	77 J.	His wife Martha, 77
3. Schwester der Frau:		
Minna Bernays	73 J.	His wife's sister, Minna Bernays, 73
4. Tochter Anna	42 J.	Daughter Anna, 42
5. Sohn Dr. Martin	48 J.	Son Martin, LL.D., 48
6. Dessen Frau Esti	41 J.	Son's wife Esti, 41
7. Dessen Sohn Walter	16 J.	His son Walter, 16
8. Dessen Tochter Sophie	13 J.	His daughter Sophie, 13
9. Enkel Ernst Halberstadt	24 J.	Grandson Ernst Halberstadt, 24
10. Verheiratete Tochter		
Mathilde	50 J.	Married daughter Mathilde, 50
11. Deren Mann R. Hollitscher	62 J.	Her husband R. Hollitscher, 62
12. Leibarzt seit 9½ Jahren		Dr. Max Schur, 41, personal physician
Dr. Max Schur, 41 J., mit		for 9½ years, with
13. Frau und zwei kleinen Kindern		Wife and two small children
14. langjährige Hausgehilfin		Paula Fichtl, 36, housekeeper for
Paula Fichtl, 36 J.		many years.
		April, 1938

very old people withstood journeys overseas at that time, frequently under most primitive conditions.

Shortly after receiving our permits, which fixed the date of departure, I came down with severe phlegmonous appendicitis. I was desperate, and tried to wait for a few hours, but eventually had to be operated on, from a medical point of view somewhat too late, and certainly too late for our timetable! I telephoned Anna Freud, who was greatly concerned. I saw her before the operation, and we discussed the possibility of my not being able to go with them. I tried to get up on the fifth day after the operation, but collapsed. Anna came again and told me that they had to leave; it was too risky to wait. We decided that Dr. Josefine Stross, now the pediatric consultant of the Hampstead Child-Therapy Clinic, should accompany them in my place and act as my substitute until I could follow.

Freud left on June 4, 1938, and all went well. I knew full well that he could not possibly have waited any longer, but I nonetheless felt lonely and abandoned as never before. I had in the meantime developed an abscess in the incision, which had to be operated on, after which, as soon as it was at all medically feasible, I was taken to the train in an ambulance. There were some ominous inquiries from the Gestapo at the hospital,[6] and the roaring reception which Freud had received in France and England, and the publicity given to his arrival there in the press, would have made any further delay dangerous for me. We left on June 10, probably just in the nick of time.

The "Aryan" surgeon who had operated on me had given me the necessary certificates to discourage the border police from searching my bandages for hidden money or jewelry. The trip, fortunately, was uneventful. The train passed through Salzburg into Germany on one of those enchanting spring days when the foothills of the Alps glow in the glorious sunset. The border control was courteous.

I shall never forget our overwhelming relief when we saw the first

---

[6] For weeks before this, I had had to report my whereabouts every three days to the police precinct nearest our home. The Gestapo knew of the date of our planned departure, and we had failed to notify the police of my emergency hospitalization. Two or three days after Freud's departure, a Gestapo agent called at the hospital to find out if I was there, whether or not my illness was genuine, and when I intended to leave the country. My wife and I had some rather bad moments when the nurse (a very friendly Catholic nun, who knew me) burst into the room blurting out that the Gestapo was making inquiries. On June 8, my wife was called down once again to a tax office to explain some new details added to our *Unbedenklichkeitserklärung*—the devilish form which certified that one was not a suspicious citizen. One's tax status was an essential part of this certification.

French border officials and the train rolled over the Rhine bridge. We were free and safe! Marie Bonaparte was waiting for us at the station, and took us to her home, where I convalesced until I could proceed to England. Recuperating of course meant more than the healing of my abdominal wound. What an unbelievable contrast it was to be out of the world of madmen, who had the power of decision about one's very existence, and to be surrounded by loving care and respect in the beautiful home of Marie Bonaparte! Even my little children (five and two and a half) understood the difference.

27

THE LAST CHAPTER

Freud in the meantime had settled in London. The letter he wrote to Marie Bonaparte after his arrival there deserves to be quoted in full, because it shows how much "life" was still left in him:

June 8, 1938

My dear Marie,
The first letter written on the desk framed by your terra cotta figurines, in a room with a view on the garden, which you will certainly like, should rightly go to you because the one day in your home in Paris restored our dignity and morale. After having been wrapped in love for 12 hours, we left proud and rich,[1] under the protection of Athena.[2] But perhaps it doesn't make much sense to thank you or tell you what you already know. You probably want to hear what's new.

There is plenty new here, most of it beautiful, some of it very beautiful. The reception at Victoria Station and then [that] by the newspapers these first two days has been kind and even enthusiastic. We are flooded with flowers. The letters are interesting: only three autograph collectors;

[1] Marie Bonaparte had given Freud the money she had been holding for him. He then insisted on repaying the "ransom" money she had advanced.

[2] On Freud's arrival in Paris, Marie Bonaparte gave him one of his favorite pieces, a little antique Greek statue of Athena, which she had smuggled out for him, with the following note:

Die Athene—
Ruhe! Vernunft!
Grüsst die Ausreisenden
aus der tollen Hölle!

Athena—
Peace! Reason!
Greets those who have fled
from the mad inferno!

504

one woman painter who wants to do my portrait after I have rested; also a single touching request for a consultation from a daughter for her mother, who has been declared incurable; furthermore, an advertisement from an enterprising delicatessen. In addition to this, greetings from most of the members of the English [Psychoanalytic] group, from some scientific and other Jewish societies, and as the *pièce de résistance* a rambling four-page telegram from Cleveland, Ohio, signed by "citizens of all faiths and professions," a most respectful invitation, backed by all kinds of promises, to make our home among them (we will have to answer that unfortunately we have already unpacked).

Finally, and this is something characteristic for England, numerous letters from strangers who just want to tell us how glad they are that we have arrived in England and that we are now safe and at peace. Really, it is as though our cause were also their cause.

My heart hasn't been too eager to function these last few days, as was the case in Paris. Our little doctor [Dr. Josefine Stross] has been watching over it very well, and it seems to be improving quickly. . . .

Your cigars are certainly harmless, even if not very tasty. So far I have not yet found anything similar here.[3]

I could go on writing for hours without exhausting the topic. But enough for now. With most cordial greetings,

Your
Freud [1]

This letter clearly shows Freud's elation over his escape and the enthusiastic reception he had received in London. There were of course many worries—his sister-in-law Minna, who had left Vienna before him, now had pneumonia and he had not yet seen her. In addition, the news about the mounting terror in Austria was very depressing.

The letter to Marie Bonaparte had been preceded by one to Eitingon in Jerusalem. After a description of the trip to London Freud had written poignantly:

It is hardly an accident that [in this letter] I have remained so matter-of-fact up to now. The emotional climate of these days is hard to grasp, almost indescribable. The feeling of triumph on being liberated is too strongly mixed with sorrow, for in spite of everything I still greatly loved the prison from which I have been released. . . . the happy anticipations of a new life are dampened by the question: how long will a fatigued heart be able to accomplish any work?—Under the impact of the illness on the floor above me (I haven't been allowed to see her [Minna] yet) the pain in the heart turns into an unmistakable depres-

---

[3] Freud never liked denicotinized cigars. He soon found some "tasty" ones!

sion. But all the children, our own as well as the adopted ones, are charming. Mathilde is as efficient here as Anna was in Vienna; Ernst really is what he has been called, "a tower of strength," Lux and the children are worthy of him; the two men, Martin and Robert, are holding their heads high again. Am I to be the only one who doesn't cooperate and lets his family down? My wife, moreover, has remained healthy and undaunted [L. 299*].

This was perhaps the only occasion on which Freud admitted how much—in spite of everything—he had loved Vienna.

After Freud's arrival in London many men of letters, science, and art began to speculate once again about Freud's possible eligibility for a Nobel prize. Arnold Zweig wrote to Freud about it, and Freud's answer of June 28, 1938, began: "Don't let yourself be driven crazy over the chimera of the Nobel prize." After pointing out that under the circumstances none of the officials on the Nobel prize committee would dare to challenge Nazi Germany by giving the award to him,[4] he continued:

We're feeling very well here, would feel very well if the unnerving news from Vienna, the continual requests for help, which only remind one of one's own helplessness, didn't stifle all feelings of well-being. . . .

I am writing with pleasure the third part of the Moses. Just half an hour ago the mail brought a letter from a young Jewish American in which I am asked not to rob his poor unfortunate people of the only comfort left to them in their misery. The letter was nice and well-meaning, but what an overestimation! Am I really to believe that my dry essay would disturb the faith of even one . . . person. . . .

I had several interesting visitors. . . . The most enjoyable was the visit of two secretaries of the Royal Society, who brought me the holy book of the Society so I could place my signature in it, because a new infirmity . . . is interfering with my leaving the house. They left with me a facsimile of the book, and if you were here with me I could show

---

[4] Freud was perhaps not quite accurate in his evaluation of the courage of the officials of the Nobel prize committee. In 1935 the Nobel Peace Prize was awarded to Ossietzky, a prominent German pacifist and editor of the leftist publication *Die Weltbühne*, who had been interned since 1933 in a German concentration camp. This award produced a violent outcry in the Nazi press.

Freud's name had been submitted several times for the Nobel prize in medicine. However, among the medical prize winners Freud had only two warm supporters; the pharmacologist Otto Loewi and the otologist Barany, plus the lukewarm acquiescence of Wagner-Jauregg, chairman of the department of psychiatry at the Vienna Medical School. The world of European academic medicine, with very few exceptions, had not accepted psychoanalysis. And although Freud had received the Goethe prize for an essay quite literary in character, it was difficult to consider him for the Nobel prize in literature.

you the signatures of I. Newton and Charles Darwin. Good company!
With most cordial greetings to you, your wife and children,
Your
Sigm. Freud
P.S. I have to get used to a new signature, because I have been informed
that only a lord signs his surname alone. All in all, an odd country.

Freud was evidently enjoying his adopted country. Since his youth
he had looked upon England as the cradle of democracy and freedom
of thought. To be a member of the Royal Society, in the company of
Newton and Darwin, obviously pleased him.

Freud liked the house he was temporarily occupying, which was
near Regents Park. Not only was he working on the third part of
Moses, but he had also started to write an essay which was published
posthumously as *An Outline of Psycho-Analysis* (1940). As he had
done so often in the past, he underplayed the importance of this work,
as for example in a letter to Marie Bonaparte. The writing proceeded
slowly and Freud never completed the work, but it turned out to be a
most lucid and profound formulation of psychoanalytic theory brought
up to date.

When I arrived in London on June 15, 1938, I learned that during
his trip Freud had had some minor cardiac symptoms, which were to
continue all through June. He also had for a short time an irritable
bladder (this was the "new infirmity" referred to in his letter of June
28 to Arnold Zweig).

I keenly felt the overwhelming responsibility which now rested
squarely on my shoulders. Pichler had referred Freud to an oral surgeon, a Dr. Exner, whom he considered to be an excellent surgeon and
technician. However, he carefully and tactfully indicated that Exner
might be lacking in experience with such complex oral pathology.
Only Anna Freud and I knew how insidious was the onset of each new
lesion. I was also fully aware of the fact that the tendency of the past
two years had been toward full-fledged malignancy, in contrast to the
prevalence of precancerous lesions in previous years. In addition, the
latest lesions were high up in the oral cavity and hard to reach. There
was hardly any normal lining left, and Freud was by now 82! The
possibility of further surgery was limited.

We tried to set up the usual routine. It was the Berggasse all over
—only much nicer and more comfortable. The Home Office had
graciously granted me permission to function officially as Freud's physician even before I had passed the required examinations. I saw Freud

almost daily. Late in July I noticed a suspicious swelling. While this one was due to a local periostitis, early in August I saw two more lesions develop within a few days. First it was a smaller one in front of the area of the last operation, wartlike, resembling a leukoplakia. Exner could not imagine that such a lesion could be significant, and I had to be quite insistent. He listened with a mixture of disbelief and annoyance to the statements of a "foreigner," and an internist to boot! We missed Pichler badly. I wrote him several urgent letters, asking if he would be willing to come to London, if necessary. Pichler immediately expressed his willingness to come to London.

Throughout the first weeks of August no decision could be reached. Exner continued to be skeptical and demanded X-rays of the bones, which, as was to be expected, were negative.

Even Freud had become somewhat angry with me, as I was to learn much later when, in 1964, I read his correspondence with Marie Bonaparte. In one of these letters [2] he accused me of being an alarmist, of contacting Pichler on my own authority, etc. At the same time he acknowledged that he would probably not escape further surgery, especially since Marie Bonaparte had written to him (on August 18, 1938) that Professor Rigaud of the Institut Curie in Paris also advocated electrocoagulation of even a slightly suspicious lesion.

During all this time, Freud was working and writing, finishing the third part of *Moses* and going ahead with the *Outline*.

In a comparatively short letter to Marie Bonaparte written on August 22, 1938, Freud discussed her paper "Time in Life, Dream, and Death," and suggested a possible metapsychological approach to the concepts of time, space, and causality in their relation to the ego apparatus of perception and consciousness.[5]

Unfortunately, these weeks were to mark the end of Freud's creative activity. At the end of August a large area began to be prominent behind the area of the last operation, more ominous because harder to reach. I knew that this was the beginning of a papilloma. Now Anna and I decided to ask Pichler to come to London. By that time Freud

[5] A passage in a letter to Marie Bonaparte written on November 12, 1938 on the subject of this paper shows how little Freud was given to wild speculation, vanity, or lack of introspection, as some have claimed: "Your comments on 'time and space' have come off better than mine would have—although so far as time is concerned I had not fully informed you of my ideas. Nor anyone else. A certain dislike of my subjective tendency to grant the imagination too free a rein [in scientific research] has always held me back. If you still want to know, I will tell you next time you come" [L. 309*].

had also overcome his reluctance, as he indicated in a letter to Marie Bonaparte of September 4. Having earlier criticized me for being an alarmist, he now wrote her with his unfailing, exemplary fairness that at this point "all three," i.e., Exner, an English radium specialist, and myself, were insisting on surgery, and that he was reluctantly giving his assent.

It was early in September of 1938. The Czechoslovakian crisis, which was to culminate a few weeks later in the Munich settlement, was nearing its climax. In many respects this was a race against time.

Pichler arrived in London on September 7. He, too, was less concerned with the area in front of the last surgery, although it was the larger of the two lesions, than with the posterior one. He stressed the urgency of surgery, not only because of the character of the lesion, but also because of its location. Any further growth of the posterior lesion would make it even less accessible. He pointed out that even now he would have to make a large external excision through the cheek and lips, and asked if I thought Freud's heart could take the strain. I voiced my conviction that it was safe to go ahead, but we left the final decision to Freud, who gave his consent. The absolute confidence he had in Pichler made it easier for him. Pichler operated at the London Clinic. His report shows how extensive the surgery had to be.

September 8: Surgery at the London Clinic, Devonshire Place. Induction [of general anesthesia] by [intravenous injection of] Evipal [an equivalent of sodium pentothal] and continuation with nitrous oxide through a nasal catheter. Splitting of the lip and carrying of the incision up along the nose, so that for once there is good access. Then excision of the tumor of the cheek with the diathermy needle, and eventually also of all the pathological tissue posterior to and above the *ramus ascendens*. Excision of large pieces of very hard, firm tissue. These do not look microscopically like carcinoma [frozen sections were examined during the surgery], but like scar tissue. They were removed up to the healthy, soft muscle, although not in every place securely into non-affected tissue. Finally, the anterior fixated edge of the *ramus ascendens* was also exposed and coagulated to the extent of 1.5 cm. Upon ascertainment that everything had been removed, insertion of the prosthesis, the wound cavity insufflated with orthoform and packed with 5% iodoform gauze.

September 8, P.M.: The patient has already done some reading and is feeling quite well.

September 9: Visited in the morning. [Patient] slept well.

Everything in fine order. Therefore flew back home at 11 A.M.

Such surgery was possible because at that time the technique of general anesthesia was more advanced in the United States and England than on the Continent. Freud tolerated the anesthesia and the more extensive surgery exceedingly well. Pichler left on September 9, because Freud seemed to be recovering uneventfully. This time the pathology report revealed "only" precancerous lesions, which caused Exner to comment that perhaps the surgery had been superfluous after all. This comment made me more keenly aware of the load of my responsibility. I missed Pichler, and kept up my correspondence with him as long as possible.

Anna Freud sent a report to Marie Bonaparte on the evening of the operation. Her last sentence expressed the feelings of all of us:

> We spent a few very uncomfortable days until we knew that it really had to be done, that we wanted Pichler, that he could come that fast. He behaved exceedingly well.
> I am very glad that it is already today, and no longer yesterday.

Freud went home after a few days and began to recover, but slowly. The area where the bone had been coagulated was partly necrotic, slow to heal, and very painful.

Freud moved to his permanent home at 20 Maresfield Gardens on September 27, 1938. In the meantime his furniture and collection had arrived from Vienna. Anna and Paula Fichtl had arranged everything in such a way that all his favorite art objects had the same position in the new room as in their old surroundings. Only the room itself was bigger and sunnier, with direct access to the garden. Freud eventually died in that room, and it has been kept virtually unchanged, affording every visitor a small glimpse of its distinguished occupant.

Freud's recovery continued, but he was extremely tired. Very occasionally his mood showed more than fatigue. The best description of his state can be found in the letter to Lou Andreas-Salomé written 13 years earlier, on March 10, 1925 (see Chapter 15).

This state did not last long. The changes were evident mainly with regard to the external events of those weeks, and not in his personal relations. His letters still showed a full scale of emotions.

This was the time of the Munich crisis, when everyone in London (with the probable exception of Chamberlain and his advisors) felt that war might break out at any moment. Then came the pact, bringing in its wake a mixture of relief and terrible let-down to everyone who recognized it for what it was.

Freud read the newspapers regularly; his comments were wise and to the point, but "the resonance was missing." Such very subtle changes were of course not recognizable to anyone who did not know him intimately.

The first letter from Maresfield Gardens was to Marie Bonaparte on October 4, 1938. It contained several errors, which were an indication of his fatigue:

. It cannot be long as I can hardly write, any more than I can talk or smoke. This operation was the worst since 1923. . . . I am abominably tired and weak in my movements, although I began yesterday with three patients, but it is not going easily [3].

Arnold Zweig came to visit Freud and stayed for several weeks.[6] Freud was happy to see him, but Zweig had so much to tell about his life and work, both men knowing full well that this was probably the last time they would see each other, that Freud was occasionally quite exhausted, although he never complained.

October and November were uneventful. Freud did not even catch his usual November cold. There was only one painful area of bone necrosis from the last operation, where some chips were expected to come out. Otherwise the surface was smooth, with less crust formation.

The German edition of *Moses and Monotheism* had been published in Holland in August, 1938, and Freud was more than eager to see the publication of an English edition, for which Mrs. Jones, with the help of her husband, was preparing the translation. The following letter to Jones, written on November 1 of that year, is pertinent here:

Dear Jones,
I greatly regretted that your cold forced you to keep away from me yesterday, and I was then really dismayed to learn that you would not be able to finish the translation of my *Moses* before February or March [1939]. I know that your time is very valuable, your conscientiousness very great, and that you have many things to do which are at least as important as this. I am mindful, however, that you took this new burden upon yourself voluntarily, without my asking you to. I understood your undertaking this, of course, as a special kindness toward me and a mark of distinction for the book.
    The prospect of a delay is disagreeable to me in more than one respect. First of all, a few months mean more to me than to someone else

[6] It was then that I met him personally for the first time, and had long talks with him.

if I persist in my understandable wish to see the finished [i.e., published] book with my own eyes [4].

By its very formality, this letter betrays Freud's disappointment and even anger toward Jones. But it also shows that he had sustained his eagerness to see the book published in England before his death. By now utterances of this kind were no longer expressive of the old preoccupation with possible death dates, but indicated Freud's realistic appraisal of his life expectancy.

In November, Zweig suffered a severe car accident shortly after his return to Palestine. He was unconscious for several days, and Freud was greatly relieved when Eitingon sent him a telegram saying that Zweig was out of danger.

Autumn was unusually beautiful and mild in London that year. Freud enjoyed the lovely garden, to which he had access from his study. He could now see four patients daily, and receive visitors. He was still reading extensively.

In the first week of December I noticed, in the area of the necrotic bone which I had been watching apprehensively, a definite, very sensitive swelling that looked like an inflammatory process. The secretion became foul, and Freud had intense pain. All this happened just a few years before the discovery of antibiotics, and it is deeply frustrating to realize that so much suffering might have been prevented had the discovery come about a short time earlier. We hoped that a necrotic bone chip would come out, and waited for it impatiently.

On December 13, 1938 Freud wrote to Arnold Zweig, who by then had more or less recovered from his accident:

Dear Master Arnold,
Eitingon of course did not fail to report about you, but it is entirely different to see your handwriting again. . . . And why must we in this way be reminded of the uncertainty of our life, of which we are convinced in any case. I was also greatly concerned about your son who was driving the car. . . . Happy to learn that he wasn't even accidentally responsible [for the accident]. May the devil not forget, when he's looking around among the English, to pick up that drunken officer too.

Not much new with us. It could be quite comfortable if it weren't for this and that, and a lot of other things too . . . [these dots in the original].

I am still waiting for a second bone which, like the first one, is supposed to detach itself from me [a tiny splinter had come out some weeks earlier].

On December 19 Freud wrote a letter to Eitingon, which I found painful to read 25 years later:

I have not yet thanked you for your conscientious reports about our Arnold Zweig. In the meantime I have also received a first letter from him, quite illegible, but gratifying nevertheless. At least one piece of good news . . . I am waiting like a hungry dog for a bone which has been promised to me, only it is supposed to be one of my own. I am now working four hours a day [5].

Even under these circumstances Freud would not begin a letter by mentioning problems of his own. And when he did report his painful expectations, he was still able to make use of "gallows humor" to turn a painful or even potentially tragic situation into a bitter joke.

Around Christmas the pain was becoming more localized, and I could now clearly see and feel a bone chip ready to come out. On December 28, I was able to remove a sizable sequestrated bone chip. This immediately brought considerable relief, and also some new hope. I shall not easily forget Freud's reaction of gratitude, which needed no words but was expressed by the look on his face and an especially warm handshake. I immediately reported the situation to Pichler, and the year was thus closing on a somewhat hopeful note.

The day before this, on December 27, Freud must have felt a trifle better and had written two remarkable letters. One had been to Marie Bonaparte, who was then on a trip to Egypt:

My dear Marie,
Your letter with the beautiful photos from the Museum arrived while we were still considering whether to send the answer to your kind Christmas telegram to Athens or to Egypt. Now it has turned into New Year's wishes and will be addressed to the latter. However, I am rushing an answer to Athens.

Yes, we did freeze here, and the ever green English lawn is thickly covered with white snow—a magnificent winter landscape in front of my window overlooking the garden. We dare not imagine what London will look like when all this snow turns to water!

Christmas was peaceful, except for the usual news of death and suicide from Vienna. My bone is still content to stay with me, but not I with it. Schur is very good, but cannot help.

Yesterday I finished reading the first proofs of the German *Moses*. My English translators [the Joneses] are in Mürren [Switzerland].

The Sinai does not deserve your interest. You know that the mountain of Jahweh was not on the peninsula, but in western Arabia; and a handing down of the law on Sinai simply never occurred. See my *Moses,* which alternately impresses and greatly displeases me.

To miss Jerusalem would be a pity. You know that on this trip you are also seeing *for me,* the "travel-paralyzed" [a novel word combination] [6].

On the same day he wrote still another particularly poignant letter, this one to a Rachel Berdach (Bardi):

Dear Madam (or Miss?)
Your mysterious and beautiful book [*The Emperor, the Sages, and Death*] has pleased me to an extent that makes me unsure of my judgment. I wonder whether it is the transfiguration of Jewish suffering or surprise that so much psychoanalytical insight should have existed at the court of the brilliant and despotic Staufer [Friedrich II, von Hohenstaufen] which makes me say that I haven't read anything so substantial and poetically accomplished for a long time!

And with it such a diffident letter! Can it be that your modesty causes you to underrate your own value? Who are you? Where did you acquire all the knowledge expressed in your book? Judging by the priority you grant to death, one is led to conclude that you are very young.[7]

Won't you give me the pleasure of paying me a visit one day? I have time in the mornings.
                         Yours very sincerely,
                              Freud [L. 311*].

It was not until 1964, after I had finished the first draft of this book, that I read Rachel Berdach's remarkable book, and was able to understand what it must have meant to Freud at that time in his life, and why he responded to it as he did.

The impact of an external stimulus depends on the constellation of factors existing in our inner life. The impact will be intensified if the nature of the sudden external stimulus plays into an internal conflict on some level. In the last days of 1938 the balance between Freud's wish to continue the struggle and his wish to give up was a very tenuous one. There was little reasonable hope for even a limited period of comfort, a true extension of life rather than a mere prolongation of life-in-death. A new year was approaching, which Freud knew would probably be his last.

[7] This was an error. Rachel Berdach was then 60 years old. However, she had actually conceived the book when she was very young; so Freud's surmise was quite accurate.

It was at this point that Freud read Rachel Berdach's book, which blends form and content in a unique way. When I first read this work, after learning of its existence from Freud's letter of December 27, 1938, to its author, I attributed the profound impact it had on me to my knowledge of, and empathy with, Freud's state of mind and body at the time he himself was reading it. However, I have reread the book several times since, and while it is difficult for me to hold this factor in abeyance, I have each time been deeply moved and filled with admiration.

The book takes us back to the 13th century, the period of the last crusades, the dawn of the Renaissance, when antagonism was growing between the Popes and the German rulers of the Holy Roman Empire. The two principal figures are the Holy Roman Emperor Frederick II and Rabbi Jacob Charif BenAron. While Frederick II's reign predated the Renaissance proper, he was in many respects a true "Renaissance man," combining political astuteness and power with culture and a thirst for knowledge. He not only built palaces and cathedrals, but tried to establish a new center for the advancement of science and art. He collected newly recovered ancient art, books in all languages, especially Arabic, Hebrew, Greek, etc. He brought together the "wise men" of various cultures—Arabs, Jews, Greeks—to study and exchange views on science, medicine, astronomy, and astrology. He himself spent much time with them and did not hesitate to encourage an exchange of ideas between these "heretics" and high-ranking representatives of the Catholic Church in residence at the Court.

Out of their colloquiums, the figure of Rabbi BenAron gradually emerges as the dominant one. The book begins with his funeral and ends with his death. And it is death, its mystery, the fear it evokes, the way it is interpreted by the various "wise men"—believers, doubters, heretics, young, and old—which is the main theme of the beautiful parables, allegories and tales of human suffering, weakness, and greatness which enrich the conversations in the imperial palace.

Some of the most poignant passages describe in poetic language what Freud dealt with in "Thoughts for the Times on War and Death" —the impact of the reality of death.

In the course of a disputation between a bishop and an Arab physician, the latter explains why, as a healer, he is revolted by the legend of Christ's miraculous resurrection of Lazarus: having been brought back to life, Lazarus had to face death a second time, an unimaginable horror. What we can only surmise, Lazarus actually experienced, and he was thenceforth doomed to live with that knowledge.[8]

When Frederick was excommunicated for making a truce with the Moslems after a Crusade he had led, and was thus excluded from receiving the sacraments of the Church, this heretic asked his fatherly friend, a firmly believing Archbishop, if he would administer the last rites when the time came, even if the ban had not yet been lifted. The priest assured him that he would not be forsaken, but would be given the necessary sustenance for his journey. The promise was kept.

Did Freud feel this request of Frederick's to be akin to his own appeal to me to help him when his time had come?

Frederick's guest BenAron had a young student, an ardent believer and poet, who was his only companion after he left the Emperor's court to return to the city where his wife and infant son had died. The rabbi loved this young man as a son, and suffered deeply when the latter died, leaving behind some notes containing crucial questions which he had been pondering. Do animals sense when they are near death? Is man alone cursed with the knowledge of death in the midst of life? Why has man not been granted ignorance?

The book ends with the description of BenAron's death. He awakens one night, struck by an uncanny silence. Running through the town and the surrounding frozen countryside, he finds that every living thing has died. Only he has been left behind by the Angel of Death. He dies, unable to utter a last despairing cry that the Angel take him along with the rest.

The special appeal of this book is in its aesthetic quality, which makes the theme of death neither morbid nor nihilistic. Perhaps it describes the splendor of true humility.

The impact which this work must have had on Freud at the time in his life when it came to his attention was only in part reflected in his letter to the author, where he expressed chiefly his delight at her "mysteriously beautiful book" and his amazement at her deep insight. But why his assumption that Rachel Berdach must have been young?

---

[8] This problem has been shifted today, from the realm of religious and philosophical debate to the realm of actuality by the refined practice of resuscitating medically dead people. New experiments in deep-freezing dying victims of incurable diseases to await eventual cures and "resurrection" will make this question one to be urgently considered. Already an international cryological society has been formed to foster such experiments.

Did he think that only the young would dare to know and write so much about death and dying[9]

Freud was able to enjoy the richness and beauty of this book, but it probably also revived the thoughts he had expressed in "Thoughts for the Times on War and Death," "On Transience" (Chapter 11), his metapsychological explanations of the fear of death in his works of the 1920s, and, finally, his letter to Marie Bonaparte of December 6, 1936 (Chapter 24). This holds true particularly for the episodes of the book which I have described in some detail above.

Unfortunately, the improvement in Freud's condition did not last long. Around the middle of January, 1939, there appeared a new swelling close to the area of bone necrosis and still higher up and further back in the oral cavity. At first it looked like another bone necrosis, but soon the lesion took on an appearance which looked ominous to me. Exner made light of my anxiety, but it did not look to me like a leukoplakia or papilloma. I believed it to be an epithelioma, and knew that with this localization further surgery would be impossible. Thus, for the first time, nothing was left but constant observation. Freud knew that we had some suspicions. Around the beginning of February I was convinced of my diagnosis, but in view of Exner's insistence that it was an inflammatory lesion I asked for a consultation. On February 10 Freud was seen by the prominent surgeon Trotter, a Fellow of the Royal Society of Medicine, who was Jones's brother-in-law. It was not really surprising, but nonetheless somewhat exasperating, to see that even Trotter, whose superior knowledge and experience could not fail to impress me, initially had difficulties in evaluating the lesion. This would probably have been true for anyone who had not had a decade of observing lesions of all kinds, under the guidance of a man like Pichler, as I had done. Trotter finally admitted that the lesion might be suspicious, but advocated

---

[9] In his introduction to the English translation of *The Emperor, the Sages, and Death*, Dr. Theodor Reik indicates (with the author's permission) that he treated Rachel Berdach psychoanalytically prior to the publication of her book, which she had conceived verbatim many years earlier without having been able to bring herself to have it published. She did so only in 1938, after she had completed her analysis. Dr. Reik also indicates that she had early in life lost a person very dear to her, which both accounted for her preoccupation with the problem of death and prevented her from putting down on paper what she carried in her head for so many years.

Rachel Berdach met Freud early in 1939, after receiving his letter. Regrettably, no record of these meetings has been preserved.

further observation. On February 11 I sent an "S.O.S." to Pichler, telling him that because of the location surgery would be impossible, and asking both for his opinion and for the notes on the amount of radiation Freud had received to date. Pichler strongly advised electro-coagulation, even if this could not be radical, in place of radium therapy.

Within the next week the lesion became so typical that there was no doubt left in my mind. The next consultation with Trotter and Exner was still more disappointing. Trotter was slightly indignant, and I— the internist and foreigner—was in a very difficult position indeed. Yet I pressed for a decision and eventually, on the suggestion of Marie Bonaparte who had been in London for some weeks, arranged for a consultation with Dr. Lacassagne, the successor to Rigaud at the Institut Curie in Paris. Lacassagne saw Freud in London on February 26, and made an excellent impression on all of us. He called the lesion most suspicious and asked for a biopsy, X-rays of the bone structure, and a surgical opinion as to the feasibility of another operation, as he had doubts about any prolonged remission from radiotherapy. He indicated that in the event of a positive biopsy and the refusal of surgery by the surgeon and/or Freud he would recommend radiotherapy, but suggested intensive X-ray treatment as a first step, explaining that radium would have to be applied directly to the lesion and was more likely to cause severe necrosis than X-ray treatment, which could be centered upon the lesion but make use of different skin fields and thus reduce the danger of tissue necrosis. He did not favor a prior electrocoagulation because of the increased danger of postradiation necrosis due to additional tissue damage. He cautioned me not to expect a lasting result, but hoped for a remission and recommended local radium treatment only as supplementary treatment for any residual lesion not responding to X-ray therapy.

The biopsy was performed on February 28, 1939. It was positive— a typical malignant epithelioma. X-rays did not show any bone involvement. The lesion, as indicated, was so high up—not far from the base of the orbita—that an operation did not seem feasible. Yet we consulted again with Dr. Trotter and the E.N.T. surgeon Dr. Harmer. The unanimous decision was that surgery would be too risky and in any case probably useless. I also doubt that Freud would have given his consent for extensive surgery this time. Radiotherapy was started immediately by the English radiologist Dr. Finzi. The daily sessions at Finzi's office were a great strain on Freud. He had unpleasant reactions—fatigue, slight dizziness, headache, and eventually he began to lose his beard and bleed from the mouth. It was hard to detect the source of this bleeding, but it occurred almost daily and was bothersome and weakening. Freud was rather worried about it. He quoted from Faust: "Blut ist ein besonderer Saft" ("Blood is quite a special fluid"). One time when I saw him during such a hemorrhage I detected a tiny telangiectasis of the upper lip as the source. This was very easy to eliminate, and Freud, who was usually not prone to express his feelings, was embarrassingly demonstrative in his gratitude. This was probably a measure of his worry about the repeated loss of blood, reinforced by his memories of 1923.

A few letters will illustrate Freud's reactions to these events. He wrote to Arnold Zweig on February 20, 1939, after commenting on the fact that Zweig would leave Palestine shortly:

> . . . I must overcome my present disinclination and give you a written report after all; unfortunately about my own state of health, which threatens to become interesting. Since the operation in September I have been suffering from pains in the jaw which are slowly but steadily becoming more intense, so that I cannot get through the day's tasks and the night without hot water bottles and higher doses of aspirin. At one time a big bone chip had already been expelled and we are waiting for the repetition of this process to put an end to this episode, but so far in vain. Now one is at a loss, does not know whether this is basically a harmless delay or the progress of the uncanny process which we have been fighting for 16 years.
>
> . . . Princess Marie, who has spent the last few weeks with us, has gotten in touch with the Parisian authority on radium. . . . He [Lacassagne] is ready to come to London . . . if the diagnosis is settled beyond any doubt. . . . I might travel to Paris with Anna and Dr. Schur to stay for about four weeks at the hospital connected with the Radium Institute. For the time being, however, I know nothing definite and can very well imagine that the whole thing is the beginning of the end, which in any event is always lying in wait for us. In the meantime I have these paralyzing pains.

It was not only the pain which was paralyzing, but also the uncertainty. Until the diagnosis was "officially" confirmed, I told Freud only of our suspicions.

The letter ended on a note of reassurance to Zweig that the latter's accident would leave no aftereffects, and with some comments on the latest novel Zweig was writing.

By the time Freud wrote to Eitingon on March 5, 1939, he already knew the results of the biopsy and spoke about them.

I have not written to you for quite some time, not only because writing, like most other activities, has become too troublesome [literally: sour], but also because the situation was too uncertain. Now we more or less know where we stand. A biopsy disclosed that we are really dealing with a new attempt by the cancer to take my place again. For quite a while we vacillated in deciding on the various possibilities of defense, but now we all have agreed on external X-ray treatment, from which everyone involved—I do not know whether I should include myself— expects good results. Tomorrow the local radiologist, a Dr. Finzi, to whom they want to turn over my case, is supposed to visit me. I hope he does not refuse as the other specialists have done. I am of course very satisfied that surgery and the trip to Paris have been abandoned. X-ray is after all more sparing of me, it gives a kind of life insurance for several weeks, and probably permits the continuation of my analytic work during that time. . . . My personal physician Schur is conducting himself with great dedication. I regret that I should be writing to you about nothing else, but that is what you wanted to know about me. Furthermore, aside from this, we are expecting the German *Moses* within the next few days. Cordial greetings to you and Mira.

> Your
> Freud

P.S. Martin Buber's pious phrases won't do much harm to *The Interpretation of Dreams*. The *Moses* is much more vulnerable, and I am prepared for an onslaught by the Jews against it [7].

The last letter Freud wrote to Arnold Zweig (there were so many lasts during those days!), written on the same day as the preceding one to Eitingon, is noteworthy for many reasons. Freud advised Zweig, who could not adjust to life in Palestine, to go to the United States rather than to England. Then he remarked:

I cannot easily guess what "comforting explanations" you say you discovered in my *Discontent*.[10] That book has by now become a stranger to me. I am just waiting for the *Moses* which is supposed to come out in March, and then I no longer need to be interested in any book of mine until my next incarnation.

I had some unpleasant weeks, not only illness and pain, but complete indecision about the next measures to be taken. Surgery and radium treatment (in Paris) were finally discarded and external X-ray therapy was decided on; it will start tomorrow. (There no longer is any doubt that it is a new advance of my dear old cancer, with which I now have been sharing my existence for 16 years).

Now comes a sentence that contains two meaningful parapraxes. I am therefore repeating this sentence in German:

---

[10] *Civilization and Its Discontents* (1930b).

Wer *damals* der Stärkere sein *würd* konnte man natürlich nicht vorhersagen [my italics].

A literal translation of this sentence would make no sense. "Who in the *past will be* [or: *would have been*] [*würd* is not an actual word] the stronger, one of course cannot foresee." The correct wording of the conscious thought would have been: "Wer *diesmal* der stärkere sein *wird* kann man natürlich nicht vorhersagen." "Who will be the stronger this time, one obviously cannot foresee."

The word *diesmal* (this time) was replaced by *damals* (in the past); *würd* is an obvious condensation of *wird*—will be—and *würde*—would have been. The interpretation of these parapraxes is evident. The wish to live was still there—"Let me turn the clock back 16 years, when *I* was still the stronger one." However, the doubt, the reality, probably also the wish for final rest account for the change of *wird* to the nonexistent *würd*.

Freud's metaphor about his "neoplasm" in the letter to Fliess of February 19, 1899 (see Chapter 5) seems uncanny in the light of these letters to Eitingon and Arnold Zweig, written so many years later.

The malignancy initially responded surprisingly well to the X-ray therapy. The pain subsided quite rapidly. On March 20, 1939, Freud wrote to Marie Bonaparte:

> I must once again express my regret that I could devote myself to you so little when you were staying with us.[11] Perhaps it will work out better next time—if there is no war[12]—because my pains still seem to be staying away. Dr. Harmer, who has just visited me, finds that the treatment had a distinct influence on the appearance of the affected areas [8].

The whole letter sounded somewhat hopeful, and this was also reflected in Freud's handwriting and in the fact that he did not start the letter by discussing his own health, something he disliked doing.

The *Moses* book arrived. Ever since I had been acting as Freud's physician he had always given me an author's copy of his publications. I had never asked for, and never received, an inscription. This time, after handing me a copy of *Moses*, Freud hesitated for a moment and then said: "Let me have it back for a moment." He took the

[11] During the weeks of indecision, Marie Bonaparte stayed in London at Freud's home.

[12] This was the week the Germans occupied all of Czechoslovakia, thereby putting an end to Chamberlain's vain hope for "peace in our time."

book and wrote on the flyleaf: "Seinem Doktor—Verf. [asser]. März 1939." "To his doctor—the Author. March, 1939." He handed it back to me with his face reflecting deep thought and resignation. No words were needed to indicate what he meant: "This is my last book, and you should have the inscription as a momento." He knew that I understood. Much later Anna told me that he had done the same with her copy.

The improvement continued, and early in April the whole area looked much better. Some additional small doses of radium were applied locally. We started to breathe easier and to hope that the result might after all last for some time.

I was now faced with an extremely difficult and painful decision. After Munich I had decided to remain in England only as long as Freud was still alive, and then to emigrate to the United States. As mentioned earlier, I had previously applied for a visa while still in Vienna, but had forfeited it when I received a permit to go to England. After the Munich crisis I reapplied for an American visa, and my application was processed under the initial quota number. On Christmas Eve of 1938 I was notified by the American Consulate in London that I was now eligible for an immigration visa. Due to the complicated American quota regulations I would have to take this visa or lose my quota number, which would mean an endless postponement of my emigration once I was ready to leave England. I had been born in what was then Poland, and the Polish quota was now filled for years to come. Yet I could not leave Freud in the condition he was in at the beginning of 1939, and requested an extension of my visa. I was given a final extension to the end of April, just at the point where Freud was beginning to improve under the influence of the X-ray treatments. When his condition was much improved, I decided to take my family to the United States, apply for my "first papers," take the New York State Boards for my medical license, and return to London at the earliest possible moment.

Freud helped me with all the necessary formalities. He wrote letters on my behalf to the American Consulate and to friends in the United States, asking them to help speed matters up there. Yet I knew that he did not quite approve of my decision, not only because he had a certain prejudice against the United States (to the extent that he was able to nurse prejudices) since his 1909 trip, but because he was used to me and in a sense dependent on me, and he probably felt that I was deserting him, or worse, giving up on him.

In my report to Jones on this episode, which the latter used for the last chapters of his biography, I remarked in this connection: "I know that I was not just projecting my own guilt feelings." Freud's letters of that period, which will be quoted presently, proved that I was right.

When I was actually leaving, Freud was softer and more forgiving, and gave me his "blessing."

I had "trained" Dr. B. Samet, a friend of mine and a former associate of Freud's cardiologist friend Braun, to substitute for me as far as possible during my absence.

We sailed on April 21, 1939, for New York. A letter written by Freud to Marie Bonaparte on April 28 reflected, among other things, his reaction to my departure:

> I have not written to you for quite some time, while you have been swimming in the blue sea [the Mediterranean at St. Tropez]. I assume you know why, and will also recognize the reason from my handwriting. (Not even the pen is the same any more; it has left me like my physician and other external organs.) Things are not going well with me. My illness and the sequelae of the treatment both have a share in the causation, but I do not know in what proportion. One has tried to draw me into an atmosphere of optimism: the cancer is shrinking, the reactive manifestations are temporary. I do not believe it, and dislike being deceived.
>
> Some intervening complications that would cut short the cruel process would be very welcome.
>
> Should I really look forward to seeing you soon again in May? [9]

Even in this sad letter Freud thought of calling to Marie Bonaparte's attention a Hungarian refugee writer who had asked for her help, and to comment on the health of her daughter, Princess Eugénie.

Freud had always trusted me to tell him the full truth, but he did not have the same confidence in the other physicians who were in charge of him. It did not lessen my guilt feelings about leaving him to read this letter many years later.

Once in New York, I tried frantically to shorten my stay. With the help of Dr. Ruth Mack-Brunswick and her father, Federal Judge Julian Mack, who had informed the authorities about the special situation I was in, I had hopes of obtaining my "first papers" in a much shorter time than was usual. I was receiving regular reports from Anna and Dr. Samet which, in May, were still encouraging. A letter of Freud's to Marie Bonaparte written on May 18, 1939, confirmed that he was feeling better. I was told how much he was enjoying the spring, the flowers, the garden. Then in June the reports began to get gloomier: pain, severe X-ray reactions, and perhaps bone necrosis in the zygomatic bone. Around June 15, I received my first papers. On June 16, Freud wrote to Marie Bonaparte (who had in the meantime been to London):

> My dear Marie,
> The evening before last I was ready to write you a long letter of condolence on the occasion of our old Tattou's[13] death, and then to prepare you for the fact that on your next visit I would listen eagerly to whatever you might tell me about your new papers, and throw in a word here and there whenever I believed that I could supplement something. The two nights that followed again cruelly destroyed my expectations. The radium has once again begun to eat away at something, causing pain and toxic manifestations, and my world is what it was previously: a small island of pain floating on an ocean of indifference.
>   Finzi continues to assert his satisfaction. His answer to my last complaint was: "In the end you, too, will be satisfied." So he is luring me half against my will into continuing to hope and in the meantime into continuing to suffer.

Could there have been a more tragic expression of Freud's and everyone's conflict than this last sentence? It was this conflict which had come through in the slips of the pen Freud had made in his last letter to Arnold Zweig. Freud was here paraphrasing the last stanza of Goethe's poem "Der Fischer":

> Halb zog sie ihn, halb sank er hin
> Und ward nicht mehr gesehn.

> Half she drew him in and half he sank down,
> And he never more was seen.

In this way he indicated that he would meet the same end as the mermaid's victims.

Freud continued this letter with some wise interpretations concerning Marie Bonaparte, and ended on a positive note:

> I hear that the German *Moses* has already sold 1800 copies. Most cordially, and with warm-weather-wishes[14] for as long as you are at the seashore.
>   Your
>   Freud [10]

13 One of Marie Bonaparte's chows.
14 Another of Freud's masterful uses of word combinations; the "warm" applies to both the weather and the wishes.

This was the last letter Freud wrote to Marie Bonaparte.

I took my New York State Boards during the last week of June, and sailed on the first boat back to England, arriving in London on July 8, 1939. I found Freud looking much worse. He had lost weight and was somewhat apathetic, at least as compared with his usual mental vigor. The skin over the right cheekbone was slightly discolored. He had lost most of his beard on the right side due to the X-ray treatments. In the region of the last lesion, there was foul necrotic tissue. I also had the definite impression that a new carcinomatous ulceration had developed behind and slightly upwards of the old lesion, in the direction of the base of the orbita. The bone was extremely tender, and there was a fetid odor.[15]

Again the thought communication existing between Freud and myself required no words. He knew what I thought; I knew what he knew. He did not believe that it was only bone necrosis, and I could not contradict him. We concentrated on mouth hygiene, proper nutrition and tonics, and on the alleviation of his suffering. This was becoming increasingly more difficult, inasmuch as Freud hated barbiturates and opiates. He thought of morphine only as a last resort, when he finally had to give up. So we had once again to resort to Orthoform, which relieved the surface pain of the ulceration but not of the bone necrosis. His usually sound restorative sleep was now beginning to fail him. Anna, who besides her normal routine of seeing patients, training, and organizing the exodus of the whole continental group, was more or less on 24-hour-duty, had to apply Orthoform

---

[15] And yet only a few days earlier, Dr. Finzi had written the following amazing report to Dr. Lacassagne, which I found among Marie Bonaparte's papers:

> 107, Harley Street—W. 1
> July 5th, 1939

Dear Lacassagne,
Princess Hélène told me you would like a word as to the progress Professor Freud is making. The growth is very greatly improved since the treatment and there is now a large cavity where it was previously filled up with growth. Unfortunately there is still considerable sepsis there which gives him a lot of pain and this pain makes him very tired. He absolutely refuses to let us give him any pain-relieving medicament of any sort except aspirin and the result is that he has bad nights and gets very weak. There probably still remains a small remnant of growth high up anteriorly, but I cannot be quite sure of this yet. What he really requires is some psychological treatment to enable him to make a pact with some other medicament similar to that which he has with aspirin, but I dare not suggest this to him.

> With kindest regards.
> Yours very sincerely
> Dr. Finzi

several times during the night. Occasionally Freud took an aspirin or Pyramidon. Throughout July he continued to see a few patients, to read, and to keep as much as possible to his daily routine. He also tried with desperate energy to eat.

Some time late in July Freud had a nocturnal attack of left ventricular failure with "cardiac asthma." In this emergency I was able to give prompt help, and from that point on he "forgave" me my trip to the United States. Whereas during the first weeks after my return some of the old intimacy had been missing, the earlier relationship was now restored. I was greatly relieved, partly because of my own feelings but mainly because I knew that this would be essential to him during the last, most trying chapter which was about to start.

Cardiac treatment had to be instituted and the medication did not help his already poor appetite.

During August everything went downhill rapidly. There could be no doubt about an extended recurrence with ulceration. The discoloration of the cheek became more and more marked, indicating the development of a skin necrosis. The foetor became more and more unbearable, and could not be controlled with any kind of mouth hygiene. It was apparent that the odor was coming from the necrosis of the bone. Again I must point out that no antibiotics were available at that time to help control this condition.

Freud became more and more fatigued, growing weaker by the day. He now had to make the most painful decision of all—to give up seeing patients. He was still able to give Anna a resume of the cases which showed his full mastery, but there were now moments when sheer fatigue dulled his alertness. He was still trying to eat, but he rested most of the day. His study also became his sick bay, and from his bed he could see the garden with the flowers he loved. However, the chow to which Freud was so attached could not tolerate the smell, and could not be prodded into coming near him. When brought into the room the dog crouched in the farthest corner. Freud knew what this meant, and looked at his pet with a tragic and knowing sadness.

Marie Bonaparte visited him for the last time between July 31 and August 6, 1939. It was a sad, silent leave-taking. Freud commented to me later how fortunate he was in having found so many valuable friends.

Late in August there was another leave-taking, this time from his granddaughter Eva, Oliver's daughter, whose visit to London (she was then living in France) Freud greatly enjoyed. He showed a special tenderness toward this charming girl, then 15 years old, who was to perish toward the end of the war in 1944.

The illness continued to take its unrelenting course. The skin over the cheekbone became gangrenous, eventually creating a hole and open communication between the oral cavity and the outside. This brought temporarily a slight lessening of the pain—or rather, the whole area became somewhat more accessible to Orthoform applications—but the odor became even worse. Freud's bed had to be covered with a mosquito netting because flies were attracted by the smell.

In the meantime the war had started. It had been anticipated that air raids might start with the beginning of hostilities. In order to be on hand in any eventuality I moved into Freud's home around September 1, while my wife and children went to a "safe" place in the country. Freud was reading the papers and was fully aware of the impact of events. But he was already "far away." The detachment which I described earlier in connection with the Munich crisis was much more pronounced. After a broadcast which mentioned the old idea that this was a war to end all wars, I asked him: "Do you believe that this is the last war"? He answered dryly: "My last war."

During the first air-raid alarms Freud's bed was moved to the "safe" zone of the house. He followed with a certain interest the steps that were taken to safeguard his art collection and manuscripts. He still followed a certain routine, and never forgot until the day before his death to wind either his watch or a desk clock which required winding once a week! In a way this tiny detail was typical of the disciplined organization of his mind. Nothing changed in his unfailing friendliness. Not once in all that time did I witness any impatient or angry reaction toward any person in his environment. He still asked how my children were reacting to evacuation, and suggested to me reading material from his library, recommending among other things certain works by Albert Schweitzer, whom he held in high esteem.

It was becoming more and more difficult to feed him. He was suffering badly, and the nights were miserable. He could hardly leave his bed and gradually became cachectic. Anna and I were taking turns applying Orthoform, but he was not yet receiving any real sedation. It was an agonizing experience not to be able to alleviate his suffering, yet I knew that I had to wait until he asked me to do so.

The final phase began when reading became difficult. Freud did not read at random, but carefully selected books from his library. The last book he read was Balzac's *La Peau de Chagrin (The Fatal Skin).*

When he finished it he remarked casually to me: "This was the proper book for me to read; it deals with shrinking and starvation."

La Peau de Chagrin was written in the spirit of romanticism under the influence of Goethe's *Werther* and *Faust,* of Hoffmann's *Fantastic Tales,* and of Byron. Both Balzac's hero, Raphael, and Goethe's Faust make a pact with the devil. Raphael is given a magic but fatal skin of a wild ass. All his wishes will be fulfilled—but with every fulfilled wish the skin will shrink, and along with it his life. Raphael cannot *master* his wishes and tries in vain to deny them. He cannot master his fear of death, and dies in hopeless panic.

Faust, on the other hand, dies only after having achieved, at least in a vision, his ultimate goal—the reclaiming of land from the fury of the ocean—in Freud's words, from the Zuyder Zee.

Since I had not read the *Peau de Chagrin* or Freud's letters at that time, I was unaware of how meaningful that statement was and why he had made it to me. The theme of the shrinking skin echoes Freud's words about his dying father written in 1896: "he . . . is steadily shrinking towards . . . a fateful date." The unconscious is immortal, Freud had said. It retains all memories. How uncanny that he should have chosen to read this book before writing "finis" to his own story!

Freud too, had accomplished all the reclamation work possible for him. In contrast to Raphael, he had overcome all his fears, as far as this is humanly possible. But he was so desperately tired that he had only one wish left, one that can best be expressed in the words of one of Goethe's most beautiful poems:

> Der Du von dem Himmel bist
> Alles Leid und Schmerzen stillest,
> Den, der doppelt Elend ist.
> Doppelt mit Erquickung füllest.
> Ach, ich bin des Treibens müde
> Was soll all der Schmerz und Lust
> Süsser Friede
> Komm, ach komm in meine Brust.

> You who come from Heaven
> Allaying every pain and grief
> Fill with doubly measured calm
> One who doubly wretched is.
> How tired am I of this struggle,
> Why this senseless pain and joy?
> Come, sweet peace,
> Come, oh come into my breast.

On the following day, September 21, while I was sitting at his bedside, Freud took my hand and said to me: "Lieber Schur, Sie erinnern sich wohl an unser erstes Gespräch. Sie haben mir damals versprochen mich nicht im Stiche zu lassen wenn es so weit ist. Das ist jetzt nur noch Quälerei und hat keinen Sinn mehr." ("My dear Schur, you certainly remember our first talk. You promised me then not to forsake me when my time comes. Now it's nothing but torture and makes no sense any more.")

I indicated that I had not forgotten my promise. He sighed with relief, held my hand for a moment longer, and said: "Ich danke Ihnen" ("I thank you"), and after a moment of hesitation he added: "Sagen Sie es der Anna" ("Tell Anna about this"). All this was said without a trace of emotionality or self-pity, and with full consciousness of reality.

I informed Anna of our conversation, as Freud had asked. When he was again in agony, I gave him a hypodermic of two centigrams of morphine. He soon felt relief and fell into a peaceful sleep. The expression of pain and suffering was gone. I repeated this dose after about twelve hours. Freud was obviously so close to the end of his reserves that he lapsed into a coma and did not wake up again. He died at 3:00 A.M. on September 23, 1939.

Freud had said in his "Thoughts for the Times on War and Death":

> Towards the actual person who has died we adopt a special attitude: something like admiration for someone who has accomplished a very difficult task.

APPENDIX: NOTES
ON UNPUBLISHED MATERIAL

CHAPTER 1

1. April 25, 1885 [letter to Martha Bernays]

Samstag 25. April 1885

Mein geliebtes Marthchen

Lustgarten, mein Arzt, hat einen Modus ausfindig gemacht, wie ich Dir schreiben kann. Dieser Brief samt Couvert wird für einige Stunden in einen Trockenkasten von 120° C gelegt werden, in dem er all seiner gefährlichen Eigenschaften verlustig gehen soll. Nicht wahr, die Art Censur wird uns nicht schaden?

. . . .

Ich habe wol die echten Blattern, aber nicht die rechten, weisst Du, nicht wie Du Dir's nach der Jugenderinnerung vorstellen wolltest. Ich habe keine einzige Pustel, vielleicht fünf charakteristische "Wimmerl"—es giebt kein deutsches Wort dafür—und ein Dutzend kleinerer Knötchen; von Entstellung, Narben, Fieber u. dgl. ist gar keine Rede. Ich war auch nie zu Bette. Aber ich bin doch krank, zu Zeiten ausserordentlich schwach, das Essen schmeckt mir gar nicht u. ich kann nur am Vormittag was lesen. Der Nachmittag wird mir qualvoll, weil ich matt, arbeitsunfähig u. ruhelos bin, abends stellt sich's wieder her. Meine Bedienerin ist sehr brav, aufmerksam u. intelligent; u. ich bin im Ganzen doch noch recht froh, erstens dass meine vorgängige Erschöpfung keine psychologische, sondern die Folge einer Krankheit war, u. zweitens dass die böse Krankheit, mit der ich mich als Arzt doch auseinandersetzen muss, mich so gütig behandelt hat.

. . . .

CHAPTER 2

1. October 18, 1893 [letter to Wilhelm Fliess]

Ich hätte viel über Nase und Sexual. (2 Themata) zu schreiben. Dass Du wenig von der Art siehst, zeugt doch von einer vorherigen Auslese des Materials. Ich habe jetzt keinen grossen Andrang und doch die schönsten Fälle, bin auch ein Stück weiter. Eine Beobachtung von Flimmermigraine bei Onanisten werde ich Dir nächstens mittheilen, leider *ohne* Nasenbefund. . . .

Mit meinem Herzbefinden denke ich Dir keineswegs durchzugehen. Es ist jetzt viel besser, nicht durch mein Verdienst, denn ich rauche arg in Folge der Aufregungen der letzten Zeiten, die reich daran waren. Ich glaube, es wird nächstens arg wiederkommen. Im Rauchen werde ich einer Vorschrift von Dir peinlich folgen, ich habe es schon einmal getan als Du Dich (Bahnhof—Wartenzeit) darüber äussertest. Es fehlte mir freilich sehr. Ein arg [crossed out], akuter Schnupfen hat die Sache nicht verschlimmert.

2. November 17, 1893 [passage of L. 15]

Deinem Rauchverbot folge ich nicht; *hältst Du es denn für ein grosses Glück sehr lange Jahre elend zu leben?* Ich bin aber von den betreffenden Sensationen sehr wenig belästigt.

3. April 19, 1894 [passage of L. 17]

Deine Bemerkung über Tagebuch werde ich mir merken. Du hast Recht.

Frau Dr. Fr. hat mir auch nicht besonders gefallen. Vielleicht tue ich ihr unrecht wenn ich sie als Fleischspeise "Gans" und als Gemüse "Z'widerwurzen" klassificiere. Dass ihr die Analyse unangenehm war, glaube ich gerne, damit hat sie nur den Gedanken der Abwehr bestätigt, sie ist mir auch das dritte Mal ausgekniffen. . . .

Den vielen Neuigkeiten, die Du ankündigst entspricht wol endlich fast ungestörtes Wolbefinden bei Dir. Über die Ätiologie Deines zweiten Kopfschmerzes habe ich nachgedacht. Ich glaube nicht recht daran. Willst Du Dich nicht lieber an die Siebbeinzellen halten?

Fratzen und Frau sind wol, letztere ist nicht die Vertraute meiner Sterbedelirien. Wol für alle Fälle überflüssig.

4. April 25, 1894 [letter to Wilhelm Fliess]

Mein lieber Freund

Du hast so liebenswürdig geschrieben, dass ich Dich nicht warten lassen kann, bis ich etwas zu sagen habe; sondern aus der Alltäglichkeit heraus Nachricht geben muss.

Ich halte Dich für sicherlich competenter für Differentialdiagnose in diesen heikeln Dingen als wen anderen und habe mich also in der Auffassung meiner Affektion wieder irre machen lassen. Breuer z.B. hat die nicht toxische Herzaffektion ruhig gelten lassen. Eine Dilatation soll ich nicht haben, gespaltene Töne, Arrythmie udgl. dauern fort trotz Abstinenz. Die Libido ist längst überwunden. 1 Gramm Digitalis in 2 Tagen hat die subjectiven Beschwerden sehr herabgesetzt und soll auch die Arrythmie beeinflusst haben, die ich zwar immer spüre so oft ich für meinen Puls eine Resonanz finde. Meine Verstimmung, Mattigkeit, Arbeitsunfähigkeit und das bischen Dyspnoe sind eher ärger geworden.

Dies der "Status idem." Dass ich diese schöne Welt nicht verlasse, ohne Dich zum persönlichen Abschied hieherzucitiren steht mir schon seit Beginn meines Krankheitsgefühles fest. Ich glaube auch nicht, dass ich demnächst in die Lage kommen werde von dieser Deiner Erlaubniss Gebrauch zu machen, aber die Quälerei und das nutzlose Verstreichen der Gegenwart gehen mir mehr zu Leide als was etwa an der Prognose unbefriedigend ist.

In wenigen Tagen schicke ich Dir ein paar Seiten Rohmaterial, eine rasch
aufgezeichnete Analyse, in der man bis auf den Grund der Neurose sehen kann.
Zu der Zusammenstellung für Dich konnte ich mich noch immer nicht haben,
ärgere mich sehr darüber. Das war doch sonst anders. Die sociale und wissenschaftliche Windstille macht mir allerlei Sorgen. Wenn ich in der alltäglichen
Arbeit bin, geht es mir am Besten.

Ich hoffe Du bist wenigstens wol. Ich glaube eine Stunde lang habe [ich] mich
in diesen Tagen doch über meine Krankheit gefreut. Das muss gewesen sein, als
ich Deinen Brief bekam.

Ich grüsse Dich und Deine liebe Ida herzlich und die Meinigen stimmen ein.

Dein

Dr. Sigm. Freud

5. May 6, 1894 [letter to Wilhelm Fliess]

Den Leitfaden der Neurosen konnte ich noch nicht fertig machen. Es geht mir
besser, zeitweise selbst viel besser, aber noch kein halber Tag war frei von
Beschwerden und Stimmung und Leistungsfähigkeit sind recht darnieder. Ich
halte es doch nicht für Nikotin, habe zuf[ällig] in letzter Woche *viel ähnliches*
in [der] Praxis gesehen, glaube es ist rheumatische Myocarditis und man wird es
nicht recht los. Rheumatische Muskelschwielen an anderen Körperstellen habe
ich in letzten Jahren wiederholt gehabt.

Im Sommer möchte ich ein wenig zur Anatomie zurückkehren,* es ist doch
das einzig Befriedigende.

6. May 21, 1894 [passage of L. 18]

Liebster Freund,
Liebster, im Ernst, denn ich finde es rührend dass Du Dich so eingehend mit
meinen Zuständen zu einer Zeit beschäftigst, da Du entweder sehr beschäftigt
oder nicht sehr wol oder vielleicht beides bist. Es war eine Lücke in Deinen
Briefen, die mir bereits unheimlich vorkam. . . . Dann kam Dein Brief mit der
sorgfältigen Widerlegung aller meiner internistisch-dilettantischen Phantasien,
aber ohne ein Wort über Dein Befinden. Ich habe lange schon gemerkt, dass
Du Leiden besser und würdiger erträgst als ich, der in der Stimmung ewig
flackernde.

Ich verspreche Dir einen ausführlichen Krankenbericht nächstens; es geht mir
besser, aber weit von gut, wenigstens arbeite ich wieder. Heute will ich mir
eine gute Stunde machen und nur Wissenschaft mit Dir plaudern. Es ist eben
keine besondere Gunst des Schicksals, dass ich ungefähr 5 Stunden im Jahr für
Gedankenaustausch mit Dir habe, wo ich den Anderen kaum entbehren kann
und Du der einzige Andere, der *Alter,* bist.

Morgen schicke ich die Henne mit den fünf Küchlein nach Reichenau und
in der traurigen Einsamkeit nachher . . . werde ich öfter den Vorsatz ausfüh-
ren, Dir wenigstens zu schreiben. . . .

M. D. war doch eine Perle? Sie kommt nicht in die Sammlung mit Breuer,
weil das zweite Stockwerk, das des sexuellen Momentes, dort nicht enthüllt
werden soll. Die Krankengeschichte, die ich jetzt schreibe—eine Heilung—
gehört zu meinen schwersten Arbeiten. Du wirst sie vor Breuer bekommen,
wenn Du sie rasch zurücksenden willst.

Unter den trüben Gedanken der letzten Monate kam der, die sexuelle These

---

* See footnote 23 in Chapter 2.

nicht mehr erweisen zu können, an zweiter Stelle, gleich nach Weib und Kindern. Man möchte doch nicht gleich und nicht ganz sterben.

7. June 22, 1894 [passage of L. 19]

Die letzte Krankengeschichte schicke ich Dir heute, am Stil wirst Du merken, dass ich krank war. Zwischen die 4. und 5. Seite fällt das Geständniss meiner lange verheimlichten Beschwerden. Die Sache selbst ist wol sehr lehrreich, war für mich entscheidend.

Der Sommer soll mir willkommen sein, wenn er bringt, wonach ich mich seit Jahren sehne, ein paar Tage mit Dir ohne arge Störung. . . . Das Leben kommt mir meistens so unsicher vor, dass ich geneigt bin, lange verhaltene Wünsche nicht mehr aufzuschieben. Andere Reisen werden daneben zurücktreten müssen, denn dies Jahr war ein combiniert schlechtes, hat ausser der Krankheit auch materiellen Ausfall gebracht. Auf ein paar Tage könnte ich natürlich doch kommen; auf das Steigen habe ich "mit schwerem Herzen"—wie sinnreich der Sprachgebrauch ist—verzichtet. Wenn Du mir's also richten kannst, dass ich nicht sehr weit zu reisen habe und dann mit Dir (dabei denke ich immer Deine Frau mit . . .) wirklich allein bin, dann sehen wir uns heuer Dank meiner Unlust zu weiterem Aufschub.

Nun folgt meine Krankengeschichte in ungeschminkter Wahrheit mit allen Details, auf die ein elender Patient Werth legt und die es wahrscheinlich nicht verdienen.

Vom Tage Deines Verbots an habe ich 7 Wochen nicht geraucht. Es ging mir, wie erwartet zuerst unerlaubt schlecht, Herzbeschwerden mit Verstimmung und dabei das gräuliche Elend der Abstinenz. Letztere ging nach etwa 3 Wochen vorüber, erstere ermässigten sich nach etwa 6 Wochen, aber ich blieb complet arbeitsunfähig, ein geschlagener Mann. Nach 7 Wochen begann ich—gegen mein Versprechen an Dich—wieder zu rauchen und dabei hat folgendes mitgewirkt.

1) Gleichzeitig sah ich Kranke mit fast identischen Zuständen in denselben Jahren, die entweder nicht geraucht hatten (2 Frauen) oder das Rauchen aufgegeben hatten. Breuer dem ich wiederholt sagte, ich halte die Affektion nicht für Intoxicatio nicot. gab es endlich zu, verwies auch auf die Frauen und so wurde mir das Motiv entzogen, das Du so treffend in einem früheren Brief bezeichnet hast: Man kann dem nur entsagen, wenn man die feste Überzeugung hat, es sei die Ursache des Leidens.

2) Von den ersten Cigarren an war ich arbeitsfähig und Herr meiner Stimmung, früher war die Existenz unerträglich. Auch habe ich nicht bemerkt, dass die Beschwerden sich nach 1 Cigarre gesteigert hätten.

Ich rauche jetzt mässig, bin langsam bis zu 3 *pro die* gestiegen, es geht mir sehr viel besser als früher, eigentlich progressiv besser, nicht gut natürlich. Ich will den Zustand schildern.

Etwas Arrythmie scheint immer zu sein, aber Steigerungen zu einem Delirium cordis mit Beklemmungsgefühl kommen nur in Anfällen, die jetzt keine Stunde dauern, fast regelmässig nach dem Mittagessen. Die mässige Dyspnoe beim Stiegensteigen ist weg, der linke Arm ist seit Wochen schmerzfrei, die Brustwand noch recht empfindlich, Stufe [? not clearly legible]. Druckgefühl, Brennen fehlen keinen Tag. Objektiv soll nichts nachweisbar sein, ich weiss es ja nicht. Schlaf und alle andere Funktionen ungestört, Stimmung beherrsche ich sehr gut, fühle mich allerdings gealtert, schwerfällig, nicht gesund. Digit[alis] hat mir ausgezeichnet gethan. . . .

Was mich quält ist die Unsicherheit, wie die Geschichte zu nehmen ist. Mir wäre es [a word crossed out] peinlich Hypochondr[ische] Beurtheilung zu verrathen, ich habe aber keine Anhaltspunkte es zu entscheiden. Mit meiner Behandlung hier bin ich sehr unzufrieden. Breuer ist voll scheinbarer Widersprüche. Wenn ich sage, es geht mir besser, kommt die Antwort: Sie wissen gar nicht, *wie* gern ich das höre. Das sollte auf eine ernste Affektion schliessen lassen. Frage ich ein andermal, was es eigentlich ist, so kommt die Antwort: Nichts, jedenfalls etwas was vorüber ist. Übrigens kümmert er sich um mich gar nicht, sieht mich 2 Wochen lang nicht, ich weiss nicht, ist das Politik oder wirkliche Gleichgiltigkeit oder vollberechtigt. Im Ganzen bemerke ich, dass ich behandelt werde wie ein Kranker mit Ausweichen und Beschwindeln, anstatt dass man mich zur Ruhe brächte, indem man mir alles sagt, was über dergleichen zu sagen ist, das heisst, was man weiss.

Es wäre mir die grösste Erleichterung, könnte ich Deine Auffassung getheilt haben oder noch theilen, selbst eine neue Abgewöhnung würde mir jetzt minder schwer fallen, aber es kommt mir als *sacrifizio d'intelletto* vor, ich bin zum ersten Mal in irgend etwas anderer Meinung als Du. Bei Breuer habe ich's leichter, der sagt gar keine Meinung.

Das Beispiel von *Kundt* hat mich weniger geschreckt, wer mir die 13 Jahre bis 51 Jahre garantieren könnte, der würde mir die Cigarre nicht verleidet haben. Meine Compromissansicht, für die ich keine wissenschaftliche Begründigung habe, ist die, dass ich noch 4-5-8 Jahre an wechselnden Beschwerden mit guten und schlechten Zeiten leiden und dann zwischen 40 u. 50 an einer Herzruptur schön plötzlich verenden werde; wenn es nicht zu nahe an 40 ist, ist es gar nicht so schlecht.

Du wirst mich nur unendlich verpflichten, wenn Du mich definitiv aufklärst, ich glaube nämlich im Geheimen, dass Du sehr genau weisst, was es ist und das Rauchverbot, das ja relative Berechtigung hat, nur in gewohnter Strenge und wegen der erziehlichen und beruhigenden Verwerthbarkeit, so absolut erlassen hast.

Also jetzt genug, es ist sehr traurig sich soviel mit sich abgeben zu müssen, wenn man über soviel Interessanteres schreiben könnte.

Zwischen Deinen Zeilen lese ich, dass Du mit Deinen Kopfschmerzen nicht sehr zufrieden bist und ärgere mich über unsere Unwissenheit. Von den Arbeiten schreibst Du nichts, offenbar hat es den Anschein, als zeigte ich für sie kein Interesse, ich bitte Dich nur anzunehmen, dass ich bloss kein Urtheil über die doch thatsächlich begründeten Dinge habe.

8. July 14, 1894 [letter to Wilhelm Fliess]

Liebster Freund,

Nektar und Ambrosia ist mir Dein Lob, da mir sicher bekannt ist, wie schwer Du es vergibst, nein richtiger, wie ernst Du es empfindest, wenn Du es vergibst. Seither habe ich, mit Abstinenz beschäftigt, wenig geleistet; eine andere Darstellung der Angstneurose, die ich aber Breuer gegeben. Fräulein Elisabeth v. R. hat sich inzwischen verlobt.

Mein Zustand, ich fühle mich jetzt verpflichtet, nicht den Verdacht zu erwecken, als wollte ich zurückhalten, [ist] folgender. Von Deinem Brief am Donnerstag vor 14 Tagem Abstinenz, die 8 Tage gehalten hat, am nächsten Donnerstag, in einem unbeschreiblich öden Moment eine Cigarre, dann wieder 8 Tage Abstinenz, nächsten Donnerstag wieder eine, seither wieder Ruhe. Kurz es bildet sich eine Institution, eine Cigarre in der Woche zur Erinnerungsfeier Deines Briefes, der mich des Tabaksgenusses von Neuem beraubt. Praktisch dürfte sich das von der Abstinenz nicht erheblich unterscheiden. . . .

Befinden unverändert, Ende voriger Woche musste ich [mich] wieder zu Digitalis entschliessen. Der Puls war wieder deliriös. . . . Unter Digitalis geht es dann gut, aber nicht behaglich. Soll ich Digitalis oft nehmen oder selten? Ich verspreche zu folgen. . . .

Dein Kopfschmerz verursacht mir ohnmächtige Kränkung. . . .

Herzlichsten Gruss . . .
Sigm. Freud

9. Undated [letter to Wilhelm Fliess]

Lieber Wilhelm,
Ich verstehe ja viel zu wenig davon um Deine so sichere Entgegnung beurtheilen zu können, aber das indicium sagt mir, dass ich physiologische Gründe genug habe, Deinen Anordnungen nachzukommen und so beginne ich heute eine zweite Abstinenzperiode, die hoffentlich andauern wird, bis wir uns im August wiedersehen.

Herzl. Gruss
Dein S.

10. August 18, 1894 [passage of L. 20]

Ich werde von jetzt ab nur Gutes prophezeien und Recht damit behalten wie mit der letzten bösen Vorhersage.

11. August 23, 1894 [letter to Wilhelm Fliess]

Am Donnerstag nach unserer Trennung hatte ich notgedrungen einen 4 stündigen Marsch von Weissenbach nach Ischl, Nacht, Einsamkeit, strömender Regen, Eile—ich habe es sehr gut vertragen.

12. February 12, 1929 [letter to Wilhelm Fliess; from the Arents collection, New York Public Library, Astor, Lenox and Tilden Foundations]

Ich begann mit 24 Jahren zu rauchen, zuerst Cigaretten, bald aber ausschliesslich Cigarren, rauche auch noch heute (72½ J.) und schränke mich in diesem Genuss sehr ungern ein. Zwischen 30 und 40 Jahren musste ich des Rauchen durch 1½ Jahre aufgeben wegen Herzstörungen die vielleicht Nikotinwirkung, wahrscheinlich aber Folge einer Influenza waren. Seither bin ich meiner Gewohnheit oder meinem Laster treu geblieben und meine, dass ich der Cigarre eine grosse Steigerung meiner Arbeitsfähigkeit und eine Erleichterung meiner Selbstbeherrschung zu danken habe. Vorbild war mir mein Vater, der ein starker Raucher war und bis in sein 81stes Lebensjahr blieb.

Sigm. Freud

CHAPTER 3

1. February 7, 1894 [passage of L. 16]

Über Deinen Kopfschmerz bin ich ruhiger, seitdem ich eine Äusserung von Scheffer in Bremen erhalten habe, die volle Genesung verspricht. Ich war so unverschämt, mich direkt an ihn zu wenden.

2. August 23, 1894 [letter to Wilhelm Fliess]

Liebster Freund,

Du hast starke Kopfschmerzen und rechnest mit einer Nachoperation; das klinge mir trüb und verdriesslich, wenn ich nicht so ganz Deine Hoffnung theilen würde, dass Du auf dem eingeschlagenen Weg frei von *Deinen* Kopfschmerzen wirst. Nur versprich mir gleich Eines, den Faktor nicht zu vergessen, der unmittelbar vor dem Knoten "Kopfschmerz" steht und der rein nervöser Natur ist. Mit andern und mal auch klareren Worten, dass Du mir versprichst, diesmal Monate über die Narben vergehen zu lassen, ehe Du an die Arbeit in Berlin gehst.

Wir schreiben oder reden noch darüber.

3. August 29, 1894 [passage of L. 21]

Liebster Freund,

Das ist doch nicht mehr schön, gehst Du mir denn ganz im Eiter auf? Wieder und wieder operieren; zum Teufel, nur werd einmal fertig, da hat* die alte Frau, der Deine Kopfschmerzen vor Jahren nicht gefallen haben, und die mir jenen merkwürdigen Brief geschrieben hat eigentlich sehr im Rechte. Aber was soll ich dazu? Ich wollt' ich wäre ein "Doktor," wie die Leute sagen, ein Arzt und Heilkünstler, um dergleichen zu verstehen und Dich in solchen Lagen keiner fremden Hand überlassen zu müssen. Leider bin ich es nicht, Du weisst es. Ich muss mich auf Dich verlassen, hierin wie in allem Übrigen, ich muss hoffen, dass Du auch *Dich* zu behandeln verstehst und auch bei *Dir* denselben Erfolg haben kannst, wie bei andern (mich eingeschlossen).

Dass dabei unser Wiedersehen entzwei geht, ist auch nicht schön. Eine zeitweilige Hoffnung hinterlässt mit einen unerfüllten Anspruch.

4. April 11, 1895 [not published in *Origins;* partially published in Schur, 1966a, p. 63f.). Only the unpublished portion of this letter is given here]

Die Wissenschaft geht halbwegs, d.h. nichts Neues, kein Einfall und keine Beobachtung. Mit der Psychologie habe ich mich gründlich überarbeitet und lasse sie jetzt stehen. Nur das Buch mit Breuer geht vorwärts, wird in etwa 3 Wochen fertig vorliegen.

So war von Dir noch gar nicht die Rede. Ich entnehme, dass Du gerade begonnen hast, Dich wieder zu fühlen. Halt jetzt einmal recht lange aus! Dein Kopf ist doch gut. *Das* wäre erreicht! das darf ich jetzt doch glauben?

5. April 20, 1895 [not published in *Origins;* partially published in Schur, 1966a, p. 63f. Only the unpublished portion of this letter is given here]

In Betreff meines Leidens möchte ich, dass Du Recht behieltest, dass der Anteil der Nase ein grosser, der des Cor ein kleiner sein möge. Nur ein sehr strenger Richter wird mir verübeln, dass ich bei dem Puls und der Insufficienz oft das Gegentheil glaube. Deinen Vorschlag *jetzt* nach Berlin zu kommen, kann ich nicht annehmen, ich bin nicht in den Verhältnissen, mir Fl. 1000-1500 für eigene Gesundheit, oder auch nur die Hälfte davon zu gestatten, und nicht demoralisiert genug, auf Deine Andeutung den Verlust zu ersparen einzugehen. Ich denke ich muss es auch nicht. Wenn das Empyem die Hauptsache

---

* "Hat" is a grammatical error here. The sentence should read either "war . . . im Recht" or "hat . . . recht."

ist, so entfällt der Gesichtspunkt der Gefahr und die Beschwerden durch einige Monate fortgesetzt, werden mich nicht umbringen. Wenn aber eine Herzaffektion das Wesen ausmacht, dann kannst Du mir ja nur Beschwerden beseitigen und ich sehe der Gefahr dann warnungslos entgegen, was ich nicht mag.

Heute kann ich schreiben, weil ich bessere Hoffnung habe; ich habe mir aus einem elenden Anfall mit einer Cocainpinselung herausgeholfen. Nicht verbürgen kann ich, dass ich nicht über 1-2 Tage für eine Ätzung oder Galvanisierung komme, aber auch das gienge momentan nicht. Am Liebsten wäre mir, Du giengest darauf ein über das Thema Herz nichts mehr wissen zu wollen.

Ich freue mich jetzt Anspruch zu haben, wieder viel und von Dir zu hören. . . .

Herzlichst,
Dein Sigm.

6. April 26, 1895 [letter to Wilhelm Fliess]

Es ist mir komischerweise nicht unerfreulich ergangen. Den letzten grauslichen Anfall habe ich durch Cocain merklich zu Ende gemacht, seither ist es gut und es kommt massenhafter Eiter. Ich habe offenbar noch L[inks] ein Keilbeinempyem, mit dem ich natürlich sehr glücklich bin. Auch ihr, meinem und Deinem Quälgeist, scheint es jetzt gut zu gehen. . . .

7. April 27, 1895 [passage of L. 23]

(1) Ich befinde mich wol, (2) entleere reichlichen Eiter, (3) ich befinde mich *sehr* wol. Ich will also gar keine Herzaffektion mehr haben, nur die "Behandlung" durch das Nicotin. Wirklich ich habe viel ausgestanden und ich kann doch nicht jetzt abkommen, bei der harmloseren Diagnose viel eher nicht als bei der schwereren. Aber ich komme und lasse mir von Dir helfen.

8. May 25, 1895 [passage of L. 24]

Nun zu meinem Nasenleiden. Ich habe überaus reichlich geeitert und dabei gieng es mir glänzend. Jetzt ist die Eiterung fast versiegt und es geht mir noch immer sehr gut. . . .

9. June 22, 1895 [letter to Wilhelm Fliess]

Heil, teurer Wilhelm! Möge Deine liebe, gute und starke Frau, bei der bisher Hoffnung und Erfüllung immer zusammentrafen auch als Mutter der Liebling des Schicksals werden. . . .

Ich komme also Anfangs September. Wie ich es anfangen werde, Dich dann wieder zu entbehren, weiss ich nicht. Es geht mir mit dem Rauchen arg genug. . . .

Deine Entdeckung dann in Ehren, Du wärst der stärkste Mann, hältest die Zügel der Sexualität in der Hand, welche die Menschen regiert, könntest alles machen und alles verhüten. Darum glaube ich die zweite frohe Botschaft noch nicht, die erste glaube ich, es ist auch leichter. . . .

10. July 24, 1895 [letter to Wilhelm Fliess]

Daimonie warum schreibst Du nicht? Wie geht es Dir? Kümmerst Du Dich gar nicht mehr, was ich treibe? Was macht die Nase, die Menstruation, der

Wehenschmerz, die Neurosen, die liebe Frau und das keimende Kleine? Heuer bin ich nun krank und muss zu Dir kommen; was soll denn werden, wenn wir zufällig ein Jahr lang beide gesund sind? Sind wir nur Unglücksfreunde? Oder wollen wir auch die Erlebnisse ruhiger Zeiten mit einander theilen?

Wohin geht Ihr jetzt im August? Wir leben auf dem Himmel sehr zufrieden.

Herzlichste Grüsse,
Dein
Sigm.

11. October 8, 1895 [passage of L. 29]

Liebster Wilhelm,
Eine Nachricht von Dir war mir bereits Bedürfniss, denn ich hatte bereits den selben irrenden Schluss gezogen, dass Dein Schweigen—Kopfschmerz bedeutet. Es wurde mir wieder behaglicher, als ich—nach langer Zeit—wieder ein Stück wissenschaftliches Materials von Dir in Händen hielt. Ich habe erst nur hineingeblickt und fürchte an dem Respekt vor so viel ehrlichen und feinsinnigen Material wird meine theoretische Phantasie zu Schande werden. . . .

Wie es mir herzwärts ergangen? Nicht besonders, aber nicht so arg wie in den ersten 14 Tagen. Meine Aufmerksamkeit war diesmal gar nicht dabei. . . .

12. November 29, 1895 [passage of L. 36]

Teurer Wilhelm,
Mir geht es ganz überraschend wol *wie seit Beginn der Geschichte nicht.* Ich habe auch keinen Eiter, sondern sehr viel schleimiges Sekret. Habe übrigens nie am Erfolg Deiner *kleinen* Eingriffe gezweifelt, mir also das Wolbefinden verdient [my italics].

CHAPTER 4

1. February 13, 1896 [passage of L. 41]

Mein Befinden verdient nicht Gegenstand der Nachfrage zu sein. Die linksseitige Eiterung hat in letzter Woche recrudescirt, Migrainen ziemlich häufig, die nothwendige Abstinenz thut mir kaum sehr wol. Ich bin rasch grau geworden.

2. March 1, 1896 [passage of L. 42]

Dass man Alles was man im Leben genossen hat, so theuer bezahlen muss, ist entschieden keine schöne Einrichtung. Wird es uns Beiden *auch so* ergehen?

3. March 16, 1896 [passage of L. 43]

Theurer Wilhelm,
Die Depression über Deinen Kopfschmerz-Kalender habe ich eigentlich noch nicht überwunden. Ich kann mich etwa darüber freuen, dass Ostern weit weg von dem Termin fällt den Du als den kritischsten unterstrichen hast. Sonst ersehe ich ja leider, dass jeder dritte Tag für Dich Kopfweh bringt. Aber wie die Kaiser einen unbezweifelten Einfluss auf das Wetter nehmen, so habe ich Deine Kopfschmerzen durch meine Gegenwart günstig stimmen können und hoffe darum auf schönes Wetter für unsere Zusammenkunft.

4. April 16, 1896 [letter to Wilhelm Fliess]

Liebster Wilhelm,

. . . den Kopf voll von Terminen und Summationsahnungen, stolz auf manche Anerkennung und mit einem frechen Gefühl von Selbstständigkeit bin ich zu gutem Wolbefinden zurückgekehrt und bin seither sehr faul gewessen, weil sich das zur intensiven Arbeit nöthige Mittelelend nicht einstellen will. Nur einige wenige aus der täglichen Arbeit aufsteigende Ahnungen über das Zwischenreich habe ich zu verzeichnen wie im Allgemeinen die Verstärkung des Eindrucks, dass *alles* so ist, wie ich es vermuthe und dass sich also alles klären wird. Darunter eine ganz überraschende Aufklärung über die Blutungen bei der Emma, mit denen Du Deine Freude haben wirst. Ich habe die Geschichte schon errathen, warte aber mit der Mittheilung bis die Patientin selbst nachgekommen ist.

Deiner Aufforderung gemäss habe ich die allseitige Isolirung in Angriff genommen und finde sie eine leichte Entbehrung. Von früher steht allerdings noch aus, dass ich Dienstag einen Vortrag im psychiatrischen Verein zu halten habe. . . .

Von mir notire ich Migraine, Nasensekretion und Anfälle von Todesangst wie heute, woran aber Tilgner's Herztod mehr Schuld tragen mag, als der Termin. Die Tabakmässigkeit hast Du mir sehr gefördert, wie ich überhaupt seit unserer Entrevue gefestigt und zusammengepasst bin. Es that mir sehr wol und sehr noth. Wahrscheinlich überrasche ich Dich nächstens einmal mit einem psychologischen Fetzen, jetzt bin ich höchst schreibfaul. Jede Spur Alkohol macht mich übrigens ganz dumm.

5. April 26, continued on April 28, 1896 [letter to Wilhelm Fliess]

Ein Vortrag über Ätiologie der Hysterie im Psychiatrischen Verein fand bei den Eseln eine eisige Aufnahme und von Krafft-Ebing die seltsame Beurteilung: Es klingt wie ein wissenschaftliches Märchen. Und dies, nachdem man ihnen die Lösung eines mehrtausendjährigen Problems, ein caput Nili aufgezeigt hat!

6. June 30, 1896 [passage of L. 48]

Mein Theurer Wilhelm,

Du hast mich gelehrt, dass hinter allem Volkswahnwitz ein Stück Wahrheit lauert und ich kann Dir ein Beispiel dafür liefern. Gewisse Dinge soll man nicht einmal im Scherz sagen sonst werden sie zu Ernst. So schrieb ich Dir unlängst, es sei eigentlich kein Bedürfnis nach einem Congress und heute habe ich Dir von einem ernsten Hindernis zu berichten, dass [a slip; the word should be *das*] sich dem nächsten—oder wenigstens der Zeitbestimmung für ihn— entgegenstellt.

7. July 15, 1896 [letter to Wilhelm Fliess]

Mein Theurer Wilhelm,

Eben Deinen Brief erhalten und mich sehr gefreut, was ich alles von Dir hören werde. Schade nur, dass ich nicht sicher weiss wann. Es liegt nämlich so: der Alte hat Blasen und Mastdarmlähmung, lässt in der Ernährung nach und ist dabei geistig überfrisch und euphorisch. Ich glaube wirklich, dass es seine letzte Zeit ist, kenne aber nicht seinen Termin und getraue mich nicht weg, am wenigstens über 2 Tage und auf einen Genuss, dem ich ganz nachhängen möchte. Dich in Berlin treffen, einige Stunden den neuen Zauber von Dir hören und dann plötzlich auf eine Nachricht Tag oder Nacht zurückreisen [zu] müssen, die doch dazu ein blosser Schreckschuss gewesen sein kann—dem möchte ich gerne ausweichen und dieser Furcht opfere ich das brennende Bedürfnis wieder einmal ganz zu leben mit dem Kopf und dem Herzen zugleich, *Zoon Politikon* zu sein und zu alledem noch Dich zu sehen. . . .

Der Zustand des Alten deprimiert mich übrigens nicht. Ich gönne ihm die wolverdiente Ruhe, wie er sie selbst wünscht. Er war ein interessanter Mensch, innerlich sehr glücklich; er leidet jetzt sehr wenig, löscht mit Anstand und Würde aus. Ein langes Krankenlager wünsche ich ihm nicht, auch meiner ledigen Schwester nicht, die ihn pflegt und dabei leidet.

8. September 29, 1896 [letter to Wilhelm Fliess]

Theurer Wilhelm!
Ich hoffe Dich mit Weib und Sohn wieder auf's behaglichste in die schönen Räume von der Hstr.* eingefügt und emsig an der Beobachtung und Berechnung neuer Perioden à 28 und 23. . . . Ich schreibe Dir erst heute, weil eine Influenza mit Fieber, Eiter und Herzbeschwerden mein Wolbefinden plötzlich gebrochen hat, so dass mir erst heute wieder etwas von möglicher Gesundheit ahnt. Ich möchte so gerne bis zur berühmten Altersgrenze circa: 51 aushalten, und ein Tag war dabei, der mir's nicht wahrscheinlich machte. Die Infektion erhaschte mich am letzten kritischen Temin 24/9, so dass ich am 25** heiser und luftlos war, gleichzeitig legte sich Martin mit einer Angina. Jetzt aber athme ich wieder auf. . . .

Die Frau meines Freundes R. habe ich in Cur genommen und wieder gesehen, wie in der Hysterie Alles klappt und stimmt, dass es eine helle Freude ist. . . .

Mein Vater liegt wol auf dem letzten Bett, er ist zeitweise verworren und schrumpft stetig ein bis zu einer Pneumonie und einem grossen Termin.

Mit allerherzlichstem Gruss
Dein
Sigm.

9. October 9, 1896 [letter to Wilhelm Fliess]

Mein Befinden hat sich nicht mehr recht gehoben, gerade die Herzbeschwerden spielen nicht die grosse Rolle, ich habe keinen Anlass Dich um sofortige Behandlung zu bitten. . . .

Der Zustand meines Alten wird meine Theilnahme wahrscheinlich auf das mindeste beschränken.

Du weisst ich lache nicht über Phantasien wie die der historischen Perioden und zwar weil ich keinen Grund dazu sehe, an diesen Einfällen ist etwas, es ist die symbolische Vorahnung unbekannter Realitäten, mit denen sie etwas gemeinsam haben. Da dann nicht einmal die Organe dieselben sind, kann man sich der Anerkennung himmlischer Einflüsse nicht mehr entziehen. Ich beuge mich vor Dir als Ehren-Astrolog. . . .

Ich bin mit meinen Curen jetzt sehr zufrieden; noch 1-2 Jahre und ich kann die Sache in Formeln fassen, die jedem mitzutheilen sind. In vielen trüben

---

* Heydtstrasse, Fliess's new address in Berlin.
** See footnote 9 in Chapter 4 for several slips in numbers.

Stunden hält mich diese Aussicht und die Befriedigung über das bereits Gewonnene hoch aufrecht.

10. October 26, 1896 [passage of L. 49]

Dass Dein Geburtstag auf den 24. Oktober fällt, habe ich erst heuer erfahren.

11. November 2, 1896 [passage of L. 50]

Mit Herz und Nase bin ich wieder zufrieden.

12. November 22, 1896 [letter to Wilhelm Fliess]

Liebster Wilhelm,
Als Erstem aus der neuen Behausung schreibe ich Dir. . . .
Die Arbeiten in der Hysterie gehen gut vorwärts, ich stehe wegen 4 neuer Curen in Unterhandlungen, die ein Resultat in keinem Fall ergeben dürften; es ist aber doch reichlicher zu thun. Stimmung und Lebensfreudigkeit geht mir ganz ab, dafür notire ich fleissig die Gelegenheiten, wann ich mich mit den Zuständen nach meinem Tod beschäftigen muss. Wieder ein Thema, das man nicht zu ausgiebig behandeln darf, wenn man seinen Freund und einzigen Correspondenten liebt. . . .
Martha hat wieder Glänzendes geleistet, so dass ich keine Ordination zu versäumen brauchte. Jetzt geht die Unordnung oben an. Die zweite Generation ist sehr zufriedenstellend. . . .

13. December 4, 1896 [passage of L. 51]

Meine böse Zeit ist typisch abgelaufen . . . und [ich] interessire mich gar nicht für das Leben nach dem Tode.

14. February 8, 1897 [passage of L. 58]

Dass ich der "Niemand" in Wien bin, der Deine Reihen glaubt, weisst Du wol.

15. March 29, 1897 [letter to Wilhelm Fliess]

Mein Theurer,
. . . Herzlichen Dank für Deinen Vortrag, er enthüllt eine unglaubliche Macht der Gedankencondensation, und führt in 20 Minuten durch's Weltall. . . . Ich lechze nach den Tagen von Prag. . . .

16. May 2, 1897 [passage of L. 61]

Karte und Telegramm unterdess erhalten und bedauert dass der Congress Dir nicht gebracht was er mir hat, Vergnügung und Auffrischung. Ich bin seither in continuirlicher Euphorie und arbeite wie ein Jüngling.

17. June 18, 1897 [letter to Wilhelm Fliess]

Ich sehne mich sehr nach dem Ende der Saison. . . . Allmälich wird man die Frage in Angriff nehmen dürfen, wann wir uns im Sommer sehen können. Ich brauche einen neuen Impuls von Dir, nach einer Weile geht er mir aus. Nürnberg hat mich für 2 Monate in Gang gebracht.

18. October 3, 1897 [passage of L. 70]

Doch danke ich Dir jedesmal für jedes kleine Stückchen, das Du so uneigennützig zu mir gelangen lässt, z.B., die Bemerkung über den Zusammenhang von Infektion und Conception bei Mutter und Tochter sind mir höchst bedeutsam erschienen, weil diese ja nur durch eine Bedingung im ewigen Leben des Keimplasmas, nicht durch eine solche im Einzelleben erklärt werden können. Weil sie also von der absoluten Zeit, nicht von der Lebenszeit abhängen müssen. Es ist mir dann eingefallen, dass dies doch nicht notwendig ist, wenn die Infektion bei der Mutter durch eine Zeiterfüllung von der Formal a. $28 + b$. 23 gegeben ist und die Conception bei der Tochter durch einen ähnlichen Ausdruck, so muss auch die Differenz beider wieder eine ähnliche Formel ergeben, ohne dass zwischen Infektion hier und Conception dort eine besondere Beziehung zu bestehen brauchte. Ob dies ein Unsinn ist, kann ich nicht übersehen. Ich müsste dazu Deine "zeitliche Disposition" schon kennen.

19. October 31, 1897 [passage of L. 73]

Ich bin so froh wieder Nachricht von Dir zu haben (die Dritte seit Berlin), dass ich alle Vergeltungsideen verscheucht habe. Und dass etwas Ganzes bei Dir zusammenkommt und biologische Typen sich herausstellen wie Deine Parallele zwischen Geburt und Erwachsenerkrankung scheint mir entzückend und ein Versprechen für viel mehr in nächster Zukunft zu enthalten.

20. December 3, 1897 [passage of L. 77]

Gestern abends war Deine liebe Frau . . . bei uns und hat uns die kurze Illusion eines erfreulichen Zusammenlebens gebracht und mit ihrem Verschwinden wieder mitgenommen. Solche Unterbrechungen der Einsamkeit wirken wolthätig, indem sie mahnen wie schwer der Verzicht eigentlich fällt, und wie unrecht man thut, sich an ihn zu gewöhnen.

21. December 12, 1897 [passages of L. 78]

So wie Du schreibt nur, wer sich im Besitze der Wahrheit weiss. Ich bin aiso furchtbar neugierig auf Breslau und werde mit allen Ohren horchen. Selber bringe ich nichts mit, ich bin auch durch eine öde und nebelige Zeit gegangen und leide jetzt selbst empfindlich unter [Nasen] Eiterungen und Verstopfungen, bin kaum jemals frisch. Wenn es sich nicht bessert, werde ich Dich bitten mir in Breslau eine Ätzung zu machen.

. . . Es wird eine Erquickung für mich sein, harmlos und ernsthaft mit Dir zu plaudern, nachdem ich wieder Monate lang die meschuggensten Sachen unausgeleert in meinem Kopf beherbergt habe und sonst keinen vernünftigen Menschen spreche. Wieder ein Schluck Punsch mit Lethe.

22. December 29, 1897 [passages of L. 80]

Zurück und wieder eingespannt, mit dem köstlichen Nachgeschmack unserer Breslauer Tage. Bi-Bi tönt es mir in den Ohren; es geht mir noch zu gut um ernstlich zu arbeiten.

. . . Mit meinem Femininen ein Wort zu reden habe ich noch nicht Zeit gefunden.

Meine Nase ist brav und lässt sich bedanken.

23. January 4, 1898 [passages of L. 81]

Ich schicke Dir heute No. 2 der Δ$_\rho$εKKOLD gischen* Berichte, einer sehr interessanten von mir für einen einzigen Leser herausgegebenen Zeitschrift. Die zurückgebliebene No. 1 enthält wüste Träume, die Dich kaum interessieren dürften, zu meiner noch ganz im Dunkel tappenden Selbstanalyse. Um Rücksendung wird gebeten wegen späterer Einsicht, doch keineswegs in nächster Zeit. Wie immer war die nächste Woche nach unserer Aussprache für mich eine sehr fruchtbare. Dann folgten einige öde Tage mit lausiger Stimmung und in die Beine dislocirten Kopf- (Oder Herz-) Schmerzen. Seit heute morgens volle Aufhellung. . . .

Auf meiner Seite im Tunnel ist es recht dunkel, Dir scheinen auch bei dieser Arbeit die Sonne und die Sterne.

24. January 16, 1898 [passage of L. 82]

Es thut mir leid, dass unsere Zustände diesmal nicht parallel geblieben sind. Ich war wol und fidel. Hoffentlich jetzt schon auch Du.

Anbei die 3te Nr. der Δ$_\rho$ . . .

25. January 22, 1898 [letter to Wilhelm Fliess]

Diese Unart meiner Organisation, mich plötzlich aller meiner geistigen Hilfsquellen zu berauben, ist mir das schwerst Erträgliche im Leben.

26. January 30, 1898 [letter to Wilhelm Fliess]

Die Symmetriebahnen und die Zahlenverhältnisse der Geburtsrelationen machen natürlich grossen Eindruck. Wenn das aus seiner Vereinzelung zum Gebäude zusammengesetzt ist, wird es viel Staunen der Wanderer erregen.

Der Güter Höchstes, kommt mir manchmal vor, ist entweder die Stimmung oder die geistige Klarheit.

27. February 9, 1898 [passage of L. 83]

Im übrigen bin ich ohne jeden Grund glänzend aufgelegt und habe mein Tagesinteresse gefunden. Ich bin tief im Traumbuch.

28. April 14, 1898 [passage of L. 88]

Beiliegend ein Brief, der folgende Geschichte hat: In der letzten Nummer der *Wiener Klinischen Rundschau* war eine Kritik Deines Buches zu lesen von einem gewissen "Ry.," ein Muster jener Art von Unverschämtheit, die der absoluten Ignoranz eigen ist. Ich habe Paschkis einen unsanften Brief mit der Bitte um Aufklärung geschrieben. Hier die loyale aber sterile Antwort. Ich will nichts weiter thun ohne Dich gefragt zu haben. Was gedenkst Du thun zu lassen? Es gäbe mehrere Wege Genugtuung zu schaffen.

29. April 27, 1898 [letter to Wilhelm Fliess]

Ich war so ungeschickt warten zu wollen, bis die Sache mit Paschkis erledigt ist. Sie ist es jetzt dadurch, dass ich meine Beziehungen zur *Klinischen Rundschau*

* See footnote 41 in Chapter 4.

gelöst und meinen Namen von der Liste der Mitwirker auf ihrem Titel zurück-
gezogen habe. Es war Absicht, dass ich Dir die grausliche Kritik nicht geschickt
habe. Ich glaube wir können die Geschichte jetzt fallen lassen.

30. May 1, 1898 [passage of L. 89]

Das mit den zwei Zeigern der Lebensuhr klingt wieder so vertraut und selbst-
verständlich, dass es eine unerhörte Neuigkeit und wunderschöne Wahrheit
sein dürfte. Der Mai ist gekommen, also Ende Mai werde ich's hören. Ich bin
wie verschmachtet, irgend ein Quell in mir trocknet ein und alles Empfinden
wird so dürr. Ich will nicht zuviel beschreiben; es sähe sonst dem Klagen zu
sehr gleich, Du wirst mir sagen, ob es das Alter, ob nur eine der vielen perio-
dischen Schwankungen ist.

Es macht mir den Eindruck, als ob Du das Geschlecht Deines nächsten
Kindes bestimmt hättest, so, dass diesmal Paulinchen eine Wahrheit werden
könnte.

31. May 18, 1898 [letter to Wilhelm Fliess]

Ich bin so unendlich froh, dass Du mir einen Anderen schenkst. . . . Ganz
ohne Publikum kann ich nicht schreiben, kann mir aber ganz gut gefallen lassen,
dass ich es nur für Dich schreibe.

32. July 30, 1898 [letter to Wilhelm Fliess]

Lass Dich nicht abhalten mir von den Ellipsen zu schreiben, wiewol ich eben
ein so unvernünftiges Stück der meinigen passiere. Denn jeder soll geben was
er hat, ohne Rücksicht auf den Anderen. Ich mache es auch so; die Zwang-
losigkeit in der man sich fühlt, macht den Hauptreiz des Briefschreibens aus.

Ich möchte Dir so gerne geben, was *Du nicht* hast: den freien Kopf; aber
Du weisst, das geht nicht. Das Unfertige in Deinen Funden stört mich gar
nicht; Du weisst ich denke nicht nach, reagiere, geniesse, staune und mache
mir Erwartungen. Tragzeiten sind bald um, das ist wol Dein Trost bei Ida's
Befinden. Ferien leider auch.

CHAPTER 5

1. October 9, 1898 [letter to Wilhelm Fliess]

Das Behagen das aus Deinen Briefen hervorleuchtet thut wol und theilt sich mit.
Merk auf, wie bald Paulinchen sich als die Reincarnation Deiner Schwester
Dir enthüllen wird. . .

2. October 23, 1898 [passage of L. 99]

Meine Schwester Rosa hat am 18. October ein Mädchen geboren, beide sind
wol.

3. October 30, 1898 [letter to Wilhelm Fliess]

Nachdem ich meinen letzten Glückwunschbrief abgeschickt, machte ich mir
Vorwürfe, darin von der traditionellen Formulierung, die Alles, was Leiden

oder Krankheit bedeutet, bis auf die letzte Spur getilgt haben will, abgewiechen zu sein. Ich wollte rationell scheinen, und dem was doch nicht zu vermeiden ist, einen Platz und eine Funktion zum Guten einräumen. Es war ein Unsinn, denn das Wünschen wird durch keine solche Correctur vernünftig. Über Deine erste Andeutung, dass Du Dich neuen experimentellen Qualen aussetzen willst, las ich unaufmerksam hinweg und so war ich sehr überrascht, so bald nachher die Nachricht von der Operation zu hören. . . .

4. December 5, 1898 [passage of L. 100]

Infolge Deines Krankseins habe ich, wie Du gemerkt, auch auf den Gedankenverkehr mit Dir verzichtet, in den soviel hineingegangen ist; ein neues Stück Resignation. Gelegentlich sehnte ich mich nach einem kräftigen und süssen Tropfen Traubensaft—wenn es doch "Punsch mit Lethe" nicht sein kann—aber ich schämte mich mir ein neues Laster zuzulegen.

5. December 20, 1898 [letter to Wilhelm Fliess]

Selten sind mir 3 getrennte Monate so lang erschienen wie diese letzten.

6. January 3, 1899 [passage of L. 101]

Ich bin doch der erste, der Nachricht von sich giebt. Nach dem Untergang des Meteors giebt es einen Lichtschein, der den trüben Himmel auf lange hinaus erhellt. Er ist für mich noch nicht verlöscht. In der Helligkeit habe ich dann auch plötzlich einiges erblickt. . . .

7. February 6, 1899 [passage of L. 104]

Der arme S. erinnert mich in Deiner Darstellung an einen der ärgerlichsten Punkte unserer modernen Medizin.

8. February 19, 1899 [passage of L. 105]

Also es geht Dir ebenso, brauche ich mich nicht zu schämen. Auch Du beginnst Briefe am 11., die Du erst am 16. fortsetzen kannst, und am 16. kannst Du von nichts Anderem schreiben als von der einen ungeheuerlich grossen, für die Kräfte des armen Menschen allzuschweren Arbeit, der jede Regung des Denkens gehört und die allmählich alle anderen Fähigkeiten und Empfänglichkeiten aufsaugt, eine Art von Neoplasmagewebe, das sich in's menschliche infiltriert und es dann ersetzt. Beinahe habe ich's noch besser—oder schlechter. Arbeit und Erwerbsthätigkeit fallen bei mir zusammen, ich bin ganz Carcinom geworden. Das Neugebilde trinkt in seinen letzten Entwicklungsstadien gerne Wein; heute soll ich in's Theater; es ist aber lächerlich, gleichsam also wollte man auf's Carcinom transplantieren. Da haftet nichts, und meine Lebensdauer ist von nun an die des Neoplasmas.

9. May 25, 1899 [letter to Wilhelm Fliess]

Montag früh bin ich mit Schwager H. auf die Rax wie in alten Zeiten, 3½ Stunden hinauf, 2½ zurück. Allein die Rax ist viel höher geworden, seit ich sie zuletzt bestiegen, mindestens 500 Meter. Mein Herz hat es vortrefflich ertragen.

10. June 27, 1899 [passage of L. 109]

Schönen Dank für den unverdient reichhaltigen Brief. Ich bescheide mich zu warten, die sonstige Klage über die unaufhebbare Entfernung habe ich mir resigniert abgewöhnt. Ich hoffe Dein Weg wird Dich noch weiter führen und noch tiefer und als neuer Kepler wirst Du uns die ehernen Regale des biologischen Getriebes enthüllen.

11. October 4, 1899 [letter to Wilhelm Fliess]

Die schmerzliche Empfindung des von sich Gebens, was einem allein zu eigen war, schilderst Du treffend. Die war es wol auch, die mir das Werk so verleidet hat. Seitdem gefällt es mir, gewiss nicht gut, aber weit besser. Ich musste es noch peinlicher verspüren, da es nicht Gedanken- sondern Gefühlseigentum war, was sich loslöste. Zur Hysterie ist es nun weit. In Zeiten wie diesen regt sich in mir keine Arbeitslust. . . .

Leben und Krankheit sind wieder eingezogen. Das erste Opfer—Ernst—ist aber wieder erholt. Die anderen sind noch wol.

Meine Stimmung hält sich noch tapfer, das Datum des nächsten Zusammenbruches theile ich Dir dann für Deine Berechnungen mit. Es sind das wirklich primäre periodische Schwankungen, denn 2 Wochen Unthätigkeit und ⅕ Erwerb—¼ reichten als äussere Aetiologie schon hin.

CHAPTER 6

1. November 9, 1899 [letter to Wilhelm Fliess]

Ich habe mich immer anders benommen; seit Wochen jammere ich Dir vor, wo ich Anlass dazu habe, auf die Gefahr hin Dich abzustossen, in der Erwartung, dass es Dich nicht abstossen wird, wenn ich Dir auch gewiss lieber Gutes und Hoffnungsvolles mittheilen möchte.

2. December 29, 1899 [poem addressed to Fliess]

Heil

Dem wackeren Sohn, der auf des Vaters Geheiss
Zum richtigen Zeitpunkt erschienen.
Ihm Gehilfe zu sein und Mitarbeiter der heiligen Ordnung.
Heil aber auch dem Vater, der kürzlich vorher tief in
    der Rechnung gefunden
Die Macht zu dämmen des Frauengeschlechts
Und sein Theil Gesetzesfolgschaft zu tragen;
Nicht mehr bezeugt durch den heimlichen Schein
    wie die Mutter
Ruft die höheren Mächte er auch für sein Anrecht,
    den Schluss, den Glauben und Zweifel;
Also steht kraftgerüstet, dem Aufwand des Irrtums gewachsen,
Am Ausgang der Vater von unendlich gereifter Entwicklung.
Stimmen möge die Rechnung, als Arbeitserbe vom Vater
Sich übertragen dem Sohn und durch die Jahrhunderte Scheidung
Knüpfen zur Einheit im Geist, was im Wechsel des Lebens zerfällt.

3. February 1, 1900 [letter to Wilhelm Fliess, unpublished except for one paragraph in Jones (Vol. 1, p. 348)]

Theurer Wilhelm,

Die Ahnung von etwas Unheimlichem hat also Recht behalten. Ich finde es arg, dass das Intervall so kurz ist. Vielleicht gehören aber die beiden Anfälle zusammen und nachher geht es dauernd gut. Es ist sehr schmerzlich; ich weiss auch nichts mehr darüber.

Martin hatte sich am 14.* Jänner zwischen 2 - 3 Uhr nachmittags mit akutem Krankheitsbeginn gelegt. Er ist der einzige Fall geblieben, ist wieder wol. Die Beobachtungsreihe bricht diesmal jäh ab. Auf ein anderes Mal.

Wenn wir in einer Stadt lebten—die müsste aber Berlin sein, nicht Wien— wäre manches anders geworden und ich glaube, ich wäre gar nicht in die Verlegenheit gekommen oder bald aus ihr heraus. Darum habe ich ja unsere Trennung so oft bedauert. Leider ändert das nichts. Vielleicht, dass für mich und für meine Cur harte Zeiten kommen. Im Ganzen habe ich ja schon oft bemerkt, dass Du mich sehr zu überschätzen pflegst. Die Motivirung dieses Irrtums nimmt den Vorwurf wieder weg. Ich bin nämlich gar kein Mann der Wissenschaft, kein Beobachter, kein Experimentator, kein Denker. Ich bin nichts als ein Conquistadorentemperament, ein Abenteurer, wenn Du es übersetzen willst, mit der Neugierde, der Kühnheit und der Zähigkeit eines solchen. Solche Leute pflegt man nur zu schätzen, wenn sie Erfolg gehabt, wirklich etwas entdeckt haben, sonst aber sie bei Seite zu werfen. Und das ist nicht so ganz ungerecht. Gegenwärtig bin ich aber vom Glück verlassen, ich finde nichts Rechtes mehr.

Eine liebenswürdige und feinsinnige, etwas verschwommene, Kritik des Traumbuches findet sich in No. 17 der "Nation" von J. J. *David,* einem persönlich Bekannten. Löwenfeld habe ich zugesagt, einen kurzen Auszug aus dem Buch als Heft der neuen "Grenzfragen des Nerven- und Seelenlebens" zum Sommer fertig zu machen.

Ich finde die Wissenschaft immer schwieriger. Am Abend möchte ich gerne etwas, was aufheitert, erfrischt und weggräumt, bin aber immer allein.

Das Hohenzollermuster ist lustig. Natürlich steigen in dem Ignoranten allerlei, auf einen idealen Congress sich bescheidende Fragen auf. Warum schiebt die Gesetzmässigkeit die *Differenz* vor? Ich hoffe, auch an Deiner Arbeit hätte ich ganz anders Antheil genommen, wenn ich in Berlin lebte. So entfremden wir uns einander von unserem Eigensten her.

Ich habe mir jetzt den Nietzsche beigelegt, in dem ich die Worte für vieles, was in mir stumm bleibt, zu finden hoffe, aber ihn noch nicht aufgeschlagen. Vorläufig zu träge.

Denk'** daran, dass ich mir bei dem Ausbleiben Deiner Briefe regelmässig die düsternsten Erwartungen gestalte und schreib' bald

Deinem
Sigm.

4. March 11, 1900 [passage of L. 130]

Mit der Zunahme meiner Unfreiheit und Deiner Gebundenheit, bei dem unerquicklichen Stoff, der sich mir jedesmal in die Feder drängt, bei der Aussicht,

---

* Freud inserted above the number 14: "5 x 28²–10 x 23."
** The "Du" is crossed out.

von Dir und den Deinigen noch weiter abgedrängt zu werden durch die bevorstehende Verbreuerung, es wäre ganz sinnlos, wollte man den Einfluss solcher Momente und den der Frauen überhaupt auch auf unsere Beziehungen läugnen.*—Kurz unter all diesen Erwägungen nahm ich mir vor meine Ansprüche an Dich einzuschränken. Daher dann mein längeres Schweigen, das ich als Warten auf eine Antwort hinstellen konnte.

5. March 23, 1900 [passage of L. 131]

Im Sommer oder Herbst, nicht später, werde ich Dich sehen, sprechen, und Dir dann auch alle Rätsel des Grafen Oerindur aufklären. Du wirst Dich überzeugen es ist blos compliciert. . . . Dann wollen wir auch das pro und contra der Nasentherapie erörtern, am liebsten gleich am Object.

6. April 28, 1900 [letter to Wilhelm Fliess]

Ja siehst Du ein, dass sich Rom nicht forcieren lässt? Ich habe oft so eine fatalistische Überzeugung, die meiner Trägheit dann sehr wohl dient.

7. October 23, 1900 [letter to Wilhelm Fliess]

Theurer Wilhelm,
Nur einen herzlichen Glückwunsch, einen freundschaftlichen Händedruck über bie Entfernung Berlin-Wien. Keine Gabe wie im Vorjahr, wo ich Dich mit dem Erstling des Traumbuches begrüssen konnte. Möge Alles, und mögen Alle bei Dir gedeihen und Euch für den nothwendigen Niedergang älterer Formationen entschädigen. Auch die Arbeit als organisch wachsendes Gebilde, sei in diesem Wunsch eingeschlossen. . . .
Herzlichst
Dein Sigm.

8. November 25, 1900 [letter to Wilhelm Fliess]

Meine Ahnung, dass Dein langes Schweigen etwas Böses bedeutet, war also richtig. Ich bin dies von früheren Zeiten her gewöhnt, wo es zu bedeuten pflegte, dass es Dir selbst *sehr* schlecht geht. Das also zum Glück nicht mehr!

Ich selbst hätte nicht so lange mit der Anfrage gewartet, wenn ich mir nicht zu Beginn der heurigen Briefverkehrsaison versprochen hätte, das viele Jammern gegen Dich durchaus zu vermeiden. Du siehst, wie bald man dann ausser Kenntnis von einander gerät; schreibst Du doch selbst: "ich habe nicht geantwortet, weil ich nichts zu berichten hatte, wenigstens nichts Erfreuliches." Wenn man darauf warten müsste! Also vielleicht ein Mittleres, nur wenig jammern und doch öfter schreiben.

Deine Nachricht hat mich sehr geschmerzt. Das erlischt also nicht, sondern tritt periodisch vor und zurück und setzt wahrscheinlich in jeder Phase des Vordringens ein neues Stück an. Ich glaube, es ist immer so bei Paranoia, es giebt dabei keine andere Art der Heilung als Zurücktreten mit Festhaltung der Verdrängung. Dabei ist die periodische Natur noch ein Segen. . . .

In der Arbeit ruht es nicht gerade, geht wahrscheinlich unterirdischer Weise ordentlich vorwärts; es ist aber gewiss keine Zeit der Ernte, der bewussten

---

* The correct spelling is *leugnen.*

Bewältigung. Überraschende Funde werden wohl überhaupt nicht mehr kommen. Die Gesichtspunkte sind wahrscheinlich alle schon beisammen, fehlt nur noch die Ordnung und die Einzelausführung. Eine Aussicht die Zeitdauer der Behandlungen wesentlich zu verkürzen, sehe ich nicht, der Umkreis der Indikation wird sich kaum erweitern lassen.

Ganz unbestimmt, wann ich zur Darstellung kommen werde, wenn überhaupt. Diesmal darf kein Irrtum, keine Vorläufigkeit mehr dabei sein, also Horazens Regel: *nonum prematur in annum.* Überdies wer interessiert sich dafür? Wer fragt darnach? *Cui bono** soll ich die Arbeit unternehmen? Ich bescheide mich bereits zu leben wie ein Fremdsprachiger oder wie Humboldts Papagei! Der Letzte seines Stammes—oder der Erste und vielleicht Einzige zu sein, das sind sehr ähnliche Situationen.

. . . Lass mehr von Dir hören und sei herzlich gegrüsst von Deinem
Sigm.

9. January 1, 1901 [letter to Wilhelm Fliess]

Mein Theurer,
Ich werfe die Psychopathologie des Alltagslebens bei Seite um Dir unmittelbar zu antworten, nachdem Dein Brief endlich das beängstigende Schweigen gebrochen hat. Ich konnte mich nicht entschliessen Dich nochmals um Nachricht zu drängen, wenn Du so deutlich zeigtest dass Schreiben Dir lästig war und kein Bedürfnis nach Mittheilung Dich bewegte. Ich habe mir auch die richtige Erklärung für das sonst unerklärliche Phänomen gegeben und meine tiefe Vereinsamung darum verhältnissmässig ruhig ertragen. Ich konnte mir denken, wie Dich die Erkrankung Deiner Mutter ergreifen musste. Selbst gegen alle Logik, denn ich weiss, Du hast lange nichts an ihr verloren, aber gerade darum um so stärker.

Ich bin jetzt ganz zufrieden, dass ich Weihnachten nicht nach Berlin gekommen bin. . . .

Die Anwesenheit Deiner Frau und die wenigen Viertelstunden Gespräch mit ihr kann ich doch nicht leicht vergessen. Um so trauriger, dass ich die Hoffnung sie wiederzusehen mit einem "Leider" begründen muss. Ich frage Dich nun, sollen wir mit unserem Briefverkehr auf eine Zeit warten, die keinem von uns beiden etwas Schweres bringt? Und heisst das nicht zu anspruchsvoll und zu wenig freundschaflich sein? . . .

10. June 9, 1901 [not published in the Fliess correspondence; for the German original, see Schur, 1966a, p. 71f.]

11. July 4, 1901 [unpublished passage of L. 144]

Von den traurigen Veränderungen in Kaltenleutgeben bin ich natürlich gut unterrichtet. Wir werden in nächster Woche hinausfahren und dort auch Königstein besuchen, dessen Tochter dort ihr erstes Kind erwartet.

"Geburt und Tod" u. s. w.

Deine Mutter quäll** sich wol schrecklich. Die Darstellung, warum der eine plötzlich in voller Kraft abstirbt, der andere sich bis ins Letzte zersetzt, stelle ich

---

* See footnote 17.
** This is a slip. Freud meant "quält."

mir nach Deinen Andeutungen sehr interessant vor. Merkwürdigerweise sind wir mit beiden Verlaufsarten unzufrieden.

12. August 7, 1901 [passage of L. 145]

So auch an dem Urtheil über Breuer. Ich verachte ihn längst nicht mehr, ich habe seine Stärke gefühlt. Ist er bei euch tot, so wirkt er noch posthum. Was thut Deine Frau anders, als im dunklen [crossed out] Zwang die Anregung ausarbeiten, die Breuer ihr damals in die Seele gelegt, als er ihr Glück dazu wünschte, dass ich nicht in Berlin lebe und ihre Ehe nicht stören kann?

Bei Breuer hast Du auch gewiss ganz recht mit *dem* Bruder. Ich theile aber Deine Verachtung der Männerfreundschaft nicht, wahrscheinlich weil ich in hohem Grade Partei bin. Mir hat, wie Du ja weisst, nie das Weib im Leben den Kameraden, den Freund ersetzt. Wäre Breuer's männliche Neigung nicht so verschroben, so widerspruchsvoll ist,* wie alles Seelische an ihm, er gäbe ein schönes Beispiel, zu welchen Leistungen sich die androphile Strömung beim Manne sublimieren lässt.

CHAPTER 7

1. April 16, 1909 [letter to Carl G. Jung published in part in Jung, 1961, pp. 361ff.].

Lieber Freund,
Von Venedig aus, wohin ich einen Osterflug gerichtet hatte, in der vergeblichen Erwartung, mir vorzeitig etwas Frühlingsgefühl und Erholung zu schaffen, schrieb ich Ihrer Frau eine Karte weil ich meinte, Sie seien schon auf dam Rad in Oberitalien.

Es ist bemerkenswert, dass an demselben Abend, an dem ich Sie förmlich als ältesten Sohn adoptierte, Sie zum Nachfolger und Kronprinzen—*in partibus infidelium*—salbte, dass gleichzeitig Sie mich der Vaterwürde entkleideten, welche Entkleidung Ihnen ebenso gefallen zu haben scheint, wie mir im Gegenteil die Einkleidung Ihrer Person. Nun fürchte ich bei Ihnen wieder in den Vater zurückzufallen, wenn ich von meiner Relation zu dem Klopfgeisterspuk spreche; muss es aber thun, weil es doch anders ist, als Sie sonst glauben könnten. Ich leugne also nicht, dass Ihre Mitteilungen und Ihr Experiment mir starken Eindruck gemacht haben. Ich nahm mir vor nach Ihrem Weggang zu beobachten und gebe hier die Resultate. In meinem ersten Zimmer kracht es unausgesetzt, dort wo die zwei schweren ägyptischen Stelen auf den Eichenbrettern des Bücherkastens aufruhen, das ist also zu durchsichtig. Im zweiten dort wo wir es hörten, kracht es sehr selten. Anfangs wollte ich es als Beweis gelten lassen, wenn das während Ihrer Anwesenheit so häufige Geräusch sich nach Ihrem Weggang nie wieder hören liesse—aber es hat sich seither wiederholt gezeigt, doch nie im Zusammenhang mit meinen Gedanken und nie, wenn ich mich mit Ihnen oder diesem Ihrem speziellen Problem beschäftigte. (Auch jetzt nicht, füge ich als Herausforderung hinzu.) Die Beobachtung wurde aber alsbald durch anderes entwertet. Meine Gläubigkeit oder wenigstens gläubige Bereitwilligkeit schwand mit dem Zauber Ihres persönlichen Hierseins dahin; es ist mir wieder aus irgend welchen inneren Motiven ganz unwahrscheinlich,

---

* This is a slip: the word "ist" is superfluous.

dass irgend etwas der Art vorkommen sollte; das entgeisterte Mobiliar steht vor mir wie vor dem Dichter nach dem Scheiden der Götter Griechenlands die entgötterte Natur.

Ich setze also wieder die hörnerne Vater-Brille auf und warne den lieben Sohn kühlen Kopf zu behalten und lieber etwas nicht verstehen zu wollen als dem Verständnis so grosse Opfer zu bringen, schüttle auch über die Psychosynthese das weise Haupt und denke: Ja so sind sie, die Jungen, eine rechte Freude macht ihnen doch nur das, wo sie uns nicht mitzunehmen brauchen, wohin wir mit unserem kurzen Atem und müden Beinen nicht nachkommen können.

Dann werde ich mit dem Rechte meiner Jahre geschwätzig und erzähle von einem anderen Ding zwischen Himmel und Erde, das man nicht verstehen kann. Vor einigen Jahren entdeckte ich bei mir die Überzeugung, dass ich zwischen 61 und 62 sterben würde, was mir damals noch als lange Frist vorkam. (Heute sind es nur noch 8 Jahre.) Ich ging dann mit meinem Bruder nach Griechenland und nun war es direkt unheimlich, wie die Zahl 61 oder 60 in Verbindung mit 1 und 2 bei allen Gelegenheiten von Benennung an allen gezählten Gegenständen insbesondere Transportmitteln wiederkehrte, was ich gewissenhaft notierte. Gedrückter Stimmung hoffte ich im Hotel zu Athen, als man uns Zimmer im ersten Stock anwies, aufzuatmen; da konnte Nr. 61 nicht in Betracht kommen. Wohl, aber ich bekam wenigstens Nr. 31 (mit fatalistischer Licenz doch die Hälfte von 61-62), und diese klügere und behendere Zahl erwies sich in der Verfolgung noch ausdauernder als die erste. Von der Rückreise an bis in ganz rezente Zeiten blieb mir die 31 in deren Nähe sich gerne eine 2 befand, treu. Da ich auch Regionen in meinem System habe, in denen ich nur wissbegierig und gar nicht abergläubisch bin, habe ich seither die Analyse dieser Überzeugung versucht, hier ist sie. Sie entstand im Jahre 1899. Damals trafen zwei Ereignisse zusammen. Erstens schrieb ich die Traumdeutung (die ja mit 1900 *vor*datiert erschienen ist), zweitens erhielt ich eine neue Telephonnummer, die ich auch noch heute führe: 14362. Ein Gemeinsames zwischen diesen beiden Thatsachen lässt sich leicht herstellen im Jahre 1899, als ich die Traumdeutung schrieb, war ich *43* Jahre alt. Was lag also näher, als dass die anderen Ziffern mein Lebensende bedeuten sollten, also 61 oder 62.—Plötzlich kommt Methode in den Wahnwitz. Der Aberglaube, dass ich zwischen 61 und 62 sterben werde, stellt sich als aequivalent der Überzeugung heraus, dass ich mit der Traumdeutung mein Lebenswerk vollendet habe, nichts mehr zu machen brauche und ruhig sterben kann. Sie werden zugeben, nach dieser Erfahrung klingt es nicht mehr so unsinnig. Übrigens steckt geheimer Einfluss von W. Fliess darin; im Jahre seines Angriffs brach auch der Aberglaube los. Sie werden die spezifisch jüdische Natur in meiner Mystik wiederum bestätigt finden. Sonst bin ich geneigt nur zu sagen, dass Abenteuer wie das mit der Zahl 61 durch zwei Momente Aufklärung finden, erstens durch die vom Unbewussten enorm gesteigerte Aufmerksamkeit, die Helena in jedem Weibe sieht, und zweitens durch das unleugbar vorhandene "Entgegenkommen des Zufalls" das für die Wahnbildung dieselbe Rolle spielt, wie das Somatische Entgegenkommen beim hysterischen Symptom, das sprachliche beim Wortwitz.

Ich werde also im Stande sein, von Ihren Complexspuk-Forschungen wie von einem holden Wahn, den man selbst nicht teilt, mit Interesse weiters zu vernehmen. Mit herzlichen Grüssen

für Sie, Frau und Kinder Ihr

Freud

CHAPTER 9

1. October 6, 1910 [paragraph from letter to Sandor Ferenczi]

Gewiss schrieb ich aber noch nicht, dass ich den Schreber einmal durchgearbeitet, den Kern unserer Paranoiaannahmen bestätigt gefunden und allerlei Anlass zu ernsthaften Deutungen habe.

2. February 17, 1911 [Letter to Carl G. Jung]

Lieber Freund,
  Ich sehe, Sie glauben mir nicht und halten mich für einen Periodiker, der durch den Ablauf seiner Zeit plötzlich die Welt rosig zu sehen genötigt ist. So muss ich Ihnen denn weitere Einzelheiten geben. Bei Tag war ein Gasgeruch nicht zu verspüren weil bei geschlossenem Hahn die Ausströmung nicht stattfand. Wenn ich aber am Abend von 10-1^h bei der Schreibtischlampe sass, strömte das Gas aus der Lockerung zwischen dem metallenen Gasrohr und dem Kautschukansatz, der zum übersponnenen Lampenrohr führt. An dieser Stelle schoss bei der Untersuchung eine Flamme empor. Ich roch nichts, weil ich in Zigarrenrauch eingehüllt da sass während sich das Gas langsam in die Atmosphäre mengte. Ich bin noch heute sehr stolz darauf, dass ich die sonderbaren Kopfschmerzen, die gerade bei der Arbeit am Abend kamen oder sich verstärkten, und die lästige Schwerbesinnlichkeit bei Tag, so dass ich mich beständig fragen musste, wer hat denn das gesagt, wann ist das vorgefallen etc., nicht auf Neurose bezog. Dagegen gestehe ich, mich auf arteriotische Zustände resigniert zu haben. Nun ist der ganze Spuk spurlos geschwunden. Die Kopfschmerzen zogen innerhalb 3 Tagen nach dem Austausch des Ansatzstückes langsam ab.

3. November 26, 1912 [letter to Sandor Ferenczi]

Jung verabschiedete sich um 5 Uhr mit den Worten: Sie werden mich ganz bei der Sache finden. Wir blieben bis zu den Abschiedszeiten beisammen. Leider hatte ich keinen guten Tag. Von der Woche und einer schlaflosen Nacht im Waggon müde bekam ich bei Tisch einen ähnlichen Angstanfall wie damals im Essighaus in Bremen, wollte aufstehen und wurde für einen Moment ohnmächtig. Ich erhob mich aber selbst und hatte noch einige Zeit Übligkeiten, abends löste es sich mit Kopfschmerz und Gähnen. . . . Die Nacht nach Wien schlief ich vortrefflich und kam ganz wohl hier an.

4. November 28, 1912 [passage from letter of Sandor Ferenczi to Freud].

Ich weiss nicht wie ich dazu kam, Tatsache ist aber, dass ich dieser Tage daran dachte, ob sich Ihr Bremer Unwohlsein in München nicht wiederholen wird. (Damals deuteten wir es als Reaktion auf Jung's Apostasie vom Antialkoholismus.)

5. December 9, 1912 [Letter to Sandor Ferenczi]

Ich bin wieder sehr arbeitsfähig, habe den Schwindelanfall in München gut analytisch erledigt und selbst die lang verhinderte dritte Übereinstimmung begonnen. Alle diese Anfälle weisen auf die Bedeutung frühzeitig erlebter Todes-fälle hin. (Bei mir ein Bruder sehr jung gestorben, als ich wenig über 1 Jahr war.) Die Kriegsstimmung beherrscht unser tägliches Leben, meine Praxis sie noch nicht berührt, aber es kann mir passiren, gleichzeitig 3 Söhne im Feld zu haben.

CHAPTER 11

1. January 21, 1920 [passage of letter to Max Eitingon]

T. F. ist gestern gestorben, friedlich von seinem unheilbaren Leiden erlöst. Für unsere Sache ein schwerer Verlust, für mich ein scharfer Schmerz, den ich aber im Laufe der letzten Monate assimilieren konnte. Er hat seine Hoffnungslosigkeit mit heldenhafter Klarheit ertragen, der Analyse keine Schande gemacht.

Als er Ihren Brief bekam, in dem Sie ihn als Mitglied des Komités begrüssten, weinte er und sagte: Ich weiss, der wird mein Nachfolger. Dabei deutete er auf den Komitéring, den er von mir erhalten hatte. Er hatte mit gewohntem Scharfsinn richtig geraten, ich hatte Ihnen diesen Ring bestimmt, der einen besonders interessanten Stein hat, und bemühte mich darum um keinen anderen für Sie. Einige Zeit später legte or wirklich den Ring ab und gab den Auftrag, ihn mir nach seinem Tode zurückzustellen.

2. January 23, 1921 [passage of letter to Max Eitingon]

". . . sonst kann ich vom Urteil nicht abgehen, dass es ein Leckerbissen ist, freilich Caviar für's Volk, das Werk eines Rabelais ebenbürtigen Kopfes."

The expression, "Caviar für's Volk" is quoted from a German translation of Shakespeare's *Hamlet*. The original English wording is, ". . . caviar to the general."

CHAPTER 12

1. July 18, 1920 [letter to Max Eitingon]

Das "Jenseits" ist endlich fertig geworden. Sie werden bestätigen können, das es halbfertig war, als Sophie lebte und blühte.

2. May 27, 1920 [letter to Max Eitingon]

Ich korrigiere und vervollständige jetzt das "Jenseits," das des Lustprinzips nämlich, und befinde mich wieder in einer leistungsfähigen Phase. *Fractus si illabatur orbis impavidum, ferient ruinae.* Alles nur Stimmung, so lange sie anhält.

3. March 27, 1921 [letter to Max Eitingon]

Für das "Jenseits" bin ich genug gestraft worden, es ist sehr populär, bringt mir Mengen von Zuschriften und Lobsprüchen ein, ich muss da etwas sehr Dummes gemacht haben.

4. March 29, 1921 [Letter to Max Eitingon]

Bei der Schwierigkeit organischer Selbstbeurteilung weiss ich natürlich doch nicht, ob ich die Freunde vom Comité auffordern soll, sich jetzt schon an den Gedanken der Arbeitsfortsetzung ohne meinen Anteil zu gewöhnen. Jetzt schon oder ein wenig später, das ist ja die ganze Frage.

CHAPTER 13

1. July 3, 1899 [passage of L. 110]

Unheimlich, wenn die Mütter wackeln, die einzigen, die noch zwischen uns und der Ablösung stehen.

2. September 26, 1923 [letter to Max Eitingon]

Ich kann heute Ihr Bedürfnis Neues von mir zu erfahren befriedigen. Es ist beschlossen worden, dass ich eine zweite Operation zu bestehen habe, eine partielle Oberkieferresektion, da das liebe Neugebilde dort aufgetaucht ist. Die Operation wird Prof. Pichler machen, der grösste Könner in diesen Dingen, der auch die Prothese für nachher anfertigt. Er verspricht, dass ich in etwa 4-5 Wochen gut werde essen und sprechen können, so dass ich den Beginn meiner Behandlungen vorläufig auf den 1. November verschoben habe.

CHAPTER 15

1. March 22, 1924 [letter to Max Eitingon; published in Part in Jones, Vol. 3, p. 101f.]

Ich kann mich nicht wie sonst auf Ihr Herkommen freuen, denn ich sehe voraus, dass es Ihnen Enttäuschungen bringen wird. Auch Sie gehören ja zu denen, die nichts davon wissen wollen, dass ich nicht mehr derselbe bin. Ich bin aber in Wirklichkeit müde und ruhebedürftig, schlage kaum die 6 Stunden Analyse heraus, halte alles Weitere von mir fern. Das Richtige wäre, Arbeit und Verpflichtungen aufzugeben und in einem stillen Winkel auf das natürliche Ende zu warten. . . . Ich bin auch beständig durch irgend etwas gequält. . . . Es stellt sich so einfach vor, ein Stück Kiefer durch eine Prothese ersetzen und alles ist in Ordnung. Aber die Prothese selbst ist nie ganz in Ordnung, die Versuche zu ihrer Verbesserung auch noch nicht abgeschlossen. Meine rechte untere Gesichtshälfte (Nase und Ohrläppchen besonders) ist schwer hypaesthetisch, das rechte Ohr ist durch Verzerrung und Verschluss der Tuba ausser Funktion, ich höre auf dieser Seite nichts als ein beständiges Rauschen und bin sehr gestört, wenn in einer kleinen Gesellschaft mehrere Personen anzuhören sind. Meine Spache ist verständlich geworden, reicht für's Gewöhnliche aus, soll auch noch weiter gebessert werden. Kauen und Schlucken kann ich natürlich, aber mein Essen verträgt keine Zuschauer. Ich schreibe Ihnen das alles, erstens damit Sie es wissen, und zweitens um Ihnen zu ersparen, hier nach meinem Befinden zu fragen.

2. August 2, 1924 [letter to Max Eitingon]

Kommen Sie nur und mit Frau, wenn sie Lust dazu hat. Ich habe es hier sehr behaglich, bin ausgeruht und nicht mehr so menschenscheu. Aber erwarten Sie nicht, mich "beschwerdefrei" zu finden. Ist das überhaupt möglich in meiner Situation? Noch immer ist mir Essen, Trinken und Sprechen eine mit bewusster Anstrengung zu lösende Aufgabe. Der Missempfindungen sind so viele, sie wechseln Örtlichkeit und Qualität so ausgiebig, dass genug Raum bleibt für dumpfe Befürchtungen hinter ihnen und sie nehmen mich so in Anspruch, dass mir nur ein Bruchteil von Interesse übrig bleibt für die Eindrücke des Tages. Am besten, wenn Sie mich also niemals fragen, wie es mir geht. Von einer entscheidenden Änderung, die in einigen Wochen nicht wahrscheinlich ist, würde ich selbst nicht schweigen.

3. April 1, 1925 [letter to Max Eitingon]

Ich habe ermüdende Zeiten hinter mir, unausgesetzte Arbeit zur Verbesserung meiner Prothese (wieviel lieber verschreib ich mich: Hypothese), das "entsprechende Sanierungselend," die Aufzehrung aller frei beweglichen Energie durch Organbesetzung, wie sie von den unglaublich reichhaltigen Paraestesien gefordert wird. Heute sind wir so weit, dass die groben Beschwerden beseitigt sind, die feineren reichen dann noch hin, mich missmutig zu machen. Von drei zärtlichen Frauenzimmern umringt und beobachtet, habe ich nicht viel Freiheit zu jammern und gute Gelegenheit, mich in der notwendigen Selbstbeherrschung zu üben. Aber man wird müde dabei.

CHAPTER 16

1. March 28, 1926 [letter to Max Eitingon]

Ich sehe nun, da ich einmal angefangen habe, vom Intimsten zu schreiben, muss ich auch fortsetzen und weiter berichten, dass der Aufenthalt in meiner "Riviera" mir sehr wohl gethan hat, was Aussehen, Körpergewicht und subjektives Befinden betrifft. Die Herzsensationen sind nicht ganz vergangen, aber doch geringfügig geworden, ich kann längere Zeit ohne Schmerzen gehen und neige jetzt dazu, den Zustand als einen episodischen zu betrachten, wie mein schlauer Internist—Braun—mir vorredet. Damit treten nach bekanntem allgemein menschlichem Vorbild auch die "Sorgen" in den Hintergrund.

2. April 27, 1926 [letter to Marie Bonaparte]

Ich muss meine Morgenfahrten in den Wiener Frühling fortsetzen und finde es wirklich schön. Wie schade, dass man alt und krank werden musste, um diese Entdeckung zu machen. Wie gut dass Sie in Ihrem Garten nicht so lange zu warten brauchten!

Kennen Sie übrigens das kleine Frühlingsgedicht von unserem Uhland? Es giebt wie kein anderes die Frühlingsstimmung wieder. Ich habe es nicht ganz sicher und vollständig im Gedächtniss, aber ich will was ich erinnere, daraus citieren:

> Die Welt wird schöner mit jedem Tag.
> Man weiss nicht was noch werden mag.

Das Blühen will nicht enden,
Es blüht das fernste, tiefste Tal.
Nun, liebes Herz, vergiss der Qual,
Nun muss sich alles, alles wenden.

Ich bin noch immer sehr tugendhaft.

Sehr herzlich
Ihr
Freud

Chapter 17

1. February 16, 1927 [letter to Max Eitingon]

. . . zweitens will ich Ihnen dafür danken, dass Sie mir wiederum die gute
Zigarre geschickt haben, schon 150 Stück seit der ersten Probe. Ich habe seit
langen Jahren nichts so Angenehmes und Bekömmliches zum Rauchen gehabt
und da es nicht meine Absicht ist, für den kurzen Lebensrest auf diese Genuss-
quelle zu verzichten, bitte ich Sie auch künftighin die Gelegenheit für weitere
Sendungen wahrzunehmen.

. . . Meine neue Prothese verzögert sich immer mehr, ich habe ja auch
keine Sicherheit, dass sie viel besser werden wird, und einstweilen lebe ich sehr
unbequem.

2. April 14, 1927 [letter to Max Eitingon]

Ich danke Ihnen sehr für die neue Zigarrensendung, die Ernst hoffentlich
jedesmal begleicht. Natürlich verlangt man, dass ich weniger rauchen soll.
Meine neue Prothese, in manchen Stücken besser, ist in anderen doch eine
Enttäuschung.

3. June 6, 1927 [letter to Max Eitingon]

Auch Sie unter den Schwärmern! Jenes "fast" dankt seinen Ursprung einer
noch immer nicht aufgegebenen Illusion, dass es Pichler gelingen wird, den
letzten Anstoss zu beseitigen und dass ich dann wieder mit Menschen verkehren
kann, ohne an die Stelle am Kiefer mehr zu denken als an den Menschen.
Aber die letzte Stelle ist immer nur die vorletzte und unterdess kommt Neues
hinzu, so jetzt eine Periostitis, mit der ein Zahn ankündigt, dass er nicht mehr
Lust hat, an der Last mitzutragen, und so geht diese den Weg aller anderen
Illusionen.

4. August 5, 1927 [letter to Marie Bonaparte]

Es war eine sehr garstige Nachricht, dass die Kleine ein Rezidiv durch-
zumachen hat. Hoffentlich überwindet sie Alles. Mein altes Vorurteil, dass
Krankheit überflüssig ist—die Notwendigkeit des Todes sehe ich ein—verstärkt
sich immer wieder.

Es ist das alte Problem, das in Dostojewski's "Grossinquisitor" in grandioser
Weise aufgeworfen wird ob die Menschenkinder etwas von ihrer Freiheit
haben können und ob nicht ein überlegener Absolutismus das heilsamste für

sie ist—Problem ja, aber wo die Lösung? Wo findet sich die Garantie für die Überlegenheit?

5. July 1, 1928 [letter to Ernest Jones]

Ich habe unter Pichlers Bemühungen mir eine bessere Prothese zu schaffen im letzten Jahre sehr gelitten und der Effekt ist sehr wenig befriedigend. So habe ich denn endlich dem Andrängen von vielen Seiten nachgegeben, mich an einen anderen zu wenden. Es ist mir nicht leicht geworden, denn im Grunde ist es doch ein Abfall von einem Menschen, dem ich bereits 4 Jahre Lebensverlängerung verdanke. Aber es ging nicht mehr weiter. Prof. Schroeder in Berlin hat vorige Woche seinen Assistenten hergeschickt, mich zu begutachten, und mir dann versprechen lassen, dass er mir in ungefähr 4 Wochen etwas besseres machen wird. Es wurde verabredet, dass ich im September zu ihm nach Berlin komme.

6. March 11, 1928 [letter to Ernest Jones]

Meine schmerzliche Teilnahme geht über das eigene Erleben. Ich erkenne, mir wurde der Trank in zwei Portionen vorgesetzt, den Sie auf einmal leeren mussten. Sophie war zwar eine liebe Tochter, aber kein Kind. Erst als drei Jahre später, Juni 1923, der kleine Heinele starb, wurde ich auf die Dauer lebenssatt. Ganz merkwürdig ist eine Übereinstimmung zwischen ihm und Ihrer Kleinen. Er war auch von überlegener Intelligenz und unsäglicher seelischer Anmut und er sprach wiederholt davon, dass er bald sterben werde! Woher wissen es diese Kinder?

Sie und Ihre liebe Frau sind natürlich jung genug, um die Fühlung mit dem Leben wieder zu gewinnen.

7. May 3, 1928 [portion of letter to Ernest Jones]

Sie rühren daran, dass ich in wenigen Tagen 72 Jahre alt sein werde. . . .

Sie wissen, dass ich mir's ausgemacht habe, bis zum 75sten solle kein Geburtstag von mir gehalten werden und können leicht verstehen, welche Erwartung sich dahinter verbirgt. Nichtsdestoweniger darf ich vermuten, dass der Verlag mir zu diesem Tag den XI. Band meiner Gesammelten Schriften überreichen wird. Und das lasse ich mir noch gefallen.

"Jung" und "Alt" scheinen mir jetzt die grössten Gegensätze, deren das menschliche Seelenleben fähig ist, und ein Verstehen zwischen den Repräsentanten beider ausgeschlossen. . . . Sollte ich diese Erde noch länger zieren dürfen, so erwartete ich mit Bestimmtheit zu erfahren, dass Sie Beide den grausamen Schlag wie junge Menschen überwunden haben.

CHAPTER 18

1. January 10, 1930 [letter to Max Schur]

Lieber Herr Doktor,

Ich bin in Verlegenheit wie ich auf die mir zugeschickte Jahresrechnung reagieren soll. Wenn ich dieselbe der Ärztekammer vorlege, werden Sie wahrscheinlich wegen standeswidriger Geringschätzung ärztlicher Leistungen zur

Rechenschaft gezogen werden. Ich fühle dass Sie sich dem Kontrakt entzogen haben, der unseren formellen Beziehungen zu Grunde liegt, möchte diese Rechnung nicht bezahlen und lege Ihnen nahe mir eine angemessenere zu schicken.

In herzlicher Ergebenheit
Ihr
Freud

2. May 1, 1930 [letter to Max Eitingon]

Es ist richtig, dass Herz- und Darmzustände mich genötigt haben, das Sanatorium aufzusuchen, d.h., dem Arzt nachzugeben, der es durchaus verlangte. Hier habe ich eine rasche und ordentliche Erholung erreicht, nicht durch irgend welchen therapeutischen Zauber, sondern durch irgend einen Akt schmerzhafter Autotomie. Es sind jetzt 6 Tage, dass ich nicht eine Zigarre mehr geraucht habe, und es ist unleugbar, dass ich diesem Verzicht mein Wohlbefinden verdanke. *Aber es ist traurig.*

3. September 9, 1930 [letter to Max Schur]

Mein Befinden ist im ganzen befriedigend, vom Herzen keine Äusserung. . . . Auf der Schuldseite: eine Zigarre täglich, seit gestern zwei.

4. June 1, 1931 [letter to Max Eitingon]

Ihre Frage nach den Zigarren entlockt mir das Geständnis, dass ich wieder rauche. Mit Rücksicht auf mein Alter und das Mass von Unbehaglichkeiten, das ich täglich zu ertragen habe, erschien mir die Abstinenz und die etwa an sie geknüpfte Chance nicht gerechtfertigt.

5. July 13, 1931 [letter to Max Eitingon]

Ich danke Ihnen sehr für Ihre Vorräte. Im Ärger über nicht weichendes Missbehagen sündige ich wieder mehr und war schon recht knapp.

6. July 25, 1931 [letter to Max Eitingon]

Die Reisesperre wird gewiss auch meine Versorgung mit Rauchzeug erschweren. Da ich den Grundsatz angenommen habe, dass man sich nach 75 nichts versagen soll, sind meine Vorräte in rascher Schrumpfung.

CHAPTER 20

1. April 12, 1931 [letter to Max Eitingon]

Seit der letzten Operation und der letzten Katarrhinfektion hat sich eine nachhaltige Verschlechterung in den Verhältnissen um die Prothese und eine deutliche Niveaufallung* meines Allgemeinbefindens hergestellt, die mir Ge-

---

* This word is an incorrect combination of *Niveau* (level) and a nonexistent noun *Fallung,* which Freud obviously constructed from the verb *fallen* (fall, decline). Having only transcripts of the Eitingon correspondence at my disposal, this seemed to me at first to be an error in the transcript. However, I then noticed the similarity

danken an irgendwelche Feierlichkeiten noch verhasster machen. Ich schliesse, um Ihnen weiter Proben meiner Stimmung zu ersparen.

2. April 16, 1931 [letter to Max Eitingon]

Ich bin mit mir gegenwärtig nicht zufrieden. Angesichts einer neuen Unsicherheit und Drohung habe ich meine überlegene Indifferenz eingebüsst, werde sie aber bald wieder haben, gewiss sobald die Lage geklärt sein wird. Ich habe seit diesem Herbst wie Sie wissen, zwei kleinere Operationen im Mundgebiet gehabt. Die erste, weil ein Teil der alten Narbe verdächtig schien, die histologische Untersuchung wies angeblich die volle Unschuld nach. Bald nachher zeigte sich am Rand der neuen Narbe eine polypartige Erhebung, auf deren sofortiger Entfernung Pichler (7 Febr.) bestand. Die Veränderungen durch den Heilungsprozess nach diesem Eingriff sind bis heute nicht überwunden, aber ich habe seither keinen erträglichen Tag mehr gehabt. Nun hat sich wenige Tage nach dieser zweiten Operation die Schleimhaut zu einer mächtigen Falte aufgeworfen, die dem Chirurgen wiederum missfällt. Seine Rede ist, das ist gewiss nicht bösartig, aber es kann so werden, und warum soll man nicht das noch harmlose Vorstadium entfernen. Meine beiden Leibärzte und ich selbst antworten, weil man keine Sicherheit hat, dass sich solche Faltenbildungen oder Wucherungen auch nach der neuen Operation, vielleicht grade darum bilden werden, während es sicher ist, dass ein monatelang anhaltendes Elend die Folge sein wird. Es ist aber schwer, gegen eine Autorität wie Pichler zu streiten. Wir sind auf die Auskunft verfallen, eine Radiumbehandlung als Alternative in Betracht zu ziehen, und da in Wien niemand ist, dem man darin genug Erfahrung zutraut, ist Dr. Schur auf die Idee gekommen, Prof. Rigaud in Paris, der als der beste Kenner dieser Dinge gilt, zu einem Gutachten einzuladen. Die Verhandlungen mit ihm, der augenblicklich in Locarno ist, gehen über die Prinzessin, die mit ihm befreundet ist. Nun wird erwartet, dass er zusagen und bald hier eintreffen wird. Er soll entscheiden, ob diese Papillären Erhebungen pathogene Bedeutung haben, ob und in welcher Weise sie mit Radium behandelt werden sollen und was man dabei an Gefahren riskiert. Vielleicht wird aus alledem nichts und ich muss mich wieder dem Messer unterwerfen. Auf alle Fälle können Sie es verstehen, wenn ich in den nächsten Wochen weder in der Stimmung noch in der Verfassung sein werde, mich an Feierlichkeiten zu beteiligen.

3. April 21, 1931 [letter to Max Eitingon]

Der Franzose (Rigaud) will nichts von mir wissen. Wenn es sich nicht um unzweifelhaft malignes Gewebe handelt, soll man Radium nicht anwenden. Nachdem wir noch eine Besprechung mit dem Röntgenologen Holzknecht gehabt haben, muss ich mich Pichler ohne Einschränkung unterwerfen. Die Operation wird Donnerstag oder Freitag stattfinden. Ich bin jetzt ganz auf ihn eingerichtet. Von den Zigarren will ich noch mitteilen, dass die kleinen— Perle—sich recht bewährt haben. Mein Vorrat ist nicht mehr gross. Wenn der Berchtesgadener die Soberanos nicht liefern kann, so bin ich bereit, die einmal als Ersatz angebotene recht gute Reina Cabana anzunehmen.

---

in the construction of the equally nonexistent nouns *Pressung-Brennung,* which Freud used in his letter of April 19, 1894, when he described his most severe attack of anginal pains with paroxysmal tachycardia. Both letters were written during a period of severe stress.

4. May 10, 1931 [letter to Marie Bonaparte]

Geben Sie sich heute mit einem kurzen Dankbrief zufrieden. Ich bin noch recht unter der Höhe, und habe diesmal gewiss einen grossen Schritt aus dem Kreis des Lebens heraus getan. . . . .
Ich habe mich sehr mit ihr gefreut, fühle mich auch sonst ungefähr wie ein Urgrossvater und kann sogar noch weiter . . . ein Bedauern hervorrufen, dass man mir keines der schönen Gefässe ins Grabgewölbe mitgeben wird.

5. September 18, 1931 [letter to Marie Bonaparte]

Mein Freund Dr. Oskar Rie ist gestern gestorben. Vor 45 Jahren, als ich jung verheiratet (1886) die Ordination für nervenkranke Kinder eröffnete kam er zu mir erst Doctorand als Assistent, wurde dann der Arzt unserer Kinder und unser Freund mit dem wir durch 1½ Menschenleben Alles teilten. Eine seiner Töchter, Marianne [Kris] ist wie Sie wissen Analytikerin geworden, die andere hat einen Analytiker [Dr. Hermann] Nunberg geheiratet, dadurch wurde die Beziehung wo möglich noch inniger. Es ist ein unabwendbares Schicksal, seine alten Freunde sterben zu sehen. Genug wenn man nicht dazu verurteilt wird die Jugend zu überleben.

Pichler arbeitet täglich an meinen drei Prothesen, hat sie soweit gebessert, dass ich schon mit allen rauchen, mit zweien sprechen kann. Ganz befriedigend ist noch keine. Es ist mit ihnen wie mit der Jagd nach dem Glück; man meint man hat es schon erhascht oder* und immer wieder ist es weg.

6. October 27, 1931 [letter to Max Eitingon]

Pichler arbeitet immer noch an meinen Prothesen und wird mir hoffentlich etwas Erträgliches machen können. In der Reihe der kleineren und grösseren Beschwerden meines Alters gibt es—bald sagte ich: natürlich—keine Pause. Ihre Sendungen habe ich dankend erhalten, habe noch Raum für mehr. "I won't be plucked of my feathers" hat in einer zum Verzicht auffordernden Lage Lord Bacon gesagt.

7. November 15, 1931 [letter to Max Eitingon]

Wenn ich von mir selbst reden soll, ich habe mehr gehabt als eine einfache Magenverstimmung, es war eine arge Magendarmrebellion—unbekannt woher —in deren Verlauf ein mehrstündiger Kolonkrampf mich sogar zwang, eine Analysenstunde plötzlich abzubrechen, was mir bisher nur einmal im Leben zur Not geworden war. Voll hergestellt bin ich auch heute nicht, aber ich bin so vorbereitet darauf, wenn es nicht das ist, wäre es etwas anderes.

Von internen Beschwerden bin ich jetzt einmal frei und die der Prothese sind auf das gewöhnliche Mass eingeschränkt. Die merkwürdige Veränderung des Lebensgefühls, die unabhängig von Wohlsein und Kranksein nebenher geht, kann man nur andächtig zur Kenntnis nehmen.

8. November 29, 1931 [letter to Marie Bonaparte]

Ich habe durch Ruth gehört, dass die Krankheit eingebrochen ist und da ich solange keinen Brief von Ihnen erhalten habe, bitte ich Sie um baldige Benachrichtigung, hoffentlich des Inhalts, dass alles wieder gut ist.

---

* A rare instance of a word crossed out—and just at this point!

Dieser Monat war eine elende Zeit, ich war unausgesetzt krank, mit der Prothese oder an anderen Dingen, und draussen hatten wir den Schreck, mit der lebensgefährdenden Melaena neonatorum der Kleinen von Marianne Kris, das Kind ist aber durch Bluttransfusion gerettet worden. . . .

9. December 14, 1931 [letter to Max Eitingon]

Ich rauche wieder herzhafter und sehe mit Bangen beide letzten Berchtesgadener Kistchen der Erschöpfung nahe. Und während Ihrer Abwesenheit?

CHAPTER 22

1. January 5, 1933 [letter to Max Eitingon]

Mit Ihrem Vater ist es mir merkwürdig gegangen damals, als Sie von einer Störung während der Operationsheilung berichteten, verlor ich das Zutrauen, und da bereitete sich die Erwartung vor, die sich später, als Sie seine Herstellung mitteilten, in dem Ausdruck Luft machte, es sei doch wenigstens Zeit gewonnen. Wenn Sie sich an diese Stelle in meinem Brief erinnern können! Nun, es war zu wenig Zeit gewonnen worden. Mir schwebte vor, dass wir doch alle zum Tod verurteilt sind, die Alten unter uns mit besonders kurzer— Bewährungsfrist.

2. March 21, 1933 [letter to Arnold Zweig]

Die schweren Zeiten machen mich verzagt. . . . Um mich selbst brauche ich ja keine Sorgen zu haben. Wie mein pessimistischer und zehn Jahre jüngerer Bruder unlängst sagte, unser Alter ist unser bestes Aktivum.

3. May 9, 1933 [letter to Marie Bonaparte]

Meine liebe Marie,
   Gern wäre ich mit Ihnen in Corsika gewesen, hätte mich miterfreut an der Schönheit der Landschaft und der Wärme des Empfanges. . . .
   Mein Geburtstag war anstrengend, überreich an Blumen Briefen und Telegrammen; von Geschenken hatte ich die Meisten abgehalten, Sie allerdings nicht. Ihr Kamel prangt bereits neben anderen Chinoiseries . . . hier im Zimmer. . . . Am Vormittag dieses Tages hatte ich einen Anfall von Schwindel, der mich fast umwarf, ohne Trübung des Bewusstseins. Dr. Schur, der zufällig gleich darauf kam, machte nichts daraus. Die Diagnose behauptete der Schwindel sei vestibulär und Folge von Nikotin. Ich bin seither auf drei Zigarren eingeschränkt, fühle mich aber wirklich nicht wohl seither ob es nun Abstinenz oder etwas anderes ist. . . .
   Sind Ihre beiden Kinder noch in Dänemark? Leider ist Dänemark nicht mehr der einzige Staat in dem etwas faul ist.

4. June 6, 1933 [letter to Marie Bonaparte]

Ich denke nicht daran etwas Neues zu schreiben. Keine Stimmung, kein Stoff, kein Publicum, zu viel gemeine Sorgen. Die politische Lage haben Sie selbst erschöpfend beschrieben. Mir scheint es, nicht im Krieg haben Lüge und Phrase so uneingeschränkt geherrscht. Die Welt wird ein grosses Zuchthaus, die ärgste Zelle ist Deutschland. . . .

Selbst nicht mehr recht lebenskräftig erscheint mir diese Welt als zum nahen Untergang bestimmt. Ich denke gerne daran, dass Sie noch wie auf einer Insel der Seeligen wohnen.

5. August 18, 1933 [letter to Arnold Zweig]

Was bei mir vorgeht? Ich füge mich der Natur, die mich altern lässt, in Eile jetzt, in den letzten drei Monaten mehr, als in den letzten drei Jahren. Alles herum ist trüb und zum Ersticken dumpf. Die Wut speichert sich auf und zehrt am Gehäuse. Wenn man etwas Befreiendes tun könnte! . . .

Die Frauen des Hauses halten besser aus, sie sind ja das beständigere Element, der Mann ist, biologisch mit Recht, hinfälliger.

6. December 7, 1933 [letter to Marie Bonaparte]

Heute fällt ein anderer [Geburtstag], Martins. Keine Kinder mehr und selbst ist man bereits überzählig, ausserhalb des Lebensstromes! . . .

Meine Existenz ist wieder um ein Stück eingeschränkt worden. Dass ich nicht ausgehe, ist grade jetzt kein Verlust. Es ist bitter kalt und unfreundlich draussen. Ob ich etwas schreibe? Nein, ich glaube auch nicht, dass ich noch werde. Ich rauche eine kleine, entnervte Zigarre im Tag.

Von Bullitt keine direkten Nachrichten. Unser Buch wird das Licht der Welt nicht erblicken.

7. February 19, 1934 [letter to Marie Bonaparte]

Nochmals herzlichen Dank für Ihre wiederholte Einladung. Es ist natürlich unschätzbar zu wissen, dass es einen schönen Ort giebt, an dem man gern aufgenommen sein würde, bis man ein neues Heim gefunden hat. . . .

Die Zukunft ist nicht vorauszusehen. . . . Wenn die Nazis hieher kommen und mit ihnen eine Rechtlosigkeit wie in Deutschland, dann muss man natürlich fort.

CHAPTER 23

1. May 2, 1934 [letter to Marie Bonaparte]

Meine liebe Marie,
Wir sind jetzt umgezogen und eingeordnet XIX. Strassergasse 47, und ich kann daran gehen meine Briefschulden abzutragen. An Sie zuerst. Es ist märchenhaft schön hier, ich möchte unbekannter Weise die Konkurrenz mit Ihrem St. Cloud aufnehmen. . . .

Ich schreibe nichts, dazu gehört doch ein gewisses Mass von körperlichem Behagen, das ich nicht mehr aufbringe und auch eine freundlichere Einstellung zur Umwelt, als man sie jetzt haben kann. Es hilft wenig, dass man genau weiss, wie gleichgiltig für das Weltgeschehen das eigene Befinden ist, man bleibt der Sklave seiner Empfindungen und das einzige was man leisten kann ist sein Missvergnügen für sich zu behalten.

2. October 14, 1935 [letter to Arnold Zweig]

Lieber Meister Arnold,
Es ist doch schön, dass man einem starken Mann mit einigen Worten eine so
grosse Freude bereiten kann, und dabei handelt es sich gar nicht um ein
freundliches Geschenk, sondern um den Versuch zur Abtragung einer Schuld.
Ausser mir, meine Tochter und meinem Sohn gibt es noch eine Person in
meiner nächsten Nähe, die Ihr Werk geniesst, und ich möchte sagen unter ihm
stöhnt. Es ist mein Leibarzt, Dr. Max Schur, ein sehr tüchtiger Doktor, so tief
empört über die Vorgänge in Deutschland, dass er keine deutschen Medika-
mente verschreibt. Ich muss ihm immer wieder von Ihnen erzählen. . . .
In wenigen Tagen ziehen wir wieder in die Stadtwohnung. Es war eine herrliche Herbstzeit, mein Befinden eher besser. Krieg oder Kriegsspannung kann
alle unsere analytische Arbeit in Wien ersticken.

3. August 18, 1933 [letter to Arnold Zweig]

Man wehrt sich in jeder Form gegen die Kastration, hier mag sich noch ein
Stückchen Opposition gegen das eigene Judentum schlau verbergen. Unser
grosser Meister Moses war doch ein starker Antisemit und macht kein Ge-
heimnis daraus. Vielleicht war er wirklich ein Ägypter.

CHAPTER 24

1. March 26, 1936 [letter to Marie Bonaparte]

Ob Sie auch zum 6. Mai hieher kommen sollen? Es würde mich gewiss sehr
freuen; aber es wäre nur ein Akt der Pietät. Wir hätten nichts davon. Ich
vermute, es werden viele kommen, Eitingon, Jones, Laforgue, Landauer unter
Anderen. Jeder wird etwas von mir erwarten und ich werde nicht leistungsfähig
sein. Mein Allgemeinbefinden hat in letzter Zeit deutlich einen Schritt nach
abwärts gemacht. Gestern hatte ich eine schwere Migraine, ganz ungewöhnlich
bei mir, und ich mach noch heute allerlei verworrenes Zeug wie Sie an Brief
und Addresse gemerkt haben werden. Ich bin reizbarer und empfindlicher gegen
schlechte Nachrichten als sonst. Minna hat sich gestern an beiden Augen wegen
Glaukom operieren lassen, sie hatte es bis zu letzt verheimlicht. Wir hoffen es
geht gut aus.
    Aus Leipzig kommt die Nachricht, dass die Staatspolizei einen grossen Teil des
psa. Bücherlagers bei Volkmar konfisciert hat, beinahe eine Katastrophe für den
armen Verlag. . . .

CHAPTER 25

1. December 1, 1936 [letter to Marie Bonaparte]

Ich habe die letzten paar Tage unter der Ausbreitung meines chronischen
Katarrh in Luftröhre und Bronchien gelitten. Nichts eigentlich Arges, aber bei
jedem Kranksein drängen sich neue Anzeichen des Altersverfalls vor. Man kann
das als unvermeidlich nur zur Kenntniss nehmen und darf keinen Zoll von
Mitgefühl dafür einfordern. 81½ war die Lebensgrenze die Vater und Bruder
erreicht haben; mir fehlt dahin noch ein Jahr. . . .

P.S. Wenn Sie allmächtig sind lassen Sie sich eine der Korxi im Museum schenken, für mich!

2. January 1, 1937 [portion of letter to Marie Bonaparte]

An den Erwähnungen intimer Vorgänge und Beziehungen fehlt es auch nicht und manches wie die Vorwürfe mit denen die Freundschaft zusammenbrach ist in der Erinnerung besonders peinlich.

3. May 16, 1937 [letter to Marie Bonaparte]

Ein wunderbarer Frühling ist hier über uns gekommen. Der Garten war noch nie so schön. Leider wird mir der Genuss durch die andauernden Schmerzen gestört. . . . Es sind schon 3½ Wochen seit dem Eingriff. Ich schreibe darum auch nicht mehr.

CHAPTER 27

1. June 8, 1938 [letter to Marie Bonaparte]

Meine liebe Marie,

Der erste Brief geschrieben auf dem von Ihren Terrakotten eingerahmten Schreibtisch in einem Zimmer dessen Gartenaussicht Ihnen gewiss gefallen wird, sollte von rechtswegen Ihnen gehören denn der eine Tag in Ihrem Haus in Paris hat uns Würde und Stimmung wiedergegeben; nachdem wir 12 Stunden lang in Liebe eingehüllt wurden, sind wir stolz und reich unter dem Schutz der Athene abgereist! Aber es hat vielleicht nicht viel Sinn Ihnen zu danken oder Ihnen zu erzählen, was Sie schon wissen. Sie werden Neues erfahren wollen.

Neues ist hier genug, das meiste schön, einiges sehr schön. Der Empfang in Victoria Station und dann von den Zeitungen dieser ersten zwei Tage war liebenswürdig, ja enthusiastisch. Wir schwimmen in Blumen. Interessant die Zuschriften: nur 3 Autographensammler, 1 Malerin die mich porträtieren will wenn ich ausgeruht bin, auch nur 1 rührende Konsultation einer Tochter, für ihre als unheilbar verurteilte Mutter, ferner eine Annonce eines grosszügigen Delikatessengeschäftes. Sonst die Begrüssungen durch die meisten Mitglieder der englischen Gruppe, einige gelehrte und andere jüdische Gesellschaften, als pièce de résistance ein weitläufiges Telegramm auf vier Blättern aus Cleveland, Ohio, gezeichnet von "citizens of all faiths and professions," höchst respektvolle Einladung unter allen Versprechungen, unser Heim bei ihnen aufzuschlagen. (Wir werden antworten müssen, dass wir leider schon ausgepackt haben!)

Endlich, und das ist das für England besondere, reichliche Zuschriften von fremden Leuten, die nur sagen wollen wie sehr sie sich freuen dass wir in England angekommen, dass wir jetzt in Sicherheit und Frieden sind. Wirklich, als ob unsere Sache auch ihre Sache wäre.

Mein Herz war, wie in Paris, auch diese Tage, nicht leistungslustig, unsere kleine Ärztin hat brav gewacht und es scheint sich rasch zu bessern. . . .

Ihre Zigarren sind sicherlich unschädlich, wenn auch nicht sehr schmackhaft. Ich habe hier noch nichts Ähnliches gefunden.

So könnte ich noch Stunden lang schreiben, ohne den Stoff zu erschöpfen. Aber genug, mit herzlichstem Gruss

Ihr

Freud

2. August 20, 1938 [letter to Marie Bonaparte]

Meine liebe Marie
Es tut mir leid so frühzeitig Alarm geschlagen zu haben. Schur hatte die Schuld der eigentlich eigenmächtig Pichler geschrieben, sein Herkommen angeregt hatte. Er antwortete natürlich er sei für die Entfernung der betreffenden Stelle. Unterdess ist wieder abgeblasen worden. Die Stelle scheint zurückzugehen alle hier befragten Ärzte halten sie für unverdächtig (Dr. Exner, Pichler's ehemaliger Assistent u. der von ihm empfohlene Vertreter ein Dr. Gottwald Schwarz aus Wien, ein hochangesehener Röntgenolog) Es ist beschlossen worden derweil nichts zu tun, abzuwarten. Schur ist auch mit einem Mal durchaus optimistisch. Er gesteht zu, dass Pichler wiederholt das Wolbefinden des Patienten der Vorsicht geopfert hat. . . .

3. October 4, 1938 [letter to Marie Bonaparte]

Er kann nicht lange sein, denn ich [kann omitted in original] kaum schreiben, nicht besser als sprechen oder rauchen. Diese Operation war [letter crossed out in original] die schwerste seit 1923. . . . Ich bin abscheulich müde und schwach in Bewegungen, habe zwar gestern mit 3 Patienen begonnen aber es geht nicht leicht.

4. November 1, 1938 [letter to Ernest Jones]

Dear Jones,
Ich habe es gestern lebhaft bedauert, dass Ihre Erkältung Sie genötigt hat, sich von mir fern zu halten, und ich war dann sehr bestürzt zu hören, Sie würden die Übersetzung meines Moses nicht vor Februar oder März zu Ende bringen können. Ich weiss, Ihre Zeit ist sehr wertvoll, Ihre Gewissenhaftigkeit sehr gross und Sie haben noch allerlei Anderes, was mindestens ebenso wichtig ist, zu thun. Aber ich denke daran, dass Sie sich freiwillig diese neue Belastung auferlegt haben, ohne dass ich Sie dazu aufgefordert. Ich erblickte allerdings in Ihrem Unternehmen eine besondere Liebenswürdigkeit für mich und eine Auszeichnung für das Buch.
Der Aufschub, den Sie mir in Aussicht stellen, ist mir in mehr als einer Hinsicht unangenehm. Vor allem bedeuten einige Monate für mich mehr als für einen anderen, wenn ich den begreiflichen Wunsch festhalte, das Buch noch selbst fertig zu sehen. ,

5. December 19, 1938 [letter to Max Eitingon]

Ich habe Ihnen noch nicht für Ihre gewissenhafte Berichterstattung über unseren Arnold Zweig gedankt. Seither habe ich auch einen ersten Brief von ihm erhalten, recht unleserlich, aber doch erfreulich. Wenigstens hier ein Stück gute Nachricht. . . . ich warte auf einen mir versprochenen Knochen wie ein hungriger Hund, nur dass es ein eigener sein soll. Ich arbeite jetzt 4 Stunden täglich.

6. December 27, 1938 [letter to Marie Bonaparte]

Meine liebe Marie,
Ihr Brief mit den schönen Bildern aus dem Museum kommt während wir noch überlegen, ob wir auf [Ihr] liebes Weihnachts Telegramm nach Athen oder nach

Egypten antworten sollen. Jetzt wird es sich also in einen Neujahrs-Wunsch nach dem letzteren verwandeln. Ich antworte Ihnen aber noch umgehend nach Athen.

Ja, wir haben gefroren und der ewig grüne englische Rasen ist dick mit weissem Schnee bedeckt. Herrliche Winterlandschaft vor meinem Fenster in dem Garten. Man getraut sich nicht zu denken wie London aussehen wird, wenn all das zu Wasser wird.

Weihnacht war ruhig bis auf die gewohnten Nachrichten von Tod und Selbstmord in Wien. Mein Knochen fühlt sich noch wohl bei mir, ich nicht mit ihm. Schur ist sehr brav, kann aber nicht helfen.

Die erste Korrektur des deutschen Moses habe ich gestern fertig gestellt. Meine englischen Übersetzer sind in Mürren.

Der Sinai verdient Ihr Interesse nicht. Sie wissen, der Berg Jahves war nicht auf der Halbinsel, sondern im westlichen Arabien und eine Gesetzgebung am Sinai hat es überhaupt nicht gegeben. Siehe meinen Moses, der mir abwechselnd imponiert und sehr missfällt.

Jerusalem zu versäumen wäre schade. Sie wissen, Sie sehen auf dieser Reise *auch für mich,* den Reise-gelähmten.

7. March 5, 1939 [letter to Max Eitingon]

Ich habe Ihnen längere Zeit nicht geschrieben, nicht nur weil mir das Schreiben wie die meisten anderen Tätigkeiten zu sauer wurden, sondern auch weil die Situation zu unklar war. Jetzt sind wir ungefähr orientiert. Eine Probeexzision hat ergeben, dass es sich wirklich um einen Versuch des Carcinoms handelt, sich wieder an meine Stelle zu setzen. Man schwankte lange zwischen verschiedenen Möglichkeiten der Verteidigung . . . nun haben wir uns alle auf Röntgenbestrahlung von aussen geeinigt, von der sich die Beteiligten—ob ich mich einschliessen soll, weiss ich nicht, Gutes erwarten. Morgen soll der hiesige Röntgenologe, ein Dr. Finzi kommen, dem man meinen Fall übergeben will. Hoffentlich lehnt er nicht ebenso ab wie andere Fachmänner. Ich bin natürlich sehr zufrieden damit, dase die Operation und die Reise nach Paris verworfen worden sind. Röntgen ist doch weit schonender, gibt eine Art von Lebenssicherung für mehrere Wochen und gestattet wahrscheinlich eine Fortsetzung der analytischen Tätigkeit während dieser Zeit. . . . Mein Leibarzt Schur benimmt sich sehr aufopfernd. Es tut mir leid, dass ich Ihnen nichts anderes schreiben soll, aber das haben Sie ja von mir wissen wollen. Sonst noch, dass der deutsche Moses in den nächsten Tagen erwartet wird. Ich grüsse Sie und Mira herzlich.

Ihr
Freud

P.S. Martin Bubers fromme Redensarten werden der Traumdeutung wenig schaden. Der Moses ist weit vulnerabler und ich bin auf den jüdischen Ansturm gegen ihn vorbereitet.

8. March 20, 1939 [letter to Marie Bonaparte]

Ich muss nochmals meinem Bedauern Ausdruck geben, dass ich mich Ihnen so wenig widmen konnte, als Sie bei uns lebten. Vielleicht geht es nächstes Mal besser—wenn kein Krieg kommt—denn meine Schmerzen scheinen weiter auszubleiben. Dr. Harmer, der eben hier war, findet einen deutlichen Einfluss der Behandlung auf das Aussehen der kranken Stellen.

9. April 28, 1939 [letter to Marie Bonaparte]

Ich habe Ihnen lange nicht geschrieben, während Sie im blauen Meer gebadet haben. Ich nehme an Sie wissen warum, erkennen es auch an meiner Schrift. (Nicht einmal die Feder ist dieselbe, sie hat mich verlassen wie der Leibarzt und andere externe Organe). Es geht mir nicht gut, mein Leiden und die Folgen der Behandlung teilen sich in die Verursachung in einem mir unbekannten Verhältnis. Man hat versucht mich in eine Atmosphäre von Optimismus zu ziehen: Das Carcinom ist in Schrumpfung, die Reaktionserscheinungen sind vorübergehend. Ich glaube nicht daran und mag es nicht betrogen zu werden. . . .

Etwas Interkurrentes, was den grausamen Prozess kurz abschneidet wäre sehr erwünscht.

Soll ich mich noch darauf freuen, sie bald im Mai wiederzusehen?

10. June 15, 1939 [letter to Marie Bonaparte]

Meine liebe Marie,

Vorgestern abends war ich daran, Ihnen einen langen Trostbrief zu schreiben zum Tode unseres alten Tattous und dann Sie darauf vorzubereiten, dass ich bei Ihrem nächsten Hiersein eifrig lauschen würde, was Sie von neuen Arbeiten erzählen, bereit hie und da ein Wort hinzuwerfen wo ich glaube, dass ich etwas dazu ergänzen kann. Die zwei folgenden Nächte haben meine Erwartungen wieder grausam zerstört. Das Radium hat wieder etwas aufzufressen begonnen, unter Schmerzen und Vergiftungserscheinungen, und meine Welt ist wieder was sie früher war, eine kleine Insel Schmerz schwimmend auf einem Ozean von Indifferenz.

Finzi fährt fort seine Zufriedenheit zu betheuern. Auf meine letzte Klage hatte er die Antwort: am Ende werden Sie auch zufrieden sein. So verlockt er mich halb gegen meinen Willen, weiter zu hoffen und unterdess weiter zu leiden. . . .

Vom deutschen Moses sollen schon 1800 Exemplare verkauft sein. Herzlichst und mit warmen Wetterwünschen, solange Sie am Meer sind

Ihr
Freud

REFERENCES

Abraham, K., *see* Freud/Abraham

Andreas-Salomé, L. (1958 [1912-1913]), *The Freud Journal of Lou Andreas-Salomé* (translated by S. Leavy from *In der Schule bei Freud*). New York: Basic Books, 1964.

———— *see also* Freud/Andreas-Salomé.

Bakan, D. (1958), *Sigmund Freud and the Jewish Mystical Tradition*. New York: van Nostrand.

Balzac, H. de (1831), *La Peau de Chagrin [The Fatal Skin]*. Paris: Gallimard, 1966.

Benjamin, J. D. (1961), The Innate and the Experiential. In: *Lectures in Experimental Psychiatry*, ed. H. W. Brosin. Pittsburgh: University of Pittsburgh Press, pp. 19-42.

Berdach, R. (1962), *The Emperor, the Sages, and Death,* tr. W. Wolf. New York: A. S. Barnes.

Bernfeld, S. (1946), An Unknown Autobiographical Fragment by Freud. *Amer. Imago, 4*:3-19.

———— (1949), Freud's Scientific Beginnings. *Amer. Imago, 6*:163-196.

———— & Bernfeld, S. C. (1944), Freud's Early Childhood. *Bull. Menninger Clin., 8*:107-115.

Binion, R. (1968), *Frau Lou.* Princeton: Princeton University Press.

Binswanger, L. (1956), *Sigmund Freud: Reminiscences of a Friendship.* New York & London: Grune & Stratton, 1957.

Bonaparte, M. (1933), *The Life and Works of Edgar Allen Poe.* London: Imago Publishing Co., 1949.

Breuer, J. & Freud, S. (1893-1895), Studies on Hysteria. *Standard Edition, 2.*

Brome, V. (1968), *Freud and His Early Circle.* New York: Vincent Morrow.

Chertok, L. (1968), The Discovery of the Transference. *Int. J. Psycho-Anal., 49*:560-576.

Deutsch, F. (1956), Reflections on Freud's One Hundredth Birthday. *Psychosom. Med., 18*:279-283.

Deutsch, H. (1933), The Psychology of Manic-Depressive States, with Particular Reference to Chronic Hypomania. *Neuroses and Character Types.* New York: International Universities Press, 1965, pp. 203-217.

D[oolittle], H. (1956), *Tribute to Freud.* New York: Pantheon.

Eissler, K. R. (1959), The Function of Details in the Interpretation of Works of Literature. *Psychoanal. Quart., 28*:1-20.

———— (1963), *Goethe,* 2 Vols. Detroit: Wayne University Press.

———— (1964), Mankind at Its Best. *J. Amer. Psychoanal. Assn., 12*:187-222.

Ekstein, R. (1949), A Biographical Comment on Freud's Dual-Instinct Theory. *Amer. Imago,* 6:213.

Erikson, E. H. (1967), [Book Review of] Freud, S. & Bullitt, W. C. *Thomas Woodrow Wilson. Int. J. Psycho-Anal.,* 48:462-468.

Fliess (1897), Beziehungen zwischen Nase und weiblichen Geschlechtsorganen. Leipzig, Vienna: Deuticke.

—— (1906), *In Eigener Sache: Gegen Otto Weininger und Hermann Swoboda.* Berlin: E. Goldschmidt.

Freud, S. (1888-1889), Translation of H. Bernheim's *Die Suggestion und ihre Heilwirkung* [1887]. Leipzig & Vienna: Deuticke.

—— (1891), *On Aphasia.* New York: International Universities Press, 1953.

—— (1892), Translation of H. Bernheim's *Neue Studien über Hypnotismus, Suggestion und Psychotherapie* [1891]. Leipzig & Vienna: Deuticke.

—— (1895), Project for a Scientific Psychology. *The Origins of Psychoanalysis.* New York: Basic Books, 1954, pp. 347-455.

—— (1899), Screen Memories. *Standard Edition,* 3:301-322.

—— (1900), The Interpretation of Dreams. *Standard Edition,* 4 & 5.

—— (1901a), On Dreams. *Standard Edition,* 5:631-686.

—— (1901b), The Psychopathology of Everyday Life. *Standard Edition,* 6.

—— (1905a [1901]), Fragment of an Analysis of a Case of Hysteria. *Standard Edition,* 7:3-122.

—— (1905b), Three Essays on the Theory of Sexuality. *Standard Edition,* 7:125-245.

—— (1905c), Jokes and Their Relation to the Unconscious. *Standard Edition,* 8.

—— (1907a [1906]), Delusions and Dreams in Jensen's *Gradiva. Standard Edition,* 9:3-95.

—— (1907b), Obsessive Actions and Religious Practices. *Standard Edition,* 9:115-127.

—— (1907c), Contribution to a Questionnaire on Reading. *Standard Edition,* 9:245-247.

—— (1908 [1907]), Creative Writers and Day-Dreaming. *Standard Edition,* 9:141-153.

—— (1909a), Analysis of a Phobia in a Five-Year-Old Boy. *Standard Edition,* 10:3-149.

—— (1909b), Notes upon a Case of Obsessional Neurosis. *Standard Edition,* 10:153-318.

—— (1910), Leonardo da Vinci and a Memory of His Childhood. *Standard Edition,* 11:63-137.

—— (1911a), 'Great Is Diana of the Ephesians.' *Standard Edition,* 12:342-344.

—— (1911b), Formulations on the Two Principles of Mental Functioning. *Standard Edition,* 12:213-226.

—— (1911c), Psycho-Analytic Notes on an Autobiographical Account of a Case of Paranoia (Dementia Paranoides). *Standard Edition,* 12:3-82.

—— (1913a), The Theme of the Three Caskets. *Standard Edition,* 12:289-301.

—— (1913b [1912-1913]), Totem and Taboo. *Standard Edition,* 3:1-161.

—— (1914a), On the History of the Psycho-Analytic Movement. *Standard Edition,* 14:7-66.

—— (1914b), The Moses of Michelangelo. *Standard Edition,* 13:211-236.

―――― (1915a), Instincts and Their Vicissitudes. *Standard Edition,* 14:111-140.

―――― (1915b), Repression. *Standard Edition,* 14:141-158.

―――― (1915c), The Unconscious. *Standard Edition,* 14:159-215.

―――― (1915d), Thoughts for the Times on War and Death. *Standard Edition,* 14:273-302.

―――― (1916a [1915]), On Transience. *Standard Edition,* 14:303-307.

―――― (1916b), Some Character-Types Met with in Psycho-Analytic Work. *Standard Edition,* 14:309-333.

―――― (1916-1917 [1915-1917]), Introductory Lectures on Psycho-Analysis. *Standard Edition,* 15 & 16.

―――― (1917a [1915]), Mourning and Melancholia. *Standard Edition,* 14:237-260.

―――― (1917b), A Difficulty in the Path of Psycho-Analysis. *Standard Edition,* 17:135-144.

―――― (1917c), A Childhood Recollection from *Dichtung und Wahrheit. Standard Edition,* 17:145-156.

―――― (1918 [1914]), From the History of an Infantile Neurosis: *Standard Edition,* 17:3-123.

―――― (1919), The 'Uncanny.' *Standard Edition,* 17:217-252.

―――― (1920), Beyond the Pleasure Principle. *Standard Edition,* 18:3-64.

―――― (1921), Group Psychology and the Analysis of the Ego. *Standard Edition,* 18:67-143.

―――― (1922), Dreams and Telepathy. *Standard Edition,* 18:195-220.

―――― (1923), The Ego and the Id. *Standard Edition,* 19:3-66.

―――― (1924a), The Economic Problem of Masochism. *Standard Edition,* 19:157-170.

―――― (1924b), The Dissolution of the Oedipus Complex. *Standard Edition,* 19:173-179.

―――― (1925a [1924]), A Note upon the 'Mystic Writing Pad.' *Standard Edition,* 19:227-232.

―――― (1925b [1924]), An Autobiographical Study. *Standard Edition,* 20:3-74.

―――― (1926a [1925]), Inhibitions, Symptoms and Anxiety. *Standard Edition,* 20:77-175.

―――― (1926b), The Question of Lay Analysis. *Standard Edition,* 20:179-258.

―――― (1927a), The Future of an Illusion. *Standard Edition,* 21:3-56.

―――― (1927b), Postscript to: The Moses of Michelangelo [1914b]. *Standard Edition,* 13:237-238.

―――― (1930a), The Goethe Prize. *Standard Edition,* 21:205-212.

―――― (1930b [1929]), Civilization and Its Discontents. *Standard Edition,* 21:59-145.

―――― (1933a [1932]), Why War? *Standard Edition,* 22:197-215.

―――― (1933b [1932]), New Introductory Lectures on Psycho-Analysis. *Standard Edition,* 22:3-182.

―――― (1936), A Disturbance of Memory on the Acropolis. *Standard Edition,* 22:239-248.

―――― (1937a), Analysis Terminable and Interminable. *Standard Edition,* 23:209-253.

―――― (1937b), Lou Andreas-Salomé. *Standard Edition,* 23:297-298.

——— (1939 [1934-1938]), Moses and Monotheism. *Standard Edition*, 23:3-137.

——— (1940 [1938]), An Outline of Psycho-Analysis. *Standard Edition*, 23:141-207.

——— (1941[1921]), Psycho-Analysis and Telepathy. *Standard Edition*, 18:173-193.

——— (1950 [1887-1902]), *The Origins of Psychoanalysis*. New York: Basic Books, 1954.

——— (1960a), *The Letters of Sigmund Freud*, ed. E. L. Freud. New York: Basic Books.

——— (1960b), *Briefe: 1873-1939*. Frankfurt: Fischer.

———/Abraham K. (1965), *The Letters of Sigmund Freud and Karl Abraham, 1907-1926*, ed. H. C. Abraham & E. L. Freud. New York: Basic Books.

———/Andreas-Salomé, L. (1966), *Briefwechsel*. Frankfurt: Fischer.

——— & Bullitt, W. C. (1967), *Thomas Woodrow Wilson: A Psychological Study*. Boston: Houghton-Mifflin.

———/Pfister, O. (1963), *Psychoanalysis and Faith*. New York: Basic Books.

——— & Rie, O. (1891), Cerebrale Kinderlähmung und Poliomyelitis infantilis. *Wien. klin. Wschr.*, 41:193-196, 244-246, 292-294. Also: Klinische Studien über die halbseitige Cerebrallähmung der Kinder. *Beiträge zur Kinderheilkunde*, Heft 3 [ed. M. Kassowitz].

———/Zweig, A. (1968), *Briefwechsel. Frankfurt. Fischer*. [All letters cited appear in my own translation.]

Friedman, L. J. (1966), From *Gradiva* to Death Instinct. *Psychoanal. Forum*, 1(1):46-53.

Gardner, M. (1966), Mathematical Games: Freud's Friend Wilhelm Fliess and His Theory of Male and Female Life Cycles. *Sci. Amer.*, 215(1):108-113; 215(2):99.

Gicklhorn, R. (1969), The Freiberg Period of the Freud Family. *J. Hist. Med. & All. Sci.*, 24:37-43.

Goethe, J. W. von, *Faust*, tr. W. Kaufman. New York: Doubleday, Anchor Books, 1963.

——— Urworte, Orphisch. *Gesammelte Werke*, 15:180-181. Leipzig: Insel Verlag, 1923.

Greenson, R. R. (1967), *The Technique and Practice of Psychoanalysis*, Vol. 1. New York: International Universities Press.

Grossman, C. M. & Grossman, S. (1965), *The Wild Analyst*. London: Barrie & Rockliff.

Hartmann, H. (1939), *Ego Psychology and the Problem of Adaptation*. New York: International Universities Press, 1958.

Jones, E. (1953-1957), *The Life and Work of Sigmund Freud*, 3 Vols. New York: Basic Books.

——— (1960-1962), *Das Leben und Werk von Sigmund Freud*, tr. K. Jones. Bern & Stuttgart: Hans Huber.

Jung, C. G. (1961), *Memories, Dreams, Reflections*, ed. A. Jaffé. New York: Pantheon.

King, J. L. & Jakes, T. H. (1969), Non-Darwinian Evolution. *Science*, 164:788-798.

Kris, E. (1950), Introduction and Footnotes to *The Origins of Psychoanalysis* by S. Freud. New York: Basic Books, 1954.

———— (1952), *Psychoanalytic Explorations in Art.* New York: International Universities Press.

Lehmann, H. (1966), A Conversation between Freud and Rilke. *Psychoanal. Quart.,* 35:423-427.

Lewin, B. D. (1932), Analysis and Structure of a Transient Hypomania. *Psychoanal. Quart.,* 1:43-58.

———— (1950), *The Psychoanalysis of Elation.* New York: Norton.

Lorenz, K. (1963), *On Aggression* (translated by M. K. Wilson from *Das Sogenannte Böse*). New York: Harcourt, Brace & World, 1966.

Nunberg, H. & Federn, E., eds. (1962-1967), *Minutes of the Vienna Psychoanalytic Society,* 2 vols. New York: International Universities Press.

Peto, A. (1969), Terrifying Eyes. *The Psychoanalytic Study of the Child,* 24: 197-212.

Pfenning, A. R. (1906), *Wilhelm Fliess und seine Nachentdecker: Otto Weininger und H. Swoboda.* Berlin: Selbstverlag.

Pfister, O., *see* Freud/Pfister.

Pollock, G. H. (1968), The Possible Significance of Childhood Object Loss in the Josef Breuer-Bertha Pappenheim (Anna O.)-Sigmund Freud Relationship. *J. Amer. Psychoanal. Assn.,* 16:711-739.

Putnam, J. J. (1915), *Human Motives.* Boston: Little, Brown.

Rank, O. (1914), Der Doppelgänger. *Imago,* 3:97-164.

Ritvo, L. B. (1965), Darwin as the Source of Freud's Neo-Lamarckianism. *J. Amer. Psychoanal. Assn.,* 13:499-517.

Rosen (1969), Sign phenomena and their relationship to unconscious meaning. *Internat. J. Psycho-Anal.,* 50:197-207.

Sachs, H. (1944), *Freud: Master and Friend.* Cambridge: Harvard University Press.

Sajner, J. (1968), Sigmund Freuds Beziehungen zu seinem Geburtsort Freiberg (Pribor) und zu Mähren. *Clio. Medica,* 3:167-180.

Schur, H. (1966), An Observation and Comments on the Development of Memory. *The Psychoanalytic Study of the Child,* 21:468-479. New York: International Universities Press.

Schur, M. (1949), Letter to the Editor. *Bull. Amer. Psychoanal. Assn.,* 5(2):74.

———— (1953), The Ego in Anxiety. In: *Drives, Affects, Behavior,* Vol. 1, ed. R. M. Loewenstein. New York: International Universities Press, pp. 67-103.

———— (1955), Comments on the Metapsychology of Somatization. *The Psychoanalytic Study of the Child,* 10:119-164. New York: International Universities Press.

———— (1965), Editor's Introduction. In: *Drives, Affects, Behavior,* Vol. 2, ed. M. Schur. New York: International Universities Press, pp. 9-20.

———— (1966a), Some Additional "Day Residues" of the "Specimen Dream of Psychoanalysis." In: *Psychoanalysis—A General Psychology,* ed. R. M. Loewenstein, L. M. Newman, M. Schur, & A. J. Solnit. New York: International Universities Press, pp. 45-85.

———— (1966b), *The Id and the Regulatory Principles of Mental Functioning.* New York: International Universities Press.

———— (1968), Discussion of: V. Rosen, Sign Phenomena and Their Relationship to Unconscious Meaning. New York Psychoanalytic Society, October 29.

———— (1969), The background of Freud's "disturbance" on the Acropolis. *Imago,* 26:303-323.

———— & Ritvo, L. B. (1970a), The Concept of Development and Evolution in Psychoanalysis. In: *Development and Evolution of Behavior,* Vol. 1, ed. L. Aronson, D. Lehrman, T. S. Rosenblatt, & E. Tobach. San Francisco: W. H. Freeman.

———— ———— (1970b), A Principle of Evolutionary Biology for Psychoanalysis: Schneirla's Evolutionary and Developmental Theory of Biphasic Processes Underlying Approach and Withdrawal and Freud's Unpleasure and Pleasure Principles *J. Amer. Psychoanal. Assn.,* 18:422-439.

Stewart, R. S. (1967), [Review of] Freud, S. & Bullitt, W. C. *Thomas Woodrow Wilson. New York Times Book Reviews,* Jan. 29.

Stewart, W. (1967), *Psychoanalysis: The First Ten Years 1888-1898.* New York: Macmillan.

Stone, L. (1961), *The Psychoanalytic Situation.* New York: International Universities Press.

Travell, J. & Bigelow, N. H. (1947), Role of Somatic Trigger Areas in the Patterns of Hysteria. *Psychosom. Med.,* 9:353-363.

Ullman, M. (1965), An Experimental Approach to Dreams and Telepathy. *Arch. Gen Psychiat.,* 14:605-613.

Weininger, O. (1902), *Geschlecht und Charakter.* Vienna & Leipzig: Braumüller. *Sex and Character.* London: W. Heinemann, 1906.

Williams, R. & Storrs, E. E. (1968), A Study of Monozygous Quadruplet Armadillos in Relation to Mammalian Inheritance. *Proc. Nat. Acad. Sci.,* 60:910.

Wittels, F. (1924), *Sigmund Freud.* New York: Dodd-Mead.

Zweig, A. (1934), *Bilanz der deutschen Judenheit: ein Versuch.* Amsterdam: Querido Verlag. *Insulted and Exiled: The Truth about the German Jews.* London: Miles, 1937.

———— (1936), Apollon bewältigt Dionysos. *Das Neue Tagebuch* (Paris), 18:425-428.

Zweig, S. (1931), *Die Heilung durch den Geist: Franz Anton Mesmer, Mary Baker Eddy, Sigmund Freud.* Leipzig: Inselverlag.

———— (1933), *Mental Healers.* New York: Viking Press; London: Cassell.

———— see *also* Freud/Zweig

NAME INDEX

SUBJECT INDEX

579